AHI

Persian Gulf States
country studies

Foreign Area Studies
The American University
Edited by
Richard F. Nyrop
Research completed
August 1984

On the cover: An Arab dhow, famous for long ocean journeys
in the past; still in use, but rapidly disappearing

Second Edition, 1984; First Printing, 1985

Library of Congress Cataloging in Publication Data

Main entry under title:

Persian Gulf states

    (Area handbook series) (DA pam   ;   550–185)
    Rev. ed. of: Area handbook for the Persian Gulf
states. lst ed. 1977.
    "Research completed August 1984."
    Bibliography: p.
    Includes index.
    1. Persian Gulf States. I. Nyrop, Richard F.
II. American University. Foreign Area Studies
III. Area handbook for the Persian Gulf states.
IV. Series. V. Series: DA pam ;   550–185
DS247.A13P47   1985   953'.6   85–6089

Headquarters, Department of the Army
DA Pam 550–185

For sale by the Superintendent of Documents, U.S. Government Printing Office
Washington, D.C. 20402

Foreword

This volume is one of a continuing series of books prepared by Foreign Area Studies, The American University, under the Country Studies/Area Handbook Program. The last page of this book provides a listing of other published studies. Each book in the series deals with a particular foreign country, describing and analyzing its economic, national security, political, and social systems and institutions and examining the interrelationships of those systems and institutions and the ways that they are shaped by cultural factors. Each study is written by a multidisciplinary team of social scientists. The authors seek to provide a basic insight and understanding of the society under observation, striving for a dynamic rather than a static portrayal of it. The study focuses on historical antecedents and on the cultural, political, and socioeconomic characteristics that contribute to cohesion and cleavage within the society. Particular attention is given to the origins and traditions of the people who make up the society, their dominant beliefs and values, their community of interests and the issues on which they are divided, the nature and extent of their involvement with the national institutions, and their attitudes toward each other and toward the social system and political order within which they live.

The contents of the book represent the views, opinions, and findings of Foreign Area Studies and should not be construed as an official Department of the Army position, policy, or decision, unless so designated by other official documentation. The authors have sought to adhere to accepted standards of scholarly objectivity. Such corrections, additions, and suggestions for factual or other changes that readers may have will be welcomed for use in future new editions.

William Evans-Smith
Director, Foreign Area Studies
The American University
Washington, D.C. 20016

Acknowledgments

The authors are indebted to numerous individuals in various agencies of the United States government and in international, diplomatic, and private organizations in Washington, D.C., who gave of their time, research materials, and special knowledge on Middle Eastern affairs and the countries covered in this book to provide data and perspective. The authors also wish to express their appreciation to members of the Foreign Area Studies staff who contributed to the preparation of the manuscript. These include Denise Ryan, Andrea T. Merrill, Lenny Granger, and Dorothy M. Lohmann, who edited the manuscript; Harriett R. Blood and Gustavo Adolfo Mendoza, who prepared the graphics; and Gilda V. Nimer, who provided valuable bibliographic assistance. The authors appreciate as well the contributions of Ernest A. Will, publications manager, and of Charlotte Benton Pochel, who typed the manuscript. The book was phototypeset by Margaret Quinn. The efforts of Eloise W. Brandt and Wayne W. Olsen, administrative assistants, are also sincerely appreciated.

Special thanks are owed to Marty Ittner, who designed the book cover and the illustrations on the title page of each chapter. The inclusion of photographs in this study was made possible by the generosity of various individuals and public and private organizations. The authors acknowledge their indebtedness especially to those who provided work not yet published.

Contents

Laraine Newhouse Carter

PRE-ISLAMIC ARABIA—The Civilizations of Prehistoric Arabia—Ancient Seafaring in the Gulf—Pre-Islamic Internal History—The Arabian Social Structure—ISLAM: EMERGENCE AND DEVELOPMENT—Conversion in the Gulf—Tenets of Islam—The Gulf During the Medieval Period—Internal Organization—The Early Period—The Ibadi Movement—THE ENTRANCE OF THE EUROPEANS INTO THE GULF—The Portuguese—Dutch and English Involvement—Piracy—THE FOUNDING OF THE MODERN GULF POLITIES: GULF STATES IN THE EIGHTEENTH AND NINETEENTH CENTURIES—The Wahhabi Movement—Internal Migrations and Political Developments—The Trucial Coast: The Qawasim and the Bani Yas—Developments in Oman—THE TWENTIETH CENTURY—British Governmental Transition—Gulf Development Before Independence—Internal Developments in Oman—THE NEW AGE: CHANGING PATTERNS IN THE RELIGIOUS AND SOCIAL SYSTEMS—Foreign Workers—Settlement Patterns—The Family—Marriage and Divorce—Women—SOCIAL SYSTEMS OF THE GULF COUNTRIES—Kuwait—Bahrain—Qatar—United Arab Emirates—Oman

Darrel R. Eglin and James D. Rudolph

GEOGRAPHY—POPULATION—EDUCATION—Development of Education—The Educational System—HEALTH AND WELFARE—THE ECONOMY—The Oil Industry—Role of Government—Labor Force—Agriculture—Industry—Finance—Foreign Trade and Balance of Payments—THE POLITICAL SYSTEM—The Constitutional Monarchy—Politics and the Social Order—FOREIGN RELATIONS

Laraine Newhouse Carter

GEOGRAPHIC AND DEMOGRAPHIC SETTING—Climate—Population—Work Force—Education—Health—Social Security—THE ECONOMY—Agriculture—Petroleum

EMIRATES—Background—Independence and Unification—
Organization of Forces—OMAN—Background—Rebellion
and Coup—Organization and Missions of Forces

List of Figures

Preface

The overthrow of the shah of Iran in 1979 and the outbreak of the Iran-Iraq War in September 1980 were matters of major importance to the region and the world, but the events were of immediate and growing concern to Iran and Iraq's five small neighbors: Bahrain, Kuwait, Oman, Qatar, and the United Arab Emirates (UAE). In 1981 the rulers of these Arab monarchies joined with the Saudi Arabian monarchy to form the Gulf Cooperation Council (GCC). The members of the GCC have since embarked on numerous joint socioeconomic and political ventures, and they have used the GCC to channel massive financial and other assistance to Iraq. In addition, by late 1984 the GCC members had engaged in two joint military exercises, and observers anticipated that military cooperation within the GCC would probably increase throughout the 1980s.

Persian Gulf States: Country Studies replaces the *Area Handbook for the Persian Gulf States* published in 1977. Like its predecessor, the present book is an attempt to treat in a compact and objective manner the dominant historical, social, economic, political, and national security aspects of the contemporary societies. Sources of information included scholarly books, journals, and monographs; official reports and documents of government and international organizations; foreign and domestic newspapers and periodicals; and interviews with individuals having special competence in the affairs of the separate countries and of the region. Relatively up-to-date economic data were available for some countries, but not for others, and the sources were not always in agreement. Most demographic data should be viewed as estimates.

Brief comments on some of the more valuable sources for further reading appear at the conclusion of each chapter; the Bibliography is located in the back of the book. Measurements are generally given in the metric system; a conversion table is provided to assist those who are unfamiliar with the system (see table 1, Appendix A). English usage follows *Webster's Ninth New Collegiate Dictionary*.

The transliteration of Arabic words and phrases posed a problem. For many of the words—such as Muhammad, Muslim, hadith, and shaykh—the authors followed a modified version of the system adopted by the United States Board on Geographic Names and the Permanent Committee on Geographic Names for British official use, known as the BGN/PCGN system; the modification entails the omission of diacritical markings and hyphens. In numerous instances, however, the names of persons or places are so well known by another spelling that to have used the BGN/PCGN system might have caused confusion. For example, the reader will find Mecca rather than Makkah, Oman rather than Uman, and Doha rather than Ad Dawhah. In addition, although the five governments officially reject the use of the term *Persian Gulf*—as do other Arab governments—and refer to that body of water as the Arabian Gulf, the authors followed the practice of the United States Board on Geographic Names by using *Persian Gulf* or *Gulf*.

Arab names are frequently confusing to the Western reader, but they should be viewed as a genealogical chart. For example, the name of the heir apparent in Qatar is Shaykh Hamad bin Khalifah Al Thani. The term *shaykh* is an honorific that is adopted by the male members of noble families, religious scholars, and other prestigious individuals; the term *bin* (or *ibn*) means "son of" and Al Thani is the name of the ruling family of Qatar. Hamad, who is addressed as Shaykh Hamad, is, as the name indicates, the son of Khalifah of the Al Thani family. Should Hamad feel the need to do so, he could include the names of his forebears to show his lineage, i.e., Hamad bin Khalifah bin Hamad bin Abdallah bin Qasim bin Muhammad Al Thani. (The word *bint* means "daughter of," and the word *bani* means "sons of," hence tribe or clan. A Gulf Arab woman rarely takes her husband's name; women's names, like men's, usually include the father's name and possibly the name of the family, clan, or tribe.)

Many names—such as Rahim, Rahman, Azam, and 96 others—are designations of the attributes of God. A common name among peninsular Arabs and of Muslims elsewhere is Abd al Aziz. *Abd al* means "servant" or "slave of"; *Aziz* means "powerful" or "precious"; the name therefore literally means the slave or servant of the Powerful (God). The name Muhammad, the Prophet or Messenger of God, is probably the most widely used name for males in the world.

Figure 1. *The Persian Gulf States of Bahrain, Kuwait, Oman, Qatar, and the United Arab Emirates, 1984*

Introduction

THE SECURITY AND WELL-BEING of the five small Arab countries on which this book focuses—Bahrain, Kuwait, Oman, Qatar, and the United Arab Emirates (UAE)—continued in the mid-1980s to be inextricably involved with the affairs and actions of the other littoral states of the Persian Gulf: Iran, Iraq, and Saudi Arabia. Iraq's invasion of Iran in September 1980 and the ensuing Iran-Iraq War, therefore, occasioned immediate concern within the other Gulf governments. The armed forces and military equipment of either belligerent far surpassed those of the smaller states. In the 1960s and 1970s the revolutionary, anti-monarchical regime in Baghdad had laid claim to parts of Kuwait, and the shah of Iran had asserted Iranian rights to Bahrain and parts of other Gulf states (see Disputes and Perceived Threats, ch. 7). The fundamentalist and expansionist Shia (see Glossary) religious leaders who seized power in Tehran in 1979 in the wake of the shah's downfall not only did not repudiate the shah's territorial claims but also repeatedly proclaimed their animosity toward the Sunni (see Glossary) monarchies across the Gulf, monarchies that they depicted as pro-American and un-Islamic. Whereas the oil-importing countries of the world were concerned primarily with the impact of the war on oil supplies and prices, the oil-exporting states of the Arabian Peninsula feared that a victory by either Iran or Iraq might lead to a military threat to their oil fields and to their survival and independence.

In the mid-1980s an estimated 60 percent of the world's proven oil reserves were located in or offshore of the eight littoral states, and most of their oil exports were shipped to world markets through the Strait of Hormuz, the choke point on the sea-lanes to the Gulf of Oman and the Indian Ocean (see fig. 21). The six societies on the peninsula possessed about three-fifths of the region's reserves but only a small fraction of its population. The populations of Iran and Iraq—over 40 million and 14 million, respectively—dwarfed those of the societies on the peninsula. In addition, the small amirates on the western shore of the Gulf included within their boundaries relatively huge numbers of aliens. Although estimates varied in mid-1984 foreigners accounted for nearly 60 percent of Kuwait's population of about 1.5 million, almost 80 percent of the UAE's 1.2 million, and between 60 and 80 percent of Qatar's approximately 270,000. Nearly 30 percent of Bahrain's 395,000 were foreigners, as were between 25 and 48 percent of Oman's estimated 950,000. Moreover, significant percentages of the populace in Kuwait, Bahrain, Qatar, and the UAE consisted of Shia, thus constituting, in the opinions of the various governments, potential fifth columns for the Iranian ayatollahs (see Social Systems of the Gulf Countries, ch. 1).

In January 1981, only four months after the outbreak of the war, the monarchs on the peninsula agreed to coordinate and unify their economic, political, social, and defense policies in a formal way. On May 24, 1981, the six heads of state met in Abu Dhabi, the capital of the UAE, and signed a charter establishing the Gulf Cooperation Council (GCC). Most foreign observers assumed that a major goal of the signers would be to achieve a close military relationship, but the early efforts of the GCC members were directed largely toward socioeconomic cooperation and joint financial enterprises. In addition, the members used the GCC to channel huge financial subventions to Iraq (see Organization and Structure, Appendix C). By late 1984 the GCC members reportedly had transferred in excess of US$35 billion to the Iraqi regime (see Impact of the Iran-Iraq War, ch. 7).

Although the armed forces of some of the member states engaged in brief, bilateral military training missions, it was not until October 1983 that military units from all GCC members participated in a joint military exercise. The operation, called Shield of the Peninsula (Dir al Jizira), was held in the UAE, and the defense officials and military commanders subsequently declared that the exercises had been an excellent training and learning experience (see Military Aspects of the Gulf Cooperation Council, ch. 7).

During 1984 the senior military commanders and defense ministers met with some frequency. In mid-September the GCC defense and foreign ministers held a joint ministerial conference at a Saudi military base in southwest Saudi Arabia. The official press release after the meeting declared that the results of the proceedings would remain secret, but the government-owned Saudi news agency announced that the ministers had "forged . . . a joint defense policy" for review by the Supreme Council, i.e., the GCC heads of state, in a meeting scheduled for November 27–29, 1984, in Kuwait. A Kuwaiti newspaper reported that Kuwait's defense minister had stated that the defense policy provided for a joint naval command center at the Saudi Gulf port of Al Jubayl and that the center would be tied into a communications and command system linking the armed forces of the member states. The defense minister was also quoted as asserting that a "GCC joint deployment force" consisting of two brigades would man an air defense system at Shuayb al Batin, about 360 kilometers north of Jiddah, Saudi Arabia.

Between October 10 and October 23, units of the GCC armed forces carried out another joint military exercise—Shield of the Peninsula II. The manuevers were held in Saudi Arabia near Hafar al Batin, the site of King Khalid Military City; the hosts built a huge tent city for the participants and observers, including a command and communications center and a field hospital. According to official press reports, the exercise focused on joint planning and a testing of joint command, communications, and coordination in simulated combat conditions. The field exercises included parachute drops of men and equipment, night operations, and "defense and attack operations involving the use of live ammunition by land and aerial forces."

In late October and early November various GCC ministerial councils and special bodies held numerous meetings in preparation for the Supreme Council meeting, which was usually described as the fifth summit conference. These conferences included meetings of the oil and mineral resources ministers and of the GCC's Finance and Economic Cooperation Committee and the Gulf Investment Corporation (see Economic Cooperation, Appendix C). The defense, foreign, and planning ministers also held meetings in preparation for the summit conference.

The official briefings at the conclusion of the summit conference quite understandably focused on the decisions reached. The heads of state extended the appointment of the GCC secretary general, Abdullah Yakub Bisharah, to November 1988 and confirmed that the sixth summit conference would be held in Muscat, Oman, in November 1985. The council decided to continue financial and other aid to Bahrain and Oman at unspecified levels. It also approved continued study and planning for an interstate natural gas pipeline system and a GCC railroad. The council agreed that nationals of one state may buy and own real property in any other member state. The heads of state endorsed the continuation and expansion of joint purchases and stockpiling of various foodstuffs, and they requested early adoption of a common tariff to encourage and protect domestic industries.

The Supreme Council nevertheless again failed to reach agreement on a comprehensive defense policy. According to official reports, the heads of state were extensively briefed by their defense advisers on the status of the Iran-Iraq War. They were acutely aware that during the first four years of the war perhaps as many as 900,000 combatants had been killed, wounded, or captured, a number almost equal to the population of Oman and larger than the combined populations of Bahrain and Qatar. They were also briefed on the ongoing Soviet occupation and war in Afghanistan, including the upgrading and expansion of two airfields in that country, one near Herat and the other some 400 kilometers to the south, and the fact that the air fields lie only 900 to 1,400 kilometers from the oil fields, ports, and other installations on the Arab side of the Gulf.

To the disappointment of some members, the heads of state agreed only on the establishment of a "strike force" that will go to the assistance of a member under clear threat of external aggression. According to a GCC spokesman, the force will consist of units in each member's armed forces that are to be ready to respond to a request for help. The Supreme Council failed to adopt the "joint defense policy" that the defense ministers had drafted, and it made no public reference to a unified command for the strike force or to a joint naval command.

According to informed observers, some of the smaller states wished to move ahead on joint defense planning and consultation but were unwilling to enter into a formal defense agreement that called for a joint command in which Saudi Arabia would perforce be the dominant participant. In addition, Oman's continuing military association with the United States and Kuwait's August 1984 purchase of US$327 million of air defense equipment from the Soviet Union—and the presence in Kuwait of 10 Soviet technicians to set up the equipment—were indications of divergent approaches. And the UAE, which had maintained close commercial relations with Iran, reportedly posed objections to a formal joint military organization that might appear to be oriented almost exclusively against Iran.

The ongoing activities within the GCC, particularly the constantly expanding socioeconomic programs, were illustrative of the vast changes of the preceding half-century. As recently as the 1930s the history and nature of the scattered societies were little known to most of the world and were of interest primarily to a few academics, diplomats, and geologists in search of oil. The noble families that ruled the thinly populated ports and oases—the inhabitants of which were overwhelmingly Arab and, with the exception of Bahrain, predominantly Sunni—were heavily dependent on subventions from the British Indian government (see The Founding of the Modern Gulf Polities: Gulf States in the Eighteenth and Nineteenth Centuries, ch. 1). The meager natural resources then available made possible only subsistence economies. Medical services were almost nonexistent, and education, with a few exceptions, was limited to rudimentary religious instruction and a few years of reading, writing, and arithmetic for the sons of the few prosperous merchant families and the noble clans. As a result of treaties signed in the nineteenth and early twentieth centuries, Britain possessed responsibility for the defense, foreign affairs, and, albeit in varying degrees, internal security of the several political entities.

In the aftermath of World War II these isolated, tribally oriented societies began to experience the first aspects of truly revolutionary change. In 1951 Britain and Oman concluded a treaty in which Britain acknowledged Oman's status as a fully sovereign nation. Kuwait severed its British connection in 1961 and in its Constitution the following year proclaimed the state a constitutional monarchy. In 1968 the British government announced its intention to reduce its military commitments east of Suez and, specifically, to terminate its treaty relationships with and obligations to the shaykhdoms on the Gulf. By the end of 1971 Bahrain and Qatar had achieved their independence as traditional monarchies, and the UAE had established itself as a federation of traditionally governed amirates (see The Twentieth Century, ch. 1). And in 1970 Oman became the Sultanate of Oman in the wake of a coup d'état in which the sultan was deposed and exiled by his son, Qaboos bin Said bin Taimur Al Bu Said, who in late 1984 continued to rule as the sultan of Oman.

By the mid-1970s each of the states had embarked on sweeping socioeconomic programs that were being paid for with earnings from their oil exports, the prices of which were steadily escalating (see Appendix B). Their revenues varied greatly; Kuwait's were enormous and those of Qatar and the UAE also substantial, whereas those of Bahrain were small and declining and Oman's were modest but growing. Nevertheless, the flow of petrodollars resulted in change on an unprecedented scale. The construction of hospitals, schools, universities, mosques, desalination plants, highways, airports, hotels, housing, and petrochemical plants fueled a building boom. Hundreds of thousands of foreigners were imported to build the new infrastructure and to staff the social, educational, and technical plants, radically altering the ethnic and religious composition of the societies. Indians, Iranians, Pakistanis, Palestinians, Egyptians, Europeans, and East Asians filled positions from the most menial to the most highly skilled and professional. In the three richest states—Kuwait, Qatar, and the UAE—the indigenous Sunni Arabs became minorities in their own societies.

In most of the states the foreigners were subject to numerous rigid controls. In Kuwait, for example, foreigners could not vote, own land or other real property, or engage in specified business, and for all practical purposes they were denied any chance of citizenship. Although the details varied, the other governments imposed similar controls on their alien populations, including provisions that the foreigners must depart the state on completion of the contract period. The newly rich amirs created welfare states in terms of social and medical services and education, and the foreigners generally enjoyed access to these facilities. In the fall of 1984, however, Kuwait announced that henceforth foreigners would be charged fees for services, and there were indications that the other states would adopt similar procedures. In addition, the UAE and Qatar enforced guidelines and procedures designed to reduce the number of illegal expatriates and to force workers to return to their homelands when their work permits expired.

Until the late 1970s the ruling families and their advisers tended to identify radical, secular Arab foreigners as the preeminent threat to their paternalistic yet absolutist regimes. They regularly endorsed and generously funded the efforts of the Palestine Liberation Organization (PLO) to secure a Palestinian homeland, but they also rigorously monitored and controlled the activities of Palestinians residing in their countries, and they allowed almost none to become citizens. During the period that Gamal Abdul Nasser dominated Egypt and was the popular hero of the Arab world, Arab foreigners employed in the Gulf states who became too ardent and vocal in their advocacy of the policies of Nasser and his fervent republicanism could expect to be expelled. The regimes were also sensitive to the activities and propaganda of the communist government of the People's Democratic Republic of Yemen (Yemen [Aden]).

In 1979 and 1980 the increasingly strident and bellicose pronouncements of Iran's new ruler, Ayatollah Ruhollah Khomeini, provoked considerable alarm within the Arab governments of the Gulf. Riots by Shia in Saudi Arabia's oil field region in 1979 and 1980, and an attempted coup by Shia in Bahrain in 1981, provided evidence that many Shia were receptive to Khomeini's advocacy of Islamic revolutions. A new element was introduced in December 1983 when a group of Iraqi Shia, whose members reportedly had been trained in Iran, bombed United States, French, and Kuwaiti offices in Kuwait's capital. In December 1984 members of the same group hijacked a Kuwaiti commercial airliner and forced the pilot to land at the Tehran airport. The hijackers said that they would blow up the aircraft unless the government of Kuwait released the 17 people whom Kuwait had arrested and convicted of the bombing incidents the previous year. Six days later Iranian personnel entered the aircraft, captured the hijackers without trouble, and released the passengers and crew. By that time, however, the terrorists had killed four passengers—two of whom were United States government officials—and abused and tortured others. Although Kuwait and other Gulf governments expressed official satisfaction with Iran's actions, several officials privately suggested that, because the terrorists had been trained in Iran, the Iranian government bore at least some responsibility for the incidents.

During the early 1980s the Gulf monarchs became aware of the serious threat to the stability of their regimes posed by indigenous groups usually described in the Western press as Islamic fundamentalists. In an article in the Fall 1984 issue of *Foreign Affairs*, Professor James A. Bill reported that one of the amirs privately commented that he "would rather deal with 10 communists than one Muslim fundamentalist." By the mid-1980s the activities of several Sunni revivalist groups had become a matter of utmost concern to the rulers.

An example of fundamentalist agitation occurred in late 1984 in Kuwait. A member of a fundamentalist student organization at the University of Kuwait asked Shaykh Abd al Aziz Baz, the senior member of Saudi Arabia's ulama (see Glossary), for his opinion on the university's coeducational system. Shaykh Baz—who has embarrassed the Saudi government by insisting that the world is flat—opined that women who attend a coeducational school are no better than prostitutes. He also castigated musicians and asserted that it is un-Islamic to photograph any living creature. Copies of the shaykh's judgment were circulated in Kuwait's mosques, and when the government launched an inquiry into the event, various fundamentalist groups charged that the government was attacking Islam.

Professor Bill uses the term Populist Islam (Islam al Shaabi) to describe the revivalist mass movement that is challenging Establishment Islam (Al Islam al Rasmi), the traditional fundamentalism of the ruling families. (Other scholars have used such phrases as "Islam from below" and "Islam from above" or "Islam of the ruled" and "Islam of the rulers" in discussing the same phenomenon.) Some adherents of Populist Islam are basically reformers, whereas others are intent on re-creating the totality of Islamic dominance and influence that they believe existed at the time of the Prophet Muhammad. Professor Bill reports that the various groups nonetheless share a rejection of Shia beliefs, a dislike of the governments of the region, and an animosity toward the United States. The real or perceived close relation between the ruling families and the United States prompts some fundamentalists to refer to Establishment Islam as Al Islam al Amriki (Islam Americana).

By the mid-1980s, to have a "pro-American" reputation was to risk being labeled as inadequately pro-Arab and, at least by implication, soft on Zionism and Israel. A majority of fundamentalists and secularists were united in a belief that the United States neither would nor could pursue a policy in the Middle East to which Israel was opposed. Put another way, Gulf Arabs tended to believe that Israel's foreign and defense policies and practices were endorsed by the United States. When in July 1980 the Israeli Knesset (parliament) formally annexed East (Arab) Jerusalem—known to Muslims as Al Quds and sacred to them because of its association with the Prophet—Arab Muslims were outraged that the United States did not force Israel to rescind an act that the United Nations (UN) Security Council declared "legally invalid." The Israeli government's policy of encouraging and subsidizing Jewish settlements in Gaza, the West Bank, and the Golan Heights continued to be bitterly resented by Gulf Arabs in the mid-1980s. The issue of the occupied territories was further inflamed in December 1981 when the Knesset extended Israeli "laws, jurisdiction, and administration" to the Golan Heights. Although the United States government criticized this de facto annexation, it joined Israel in casting the only two votes against a UN General Assembly resolution condemning the act, thus alienating moderate as well as extremist Arabs.

The growing feeling of ill will toward the United States created a dilemma for the Gulf monarchs, who had, after all, observed the overthrow of several neighboring monarchies in recent years. Their economies remained closely linked to the West in general and the United States in particular. Despite the Soviet Union's pro-Arab posture in the confrontation between the Arabs and Israel, only Kuwait maintained diplomatic relations with Moscow, and only a fraction of the foreign trade of the Gulf states involved the Soviet Union and its East European allies. Nevertheless, some observers feared that in the future at least some of the rulers will feel compelled to convey a public image of loosening or even ending the American connection.

December 28, 1984   Richard F. Nyrop

Chapter 1.   Historical and Cultural Setting

Youth dressed in traditional Omani attire

IN MID-1984 WORLD ATTENTION remained focused on the seemingly interminable Iran-Iraq War, and foreign and local observers speculated that the war might spread to the other oil-rich states on the Persian Gulf littoral. Because of their financial support of Iraq's war effort and as a result of Iranian threats, several of the Gulf states—particularly those with Shia populations—worried as much about the possibility of internal subversion as about overt attack. Bahrain had already experienced an Iranian-inspired coup attempt in December 1981. This, however, was but one of several concerns of the Gulf societies in 1984. Others included the drop in oil revenues, an increase in Islamic fundamentalism, and the effect that both might have on the expectations and aspirations of its citizen body. In the single generation since the independence that brought them control of their future and the burgeoning oil revenues, Gulf societies had changed from being largely impoverished and underdeveloped to being affluent, increasingly educated, and physically healthy. Although ruled anachronistically by paternalistic and patriarchal tribal leaders, the citizenry had taken an ever-improving standard of living as their right.

Trade—not oil—was the first medium to bring life to the Arabian shore of the Gulf. In the century before the discovery of oil and the subsequent use of oil revenues for improving economic strength and for social welfare projects, the Arab states that line the western littoral were at the most somnolent point in their long and turbulent history.

There is evidence that before human beings had migrated to the European geographic area, indigenous traders of the western coast of the Gulf were enriching the first civilizations of the Fertile Crescent both commercially and culturally. Despite periods of decline, such trade appears to have continued for millennia. Gulf trade was active during the ancient period but extraordinarily so by medieval times. In the ninth century A.D. Gulf traders were traveling to China and returning up Gulf waters to Basrah, facilitating the exchange of ideas and goods among the great civilizations of the time. The peoples of the Gulf coast, unlike the inhabitants of the interior of the Arabian Peninsula, had always been exposed to outside influences. The cultural and economic area to which the Arab Gulf states belonged was not at all limited to Arabia but included the whole of the Gulf area. Arabs and Iranians moved with nonchalance from one side of the Gulf to the other.

One persistent factor in Gulf history is the constant rivalry between merchant states and the desire for hegemony. Another factor, destined to be more fatal to Gulf trade, was the interest in the area by outsiders—Europeans, Ottoman Turks, the Wahhabis (see Glossary) of central Arabia, and the Egyptians. After the entrance of the Europeans but before European power reached its apogee in the Gulf, Hormuz—located near the Iranian coast—was for a time the foremost trading center in the world (see fig. 1). A popular Arab and Iranian saying is "If the world were a ring, Hormuz would be its jewel."

Largely because of events in Europe, the British were able to outstay the Dutch and slowly but effectively to build up power in the area. Tribal animosities and rivalries and mutual piracy among Gulf states served British interests, and by means of a series of exclusive treaties the British eventually pacified the Gulf. Although local merchants were still active, they were considerably circumscribed by these treaties. In the early years of the nineteenth century, new Gulf powers, particularly the states of Kuwait and Bahrain, were emerging and achieving great wealth through trade. Because the states had few natural resources other than pearls and date palms, maritime activity was not only the easiest way for Arab Gulf states to achieve wealth but also virtually the only way they could survive. A dramatic change in living conditions occurred, therefore, when European steamships and the associated technology began to appear in the Gulf in the 1860s. Although the Arabs were capable of hand-building ships that could carry several tons of merchandise to China and back, they had not developed industrially and could not begin to compete with the European vessels. Fossilized into their political positions and isolated from much influence by British protectorate treaties, the Arab Gulf states went into a decline and were revived only with the discovery of oil.

In the period before oil, Gulf Arabs fell back on their natural resources (meager as they were) until the values of these, too, were threatened. In the 1920s the Japanese began producing cultured pearls, and the economic well-being of Bahrain, Qatar, and much of the Trucial Coast area (since 1971 the United Arab Emirates—UAE) was reduced further. Arabs subsisted largely on minor commerce and other dealings with the Europeans who called there. The worldwide depression of the 1930s reduced traffic in the Gulf and consequently reduced income for those who provided services. The people of Dubai, deciding old ways were best, became active in smuggling gold to India.

Oil and the change in British priorities, particularly after

World War II, altered the situation. The discovery of oil and the practical utilization of wealth accruing from it were initially slow processes. Gulf Arabs were awakening from a long sleep, and the lack of immediate reform was largely the result of ignorance and underexposure to the kinds of positive social, cultural, and economic change that money could buy. The Gulf has never been a monolith, and the individual states moved at different rates depending on custom and income. A curious reversal had taken place. Oman, Ras al Khaymah, and Sharjah, once the most powerful of the Gulf entities, became the poorest.

Once the states realized their affluent position and what it could do, the traditional welfare system built into the tribal order served them well. In 1984 none of the "welfare" states emerging in the modern Gulf was socialistic; yet all that had oil money were extravagant, by any standard, in spending for the benefit of their citizens. This was not an idea introduced by the West; it was rather an expansion of the tribal belief, reinforced by Islam, that no man is rich if a member of his clan is poor.

Pre-Islamic Arabia

The Civilizations of Prehistoric Arabia

Archaeological investigations of pre-Islamic Arabia are still in an embryonic state, and the results are hypothetical and controversial at best. Through the mid-1900s few people had the physical endurance or the survival techniques crucial to investigate the area. Scarcity of water, the difficulties of desert transport, and, until the 1940s, hostile tribes made systematic research a heroic undertaking., Further, very little was known about present-day Arabia beyond its coastal settlements. Initial archaeological discoveries are often the accidental finds of explorers eager to investigate the isolated land and map its interior.

The oldest evidence of civilized man in northern Arabia is artifacts found 90 kilometers to the north of Dhahran on the coast of the Gulf (see fig. 2). Dated to 5000 B.C., they are identical with those of the Al Ubaid culture of Mesopotamia, the first people to cultivate and settle the Fertile Crescent and the ancestors of the Sumerians, the first known people to develop a high culture. If Al Ubaid culture originated in Mesopotamia, then civilization reached Arabia from the north. If, however, Arabia was the parent site, then the first known agriculturists in the region were migrants from Arabia. This would substantiate the Sumerian

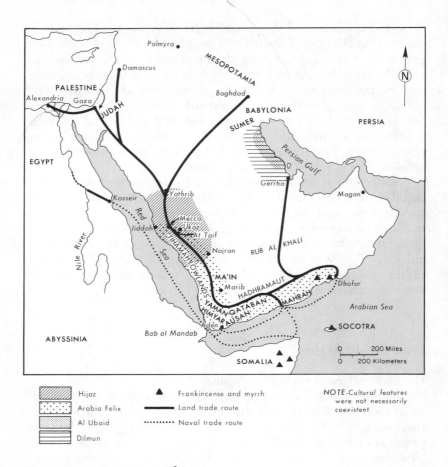

Figure 2. Ancient Arabia

myth that agriculture had been brought to Mesopotamia by a "fish-man" from the Gulf.

From about 4000 to 2000 B.C. the civilization of Dilmun dominated the eastern coast of Arabia from present-day Kuwait to Bahrain and extended some 90 kilometers into the interior to the oasis of Al Hufuf. At its zenith in 2000 B.C. Dilmun controlled the route to the Indies and was the trading link between the civilizations of the Indus Valley and those of Mesopotamia. The Mesopotamians regarded Dilmun as a holy place and its people as extraordinarily blessed. In Oman and Abu Dhabi the remains of a civilization have been found that might have been related to the

6

one at Dilmun. In Abu Dhabi, pre-Bronze Age stone buildings and settlements with elaborate tombs suggest a peaceful people and advanced cereal cultivation.

Arabia was only sparsely peopled in the interior. Until about 3000 B.C. the inland was sufficiently verdant to support both cereal agriculturists and herding peoples in the north and hunting and gathering societies in the south. As climatic conditions changed and the desert slowly encroached upon land that had supported both animal and human life, the inhabitants were forced to cling to the relatively few areas that had supplies of fresh water. Ecological constraints induced much of the population to migrate to the more hospitable lands to the north and northeast.

Ancient Seafaring in the Gulf

Some of the more tenacious and adventurous turned their backs on the inhospitable land and founded thalassocracies (maritime supremacies), greatly advancing the interchange of commodities and culture in the ancient period. Although the Gulf apparently experienced various periods of relative decline in its shipping activities, it was always numbered among the world's great trade routes. At its northernmost point the Gulf terminates near the confluence of the Tigris and Euphrates rivers. Goods transported through the Gulf from the south and later from East Africa and East Asia reached Mesopotamia and Babylon—states that, although rich in fertile land, lacked the stone, metals, and woods necessary to sustain advanced civilizations. Seafaring trade on the Gulf to these areas is documented from the third millennium.

More precise data from the second millennium indicate that Mesopotamia was then importing from three city-states in the direction of the Gulf: Dilmun, which had its headquarters on Bahrain; Magan, on the coastal curve of modern Oman lying on the Gulf of Oman; and Maluhha, which in very ancient times was in the region of Sind and the Indus Valley but by the first millennium was identified with Nubia in Ethiopia. Initially, Magan functioned as Maluhha's entrepôt. Typical Mesopotamian imports from Magan included copper, diorite, ivory, red ochre (perhaps from the island of Abu Musa), onions, bamboo, wood, and precious stones. "Fisheyes" (pearls) were also listed. Since the best pearl banks are between the tip of Qatar and Sharjah, it is likely that even at this early date pearling was a local industry. Dilmun eventually became the entrepôt for Magan and Maluhha. Dilmun's commercial power began to decline in about 1800 B.C., perhaps as a result of the invasion and devastation of the Indus Valley civilization, which disrupted trade in the region for several centuries.

Piracy flourished in the Gulf during Dilmun's decline, and Omani seafarers and merchants perforce turned their attention to Dhofar, the southern region of present-day Oman. Dhofar was one of only three producers of the highly valuable aromatic gum resin, frankincense. Frankincense, an essential element in certain ancient Jewish and pagan rituals, was burned as an offering to the gods. It was used lavishly in cremation services and, in Egypt, for embalming. For the funeral of Nero's wife an entire year's harvest was reputedly consumed. Frankincense also has healing properties; it was used as an antidote to poisons and to stop hemorrhages. From Dhofar frankincense was exported by sea from the port of Sumharam (near present-day Salalah) or transported by camel through the Hadhramaut and then usually up the land route through the Hijaz (the western coastal area of present-day Saudi Arabia).

Gulf trade did not cease completely after Dilmun's decline. Alexander the Great's admiral, Nearchos, wrote in his journal of an Arabian cape called Maketa (Ras Musandam, or the Musandam Peninsula) from which cinnamon was exported to the Assyrians. By the end of the third century B.C., Gulf trade had revived slightly. Gerrha, opposite Bahrain on the Arabian mainland, had become the most important commercial center in the area and was the local entrepôt for the fabulously wealthy kingdoms of southwest Arabia, among which were Saba (Sheba) and Himyar. At that time Magan in Oman came to be called Maazun by the Iranians, who were increasingly involved in Gulf trade. In A.D. 228 the Sassanians established their dynasty in Iran. During the Sassanian period Iranian trade in the Gulf reached its apogee, and it did not decline until the Arabs conquered Iran in the seventh century.

By the third century A.D. northern Oman's coastal districts were under Iranian control. In the fourth century the Iranians occupied Bahrain, a claim that would be resuscitated during the reign of Mohammad Reza Pahlavi and under the rule of Ayatollah Ruhollah Khomeini. When King Khosrou I invaded and occupied the Yemen in 520, southern Oman was included in the conquest. The Iranians introduced the *qanat* (*falaj* in Arabic), an ingenious irrigation system by which underground channels tap groundwater and carry it to fields several miles away. In 1984 much of Omani agriculture was still dependent on the system (see Agriculture, ch. 6).

Oman never acquired the reputation the Yemen did because it was virtually denied immediate access to the West by the vast Rub al Khali (Empty Quarter). It is clear, however, that Omanis in the pre-Islamic period were as active in long-distance sea trade between East and West as they were later and that the Gulf Arabs, particularly Omanis, played a significant role in the development of ancient trade.

Pre-Islamic Internal History

Until the advent of Islam the dominant political and commercial powers in the Arabian Peninsula were those of the south—Oman and the declining kingdoms of the Yemen. Apart from the Omani and Iranian trade colonies on the Gulf littoral and the Hijazi caravan stops that had turned into independent cities, such as Mecca and Yathrib (Medina), much of the population of Arabia was nomadic. In the first three centuries A.D. there were mass tribal relocations throughout the peninsula. Oman and the lower coast with their embryonic local industries and seafaring trade were the main objects of these migrations. The reasons for the migrations are unclear. Certainly the collapse of the dam at Marib, in the northeast of present-day Yemen Arab Republic (Yemen [Sanaa]), which had irrigated otherwise untillable land, contributed to it. There was also a great deal of social disruption. The population was increasing, and attacks by beduin on the *hadr* (settled peoples) were becoming more frequent.

Several northern beduin tribes moved south, much to the consternation of the indigenous southerners, who were already pressed for survival because of the paucity of local natural resources. It was about that time that traditions about tribal origins began to take concrete form. The tradition that has had the most serious political consequences for the Gulf concerned the difference between northern and southern Arabs. The southern Arabs entered the Islamic period with a clear sense of ethnic distinction between themselves and all other Arabs that explained the differences of language, custom, and physiognomy. Popular belief held and still holds that, although all Arabs are descended from Sham ibn Nuh (Shem, son of Noah), the "pure" or southern Arabs (Qahtani) are descended from Qahtan ibn Abir, or Hud, as he is often called, whereas the northern Arabs (called Adnani; in Oman sometimes called Nizari) are descended from Ismail (Ishmael) through Adnan. Although other Arab nationals, particularly those of tribal societies, know or think they know to which group they belong but are little concerned about it, the split is a matter of importance to Omanis and to Arabs of the lower Gulf. Many feuds in the eighteenth, nineteenth, and twentieth centuries can be traced to it.

There is little definite or reliable information about the Gulf area from the period of the decline of the great ancient peoples until the advent of Islam. Some scanty information exists for Oman because it was the most developed area of the littoral at the time. In the second century A.D. the Al Azd tribe migrated to Oman. Future imams (see Glossary) took "al Azdi" as the final part of their titles. The Al Julanda were rulers of Oman at the time of the Azdite invasion and were vassals of the Iranians. The Al Azd, a large force, ousted the Iranians for a brief period. In a short time, however, the Al Julanda ruled again from the coast in cooperation with the Iranians, while the Al Azd moved beyond the mountains, thus creating an internal division in the country that prevailed until 1970.

Also in the second or third century there was a major migration to Tuam (Buraymi Oasis) of two Adnani tribes, the Bani Said and the Bani Abd al Qais. The latter provided the ruling family for Qais, a major medieval Gulf port.

Most of the Arabs of the peninsula worshiped an astral triad. In the southern regions—Yemen and Oman—there were also Judaized Arabs, Christians, and, as a result of the Iranian presence, Zoroastrians. Judaism came to the Yemen via the Hijaz, when great numbers of Jews fled south after the destruction of the Temple of Jerusalem by Titus in A.D. 70. Theophilus Indus, the most important Christian missionary to southern Arabia, established three churches: at Sanaa, at Aden, and on the Gulf, most probably at Sohar. John, Oman's first bishop, was appointed in the fifth century; Stephen, the last known bishop, was still living in Oman in 676.

The Arabian Social Structure

The core of the social structure that characterized Gulf societies in the twentieth century was well established by the seventh century. Only those families that can trace their origins back to this period are considered noble. Before the advent of oil the typical Gulf society had consisted of a port town and its surrounding hinterland, which may have included scattered farming settlements and nomadic herding groups. In both settled and nomadic society, tribalism provided the framework for social organization. Each major tribe was associated with a territory in which it enjoyed use rights to agricultural land or pasturage and water. Settled tribes dominated villages, and specific lineages within each nomadic tribe owned particular wells and oases where lineage members gathered with their herds during the scorching summer heat. Substantial segments of most lineages lived permanently on the oases, tending the date trees and other food-bearing plants that grew there. Because village farmers also traced ties to tribes, the line between nomads and settled tribes was unclear in many cases and remains so.

In addition to having a territorial structure, a tribe is a complex social unit. Tribal social structure is based on the ramification of patrilineal ties between men. A tribe is a group of related families claiming descent from a supposed founding ancestor. Within this overall loyalty, however, descent from intermediate ancestors defines several levels of smaller groups. In cases of conflict, groups of kinsmen mass at the appropriate level of opposition. For example, the grandsons of brothers form two groups in opposition to each other, but they form one unit in opposition to the descendants of the brother of their common great-grand-father.

Tribal societies consist of larger and larger groups bound by weaker and weaker ties of loyalty. The basic unit of organization is the household. A number of households, supposedly descended from an ancestor about five generations in the past, form the lineage. Four to six lineages combine into a clan, claiming descent from a more distant ancestor. The clan figures most prominently in tribal politics. The tribe, which consists of about seven clans, was formerly the military unit. Each of the fixed descent groups goes by the name of its presumed founder, preceded by *al* (people of) or *bani* (sons of).

The positions of shaykh and amir, though the prerogatives of a particular lineage, are not, strictly speaking, hereditary. The choice of the particular individual who will assume leadership in case of a vacancy is made consensually by the heads of influential families from among candidates who have the requisite descent position. In the past the choice tended to go to a man known for his courage, leadership qualities, and, when relevant, his luck in battle. No one who lacks the requisite ancestry can aspire to tribal leadership, but ancestry alone does not determine the outcome.

Although the vast majority of the population in the typical Gulf society was sedentary, tribalism remained extremely important in the mid-1980s. Most people, whether nomads, villagers, or townsmen, claimed tribal affiliations or at least recognized the validity of such affiliations as the framework for society. The cities grew out of tribal agglomerations, and tribal ties carried considerable weight in social life, even in cities. Many towns were organized into tribal quarters, so that town geography represented social organization.

Islam: Emergence and Development

Unquestionably the event of greatest social, political, and cultural significance for the inhabitants of the Gulf and Oman was the conversion of those populations to Islam late in the seventh century. The discovery and production of oil centuries later transformed the marginally productive medieval city-states of the Gulf at a speed probably unprecedented in history; Islam has remained the bedrock of the societies, however, and modern economic concerns function to a large extent within the legal and cultural framework that is Islam's legacy.

From a religious standpoint the west coast of the Gulf is one of the most varied regions in the Muslim world. Almost every form of Islam currently practiced is represented along the Gulf; from the puritanical austerity of Ibadism to the ornate mysticism of Persian-style Shiism (see Glossary), virtually the entire theological and liturgical gamut is present. In addition, such non-Muslim religions as Hinduism and Christianity count significant numbers of adherents in this heterogeneous cluster of societies.

To state that the Gulf area abounds in religious forms is not to state, however, that each individual society contains the entire spectrum. Political and historical forces, some arising during the early centuries of Islam, have distributed the various denominations among the present-day states in such a way that most political entities display a distinctive array of religious groups. In general terms, however, it is safe to say that Islam is the dominant spiritual, cultural, and, many cases, political influence among the societies of the Gulf.

In 1984 the pervasive influence of Islam in the Gulf societies appeared to be intensifying. A resurgent Islam appeared as a response to a variety of political, economic, and psychological factors affecting Gulf societies in the 1980s. Ulama (see Glossary) and fundamentalist groups pressured governments to make changes implementing a greater measure of Islamic law in their societies. At the same time, the religious rifts that emerged in Islamic society during its early period appeared to be deepening and to be taking on a stronger political coloration than they had in centuries.

Conversion in the Gulf

In the sixth century Mecca was preeminent among the caravan cities that dotted the Hijaz. It owed its status to several factors: the presence of a major pagan pilgrimage center, the Kaabah; an intellectual center, Ukaz, nearby; and the fact that the tribe of the Quraysh, which controlled the town, was sufficiently large to be able to ensure safe passage north to the merchants who patronized them. Recently nomadic, the Quraysh found that the values that had sustained them in the desert, particularly generosity, did not transplant to the more affluent urban setting. In sixth-century Mecca, orphans were starving to death, widows were forced into prostitution, and those from more powerful clans within the Quraysh were able to terrorize weaker ones with relative impunity. Only the rudimentary tribal law, *urf*, offered minimal restraint in a basically lawless society.

In 570 A.D. the prophet of Islam, Muhammad, was born into the tribe of the Quraysh but into a weak clan, the Hashim. Muhammad's father died before his birth, and his mother, Aminah, died when he was six. Muhammad was apparently a sensitive child, humiliated by his low status and by the many privations he suffered as an orphan. He was raised by his grandfather and later by an uncle, Abu Talib, whose son, Ali, would figure prominently in the most significant split in Islam.

Muhammad began to work in the caravan business, quickly earning a reputation for dependability and fairness. At the age of 25 his employer, a wealthy widow named Khadijah, who was 15 years his senior, proposed marriage. The only child who would outlive the Prophet was Khadijah's daughter, Fatima. Muhammad's business trips took him as far north as Syria and as far south as the Yemen, where he met many Christians and Jews. Muhammad was impressed by these people, who possessed holy books that appeared to sustain them in alien environments as well as to offer them ethical guidelines for regulating their lives.

Muhammad's discomfiture concerning the moral malaise of Mecca encouraged him to meditate on these problems. In 610, at the age of 40, when Muhammad was meditating in one of the caves near Mecca, he heard the voice of the angel Gabriel, instructing him to preach the revelations that God, through the angel Gabriel, would give him. The religion Muhammad preached was Islam, which means submission to the will of God. As Muhammad explained it, Islam was not a new religion but rather the continuation and the fulfillment of the Judeo-Christian tradition.

Because Mecca's economy was based in large part on the

thriving pilgrimage business to the Kaabah shrine and to numerous pagan religious sites located there, Muhammad's vigorous and continuing censure of polytheism eventually earned him the bitter enmity of the town's leaders. Ultimately, the Quraysh boycotted Muhammad and his first converts to the extent that they could no longer obtain food supplies. This prompted the removal of the embryonic Muslim community to Yathrib, which came to be known as Medina (from Madinah al Nabi—the Prophet's city) because it became the center of his activities. This move, or hijra (see Glossary), known in the West as the hegira, marks the beginning of the Islamic era and of Islam as a force in history; the Islamic calendar, based on the lunar year, begins at the time of this move in 622. The Islamic calendar dates from the hijra because it was in Medina that for the first time the Muslim community could openly practice its faith. In Medina Muhammad continued to preach, eventually defeated his detractors in battle, and consolidated both the temporal and the spiritual leadership of all Arabia in his person. He entered Mecca in triumph in 630, smashed the idols in the Kaabah—announcing that "truth has come and falsehood has vanished"—and proclaimed that henceforth the Kaabah, stripped of its pagan accoutrements, would be a symbol of the one God. Muhammad returned to Mecca to make the pilgrimage (haj) shortly before his death in 632.

Tenets of Islam

Because of the connection with the Judeo-Christian tradition, Islam shares much of its theology: a belief in one God, creator of heaven and earth; angels; devils; heaven; hell; final Day of Judgment; a resurrection of the body; a divine life of the soul; and individual responsibility for salvation. Most of the prophets of the Old and New Testament are prophets in Islam as well. Particularly revered are those who are considered *hanifs*, true monotheists who preceded Islam, such as Abraham, Moses, Solomon, and Jesus (in Arabic, Ibrahim, Musa, Sulaiman, and Isa, respectively). Jesus, although not considered divine, is regarded as a particularly important prophet, who, according to the Quran, was more powerful than Muhammad because he could heal the sick and raise the dead. Jesus' mother, also highly regarded, is the only woman mentioned by name in the Quran. Muhammad is the "seal of the prophets," meaning there will be no more after him.

All acts prohibited by Christianity are also forbidden in Islam, with the exception that a man may marry up to four wives at one time, providing he can support them well and treat them equally. Gambling and usury are forbidden to Muslims, as is the ingestion of intoxicating substances, pork, carrion, or blood (meaning that all meat must be well cooked).

A Muslim stands in a personal relationship to God. The ulama are those who are distinguished by their knowledge of Islamic law (sharia). Additionally, the performance of the five pillars of the faith is a religious duty; for Sunni (see Glossary) Muslims they are the recitation of the testimony of faith *(shahada)*; daily prayer *(salat)*; almsgiving *(zakat)*; fasting *(sawm)*; and the pilgrimage (haj). Shia (see Glossary) Muslims add holy war (jihad) and "good thoughts, good words, and good deeds."

The *shahada* (literally, testimony) succinctly states the central belief of Islam: "There is no god but God and Muhammad is his messenger (prophet)." The *shahada*, recited in Arabic, is repeated on many ritual occasions. Pronounced with sincerity in the presence of Muslim witnesses, it converts the reciter to Islam. *Salat*, ritual prayer, enjoins the believer to pray after proper ablutions, when the call to prayer is intoned by the *muadhdhin* five times a day. Approximate prayer times are before dawn, late morning, mid-afternoon, before sunset, and evening. Prescribed prayer attitudes and prostrations accompany the prayer, which is always recited in Arabic and facing the direction of Mecca (the *qibla*). Because there is more merit in praying together than alone, men will frequently pray in a mosque (in Arabic, *masjid*, place of prostration). They must do so for the Friday noon prayers, at which time there is a sermon. The great majority of Gulf women pray at home. Shia Gulf women, however, frequently go to their *maatam*, or study centers, for prayer and religious readings during the many Shia holidays.

Zakat is a charity tax of approximately 2 percent of one's wealth paid during the month of Ramadan for the upkeep of charitable institutions. Muslims are also encouraged to make *sadakat*, or free-will gifts. Additionally, many properties contributed by pious individuals to support religious and charitable activities or institutions have traditionally been administered as inalienable religious foundations (waqfs; sing., waqf).

The ninth month of the Muslim calendar is Ramadan, a period of obligatory fasting in commemoration of Muhammad's receipt of God's revelation, the Quran. This is not a penitential fast but is performed to strengthen the believer's compassion and generosity by personally experiencing hunger, thirst, and other deprivations. Throughout the month all but the sick, the weak, pregnant and nursing women, soldiers on duty, travelers on necessary journeys, and children are enjoined from eating, drinking (including water), smoking, and sexual intercourse during the daylight hours. Those excused are obliged to endure an equivalent fast at their earliest opportunity. A festive meal breaks the daily fast and inaugurates a night of feasting and celebration. Because the months of the lunar calendar revolve through the solar year, Ramadan falls at various seasons in different years. Although fasting is a considerable test of discipline at any time of year, a fast that falls in summertime imposes severe hardships on those who must do physical work or travel in the desert. Frayed tempers and poor work performances are annual concomitants of the fast. In all Gulf states the workday is restricted to six hours a day for Muslims, and most businesses close during the afternoon hours, opening again after the daily fasting is completed. The first day following the end of Ramadan is celebrated as a religious holiday, the Id al Fitr.

Finally, at least once in their lifetime all Muslims should, if possible, make the haj to Mecca to participate in special rites held during the twelfth month of the lunar year. The rites relate to the story of Abraham's sacrifice and the tribulations of Hagar (Abraham's Arab concubine) and Ismail (Ishmael—Abraham's firstborn son) in the wilderness. In Islam it is Ismail, the son by Hagar, whom Abraham offers for sacrifice. On the tenth of the month, pilgrims (hajis) sacrifice and cook an animal, give half to the poor, and consume the remainder in honor of Abraham's sacrifice. The day of sacrifice is the most important religious holiday for Muslims, called in Arabic Id al Adha, the Great Feast, or Id al Qurban, the Feast of the Sacrifice. The day celebrates the compassionate God who requires nothing difficult of man. The haj as a whole serves to remind hajis that Muslims come from all ethnic groups and economic conditions. Because the haj rituals can only be performed in Arabic, the language acts to unify Islam's diverse members.

The Gulf During the Medieval Period

Arabia had become unified, but ironically it had to be virtually emptied to ensure unification. As in the great migrations of the past, Arabia in the immediate post-Muhammad period once again fed its people into the surrounding areas. Peasants were easier to control than refractory tribes, and the social structure and the agricultural assets of the conquered land outside the peninsula encouraged permanent settlements that were necessary in any case to secure Islamic rule. Thus, Islamic politics moved from Arabia to Damascus and, in the period between the ministry of Muhammad and the discovery of oil, Arabia became an economic backwater except for trade on the Gulf, which increased for the Arabs as the Muslim conquest expanded. Nevertheless, because Arabia was considered the homeland of the Arabs and because Mecca and Medina—Islam's holiest cities—were there, it could not be ignored. Pilgrims who made the haj had to be afforded some protection. Furthermore, control of the holy cities gave a ruler instant prestige. The political unit that kept the Hijaz secure was usually Egyptian based, and Egypt was also the source of much of the Hijazi food supply. Islamic rulers in Damascus paid off religious leaders in Arabia who might cause trouble. Arabia became a frontier zone from which political rivals emerged. During the various struggles for religious and political supremacy in Damascus and later in Baghdad, Mecca and Medina became sites for the opposition, and both cities were virtually destroyed in the tumult that ensued. For the most part social organization in Arabia continued as it had been before Muhammad's unification.

During the centuries between the Islamic conquest of the Gulf area and the founding of the modern polities in the eighteenth century, the focus of political activity was coastal. Natural resources consisted chiefly of dates, pearls, and camels. Those items were insufficient to supply even the minimal needs of the population, and the people early turned to maritime activities, imitating their Omani neighbors to the south. Favored by the Gulf's position at the center of the medieval trading route network, maritime city-states developed and vied for the trade through the Gulf.

The golden age of Gulf shipping began in the eighth century with the establishment of the Abbasid caliphate (750–1258) in Baghdad. The general economic revival in the Middle East and Europe during the eighth century and the unification of China under the Tang Dynasty during the previous century were chiefly responsible for the acceleration of trade. But the Gulf was particularly favored—over the Red Sea, for instance—because of Baghdad's position due north of the Gulf. The intrepid merchant sailors of the area went as far as China. In the middle of the eight century an Omani, Abu Ubaydah, made the first recorded round-trip from the Gulf to Canton. In incredibly flimsy but capacious boats built of local materials, Gulf Arabs regularly followed the monsoons and sailed yearly between the major centers of civilization of the medieval world.

The city of Siraf on the Iranian side of the Gulf was the

paramount trading city between 900 and 1100. The accelerated movements of the Seljuk Turks into Iraq and Iran between 1055 and 1155 contributed to Siraf's decline when the Seljuks attacked it from land and sea. Further, by the eleventh century the rise of the Fatimid caliphate in Egypt had siphoned off much of the Gulf trade and redirected it through the Red Sea. Between 1100 and 1300 Qais, an island 16 kilometers off the Iranian coast, succeeded Siraf as the chief collection and distribution emporium in the Gulf. Finally, in the late thirteenth century Hormuz became the chief center; it remained so until 1507, when it was destroyed by the Portuguese. Hormuz' reputation as a place of riches was so legendary that more than a century after its destruction Milton used it in *Paradise Lost:* "High on a Throne of Royal State, which far outshone the wealth of Ormus and of Ind, or where the gorgeous East with richest hand Show'rs on her Kings Barbaric Pearl and Gold, Satan exalted sat."

During the period of Hormuz' flourishing, Sohar and Muscat in Oman prospered greatly from their strategic position on the Gulf of Oman near the entrance to the Persian Gulf. During the early Islamic period, although the main trading cities were on the Iranian coast, Arabs were usually the towns' rulers. When there was a strong and well-organized Iranian government, they paid tribute; otherwise, they ruled quite independently. The presence of Iranians in Oman and Arabs in Iranian territory produced the ethnic mixture still prevailing on the Gulf's coasts and led to Iranian claims to islands in the Gulf and to parts of its western shore.

Internal Organization

The maritime city-states of the Gulf differed from those of other cultures in that political rule did not derive from an originally oligarchic, settled merchant class with a long history of urban living and urban institutions. The orientation of the Gulf city-states was based on the traditional political model of the desert Arabs. Usually, the dominant tribe in the area produced the city's rulers; the shaykh who ruled the tribe was the town's leader and often its most affluent merchant. The shaykh's main objects were to secure peaceful internal conditions so that trading would not be disrupted and to secure profits sufficient to maintain his own position. The ruler's income was derived from licenses for trade and pearl fishing, customs duties, and the taxation on such commodities as date palms, all of which were secondary in importance to the profits he made as a result of his own commercial transactions. The shaykh secured his political primacy by payments to his military forces, usually fellow tribesmen; tribute to larger and potentially troublemaking neighboring states; and a variety of subsidies to those in a position to challenge his authority. As has been the case for much of the Gulf's modern history, the total income of a city was the shaykh's private purse to dispense privately or in the public interest according to his discretion. The shaykh would attempt to placate nomadic tribes close to the city and to guarantee their cooperation, that is, to encourage their hiring for seasonal activities in the city in order to discourage them from making sporadic attacks on townspeople. City dwellers not directly engaged in trade dived for pearls during the season or cultivated the few arable acres on the city's periphery.

The urban institutions that existed were not the result of the ruler's initiative but were those ordained by sharia. Because of the comprehensive nature of sharia, certain protections and rights were available to the citizens, as were certain restrictions. Common tribal law, *urf*, was also a conspicuous element in the regulation of daily life but usually did not conflict with sharia.

Because rule was based on the patriarchal desert model, however, the fortunes of a city depended greatly on the strength and astuteness of its ruler. When Gulf trade experienced moments of decline, competition between cities was sufficiently fierce to provoke intertribal and intercity violence that usually took the form of piracy on the sea and produced internal confusion at home. If a weak ruler succeeded a strong one, he was soon overthrown; rapid changes in the ruling family became the norm. The flux of political configurations in the Gulf city-states was emblematic of the area until the eighteenth-century founding of the modern polities and the eventual protection of their vested interests by the European maritime powers, particularly the British.

The Early Period

During his lifetime Muhammad held both spiritual and temporal leadership of the Muslim community; he established the concept of Islam as a total and all-encompassing way of life for man and society. Islam teaches that God revealed to Muhammad the immutable principles governing decent behavior; it is therefore incumbent on the individual to live in the manner prescribed by revealed law and on the community to perfect human society on earth according to the holy injunctions. Islam traditionally recognized no distinction between religion and state; religious and secular life merged, as did religious and secular law. Muhammad appeared, however, to have left no mechanism for selection of subsequent leaders.

After Muhammad's death in 632 the leaders of the Muslim community consensually chose Abu Bakr, the father of the Prophet's favorite living wife, Aisha, and one of his earliest followers, to succeed him. At that time some persons favored Ali, who, besides being a member of the Hashimite lineage, was the Prophet's cousin and the husband of his daughter, Fatima. Ali and his supporters (called the Shiat Ali, or party of Ali) eventually recognized the community's choice, but only after Fatima's death. The next two caliphs (from *khalifa,* successor)—Umar, who succeeded in 634, and Uthman, who took power in 646—enjoyed the recognition of the entire community.

Dissatisfaction with the rule of Uthman began to mount in various parts of the Islamic empire, however. For example, the codification of the Quran, which took place under Uthman, hurt the interests of the professional Quran reciters. Some, such as those at Al Kufah in present-day Iraq, refused to accept this reform. Others accused Uthman of nepotism. Although himself an early Muslim, Uthman came from the Banu Umayyah lineage of the Quraysh, whose members had been Muhammad's main detractors in Mecca and had resisted him for a long time. The appointment of many members of this house to official posts caused resentment among those who had claims based on earlier loyalty. Still others objected to corruption in financial arrangements under Uthman's caliphate.

Ali, his claim to the caliphate frustrated, became a perfect focus for dissatisfaction. In 656 disgruntled soldiers killed Uthman. After the ensuing five years of civil war, known in Islamic history as *fitnah* (trials), the caliphate finally devolved on Ali. But Aisha, who had long been a bitter foe of Fatima and Ali, objected, demanding that Uthman's killing be avenged and his killers punished by the Hashimites. She helped rally opposition to Ali's caliphate.

The killers insisted that Uthman, by ruling unjustly, had relinquished his right to be caliph and deserved to die. Ali, whose political position depended on their action and their support, was forced to side with them. From his capital at Al Kufah he refused to reprimand the killers.

At this point Muawiyah, the governor of Syria and a member of the Banu Umayyah, refused to recognize Ali's authority and called for revenge for his murdered kinsman, Uthman. Ali attacked, but the ensuing Battle of Siffin was inconclusive.

Muawiyah's soldiers advanced with copies of the Quran on their spears, thus calling symbolically for God to decide or for the question to be submitted to arbitration. Ali agreed to this settlement, and each side selected an arbitrator.

Some of Ali's supporters, however, rejected the notion that the caliph, the Prophet's successor and head of the community, should submit to the authority of others. By so doing, they reasoned, he effectively relinquished his authority as caliph. They argued that, according to Quranic teaching, rebels must be brought to obedience by force; arbitrating the dispute with the rebellious Muawiyah was therefore wrong. They further argued that the question of Uthman's right to rule had been settled by war during the *fitnah*. When Ali insisted on his course, this group, which came to be known as the Kharadjites (those who seceded), withdrew to Harura near Al Kufah and chose their own leader.

The arbitration went against Ali in 658. He refused to accept the decision but did not renounce the principle of arbitration. At this point the Kharadjites became convinced that personal interest, not principle, motivated Ali. His support dwindled among all elements of his followers. He tried to attack Syria, but Muawiyah repulsed him. Ali also engaged in numerous battles with the Kharadjites, including a massacre at Nahrawan in which most of them were killed. In revenge for the slaying of his wife's family in this raid, the Kharadjite Abd ar Rahman ibn Muljam al Muradi murdered Ali in 661.

Ali's death ended the last of the so-called four orthodox caliphates and the period when the entire community of Islam recognized a single head. Muawiyah then proclaimed himself caliph from Damascus. The Shiat Ali, however, refused to recognize Muawiyah or the Umayyad line. They withdrew and in the major schism of Islam proclaimed Hassan, Ali's son, the caliph. Hassan, however, eventually relinquished his claim in favor of Muawiyah and went to live in Medina, supported by wealth apparently supplied by Muawiyah.

The claims of the Alid line and its supporters did not end here. In 680 Yazid succeeded to the caliphate while his father, Muawiyah, was still alive. Ali's younger son, Husayn, refused to recognize the succession and revolted at Al Kufah. He was unable to gain widespread support and was killed, along with a small band of his soldiers, at Karbala in present-day Iraq in 680. To the Shia, Husayn then became a martyred hero—the tragic reminder of the lost glories of the Alid line and the repository of the special claim by the Prophet's family of presumptive right to the caliphate. The political victor of this second period of *fitnah* was Marwar of the Umayyad line, but Husayn's death aroused increased interest among his supporters, enhanced by feelings of guilt and remorse and a desire for revenge.

Although they did not gain political preeminence in the world Muslim community, supporters of the Alid cause became if anything more fervent in their beliefs. As they had since the earliest days of the caliphate, Ali and his family served as a lightning rod for discontent. With continued conquests the number of Muslims from non-Arab cultural backgrounds grew. It was inevitable that their religious values, quite foreign to the austere faith born in the Arabian desert, should demand some outlet. In the words of Israel Friedlaender, an authority on Shia history, the Alid cause permitted conquered peoples to "smuggle into Islam some of their most cherished ideas which were essentially un-Islamic and for the most part even anti-Islamic." By this he means that they contradicted the strict, rationalist monotheism of early Islam.

The Shia founded their objections to the Umayyad and later non-Shia caliphs on the notion that members of the house of Muhammad, through Ali, were most appropriate successors to his position as both political leader and, more important, imam or prayer leader. Many believed that Ali, as a close associate, early had a special insight into the Prophet's teachings and habits. In addition, many felt that he deserved the post because of his personal merits and, indeed, that the Prophet had expressed a wish that Ali succeed him. In times these views became transformed for many Shia into an almost mystical reverence for the spiritual superiority of Ali's line. Some Shia also believe that Muhammad had left a written will naming Ali as his successor but that it had been destroyed by Ali's enemies, who then usurped leadership.

Because the correct selection of the imam was the crucial issue over which the Shia departed from the main body of Sunni Islam, the choice of later successors also became a matter of conflict. Disagreements over which of several pretenders had the true claim to the mystical power of Ali precipitated further schisms.

The early political rivalry remained active as well. Shiism eventually gained political dominance in Iraq and Iran, as well as in present-day Yemen (Sanaa); Shia are also numerous in Syria and are found in small numbers in most present-day Muslim countries. They constitute more than half the Muslim population of Bahrain.

The early Islamic polity was intensely expansionist, fueled

both by fervor for the new religion and by economic and social factors. Conquering armies and migrating tribes swept out of Arabia. By the end of Islam's first century, Islamic armies had reached far into North Africa and eastward and northward into Asia.

Although Muhammad had enjoined the Muslim community to convert the infidel, he had also recognized the special status of the People of the Book—Jews and Christians—whose revealed scriptures he considered contributory to Islam. These peoples, approaching but not having achieved the perfection of Islam, were spared the choice offered the pagan—conversion or death. Jews and Christians in Muslim territories could live according to their own religious law and in their own communities. This status entailed recognition of Muslim authority, a special tax *(jizya)*, and prohibition of proselytization among Muslims.

The first centuries of Islam saw the community grow from a small and despised cult to a powerful empire ruling vast domains. This time also saw the evolution of the sharia, a comprehensive system of religious law, to regulate life in the community. Derived from the Quran and the hadith (see Glossary) by various systems of reasoning, four schools of religious law—the Hanafi, Shafii, Maliki, and Hanbali—are generally recognized; each orthodox Muslim theoretically acknowledges the authority of one of them.

With the passage of centuries Islam gradually absorbed influences from sources other than the prophetic revelation. Bands of mystics, or Sufis (from *suf*, wool, referring to their rough clothing), sprang up in various countries, claiming to achieve communion with God through various ecstatic or irregular means. Sufi orders gradually arose among both Sunnis and Shiites, and recognized leaders taught particular mystic ways to experience union with God. Sufism gained acceptance in large parts of the Islamic world. In most regions people fell away from the singularly austere cult preached by the Prophet Muhammad and adopted practices that softened it and made it more personal and emotional.

Sufi religious life generally centers on orders, or brotherhoods, that follow a leader, or shaykh, who teaches a mystical discipline known as a *tariqa* (way). Such aids to achieving ecstasy as whirling, dancing, and music figure prominently in many Sufi orders.

The Ibadi Movement

Present-day Ibadis, the dominant religious group of Oman,

continue the tradition of the moderate wing of the Kharadjite movement. Found in North and East Africa and Iran as well as in Oman, they are the world's only remaining Kharadjites.

Soon after their withdrawal to Harura, the Kharadjites elected Abdallah ibn Wahb al Rasib as their leader. Others joined the group in fair numbers, especially after the results of the arbitration became known. A substantial body of people left Al Kufah, where Ali's army had camped during the arbitration truce, and joined the Kharadjite camp, now on the Nahrawan canal. After Ali's devastating raid on Nahrawan in 658, the Kharadjite opposition continued in scattered uprisings.

In the face of continued violence and fanaticism among their fellows, some Kharadjites adopted a quietist position, opposing the indiscriminate continuation of holy war. Abu Bilal Midras ibn Udaiya al Tamimi was leader of this group by 670. After his murder in 681 leadership of the moderates eventually passed to Abdallah ibn Ibad al Murri al Tamimi. Little is known of the life of the man from whom Ibadism took its name except that in 683 he and his father came from Najd in present-day Saudi Arabia to help defend Mecca against a general of Caliph Yazid. Late in that year Ibn Ibad traveled to Basrah in present-day Iraq, where a sizable body of Kharadjites had settled. Basran followers of the Kharadjite leader Nafi bin Azraq, who were known as Azraqis, left Basrah to help in the defense of Mecca, but Ibn Ibad, his adherents, and other moderates remained in Basrah. A split in the moderate ranks occurred when Abdallah ibn al Saffar, leader of a group known as the Sufris, asserted that non-Kharadjite Muslims should be viewed as *mushrikun*(polytheists). Ibn Ibad rejected this notion, and the Sufris left Basrah.

The Kharadjites lost political control of Basrah, and the Ibadis entered a state of *kitman* (concealment) during which Ibn Ibad headed what scholars have described as a shadow government. By the end of Islam's first century, however, the growing radicalism of the Ibadis of Basrah had so alienated the governor that he banished the sect—now headed by Ibn Ibad's successor, the Omani scholar Djibir bin Zaid al Azdi—to Oman on the Gulf. Even in the early days of Kharadjism, followers of Abu Bilal had lived in Oman. The arrival of Djibir bin Zaid and other important scholars greatly increased Ibadi influence in Oman, and Nazwa became a religious center.

Little is known of the doctrines of the early Ibadis. Contemporary Ibadis, like other Kharadjites, feel obliged by Quranic doctrine to elect their leader, or imam. Unlike other Muslims, they do not restrict the choice of leaders to members of the

*Fort Jalali, on harbor near Muscat, Oman,
built by Portuguese in fifteenth and sixteenth centuries*

Quraysh or descendants of Ali but believe that any worthy Muslim may be elevated to leadership, regardless of ancestry. They also feel an obligation to overthrow an imam who acts improperly. As a consequence they accept as legitimate the caliphates of Abu Bakr and Umar, the first seven years of the rule of Uthman, and the rule of Ali only until the arbitration. They accept none of the Umayyad caliphs.

Selection of the imam, who acts as religious and military leader and judge, is the responsibility of the community's scholars, as is the power to depose a leader who rules improperly. As long as he follows the Quran and Sunna, however, an imam has absolute power. Removal of an imam accused of improper behavior requires the supposed wrongdoer to meet with the ulama, who determine whether grounds for the accusations exist. If the imam is found to be at fault, he is offered the opportunity to repent. Failure to do so results in removal from office.

In their relations with other Muslims, Ibadis adopt one of two attitudes: *wilaya* (friendship and cooperation) with those they regard as true believers and *baraa* (hostility) toward all others. Unlike other Kharadjites, however, they regard non-Kharadjite Muslims as *kuffar* (infidels; sing., *kafir*) rather than as *mushri-kun*. Consequently, they do not permit killing of other Muslims on solely religious grounds. Ibadi doctrines even permit marriage with non-Ibadi Muslims.

The Ibadi community can exist in one of several states determined by the ulama. The state of *kitman* occurs during periods of persecution, when individual Ibadis are free to practice *taqiyya* (religious dissimulation) to hide their true religion and thus save their lives. In the state of *difa* (danger) a special *imam al difa* is appointed to lead the defense. When the Ibadis count themselves half as strong as their adversaries in men, arms, supplies, and so forth, they may pass into the state of *zuhur* (manifestation), at which time an imam is openly elected.

The Ibadis are also distinguished by a strict and puritanical ethical code that rejects frivolity and all innovations in worship. Though ascetic, they nevertheless accept mysticism. Commission of a capital sin removes one from the community of good Muslims and places him among the despised *kuffar*.

The Entrance of the Europeans into the Gulf

The Portuguese

Although Gulf Arabs, particularly the Omanis, had a virtual monopoly on East-West trade, European powers early entered the competition. The Venetians made a commercial treaty with the Abbasid caliph in Baghdad and had business centers in Damascus and Aleppo. When Fatimid Egypt became the predominant Muslim power in the twelfth century, the Venetians established themselves in Alexandria and, in exchange for spices and other Eastern delicacies, supplied the Fatimids with munitions, wood, and slaves. The Genoese to a lesser extent also benefited from Arab trading routes established with the East, but by the fourteenth century they were forced to reduce their trading commitments. The Venetians then were the sole corporate link between the Muslim world and Europe until the end of the fifteenth century.

The capture of Constantinople by the Ottomans in 1453 limited Venetian trade to the Red Sea, but the final blow to their Eastern trading activities was delivered by the Portuguese, who entered the Indian Ocean in the last years of the fifteenth century. Vasco da Gama sojourned at many Arab colonies on the east coast of Africa during his voyage in 1497. At Malindi he requested a noted Arab navigator, Ahmad ibn Majid, to sail him to Calicut. Thus familiarized with the vagaries of the monsoons and coastal hazards, the Portuguese were able to divert eastern trade around the Cape of Good Hope to the Mediterranean.

The chief object of the Portuguese venture was to monopolize the trade in spices and other Eastern luxuries to which the Portuguese had become accustomed during the Muslim occupations. The crusading mentality also figured in the Portuguese exploration. At least that is one explanation for the wholesale atrocities committed by da Gama on unarmed pilgrims making their way to Mecca. The Portuguese were by no means supported in their ventures by the Christian West. The Venetians, whose commercial interests were also damaged, allied in vain with the Egyptians against the Portuguese. The king of Portugal, bearing the title "Lord of the Conquest, Navigation, and Commerce of India, Ethiopia, Arabia, and Persia," sent Francisco de Almeida to act as governor of the Portuguese settlements in the East. In 1506 Alfonso de Albuquerque started on his journey to India, where he replaced de Almeida as viceroy and governor of India.

Before reaching India, Albuquerque secured the Portuguese position in the Gulf. He had been given instructions to obstruct Egyptian and Venetian trade in the Red Sea, but he was aware that to blockade the Red Sea effectively he first had to secure a position in the Gulf. He seized the island of Socotra in the Arabian Sea as a convenient midway point. After destroying every Arab ship in his compass, he captured Kalhut, Qurayyat, Muscat, Suhar, Khor Fakkan, and finally Hormuz, the premier city of Gulf trade. The first of a series of Portuguese forts to be strung along the lower Gulf was erected at Hormuz. Albuquerque's initial stay at Hormuz was very short. Troubled by fractious Portuguese crews, he resumed his voyage to India, and Hormuz was temporarily abandoned. Because it was too strategic a position to be neglected for long, Hormuz was retaken by the Portuguese in 1515.

The Portuguese set the example to be followed by the English in not interfering with local rule. After a series of local uprisings when the Portuguese attempted to administer the customhouses directly, a treaty between the shaykh of Hormuz and the Portuguese was signed on July 23, 1523, at Minab. The shaykh of Hormuz thereby not only was "protected" by the Portuguese but also was under their direct control. However, the shaykh was confirmed in controlling the internal affairs of Hormuz and the other Gulf states under his suzerainty. In 1538 and 1550 the Turks made sporadic attempts, often with local assistance, to dislodge the Portuguese. Portuguese control remained firm, however, until the early seventeenth century, when a combination of factors made their position untenable.

Dutch and English Involvement

In the late sixteenth century Holland and England began to investigate the possibilities of their countries' involvement with Gulf trading activities. John Newberrie of London visited Hormuz in 1580 and returned there three years later with Ralph Fitch. The Dutch decision to raise the price of pepper by almost threefold caused great consternation in English mercantile circles. After Fitch published a memoir of his Gulf visit, London merchants were sufficiently encouraged to form the East India Company in 1600.

The English venture coincided fortuitously with the accession to the Iranian throne in 1587 of Shah Abbas I, who decided that the Portuguese presence on the coast of his dominions was a severe irritation. The Portuguese had never distinguished themselves by diplomatic niceties in the Gulf and had steadfastly refused to pay the relatively small tribute that Iran had always demanded of those who ruled its Gulf trading towns. In 1602 Shah Abbas evicted the Portuguese from Bahrain, and between 1608 and 1615 he tried ineffectually to drive them from Hormuz. During those years the English had slowly been acquiring prestige and making friends at the Iranian court. Sir Anthony Sherley and his brother Robert had entered the private service of the shah in 1600. When in 1617 Edward Connack carried a letter to the shah from King James I asking for support for the East India Company, he was extremely well received. The shah promised them the port of Jashk from which to trade, granted the English sole control of all silk leaving Iranian ports, and provided for the permanent presence of an English ambassador at court.

The Portuguese, who were experiencing increasing difficulties in maintaining their position—in part because of their annexation by Spain in 1581—attempted unsuccessfully to block the ships of the East India Company from entering the Iranian port of Jashk. In 1622 an English-Iranian attack on the Portuguese garrison at Hormuz and a post on the island of Qeshm resulted in victory and an agreement that customs collected in Qeshm and Hormuz would be shared by the Iranians and the East India Company. The English established their headquarters at Bandar

Abbas, which became the center for political and commercial activities in the Gulf for the next 150 years.

Total reclamation of Portuguese-held areas was slow but inevitable. The Iranians reclaimed Khor Fakkan and held it for one year; the Portuguese then recaptured it but were ousted by Arab troops under the leadership of the first imam of the Yaruba Dynasty in Oman, Nasir bin Murshid. In 1643 Nasir took Sohar, and by 1650 the Portuguese were coerced to abandon Muscat. Only Kunj in southern Iran was left to them.

The Dutch presence in the Gulf lasted only 133 years but was extraordinary lucrative for them. The United Dutch East India Company, formed shortly after its English equivalent, was the first public corporation in the world, that is, the first to offer issued shares of ownership in a general public offering, and this undoubtedly contributed to its initial success. Stockholders at home put continued pressure on the Dutch government to support the company's activities, whereas the English East India Company had at first to depend entirely on its own resources. The Dutch were given organizational support in the Gulf by the English in return for Dutch assistance in an anti-Portuguese military engagement in 1625. The Dutch, too, used Bandar Abbas as their center. The Dutch had a much wider trading network than the English because of their earlier development of East Asian trade, and consequently they prospered much more. An English-Dutch war in Europe (1653–54) was extended to the Gulf, and the English incurred severe losses. Mercantile supremacy passed to the Dutch, and by 1680 their strong presence in both Basrah and Bandar Abbas secured the Gulf as a "Dutch lake." The English bided their time, and the decline of Holland in the eighteenth century progressively diluted Dutch influence in the Gulf. Bandar Abbas was relinquished in 1759, and, when Kharg Island was abandoned in 1765, the Dutch presence was effectively ended in the Gulf (see fig. 3).

Piracy

From the end of the seventeenth century until 1778, chaos reigned in the Gulf. Piracy was a long-established tradition, recorded from Assyrian times. In the modern period the Arabs, particularly the Omanis, were the first pirates to attain general notoriety. It is doubtful whether the word *pirate* can be used as a designation for people using the only means at hand to defend their land from foreign occupation and therefore exploitation, but such was the name given by Europeans who themselves were exceed-

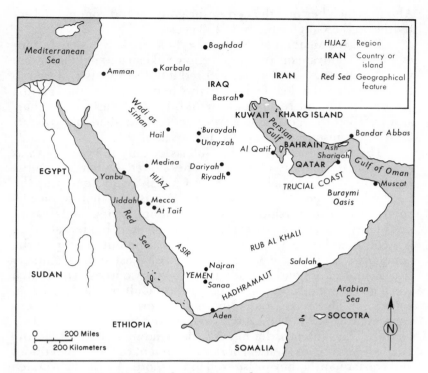

Figure 3.   The Gulf in the Nineteenth Century

ly active in piracy in the Gulf and elsewhere.

Negative contacts of the English with the Dutch and briefly with the French added to the general instability. By 1688, even though piracy had by no means reached its apogee in the Gulf, it was unthinkable that the English could maintain a solely commercial presence there and survive. The English government therefore ceded the island of Bombay to the East India Company. The English were to protect Portuguese holdings in the East Indies in return for their evacuation of the island. To protect themselves and their commitments to the Portuguese, the company was permitted to organize a civil administration and to acquire troops. The East India Company merged with "new" companies in 1708 to form the United Company of the Merchants of England Trading to the East Indies.

Residents   representing   the   conglomerate   had   consular power and rank. Presumably either to increase incentive or to encourage loyalty, residents were required to invest their personal financial resources in some aspect of trade. This caused complications when personal interests deviated from company policy.

Ineffectual as these measures were, they set a precedent for further political and military establishments in the area. By 1763 British merchants were very much in need of such establishments. From the end of the Safavi Dynasty in Iran in 1722, a period of almost unbroken internal chaos and anarchy had prevailed, and Bandar Abbas was definitely unsafe. With the consent of the shah at the time, Karim Khan Zand, the company moved its center to Basrah, and a new trading post was formed at Bushire (present-day Bushehr). Karim gave the company freedom from taxation and the sole right to import woolens into Iran and assured the company that no other European power would be permitted to establish a port there. The Bushire Residency became autonomous in 1778, and the British Residency in the Gulf, dating from that event, remained headquartered at Bushire until it was moved to Bahrain in 1946.

The Founding of the Modern Gulf Polities: Gulf States in the Eighteenth and Nineteenth Centuries

While the British were relocating their trading posts and solidifying their relationship with Iran, the Gulf Arabs were involved in a highly turbulent period of mass migrations to the north and central parts of the Gulf, local wars, a major religious movement, and civil war in Oman. Because of the hitherto unstable political rule in Arabia and because the Arab tribes of the peninsula had never seemed able to remain united long enough to inflict long-term damage to European interests, little attention was paid initially to events that proved to be momentous.

The Wahhabi Movement

As a result of its isolation, central Arabia became a backwater after the movement of the Islamic capital from Medina to Damascus. Coastal events hardly penetrated Najd (in which modern Riyadh is located) in central Arabia. Although the population was Muslim, pre-Islamic practices reappeared. People in the Arabian Peninsula, particularly in the interior, resumed veneration of trees and stones, though maintaining their identification with the Muslim community.

Various holy men, especially those who claimed descent from the prophet, achieved reputation for exceptional spiritual or magical powers. Pre-Islamic beliefs in the inheritance of special spiritual powers in certain family lines blended smoothly into popular Islam. Stories of holy men circulated, and people began visiting these individuals or their graves to seek cures, fulfillment of wishes, or other favors.

Such practices were viewed with particular abhorrence by a religious scholar born in 1703 in the town of Unaynah in Najd. A descendant of generations of Hanbali qadis (religious judges), Muhammad bin Abd al Wahhab followed the family tradition of religious studies and traveled to Medina, Basrah, and Damascus, among other places. Even as a young man he showed signs of unusually extreme orthodoxy. Having studied widely and having reportedly dabbled in Sufism, he returned to his native town, where his family was prominent. There he began to preach his own views based on the teachings of the controversial and extremely conservative Hanbali legal scholar Taki al Din Ahmad bin Taimiya, whose ideas went far beyond the Hanbali norm in strictness and literalness of interpretation. Like his spiritual mentor, Abd al Wahhab attracted unfavorable reaction because of the unusual severity of his teachings. He eventually left Unaynah with his considerable household and property and was received into the village of Dariyah, which was ruled by Muhammad bin Saud.

Abd al Wahhab quickly put into effect Taimiya's teaching that the ulama should combine with the *umara* (powerholders; sing., amir) to create a true Muslim society. In 1744 he and Saud concluded a pact stating that the Al Saud (House of Saud) would adopt, fight for, and propagate the Wahhabi doctrines and that in all conquered territory the Al Saud would hold political power and the Al ash Shaykh would hold religious power. (In this usage *Al* means "house of" or "family of.") Thus came into being the partnership that harnessed Wahhabi religious fervor to Saudi dynastic expansionism and that resulted immediately in the creation of a kingdom in Najd and eventually in the development of the modern state of Saudi Arabia.

Abd al Wahhab took a literalist view of the Quran and, like Taimiya before him, believed that the absolute and incomparable unity of God was the core of true Islam. Thus, the worst sin was *shirk*, the association of anything with God or the worship of anything besides him; such practices and beliefs denied God's basic nature. An important cause of *shirk*, Abd al Wahhab believed, was the adoption of *bida* (innovations)—practices not sanctioned by the Prophet or his followers earlier than the third century of

Islam. Some of these supposed innovations in fact predated Islam, but Abd al Wahhab denounced them as ungodly later accretions. Prominent among them were the customs of visiting saints and tombs and the veneration of trees and rocks. Forbidden *bida* also included rendering improper honor to the Prophet Muhammad, as well as the custom of celebrating his birthday. Particularly forbidden was the invocation of the names of the Prophet or of saints in prayer in the hope that they would intercede with God. The Wahhabis believed that, although Muhammad can intercede with God, he does so not in answer to specific requests but only in the case of an exemplary believer.

All special relationships with God are absolutely rejected, whether they involve Sufis, saints, or Shia imams, as are all ecstatic practices believed to foster such relationships. Access to God is provided only through prayer and obedience to duty, and that access is equal for all true believers. Abd al Wahhab accepted such Hanbali beliefs as the literal truth of the Quran, the ungodliness of knowledge not derived from it or the hadith, and the predestination of human events. He went beyond Hanbali teachings, however, in rejecting smoking, shaving, and strong language; requiring rather than merely encouring attendance at public prayer; enforcing payment of *zakat* on so-called secret profits; demanding evidence of good character in addition to acceptance of beliefs for admission to the Muslim community; and forbidding minarets, embellishments of tombs, and such aids to prayer as the rosary. He also insisted on strict enforcement of the sumptuary laws established by the Prophet and banned activities he deemed godless frivolity, such as music and dancing.

Unity for Abd al Wahhab implied not only the absolute oneness of God but also the absolute singularity of the believer's devotion. The sole duty of human life is to serve and obey God with a resignation that accepts what comes as God's will. Service, furthermore, must be rendered strictly according to God's law. The believer's spiritual zeal thus combines with punctilious obedience to form total submission to God. In the words of Henri Laost, an authority on Hanbali law, Wahhabism implies "the most perfect sincerity placed at the service of the law."

For Abd al Wahhab any other approach to God constituted *shirk*. Worse even than non-Muslims were Muslims of other sects or schools; by claiming to follow the true religion of God while practicing polytheism, Abd al Wahhab believed, they practiced hypocrisy. The duty of the good Muslim was to stamp out such mockeries of true religion. As they gained power, therefore, the Wahhabis proved to be iconoclasts. In 1801 they shocked much of the Muslim world, for example, by defacing the tomb of the martyr Husayn at Karbala, a particularly holy shrine to the Shia.

A Wahhabi does not practice his religion as an isolated individual. Like other Muslims, Abd al Wallab viewed the community as the ideal vehicle for enforcement of God's law. Law is the acting out of faith; Islam is the fulfillment of law. Wahhabis interpret the concept of jihad to include the obligation of the community to enforce the law and the reciprocal obligation of the believer to obey the constituted authority of the Wahhabi imam except where such obedience would lead to straying from the law. The leader, therefore, has the right and duty to prevent sin, frivolity, and indecency and to enforce such ritual acts as fasting, attendance at prayer, and payments of *zakat*.

Within their communities Wahhabis believe in the social equality of believers. The only permissible social distinction is between "true" Muslims and others. A Wahhabi ideally strives for the perfection of the example of the Prophet and his contemporaries, who are viewed as the noblest and most perfect of human beings. The followers of Abd al Wahhab regard his teachings so highly that they refer to the period before him as *jahaliyah* (ignorance), the term generally used within the broader Muslim community to refer to the period before Islam.

This should not be taken to imply that Abd al Wahhab's followers in any way equate him with the Prophet. Rather than preaching anything new, he sought to return Muslims to the true religion and to the *al salaf al salih* (ways of the pious ancestors). No serious scholar of Islam has accused Abd al Wahhab of heresy. Like Muhammad, however, Abd al Wahhab provided religious justification for a political movement that sought to sweep away tribal distinctions and to bind all Arabia into a unity based on religion.

After the initial successes of Saud and his immediate successors, the Wahhabi movement went into political decline until the beginning of the twentieth century and the rise of Saud's descendant, Abd al Aziz, who was sometimes referred to as Ibn Saud. A gifted leader, he harnessed religious fervor to political ambition and forged the modern nation of Saudi Arabia under the banner of the Wahhabi cause.

Internal Migrations and Political Developments

Kuwait and Bahrain

An unusually long drought that began in 1722 and the accompanying famine in the Alflaj region of Najd in central Arabia pre-

Pottery worker
Manama, Bahrain
Courtesy Aramco
World Magazine

cipitated a major migration of Arab tribes of the Adnani-Anayzah confederation, including the Utub (adjective, Utbi), to the north coastal lands of the Gulf. The area was under the domination of the Bani Khalid, whose suzerainty extended from Basrah in the north inland to the eastern part of Najd and south beyond Al Hasa to Qatar.

The Utub had for a long time been under the protection of the Bani Khalid and regularly grazed their flocks in Al Hasa. The Utub were well received, and they settled at a small town they began to call Kuwait, the diminutive of the Arabic *kut*, a fortress built near water. Kuwait did not have much to recommend it. It was almost entirely without agricultural resources and lacked a nearby source of potable water. In comparison with the rest of Bani Khalid territory, however, it had a mild climate. Further, Al Hasa, the destination of many of the migrating Anayzah tribes, was quickly becoming overcrowded.

The most influential tribe of the Utub were the Al Sabah, but they were not the only Utub to settle Kuwait. The Al Khalifa and Al Jalahima were the next in importance; at least seven other families or clans emigrated there, although not simultaneously. The town was divided into three sections, and the Al Sabah controlled all from the *wasat*, or central quarters. The exact date of the Utbi settlement is unknown. It was certainly early in the eighteenth century but probably later than 1716, a commonly given date, since neither the Al Sabah nor the Al Khalifa were clan chiefs at the time. Until 1752 the Al Sabah exerted mild internal leadership with the blessing of the shaykh of the Bani Khalid,

Sulaiman al Hamud. At Sulaiman's death in 1756, Sabah bin Jabir, ancestor of the present-day ruling house, was elected as the first recorded Utbi shaykh. There is much discussion about the reason Sabah is remembered as the first of the Utbi shaykhs, since desert Arabs are particularly gifted at remembering genealogy and can usually trace a line for many generations. It is probable that the clans did not come to be called Utub until after their major migration; Utub derives from the Arabic root *ataba*, meaning to go from place to place.

In 1766 an Utbi settlement was established by the Al Khalifa at the short-lived city of Zubarah in Qatar. At the time of the Al Khalifa settlement on Qatar, nearby Bahrain was under the suzerainty of Shaykh Nasr al Madhkur, an Omani Arab who ruled from Bushire on the Iranian coast. Hostilities between Bushire and the Utbi-held areas led to attacks by Nasr on Zubarah in 1778 and 1782. In retaliation a joint attack by the Al Sabah and Al Khalifa netted them Bahrain in 1783, a capture that obliterated Iranian influence from the Utbi sphere of influence and gave the Utub access to the richest pearl beds of the Gulf while also providing a midway point for their increasing mercantile activities. The Al Sabah, particularly, were in an excellent mercantile position because they had access to land as well as sea trade routes. Caravans from Aleppo made regular stops there, and the proceeds enabled them to build a powerful fleet. Because of excellent relations with foreign powers, particularly the British, the Utub with one exception were not forced to engage in piracy. Further, the Utbi choice of settling in relatively unoccupied areas ensured unharassed and untaxed access to land and sea trade.

Kuwait's second ruler, Abdallah al Sabah, succeeded his father in 1762 (see fig. 7). Abdallah's long and prosperous reign, which lasted until his death in 1812, set patterns for Kuwait's future political and social development that prevailed until the exploitation of oil and in some cases after it. Abdallah continued the friendly relationship with the British begun by his father. In 1793 he invited the British to Kuwait, where they remained for two years until danger to their port at Basrah was eliminated. In return the British helped defend Abdallah against Wahhabi attacks in 1795. Neither the Ottomans in Iraq nor the Iranians were strong enough to interfere with Kuwait's rising mercantile power in the eighteenth and the early part of the nineteenth centuries. Shaykh Abdallah Al Sabah (1866–92), however, recognized Ottoman suzerainty over Kuwait, although Ottoman influence was minimal. Shaykh Mubarak Al Sabah (1895–1915) had the prescience to realize that the Ottomans would soon be a substantial threat to his shaykhdom and so in 1899 signed an agreement with the British whereby Britain assumed responsibility for Kuwait's foreign affairs and for its protection from foreign powers, in exchange for which Mubarak agreed to have no direct relations with foreign powers nor to cede them any land by sale or lease. Until 1961 there were no changes of substance in the agreement. If any change occurred, it was that relations became more intimate as a result of mutual British-Kuwaiti interests.

Bahrain already had an extensive and turbulent history by the time it was captured by the Utub from Kuwait and Zubarah. The Al Khalifa initially ruled Bahrain from Zubarah but established themselves permanently in Bahrain between 1796 and 1798 as a result of devastating Wahhabi attacks directed particularly at Zubarah.

In the late eighteenth and early nineteenth centuries, it appeared that every power in the Gulf was claiming Bahrain. It had been ruled first by the Bani Abd al Qais and then successively by the Umayyads, Abbasids, Iranians, Portuguese, and southern Omani Arabs. Thus, there were many to dispute Al Khalifa claims. Claims were confused because of changing nomenclature. Until early in the sixteenth century, Bahrain was a geographic entity that included not only the present-day archipelago but also the Gulf coast from Basrah to the Strait of Hormuz.

Because of the repeated acts of piracy by the Qawasim (adjective, Qasimi), which encourged other Arab shaykhdoms to join the fray, the British made a concerted attack (their third) against Ras al Khaymah, the headquarters of the Qawasim, in 1819 (see The Trucial Coast: The Qawasim and the Bani Yas, this ch.). The Bahrainis had not entirely abstained from piratical activities but had suffered more from them than they had gained. Accordingly, in 1820 Bahrain signed the General Treaty of Peace with the British, agreeing not to engage in piracy unless they were in a declared state of war. The treaty set the precedent for other states to sign, states that were inclusively referred to as the Trucial Coast until their independence in 1971. Friendly Bahraini-British relations continued, and in 1861 the two parties signed the Perpetual Truce of Peace and Friendship, which included the issues of slavery, British trade with Bahrain, and maritime aggression.

Ottoman involvement in the Arabian Peninsula, usually nominal and concentrated in the Hijaz, became more intense when the Sublime Porte (the government of the Ottoman Empire), fearing the growing strength of the Wahhabi incursions, dispatched its vassal, Muhammad Ali Pasha of Egypt, to subdue the Wahhabis in the eastern part of the peninsula. As the Ottomans increased their activity in the area, they again put forth claims to Bahrain in 1870 and 1874. Ottoman suzerainty in the Gulf could only mean a diminution of British power there. For the benefit of both British and Bahraini interests, treaties were signed in 1880 and 1892. Shaykh Isa bin Ali Al Khalifa agreed, in a treaty similar to that which Britain had signed with Kuwait, neither to dispose of Bahraini holdings without British consent nor to establish relationships with foreign powers without British agreement. A British political agent was assigned to Bahrain in 1902. Acting for the Bahrainis, the British signed a convention with the Ottomans in 1913, ensuring Bahrain's independence as a sovereign state. In 1916 a British agreement with Abd al Aziz, future king of Saudi Arabia, ensured that he would not attempt to conquer Bahrain.

Qatar

The withdrawal of the Al Khalifa from Zubarah to Bahrain naturally decreased their power in Qatar, although the Al Khalifa returned for a short period in the nineteenth century and always kept close contact with Qatar. The most important clan in Qatar before the advent of the Al Khalifa were the Al Thani, descendants from Thani bin Muhammad bin Thamir bin Ali of the Bani Tamim, a large Adnani clan. Tradition holds that ancestors of the Al Thani migrated from Najd and settled chiefly in eastern Qatar at the Jibrin Oasis late in the seventeenth century. They eventually moved to Doha (Ad Dawhah), the present-day capital. Apparently the Al Thani were subject to the Al Khalifa until Muhammad bin Thani, shaykh of Doha, began to seek autonomy. The Al Thani were, however, powerless against the Al Khalifa until Ottoman influence increased in the eastern peninsula. The Ottomans were not concerned with direct rule of the states, realizing that such an attempt would net them little, but they did wish to establish a nominal suzerainty because of the strategic military position of states along the Gulf.

In 1872 the Al Thani became independent of the Al Khalifa when Shaykh Muhammad bin Thani became a *qaim-maqam* (Ottoman provincial ruler). Muhammad was succeeded by his son Qasim (1876–1913), who had a great vision for Qatar's future and who for a time became very influential in the peninsula. Qasim's son Abdallah (1913–49) attempted to continue the peninsular policies of his father and also remained under the tutelary direction of the Ottomans, but in 1916 he signed a treaty with Britain that was virtually identical with those signed by Kuwait and Bahrain.

*Clock tower and Grand Mosque on left,
ruler's palace on right—Doha, Qatar*

The Trucial Coast: The Qawasim and the Bani Yas

The seven Trucial Coast shaykhdoms that became the
United Arab Emirates (UAE) in 1971 had for the most part separate histories until the discovery of oil (see fig. 13). Historically,
the five lesser states, that is, those without oil or much less oil
than Abu Dhabi or Dubai, were ruled by groups that had had extensive power in the eighteenth and early nineteenth centuries.
Their piratical activities were a major instigation for the British to
control or at least pacify the Gulf by making truces with them and
other states.

The Qawasim were the rulers of Ras al Khaymah and Sharjah. For centuries the Qawasim were settled on the Iranian coast
of the Gulf and the coastal area a few kilometers due north of the
Musandam Peninsula. Suzerains of Sir, a geographical area that
can be thought of as running horizontally across the Gulf, the
Qawasim were also lords of Lingeh, Qeshm, Junj, and Luft. Because of the geographic proximity of the Qawasim to Oman and

Omani cities on the Iranian coast, their histories are intermingled. The Qawasim had made themselves so conspicuous, initially by their trade and later by the magnitude of their piratical activities, that the British in the eighteenth and nineteenth centuries referred indiscriminately to all non-European pirates as the Qawasim, whom they called Joasmees—a misnomer presumably originating from hearing Gulf Arabs pronounce the Arabic letter *qaf* with a soft *g*.

It first became apparent that the Qawasim had other interests besides trade when the Qasimi shaykh of Ras al Khaymah assisted the imam of Oman, Sultan bin Saif II, in seizing Bahrain in 1720. A few years later the Qawasim founded a port at Basidu on the island of Qeshm. Because the East India Company's headquarters were at Bandar Abbas on the mainland behind Qeshm, the British were outraged at the loss of revenue caused by ships berthing at the closer port of Basidu. Accordingly, the company's agent directed a naval foray against Basidu to secure compensation from the Qawasim.

The Qawasim, however, were not long on the defensive. Because of the confusion that prevailed in Iran during most of the eighteenth century, governors were forced to defend their own interests; dependence on the central government usually was futile, and frequently the Iranian shah would exploit a governor. Mulla Ali Shah, the Iranian admiral and governor of Hormuz, therefore sought help from the Qawasim to assist him in defending his governorship against the multitude of demands for tribute made by candidates for the Iranian throne. Marriage alliances, a traditional Gulf response to political problems, were arranged between the families of Mulla Ali Shah and the Qasimi shaykh, Rashid bin Mattar bin Qasim. The Qawasim gained great prestige among the Arabs from the various profits that accrued to them from this coalition. More important, when the Qawasim annoyed the British at Bandar Abbas, the Iranians were unable to defend British interests.

The growth of Qasimi power was threatening not only to the British but also to other Arab maritime powers, particularly the Utub of Kuwait and Bahrain and the Omanis. The Omanis and the Qawasim were engaged in almost perpetual warfare during the second half of the eighteenth century; their one truce occurred in 1773, when the Iranian shah appeared likely to be a threat to states on the Arabian coast. Conflict between the Qawasim and the Utub came about almost accidentally. Secure in their power, the Qawasim attempted in 1782 to play diplomat between the Al Khalifa and the shaykh of Bushire, who was making claims to Bahrain in the name of Iran. Unfortunately, an Utbi vessel captured and killed the crew of a Qasimi boat. The Qawasim, therefore, threw in their lot with Arabs of the Iranian coast and attacked the Utbi settlement at Zubarah.

Between 1797 and 1804 there were only three incidents between the Qawasim and the British, and the Qawasim incentive was usually to disrupt Omani trade. Situations in virtually the whole of the Arab coast changed abruptly, however, with the Wahhabi religious and military expansion from central Arabia to the east coast of the Arabian Peninsula in 1800. Since a majority of coastal Arabs were Sunni, with the one exception of Oman, there originally was some sympathy for the movement. At their zenith the Wahhabis controlled the whole of the coast from Basrah to Dibbah. Control of a territory by a religiously motivated force and permanent conversion to its tenets are entirely different matters, however, and only Qatar remained Wahhabi. At the time, however, the Qawasim responded more positively to Wahhabism than did most other Gulf Arabs. This was at least partially due to the Qawasim's rivalry with the Omanis for commercial supremacy. The Omanis, as members of the Ibadite branch of Islam, were regarded as infidels by the austere Wahhabis. Presumably the Qawasim hoped that, by aligning with the Wahhabis, they would eventually have access to the spoils that would accrue if Oman fell to the Wahhabis. Because Oman was embroiled in civil war, the Qawasim received help from one of the two Omani warring factions—the Ghafiri, who were Adnani and who, although they did not wish for a Wahhabi takeover in Oman, hoped that the Qawasim would support their cause against their internal enemies.

The Qasimi collaborations with the Wahhabi movement encouraged their wholesale piracies against the British and thus quickened the British desire to make as many firm truces along the coast as possible. Many scholars attribute the increased Qasimi piratical activities not so much to Wahhabi fervor as to British interference in the long-term war between the Qawasim and the Omanis, and particularly to the British support of the Omanis, because wholesale attacks on British vessels did not commence until after 1808, when the war began to acquire some substance. British protection of the Omanis was not owing to special allegiance to them or to a particular treaty arrangement. The chief British concern was that the Qawasim, through the Wahhabis, not monopolize Gulf trade. The Qawasim felt they had been meanly dealt with, for a British-Qasimi treaty of 1806 had ensured that the Qawasim would respect the East India Company's flag and that in return the Qawasim would not be harassed during their attempts to recoup part of their Indian trade, which they felt had been usurped by the Omanis.

Anti-British incidents in 1808 prompted a radical change in the British laissez-faire stand on the internal affairs of the Arabs. Lord Minto, the governor general of India, and Rear Admiral William Drury, the naval officer in command of the East India station, decided that the independence of Oman (threatened by Qasimi attacks) was vital to British interests. A British show of support for Oman was also necessary because Sayyid Said, the Omani shaykh, had previously shown sympathy with the French, and the British were still in a state of shock from Napoleon's incursions into Egypt in 1797 and 1798. Accordingly, in 1809 the British destroyed Ras al Khaymah as well as a few small Qasimi holdings elsewhere. The Qawasim recouped their losses, and in 1812 and 1813 they made further attacks on British vessels. Attacks on Ras al Khaymah in 1812 and 1814 were made by Sayyid Said, with assistance from the Bani Yas of Abu Dhabi. Qasimi attacks and British counterattacks continued. A particularly crushing foray was made by the British on Ras al Khaymah in 1820.

Five of the seven shaykhdoms are Qasimi, and the shaykhdoms of Ajman, Umm al Qaywayn, Sharjah, and Fujayrah were under the dominance of the shaykhdom of Ras al Khaymah for much of their history. The other two, Abu Dhabi and Dubai, were founded by the previously nomadic Bani Yas. Abu Dhabi, founded in approximately 1761, was originally valued by the Bani Yas for its fresh water and proximity to pearl-bearing oyster beds. The people of Abu Dhabi quickly learned the value of maritime pursuits, and in 1790 the shaykh of Abu Dhabi's most powerful clan, the Al Bu Falah, moved his settlement to Abu Dhabi town. Dubai, in the late eighteenth century, was also inhabited by the Bani Yas, although the port had probably been used by the Omanis for centuries. Initially, under the dominance of Abu Dhabi, Dubai—settled by the Al Bu Falasah branch of the Bani Yas—declared its independence in 1834 and soon was a serious rival to the newly mercantile clansmen in Abu Dhabi. The Bani Yas settlements, because of their late founding, did not figure importantly in the Gulf until the mid-nineteenth century, but they did ally themselves with the Omanis against the Qawasim. In 1820 the Bani Yas were among the signers of the General Treaty of Peace between Britain and the states of the Trucial Coast. Some of the towns whose shaykhs signed the treaty of 1820 have been absorbed by other powers or have undergone name changes, but the original signers were the shaykhs of Abu Dhabi, Dubai,

Ajman, Umm al Qaywayn, Jazirat al Hamra, and Hatt and Falna.

The years between 1820 and 1852 continued to be stormy ones for the British and the other signers of the treaty. Abu Dhabi and Dubai began to rise in prominence; Sharjah, formerly second to Ras al Khaymah, became more affluent, and by 1820 Ajman and Umm Al Qaywayn had come into existence. The Qawasim by no means ended their activities, but their potential to build a powerful, independent indigenous state was crushed forever by the British. In 1853 the Treaty of Maritime Peace in Perpetuity was signed by the Qawasim and Bani Yas states, and the name of the coast was changed in British records from "Pirate" to "Trucial." It also fossilized the ruling families of the states and the states themselves because they had agreed not to combat each other on the open seas. Intertribal and intratribal warfare continued, however, but the fighting was more on land than at sea. The British still refrained from interfering in internal affairs; the unusual result was a situation in which territory was not being taken, but deaths and devastation were common.

Although treaties ensured the existence of the states, they did not ensure the conditions under which they would exist, and the resolution of many tribal problems was carried into the twentieth century. In 1892 the Trucial Coast states signed an exclusive agreement stating that Britain would be their only foreign and diplomatic contact. The internal histories of the Trucial Coast states were of little interest except to those who lived there; the British were firmly in control of local events.

Developments in Oman

Oman, having a continuous history recorded from ancient times and permanent tribal residents recorded from the second century A.D., differed in religion, tribal origins, and world view from the other Arab states of the Gulf. While engaging in extensive trade and carrying out frequent forays against some rival states and making alliances with others, Omanis were also concerned with internal divisions caused by geography, tribal origins, and theological subtleties. Although some of the Gulf states have been able to overcome their differences within the virtually all-encompassing embrace of oil, internal Omani problems—particularly those that intensified during the eighteenth century—have consistently been a divisive factor.

Early in the eighteenth century the contest for the succession to the imamate became so violent that it not only solidified the divisions that already existed in Oman but also involved many of the tribes of the future Trucial Coast states. The ulama favored the election of Muhanna bin Sultan al Yaruba, who appeared to fulfill the stringent requirements for an Ibadite imam, whereas tribal leaders wished to elect a young son of the previous imam. Although Muhanna was eventually elected, the dispute acquired a life of its own. Two factions formed: the Hinawi, named for the Bani Hina tribe and its leader, Khalifa bin Mubarak Al Hinawi; and the Ghafiri, named for the Bani Ghafir and particularly for Muhammad bin Nasir Al Ghafiri, who led that faction.

The Hinawi supported the choice of the ulama, and the Ghafiri supported the choice of tribal leaders. Although the choice of imam was certainly an important one to Omanis, the question of who was rightful imam was really only the catalyst in a situation that had long been in the making.

The Hinawis were southerners, that is, Qahtanis; the Ghafiris and their supporters were Adnani. Although both groups were Ibadite, the Hinawis, descendants of original Ibadite tribes, considered themselves the preservers of orthodoxy. Oman was without an imam for various periods when a compromise could not be reached between the two groups.

In the second half of the eighteenth century, the imamate was bestowed on a member of the Al Bu Said, an ancestor of the ruler in 1984. A grandson of the first Said ruler and an imam, he made the political error (as far as the tribes were concerned) of moving his capital to Muscat. It was a wise decision, considering the commercial advantages and the fact that he could more effectively negotiate with foreign powers—both Arab and European—from a coastal town rather than from the interior. The more conservative religious leaders of the interior did not, however, see the justification for such a move and began to elect their own imams, who acquired tremendous political power and virtually ruled the imamate as a state separate from the one coalescing around Muscat. Gradually, the rulers of Oman, no longer elected as imams, assumed the secular title of sultan.

The sultans of Muscat quickly developed an amicable relationship with the British that was advantageous to both parties. The first treaty, the Agreement of Friendship, was signed in 1800. The British felt it protected them from French influence in Oman, and the Omanis felt it greatly enhanced their international prestige and importance. The sultan of Muscat was also the suzerain of Zanzibar, a few other East African coastal towns, and Gwadar on the Makran coast of Baluchistan (in present-day Pakistan).

The British gave what aid they could to Oman during the

Wahhabi incursion and, by forcibly subjugating the Qawasim, secured Oman's position. In 1822 the sultan signed the first of three treaties (the others were in 1839 and 1873) with the British to suppress the slave trade in Oman.

Although the British have always been the best Western friends of the Omanis, the United States also made overtures during this period. The Americans, by then able traders, wished to make some arrangement whereby their trade passing through Omani waters would not be so heavily taxed. In 1833 Edmund Roberts, a private merchant, arrived in Muscat, having been given the authority to make commercial treaties by the United States Department of State. He effectively negotiated the Treaty of Amity and Commerce, the first American treaty in the area. It remained in effect until 1958, when it was replaced by a similar but updated version. (In 1840 an Omani delegation arrived in New York, the first Arabs to do so officially.)

The outgoing Sultan Sayyid Said, ruler during the mid-1800s, had given many gifts to the British, among them the guano-rich Khuriya Muriya Islands. The British by that time were so closely involved in Omani affairs that the British viceroy in India, Lord Canning, adjudicated between the sultan's quarreling sons after the sultan's death in 1856. One son was given Muscat and the other Zanzibar; Zanzibar, however, was to pay an annual tribute of 400,000 Maria Theresa dollars to Muscat. Zanzibar soon stopped paying the tribute. But because the British had arranged the conditions and because they wished to maintain a stable rule in Oman, which translated into money enough to ensure the sultan's power, British India assumed responsibility for the payment, which it continued to pay until the British Foreign Office assumed the burden in 1947.

The second half of the nineteenth century saw the beginning of Oman's decline and the decline of the rest of the Gulf states. Locally built sailing ships were no competititon for European steamship lines, and the Gulf for the first time in many centuries was becoming an economic backwater. In 1873 Sultan Turki bin Said Al Bu Said, who had come to power largely through British support, signed a major agreement aimed at the suppression of the slave trade. The end of slave trading and gunrunning, the last two lines of Omani economic power, dealt the coup de grace to Omani commercial independence. The sultan was hopelessly dependent on the British and had incurred the wrath of the more conservative Ibadites of the interior, because slavery under special conditions is sanctioned by the Quran and because the interior tribes relied on gunrunning.

The British apparently were aware of the difficulties they had caused the sultan. Between 1895 and 1897 Oman was granted two loans financed by the government of British India.

Ibadite discontent, fomenting for nearly a century, found a voice in Isa bin Salih, elected imam in 1913. That same year Taimur bin Faisal Al Bu Said became sultan in Muscat. By 1915 the imam's warriors had declared jihad against the sultan and were besieging Muscat. Infantry from British India assisted the sultan's forces, and Isa bin Salih was driven back. It was a Pyrrhic victory for the sultan, who maintained only the narrow coastal strip near Muscat. In 1920 an agreement was finally reached whereby the imam's forces would not attack the coastal areas under the sultan's aegis and the sultan would not interfere in the internal affairs of the "people of Oman." A new imam was elected immediately after the death of Isa bin Salih. A long-held feeling had reached the treaty table and become fact—Oman was for all purposes two nations. Thus Oman, once indisputable leader of the world's trade and then of the Gulf's, entered the twentieth century with depleted resources and a divided kingdom.

The Twentieth Century

British Governmental Transition

As the power of the British in the Gulf grew, so did their responsibility and presence there, requiring constant readjustment of their administration. By the middle of the nineteenth century Britain was responsible for the affairs of its agents in the Gulf but until a century later delegated that responsibility. The East India Company conducted diplomatic, defensive, commercial, and administrative affairs until 1858. The government of Bombay then assumed responsibility until 1873, when the British Indian government took charge, holding it until its demise in 1947. From 1947 until December 1971 and the independence of the UAE, the Foreign Office in London handled all Gulf matters through its political resident in Bahrain and by political agents eventually established in Bahrain, Qatar, Abu Dhabi, and Dubai.

The various treaties that the British made never provided that those states would be under the sovereign power of Britain— only that Britain would regulate and conduct their external affairs. Such conditions brought a measure of security to individual states against the incursions of rivals. But "external affairs" meant the same thing to Gulf Arabs as it did to the British—the sea—and any Arab vessel on the Gulf was subject to British-drawn guidelines.

Although the treaties allegedly restricted British power and involvement to external affairs, the British gradually encroached on the internal prerogatives of the Arabs—the natural consequence of the psychological conditioning received by the Arabs, who found themselves having to defer to British restrictions every time they ventured out of port. The conditioning was reinforced by tradition, and the opinion of a political resident on internal affairs could be discounted only at the risk of military or economic sanctions or even exile for the dissident.

Robert G. Landen, an expert on Oman, writes:

> By the early twentieth century British support had become a more important prerequisite for a ruler's continuance in power than his government's popularity among his own subjects. As late as 1970 such modes of indirect rule remained valid; for instance, the British played a large role in overthrowing the rulers of Sharjah in 1965, Abu Dhabi in 1966, and Oman in 1970.

The adviser system came to be widely used in the Gulf. Initiated in 1920 in Oman, when the British organized the Muscat Levies, a British-commanded internal security force, the adviser system formed the foundation of many of the administrative practices of the Gulf states. Foreigners, at first usually British, were employed by rulers and advised them on political, economic, and social affairs. The discovery of oil increased, sometimes without warrant, the self-confidence of many rulers, who slowly began to make decisions without direct British counsel.

After World War II and particularly after the loss of India in 1947, British priorities in and attitudes toward the Gulf changed. The area was no longer necessary as a military frontier from which to protect the empire in India. Because of oil, however, the area was of great economic importance to the British, and a situation reminiscent of the first days of the British in the Gulf obtained. Battalions of British soldiers were placed in Oman, Sharjah, and Bahrain. By the 1960s, however, it was clear that the British were losing more in expenditures than they stood to gain by their vigilance. Accordingly, Britain began to grant full independence to the Gulf states. Because, among other things, of the stability of Kuwait's internal rule, it was the first to achieve independence, on June 19, 1961. In 1968 the Labour government in Britain announced that its "protection" of the Gulf would end in 1971. Bahrain became independent on August 14, 1971, Qatar on September 1, 1971, and the UAE on December 2, 1971. Although some British troops remained in Oman, the Gulf was largely depleted of British forces by the end of 1971. That did not end British interests or influence there, nor did it substantially change the respect and friendship felt by the Gulf Arabs for the British.

Gulf Development Before Independence

Although the rate of social and economic change was greatly accelerated by independence, many of the Gulf states, with the exception of Oman, were making small starts toward modernization despite the fact that at the end of World War II most of them were nothing more than impoverished fishing villages.

Kuwait's growth after World War II was rapid, although in the late 1940s it was still only a small walled town. Oil had been discovered in 1938 but was not exploited until after the war, and most of the country's social programs were developed after independence. The pace of development was so rapid afterward that Kuwait was able to give substantial aid and advice to the states of the lower Gulf that were not yet independent. Many Gulf states modeled their social welfare systems, particularly education, on Kuwait's.

Initially, the greatest postwar change in the Gulf was in the development of local military and police forces. The Trucial Oman Levies, formed in 1951 (and later called the Trucial Oman Scouts), was the first. Although a British idea and officered by British volunteers, it functioned as an internal peacekeeping force staffed by local tribesmen. By 1956 the force included approximately 1,000 men. Dubai was the first to install its own police force in 1956; Abu Dhabi was next in 1957; and in the early 1960s the other states of the Trucial Coast followed suit. By 1965 Abu Dhabi had founded its own military defense force; although small, it included army, navy, and air force divisions (see United Arab Emirates, ch. 7).

Developmental changes of a social nature in the Gulf states were initiated by the British, who began to feel that they should undertake some limited responsibility for development schemes. In 1939 the British government opened a clinic staffed by an Indian doctor at Dubai and 10 years later began building a hospital there. In 1952 a modest water resources survey and some well drilling were financed, and in 1955 the first modern school was built at Sharjah. Flushed with success, the political agent in 1955 drew up a five-year development plan. Administrative developments, such as the improvement of the court system and modern buildings for the Trucial States Council, were envisioned, but greater progress was achieved in the social sphere. By 1961 an agricultural school near Ras al Khaymah and a trade school at Sharjah were established, a teacher training clinic was opened in Bahrain, the Dubai hospital was expanded, four primary-school buildings and a handful of clinics were built, and an antimalaria campaign was begun. The second five-year plan was straitened because of economic difficulties in Britain, but in the 1962–63 period a trade school was established at Dubai, and funds were made available in Ras al Khaymah to attack the problems that had developed in the previous decade.

By 1965 both Abu Dhabi and Dubai were sufficiently affluent to assume a major portion of schemes planned by the Development Fund, and in 1966 the ruler of Ras al Khaymah became chairman of the Trucial States Council, which administered the fund. Slowly at first the Gulf Arabs, particularly the Kuwaitis, funneled money through the fund and began to make their own decisions about development priorities in the area. The Arab tendency to build on a monumental and grandiose scale was tempered by British practicality in the years before independence, which was important, considering the many urgent needs of the region.

As a result of oil produced in commercial quantities by 1932, Bahrain was the only Gulf state where modernization was in progress by 1950. Sir Charles Belgrave, resident adviser to the ruler of Bahrain between 1928 and 1956, was largely responsible for the efficient manner in which Bahrain was administered. The educational and economic levels of Bahraini citizens were the highest in the Gulf.

Although Bahrainis enjoyed many of the advantages of a welfare state, they were not able to exercise any meaningful political rights. Dissatisfaction with the lack of popular participation led in 1954 to the formation of a nationalist movement, the Committee of National Union; it was a pan-Arab alliance of students, intellectuals, oil laborers, and artisans who demanded a number of reforms, including the development of a modern code of law, the formation of a trade union and a legislative council, and the dismissal of Belgrave. A general strike led to investigation of the grievances and authorization to establish an education and health council, half of whose members were to be elected. Although elections were held in 1956, unrest continued until it came to a head during the Anglo-French and Israeli invasion of Egypt of November 1956, and widespread rioting broke out. Law and order were eventually restored, and the leaders of the movement were exiled, an action that terminated the first political movement. The outcome of the riots, however, was the removal of Belgrave and the institution of a limited measure of reform.

In an effort to create a more viable political entity, Britain in 1951 sponsored the establishment of the Trucial States Council.

Members of the council were the seven rulers of the Trucial Coast states. Britain announced its intention to remove its forces from the Gulf and other areas east of Suez by the end of 1971, triggering renewed interest among the shaykhs in the possibility of a federation. With British encouragement the seven Trucial Coast states rulers and their counterparts of Bahrain and Qatar met in Dubai in February 1968 and announced the formation of the Federation of the Arab Amirates. The Supreme Council, composed of the nine rulers, would be established and would function on the basis of unanimity. The presidency would rotate among the nine rulers. The council would draw up a charter, formulate foreign, defense, and economic policies, and design the federal laws. The agreement would become effective on March 30, 1968.

It quickly became clear, however, that the rulers of the nine states were not yet ready to implement plans to federate by March 30. At a July 1968 meeting a compromise was reached whereby the shaykhs agreed to establish the Provisional Federal Council and a number of ad hoc committees to study such issues as a common currency, a postal system, a flag, and a national anthem.

The nine shaykhs continued to meet from time to time, and the various committees made some progress on combining technical services. At a meeting in October 1969 the shaykhs finally decided to appoint Shaykh Zayid bin Sultan Al Nuhayyan of Abu Dhabi as their first president and accepted the town of Abu Dhabi as the provisional capital. No further agreement was reached concerning the materialization of the federation. Traditional tribal rivalries and distrust and the inability of the rulers to adapt to problems and concepts transcending their tribal origins impeded federation efforts. The disparity in wealth, population, and power among the Gulf states compounded the difficulties of forming a working federation.

The attitude of other Gulf rulers to Bahrain's inclusion was lukewarm, for Iran was still making claims to Bahrain. As soon as the Iranian claim was settled, Bahrain demanded a representational position based on population within the Provisional Federal Council. When the idea was rejected, Bahrain declared its independence as a state separate from any federation on August 14, 1971. Because the Qataris had not forgotten the Utbi incursions in the eighteenth century and bore a grudge because of them, they refused to be in a position less strong than Bahrain and so declared their independence on September 1, 1971. The probability of a federation appeared to be declining. The people of Ras al Khaymah, furious at their state's being given a minor role in federation affairs—considering its illustrious past—and feeling ill-used because of the lack of support from other Gulf states in regard to Iran's occupation of the Tunb Islands (which Ras al Khaymah claimed), refused to join the federation of the UAE, which was finally announced on December 1, 1971. By the next day the UAE was independent of Britain. Ras al Khaymah did not join until February 1972.

Internal Developments in Oman

The twentieth century did not appear to herald great change for Oman until 1932, when Sultan Taimur abdicated in favor of his son, Sultan Said bin Taimur Al Bu Said. Secularists judged that the direction in which Said moved the sultanate was backward; although he clashed with the Ibadites of the interior, he was basically of their conservative mind. Geographical particularism made it impossible for him to be elected imam by the Ibadites of the interior, but the office of sultan under him became a close approximation of the imamate. Ibadite restrictions were firmly enforced. Alcohol, tobacco, dancing, singing, and films were strictly prohibited. Women were forbidden to appear unveiled in public and were denied access even to the religious schools.

Said's motivation was not entirely clear. Certainly he did everything in his power to isolate his country from outside influence or even intercourse with foreigners, with few minor exceptions: a few British were employed where absolutely necessary in the government and armed forces, and American missionaries ran the country's two hospitals. The missionaries, however, restricted their activities to the purely medical. Entrance visas were denied to virtually all. The few exceptions were made mostly to employees of a British-operated oil firm. The sultan talked a great deal with his British contacts about moderation but increasingly moved away from it. Ultimately, he discouraged trade except that necessary to sustain the country at barely subsistence level.

Although the sultan was unwanted in the interior, he nevertheless decided that Muscat was too close to foreign influence and so moved his capital to Salalah in Dhofar Province. Curfews were instituted in all major towns, and city gates were locked a few hours after sunset. Strongly opposed to education, he grudgingly permitted the functioning of three boys' schools. Young men who sought higher education outside the country were routinely denied reentrance visas. Relatively speaking, Said trusted the British more than any other foreigners and also realized the need for military leaders. He therefore permitted his

51

only son, Qaboos bin Said, to attend Sandhurst. When Qaboos completed his education and returned home, however, he was promptly placed under house arrest (see Political Dynamics, ch. 6).

A new imam was elected in the interior in 1954, and he and his supporters attempted unsuccessfully to gain recognition for Oman as an independent state in the League of Arab States (Arab League). Between 1954 and 1959 forces of the sultan and the imam were in a state of constant warfare until the British, at Said's request, helped put down the revolt in 1959. The imam took sanctuary in Saudi Arabia, which had supported him just as the Wahhabis had consistently supported imams against Omani sultans.

Despite Said's paranoia and the enforced isolation of his subjects, modern ideas were spreading, particularly among the young, from the unlikely source of Saudi Arabia. On July 24, 1970, a bloodless coup by the liberals, led by the sultan's son, Qaboos, ousted Said and exiled him to Britain, where he died in 1972. In 1984 Omanis continued to say "Before Qaboos, nothing." Certainly this sums up the reign of his father and Oman's position when it finally entered the twentieth century in 1970.

The New Age: Changing Patterns in the Religious and Social Systems

The states of the Gulf represent a series of variations on a theme—the adaptation of basically similar tribally oriented Arabian societies to the varying demands and opportunities of the burgeoning petroleum economy. At the beginning of the twentieth century, all of the societies, despite some local differences, displayed similar cultural tendencies and social organization. By midcentury, however, several of the Gulf peoples had come into one of the greatest—and most sudden—windfalls in human history. The discovery that a substantial proportion of the entire world's known petroleum reserves lay along the Gulf litorral transformed several of the states from impoverished, backward shaykhdoms into world financial powers in a span of time that may be called, in historical terms, overnight. Although the Gulf states have vastly differing amounts of oil, all states have experienced vast change because of the traditional paternalism and patterns of sharing in the Gulf. The degree of change differs, however. The opportunities , pressures, and rewards of exploiting a commodity of unprecedented value fell to societies ill-equipped to deal with them, particularly because this new prosperity arrived almost simultaneously with their independence from the British. The adjustments required have therefore been—and remain—demanding. Conspicuous consumption, intrastate economic rivalry, and, in some cases, mindless imitation of the West characterized much of the late 1970s. Experts opine that many people of the Gulf are experiencing profound future shock, which in turn has engendered a crisis of identity. The transition from a pastoral and primitive mercantile culture to one dominated by high technology without, for instance, an intervening period of industrialization, has created stress for family life and the political system.

In the early 1980s as Gulf societies sought to readjust their priorities along the lines of their value systems, Islam, never unimportant, once again came to the fore. In January 1984, for instance, the Gulf states, along with Saudi Arabia, agreed on a five-year plan to implement sharia. At the same time, personal attendance had increased significantly at mosques, and fundamentalist organizations were experiencing phenomenal growth. Some of these organizations also had political agendas, reflecting the fact that Islam has never recognized a separation of church and state. The political elite felt threatened by some of the fundamentalist organizations and sought to curb their excesses.

Foreign Workers

A major feature of oil-rich postindependence Gulf societies has been the presence of large numbers of expatriates whose skills are critically necessary for the development of modern states. Foreign workers have arrived in such numbers that in several states they outnumber the citizen body. The foreigners are viewed with mixed feelings by Gulf people, who worry about their overreliance on foreign laborers and technicians and the potentially deleterious effect they have on the traditional culture and the political system. Nowhere in the Gulf states do governments encourage foreigners to remain permanently, largely for fear that they could quickly come to dominate the societies at the expense of the native populations. Naturalization rules are strict in all the states, and in many of them gaining citizenship is virtually impossible. The states also strictly control entrance of foreigners according to labor needs. Separated from local society by their alien nationalities, the foreigners are also kept separate in ordinary social life. In some cases they inhabit special districts occupied almost entirely by foreigners. Compared with the family-oriented local populations, the foreign populations contain disproportionate numbers of young, single men. Both the native populations and the foreigners themselves view the foreign population as temporary, although some foreign workers have spent more than 20 years in the Gulf states. The situation is particularly poignant for the many Palestinians who have no hope of gaining citizenship in the countries where they live and no real homeland to return to at retirement. Some states forbid foreigners to own businesses or houses; even long-term migrants must remain employees and renters.

Because the immigrants come from different countries, they represent a variety of skill levels and cultural and religious orientations. Europeans—especially British—and Americans rank at the top of the hierarchy of training and responsibility; they mainly hold positions as high-level military, technical, or business advisers. A small group, they are almost totally cut off from the local societies. The largest group of foreign residents, and the next in the job stratification, are the Arabs, although their numbers were in decline in the early 1980s. Though similar in language and basic culture to the host population, the group is internally stratified by occupation. People from northern Arab countries tend to bring a relatively high level of education and professional skills. Palestinians are active in numerous white-collar fields, including communications, government, business, education, and medicine, as are Lebanese, Syrians, and Iraqis. Egyptians belong overwhelmingly to the teaching profession and constitute a high proportion of the teachers in the public school systems, and many work at white-collar government jobs. Jordanians hold many important posts in the military. Southern Arabians, such as Yemenis, come from countries much poorer in educational resources and therefore tend to be less skilled. They are found throughout the Gulf states as laborers and mercenary soldiers.

Those from the Arabic- and Farsi-speaking regions of southern Iran, some of whom have lived along the Gulf for generations, include a number of the wealthiest merchants. Farsi speakers from northern and central Iran arrived more recently in the Gulf area and have been active in commerce on a smaller scale. Small and marginal merchants and many laborers have come from the Baluchi-speaking regions of Iran and Pakistan.

The Indo-Pakistani subcontinent also provides immigrants from a variety of cultural backgrounds. Speakers of Urdu, Sindhi, and Punjabi from Pakistan are generally skilled workers, earning their living as merchants, white-collar and professional workers, and skilled tradesmen. Keralans from southern India and Pakhtuns and Baluch from Pakistan are generally unskilled, earning their living as menials.

Asians, particularly South Koreans, came into special favor in the late 1970s and early 1980s. Brought in to accomplish specific projects by contractors, Koreans were boarded together and had minimal, if any, contact with the local population. They generally finished projects ahead of schedule and were immediately returned to their country.

Female foreign workers from Sri Lanka, Thailand, India, and Seychelles, although proportionately few in number compared with the males, attracted a great deal of attention in the early 1980s. Working primarily as maids and nannies, their employment caused many local newspapers to decry the fact that non-Arabs and non-Arabic-speaking women were raising many of the children of the elite of their societies.

Settlement Patterns

Unlike most other Arab societies, the shaykhdoms along the Gulf have long been dominated by towns. More like city-states than nation-states, several are among the most urbanized polities in the world. The advent of the oil industry has increased the dominance of city occupations, city people, and city ways. Towns have expanded into cities, and the cities now boast modern skylines. New residential and commercial buildings have usurped the space formerly occupied by long-standing and well-knit communities. The physical dimensions of some towns also have changed radically. In Qatar and in Bahrain particularly, extensive land reclamation has added miles to formerly shorefront land.

Many villages remained in the early 1980s, however. Many of the men of the villages traveled to towns and cities to work, but, on the whole, village life went on much as it did centuries ago. Village women possessed modern appliances and often new housing provided by government grants and loans. The houses, however, continued to be modeled on traditional structures appropriate for a large and usually extended family.

The Family

Through all the manifold change, both in city and in village, social life has continued to focus on the family. No other institution of even roughly comparable strength exists. Family loyalty and particularism continue to pervade all aspects of life. Although education has expanded the opportunities for many and by the early 1980s had created a new and growing class of technocrats, ascribed status generally outweighs personal achievements in regulating social relations and in influencing economic well-being. And marriages continue to be arranged in a manner that would have been deemed appropriate a century ago.

The prototype of the elite reinforces this tendency. All ruling families of the Gulf states base the legitimacy of their regimes on their descent from a leading tribe or lineage long known for its nobility of ancestry. Even in the midst of tremendous social change, ruling families attempt to maintain and strengthen the ties to the strong tribes with which they claim kinship.

Arabs generally reckon kinship patrilineally, and the household is based on blood ties among men. Ideally it consists of a man, his wife or wives, his married sons with their wives and children, his unmarried sons and daughters, and possibly other relatives, such as a widowed or divorced mother or sister. At the death of the father each married son ideally establishes his own household to begin the cycle again. Because of the centrality of family life, it is assumed that all persons will marry when they reach the appropriate age; many divorced and widowed persons remarry for the same reason. In most areas adult status is bestowed only on married men and often only on fathers.

As of 1984 the extended family remained the norm, although the nuclear family household was on the increase. A majority of nuclear households, however, formed parts of extended families living in adjacent or nearby houses rather than in the same house. Landownership was frequently a determinant. With land values skyrocketing in the late 1970s and early 1980s, families that owned land found it sounder financially to build all the family houses in the same section.

In a household the individual usually endeavors to subordinate his personal interests to those of the family and to consider himself a member of a group whose importance outweighs his own. It is not common for persons other than male foreigners to live apart from a family group. Grown children ordinarily live with parents or relatives until marriage; for a young woman of a respectable family to do otherwise would be unthinkable.

Marriage and Divorce

Marriage is a family rather than a personal affair. Because the sexes do not ordinarily mix socially, especially when teenagers, young men and women have few or no acquaintances among the opposite sex. Parents arrange marriages for their children, finding a mate usually through their own family and social contacts. Among both villagers and those with tribal ties, the preferred marriage partner is the child of the father's brother or someone similarly related, and such marriages are common. If the ideal cousin marriage is not possible, marriage within the patrilineal kin group is the next choice; tribes, especially those of noble stature, traditionally practiced virtually total endogamy. The only common exception was a marriage with an outsider contracted for political reasons. Endogamous marriages in traditional society produce several advantages for all parties: the bride price *(mahr)* payments demanded for the bride's kin tend to be smaller; the family resources are conserved; little danger exists of an unsuitable match; and the bride need not go as a stranger to her husband's house. Although some men educated abroad have married foreign women, most governments officially discourage such matches. Even in societies where an emerging class system threatens the traditional tribal domination, such personal achievements as education and job prospects hardly outweigh descent as criteria in marriage arrangements.

In Islam marriage is a civil contract rather than a sacrament. Consequently, representatives of the bride's interests negotiate a marriage agreement with the groom's representatives. Although the future husband and wife must, according to law, give their consent, they usually take no part in the arrangements. A young man—or, increasingly, a young woman—might suggest to his parents whom he or she would like to marry. Men expect virginity of their brides, but no such expectation exists for bridegrooms. The marriage is registered by the bridegroom and the bride's male representative rather than by the bride. The contract establishes the terms of the union and outlines appropriate recourse in the event they are broken. Special provisions inserted into the standard contract become binding on both parties.

In Islam a man may take up to four wives at one time, provided he can treat them equally; in the 1980s few men had more than one wife. In the vast majority of cases, a second wife was taken because the first had been barren. From the point of view of the law, although not of society, a man can divorce his wife with relative ease, whereas a woman must petition a judge. Grounds for divorce for women include the inability of a husband to support his wife in the manner of her family or impotency. In the case of divorce, children stay with the mother until approximately the age of seven for sons and nine for daughters. Ultimately, however, the children belong to the father's household. Even when a woman is wealthy in her own right or employed, financial responsibility for a household resides totally with the males.

Men who work in the city may be seen in either Western clothing or the traditional male garments of the Gulf. This consists of a long white A-line garment called the *thobe*, with a head covering, either the white *gutra* or checked *kaffiyah*, held in place by the *agal*, a circle of doubled black cord. Men's traditional dress, both because of its greater comfort and out of a sense of growing national pride, was in 1984 being worn more often than Western clothes. In Oman the *gutra* or *kaffiyah* is worn wound like a turban without the *agal*, and the *thobe* is distinguished by a tassel at the front neck closing.

Common garb for urban women includes more modest versions of Western clothes but usually covered in public by an *abayah*. In Doha, Abu Dhabi, and some parts of Oman, face-veiling is the norm. It is seen in Kuwait but is becoming increasingly rare because women have been forbidden to drive while veiled. Village women dress traditionally and, as such, face-veiling is rare. Their dress is composed of two major pieces—a kaftan with long sleeves and a sleeveless overgarment, the sides of which can be pulled up to cover the head. Village girls cover their heads in public.

Women

Even in those countries that have a relatively high proportion of women in the work force, such as Bahrain and Oman, sexual segregation, to one degree or another, is the norm. Most households, poor or rich, have two living rooms or majlises, one for males and the other for females and close family friends. It is increasingly common for the more urbanized young married couples to socialize together either in the home or in restaurants.

The honor of the men of a family, which is easily damaged and nearly irreparable, depends on the conduct of the women, particularly of sisters and daughters; consequently, women are expected to be circumspect, modest, and decorous and their virtue to be above reproach. The slightest implication of unavenged impropriety, especially if publicly acknowledged, could irreparably destroy the family's honor. Although family honor resides in the person of a woman, it is actually the property of the men of her natal family. An unfaithful wife, for example, shames her father and brothers far more than her husband. Enforcement of honor, even at the cost of a sister's or daughter's life, is the obligation of the men of a family. Any social standing whatsoever, and even minimal respect, is impossible without it.

In some areas women marry in their middle teens, but, where education has become widespread, the age of marriage has risen. The young bride goes to the household, village, or neighborhood of the bridegroom's family, where she may be a stranger and where she lives under the constant surveillance of her mother-in-law. A woman begins to gain status, security, and satisfaction in her husband's family only after she produces children and, particularly, sons.

Although women's power is based largely on their relationships with male relatives, it is far from negligible. Respected women with wide social contacts in female society often act as important sources of information for their menfolk; women can gather a good deal of news about what is being thought and done in the homes they visit, whereas men are discouraged by etiquette even to discuss the female relatives of their friends. Women play crucial roles in marriage arrangements, which often carry important political overtones; their support or opposition often determines which matches come about. Their visits to their natal households serve to strengthen ties between allied men. Their labor makes male hospitality possible. Within the privacy of the family circle, women's opinions often carry weight in men's decisions. A prominent example of an influential female is Shaykha Hussa bint al Murr, mother of the ruler of Dubai; according to authorities, she exercised considerable political power during the early decades of the twentieth century.

Chiefly because of the laws of Islamic inheritance, women have accumulated significant economic power since the oil boom. Favored areas of investment for women include real estate and small businesses. During the stock market fever that enraptured Gulf society in 1982 and 1983, many women were active players.

The development of the educational system has presented women, for the first time, with options other than traditional marriage and household life. Women of all ages have reportedly responded enthusiastically to those new opportunities, both because of a desire for self-improvement and because the highly desirable modern-educated man prefers an educated wife. It is not at all clear, however, to what extent education has changed or will change the basic nature of relations between the sexes in the Gulf states.

Social Systems of the Gulf Countries

Kuwait

Kuwait probably represents the highest development of an oil economy and therefore the greatest degree of visible change. The displacement of many of the social groupings of an earlier time resulted not only from the waves of immigrants, who in mid-1984 accounted for more than 60 percent of the population, but also from deliberate government policy. During the early 1950s the government purchased the bulk of the real estate in Kuwait City at highly inflated prices. It simultaneously constructed new, planned suburbs on the city's periphery and permitted the construction of unplanned suburbs as well. The policy of assigning families to new homes has resulted in the segregation of Kuwaiti from non-Kuwaiti elements of the population. The former mostly inhabit the well-equipped, well-served planned suburbs; the latter, less desirable suburbs and shantytowns.

In addition to the ruling Al Sabah Dynasty, which traces its descent from eighteenth-century members of the Anayzah confederation, about 180 other prominent families, called *asilin* (sing., *asil*), also claim social prominence because of their descent from noble tribes. These families use the prefix *al* before their names.

Well over 90 percent of native Kuwaitis are Sunni, as are most non-Kuwaiti Muslims in the country. The royal family and the courts generally follow the Maliki rite. Other religions tolerated in the state include the Shiism of Iranians and some Iraqis and the Protestant and Roman Catholic Christianity practiced by Europeans employed in the country.

Despite this tribal background, however, social change is the hallmark of contemporary life in Kuwait. Rapid economic growth has diluted many of the social relationships that once supported a largely tribalized society. The growth of the Kuwait City complex and the industrial towns of the southeast has reinforced the country's traditional urban character. The bonds of tribe have been greatly eroded in the towns, and only a fraction of the population continues to live in the deserts. Class relationships have also changed. The native-born unskilled worker has largely disappeared, his place being taken by foreigners.

Class and class consciousness have emerged as important new elements in Kuwaiti society. The development of a comprehensive, free educational system has removed all social barriers to white-collar occupations for Kuwaiti citizens. Government policy of giving citizens preference over noncitizens in competitions for jobs has produced a situation in which no qualified citizen faces any difficulty in finding desirable employment for which he is better paid than a non-Kuwaiti doing similar work. Some observers have stated that the favorable economic situation has destroyed the willingness of Kuwaitis to accept undesirable jobs or even to remain in school if it proves difficult or unpleasant.

Because they enjoy a virtual monopoly on business opportunities, Kuwaitis have profited enormously in a number of endeavors subsidiary to the main source of wealth. Fortunes have been made in importing, real estate, the stock market, and a number of other fields. The government's land purchase scheme of the 1950s had as one of its goals placing substantial amounts of capital in the hands of owners of buildings. The families of noble merchants that dominated the economy in the era before petroleum were the chief beneficiaries of the program and of the unprecedented business opportunities that developed soon afterward. One of the most successful has been the Al Ghanim, who transformed a prosperous but traditional trading company into a modern multinational corporation with holdings in the United States and projects in a number of other countries.

Although such families have grown markedly wealthier and more powerful on the international scene, they have lost considerable ground relative to the royal family, which, because it controls the country's enormous oil income, has seen its own power increase astronomically at home and abroad. In addition to these wellborn beneficiaries, numerous ambitious Kuwaitis of more modest social origin have also been able to achieve prosperity. Although personal connections still count heavily in business life, personal ability has increased in importance in the bureaucratic atmosphere promoted by the Kuwaiti economy.

One important change reflecting the country's growing modernization is the new attitude toward women, who are increasingly being liberated from the restraints of custom. Although they do not yet have the vote, they are being educated and trained for such careers as physicians and teachers. The younger Kuwaitis are the beneficiaries of modern education and have a better knowledge of the outside world than their parents, but they have never known anything but affluence and are less appreciative of the government's sweeping paternalism. Throughout the country, isolation and provincialism are breaking down because of automobiles, radios, and television sets.

Bahrain

In many ways Bahrain is the most socially advanced Gulf state. Education in Bahrain was a generation ahead of the rest of the Gulf, and many Bahraini families are now in their third generation of college graduates. Although Bahrain was the first Gulf state to discover oil, it was soon obvious that the amount was relatively small. Fortunately, this resulted in the very early diversification of the economy, which has been better able to absorb economic shock. In the pre-oil period, Bahrain had a well-defined social hierarchy, extending downward from the leading shaykhs through the leading merchants and small shopkeepers to the cultivators and the ex-slaves and migrants who served as pearl divers and fishermen. But with the gradual extension of education that has accompanied modernization, a new middle class has developed, counting bureaucrats, bankers, teachers, and students among its ranks.

In the mid-1970s the Al Khalifa family, the ruling dynasty, stood at the top of the hierarchy of power and influence, followed by the leading commoners. Before World War II this group had consisted primarily of pearl merchants, but it has since come to include merchants in a broad spectrum of pursuits.

Because Bahrain, unlike other states in the Gulf, has a majority Shia population, the Shia have had their own law courts, and the leaders of organized religious groups occupy a more prominent position than elsewhere (see The Constitutional Experiment, ch. 3). The ruling family is Sunni of the Maliki school, and most judges and other government officials have traditionally come from this group. The Shia, formerly mainly farmers and fishermen, have also begun to join the urban working class in substantial numbers. There are quite a few wealthy Shia merchants whose families emigrated from Iran one or two generations ago.

The population of Bahrain is nearly 100 percent settled and nearly 80 percent urban; over 50 percent of the population lives in Manama, the capital city. In 1984 foreigners composed about 30 percent of the population and, except for relatively small numbers of Americans and British in high-level technical and management positions in the oil industry and elsewhere, foreigners were concentrated in laboring jobs and in the services sector. Because of its strong commitment to education, Bahrain has for some years produced a surplus of aspirants to white-collar jobs (see Education, ch. 3). To reduce unemployment among young Bahrainis entering the white-collar labor market for the first time, the government has adopted the policy of replacing foreigners in white-collar positions with Bahraini citizens.

Ministry of Foreign Affairs, Doha, Qatar

Women form 6 percent of the work force and are employed mainly as physicians, teachers, secretaries, accountants, engineers, and brokers. In 1984 the norm was that women from the upper and middle classes would receive a college education.

Qatar

The ruling Al Thani family dominates Qatar not only by its power and social prominence but also by its size. One authority characterized it as "vast"; estimates of family membership range as high as 20,000 people, of whom 500 rate the title shaykh, out of a population numbering between 250,000 and 290,000 in the 1980s. The Al Thani family also supports a large number of retainers, many of whom occupy positions of social and political prominence.

Unlike the cities of Bahrain, which had been centers of trade, pearling, and boatbuilding before the era of petroleum, Doha—the capital and largest city—was little more than a sleepy fishing village without any deep-water facilities and little in the way of a commercial tradition. Crude oil production in Qatar began in 1949, and since that time Doha has been transformed into a modern city, boasting new roads and houses, water and electrical services, and other modern amenities. Commercial activity has expanded phenomenally.

Although no tradition of commerce existed before the discovery of oil, a number of Qatari nationals have emerged as substantial merchants, but a vast majority of the small- and medium-sized merchants are foreign, mainly of Iranian origin. Foreigners compose a majority of the work force. Qataris, who in past generations earned their living in pearling, fishing, a small amount of pastoral nomadism, and an even smaller amount of farming at the subsistence level, are rapidly disappearing from the manual labor force. The advent of oil wealth has allowed them to hire foreigners to do work that citizens consider unpleasant or undignified. Pakistanis and Indians, both Muslim and Hindu, make up the majority of foreigners, although substantial numbers of Palestinians and somewhat fewer Egyptians are also present.

The native population is Sunni Muslim of the Wahhabi persuasion. They follow the Hanbali legal school. Iranian merchants in Qatar appear to be evenly divided between Sunni and Shia.

United Arab Emirates

The UAE is a federation of seven small shaykhdoms (see fig. 13). Two of them, Abu Dhabi and Dubai, experienced rapid development in the early 1970s. Oil production began in Sharjah in mid-1974 and the influx of oil revenues, as well as its contiguous position to Dubai, caused significant change, particularly in its infrastructure. In the mid-1980s foreign observers doubted that significant amounts of oil would be found in the other four shaykhdoms—Ras al Khaymah, Ajman, Umm al Qaywayn, and Fujayrah—although exploration was continuing. The last three, moreover, are so small that one authority characterized them as "village states." Ras al Khaymah and Fujayrah, however, have become popular resorts.

The populations of Ajman, Dubai, and Umm al Qaywayn are nearly entirely settled; between 85 and 95 percent of the populations of the remaining shaykhdoms are settled. Beduin constitute the remainder. Traditionally, the coastal people earned their living as sailors, pearlers, and traders; the inland peoples, as camel herders and small-scale farmers. Although the population of the UAE as a whole has grown dramatically as a result of immigration, the foreign workers are not evenly distributed among the shaykhdoms.

Abu Dhabi

The passing of traditional society is clearly seen in Abu Dhabi. As late as the early 1960s there were essentially three kinds of inhabitants, each engaged in economic activities of long standing: coastal and island settlers, who were engaged principally in fishing, pearling, and trade; oasis dwellers, who depended on subsistence cultivation; and beduin pastoralists, who roamed the mainland in search of water and grazing land. The development of the petroleum industry, after the discoveries in 1960, led to critical shifts in the social pattern. Abu Dhabi's inhabitants have gradually been drawn into wage-earning jobs in petroleum exploitation, construction, and services. Tribal life is breaking down in the face of increased social mobility, the growth of a money economy, and state programs in health, education, and housing.

Nevertheless, Abu Dhabi has more tribal groups than any other shaykhdom in the UAE. Although mainly settled at oases in the interior, they include some nomads. The most important tribal grouping is the Bani Yas, a confederation of 15 tribes, one of which includes the ruling Al Nuhayyan Dynasty. The Al Nuhayyan originated in the Liwa Oasis (Al Jiwa) and is also associated with the settlement of Al Ayn in the Buraymi Oasis, where some members moved in the 1800s. A section of the tribe migrated from Liwa to the coast in the 1700s, although most members remained behind. When oil production began in the 1960s, however, members began to move from Liwa to Abu Dhabi, where the capital had long been located. The move ultimately resulted in the highly unusual phenomenon of a major tribe's changing its primary geographic identification. Although Al Nuhayyan influence remains strong in the interior, the lineage is concentrated on the coast.

Other important tribal groups are the Dhawahir, a confederation of 15 tribes that is important at Al Ayn, and the Awamir, who are found west of the Buraymi Oasis and south of Al Dafrah (Dafir). Government policy favors the settlement of the country's remaining nomads; a new town has been constructed for this purpose near Liwa.

In comparison with the royal family, the merchants of Abu Dhabi are not a very powerful class, although they have become very wealthy. They and the Abu Dhabians employed in the oil industry are, however, the only citizens working in the modern sector. Development of a new middle class has begun. The university-trained men in the country have been assimilated into the more traditionally based elite. The substantial working class at the bottom of society consists of foreigners.

Dubai

Dubai is the commercial hub and largest town in the UAE, a center for entrepôt trade, a thriving port, and a market for tribesmen from Oman. Oil was discovered as recently as June 1966. Dubai owes its existence as a permanent town and its development as a commercial center to the fact that it was the only deepwater port along the coast.

The ruling Al Maktum Dynasty, which belongs to the Al Bu Falasah segment of the Bani Yas, has taken full advantage of the state's commercial dominance. The ruler is the leading merchant, the largest shareholder in the telephone and electric companies, and the owner of shipping and land interests. Nonroyal merchants also figure prominently in society; many more of the immigrants are merchants than in the other shaykhdoms.

Other Amirates

The other, smaller amirates have experienced the least social change. Because of its past prominence as a British headquarters, Sharjah has the highest per capita rate of university graduates in the UAE. In the early 1970s it had difficulty in employing its educated population, but in 1984 the booming economy reportedly provided nearly full employment.

Tribalism is important in these shaykhdoms. The smaller amirates have experienced less social upheaval and retain their tribal character, although increasingly their young men are entering the work force as technocrats. Tribal units are less tied to modern political entities than elsewhere in the Gulf. Different branches of the Qawasim tribe rule in Sharjah and Ras al Khaymah, for example, although in Sharjah they are a large tribe and in Ras al Khaymah a relatively small one. The rulers of the other amirates belong to the most important tribes in their respective states, but the tribes are to some extent also scattered among the other political entities.

The majority of the native population is Sunni of the Maliki legal school. About one-half of the population of Al Ayn on the Saudi Arabian and Omani borders is Wahhabi Sunni. There is also a concentration of Sunnis of the Shafii school in Fujayrah.

Oman

Oman straddles the corner of Arabia, lying along both the Gulf and the Arabian Sea. Thus, it shares features with the amirates to the north and with the Yemens to the west. The country has a long tradition of isolation and localism, and the ethnography of its hundreds of tribes is little known. Traditionally, the family and the tribe were the dominant social institutions, and no higher institutions or organizations bound the disparate groups into a single people. The territory's inhabitants range from residents of cosmopolitan port cities to isolated tribesmen speaking aboriginal tongues.

Although the population is estimated to be predominantly Arab, there are significant concentrations of non-Arabs, particularly in the neighboring coastal towns of Muscat and Matrah, where non-Arabs predominate. The Baluch, who are Sunni—originally inhabitants of the sultan's former possession of Gwadar on the coast of Pakistan—were introduced into the country as mercenaries. Many are still in the sultan's service, but others are found in various seafaring occupations along the coast. A very few have settled in the interior and have been assimilated by the Arabs. Muscat and Matrah also have large numbers of Indians, both Hindu and Muslim, descended from the early merchants and traders who emigrated to the sultanate during its heyday as a maritime empire. Probably the largest minority group is Negro. For several centuries Muscat was an important entrepôt for the slave trade; many Negroes still serve as retainers for the sultan, tribal shaykhs, and other dignitaries. Other Negroes are employed most frequently as fishermen and pearl divers.

According to the tradition of the country, the Arab majority divides into two principal tribal factions: the descendants of the first Arab settlers, identified by several designations, including Yamaniyah, Azdi, Qahtani, and, in the eighteenth century, Hinawi; and the scions of the second wave of Arab settlers, known as Nizari, Adnani, and, in the eighteenth century, Ghafiri. The first Omanis were of southern or Yemeni origin; the later arrivals, who were from the north and central portions of Arabia, began to push into Oman sometime in the fifth century. For nearly 1,500 years the two groups have been feuding, and the feud is still an important factor in internal politics.

Generally, the Ghafiri predominate in the northwestern districts, and the Hinawi are more powerful in the southeast. Over the centuries, however, a great deal of intermingling has taken place, so that often a village is split between subgroups of tribes affiliated with the warring factions.

Although the ruling house and the majority of ordinary Omanis are Ibadi Muslims, it should be emphasized that the Hinawi-Ghafiri split, in spite of its ethnic antecedents, is primarily a religious division in present-day Oman. The Hinawi have been closely associated with the Ibadi version of Islam, which has been thĕ pillar of Omani particularism over the centuries (see The Ibadi Movement, this ch.). The Ghafiri, although often affiliated with Ìbadi Islam, have traditionally been more receptive to outside influences. There are several Ghafiri tribes whose religion is Sunni Islam, and a few others have adapted the Wahhabi practices traditionally connected with Saudi Arabia.

Tribalism remains the most important source of social identity for the majority of the people. Of the many scores of tribes and subtribes found in the country, the most important are the Al Bu Said, the royal tribe; the Bani Ghafir, Bani Amr, and Hawasin of inner Oman; the Sunni Shihuh and Habus of the Musandam Peninsula; the Janabah of Masirah Island; the Duru of Dhahirah in the north; the Sunni Bayt Kathir, Mahrah, and Qara of Dhofar near the People's Democratic Republic of Yemen (Yemen [Aden]) border; and the Al Hirth of Ash Sharqiyah.

Of considerable ethnographic interest are the Sunni Shihuh and Qara, who speak non-Arabic Semitic languages and apparently are descendants of an indigenous population displaced by Arab invaders. The Shihuh are seminomadic, moving each year between winter lodgings in the mountains and summer lodgings on the coast. Different social groupings come into play in the two kinds of settlements—winter settlements are inhabited by one extended family each, and summer settlements by several related extended families.

The Qara and other peoples of the Dhofar region are more oriented to local groupings or to tribal fellows in Yemen (Aden) than to the regions to the east. Only in the immediate area of the coastal towns do ties with the rest of the country gain importance.

The tribes formerly exercised substantial political leverage over the towns throughout the country. Tribal leaders received large subsidies to refrain from raiding certain towns or caravans originating from them. Travelers and merchants paid tribute to local shaykhs when crossing tribal lands. The revenue accruing to tribal leaders enabled them to exercise control over the far-flung branches of their tribes. They could afford to be generous and thus commanded widespread allegiance. With the advent of modern transportation in the 1970s, however, the countryside has become more accessible. As a result, the towns became more influential and the tribes' power declined.

The development of the oil industry and the growing strength of the central government have hastened the decline of the tribes' power. As development projects and bureaucratic organizations grow, the tribes are being drawn into a more national orbit. A significant migration from tribal areas to cities has begun, and the sharp cultural differences between the interior and the coast have begun to lessen. The power of tribal leaders in matters beyond their immediate locality has declined, although they remain important in local affairs.

Education is providing a natural vehicle for the development of loyalties to group beyond the family and the tribe. By 1984 politicized youth clubs supervised by the Ministry of Labor and Social Affairs constituted one of the first examples of voluntary associations in the country.

At the national level the most important social stratum is the ruling family. A few expatriates, mainly British, occupy positions of importance in the military, the oil industry, and the development program and enjoy the sultan's favor. About 12 merchant houses constitute the commercial elite that forms the next stratum. These families control import franchises and are active in various enterprises other than oil. Nearly all these families are of foreign extraction—mainly Iranian, Indian, or Pakistani. Not one of the 10 most important mercantile houses adheres to Ibadi Islam; most are Shia, but the group includes Sunnis and Hindus.

A small urban group of growing importance is made up of the modern-educated intellectuals; in the early 1970s about a dozen were graduates of foreign universities, and a number of others had studied at secondary schools in Africa, Aden, and elsewhere. By the mid-1980s this group had expanded significantly (see Education, ch. 6). Such persons often find themselves in cultural conflict with the traditional Ibadi religious elders. Former slaves of the sultan, who number about 2,000, also form a group of some importance. Many remain in his service and enjoy close ties to the palace.

Foreigners and minority groups are concentrated in the port cities of Muscat and Matrah. Indians, Pakistanis, and Baluch constitute the most important minorities. Indians and Pakistanis tend to work in commerce, artisan crafts, the military, and the government. Baluch mainly work as soldiers, farmers, laborers, and fishermen. The Indian community includes Christians from Goa and Kerala, who mainly hold white-collar jobs; Sikhs from the Punjab, who work as electricians, carpenters, and in other skilled trades; and Hindu merchants.

* * *

Information on the period before the founding of the Gulf states in the eighteenth century is scant. Excellent summaries may be found, however, in books that have a later focus. Ahmad Mustafa Abu-Hakima's *History of Eastern Arabia, 1750–1800* is particularly valuable because of his perusal of all Arabic sources and discussions of their validity. Arnold Talbot Wilson's classic, *The Persian Gulf: An Historical Sketch from the Earliest Times to the Beginning of the Twentieth Century*, remains an important and heroic attempt at sorting out the complex dynamics of premodern Gulf history. *Oman since 1856*, by Robert G. Landen, is the most thorough and scholarly study of the internal and external affairs of Oman and contains an excellent study of Oman's early period. Two key works concerning the British in the Gulf are J.B. Kelly's weighty and meticulous book *Britain and the Persian Gulf, 1795–1880* and Donald Hawley's *The Trucial States*. Hawley's work is superb for the general reader because he comprehensively covers the history of the area, including the murky period between World War I and independence.

Books that are valuable reading for the contemporary period are K.G. Fenelon's *The United Arab Emirates: An Economic and Social Survey;* David E. Long's *The Persian Gulf: An Introduction to Its People, Politics, and Economics;* John Duke Anthony's *Arab States of the Lower Gulf: People, Politics, and Petroleum;* Jacqueline S. Ismael's *Kuwait: Social Change in Historical Perspective;* and Frauke Heard-Bey's *From Trucial States to United Arab Emirates: A Society in Transition*.

Sources on the religious life of the Gulf are uneven in both quantity and quality. An adequate, if hardly ample, quantity of material exists on the Ibadis and the Wahhabis, but information on other, more common forms of Islam as practiced in the Gulf is very scanty. For Oman and the Ibadis, T. Lewicki's article in *The Encyclopedia of Islam* and Roberto Rubinacci's "The Ibadis" provide good introductions. George Rentz' article, "The Wahhabis," serves a similar purpose. Very brief summaries of the religious situation in the Persian Gulf are available in Anthony's *Arab States of the Lower Gulf* and Long's *The Persian Gulf*. Philip K. Hitti provides a clear discussion of the basic tenets and values of Islam in *Islam: A Way of Life*. For a comprehensive, challenging history of the founding of Islam, the *fitnah* period, and later de-velopments, the first volume of Marshall G.S. Hodgson's magisterial *The Venture of Islam* is highly recommended.

Information on the social organization of the Persian Gulf states is scattered and incomplete. Useful sources, though some-what limited in their approach to social structure, are Anthony's *Arab States of the Lower Gulf* and *Political Dynamics of the Sul-tanate of Oman*. Also useful are Hassan A. Al-Ebraheem's *Kuwait: A Political Study*, Emile A. Nakhleh's *Bahrain: Political Development in a Modernizing Society*, and Cora Vreede-De Stuers' "Girl Students in Kuwait." Louise E. Sweet presents a summary of ethnographic knowledge through the late 1960s in "The Arabian Peninsula" in *The Central Middle East*. (For further information and complete citations, see Bibliography.)

Chapter 2. Kuwait

Crest of the State of Kuwait

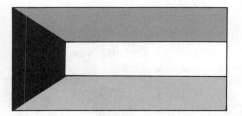

Country

Formal Name: State of Kuwait.

Short Form: Kuwait.

Term for Citizens: Kuwaiti(s); adjectival form, Kuwaiti.

Capital: Kuwait (Kuwait City frequently used to distinguish it from country).

Flag: Three horizontal stripes (green, white, and red from top to bottom) joining a black trapezoid at staff side.

Geography

Size: About 17,818 square kilometers.

Topography: Mainland and islands desert.

Climate: Hot and humid, scant rainfall.

Boundaries: Mostly defined; boundary dispute with Iraq seemingly resolved.

Society

Population: About 1.5 million in mid-1984, although estimates vary. Foreigners accounted for 49 to 65 percent of total.

Education: Free to all citizens and many foreigners from pre-school through university. Literacy rate about 70 percent for

Kuwaitis, about 75 percent for foreigners.

Health: National comprehensive health care system extensive and continuing to expand and improve. Ratio of one physician for every 619 residents, one of best in world.

Ethnic Groups: Most Kuwaitis are Arab. Foreign community includes large Arab contingents, especially Palestinians and Egyptians, as well as Indians, Iranians, and Pakistanis.

Religion: Most Kuwaitis are Sunni (see Glossary) Muslims, as are most Palestinians, Egyptians, and Pakistanis. Between 20 and 24 percent of citizens are Shia (see Glossary) Muslims.

Economy

Gross Domestic Product (GDP):   US$27.6 billion in 1980 and US$24.3 billion in 1981; US$20,079 per capita in 1980 and US$16,518 in 1981.

Oil Industry: 63 percent of GDP in 1981, 97 percent of government revenues in 1982, and 93 percent of commodity exports in 1980. Crude oil production 823,000 barrels per day (bpd) in 1982 and 1.06 million bpd in 1983.

Industry: About 4 percent of GDP in 1981. Largest industries petrochemicals and building materials.

Agriculture: Little farming—mostly vegetables and fruits. Most food imported.

Exports: US$15.7 billion in 1981; mostly crude oil and refined products. Asia and Western Europe main markets.

Imports: US$6.7 billion in 1981—largely such finished products as appliances and vehicles from industrialized nations, particularly Japan, United States, and Western Europe.

Exchange Rate: One Kuwaiti dinar (KD) per US$3.43 average in 1983.

Government and Politics

Government: 1962 Constitution specifies "herediatary amirate" and fixes succession among male "descendants of the late Mubarak Al Sabah." Members of Al Sabah dominant force in 50-member National Assembly, sole elected legislative body functioning on Arabian Peninsula in 1984.

Politics: Al Sabah family dominates political events, but several other noble merchant families also powerful. Major social and political problems center on cleavages between Kuwaiti minority and non-Kuwaiti majority. In mid-1980s various Sunni and Shia fundamentalist groups also agitating for power.

Foreign Relations: As of mid-1984 major foreign policy efforts continued to be directed within context of Arab allies—particularly Gulf Cooperation Council (GCC)—but Kuwait tended to take a more aggressively nonaligned stance than other GCC members and was expanding relations with Soviet Union and members of Warsaw Pact. In addition to GCC, Kuwait belongs to more than 20 international organizations, including United Nations, League of Arab States (Arab League), Nonaligned Movement, and Organization of the Islamic Conference.

National Security

Armed Forces: Estimated strengths in early 1984: army, 10,000; navy, 500; and air force, 1,900. Service voluntary. Army well equipped with tanks, self-propelled artillery, and armored personnel carriers; increasing its antitank capabilities. Navy, formerly only coastal patrol, will acquire several guided missile craft in 1984. Air force combat aircraft included McDonnell Douglas Skyhawks and French Mirages.

IN THE MID-1930s Kuwait was a poor shaykhdom whose people secured a meager living from fishing, pearling, and trading with neighboring Persian Gulf societies. The state's defense and external affairs were in the hands of the British, who also provided the ruling family—the Al Sabah—a small yearly stipend. A half-century later Kuwait possessed one of the highest per capita incomes in the world and a system of social services—including free public education and medical care—that placed it among the most advanced welfare societies.

Kuwait's enormous wealth derives from its sole valuable natural resource—oil—and the acumen with which the country's rulers have invested the money earned from oil. In the mid-1980s Kuwait's earnings from its foreign investments, tanker fleet, and other financial and commercial enterprises about equaled and at times exceeded the revenues earned directly from oil exports. The government has used its vast treasure to build roads, ports, schools, hospitals, and housing, to expand and modernize its national security forces, and to make large loans and gifts to other nations. Furthermore, the severe water shortage that had plagued Kuwait for centuries was eliminated with the construction of a huge desalination system.

These dramatic socioeconomic transformations have not been without problems. By the mid-1980s almost three-fifths of the population were non-Kuwaitis. The largest non-Kuwaiti group consisted of Palestinians, most of whom carried Jordanian passports. The nation's strict naturalization law precluded almost all resident aliens from ever acquiring citizenship, and the law and related legislation ensured that the economy, the government, and the national security forces would stay under direct Kuwaiti control. The manifest inequality of treatment and opportunity between citizens and aliens continued to breed resentment, a feeling that was intensified by the obvious fact that the skills of the foreigners remained essential for the functioning of the socioeconomic system and for critical aspects of the government.

In 1984 Kuwait operated as a constitutional monarchy in the sense that the head of state was a monarch and the system of government was based on the Constitution, which was promulgated in 1962. Since independence in 1961, the most significant political innovation has been the gradual acquisition of power and prestige by a popularly elected legislature, which the amir (ruler) has nonetheless prorogued on occasion. In addition, Kuwait has established a secular legal system, unique among the Gulf states.

The monarchy is hereditary within the Al Sabah family, and the reigning monarch is by the Constitution designated the Amir of Kuwait. In mid-1984 the amir was Shaykh Jabir al Ahmad al Jabir Al Sabah; his designated successor was the prime minister, Shaykh Saad al Abdallah al Salim Al Sabah. Within the Al Sabah family only male descendants of Shaykh Mubarak Al Sabah, who reigned from 1896 to 1915, are eligible to become amir. In practice only two branches of Shaykh Mubarak's lineage were important in this selection process: Al Jabir and Al Salim. Amir Jabir is of the Al Jabir branch, and Prime Minister Saad is of the Al Salim branch.

Geography

Located at the northwestern corner of the Gulf, Kuwait is bounded on the east by the Gulf, on the north and west by Iraq, and on the south and southwest by Saudi Arabia (see fig. 4). The area of the state is about 17,818 square kilometers, somewhat less than the size of New Jersey. Included in this territory are a number of large offshore islands, the largest of which is Bubiyan, separated from the mainland by a narrow waterway. Of these islands, only Faylakah at the mouth of Kuwait Bay is inhabited. This island is believed to have been a center of civilization in antiquity and is the site of an ancient Greek temple built by the forces of Alexander the Great. The country's only prominent geographic feature is Kuwait Bay, which indents the shoreline for about 40 kilometers, providing natural protection for the port of Kuwait and accounting for nearly half the state's shoreline.

The northern border with Iraq dates from an agreement between Kuwait and the Ottoman Empire in 1913 that, though never formally ratified, was accepted by Iraq when that country became independent in 1932. (In the 1960s and again in 1976 Iraqi governments made claims to Kuwaiti territory.) The boundary between Kuwait and Saudi Arabia was set by the Treaty of Uqair in 1922, which also established the Kuwait-Saudi Arabia Neutral Zone. In 1966 Kuwait and Saudi Arabia agreed in principle to divide the Neutral Zone; the partitioning agreement making each country responsible for administration in its portion was signed in December 1969. The resources in the area, since known as the Divided Zone, were not affected by the agreement, and the oil from onshore and offshore fields continued to be shared ·

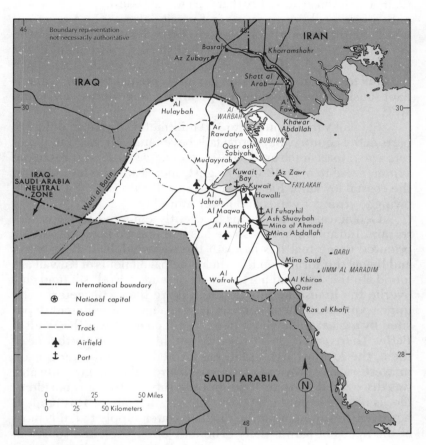

Figure 4. Kuwait, 1984.

equally between the two countries.

Most of Kuwait consists of waterless desert. There is one small oasis at Al Jahrah at the western end of Kuwait Bay, however, and a few wells in the coastal villages. There are no permanent streams, but a few wadis are filled by winter rain. Notable among these is the Wadi al Batin, the broad shallow valley forming the western boundary of the country. At Ar Rawdatyn in the north several shallow wadis converge and provide a temporary repository for winter floodwater, which quickly evaporates or sinks into the porous subsoil.

The climate is somewhat less severe than in other parts of the

Gulf. The intense humidity that is characteristic of the region lasts only a few weeks of the year in Kuwait—usually in August—at which time temperatures regularly exceed 43°C and have been known to exceed 54°C. Sand and dust storms are frequent in the summer, when the *shamal*, a strong northeast wind, blows down the Gulf from Iran. Winters are generally pleasant. There is abundant sunshine, and daytime temperatures range between 7°C and 16°C.

Rainfall varies from 75 to 150 millimeters a year in different parts of the country, but actual falls have ranged from 25 millimeters a year to as much as 325 millimeters. Sea temperatures in the summer rise to over 32°C in August, increasing the humidity on the coastal lowland. Farther inland the climate is more favorable owing to stronger winds and lower humidity.

Geologically, the land is a recently emerged and youthful terrain. In the south, limestone has been raised in a long, north-oriented dome that lies beneath the surface debris. It is within and below this formation that the principal oil fields of Kuwait are found. In the west and north, layers of sand, gravel, silt, and clay overlie the limestone to a depth of more than 210 meters. The upper portions of these beds are part of a mass of sediment deposited by a great wadi whose most recent channel was the Wadi al Batin. There are at least two structural highs in the north; one of them, the Ar Rawdatyn uplift, has formed a groundwater trap on its western side. Kuwait's principal source of fresh groundwater was discovered there in 1960, but the supply, though considerable, is not sufficient to support extensive irrigation. It is tapped, however, to supplement the distilled water supply that fills most of the needs of Kuwait City. The only other exploited source of groundwater is the permeable zone in the top of the limestone of the Ash Shuaybah field south and west of Kuwait City. Unlike the Ar Rawdatyn deposit, Ash Shuaybah water is saline. Several million gallons a day of this brackish water were produced for non-drinking purposes, and in the mid-1980s a vast supply remained (see Industry, this ch.).

Population

The 1980 census reported the total population as 1,357,952. Of that number, 792,339 (about 58.3 percent) were identified as non-Kuwaiti (see fig. 5). The comparable figures in the 1975 census had indicated a total population of 994,837, of which 552,749 (about 55.5 percent) were foreigners.

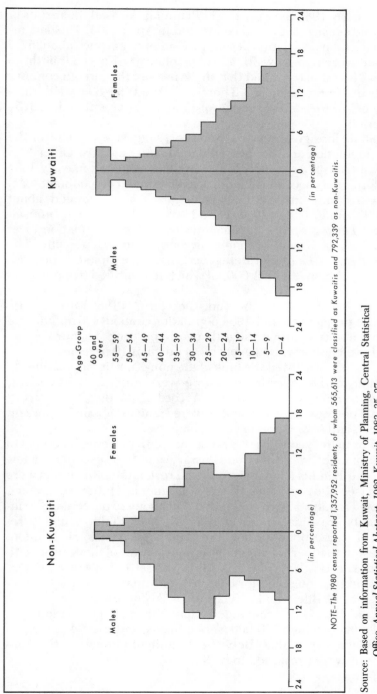

Source: Based on information from Kuwait, Ministry of Planning, Central Statistical Office, *Annual Statistical Abstract, 1982,* Kuwait, 1983, 35–37.

Figure 5. Kuwait. Age-Sex Pyramid, Census 1980.

In early 1984 the Ministry of Planning released the results of a sample census that it had conducted in April 1983. The data indicated a total population of about 1.5 million, of which about 57.5 percent were non-Kuwaiti, a decline of nearly 1 percent in three years. The ministry stated that the growth of the foreign community had averaged almost 3.3 percent in the 1980–83 period, markedly below the annual average of almost 8.8 percent in the 1975–80 period.

Some foreign observers, however, suggest other data for the total population and the percentage of non-Kuwaitis. Officials in one United States agency, for example, speculated in early 1984 that foreigners accounted for nearly 65 percent of a population of about 1.6 million and that Palestinians alone totaled about 350,000, or more than 20 percent. In its April 1983 issue, *International Demographics* estimated that the population was 1,562,190, of which foreigners accounted for 61 percent. The United States Central Intelligence Agency estimated the mid-1983 population at 1,652,000, of which it identified 61 percent as non-Kuwaiti.

The most that may be said, therefore, is that Kuwait's official data projected a mid-1984 population of about 1.6 million and an annual rate of growth slightly over 3 percent. That projection may have been low, however, by as much as 10 percent.

Arabs constituted the bulk of the non-Kuwaiti population. In addition to the Palestinians, there were numerous Egyptians, Iraqis, Syrians, and Lebanese. According to the 1980 census, about 8 percent of the foreigners were Iranians, about 7.5 percent Indians, and over 6 percent Pakistanis.

For many years observers estimated that about 10 percent of the population was Shia (see Glossary) and that, except for a few thousand Hindus and Christians, the rest of the inhabitants were Sunni (see Glossary) (see Tenets of Islam, ch. 1). In recent years, however, analysts have concluded that about 25 percent of the inhabitants are Shia. In early 1984 Michael Field, a highly respected correspondent for the *Financial Times* of London, suggested that perhaps as many as one-quarter of the Kuwaiti citizens are descendants of Iranian Shia who settled in Kuwait before 1920 and thus qualified for citizenship. American political scientist James A. Bill, who in 1982 and 1983 conducted four research trips to the Gulf, concluded that Kuwait's population was 1,370,000, of which 570,000 were citizens, and that 24 percent of the citizens were Shia. Between 15 and 20 percent of the non-Kuwaitis were presumed to be Shia.

Education

Prominent among the nation's efforts to transform a traditional society into a modern, industrial country has been an ambitious, expensive program to develop universal education. In FY (fiscal year) 1982 education was the second largest government expenditure item, exceeded only by the combined expenditures for defense and general public services. Expenditures on public education in both current and capital accounts were about KD222 million (for value of the Kuwaiti dinar—see Glossary). In addition, over KD38 million was spent on university education in FY 1982. Expenditures on this scale have produced in only a few decades a totally subsidized system that is one of the best in the Middle East. Whereas there were 198 teachers and 4,665 students in the public schools in FY 1949, there were 24,367 teachers and 355,512 students in FY 1982, and the expansion in the number and size of the educational facilities has been equally impressive.

Public education is free to Kuwaiti citizens and many foreigners from the kindergarten through the university level. The government absorbs the costs of books, clothing, meals, and transportation and pays parents an allowance that increases when a child reaches the secondary-school level. The government also subsidizes hundreds of students in universities abroad. In addition to providing education to its own residents, Kuwait attracts university students from the Gulf area and elsewhere in the Middle East and has become a leading center of education.

As a result of these efforts, the literacy rate has continued to increase. Including all residents over the age of 10, the literacy rate at the time of the 1980 census was 71 percent—about 75 percent for men and 65 percent for women. Foreigners had somewhat higher literacy rates than citizens; 75 percent of the non-Kuwaiti men and 73 percent of the non-Kuwaiti women were literate, whereas 73 percent of the Kuwaiti men and 51 percent of the Kuwaiti women were literate. Because persons who claimed only an ability to read were included among literates, it is likely that the actual level of functional literacy was somewhat lower than the figures indicate. Moreover, whereas 87 percent of those in the 10-to-14 age-group were literate, less than 38 percent of those aged 50 and over claimed to be literate.

Development of Education
Kuwait's first modern educational institution, Al

Mubarakiyya, was founded by a group of merchants under the patronage of the ruler in 1912. Until that time instruction was available only under religious tutors who gave lessons to individuals or to groups. Training generally consisted of reading, writing, memorizing the Quran, and other elementary studies in religion. The Al Mubarakiyya school, however, was intended to supply clerks trained in modern commercial skills. In addition to religious studies, therefore, it originally offered arithmetic and letter writing. Teachers brought from Palestine added history, geography, and drawing to the curriculum. Supported by contributions from local merchants, the school had scanty facilities and often used texts written by the teachers. In 1921 Al Ahmadia school, the first to offer English, was founded, and in 1927 the first girls' school was opened, offering Arabic, home economics, and Quranic studies. When the worldwide depression caused a drop in the pearl market—then the mainstay of the economy—the merchants found it impossible to continue, and Al Mubarakiyya closed.

The modern period in Kuwaiti education began in the 1930s, when an educational mission from Palestine arrived and Kuwaitis began sending boys abroad for schooling. By the mid-1930s the economy again required a steady supply of clerks, and in the 1936–37 school year four primary schools—three with a total of 600 boys and one with 140 girls—were established. A new tax-supported education department was founded in 1936 to supervise the state schools. In that year teachers from Egypt, Lebanon, Iraq, Syria, and Palestine introduced secondary education, using a syllabus from Palestine.

From this small base, education developed gradually until the 1950s. Serious expansion got under way when the proceeds from oil began flowing into the national treasury. Various special education facilities developed during the 1950s and 1960s. The first kindergartens and the first technical college were established in the 1954–55 school year. The college opened with 80 students studying such fields as auto mechanics and air-conditioning and grew to over 12 fields, including chemical engineering. Special education was established the following year, when 36 children enrolled in the Institute for the Blind; in 1973 there were 11 institutes with 1,644 students for deaf or otherwise handicapped children. Adult education began for men in 1958 and for women in 1963. In 1962 the education department was upgraded to a ministry. As of the mid-1980s the most dramatic achievement in Kuwaiti education had been the opening of a university.

The relatively small number of educated Kuwaitis and the

rapid growth in curriculum and enrollment have required continuing dependence on foreign teachers—mainly Egyptians, Jordanians, and Palestinians. In 1982 only 6,478 of the country's 24,367 teachers were Kuwaitis; they taught mainly in the primary grades, where they constituted over half the faculty. Government policy favors the gradual replacement of foreign teachers by Kuwaitis, but achievement of the government's goal is far in the future.

The Educational System

Since 1957 Kuwait has followed a program of two years of kindergarten, four years of primary, four years of intermediate, and four years of secondary school. Since 1965 education has been compulsory for Kuwaitis between six and 14 years of age. Paralleling the intermediate and secondary segments of the secular curriculum is a religious institute for boys. Private schools, teaching in Arabic and foreign languages, exist at all levels as well. Enrollment and facilities in all institutions have been growing rapidly (see table 2; table 3, Appendix A).

Because essentially all economic and social barriers have been removed, all Kuwaitis may attend school; for non-Kuwaitis, it is somewhat more difficult. Although the government encourages the education of foreign children and admits them to government schools when space is available, in the 1981–82 school year perhaps 30 percent of the non-Kuwaiti students attended private schools. The government provides subsidies and technical assistance to the private schools, sells them books and other materials at cost, and inspects them for adherence to government standards.

At the apex of the educational system is the University of Kuwait, which the government established in 1966. In its first school year the university had 242 male students and 176 female students in an affiliated women's college. By the early 1980s the university enrolled over 10,000 students (see table 4, Appendix A). Kuwaiti citizens made up over 75 percent of the student body, 57 percent of which consisted of women. Over 2,200 Kuwaitis were attending universities and colleges abroad in 1982—almost 1,500 of them in the United States.

Health and Welfare

The development of the health care system and resultant improvement in health conditions paralleled the country's developing wealth and contact with the outside world. In the first decade of the twentieth century, the country remained what G.E. Ffrench, an authority on Kuwait, terms "premedical"; it had essentially no effective health care and suffered an infant mortality rate of over 120 per 1,000 live births and a general mortality rate of over 25 per 1,000. Natural increase was close to zero. In 1909 an American physician representing the Arabian American Mission of the Dutch Reformed Church arrived in Kuwait. By 1911 he and a small staff had organized a hospital for men and by 1919 a small hospital for women. In 1934 the 34-bed Olcott Memorial Hospital was opened. Between 1909 and 1946 Kuwait experienced some improvement in health conditions. General mortality stood between 20 and 25 per 1,000 and infant mortality between 100 and 125 per 1,000 live births.

In 1946 a state health plan supplemented the efforts of the mission facilities and the Kuwait Oil Company (KOC), and between then and 1950 general mortality fell to between 17 and 23 per 1,000 and infant mortality to between 80 and 100 per 1,000 live births. During that period the country had approximately one physician per 25,000 people.

Between 1950 and 1955 a national health system developed rapidly. Hospital beds numbered more than 1,000, and the effects of the expansion of facilities were visible in a drop in general mortality, which fell to between 12 and 18 per 1,000, and in infant mortality, which fell to between 50 and 75 per 1,000 live births. As the health care system grew in size and comprehensiveness throughout the 1950s and 1960s, mortality rates approached those experienced in developed countries. The infant mortality rate of 35 to 45 per 1,000 in the late 1960s resembled that of Britain after World War II, and the general mortality rate stood between 10 and 15 per 1,000.

The government's current expenditures for health in FY 1982 were about KD162 million. These funds supported 14 hospitals and sanitariums, 55 clinics, 105 dental clinics, 17 maternity centers, 28 pediatric centers, 23 preventive health centers, and 480 school clinics. The funds also paid for over 14,000 medical personnel, including over 2,100 physicians and almost 6,000 nurses. There was one physician for every 619 residents and one nurse for every 220 residents, a ratio that few societies can match.

Over 82 percent of the physicians employed by the government were foreigners. The largest non-Kuwaiti contingent— some 42 percent—came from Egypt; almost half of the female physicians were Egyptians. Most of the approximately 200 physi-

Fishing dhows

Camels—ships of the desert

cians in the private sector were also foreigners.

By the mid-1980s some major health problems that had previously plagued the country had been brought under control or eliminated. As a result of the worldwide campaign by the World Health Organization, smallpox had disappeared. Of the 13,080 cases of infectious diseases reported by the health care centers in 1981, the largest category was measles (2,598 cases), followed by salmonella (2,388), mumps (2,170), and infectious hepatitis (1,741). In addition, there were 819 registered cases of tuberculosis, but because only 252 of the cases were female, observers concluded that not all cases were being reported.

By 1980 infant mortality had fallen to 22.3 per 1,000 live births for non-Kuwaiti females and 25.8 per 1,000 for non-Kuwaiti males. The comparable figures for Kuwaiti females and males were 29.3 and 33.3, respectively, per 1,000. The largest recorded causes of death in 1981 were diseases of the circulatory system (1,388 deaths), followed by "accidents, poisoning, violence, and others" (1,111 deaths), neoplasms (412 deaths), and respiratory diseases (386 deaths).

In addition to a comprehensive system of health care, the government provided residents with one of the world's most encompassing welfare programs. Payments were made to the disabled, the senile, students' families, widows, unmarried women over the age of 18, orphans, the poor, and the families of prisoners. In FY 1982 the government's current expenditure budget provided KD56.2 million for social security and welfare services and KD79 million for housing and community affairs and services. In addition, over KD43 million was allocated for recreational, cultural, and religious affairs and services.

The Economy

After their migration to Kuwait Bay in the early 1700s, Kuwaitis were forced by the scant rainfall and limited water for irrigation of crops to look seaward for economic development. Boatbuilding flourished, and Kuwaiti craft became known throughout coastal Arabia for their quality. These craft with Kuwaiti sailors plied the waters of the Gulf, the Arabian Sea, and the Indian Ocean. Pearling was also a large-scale activity until the rise of the cultured pearl industry in Japan in the 1920s. The good harbor in Kuwait Bay and other maritime activity led to the development of a vigorous merchant class in Kuwait City. During the eighteenth and nineteenth centuries, the city rivaled Basrah in Iraq as an entrepôt for the trade between India and parts of the Middle East. The legacy of seafaring and trade gave the Kuwaiti people an aptitude for commerce and a propensity to look abroad that continued into the 1980s.

Although maritime activities provided employment in early Kuwait, incomes were low and life harsh except for a few merchant families who became wealthy. Even the ruling family had a very limited income. In the mid-1930s the entire budget for the palace and all of the royal family was the equivalent of about US$7,500 a year and was contributed directly or indirectly by the merchant families. In FY 1939 the average per capita income in the country was estimated at the equivalent of about US$35 a year, and total public revenue, two-thirds of which came from import duties, amounted to US$290,000. Some observers attributed the resourcefulness and independent spirit of the Kuwaiti people to their struggle for survival under adverse conditons.

Conditions began to change after oil was found in 1938. Oil field activities created jobs at much higher pay than many traditional pursuits, attracting Kuwaitis from labor-intensive, low-income sectors of the economy and workers from other countries. World War II held up development of the fields. Commercial production of crude oil began in 1946, ushering in a construction boom. More workers were attracted from abroad, and by the 1950s foreigners outnumbered Kuwaitis in the work force. By 1948 oil revenues had reached about US$6 million, sufficient for the government to begin public projects to improve living conditions. In 1949 construction began on a public hospital, a government building, schools, and roads.

The government was not prepared for the changes that occurred; there was little government when oil was discovered, and little was needed. Initial public projects were started with minimal basic planning and often from simple sketches. Public administration developed in response to the increasing flow of oil revenues. But one basic change occured with the first oil company payment: the oil revenues were paid to the amir, concentrating in his hands and, subsequently, those of other government officials, the distribution of funds. The position of the amir was enhanced relative to other segments of the society, and he was freed of dependence on financial support or taxes from the rest of the community.

Oil revenues continued to mount. By the 1960s Kuwait had become the richest country in the world (wealth being measured in terms of national income per capita). The rapid escalation of crude oil prices and revenues per barrel greatly increased the government's income in the 1970s and early 1980s. Oil revenues jumped from US$1.8 billion in FY 1974 to US$8.3 billion in FY 1975. By FY 1980 government income from oil reached nearly US$21.7 billion, and in 1981 gross domestic product (GDP) amounted to US$24.3 billion. GDP on a per capita basis was about US$16,500, making the average Kuwaiti the world's wealthiest—except, perhaps, for the citizens of Qatar.

The flow of oil revenues created a problem unusual to most governments in the world—what to do with all the money. By the early 1980s Kuwait had an extensive welfare program, exceeded perhaps by no other country. Citizens received free medical services from modern facilities, free education through the university level, and subsidized food, housing, utilities, and transportation, for example. Noncitizens, however, benefited much less, and many resented their disadvantaged position despite having worked many years in the country. In the 1970s the government invested heavily in a gas-gathering system and downstream (see Glossary) facilities for refining, petrochemicals, and petroleum marketing. Even with the various expenditures a substantial surplus of funds accumulated over the years, which the government invested in overseas assets.

By the early 1980s Kuwait's economy was far different from that of 40 years earlier. In 1981 the oil industry (including refining) dominated the economy, contributing 63 percent of GDP (see table 5, Appendix A). The other major activity was public administration and social service, which accounted for about 10 percent of GDP. Trade contributed 7 percent of GDP and financial services a similar percentage. Industrial activity and construction each amounted to 4 percent of GDP. The remaining sectors made minor contributions to value added—particularly farming and fishing, which accounted for 0.3 percent of GDP. Apart from the oil industry but because of oil revenues, the economy was predominantly service oriented. The distribution of oil revenues among the population accounted for part of the services and also stimulated distribution and sale of imported goods and financial transactions, including real estate and stock market speculation (see Finance, this ch.). The traditional commercial orientation of the more prosperous Kuwaitis persisted in the 1980s, causing interest and investment in industry or agriculture to be the choice of relatively few.

Once exports of oil began in the late 1940s, economic development became nearly continuous. Until 1972 much of the expansion resulted from increasing crude oil production, but oil production peaked in that year. For the rest of the 1970s, oil production was substantially lower, but higher revenues per barrel financed continued economic growth (see table 6, Appendix A). In late 1980 a surplus of oil relative to demand began to emerge on world markets, and this persisted in 1984. More important, oil revenues declined from US$21.7 billion in FY 1980 to US$9.7 billion in FY 1982. Although data were unavailable, economists expected that oil revenues remained low or declined a little in FY 1983.

Economic activity slowed after 1980. GDP fell 9 percent in 1981 and probably further in 1982 and 1983. A crash of the unofficial stock market in mid-1982 contributed to the diminished economic activity (see Finance, this ch.). Although budget revenues dropped sharply during the recession of the early 1980s, officials largely sustained government spending by drawing on investment income from assets abroad (see Role of Government, this ch.). By maintaining government expenditures the economy was spared the worst effects of the recession. By 1984, however, some mild austerity measures had been introduced to limit the growth of expenditures. Although many economists considered the economy sound and stable because of the country's foreign assets, observers wondered about the population's reaction if further austerity measures were required by continuing low demand for Kuwait's oil in world markets for a few more years.

The Oil Industry

Kuwait is the classic example of an oil shaykhdom. A sleepy maritime settlement whose inhabitants eked out a bare existence by traditional pursuits in a harsh environment emerged in little more than a generation into one of the world's wealthiest countries on a per capita basis. The oil industry dominated the economy, contributing 63 percent of GDP (FY 1981), 97 percent of government revenues (FY 1982), and 93 percent of commodity exports (FY 1980). Kuwait was also blessed with large oil deposits, although official estimates of oil and gas reserves were not available in mid-1984. The authoritative *Oil and Gas Journal* estimated the country's recoverable crude oil reserves (including the Divided Zone) at nearly 66.8 billion barrels at the beginning of 1984, sufficient to last more than 160 years at the 1983 production level. Other publications frequently mentioned reserves of 70 billion barrels or more. For the beginning of 1984 the *Oil and Gas Journal* listed the country's gas reserves at nearly 1.1 trillion cubic meters, nearly all of which was associated with crude oil reserves.

Discovery and Development of Oil

For centuries oil seepages in the desert indicated oil below, but the amount and quality could be determined only by drilling. The natural seepages interested oilmen, and in 1911 a company, which in 1954 was to be renamed British Petroleum (BP) and which was developing oil fields in Iran, requested permission to negotiate a concession from Kuwait. The British government refused the request, saying that the area was too troubled. In 1913 the British government sent men to inspect the seepages and make a geological survey. The ruling shaykh also reaffirmed a previous stipulation that he would grant a concession only to a group recommended by the British government. World War I interrupted another effort by BP to negotiate a concession. By this time the British government had purchased 51 percent ownership in BP as part of an effort to ensure oil supplies for its Royal Navy.

In the 1920s the Gulf Oil Corporation of the United States began to seek concessions in the Gulf to overcome its lack of crude oil sources. British treaties with most rulers in the Gulf, including Kuwait, made it difficult for non-British companies to gain access, however, even though the United States government pressured the British to provide equal treatment to American oil firms. During the 1920s BP continued attempts to obtain a Kuwait concession. In 1932 Gulf Oil and BP formed a joint company to negotiate a concesion in Kuwait, and this received British approval. The amir finally signed the concession on December 23, 1934. The concessionaire was the Kuwait Oil Company (KOC), owned equally by Gulf Oil and BP.

KOC began operations with surveys in 1935. Drilling started in 1936 on the north shore of Kuwait Bay, but no oil was found. The second attempt, in the desert, struck a real gusher in 1938 that subsequently was called the Burgan (Al Burqan) field, one of the largest and most productive in the world (see fig. 6). World War II halted development, and finished wells were plugged. At the end of the war, pipelines and other facilities were completed to handle 30,000 barrels per day (bpd) of crude. Commercial export of crude oil began in June 1946. Production amounted to 5.,9 million barrels in 1946 and 16.2 million barrels in 1947. KOC subsequently discovered seven additional oil fields, and production continued to increase until 1972.

Subsequent concessions contained progressively better terms for Kuwait, partly because of the entrance of small oil companies anxious to acquire crude oil sources and partly because of the activities and exchange of information among oil-producing

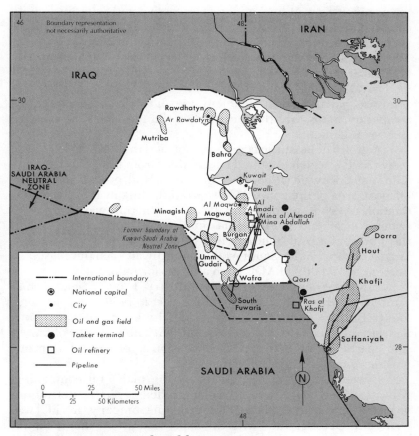

Figure 6.   Kuwait. Oil Fields, 1984

states (see Appendix B). Payments were substantially higher, the length of the concessions was shorter, schedules for relinquishing underdeveloped areas were established, and opportunities for Kuwait participation in the companies were increased.

The American Independent Oil Company (Aminoil) was the successful bidder for Kuwait's rights in the Kuwait-Saudi Arabia Neutral Zone, receiving on June 28, 1948, a 60-year concession for exploration and production. Aminoil, which was owned by a number of small American oil companies, had a joint operation with the Getty Oil Company, which held the Saudi rights in the Neutral Zone. The Arabian American Oil Company (Aramco, the main developer of Saudi Arabia's oil fields) reportedly viewed the terms given Kuwait by Aminoil as excessive and relinquished its concession in the Neutral Zone, which Getty won. Aminoil started exploratory drilling in 1949 but did not strike oil until March 1953. Production started in 1954. Production from the Neutral Zone was shared between the two countries, and Aminoil paid royalties and taxes to Kuwait and Getty to Saudi Arabia. The zone was partitioned in 1969 and does not appear on most contemporary maps, but the partitioning did not affect the concession arrangements.

A group of Japanese companies formed the Arabian Oil Company (AOC), which obtained concessions from both Saudi Arabia (1957) and Kuwait (1958) for exploration and production in the offshore area of the zone. AOC started drilling in 1959, and production of crude oil began in 1961. Production was shared between Kuwait and Saudi Arabia. Some of AOC production is from the northern tip of Saudi Arabia's Saffaniyah field, the world's largest offshore field. Saudi Arabia and Kuwait each purchased 10 percent ownership of AOC soon after its formation.

From the beginning of the oil industry, Kuwait's leaders had wanted to participate and have some part in policy and management. BP and Gulf Oil turned aside the amir's demand for a Kuwaiti on the board of directors of KOC. The Kuwaitis obtained some participation in the AOC concession agreement, but its importance was more symbolic than real.

Frozen out of oil operations by the major oil companies, Kuwait started on its own to develop proficiency in the petroleum industry. The Kuwait National Petroleum Company (KNPC) was formed in October 1960 with the expressed intent that it should become an integrated oil company. Its founding charter allowed it to engage in almost any activity touching on petroleum at home or abroad. It began with 60 percent government ownership, the remaining shares being held by private Kuwaiti investors. The government bought out the private investors in 1975.

KNPC started operations on a small scale, partly because of Kuwait's acute shortage of skilled manpower. It bought out KOC's local petroleum distribution facilities and became the sole supplier of petroleum products in Kuwait. It participated in foreign refinery operations and established subsidiaries and facilities abroad for marketing petroleum products. Departments for exploration and other aspects of field operations were established within KNPC to work with foreign companies in the concession area that KNPC had received from the government.

KNPC also built, with foreign expertise and equipment, a

modern refinery to use gas in the Burgan field—which would otherwise have been flared—in a hydrogenation process to convert crude into products and to produce sulfur as a useful by-product. Kuwait's crude is heavy and contains considerable sulfur, so the design of the refinery was excellently fitted to the local circumstances to turn out a more superior product than a normal refinery. The refinery at Ash Shuaybah was completed in 1968, but technical problems caused an unprofitable mix of products for a while. Between cost overruns during construction and a poor range of products, KNPC lost money until the problems were corrected. Nonetheless, KNPC provided important training for Kuwaitis in upper levels of management for oil company operations.

Kuwait's goal of real participation in and control over its oil industry was achieved in 1974 and 1975. In 1974 the government bought 60 percent of KOC, including the refinery and other installations, reportedly for US$112 million—presumably the net book value of the assets involved. In December 1975—backdated to March 5, 1975—the government bought the remaining 40 percent of KOC, reportedly for US$50.5 million. BP and Gulf continued to provide technical services and personnel in return for access to oil supplies and service fees. By 1980 about half of KOC's work force were Kuwaitis, many of whom held high administrative and technical positions.

In 1976 negotiations were concluded for Kuwait's purchase of 60 percent of its half-share of AOC's offshore operations. Negotiations for 60 percent of Aminoil floundered over the value of assets. In 1977 Kuwait nationalized the firm, paying compensation on the basis of an official estimate of the value of assets. Aminoil became the Kuwait Wafrah Oil Company, until 1978, when operations in the Wafra field passed to KOC, and KNPC took over the former Aminoil refinery and shipping terminal at Mina Abdallah.

In January 1980 the government created the Kuwait Petroleum Corporation (KPC) to rationalize the organizational structure of its oil industry. KPC was established as a commercial company outside of the government's budget and expenditure control system. KPC became the country's national (government-owned) integrated oil company with KOC, KNPC, the Kuwait Oil Tanker Company (KOTC), the Petrochemicals Industries Company (PIC), and the Kuwait Foreign Petroleum Exploration Company (KFPEC) as some of its more important wholly owned subsidiaries. KOC was primarily responsible for domestic exploration and production of oil and gas, and KNPC was mainly the refining subsidiary. KPC also entered joint ventures with and purchased shares in foreign companies involved in aspects of the oil business. In 1981, for example, KPC bought Santa Fe International Corporation, an American drilling and energy enginneering firm, for a reported US$2.5 billion. Other KPC activities abroad included part ownership in refineries and petrochemical plants, exploration and drilling in foreign concession areas, such as Egypt, Indonesia, and China, and purchase of retail outlets for petroleum products in Western Europe.

Government Oil Policy

Since assuming control of its oil industry in the mid-1970s, Kuwaiti officials followed moderate policies between conflicting objectives. Most Gulf oil governments, including Kuwait, believed that oil in the ground was worth more to future generations than holding such paper claims as securities and corporate shares, which were subject to price inflation, exchange rate risks, and sequestration. Kuwait officials could have limited oil production to that required for financing priority programs. Officials also actively supported the Organization of Petroleum Exporting Countries (OPEC), which at times required oil production levels below that necessary to cover government expenditures. Kuwait, for example, reduced oil production and exports during the Arab oil embargo associated with the October 1973 War launched by Egypt and Syria against Israel.

An oil production limit of 3 million bpd was set in 1973 after members of Kuwait's National Assembly questioned the accuracy of KOC estimates of recoverable reserves. The government hired foreign experts who confirmed KOC estimates, although reserve figures were not released. Nonetheless, the production limit was established, but it applied only to KOC operations because limits on production from other oil fields—those in the Divided Zone— would have required Saudi Arabia's cooperation. Former KOC fields, however, accounted for nearly all of the country's oil production. In late 1976 Kuwait's production from all fields briefly exceeded 3 million bpd. In 1976 the production ceiling was reduced to 2 million bpd, which was exceeded in early 1979, when Gulf producers increased production to compensate for the disruption of supplies from Iran (see Appendix B). Kuwaiti officials showed a responsibility to oil-consuming nations.

As surplus oil supplies appeared in world markets in the early 1980s, Kuwait's production ceiling was reduced to 1.5 million bpd, although actual production was appreciably lower, amounting to only 821,00 bpd in 1982 and about 1.06 million bpd in 1983. Installed capacity for crude oil production by 1984 was rated at about 3.2 million bpd, although sustainable maximum production over several months was about 2.8 million bpd.

As oil revenues began to mount in the early 1970s, officials decided to invest part of the funds in downstream petroleum operations. A key ingredient was a gas-gathering system to use the gases produced in association with crude oil. Until the late 1970s a considerable part of the gases had been flared. A major portion of the gas-gathering system was completed in 1979. Extension to onshore fields in the Divided Zone was finished in 1983, and construction of the system for offshore fields was scheduled to begin in 1984 or 1985. Processing facilities removed corrosive sulfur compounds, yielding sulfur as a by-product. The KNPC liquefaction plant separated the gases (consisting of methane and ethane), which provided fuel and feedstock for industrial uses from the natural gas liquids (NGL) that were further separated into propane, butane, and natural gasoline. Propane and butane were stored and shipped under refrigeration as liquefied petroleum gas (LPG). By 1984 the bulk of the gases associated with crude oil production was captured and used. When the gas-gathering system was completed to offshore fields, little gas would be flared.

In addition to the gas-gathering system, the government expanded its investment in oil refining capacity and petrochemical facilities. In 1984 an expansion was under way, costing about US$4.8 billion at two of the country's three refineries, which would raise total refining capacity to about 664,000 bpd of crude oil input by the end of 1986 as well as providing a better product mix and cleaner products. In 1982 about 10 percent of refined products and about 20 percent of LPG products were consumed locally; the remainder was exported. The major markets were East Asia, 32 percent; the rest of Asia, 20 percent; Western Europe, 16 percent; Oceania, 10 percent; and the Middle East, 9 percent. In 1983 and early 1984 KPC purchased some of Gulf Oil Company's West European marketing system, which included at least 2,800 gas stations that would in future years provide outlets for larger exports of refined products. Petrochemical plants were constructed to use the products resulting from the gas-gathering system (see Industry, this. ch.). Gas products, used for fuel and feedstock in industrial plants, were priced substantially below international prices.

The glut of oil on the world markets after 1980 created particular problems for Kuwait. By early 1984 the country's only source of natural gas was that associated with crude oil production. At the beginning of 1984 the *Oil and Gas Journal* estimated

Kuwait's gas reserves at 1.1 trillion cubic meters. As crude oil production dropped from an average of about 2.5 million bpd in 1979 to 823,000 bpd in 1982, supplies of associated gases fell from 37.3 million cubic meters per day in 1979 to less than 12 million cubic meters per day in 1983. In the early 1980s industry became increasingly short of gas supplies. Kuwait's electric power plants were able to switch to the use of fuel oil and crude oil to fire boilers. KNPC's liquefaction plant and PIC's petrochemical plants were greatly underutilized by 1983, and some operations were shut down. In 1982 and 1983 KPC had to reduce progressively export sales of LPG products.

Since 1976 Kuwait has been drilling to find reservoirs of natural gas. Many oil experts believed that the country had substantial natural gas deposits, but by 1984 drilling onshore had failed to find them. Only more oil fields were discovered. In 1984 drilling for gas included offshore areas. Officials indicated that imports of liquefied natural gas would by mid-1984 begin to relieve the gas shortage. A specialized gas tanker had been purchased to transport the gas. Observers wondered how officials would price the natural gas, because its international price was substantially above that charged for domestic gas.

By 1984 Kuwait controlled its hydrocarbon resources and had created an international oil company that rivaled other major oil companies. KPC was among the world's largest corporations and was sometimes called the "seventh sister," a reference to its having become one of the seven major international oil companies. Through its subsidiaries it was involved in all aspects of the oil industry and in many countries of the world. This was a remarkable achievement in less than a quarter of a century since the first Kuwaiti effort to enter the oil industry.

Role of Government

Under the first oil concession, payments were made to the amir. Government in the usual sense did not exist. The amir and his advisers decided how much of the oil revenues would be spent and in what way. In time ministries, budgets, financial controls, and other aspects of modern public administration were instituted, but decisionmaking remained centralized in a small group at the pinnacle of government (see The Constitutional Monarchy, this ch.). The objectives of government policies, however, remained largely unchanged between the first exports of oil and 1984.

Government officials have been keenly aware that oil is a de-

Restaurant and water towers in city of Kuwait

pleting asset, that the country had few other resources, and that preparations had to be made for the day when there would be no more oil. Almost from the beginning of oil revenues, officials spent less than the treasury received, leaving a surplus in the state's General Reserve for investment; because of the limited domestic investment opportunities, most investments were made abroad. World Bank (see Glossary) economists estimated that about a quarter of revenues were placed in foreign assets during the 1950s, although officially published data have always been vague about reserves and some other economic variables.

In 1952 an office was established in London, staffed with experienced British investment counselors who guided the government's placement of funds. In the same year investment relations were established with a large New York bank. The best known of Kuwait's investment organizations, which was copied by other oil exporters, was the Kuwait Fund for Arab Economic Development (KFAED), formed in 1961. This fund functioned as both an investment and an aid agency, providing loans for specific projects and often on concessional terms. KFAED's charter was changed in 1974, when capitalization was increased to KD1 bill-

101

ion so that it could provide funds to developing countries anywhere in the world. Loans were made to governments or to recipients for which a government guaranteed repayment. The total loans provided by KFAED between January 1963 and November 1983 amounted to KD1.2 billion and included 62 countries (see Foreign Relations, this ch.). In 1976 the Reserve Fund for Future Generations was established to invest 10 percent of annual oil revenues, although there were suggestions that in some years more than 10 percent was set aside. These funds were not to be used until many years in the future. Kuwaiti officials had established other investment relationships and were in a good position to invest profitably the surplus funds that emerged after the great increase in oil revenues in the 1970s.

Official government statements in 1984 indicated government reserves of at least US$74 billion as of June 30, 1983, with perhaps more than US$30 billion invested abroad. Maybe half was invested in the United States, and much of the remainder was placed in West European countries. Kuwaiti officials reportedly favored equity investments, holding relatively small amounts of bonds and other securities. Some government investments have gone into real estate, particularly in Britain. By the 1980s earnings from foreign investments had become substantial, amounting to an estimated US$5.5 billion in 1983. These earnings were not shown as government revenues in the budget, but many observers believed they were drawn on, beginning in 1981, to balance expenditures.

From the first oil concession the amir wanted Kuwaitis to be employed and to participate in management of companies exploiting the country's oil deposits, but officials never attempted to establish certain activities exclusively for the public sector. In fact, the private sector, including domestic and foreign investors, was encouraged in various ways to expand the economy. It was recognized that only through technological transfers and on-the-job training of Kuwaitis would the economy modernize. The government attitude remained essentially the same in 1984.

Nonetheless, in the mid-1970s a substantial public sector that was concentrated in the production and processing of crude oil and gas—including basic petrochemical products—began to emerge. Private shareholders, both foreign and domestic, were bought out in nearly all of these activities, and in one case an oil firm was nationalized. Several factors contributed to the growth of Kuwait's public sector. Developments in the international oil industry, the need to establish control over hydrocarbon resources and to gain the maximum value added as the power of international oil companies waned, the size of investments, that were needed, and the demonstrated reluctance of Kuwaiti investors to undertake large-scale industrial projects combined to push the government to take leadership in hydrocarbon-related fields. Many other oil-exporting countries followed a similar pattern. In 1984 Kuwait still did not have any activities exclusively for the public sector and continued to encourage private investment, but major oil-related industries appeared likely to remain almost completely in government ownership for several years.

From the beginning of oil revenues, officials relied on them as the main source of financing expenditures. In FY 1982 oil revenues accounted for 97 percent of budget revenues, although the budget did not include income from investments. Income tax receipts, apart from those paid by foreign oil companies, were minuscule. The only important tax consisted of duties on imports, which provided KD57 million in FY 1982, 1 percent of total revenues. Import tariffs were mostly modest. Charges for services—such as utilities, housing, and transportation—provided KD104 million, 2 percent of total revenues in FY 1982. Most of these services were substantially underpriced. As oil revenues declined in the early 1980s, pressure increased to expand sources of government revenues, but Kuwait's businessmen strongly opposed taxes. By 1984 a few prices had been raised, but no effective measures to increase revenues appreciably had been implemented.

Kuwaiti officials decided early to provide a variety of services to the population as a means of distributing the country's oil income. An elaborate welfare program evolved, providing free education and health services and large subsidies for electricity, water, fuel, housing, transportation, communications, loans, and numerous foods. By the early 1980s a serious shortage of housing had developed, however. In 1982 and 1983 officials instituted mild measures to restrain the expenditure side of the budget, such as increasing the number of students per teacher. The price of gasoline was doubled, but it still was less than half that in the United States. There was discussion of raising charges for electricity, which the population used in large quantities, to reduce the subsidy and excessive consumption. Other measures were advocated, but as of mid-1984 few appeared to have been implemented. Nonetheless, officials recognized that greater austerity and more selective subsidies might become necessary if oil revenues remained low. Development expenditures were also restrained by stretching some construction schedules and by postponing or canceling less essential projects. Data were unavailable to determine the effects on defense expenditures, which customarily were an important budget item (see Kuwait, ch. 7).

Officials traditionally used part of oil revenues to assist other countries, primarily Arab nations. Kuwait's foreign aid increased substantially as oil revenues rose in the 1970s. The aid took many forms, such as loans, joint financing, equity participation, and direct grants—particularly in support of Arab causes. KFAED was a major vehicle for extending aid but not the only one. In 1982 Kuwait's foreign aid amounted to nearly US$1.2 billion, about the same level as in 1980 and 1981. Kuwait reportedly had provided about US$6 billion to Iraq in its war with Iran, but at least part of that would have been outside of balance of payments data.

Kuwait's officials have traditionally followed a conservative fiscal policy. Development expenditures were financed from current revenue, and total expenditures were usually kept below income. This conservatism greatly lessened the damage inflicted by the downturn in the country's economic fortunes. Oil revenues fell by more than half between 1980 and 1982. Many governments would have had trouble surviving such a rapid and catastrophic fall in their main source of income. Officials talked about budget deficits in the early 1980s, but when figures were placed in the usual budget format, Kuwait retained a budget surplus between FY 1980 and FY 1983 (see table 7, Appendix A). Nonetheless, the surplus was small after FY 1981. By 1984 officials were trying to cut waste in government spending and to target subsidies and services more selectively toward those in need.

Labor Force

Kuwait's economic development was achieved in part by importing foreign workers. By 1980 non-Kuwaitis made up 79 percent of the employed labor force (see table 8, Appendix A). During the decade of the 1970s, Kuwaitis in the work force increased by the high average rate of 5.7 percent a year, but the non-Kuwaiti segment grew even faster—an average 8.1 percent a year. The critical importance of foreign workers to the economy was difficult to overstress. Non-Kuwaitis appeared prominently throughout the employment spectrum, filling professional, technical, managerial, and clerical posts—for which there were not enough qualified Kuwaitis—and industrial and menial jobs that Kuwaitis would not accept. In 1980 non-Kuwaitis held 84 percent of the 27,400 professional, technical, and managerial jobs in the country and had about a five-to-one advantage over nationals in terms of having university degrees. At the other end of the spectrum, construction, which employed large numbers of unskilled laborers, was made up of nearly 99 percent expatriates.

A major factor contributing to the reliance on foreign workers was the low educational level of Kuwaitis, reflecting the gradual development of an educational system. In 1975 illiterate Kuwaitis in the labor force amounted to 36 percent, and another 23 percent claimed ability to read and write but lacked an elementary education, leading one observer to conclude that over half of working Kuwaitis should be considered illiterate. Expansion of the educational system after the 1950s started to remedy the situation, but it was a slow and ongoing process (see Education, this ch.) The low participation of females in the work force was another important factor contributing to the reliance on foreign workers. Although Kuwaiti women were clearly more emancipated than others in the Gulf and many had taken advantage of the opportunities for education, their entrance into the labor force was slow. In 1980 Kuwaiti women constituted only 13 percent of all employed Kuwaitis.

The bulk of Kuwaitis were employed in service industries— 88 percent in 1980. The government was the largest employer in the country and employed most of the Kuwaitis in the labor force (about 47,000 in 1983). The Constitution essentially guarantees jobs to citizens, and the government implemented this through its liberal employment policy. Many Kuwaitis preferred government employment to other positions even when it meant routine tasks that often under-utilized their skills and time. Observers usually noted the country's excessive bureaucracy and over-staffing of many positions, to the extent that several people were often assigned to what should have been a single job. In 1983 there were 4.5 citizens for every civil servant. Observers and experts have long advocated reform of the civil service to reduce the inefficiency and underuse of available manpower.

In 1980 some 60 percent of the foreign workers in Kuwait were Arabs, and another 28 percent were Asians, particularly from Iran, Pakistan, and India. Americans and West Europeans accounted for about 1.5 percent, and a few hundred Africans constituted the remainder. Palestinians and Egyptians were especially prominent in professional, technical, and government work. Pakistanis and Indians tended to be skilled workers in technical jobs. Iranians and Iraqis often had menial positions in production or service activities. An influx of East Asian construction workers accompanied the construction boom of the late 1970s and early 1980s. A 1983 government survey found a substantial slowing of the increase in Kuwait's expatriate community since the

1980 census, presumably reflecting a similar reduction in the rate of growth of foreign workers in the labor force. The reduction was probably attributable to diminished development expenditures as well as completion of some of the large construction projects, which resulted in the return home of the imported construction force.

In spite of the country's heavy reliance on imported workers since the 1950s, government policy sharply discriminated against them. Most non-Kuwaitis were paid less than their Kuwaiti counterparts and often less than a Kuwaiti with few qualifications in a less responsible job. The country's social security system, including a 1976 revision, and most retirement benefits were limited to Kuwaitis. Foreigners could not own real property and usually rented in the poorer neighborhoods or sought shelter in shanties constructed of scrap materials. Modern suburban housing developments with many amenities were exclusively for citizens. Foreign workers could not form their own unions, but they could join Kuwaiti unions, although they were prohibited from running for union offices or voting. Acquiring Kuwaiti citizenship was difficult and very limited, even for highly educated expatriates who had worked for 20 years or more in Kuwait and raised families there.

The large number of expatriates created social tensions between the foreigners and the native population. Foreign workers—particularly those who had worked many years in Kuwait—resented the discrimination against them. Natives often viewed the foreign workers with suspicion, if not hostility. In order to enhance the foreign workers' stake in the country's development and to reduce departures of highly trained personnel for jobs elsewhere in the Middle East (where there was less discrimination), some observers suggested granting naturalization or permanent residency on a larger scale to foreign workers who had much needed skills. But the political climate in early 1984 was not conducive to liberalization. Seven car bombings in December 1983, involving some long-term, legal, Iraqi residents, increased the apprehension of Kuwaiti authorities over foreign workers and led to more stringent policies toward applications for work permits. The authorities faced a serious dilemma, however, in choosing between security considerations and the dependence of the economy on foreign workers.

Agriculture

Scant rainfall, little irrigation water, and poor soils have always limited farming in Kuwait. Before the discovery of oil, nomads moving livestock to the limited forage in the desert and pearling and fishing contributed much of agricultural income, but none of these occupations provided much more than subsistence. Growth of the economy and welfare measures since World War II drew workers away from traditional pursuits and lessened the role of agriculture. By 1984 agriculture, including some fishing, contributed only a small fraction of 1 percent to GDP and employed less than 2 percent of the labor force.

Kuwait's total area amounted to 1,781,800 hectares. In 1980 official data indicated 44,041 hectares were uncultivable; the bulk of the land, 1,717,910 hectares, was listed as pasture, which obviously meant primarily the scant forage available in the desert. Some 16,229 hectares were listed as fallow but not part of farm holdings; it appeared doubtful that much of the fallow land could be cultivated. Areas with trees amounted to 2,269 hectares, but this appeared too large for commercial tree crops such as date palms and presumably included substantial areas of desert scrub growth. In 1980 the area under crops amounted to 1,351 hectares, less than 0.1 percent of the country's total area. Nonetheless, the cropped area had increased by 85 percent between 1975 and 1980.

In 1980 the 1,351 hectares that were cropped belonged to 501 agricultural holdings, essentially farms. Three hundred eighteen of the holdings specialized in raising vegetables, 58 in raising poultry, and 42 in raising milk cows; the remaining 83 engaged in various farm activities. Vegetable production totaled 36,782 tons; fruits 745 tons; a form of clover for animal feed, 36,585 tons. The country's farmers supplied about half of the fresh vegetables consumed, 40 percent of the milk, over a third of the poultry, and 18 percent of the eggs. Thus, imports supplied the bulk of the population's food. The major crops were tomatoes, radishes, melons, and cucumbers, plus the clover grown for fodder. Cultivation of grains was quite limited. All cultivation depended on irrigation. Deep wells supplied most irrigation water, which had a salt content that ranged from 0.3 to 1.1 percent. Experiments were under way to use drip irrigation and hydroponics on a broader scale as well as to find salt-tolerant plants better suited to the country's brackish irrigation water.

The gross value of animal products far exceeded that of crops—by about threefold in the latter half of the 1970s. In terms of value, production of milk, eggs, and poultry meat were the most important activities. Commercial chicken raising, using prepared feed for growth, had grown rapidly since the 1960s, and poultry meat substantially exceeded the meat from sheep, goats, and cattle supplied by local producers by the early 1980s. Many dairy farms were modern and commercial, although in the early 1980s goats still provided over 40 percent of the milk produced. Nomads continued to raise sheep on coarse desert vegetation, but observers reported that such activity was declining, partly in response to government settlement programs.

Fishing was a minor but important contribution to the value added by the agricultural sector. Much of the fishing for the local market was from small boats, including many native dhows. During the 1970s, overfishing by many nations in the Gulf considerably reduced catches of fish and shrimp. Large-scale commercial fishing was mostly confined to the United Fisheries Company, which operated a fleet of more than 150 vessels (including factory ships) as far afield as the Indian Ocean, the Red Sea, and the Atlantic Ocean. United Fisheries was a large, international firm that processed and exported part of its catch, particularly frozen shrimp. The fish catch was about 4,500 tons in 1982.

Industry

Industrial development in Kuwait has always faced formidable obstacles. The lack of resources other than oil restricted the manufacturing that could be established. No metallic minerals and few suitable nonmetallic minerals had been found. For example, most of the raw materials for cement had to be imported, largely from Iraq. The limited supply of fresh water was another constraint. The small size of the domestic market restricted production for local consumption to small-scale operations. Moreover, the open economy, which was maintained before and after the discovery of oil, provided little protection from foreign competiton. Industrialists interested in large-scale production had to think in terms of foreign markets and established competitors. The small Kuwaiti labor force, possessing limited skills and a distaste for industrial work, forced the importation of foreign workers for industrial development. After the discovery of oil, labor costs escalated, and in a few years wages in Kuwait were higher than those in almost any other area of the Middle East. Wages remained high in the early 1980s. The commercial tradition in the country predisposed most entrepreneurs to invest in trade rather than manufacturing. As a result of the obstacles, industry (excluding oil refining but including electricity and water desalination) expanded slowly and contributed only 4 percent of GDP in the early 1980s, little more than it had a decade earlier.

The discovery of oil created a demand for new industries, initially satisfied by the oil company itself. Oil operations particularly needed water, electricity, and refined petroleum products, and these were the first modern industries built in the country. The government soon took over production of electricity and water, expanding the systems. Installed electric generating capacity increased from 30 megawatts in 1956 to nearly 3,000 megawatts by mid-1982. Generators were added so that installed capacity was to be 5,086 megawatts by late 1984. Production of electricity rose from 87 million kilowatt-hours in 1956 to 10 billion kilowatt-hours in 1981. Industrial use of electricity was relatively small; air-conditioning was the largest user of electricity, so that peak summer loads were over five times minimum winter loads, creating substantial idle capacity for about half the year. By 1983 charges for electricity had not been changed for over 20 years, and subsidy costs reportedly amounted to nearly US$800 million in FY 1983, probably the most expensive of the government's subsidies. Users paid about 6 percent of actual generating and distribution costs. Generators usually used gas as fuel but could switch to fuel oil or crude oil, which became necessary because of the shortage of associated gases in the early 1980s (see The Oil Industry, this ch.). Several of the power plants were associated with the desalination of seawater.

In a country without streams and few underground sources, provision of water was crucial to both inhabitants and industrial development. Before the discovery of oil and the consequent high population growth, native sailing boats had carried water from Iraq. The need for larger and regular supplies of water—no matter how costly—compelled the Kuwait Oil Company (KOC) to install the first desalination plant. In 1953 the government installed its first unit of 3.8 million liters per day. Subsequently, the government claimed that it had developed the most advanced continuously operating desalination facility in the world—one that had a capacity of 258 million liters per day in 1981. Additional capacity of 418 million liters per day was to be installed between 1982 and 1986, reflecting the rapid population increase and accelerating per capita consumption. In 1981 average per capita consumption was 197 liters of desalinated water and 76 liters of brackish water from underground sources that were added to purified water. In the same year total production was 261 million liters per day of fresh water (almost all desalinated) and 126 million liters per day of brackish water; most of the latter was used in agriculture and industry. Seawater was also supplied to industrial areas for cooling.

The petrochemical industry offered fewer obstacles to industrial development than most others for Kuwait. The industry needed relatively few workers, large capital investments, and substantial oil and gas sources—requirements that fit the country's circumstances. Despite the apparent advantages, the government moved slowly, perhaps for good reason. In 1963 the Petrochemicals Industries Company (PIC) was formed, having 80 percent state ownership. It began with modest facilities but acquired additional plants over the years through purchase of other companies and construction of new facilities. In 1976 the government bought out the private investors, and PIC became wholly government owned. In 1980 PIC became a wholly owned subsidiary of the Kuwait Petroleum Company (KPC) (see The Oil Industry, this ch.).

PIC's chemical complexes were the country's largest manufacturing plants. In 1983 PIC's three ammonia plants had a total capacity of 660,000 tons a year, and a fourth unit was to begin operating in 1984, raising capacity to about 900,000 tons a year. An ammonium sulfate plant had a capacity of 165,000 tons a year; three urea plants, 792,000 tons a year; and a sulfuric acid plant, 132,000 tons a year. (A salt and chlorine complex produced a variety of products but on a smaller scale.) A substantial part of PIC's production was ordinarily exported, and Kuwait had become an important exporter of fertilizer. In 1982 and 1983 depressed world markets for chemical products and a domestic shortage of natural gas to provide fuel and feedstock greatly restricted petrochemical production. In 1983 the ammonium sulfate units remained closed for a third year, the urea and sulfuric plants operated only for short periods, and the ammonia units produced at little more than half of capacity. In 1984 the country was to import liquefied natural gas to reduce the domestic shortage. For about a decade the government considered the development of a complex to produce ethylene and other basic petrochemical products for further processing by smaller privately owned plants into propylene and other products, but it was postponed or canceled in 1983 because of the gas shortage and poor sales prospects abroad. PIC plants obtained gas at concessionary rates from the government's KPC.

A small group of relatively large-scale businesses merged in the 1960s and 1970s; the government owned shares in some of them. The Kuwait Cement Company, for example, with an annual production capacity of 2.1 million tons in 1983, was only partially privately owned. Its production was primarily for the domestic market. The National Industries Company, 51 percent government owned, produced a variety of products, such as asbestos pipes and sheets, lime bricks, lead acid batteries, and detergents. A metal pipe company produced a variety of pipes for oil, gas, and water installations and was the largest in the Middle East, supplying domestic and foreign markets. A privately owned company produced pre-engineered steel buildings for a variety of purposes for erection at home and abroad. In the early 1980s several companies were established to produce insulation materials because the government substantially raised insulation requirements in new buildings in order to reduce electrical use for air-conditioning. A large number of companies, usually operating on a small scale, produced paints, furniture, textiles, metal products, and processed food and beverages for the domestic market.

Most of the larger industrial facilities were located in the Ash Shuaybah Industrial Estate, established in 1964 and operated by a government agency supported largely by budget funds. The agency had partially developed its 11 square kilometers at Ash Shuaybah and an additional estate area of 13 square kilometers at Mina Abdallah. The government and its agency provided such necessary facilities as roads, gas, electricity, water, sewerage, port facilities, and communications, and rented or leased industrial sites at nominal rates. Some small manufacturing establishments were located throughout the populated parts of the country.

The government provided various incentives to private manufacturers, although 51-percent Kuwaiti ownership was required. Financial aid included equity capital and loans. The Investment Bank of Kuwait was created in 1974, with 49-percent government ownership, to provide medium- and long-term industrial financing. Long-term loans were at 5 percent interest. Between 1974 and 1983 the bank provided about US$800 million to 288 projects and was an influential force in the pace and direction of industrial development. The government also provided local industry preference in government purchases (amounting to about 10 percent of price), protection from imports in selected cases, and exemption of customs duties and taxes, although foreign investors were taxed for their share of profits.

Kuwaiti businessmen argued that the government lacked an industrial strategy and that the private industrial development that had occurred resulted from the ingenuity and perseverence of local entrepreneurs. The government and private investors agreed that future industrial expansion should be in capital-intensive, advanced technology industries that limited requirements of imported labor. But economists questioned how far the country should and could go in attempting to industrialize. The returns might be larger on investments made in foreign countries that had an established industrial base. By 1984 the government and private investors already had invested substantial sums in manufacturing plants and energy facilities abroad.

Finance

Before independence in 1961, foreign monies, largely the Indian rupee in the 1930–60 period, circulated in Kuwait. At independence the Kuwaiti dinar was introduced and a currency board established to issue dinar notes and maintain reserves. In 1959 the Central Bank of Kuwait was created and took over the functions of the currency board and the regulation of the banking system.

The first bank in Kuwait was established in 1941 by British investors. Subsequent laws prohibited foreign banks from conducting business in the country. When the British bank's concession ended in 1971, the government bought 51-percent ownership. In 1952 the National Bank of Kuwait, the largest commercial bank, was founded. By 1984 there were six regular commercial banks and the Kuwait Finance House (KFH—formed in 1977), all with at least majority Kuwaiti ownership. The KFH accepted deposits and invested funds but operated under sharia (Islamic law); it could neither pay nor receive interest but shared profits from investments with its depositors. Commercial banks often had more deposits than local borrowers and conducted an important part of their business overseas. Local lending was often to reputable persons who posted little collateral and frequently did not make interest payments until they settled their loan accounts in full. Lending by name was common in Kuwait's tight-knit, family-oriented business community.

The early focus of commercial banks on foreign-trade financing led to formation of some specialized financial institutions. The government established the Credit and Savings Bank in 1965 to channel funds into domestic projects in industry, agriculture, and housing. The Industrial Bank of Kuwait—49 percent government owned—was created in 1974 to fill the gap in medium- and long-term industrial financing. Private investors formed the Real Estate Bank of Kuwait in 1973. Three large investment companies, in two of which the government held 51 percent or more of the shares, invested public and private funds at home and abroad.

In Kuwait's high-income economy a number of persons had funds from which they wanted to earn more than the usual return, and many became wealthy through luck. Real estate has been a frequent means of speculation and became so again in the early 1980s. In the 1970s an informal stock market became another active means of speculation. A crash came in 1977, and the government stepped in and provided a rescue operation for bankrupt investors. Meanwhile, in 1976 an official stock market was formed and by 1984 listed over 40 Kuwaiti firms. Trading was regulated and remained relatively stable.

By the later 1970s speculation fever again began to mount. Most attention was focused on the unofficial stock exchange, called Souk al Manakh, which dealt with companies usually registered in Gulf states other than Kuwait. By early 1982 trading was frantic and almost a national pastime. Share dealings using postdated checks, sometimes a year ahead, created a huge, unregulated expansion of credit. The postdated checks usually included a premium of 100 percent or more to get immediate ownership of the shares. Trust and confidence, or perhaps greed, made the system work. Officials were aware of the activity but possibly not of the magnitude of the speculation.

The crash of the unofficial stock market came in August 1982, when a dealer presented a postdated check for payment, which he could do by law, but the issuer of the check lacked funds for payment. A house of cards collapsed. Official investigations revealed that total outstanding checks amounted to the equivalent of US$94 billion (more than three times the GDP), involving about 6,000 investors from all levels of the population. There were ramifications in other areas. In some cases shares from the unofficial market and postdated checks were used in real estate transactions, and bank loans were involved in some speculation; commercial banks claimed they were not seriously affected by the crash. By mid-1984 the complete picture had not been unraveled, the number of bankruptcies clarified, nor the value of many assets and net worth of individuals and firms established. For over a year a substantial part of the population existed in suspended financial animation—conducting business but not sure if they were financially sound or bankrupt. The crash depressed real estate prices, credit demand, and overall business activity in Kuwait; it was a major event that contributed to the country's recession in 1983 and 1984.

The largest debtor reportedly owed a gross sum of US$10.5 billion; he was a former passport clerk and not one of the known wealthy. About nine traders accounted for two-thirds of the debt and faced possible criminal prosecution, as did 50 more traders who accounted for much of the remaining debt. At the bottom of the debt pyramid were several thousand small investors, defined as those with liabilities of up to about US$7 million; these were the dealers for groups, such as taxi drivers, hotel clerks, and barbers, who pooled their money to participate. About 300 to 400 persons represented the mid-range of indebtedness.

In 1983 government investigators believed that offsetting debts would reduce the balance to be settled to about US$24 billion. If a formula for reducing the premiums included in the postdated checks could be found, the net loss might be around US$7 billion. Meanwhile, the unofficial stock market was closed in September 1982 and use of postdated checks prohibited. (In early 1984, however, journalists reported renewed activity on the unofficial market.) The government established a US$1.8 billion rescue fund to pay cash to holders of checks worth up to US$350,000 and bonds to those holding checks up to about US$7.5 million. The government injected liquidity into the banking system so the bonds could be discounted and, to restore confidence, spent nearly US$2 billion to support shares on the official stock exchange. In addition, loans were made available, to be secured by real property or appropriate collateral, to investors to repay debts arising from postdated checks. By early 1984 the debts from the crash were still not completely clarified, let alone settled. Observers expected bankruptcies and court cases to continue for some years.

Apart from the chaos in the unofficial stock market, financial officials have regulated the financial system conservatively. Despite the swings in the country's fortunes, the effects on prices have been moderate. The rate of inflation averaged under 8 percent a year from 1977 to 1982, although this was helped by government subsidies on important goods and services. The consumer price index increased 7.8 percent in 1982, partly because of the increased price of gasoline; it increased 7.3 percent in 1981.

Foreign Trade and Balance of Payments

Foreign trade always played a key role in the economy of Kuwait. Before the discovery of oil, merchants developed a large transshipment and reexport business, which along with sales of pearls to foreign dealers yielded a substantial part of the population's income. The discovery of large quantities of oil provided a new and increasingly important export, for Kuwait needed only small amounts of petroleum products in its domestic market. Even after the discovery of oil, Kuwait's merchants continued to develop transshipment and reexport business with neighboring

Market scene in Kuwait

countries. The Iran-Iraq War, which broke out in 1980, eroded Kuwait's role as an entrepôt. By the early 1980s Kuwait's transshipment and reexport trade with Iraq, an important market, had declined substantially, contributing to Kuwait's recession.

Oil dominated Kuwait's exports, accounting in 1980 for 98 percent of the value of exports and 93 percent when reexports were included. The bulk of oil exports were traditionally in the form of crude oil. In the 1970s officials increased refining capacity to gain the value added from exports of refined products. In the early 1980s, as oil exports declined because of the world recession, refined products gained relative to crude oil exports. Officials intended that refined products would be a higher proportion of oil exports in the rest of the 1980s, although the share would depend mostly on the level of total oil exports. Asia was the main market for Kuwait's oil exports, accounting for 55 percent of their value in 1980 (see table 9, Appendix A). Japan purchased the largest amount of Kuwait's oil, followed by Taiwan and the Republic of Korea (South Korea). Countries of the European Economic Community provided the other major market, purchasing 27 percent of Kuwait's oil exports in 1980. Britain, Italy, and the Netherlands were the important customers. Kuwait exported very little oil to the United States. Brazil was the largest importer in the Western Hemisphere.

Exports of national products amounted to US$19.3 billion in 1980, and only US$355 million were non-oil commodities. About half of the non-oil commodities were a variety of manufactured goods, such as steel pipe and pre-engineered steel buildings exported largely to nearby countries. The other major non-oil export was chemical products, mainly fertilizer sold to India, China, and other Asian countries. Reexports in 1980 amounted to nearly US$1.2 billion and went primarily to neighboring countries. Reexports were predominantly manufactured goods, of which machinery and transport equipment were by far the most important. Data to determine the extent of the decline of reexports after 1980 were unavailable in mid-1984.

Kuwait's large foreign exchange earnings from oil exports and investment income largely removed any constraint on imports. Almost any commodity could be imported, and most import duties were modest. In 1980 imports amounted to US$6.5 billion, continuing the rising trend of the 1970s. Imports grouped in different ways revealed the nature of the economy. Imports for Kuwait's high-income economy were 62 percent finished products in 1980 because of the small manufacturing sector; raw materials accounted for only 9 percent and semifinished products for 29 percent. Imports grouped by intended use in 1980 showed 44 percent for consumption, 17 percent as capital goods, and 39 percent as intermediate commodities requiring further processing or assembly before final use. This latter grouping presented a better insight into the economy than the more commonly used import classification, which lumped many consumer durables, such as cars and appliances, under machinery and equipment (see table 10, Appendix A).

Kuwait's imports, which were predominantly finished products, came largely from industrialized countries (see table 11, Appendix A). In 1980 Japan had the largest share of the market (21 percent), followed by the United States (15 percent), the Federal Republic of Germany (West Germany) (9 percent), and Britain (9 percent), which together accounted for more than half of Kuwait's imports. Other West European countries, South Korea, and Taiwan supplied the bulk of the remainder. Kuwait bought mostly live animals, meat, fruits, and vegetables from its Arab neighbors.

Modest spending and development policies combined with rising oil revenues, paid in foreign currencies, have largely freed

Kuwait from balance of payments worries for more than a decade. The government and individuals accumulated surplus funds in many years, part of which was invested abroad. In the early 1980s, as oil revenues fell, earnings from overseas public and private investments supplied foreign currencies so that imports were not restricted other than by slowing government development expenditures. Some economists calculated that by 1982 foreign investment income (public and private) exceeded oil revenues, while others using different accounting procedures calculated that oil revenues still remained higher (see table 12, Appendix A).

In any event, investment income had become a very critical supplement to oil revenues to meet the country's balance of payments needs. Income from foreign investments fluctuated, however, depending on foreign interest rates and business activity. Investment income declined in 1982 from the level of the previous year, for example. Between 1980 and 1982 the government stabilized foreign aid, and public and private investors reduced the flow of funds into foreign investments, which also contributed to easing balance of payments pressures from declining oil revenues. Despite sharply changing circumstances, the country maintained a surplus on its balance of payments between 1979 and 1982.

The Political System

The modern political history of Kuwait was launched in the early eighteenth century, when a number of families of the Utbi section of the Anayzah tribe ended their migration at the location of the present-day city of Kuwait (see Internal Migrations and Political Developments, ch. 1). In 1756 these settlers decided to appoint the head of the most prestigious family among them, the Al Sabah, as their local shaykh (see Glossary), who would provide security and represent them to the ruling Ottoman Turks. For nearly two centuries afterward there would be little change in the style of rule by successive Al Sabah shaykhs. Kuwait was ruled as a dynastic, tribal shaykhdom, and the amir was chosen by senior members of the Al Sabah. Although his rule was autocratic, decisions were made after consultation with senior family members and others within the tightly knit Kuwaiti community. Merchant families in particular were consulted, for the Al Sabah relied heavily on the taxation of trade for their own livelihood. Tribal leaders were also consulted periodically when the amir held *di-*

117

waniyya (also known as majlis—see Glossary), gatherings at which those with *wasta* (roughly equivalent to influence) could make requests of the leadership.

Throughout the latter eighteenth and early nineteenth centuries, Kuwait remained an undistinguished part of the Arabian holdings of the Ottoman Empire. Being tiny and of meager wealth, Kuwait never came under direct Ottoman rule. Shaykh Abdallah Al Sabah (1866–92) recognized Ottoman suzerainty over Kuwait, however, by his payment of tribute and his acceptance of the title of Qaimaqam (Commandant) under the Ottoman administration located in Basrah (in present-day Iraq). His successor, Mubarak (1896–1915), fearing Ottoman occupation of Kuwait, signed an agreement with the British in which he agreed not to enter into any foreign relationships without British consent in return for an annual British subsidy. Henceforth, Kuwait was, in effect, protected by the British naval presence in the Gulf; this relationship was formalized in a 1914 British declaration that "the British Government does recognize and admit that the Shaykhdom of Kuwait is an independent Government under British protection."

Although Mubarak had come to power (in what was the first and last violent succession in Kuwait's history) after killing two of his half brothers, his period of rule was considered highly successful and earned him the title of "Mubarak the Great." He was able to establish that future succession would pass exclusively through his heirs. Two of his sons ruled only briefly before their deaths; the second, Salim (1917–21), sided with the Ottomans during World War I, thus incurring a blockade of Kuwait and considerable hardship for its citizens. Mubarak's grandson, Ahmad al Jabir, succeeded his uncle in 1921 and ruled successfully for nearly three decades.

Ahmad's rule had rather inauspicious beginnings, however. "On the death of Shaykh Salim," according to British historian H.R.P. Dickson, "the townspeople, tired of unnecessary war into which they had been led against their will, determined that in the future they would have some say in the affairs of state. They informed members of the Al Sabah family that they would accept as their ruler only one who would assent to a council of advisers." Ahmad did appoint a 12-member council, headed by a leading merchant, though the council barely functioned during its short life span. In the following year Kuwait's boundaries were set at the Uqair conference, attended by Abd al Aziz Al Saud of Najd in present-day Saudi Arabia and representatives of Iraq and Britain. There was little that Ahmad could do, despite his unhappiness with the results of this 1922 conference in which there had been no Kuwaiti representation.

A second call for political reform led to the establishment in 1937–38 of a 14-member Legislative Assembly composed of commoners. The new Assembly soon sought the loosening of ties between Kuwait and Britain and the redirecting of Kuwaiti revenues—which accrued directly to the Al Sabah—toward the public good. Before long the Assembly was dissolved by Ahmad, and its members were imprisoned. The very establishment of a legislative body, however, set a precedent on the Arabian Peninsula and served to foreshadow Kuwait's postindependence National Assembly.

As an alternative to the Assembly, Ahmad set up a legislative council that, though of extremely limited authority itself, did establish a number of governmental departments—each headed by a member of the Al Sabah, who ran it as a personal fiefdom—that were the nucleus of the modern governmental administration. These departments grew in size and scope under the rule of Ahmad's cousin, Shaykh Abdallah al Salim (1950–65), when massive oil revenues first became available to the government.

Abdallah also oversaw, on June 19, 1961, the termination of the 1899 agreement with the British, an act that was tantamount to Kuwait's achieving full independence. Abdallah added the title of amir to his name. Six days later President Abd al Karim Qasim of Iraq publicly claimed all of Kuwait's territory for Iraq. In response, Abdallah requested immediate British military assistance and, as gestures aimed at national concilation in the face of the Iraqi threat, asked a number of leading merchants to participate in the government and authorized the election of a constituent assembly to draft a new constitution.

The Constitutional Monarchy

On November 11, 1962, Amir Abdallah approved and promulgated the Constitution as written by the Constituent Assembly. The 183-article Constitution remained unchanged until August 1976, when four articles (concerning the dissolution of the legislature and freedom of the press) were suspended. They were reinstated four years later, however, and the Constitution remained intact during the early 1980s. In 1982 the government submitted 16 constitutional amendments that, among other things, would have allowed the amir to declare martial law for an extended period and would have increased both the size of the legislature and the length of term of office. In May 1983 the pro-

119

posals were formally dropped, however, after several months of legislative debate. Discussions continued to surface occasionally within both the executive and the legislative branches, however, on the need to amend the Constitution in light of two decades of experience with the coexistence of monarchical and democratic forms of government.

The Constitution declares that Kuwait is an Arab state. Islam is the religion of the state, and sharia is "a main source of legislation." Kuwait is further defined as "a hereditary Amirate, the succession to which shall be in the descendants of the late Mubarak Al Sabah." The system of government is defined in Article 6 as "democratic, under which sovereignty resides in the people, the source of all powers."

Before the governmental system is detailed further, the rights and duties of citizens and the social role of the state are defined in articles 7 through 49. Individual rights are extensive and include personal liberty and equality before the law, freedom to hold beliefs and express opinions, and freedom of the press. Residences are inviolable, torture and deportation of Kuwaiti citizens are prohibited, and the accused are assumed innocent until proven guilty. Also guaranteed is the freedom to form associations and trade unions. Duties include national defense, the observance of public order and respect for public morals, and the payment of taxes. The social obligations of the state expressed in the Constitution lay the basis for Kuwait's extensive welfare system (see Health and Welfare, this ch.). The state is constitutionally obligated to care for the young, ensure aid for citizens who are old, sick, or unable to work, promote public education, and care for the public health.

These rights and obligations apply only to Kuwaiti citizens, however, and legislation passed in 1959 and 1960 strictly defined citizens as those present in and before 1920 and their descendants. In the early 1980s only about 40 percent of the population were Kuwaiti citizens under this restrictive definition (see Population, this ch.). The remainder of the population are given due process under the law but have few other political and civil rights and enjoy restricted access to the benefits of the state system of welfare.

The Executive

Article 50 of the Constitution states that "the system of government is based on the principle of separation of powers" among the executive, legislative, and judicial branches. This principle is not strictly adhered to, however, for cabinet officers sit as ex officio members of the legislature. Although the executive is clearly the most powerful branch of the government, the mere existence of an elected legislature and partial adherence to the separation of powers made Kuwait the most liberal and democratic government on the Arabian Peninsula. The restraint on the power of the executive conforms to Kuwaiti tradition: the Al Sabah have never held the absolute power over decisionmaking of the Al Saud in Saudi Arabia, for example, but have always shared power with local tribal leaders and wealthy merchants.

Executive power is vested in the amir and, under him, the Council of Ministers, which by tradition is led by the amir's heir apparent, who acts as prime minister. The amir, who rules for life, is the head of state as well as supreme commander of the armed forces. He holds the power to appoint and dismiss virtually every senior executive official, including the heir apparent (who must be appointed within one year of succession of a new amir and be approved by the legislature), all cabinet officers, local governors, and officers in the armed forces. The amir also holds the power to initiate, sanction, and promulgate laws, although all laws must be approved by the legislature.

Since the death of Shaykh Mubarak in 1915, succession has alternated (with only one exception) between the two branches of the Al Sabah defined by two of Mubarak's sons, Jabir and Salim (see fig. 7). This one exception occurred upon the death of Abdallah in 1965, when instead of being passed to a cousin in the Jabir branch, the throne was passed to a half brother, Sabah al Salim. To placate the Jabirs, a large number of them were named to high government posts, and its senior member, Jabir al Ahmad al Jabir, was named as prime minister and heir apparent. Upon the death of Sabah in 1977, Jabir succeeded to the throne at age 51. The following year he named a cousin, Saad al Abdallah al Salim Al Sabah, as heir apparent, thus reestablishing the tradition of alternating succession.

Candidates for sucession are also subject to the criteria of seniority and individual competence. Outside observers attributed the extraordinary 1965 succession to these factors (that no candidate from the Jabir branch met the standards of Sabah al Salim in terms of seniority and competence) rather than to any malevolence between the two family branches. These observers noted that intrafamily quarrels surrounding succession, such as sometimes presented serious problems to other Arabian monarchies, had been quite successfully resolved by the Al Sabah after more than two centuries of continuous family rule.

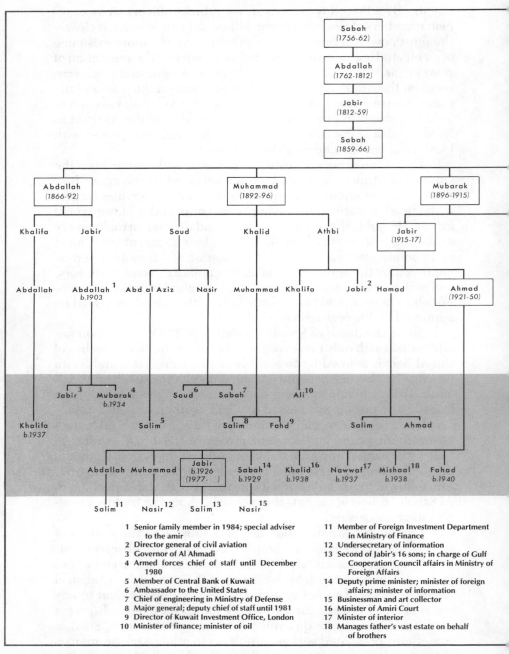

Figure 7.   Kuwait.   Abbreviated Genealogy of the Al Sabah,
with Government Positions, 1984.

1 Senior family member in 1984; special adviser
   to the amir
2 Director general of civil aviation
3 Governor of Al Ahmadi
4 Armed forces chief of staff until December
   1980
5 Member of Central Bank of Kuwait
6 Ambassador to the United States
7 Chief of engineering in Ministry of Defense
8 Major general; deputy chief of staff until 1981
9 Director of Kuwait Investment Office, London
10 Minister of finance; minister of oil
11 Member of Foreign Investment Department
   in Ministry of Finance
12 Undersecretary of information
13 Second of Jabir's 16 sons; in charge of Gulf
   Cooperation Council affairs in Ministry of
   Foreign Affairs
14 Deputy prime minister; minister of foreign
   affairs; minister of information
15 Businessman and art collector
16 Minister of Amiri Court
17 Minister of interior
18 Manages father's vast estate on behalf
   of brothers

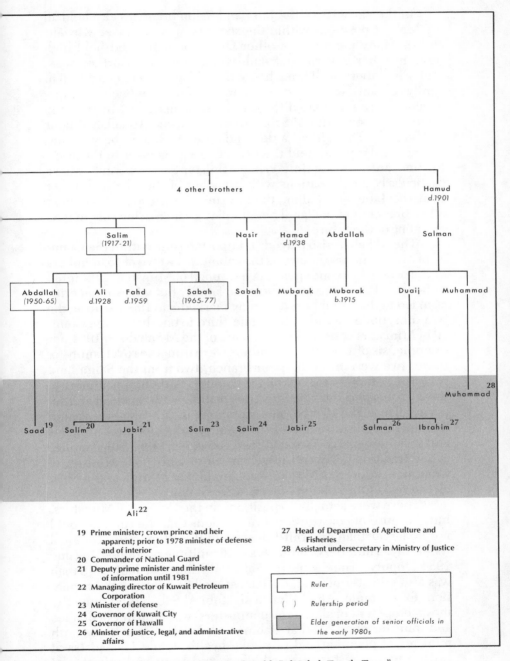

4 other brothers

Hamud
d.1901

Salim
(1917-21)

Nasir

Hamad
d.1938

Abdallah

Salman

Abdallah
(1950-65)

Ali
d.1928

Fahd
d.1959

Sabah
(1965-77)

Sabah

Mubarak

Mubarak
b.1915

Duaij

Muhammad

28
Muhammad

Saad [19]

Salim [20]

Jabir [21]

Salim [23]

Salim [24]

Jabir [25]

Salman [26]

Ibrahim [27]

Ali [22]

19 Prime minister; crown prince and heir
    apparent; prior to 1978 minister of defense
    and of interior
20 Commander of National Guard
21 Deputy prime minister and minister
    of information until 1981
22 Managing director of Kuwait Petroleum
    Corporation
23 Minister of defense
24 Governor of Kuwait City
25 Governor of Hawalli
26 Minister of justice, legal, and administrative
    affairs

27 Head of Department of Agriculture and
    Fisheries
28 Assistant undersecretary in Ministry of Justice

	Ruler
( )	Rulership period
	Elder generation of senior officials in the early 1980s

Source: Based on information from Michael Field, "Al-Sabah Family Tree,"
Financial Times, London, February 22, 1984, Sect. 4, 3.

In the early 1980s the Jabir and Salim branches also held all the highest positions within the security apparatus (see Kuwait, ch. 7). Many members of other family branches did hold high posts in other government endeavors, however. Furthermore, senior members of all branches of the Al Sabah were consulted in family councils, where the most important policies (including succession) were formulated through family consensus. In 1984 the senior member of the Al Sabah was 81-year-old Abdallah al Jabir al Abdallah. Though not a descendant of Mubarak, he was consulted regularly and held the title of special adviser to the amir. Furthermore, at that time Prime Minister Saad was said to have particularly good relations with branches of the Al Sabah other than the Jabir and Salim, thus raising the prospect that these other branches of the family might play an increasing role in government in the future.

The Al Sabah also played an important role within the Council of Ministers (also known as the cabinet). Twelve of 15 members in the original postindependence Council of Ministers appointed in January 1962 were from the royal family, but widespread criticism led to their numbers dropping markedly in 1964. During the two subsequent decades, from one-third to one-half of the Council of Ministers consisted of members of the Al Sabah. In 1984, for example, six of 15 cabinet members were from the royal family (of these, two were from the Jabir branch, two from the Salim, and two from other branches of the family). Although a minority, these six headed the key ministries dealing with financial and security affairs. The 10 other ministers were mostly highly educated technocrats put in charge of the country's development projects and social programs. Two ministers, however, were from families of the traditional Kuwaiti merchant elite. Only one, Minister of Communications Isa Muhammad Ibrahim al Mazidi, was a Shia; all the rest of the cabinet officers were Sunni.

There were actually 20 positions on the Council of Ministers, but, because of constitutional restrictions that the cabinet could not be larger than one-third the size of the 50-member National Assembly, a number of ministers held multiple portfolios. In June 1984 Deputy Prime Minister Sabah al Ahmad al Jabir Al Sabah was also minister of foreign affairs as well as minister of information, for example. Ali al Khalifa al Athbi Al Sabah (said to be the most competent of all the royal ministers) was minister of finance and minister of oil. Abd ar Rahman Abdallah al Awadi was both minister of planning and of public health, while Hamad Isa al Rujayb was minister of social affairs and labor and minister of housing. Portfolios that received the undivided attention of a cabinet official were the ministries of waqfs (religious endowments) and Islamic affairs; commerce and industry; communications; defense; education; electricity and water; interior; public works; and justice, legal, and administrative affairs. Finally, Minister of State for Cabinet Affairs Abd al Aziz Husayn, who acted as the government's chief press spokesman, also sat on the Council ŏf Ministers. The Council was headed by Saad al Abdallah al Salim Al Sabah, as it had been since 1978, when he was first appointed prime minister and heir apparent. Two ministers who were not cabinet members were Special Adviser to the Amir Abd ar Rahman Salim al Atiqi, who previously had acted as minister of finance, and Khalid al Ahmad al Jabir Al Sabah (half brother to the amir), who was minister in charge of the amir's *diwaniyya* affairs.

The Council of Ministers is constitutionally obligated to resign upon the election of a new National Assembly, which normally occurs every four years. It also resigns upon the death of an amir, when the prime minister normally succeeds to the throne and a new prime minister is named. In practice, many of the same ministers have been reappointed on these occasions, and the composition of the cabinet has remained fairly stable. For example, the new Council of Ministers formed in February 1978, following the death of Amir Sabah al Salim, contained only two new members. Five ministers were dropped from the council in March 1981 following the February National Assembly elections.

Ministers are appointed and removed by the amir upon the recommendation of the prime minister. Although the prime minister presides over meetings of the Council of Ministers, the constitutional responsibility of each minister for the affairs of his ministry is to the amir. A minister can also be subject to a vote of no confidence in the National Assembly, in which case he must resign. The prime minister is immune from such a vote, but if the National Assembly decides that it cannot work with a prime minister, the matter is referred to the amir, who must either dismiss the Council of Ministers or dissolve the National Assembly. The ministers—who under normal circumstances act as ex officio members of the National Assembly—do not vote during any such crisis between the executive and the legislature.

Many autonomous agencies and public corporations, such as the Kuwait Petroleum Corporation (KPC) and the Kuwait Fund for Arab Economic Development (KFAED), were under the authority of the Council of Ministers. Their employees, along with those of the ministries themselves, made up the bulk of the nation's civil servants. After independence the number of civil servants grew along with government revenues and the increased role of government in society. Civil servants totaled some 52,000 in 1966, 90,000 in 1972, 116,000 in 1976, and 144,000 in 1983. Non-Kuwaitis were counted on heavily to staff government posts; in 1976 they accounted for fully 60 percent of all civil servants, and in 1983 the figure had grown to 65 percent despite growing political pressures to lower this percentage by training Kuwaitis to replace the (largely Palestinian) non-Kuwaitis, who were needed to make the still-growing government apparatus function (see Labor Force, this ch.).

Local government—understandably not highly developed because of the nation's small size—was administered through the Ministry of Interior. The country was divided into four provincial governorates, each named after its principal city: Kuwait City, Hawalli, Al Ahmadi, and Al Jahrah. All governors were appointed by the amir; in the early 1980s all were Al Sabah family members except the governor for Al Jahrah, which had only become a separate administrative subdivision in the late 1970s. The primary responsibility of the governors lay in the enforcement of security in their local jurisdictions.

Another organ of local government was the 16-member (10 elected, six appointed by the amir) Municipal Council. This one council apparently had responsibility for municipal services—such as public health, garbage collection, and city planning—in all of Kuwait's cities. The Municipal Council worked closely with the governorates in such matters.

Legislature

The most remarkable aspect of the Kuwaiti governmental system is its unicameral National Assembly—the only elected legislative body in the Arabian Peninsula in the early 1980s. The authors of the Constitution, aware of the precedent set in the 1937–38 Legislative Assembly, saw the creation of an elected legislative body as an important means to widen the popular consensus and thereby further legitimize the rule of the Al Sabah at a time when the family's position was threatened by the Iraqi claim to the entire territory of the new nation. Since the January 1963 election of the first National Assembly, it has evolved into a wider role, including that of acting as a forum for political opponents of the regime. Although the Constitution affords the Assembly considerable powers, it is limited by two major restrictions: the small size of the electorate as defined by law, and the power of the amir to dissolve the Assembly virtually at will. These restrictions greatly inhibit the activities of the Assembly and have had the effect of making it, in the words of a United States Department of State publication, "a body to review government policy and programs and to make recommendations." Even at that the National Assembly provided the most open political forum among the nations of the Gulf and was responsible for Kuwait's being far ahead of its neighbors in terms of democratic institutions and the free expression of ideas.

The Assembly consists of 50 members elected to four-year terms (there are no restrictions on being reelected) and the members of the Council of Ministers, who sit as ex officio members. It is in session once a year for at least eight months. A Speaker and deputy Speaker are elected at the beginning of each new term; in 1981 former minister of public works Muhammad Yusif al Adasani was elected as Speaker until 1985. Each year new members are elected to eight standing committees within the National Assembly. Three of the more important of these are the Legislative and Legal Committee, the Financial and Economic Committee, and the Foreign Affairs Committee. Ex officio members cannot be elected to committees.

Bills may be initiated in the Assembly or within the executive branch. Bills passed by a simple majority in the Assembly must then be sanctioned by the amir before becoming law. Failing that, a two-thirds majority in the Assembly (which is extremely difficult to achieve, given that one-fourth to one-third of the members of the Assembly are, in effect, representatives of the amir) will override the amir's veto. The bill will also become law if it is introduced again the following year and is passed once more by a simple majority. Likewise, laws promulgated by the amir must be approved by a majority vote within the National Assembly. If it is not in session at the time, the law must be introduced when the Assembly is next convened. Among the most important considerations of the Assembly are the approval of each year's state budget and the approval of all treaties with foreign governments. In addition to its legislative powers, the National Assembly has the power of interpellation over members of the Council of Ministers.

The restricted nature of the electorate—voters had to be literate males over the age of 21 who could trace their descent to inhabitants of Kuwait prior to 1920—made the National Assembly representative of only a small elite within Kuwaiti society. The first Assembly was elected in 1963 by a mere 17,000 voters; in the February 1981 elections the electorate was still below 40,000. At that time it was estimated that some 90,000 Kuwaitis were eligible to vote, but fewer than half of those bothered to register.

Ninety-two percent of the nearly 412,000 registered voters participated in that election; this amounted to less than 3 percent of the nation's population of about 1.4 million.

Prior to 1981 Kuwait had been divided into 10 districts (known as constituencies) for electoral purposes, and each district elected five members to the Assembly. Before the 1981 election the country was reapportioned to create 25 constituencies, each electing two members. Some constituencies henceforth had as few as 2,000 inhabitants, and elections in such areas necessariily had the flavor of family affairs. Because there were no political parties, all candidates ran as individuals; in 1981 some 447 persons competed for 50 Assembly seats. The victors were those with the two largest pluralities in each constituency.

Although political parties were illegal, voting blocs inevitably emerged within the Assembly. The most prominent political dynamic played out in the Assembly was between those supporting the Al Sabah regime and those in opposition. The traditional opposition within the Assembly first emerged in 1965, when 12 members formed an Arab nationalist bloc that opposed the regime from a leftist, antimonarchist, and Pan-Arab point of view. Their leader was, and continued to be almost two decades later, Ahmad al Khatib of the Arab Nationalist Movement, an organization that had been founded by the radical Palestinian leader George Habash. The Arab nationalist bloc lost all but four seats in the 1967 election (which was protested to no avail by numerous persons and organizations who charged fraud), and the opposition remained weak in the Assembly elected in 1971. The 1975 elections, however, produced a National Assembly in which fully one-third of its membership was counted among the Arab nationalist bloc.

Assembly debates grew increasingly strident during 1975 and 1976. Those regarding oil policies and social policies brought public attention to the growing disparities of personal wealth within Kuwait and on occasion brought explicit verbal attacks on the ruling family. Middle Eastern politics became another central issue in the Assembly, for the Arab nationalist opposition championed the Palestinian cause. The ruling family came to view these activities as dangerous to Kuwait's internal security and contrary to its foreign policy interest. In mid-1976 the Assembly adopted a pro-Palestinian resolution that condemned Syrian involvement in the Lebanese civil war—in direct opposition to the government's officially neutral position—and on August 19 the amir ordered the National Assembly dissolved. Using a revised constitution during the next four and one-half years, Kuwait's legislature consisted of six appointed legislative committees under the Council of Ministers.

The redistricting that took place before the 1981 elections, together with new emphases that had developed in Arab politics during the previous five years, had a devastating effect on the Arab nationalist opposition in the National Assembly; every one of its candidates was defeated in February 1981. Beduin tribal leaders, traditionally the element most loyal to the Al Sabah, garnered 23 of the 50 seats being contested; loyal moderates and technocrats gained another 13 seats; members of the Shia community, which had 10 seats in 1975, won only four in 1981; and Sunni fundamentalists, a new element in the Kuwaiti political spectrum, won five seats. The fundamentalists were henceforth the only opposition in the Assembly. Between 1981 and 1984 the fundamentalists introduced numerous initiatives designed to enforce greater compliance with Islamic practices: citizenship was barred to non-Muslims, importation of alcoholic beverages was prohibited, and schoolrooms were segregated by sex. As of 1984 repeated fundamentalist efforts to amend the Constitution to make sharia the sole basis of Kuwaiti law had been unsuccessful (see Politics and the Social Order, this ch.).

The Judiciary

The Constitution guarantees the independence of the judiciary and designates the Supreme Council of the Judiciary as its highest body and guarantor of judicial independence. The constitutuional basis for the legal system, the organization of the judiciary, and the codification of law were derived from a number of sources. The framework of various other Arab states was important, particularly that of Egypt, Iraq, and Bahrain. Traces of the French legal code were borrowed from the Egyptian system, and elements of English common law entered Kuwait via Bahrain. The Kuwaiti system also relies on the Islamic legal provisions of the Majalla, the Ottoman Civil Code of 1876. In the areas of civil and personal status law, the legal system reflects the conservative and unifying force of sharia. Matters of personal status were based on the Maliki school of Islamic jurisprudence; civil codes were based on the Hanafi school (see The Early Period, ch. 1).

The lowest level of the court system consisted of four separate divisions: personal status, civil, commercial, and criminal courts. Kuwait had a number of each of these courts of first instance or, as they were sometimes known, courts of general session. At the next level was the High Court of Appeal, having two chambers—one for civil matters and the other for commercial and criminal cases. This court dealt exclusively with appeals from the lower courts. Appeals from the high court went to the Supreme Court of Appeal, which also ruled on the constitutionality of laws. The amir acted as the final source of judicial appeal and as a source of pardon, and he reviewed all convictions for capital offenses.

Two specialized courts were the Military Court, which only tried cases involving infractions of military law by members of the armed forces, and the State Security Court, which has been convened only on rare occasions in order to try political cases (see Kuwait, ch. 7). The State Security Court was first created in September 1975 and was reconvened in December 1983 in order to try 25 individuals accused of the multiple terrorist bombings perpetrated earlier that month.

The Constitution calls for the creation of two other judicial organs. The Public Prosecution Office supervises the affairs of the judicial police, the enforcement of penal laws, the pursuit of offenders, and the execution of the judgments of the court. The Council of State acts as the principal administrative body of the judiciary. It also drafts bills and regulations concerning the judiciary and renders legal advice to the citizenry.

Politics and the Social Order

Despite its small population, Kuwait had become a country of considerable social complexity by 1984, and different communities derived various levels of status depending on their religious and ethnic identities and on the date of their or their ancestors' immigration into Kuwait. Such social stratification and cleavages were common throughout the oil-rich monarchies of the Arabian Peninsula, but the communities had little, if any, political impact in other nations, where politics was closed to all but the royal families and a number of small, nonroyal elites. In Kuwait, however, the relatively democratic and open nature of the political system, manifested especially in the National Assembly, lent a significance to nonelite groups that was of considerable interest to political observers. Although organized forms of political participation common to democratic nations, such as political parties and labor unions, were not a political factor in Kuwait, other forms of popular political expression, reflecting social cleavages within Kuwait as well as those in the Middle East region as a whole, were evident.

The overriding social cleavage is between Kuwaitis and non-Kuwaitis, the majority of the latter having arrived after World

Modernistic mosque in capital city

War II to take advantage of the opportunities that accompanied the oil boom. In the late 1950s and early 1960s, when it first became apparent that the foreign population was becoming a significant and semipermanent presence in Kuwait, the government undertook legal measures to discriminate against the newer arrivals. In addition to being denied voting privileges and other political rights, those defined as non-Kuwaitis were restricted in their ownership of business and property and, although able to benefit from free education and health care, were denied other aspects of the government's welfare provisions, such as housing subsidies and pensions.

The discriminatory laws were of little concern to the vast majority of non-Kuwaitis whose access to part of Kuwait's generous welfare benefits and to local job opportunities offered them a privileged position compared with conditions in their native countries or elsewhere in the Middle East. However, among a small elite of the non-Kuwaitis, consisting largely of educated and politically aware Palestinians who were residents of several generations and held high positions in government or elsewhere, the legal discrimination was a cause of growing resentment and alienation. Although long aware of this problem built into the social and political systems, the government had done little by 1984 to alleviate this ever growing, long-term problem.

Journalism was the chosen profession of a number of the 300,000 to 350,000 Palestinians estimated to live in Kuwait in the mid-1980s. Until the promulgation of the stringent Press and Publications Law in August 1976, the press—which included five Arabic and two English-language dailies and some 20 other periodicals of less frequency—was known as freewheeling and open to the expression of a wide variety of political opinion. Although the 1976 law did not institute prior censorship, it did set down a number of pretexts under which the government could close a paper and administer other punishments for offending editors and publishers. The liberal use of the law between 1976 and 1984 had the effect of instituting self-censorship, and the press lost part of its previous vitality as a result. Radio and television were run by the Ministry of Information.

Among Kuwaiti citizens, women were the objects of legal discrimination in that they remained disfranchised in 1984. The Women's Cultural and Social Society—one of the more active of several dozen such popular organizations that occasionally assumed a politically active stance akin to lobbying—had long been headed by Lulwa Qattami and had been in the forefront of attempts to gain women the right to vote. After unsuccessful efforts in 1981 and 1982 to pass a bill in the National Assembly calling for the enfranchisement of women, Qattami and her orgnaization shifted their efforts to the courts, where they hoped that the discriminatory electoral law would be ruled unconstitutional in light of Article 29, which states that all Kuwaitis are "equal . . . in public rights and duties before the law without distinction as to sex. . . ." Although the amir and the heir apparent supported women's right to vote, the effort confronted strong public opposition that was spearheaded by the growing Sunni fundamentalist groups.

Male Kuwaitis, then, were a privileged minority. Social stratification—based on the time when an individual's ancestors arrived in Kuwait and on religion and ethnicity—did exist within this elite minority but under normal circumstances was not a cause of politically charged disputes because Kuwait's oil-based economy provided adequately for all. At the top of the pyramid was the Al Sabah, which, along with six other families whose ancestors were the original eighteenth-century settlers, held vast wealth. Unlike some other Arabian royal families, however, the Al Sabah did not habitually display their wealth and therefore rarely aroused the envy of the citizenry. At the bottom were the Shia whose ancestors had arrived before 1920 from Iran, Iraq, and eastern Arabia. After the 1979 revolution in Iran, the Kuwaiti Shia community became the object of considerable propaganda from across the Gulf, but five years later it had shown few signs of political disaffection—a phenomenon that some observers attributed to Kuwait's political system that, although Sunni-led, provided a comfortable existence to Shia citizens. Others pointed out that the major Shia cultural organizations received money from the Kuwaiti government.

This general state of social tranquillity was severely disrupted, if only temporarily, during the early 1980s by the mid-1982 crash of Kuwait's unofficial stock market, the Souk el Manakh (see Finance, this ch.). Individuals—particularly those near the bottom of the social pyramid—had invested heavily in the Souk in anticipation of quick profits, and when it crashed, the mountain of checks totaled an estimated US$94 billion. Soon afterward the government announced that it would supply funds to compensate poor individuals for part of their losses. After the initial bitterness toward the government for having allowed the Souk to crash, tensions lingered for many months over how the government's promised compensation would be distributed. Poorer groups especially feared that the crash and the compensation scheme would result in the redistribution of wealth to the very rich. Two years after the crash a number of related problems still had not been solved, although observers noted that thus far the compensation process had been largely satisfactory to small investors and that the potentially explosive tensions evident in 1982 had dissipated to a large extent.

Political phenomena elsewhere in the Middle East were also reflected in the Kuwaiti panorama. This fact could be attributed in part to the large number of Middle Eastern immigrants who, in the relatively open Kuwait political climate, could express their concerns with respect to events in their home countries. Other phenomena, such as Islamic fundamentalism and Arab nationalism, were national expressions of regionwide social and political currents.

Perhaps because Kuwait is such a small nation, its political concerns—particularly those involving matters of internal security—often involved its neighbors (see Kuwait, ch. 7). The dissolving of the National Assembly in 1976, for example, supposedly was undertaken at the urging of the conservative Saudi Arabian monarchy. It was also reported that Kuwait's rulers consulted at length with those in Saudi Arabia and other peninsular states in the wake of the December 1983 terrorist bombings in Kuwait. In a major sense these two events in Kuwait were manifestations of events elsewhere: the closing of the Assembly was linked to the civil war in Lebanon; the 1983 bombings, to the Iran-Iraq War.

In these and other instances, loyalties among non-Kuwaiti residents that varied from official Kuwaiti policies led to the government's viewing portions of the community of alien residents as a political, and potentially a security, threat. Thousands of non-Kuwaiti Arabs were reportedly deported following the closing of the Assembly; further deportations were expected in 1984 after the trial of the 25—many of whom were non-Kuwaitis—accused of participating in the December 1983 bombings.

Although Kuwaiti officials feared that the militant Shia ideology imported from revolutionary Iran would have a major impact on Kuwait's sizable Shia population, this fear had not been borne out. Instead, another type of Islamic extremism—Sunni fundamentalism—did make significant inroads into Kuwait during the early 1980s. This regionwide movement continued to grow in Kuwait after five fundamentalists were elected to the National Assembly in 1981. In 1983 elections at the University of Kuwait, for example, 14 of the 20 student societies were won by slates that were designated "Islamic." At the time officials did not view this growth with alarm; the conservative nature of most of the Islamic movement did not fundamentally threaten the status quo and served to counter popular leftist sympathies, which historically had been viewed as a threat to the stability of the monarchy.

A large number of Islamic cultural organizations were to be found in Kuwait; analysts divided the Sunni fundamentalist groups into four distinct currents. The smallest, though it was growing in the early 1980s, was Sufism (sometimes known as Islamic mysticism). Avoiding direct confrontation with authorities, it was relatively inactive politically. Another relatively small current was the so-called New Ikhwan Movement, whose largest group was the Society for Islamic Guidance. It made a special appeal to the Kuwaiti intelligentsia not only by opposing established Islam but also by criticizing the more militant and dogmatic fundamentalist groups.

The last two currents were far more influential. The Social Reform Society was the major representative of the Al Aslah current. As the Kuwaiti embodiment of Egypt's influential Al Ikhwan al Muslimun (Muslim Brotherhood), this current had been a part of Kuwaiti politics since the 1950s. Under the leadership of Umar Bahair Amiri, it gradually evolved from a position of opposition into an important component of the nation's Islamic establishment. The Speaker of Kuwait's National Assembly, Yusif al Adasani, was an active member of the Social Reform Society. If the Al Aslah was the least dogmatic of the fundamentalist currents, the Salafiyyin (literally, Forerunnerists) was the most dogmatic and extreme. Its profoundly reactionary goal was to transform society into a mirror image of that during the time of the Prophet Muhammad in the seventh century. The largest organization within the Salafiyyin current was the Society for the Revival of Islamic Heritage, led by Khalid Sultan. The Salafiyyin was perhaps the fastest growing of all fundamentalist currents, and it had a considerable impact on the debate in the National Assembly during the early 1980s.

Foreign Relations

For a nation of its small size, Kuwait had an active and diversified foreign policy; in the early 1980s it maintained formal diplomatic relations with over 90 nations. Kuwait prided itself in having an independent and pragmatic foreign policy stance that "opened its windows to the world" of both conservative and radical Arab nations and of both capitalist and communist superpowers. This stance on the nonaligned middle ground was less a matter of ideological conviction, however, than a product of Kuwait's small size, its geographic location, its military vulnerability, and the composition of its population. Since first assuming responsibility for its foreign policy from the British in 1961, the ruling Al Sabah has viewed a centrist position—from which it can appear as all things to all nations—as a key to its survival. The maintenance of national security was, indeed, Kuwait's most vital foreign policy concern. Other major concerns included the maintenance of amiable commercial relations with its oil customers and those nations in which its surplus oil revenues were deposited and the pursuit of Arab solidarity in the conflict with Israel, with particular attention paid to the Palestinian problem. A key tool in the quest for these goals was the prodigious use of its oil wealth to win foreign allies, conciliate enemies, and spread goodwill in the name of Kuwait.

Major foreign policy decisions were made by Amir Jabir and Prime Minister Saad in consultation with their senior advisers.

Minister of Foreign Affairs Sabah, who by 1984 had held that post for well over a decade, was the most publicly visible of these secondary decisionmakers and was viewed as the architect of the government's nonaligned posture. The ministers of defense and of oil also played important advisory roles in their respective areas of concern. Foreign policy debates in the National Assembly added a measure of Kuwaiti public opinion to the decisionmaking equation. In the early 1980s, for example, this factor made it more difficult for the government to continue its subventions to Syria while the latter was warring on Palestinians in Lebanon. During that time the Assembly also raised objections to supporting the Iraqi war effort while longtime border differences between Iraq and Kuwait remained unresolved.

Kuwait's security concerns centered on its relations with its three large neighbors—Iraq, Iran, and Saudi Arabia—and its efforts to avoid "being caught in the cross fire" among these frequently antagonistic regional powers. In 1984 these relations continued to be dominated by the fierce Iran-Iraq War being waged less than 100 kilometers from Kuwait's northern border (see The Impact of the Iran-Iraq War, ch. 7). Kuwait's initial stance in this conflict had been one of neutrality, but in 1981, fearing an Iranian victory, it began to support Iraq through loans that totaled US$6 billion over a two-year period and by allowing Iraqi-bound trade to enter Kuwait ports and traverse its northern border. In October 1981 Iranian jets attacked Kuwait's oil facilities at Umm al Aysh as a warning against this support of Iraq, and most Kuwaitis interpreted the December 1983 terrorist bombings in Kuwait City as another warning to be cautious in supporting Iraq.

Kuwait's support for Iraq was hardly steadfast; in fact, it feared a victory by either antagonist, for both were viewed as potential enemies. Revolutionary Iran, on the one hand, threatened all the Sunni monarchies of the Arabian Peninsula by its revolutionary propaganda aimed at foreign Shia Muslims, who in Kuwait made up over 20 percent of the population. A resurgent Iraq, on the other hand, would be in a strengthened position to press its historical territorial claim to Kuwait.

Tensions caused by its 1961 claim to the entire territory of Kuwait were greatly eased in 1963, when a new Iraqi regime granted formal recognition of Kuwait's independence. This action did not involve an acceptance of Kuwait's borders, however, and in 1973 Iraq briefly occupied a Kuwaiti border post in order to press its claim. In May 1975 Iraq, in effect, altered its claim by proposing that Kuwait cede its sovereignty over Al Warbah Island and lease half of Bubiyan Island to Iraq for 99 years. This proposal, designed to protect the approach to Iraq's second largest port at Umm Qasr, was categorically rejected by Kuwait, which argued that it would lose considerable offshore drilling rights under such an arrangement. Iraq again pressed this claim after the outbreak of war with Iran in September 1980 and the resultant closure of its primary port at Basrah. Kuwait again rejected the Iraqi claim and responded by building a causeway from its mainland to the police post on Bubiyan in order to secure its position on the island.

The stalemate in the Iran-Iraq War during the early 1980s, then, temporarily served Kuwaiti interests by distracting two potential adversaries. Kuwait feared the escalation of the war, however, particularly if it were to involve the intervention of the United States and/or the Soviet Union, and therefore called publicly for negotiations that would lead to an end to hostilities. Thus, in 1984 Kuwait called on Iran to respond to Iraq's request for a mediated solution to the conflict. Although in May of that year there was no prospect of this call's being heeded, Kuwait attempted to maintain a modicum of leverage by continuing its low-profile aid to Iraq while trying to keep its trade lines open to Iran.

The Iran-Iraq War also had the effect of strengthening Kuwait's ties with Saudi Arabia and the smaller monarchies of the Arabian Peninsula. The founding of the Gulf Cooperation Council (GCC) in May 1981 was a direct response to the outbreak of war in the Gulf (see Appendix C). Kuwait, Saudi Arabia, Bahrain, Qatar, the United Arab Emirates, and Oman saw the GCC as a forum for coordination of policies in the fields of investments, development, trade, and finance, but it was in the area of defense that the major cooperative efforts of the GCC were directed. Most of Kuwait's aid to Iraq, for example, along with that of other member states, was channeled through the mechanism of the GCC.

Although Saudi Arabia played the predominant role, Kuwait's countervailing influence—as the most politically liberal of the GCC states and the only one with diplomatic relations with the Soviet Union and its allies—was felt in the defense area. Kuwait was often criticical of Saudi Arabia for its close ties to the United States and of Oman for having granted' military base facilities to the United States within the framework of the Rapid Deployment Force (by 1984 the United States Central Command). Analysts described these as disagreements among friends, however. The relationships among the GCC states, based on common cultures and histories, similar if not identical political systems, and a common perception of the threat posed by the Iran-Iraq War and especially by an Iranian victory, remained extremely close.

The Arab-Israeli conflict was another focus of Kuwaiti attention. Although Kuwait had participated only marginally in the
several wars, its absorption of a large number of Palestinian
refugees and its financial aid to the combatant countries—particularly Egypt, Jordan, and Syria, as well as to the Palestine Liberation Organization (PLO)—made it an important actor. Kuwait
was one of the largest financial backers of the moderate Al Fatah
wing of the PLO, and Kuwaiti leaders often voiced the PLO goal
of establishing a Palestinian homeland in the territories occupied
by Israel since the June 1967 War. Al Fatah was allowed a substantial presence in Kuwait on the condition that it not involve itself in local politics. Kuwait's support for the PLO overrode its
support for the front line Arab states in the cases of Jordan in 1970
and Syria in 1983. On these occasions when Arab governments
waged war with Al Fatah, Kuwait temporarily curtailed its subventions to the governments in solidarity with the Palestinians.
Kuwait joined other Arab nations in severing diplomatic relations
with Egypt following its 1979 peace treaty with Israel. Commercial relations never ceased, however, and in 1984 there were good
prospects for a thaw in political relations as well.

Kuwait's foreign aid program was concentrated in, but by no
means limited to, the Arab Middle East. In 1974 the charter of its
major foreign aid agency, the KFAED, was amended to allow
funds to be distributed to non-Arab developing nations of Africa
and Asia. During the late 1970s slightly less than half of over US$1
billion committed annually in foreign aid went to non-Arab states,
such as India, Pakistan, Bangladesh, the Philippines, Thailand,
Mali, and Ghana. The Kuwait-based Arab Fund for Economic
and Social Development, to which Libya and Saudi Arabia also
made major contributions, was another major vehicle for Kuwaiti
foreign aid. Numerous observers have noted that although such
Kuwaiti concerns as its antipathy toward Israel and toward the
system of apartheid in South Africa are well-known to aid recipients, Kuwait's program was one of the most professionally run
and least politically motivated programs of foreign aid in the
world.

Kuwait's commercial relations were focused in East Asia,
Western Europe, and the United States. Japan was by far the
largest customer for its oil exports during the early 1980s, followed by Taiwan, South Korea, the Netherlands, Singapore, and
Britain, in that order. Although the United States was insignificant as a consumer of Kuwaiti oil, it was second only to Japan as a
source of imports (United States exports to Kuwait in 1981 and
1982 exceeded US$900 million). The United States, along with

Britain and France, were the major suppliers of military equipment to Kuwait; the Soviet Union and West Germany were minor suppliers. Finally, in the commercial field an estimated two-thirds of Kuwait's US$80 billion or more surplus from oil revenues (the profits from which had become a major source of government revenues by the early 1980s) was invested overseas. The bulk of these investments was believed to be in Britain and the United States (see Foreign Trade and Balance of Payments, this ch.).

Relations with the United States were broadly based and generally good despite some tensions over the United States role in the Middle East. During the early 1980s the quasi-official Kuwaiti media often criticized the United States military presence in and around the Gulf, expressing fears that it would accomplish little, other than to increase regional tensions and encourage the Soviets to increase its regional profile. Close United States relations with Israel were also criticized, particularly because they were felt to dampen prospects for what Kuwait termed "a just solution" to the Palestinian problem. The status of Jerusalem entered the equation of the United States-Kuwaiti relations in August 1983, when the United States nominee as ambassador to Kuwait was rejected on the grounds that he had served previously as the American consul general in Jerusalem. This incident caused increased strain in United States-Kuwaiti relations.

Kuwait argued with its fellow Arabian monarchies in the GCC that their refusal to establish diplomatic relations with the Soviet Union left them at the mercy of Untied States policies in the region. Kuwait's Soviet ties, which date back to 1963, were better explained, however, as an effort to neutralize its domestic leftist political opposition and to gain the trust of Iraq and other regional nations that had Soviet links rather than as an effort to gain leverage over the United States. The 1975 visit to the Soviet Union by Minister of Foreign Affairs Sabah and the subsequent conclusion of a Soviet agreement to sell a variety of missiles to Kuwait marked a significant departure from previous ties, which had been limited to economic, technical, and cultural cooperation. No Soviet advisers accompanied the US$400 million deal, however, and no further arms purchases were recorded until 1981. On August 15, 1984, Kuwait and the Soviet Union signed an arms agreement that provided for Kuwait's purchase of various air defense weapons and for Soviet personnel to train Kuwaitis in their use (see Kuwait, ch. 7). In September 1981 Amir Jabir made an unprecedented trip to Eastern Europe that included stops in

Bulgaria, Romania, Hungary, and Yugoslavia. Erich Honecker of the German Democratic Republic (East Germany) visited Kuwait in 1982.

Kuwait was also active in more than 20 multilateral organizations, including the United Nations (UN), the Organization of Petroleum Exporting Countries (OPEC), the Organization of Arab Petroleum Exporting Countries, the League of Arab States (Arab League), the Nonaligned Movement, and the Organization of the Islamic Conference. It was accepted as the one-hundred-and-eleventh member of the UN in 1963 and in 1978–79 served on its Security Council. In 1960 it had been a founding member of OPEC along with Saudi Arabia, Iraq, Iran, and Venezuela.

*   *   *

Kuwait: Urban and Medical Ecology, by G.E. Ffrench and A.G. Hill, presents a wealth of information on a variety of subjects. Harry Winstone and Zahra Freeth's *Kuwait: Prospect and Reality* offers a more general but still useful survey. A brief treatment of Kuwaiti education can be found in A.L. Tibawi's *Islamic Education.*

A useful but dated survey of the Kuwait economy was prepared by economists of the International Bank for Reconstruction and Development in *The Economic Development of Kuwait.* David Sapsted's *Modern Kuwait* presents a broad picture of the economy up to 1980. The article "Kuwait Adopts Measures to Adjust to the Impact of Reduced Oil Revenues," in the *IMF Survey,* August 8, 1983, contains a brief summary of economic developments. Between 1973 and 1984 the *Financial Times* of London published annual reviews of Kuwaiti developments. The Kuwait government publishes many statistical series; the *Annual Statistical Abstract* contains a broad range of data, though not as up-to-date as one would like. Many current statistics are carried in the International Monetary Fund's monthly *International Financial Statistics.*

Hassan A. Al-Ebraheem's *Kuwait: A Political Study* is an excellent introduction to the political system of Kuwait. Kuwaiti attempts to develop democratic institutions within a constitutional framework are analyzed in various works by Abdo I. Baaklini, such as "The Legislature in the Kuwaiti Political System." Kuwait's role in regional and international relations is covered in depth in Soliman Demir's *The Kuwait Fund and the Political*

Economy of Arab Regional Development and David E. Long's
*The Persian Gulf: An Introduction to Its People, Politics, and
Economics.* (For further information and complete citations, see
Bibliography.)

Chapter 3. Bahrain

Crest of the State of Bahrain

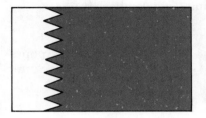

Country

Formal Name: State of Bahrain.

Short Form: Bahrain.

Term for Citizens: Bahraini(s); adjectival form, Bahraini.

Capital: Manama.

Flag: Three-fourths red field with serrated line separating white field on staff side.

Geography

Size: About 676 square kilometers.

Topography: An archipelago, of which four islands inhabited and Bahrain by far largest.

Climate: Hot and humid, little rainfall.

Society

Population: About 395,000 in mid-1984, of which about 70 percent Bahrainis.

Education: In 1984 about 85 percent of school-age children enrolled in 12-year school system. Legislation being drafted to make education (free) compulsory for at least primary cycle of six years.

Health: Free, comprehensive public health care system, plus three hospitals outside government system.

Ethnic Groups: Most Bahrainis are Arabs, although fairly large number of Iranian origin. Foreign community includes other Arabs, Iranians, Indians, Pakistanis, and smaller groups of East Asians and Europeans.

Religion: Excluding Indians, East Asians, and Europeans, population about 70 percent Shia (see Glossary) and 30 percent Sunni (see Glossary).

Economy

Gross Domestic Product (GDP):   In 1982 US$4 billion; per capita US$10,100.

Industry: Hydrocarbons and related industries, ship repair, and aluminum; in 1982 contributed about 70 percent of GDP.

Agriculture: Contributed about 2 percent of GDP in 1982.

Services: Banking and similar services contributed about 26 percent of GDP in 1983.

Exports: Total exports in excess US$3.7 billion in 1982, down 12.8 percent from 1981. Refined oil dominant export, earning about US$3.1 billion in 1982.

Imports: Total about US$3.8 billion in 1982, decrease of 9.6 percent from 1981. Machinery and transportation equipment major items at about US$702 million.

Government and Politics

Government: Ruler (amir) head of state and head of government. Shaykh Isa bin Salman Al Khalifa became amir in 1961; his son and designated successor, Shaykh Hamad bin Isa Al Khalifa, continued to serve in 1984 as defense minister. National Assembly elected 1973, dissolved in 1975; no indication in 1984 of plans to reestablish.

Politics: No political parties. Senior members of Al Khalifa and other noble families dominate political and economic decision-making.

Foreign Relations: Shaykh Isa continued in 1984 to maintain friendly relations with wide range of countries, but major activities channeled through Gulf Cooperation Council (GCC). Member of United Nations, GCC, League of Arab States (Arab League), and Organization of the Islamic Conference.

National Security

Armed Forces: Estimated strengths in early 1984: army, 2,300; navy, 300; and air force, 100. Service voluntary. Small, lightly armed army depends primarily on armored cars. Navy has two gunboats, awaiting delivery of two missile boats. Air force to acquire combat capability after delivery in 1984 of McDonnell Douglas F-4 Phantoms and Northrop F-20 Tigersharks.

THE COUNTRY'S RULER in 1984 was Shaykh Isa bin Salman Al Khalifa, who had become the head of the Al Khalifa family upon the death of his father, Shaykh Salman bin Hamad Al Khalifa, in 1961. Isa, who was born in 1933, was the tenth Al Khalifa ruler of the Bahrain Archipelago; when Bahrain secured its independence from British protection and suzerainty on August 14, 1971, Isa became the first Amir of Bahrain.

In mid-1984 the Al Khalifa continued to dominate Bahrain's government and society. Isa's brother, Shaykh Khalifa bin Salman Al Khalifa, was prime minister and head of government; Isa's eldest son, Shaykh Hamad bin Isa Al Khalifa, was defense minister and heir apparent. Six other members of the royal family served in the 17-member cabinet. The pragmatic, Western-oriented team of ministers has, with few changes, directed Bahrain's affairs since the withdrawal of the British protectorate in 1971.

The paramount family among the noble beduin tribes from the interior of the Arabian Peninsula who in 1783 expelled the Iranians from Bahrain's islands, the Al Khalifa by the late nineteenth century had adopted a form of hereditary succession. Unlike most Arab monarchies, which select the heir apparent from among the several able males within the royal family, the Al Khalifa succession is based on primogeniture. Since the rule of Shaykh Ali bin Khalifa Al Khalifa (1868–69), each ruler has been succeeded by his eldest son. The 1973 Constitution specifies that future rulers must be from the lineage of Amir Isa.

The political stability and relative economic prosperity of the royal family and Bahrain were fixed by the three men who ruled from 1869 to 1961: Shaykh Isa bin Ali Al Khalifa (1869–1932), his son Shaykh Hamad (1932–42), and his grandson Shaykh Salman (1942–61). During this period the various shaykhs signed treaties of protection with Britain, granted oil concessions to foreign companies, and laid the groundwork for the government that was formed after independence. Bahrain was the first Gulf Arab state to benefit from the discovery of oil, the first to institute general and free education and public health services, and the first to experience serious domestic unrest.

Because of the modest oil reserves of this small island state, the ruling family has linked the society's economic future to the building of a viable regional services and industrial center. In 1984 it was the Persian Gulf's principal base for banking, insur-

149

ance, and ship repair and was the Gulf's focal point for regional business operations and joint-venture industrial projects.

Bahrain enjoyed the most efficient communications system in the Gulf and was actively developing its educational sector, petroleum services, and selected industries, such as petrochemicals, aluminum smelting and extrusion, and iron ore processing. Bahrain's population was hardworking and was exposed to modern education a generation earlier than its neighbors.

Despite potentially divisive elements within its diverse society—Bahrain was the only lower Gulf state with a majority Shia population—it had the most relaxed social climate of all the Gulf states in 1984 and the one most hospitable to expatriate workers. There was some speculation as to whether this would remain the case once the causeway linking Bahrain with the Saudi Arabian mainland was completed at the end of 1985. Most observers felt, however, that the function of "social pressure value" that Bahrain serves for the Gulf, as well as the resoluteness of the Bahrain elite to shape their own, unique society, would prevail.

Since the early 1960s Bahrain has transformed itself from a remote, sleepy island—scarcely noted save for its archaeological sites, pearl fishing, and oil refinery—into a modern, sophisticated, and diversified economy. Between 1973 and 1981 the economy of Bahrain was radically transformed. This rapid and somewhat uneven economic growth typically was accompanied by high inflation and some social dislocation as living and working patterns took new forms. Many Bahrainis were not altogether displeased when the economy cooled in 1979.

New project planning between 1980 and 1983—much of it the product of joint ventures with its wealthier neighbors—once again quickened the island's economic activity. Some unified major projects originally targeted for completion in 1985 annd 1986 will be stretched out to better accommodate budgetary restraints in the light of falling oil revenues. This should prove helpful to the overall economy and should temper inflation.

Continued economic development in Bahrain depends heavily upon three factors largely beyond the control of those who manage Bahrain's affairs. Outweighing all other factors is the regional political stability that is essential for Bahrain to maintain the international business confidence necessary for its development as the mercantile and financial center of the Gulf. As the Gulf state poorest in mineral resources, it is the most economically vulnerable to any withdrawal of that confidence. Further, because regional political disputes—including the Iranian revolution—find echoes in elements within the Bahraini community,

Bahrain needs regional peace so that its social and political development can keep step with its economic growth.

A secondary, but nevertheless important, factor for Bahrain's growth is the continued ability of the other Gulf states to carry through their financial commitments to Bahrain, particularly those involving joint ventures in industrial development. Falling oil revenues and major budget deficits in neighboring states have the potential to jeopardize second-generation industrialization projects in Bahrain. Government officials, however, stated in 1984 that projects then budgeted would be carried out.

Finally, the Gulf Cooperation Council (GCC), composed of Saudi Arabia, Kuwait, the United Arab Emirates (UAE), Qatar, Oman, and Bahrain, has made a promising beginning since its foundation in May 1981 but must continue to strengthen its economic planning and cooperation. The GCC decision to make Bahrain and Oman the venue for all future GCC joint industrial projects holds great promise for both states. Also, the GCC Unified Economic Agreement, which was signed in June 1981, could encourage the development of Bahrain's embryonic light industry sector.

Geographic and Demographic Setting

Bahrain comprises an archipelago of one large and about 35 small islands situated halfway down the Gulf, 24 kilometers from Saudi Arabia's eastern coast and 28 kilometers from the coast of the Qatar Peninsula. The total area of the islands is 676 square kilometers, about four times the size of Washington, D.C. The largest is Bahrain (from the Arabic word for "two seas") Island (578 square kilometers), from which the state takes its name. It runs from north to south, is 16 kilometers across at its widest point in the north, and is 48 kilometers long (see fig. 8).

Most of the island is low-lying and barren desert. Low outcroppings of limestone form rolling hills, stubby cliffs, and shallow ravines. The limestone is covered by various densities of saline sand, capable of supporting only the hardiest desert vegetation—chiefly thorn trees and scrub. There is a fertile strip five kilometers wide along the northern coast on which date, almond, fig, and pomegranate trees are grown. The interior contains an escarpment that rises to 122 meters, the highest point on the island, to form Jabal ad Dukhan, "Mountain of Smoke," named for the mists that often wreathe its face. Most of Bahrain's oil wells are situated in the vicinity of Jabal ad Dukhan.

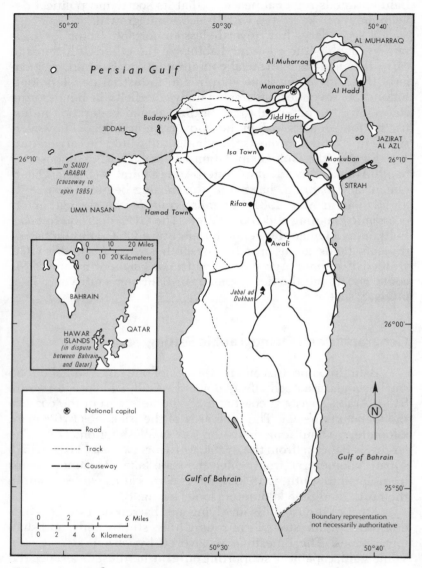

Figure 8. Bahrain, 1984

Manama, the capital, is located on the northeastern tip of the island of Bahrain. The main port, Mina Salman, is also located on the island, as are the major petroleum refining facilities and the business centers. Bahrain Island is connected by a causeway to Al Muharraq—the second largest island, on which the international airport is located—and by a bridge spanning a narrow channel to Sitrah. Other islands of significance include Nabih Salah to the east, where freshwater springs irrigate numerous date groves; Jiddah, a rocky islet that serves as a prison settlement; and Umm Nasan, the personal property of the amir and the site of his private game preserve. In addition, Jazirat al Azl, connected by a causeway to Al Muharraq, is the site of a major ship-repair and dry-dock center.

To the southeast, near the Qatar coast, lie the 16 small islands that compose the subject of a territorial dispute between Bahrain and Qatar—the Hawar Islands. The largest of these is 19 kilometers long and about 1.5 kilometers wide. Because of the similarity in shape to the island of Bahrain, it was called "Hawar," from the Arabic for young camel, to suggest that it was the offspring of the "parent" landmass. There are numerous other small islands in the archipelago, uninhabited by man, that are nesting sites for a rich variety of migrating birds.

Climate

Although the climate is relatively pleasant, temperatures ranging from 10°C to 20°C from October to April, it is characterized by intense heat and humidity during the summer, when temperatures can reach 44°C. Daily temperatures are fairly uniform throughout the islands. A dry southwest wind, known locally as the *qaws* or *shammal,* periodically blows sand clouds across the barren southern end of the island toward Manama.

The average annual rainfall is approximately 100 millimeters; no year-round rivers or streams exist. Rain tends to fall in brief, torrential bursts during the winter, flooding the shallow wadis that are dry the rest of the year and making all but major roads impassable. Little of this water is reserved for irrigation or drinking. Water is scarce in Bahrain, although a number of natural springs exist, mainly along the northern coast and in the shallow sea surrounding the islands. The underground water deposits are bacteria-free but have a high mineral content. They lie below the rock stratum and extend beneath the sea to Saudi Arabia. Desalination plants built in the early 1980s render seawater suitable for domestic and industrial use.

Population

As of mid-1984 the population was estimated at 395,000, of which 70 percent were native Bahrainis. The 1981 census had indicated a total population of 360,000. Improvement in health and welfare services has been reflected in an increasing annual rate of population growth, from 2.6 percent in 1971 to the extremely high rate of 4 percent in mid-1983. The high cost of providing housing and basic goods and commodities for such an expanding population was a serious concern of the government. The foreign labor force—39 percent—had been declining by about 7 percent a year, but the government of Bahrain expected that the proportion of non-Bahrainis would rise in the 1984–85 period because of the number of foreign workers required to implement major new projects. The high percentage of non-Bahrainis indicated the attractiveness of the labor market, especially for those who had specialized skills.

The economically active native population in 1983 was estimated at approximately 40 percent of the populace, indicating a high dependency rate in the country. Similar to many developing countries, Bahrain's population was predominantly youthful, approximately one-half the native population being under the age of 18. The majority of the work force was employed in manufacturing, oil production, trade, and service occupations, including government jobs and banking. A greater percentage of Bahrainis than non-Bahrainis were employed in clerical, sales, transportation, and communications positions. By industry, the service sector employed the largest number, followed by construction and manufacturing (see Work Force, this ch.).

Approximately 40 percent of the population in 1983 lived in Manama, the capital. This decrease from the all-time high of 66 percent in 1971 was a result of extensive government planning aimed at residential decentralization. Two new towns, Isa Town and Hamad Town, inaugurated in 1968 and 1982, respectively, have been instrumental in reducing the growth of Manama's population, as has extensive reclamation of land from the sea. Careful urban planning has spared the fertile regions to the west from residential buildup. The population in 1983 was chiefly distributed among the following towns: Manama, 121,986; Al Muharraq, 61,853; Jidd Hafs, 33,693; Rifaa, 28,150; and Isa Town, 21,275.

Although the Shia (see Glossary) in Bahrain embrace Ithna Ashari (Twelver) Shiism, the kind practiced in Iran, Bahrain's Shia have diverse origins. Descendants of the original inhabitants of Bahrain are known as Baharna. The Hassawis are those whose forebears are from Eastern Province in Saudi Arabia, chiefly the Al Hufuf or the Al Qatif oasis. The Ajami are those whose families migrated from Iran, usually within the last century. It is uncommon for any but the Ajami to have retained Farsi, though many Baharna—particularly the wealthy—had an Iranian grandmother. Marriage to an Iranian was a symbol of achievement for the Baharna in generations past. None of these groups was characterized by a specific socioeconomic level in 1984. All groups encompassed a socioeconomic status ranging from relatively poor to extremely rich. Both Ajami and Baharna counted millionaires among them in 1984. The degree of religiosity among the Shia also ranged the spectrum, from secular to deeply devout.

Not all those who originated in Iran were Shia, however. Sunnis (see Glossary) from the Zagros Mountains developed a significant population in Bahrain during the nineteenth century. Before their arrival Sunni Arabs, called *hawala,* who had migrated from Arabia and settled on the Iranian coast, recrossed the Gulf to settle in Bahrain shortly after the arrival of the Al Khalifa in the eighteenth century.

Exact figures were not available in 1984, but most sources estimated that approximately 30 percent of the native population was Sunni Muslim, the branch to which the royal family adheres. Shia were thought to comprise approximately 70 percent of the population. This higher estimate is based, in part, on the higher birthrate among the Shia.

Work Force

Because of the society's predominantly youthful population and the paucity of oil, with its concomitant economic opportunities, government planners have drawn up highly specific programs and laws to ensure employment of Bahraini nationals. Within the private sector, employers had the option of operating their own training courses or providing funds to finance training courses. A company paid a levy equal to 4 percent for every foreigner but to only 2 percent of the salary for every local employee. At the completion of a foreign worker's contract, representations were made to the hiring company to encourage them to take on more nationals.

A project known as "10,000 jobs" was an attempt in the early 1980s to identify 10,000 jobs carried out by foreigners and to provide appropriate training for Bahrainis, enabling them to replace the foreigners. The Ministry of Labor and Social Affairs projected that 30,000 jobs for men and from 8,000 to 12,000 jobs for women must be provided during the 1980s. If the goal were realized, 99,000 Bahrainis would be in the work force by 1991.

Despite such enactments, there were two to five jobs for every available Bahraini. Employers cited the fact that once hired and trained, Bahrainis often left their employment to seek higher wages. Ministry officials conceded that there was a great deal of "target employment" among Bahrainis, i.e., jobs were taken in order to secure funds to purchase a particular consumer item. Because of this flux, major industrial employers required a Bahraini national to work for one year before he or she could be accepted as an apprentice.

Bahrainis, additionally, continued to be unwilling to work for the lower wages acceptable to, for instance, an Indian trading manager. Within the private sector there also remained reluctance on the part of employers to hire Bahraini (as opposed to foreign) underlings in order to protect the confidentiality of the Bahraini family business.

The participation of Bahraini women in the work force remained greater than in any other state of the Arabian Peninsula. In 1981 they constituted 13.3 percent of the labor force, up from 3.8 percent in 1971. Bahraini women predominated in such traditionally female occupations as teaching, but in the early 1980s they began to enter banking, finance, engineering, the civil service, commerce, and administration. Bahrain's labor ministry estimated that between 800 and 1,200 women would enter the work force each year.

The government encouraged the active participation of women in the labor force by enacting one of the most pro-female labor laws in the world. Women were guaranteed 45 days of full-pay maternity leave plus 15 days at half pay. Nursing periods were provided in addition to coffee breaks. The law forbidding discrimination against working mothers was stringently enforced.

Immigration was rigidly controlled by a system of visas and residency and work permits. Acquisition of Bahraini nationality was permitted but highly restricted. An unusual feature of Bahrain's expatriate work force was the comparative absence of other Arab nationals. There were an estimated 2,500 Palestinians in the early 1980s, a fraction of the number found in other Gulf societies. The approximately 4,000 Egyptians constituted the largest Arab expatriate group. Working chiefly as teachers, they were considered a politically "safe" group, as distinguished from Arabs of the eastern Mediterranean.

Asians and Westerners dominated the expatriate component in the work force. There was an estimated total of 4,500 Britons in

Bahrain in 1984, a number that included both workers and their families, and a total of 2,000 Americans, of whom approximately one-third were in the work force. In 1983 some 105 Americans and 1,123 Britons were given work permits, in comparison with a total of 105 given to Jordanians, Lebanese, Syrians, and Palestinians. Indians and Pakistanis, who totaled approximatley 40,000 in 1984, dominated the Asian sector of the work force. In 1983 some 19,004 Indians and 3,909 Pakistanis received work permits. The majority worked as unskilled and semiskilled laborers, but a growing number were employed as low- to middle-level managers in hotels and in other parts of the private sector.

Education

Bahrain enjoys the oldest public education system in the Arabian Peninsula. Primary education for boys was introduced in 1919, and separate facilities for girls and various secondary programs were subsequently established. In 1984 there were many elite Bahraini families in their third generation of college graduates. Education was one of the largest recurrent government expenditures in the 1970s and early 1980s. Despite the intensity of government efforts, in 1984 the estimated literacy rate was approximately 45 percent, although attendance at primary and secondary schools was estimated at 85 percent.

In the 1982–83 school year there were 75,434 students and 4,450 teachers in 126 public schools. There were 48 private schools, including the United States-accredited and -operated Bahrain International School, which offered classes from primary through high school. Education in the public system was free through the secondary level; students received supplies, uniforms, meals, and transportation to and from school at no charge.

In 1983 the minister of education, Ali Muhammad Fakhru, announced sweeping changes to revolutionize the primary-school system. Classrooms were to be enlarged to contain special activities areas, and methodology was to become less formal, minimizing rote learning and replacing it to some extent with activity-based learning. Fakrhu said that his goal was to reduce the primary drop-out rate from 15 to 2 percent. In mid-1984 legislation was being drawn up to introduce compulsory education for all children between six and seventeen years of age.

Higher education in Bahrain expanded rapidly during the late 1970s and early 1980s. As of 1983 the six-year-old College of Health Services had graduated some 500 students in a wide variety of health-related fields and had plans to build a nursing center. Gulf Polytechnic, which in 1984 enrolled 2,000 students, was founded in 1968 as Gulf Technical College. By 1984 it had expanded its program to meet most technical and vocational needs in the Gulf, including computer science, engineering, and business management. One-half of the engineering students in 1984 were women, and in the business and management division the male-female ratio was one to three.

In 1983 the University College of Art, Science, and Education (UCB)—founded in 1979—had a student enrollment of 1,100 in its four-year curriculum. Education officials projected that the figure would rise to 6,000 by 1994. Among freshmen-registered students at UCB in 1983, females outnumbered males in science (60 female, 26 male); premed (32 female, 13 male); and education (108 female, 38 male).

In late 1983 the prime minister announced that Gulf Polytechnic and UCB would eventually be merged. The two campuses converged, and the merger was described by the prime minister as a way of establishing a national university in Bahrain and avoiding the costly duplication of administration and resources.

The College of Medicine of the Bahrain-based Arabian Gulf University (AGU) was scheduled to open in September 1984. The college is the first phase of the estimated US$300 to US$400 million AGU project, a joint venture of the six GCC states and Iraq. The main university site and a marine service center are planned to serve 7,000 students by the year 2000.

Education was slated to receive BD431 million (for value of Bahraini dinar—see Glossary) in the first five years of the Economic and Social Development Program, from 1982 to 1987. Capital expenditure was projected at BD7.1 million for 1984, rising to BD9.4 million in 1985, then falling to BD6 million in 1986. Recurrent expenditure for education rose from BD37.2 million in 1982 to a projected BD43 million in 1984.

Most of the expenditure will be used to build additional schools, which are estimated to cost approximately BD1 million each. The education ministry plans to build 15 schools between 1984 and 1987. The addition of these schools to the 1982–83 total of 126 schools and 4,450 teachers serving 75,434 students was estimated to meet Bahrain's educational needs in the 1980s.

Health

Free medical services, including immunization, outpatient treatment, and hospitalization, were established in Bahrain in

Children in primary school
Courtesy Ministry of Information, Bahrain

1925. Since that time such endemic and infectious diseases as smallpox, trachoma, and dysentery have been virtually eradicated, and in mid–1984 life expectancy was estimated at 65 years. In 1984 Bahrain had a modern comprehensive health care system, the facilities of which included inpatient and outpatient dental, pediatric, psychiatric, maternity, and orthopedic care. Within the state system almost all primary and secondary treatment remained free, to both nationals and expatriates.

Salmaniya Medical Center, opened in 1978, remained the core of the public health system. The center consisted of a 650-bed general teaching hospital that had accident and emergency facilities and fully equipped laboratories. Plans for Salmaniya included an expansion to 1,000 beds by 1985. More than 200 of the approximately 355 physicians within the national system work at Salmaniya. Primary health care was the responsibility of the 16 regional health centers. Ten new centers were to be added by 1986. The centers provided facilities for diagnostic services, minor surgery, dentistry, prenatal and postnatal care, and general family medical care.

Three hospitals were outside the public health system. The

135-bed Bahrain Military Hospital was reserved for the armed forces and their families. The American Mission Hospital in central Manama was the oldest hospital in Bahrain and one of the oldest in the Gulf. It was considered to have the best intensive care unit on the island. Founded and run by the United States-based Arabian Mission—a branch of the Protestant Reformed Church—this small (45-bed) but excellent hospital continued to enjoy the patronage of the elite of Bahrain, many of whom had been born there. International Hospital, an ultramodern, privately owned hospital with 23 beds, was founded with high-income patients in mind.

Various training programs, both within the country and abroad, had by the mid–1980s begun to increase the participation of Bahrainis in the medical services, although the country was still dependent on expatriate personnel. Bahraini women continued to be reluctant to enter nursing—where most positions were filled by Indians—but their number as physicians was steadily increasing because of the opportunities for medical training within the country.

Social Security

Legislation introducing a social security system was enacted in 1976. In 1984 the system continued to be run by the General Organization for Social Insurance (GOSI) and was mandatory for all companies employing at least 10 people. Seven percent of a Bahraini's salary and a further 11 percent from the employer were paid into GOSI monthly. The pension scheme was restricted to Bahraini nationals, but employers paid an extra 3 percent of their payroll to cover both Bahrainis and expatriates against accidents.

In 1983 approximately 100,000 employees were covered by the program. Of these only 20,000 were Bahraini, who eventually will receive pensions. By the end of 1983 GOSI had accumulated BD100 million in contributions.

The first pensions are due to be paid in 1986. Pensions will be based on the length of contributions, with a maximum of 75 percent of final salary or BD350 a month, whichever is less. GOSI calculated that it would need a 5.5-percent annual return on its investments to finance the program but thus far had obtained 10 percent. GOSI policy was to invest no more than 10 percent of its assets abroad, although actual placements in 1983 were one-half that percentage. The remainder was invested in Bahrain in real estate, public and private companies, government bonds, and bank deposits.

The large funds that GOSI had at its disposal made it a significant force within the economy because it functioned in a manner similar to a development fund. GOSI director Shaykh Isa bin Ibrahim Al Khalifa has directed the GOSI fund toward purposes that normally are the preserve of the state—chiefly the rescue of failing industries and companies. Future plans for GOSI included a bank that would provide low-interest loans to individuals who could not afford commercial bank loans.

The Economy

Agriculture

Scant rainfall, increasing salinity of the island's aquifers, and poor soil continue to impede the development of the agricultural sector. Nevertheless, the fundamental aims of the government's six-year agricultural plan, submitted in 1980, were to expand domestic production of foodstuffs from 6 percent to 16 percent between 1982 and 1985, to achieve self-sufficiency in egg production and 75-percent sufficiency in vegetables by 1985, and to double milk production to 30 percent of domestic requirements by 1985. In 1984 the government allocated BD2.6 million to agricultural development.

The plan was designed to save substantial amounts of natural water for irrigation. In 1984 there were 820 farms and smallholdings (less than four hectares) operated by about 2,500 farmers. The government offered various incentives to farmers to adopt new techniques for irrigation and cultivation. A drip irrigation system was introduced in 1983 in a bid to reduce the vast amount of water wasted through traditional methods.

Plastic greenhouses were being installed on selected farms. More intensive cultivation was expected from this method, which economizes on water usage and manpower as well as improving yield per holding. Farmers received a 50-percent subsidy from the government in order to keep agricultural production within the price range of the general public.

Other projects included treatment of sewage effluent for use as fertilizer, improvements in the drainage of low-lying areas, and enhanced marketing and processing facilities for locally produced agricultural goods. Continuous agricultural experimentation at the Directorate of Agriculture's Budayyi Gardens had resulted in a steady increase in the number and types of produce grown. Plants and trees were imported, and those that did well were grown in quantity for distribution to farmers.

In late 1983 more than 9,000 square meters were planted with experimental crops, including 4,000 square meters of hothouse and hydroponic units. Between 45,000 and 60,000 trees, flowers, and shrubs are grown during an 11-month growing season. Extensive nurseries produced 25,000 seedlings monthly, reducing the cost of plants to one-tenth the import price.

Skilled farm labor had become scarce by 1984 because of the higher wages and greater social status offered by other sectors, although agricultural workers represented 25 percent of the rural population in 1983. The government's policy was to encourage agricultural investment as a favorable long-term proposition. The land-tenure system, under which 60 percent of all cultivable land is leased from landlords for three-year periods, hampered efficiency and stability, however.

Imports of food and live animals cost BD64.3 million in 1982 and represented the fourth largest sector out of a total import bill of BD496.6 million. The main food imports were fruits and vegetables, BD17.8 million; meat and meat preparations, BD9.4 million; live animals, BD8.7 million; cereals and cereal preparations, BD7.7 million; and dairy products and eggs, BD7.1 million.

Fishing was similar to agriculture in its dependence on outmoded practices and its relatively low productivity per worker. In 1981 the government launched a five-year plan, budgeted at approximately BD9 million, to revitalize the industry. The plan covered both the expansion of the infrastructure and the addition of facilities, such as jetties and cold-storage centers. In 1981 the government introduced training courses that in part encouraged fishermen to abandon the traditional, small-mesh nets in favor of designs more easily repaired at sea. The courses also included instruction on engine maintenance and methods for modernizing the traditional dhow, of which about 100 remained in use in 1983. The Directorate of Fisheries' fleet of five trawlers expanded the catch and introduced new products, such as frozen fillets, to the domestic market. In 1981 the total catch was about 5,400 tons of fish and 630 tons of crustaceans.

Fish imports in 1982 totaled 879 tons, a 39-percent decrease from 1981, at a cost of BD960,000. Exports drastically declined from 219 tons in 1981 to 21 tons in 1982.

In March 1983 an oil slick emanating from a damaged oil platform in Iran's Nowruz offshore field in the northern Gulf began to leak about 4,500 barrels per day (bpd). At the height of the slick, it was estimated to contain in excess of 300,000 barrels and to cover more than 20,000 square kilometers. Although the long-term ecological impact was not certain, most marine biologists ex-

Control room of power station
Courtesy Ministry of Information, Bahrain

pected the slick to have profoundly detrimental effects on the fishing industry, particularly because the slick adhered to coral, the site of fish nurseries during the breeding season.

Petroleum Industry

The discovery of oil on June 1, 1932, and its production two years later made Bahrain the first country in the lower Arabian Gulf and Arabian Peninsula to have an oil-based economy. The Bahrain Petroleum Company (BAPCO), which was formed in 1936 and soon after became a subsidiary of the Caltex Petroleum Corporation (50 percent Socal, 50 percent Texaco), was the first modern industrial establishment in the Gulf states. For half a century BAPCO has trained Bahrainis to work in and manage a modern economy. Many of Bahrain's senior civil servants and technical personnel are former BAPCO employees. Although Bahrain is the Gulf's smallest crude producer and attempts have been made to diversify the economy, petroleum supplies the country with approximately 70 percent of its national revenue. More than one-half of the revenues, however, do not derive from Bahrain's own oil production. By agreement with Saudi Arabia, Bahrain receives half the income from the sale of crude from the offshore Abu Safah field, which lies within Saudi territorial waters adjacent to the Saudi-Bahrain boundary line, and is operated by the Arabian American Oil Company (Aramco).

In July 1980 the government announced the acquisition, for an undisclosed price, of a 60-percent share of the previously wholly Caltex-owned refinery. To manage its remaining interests in Bahrain, the Caltex Petroleum Corporation created a wholly owned subsidiary company, Caltex Bahrain. In 1984 this new company continued to carry out the local marketing of lubrication oils and to coordinate the supply and distribution functions for Caltex' remaining 40-percent share of the refinery. The Caltex/government joint-venture refining company, BAPCO, processed crude oil on behalf of the two shareholders.

In January 1981 the government established the Petroleum Marketing Unit within the Ministry of Development and Industry to market finished products from the government's share of the BAPCO refinery. Exactly one year later the Bahrain National Oil Company (BANOCO), established in 1976, took over full responsibility for the management and operation of the onshore oil-producing and -refining activities, together with all offshore exploration and development. These moves were consistent with the long-term trend in the region of national governments assuming control of production, refining, and marketing of their petroleum resources (see Appendix B).

Since 1981 Bahrain has spent approximately US$20 million searching for fresh reserves of oil (see fig. 9). As of May 1984 no major new fields had been located, and the government had postponed a decision whether to drill. Eleven dry holes had been put down onshore and offshore since 1954. In December 1983 a small offshore exploration area was reassigned to the Kuwait Foreign Petroleum Exploration Company (KFPEC). Under a 35-year production agreement Bahrain would—after recovery of costs by the foreign partners—receive 80 percent of any oil or gas found.

Annual production from Bahrain's own onshore oil field has been declining since the 1977 peak of 77,000 bpd; remaining recoverable reserves were about 430 million barrels. In 1982 Bahrain's 241 production wells yielded an average of 44,000 bpd. Pro-

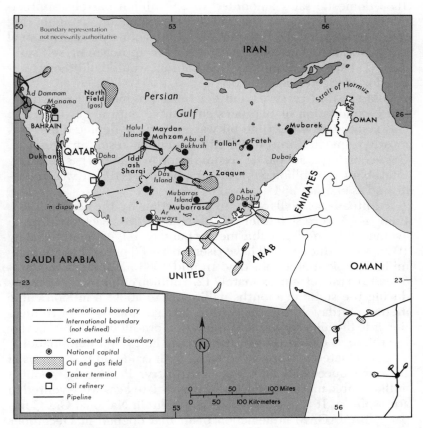

Figure 9. Oil Fields of the Lower Gulf, 1984.

duction in 1983 averaged 41,096 bpd for a total of slightly more than 15 million barrels for the year.

Bahraini crude production in early 1984 accounted for only 16 percent of the refinery's total throughput capacity of 250,000 bpd. In addition to its own crude, Bahrain's refinery processes Arabian light crude delivered by underwater pipelines from Saudi Arabia. Throughput in the first quarter of 1984 climbed to 200,000 bpd after severe drops in 1983.

Because foreign product prices remained depressed, the refining margin was unprofitable. In 1983 the possibility of BAPCO's refining for Saudi Arabia's domestic market was broached, but as of mid-1984 no contract had been signed. In

1983 domestic sales amounted to 2.6 million barrels, approximately 17 percent of the refinery's production. Neighboring states constituted over 40 percent of the country's international sales. Because many of these states were approaching self-sufficiency, it appeared unlikely that Bahrain would hold these markets for a long period.

Modest oil reserves and declining production have stimulated exploitation of Bahrian's substantial natural gas reserves. Gas associated with crude oil was essentially depleted and was mostly reinjected into the field to maintain reservoir pressure. Gas occurring as a separate accumulation in a natural gas field may total about 360 million cubic meters, but this estimate was unconfirmed as of mid-1984.

Fifteen gas wells were in production by the end of 1983. Four more were slated for completion in 1984, each yielding an average of 1.5 million cubic meters per day. It is estimated that by 1986 gas production will have risen nearly 80 percent to about 20 million cubic meters per day. In mid-1983 natural gas was produced at a rate of approximately 12.6 million cubic meters per day during the summer months, falling off to about a million cubic meters per day during the winter. The gas was used for reinjection into the oil reservoir to stimulate oil production and as fuel for the refinery, electric power generation, and water desalination.

Associated gas produced along with crude oil is the basis of Bahrain's successful liquefaction industry. Previously, about 3 million cubic meters per day of this associated gas were vented to atmosphere. It is now routed to the Bahrain National Gas Company (BANAGAS) liquefaction plant that opened in December 1979. The 75-percent government-owned company produced 985,749 barrels of propane, 890,443 barrels of butane, and 1,139,434 barrels of naphtha in 1982. The "tail gas" from the plant is piped to Aluminum Bahrain (ALBA), where it is combined with other gas to fuel the smelter's large power generators. The reserves could last 50 years if their use is retained only for these purposes and as fuel or feedstock in currently planned industrial development.

In 1980 Bahrain took a step forward toward building a petrochemical industry to complement its oil and gas production when it formed the Gulf Petrochemical Industries Company (GPIC) as an equal tripartite joint venture with Petrochemicals Industries Company (PIC) of Kuwait and Saudi Basic Industries Corporation (SABIC). Snamprogetti—a subsidiary of Italy's state hydrocarbon concern, Ente Nazionale Idrocarbure—will construct the main complex of twin plants that will produce 1,000 tons a day of ammonia and methanol.

The US$400,000 contract for the feasibility study of an even larger engineering project, the Heavy Oil Conversion Company (HOCC)—40 percent owned by Bahrain and 30 percent each owned by Saudi Arabia and Kuwait—was awarded to Lummus Engineering of Bloomfield, New Jersey. In 1983 Lummus was investigating about 30 possible plans for the project; it will recommend the three most viable plans.

Construction of the hydrocracking unit originally was planned for Bahrain's refinery and was to upgrade 80,000 bpd of the low-quality residual fuels into high-value products, such as naphtha and benzene. As a result of economic constraints, in mid-1984 the government of Bahrain was rethinking the project and considering a smaller 30,000-bpd hydrocracker.

Other Industry

Since the late 1960s the government of Bahrain has sought to create an industrial establishment that would be the basis of the Gulf's first economy not based directly on petroleum production. Such industries not only provided income from the state but also created jobs and training for Bahrainis. Additionally, they stimulated local satellite industries and workshops. The success of these new industries, however, will be linked to the petroleum sector, either directly—as with the planned ammonia/methanol plant—or indirectly, in terms of fuel. The aluminum industry is the leading example.

The Aluminum Sector

Apart from oil, aluminum is the country's most securely established industry. ALBA, formed in 1971, produces aluminum for its four investors: the government of Bahrain, 57.9 percent; Saudi Public Investment Fund, 20 percent; Kaiser Aluminum Bahrain, 17 percent; and Breton Investment, 5.1 percent. Despite the depression in the metals market in the early 1980s, ALBA operated at full capacity (170,000 tons) in 1982 and showed a finished production figure of 170,960 tons. This represented an increase of 29,644 tons over 1981. Continuing its stockpiling policy, ALBA set a 1983 production target slightly higher than the 1982 production figure. In 1983 ALBA doubled its billet capacity at a cost of US$4 million and began to modernize its original facilities as part of a six-year, three-phase program.

In 1983 raw materials came from the following countries:

Australia (340,000 tons of alumina); Italy (6,000 tons of fluoride); Japan (3,100 tons of cryolite); the United States (88,000 tons of petroleum coke); and Australia and the Federal Republic of Germany (West Germany) (23,000 tons of pitch). Alloys for billet and rolling slab came mainly from Europe. The raw materials were paid for at agreed-upon prices as part of a 20-year contract that will terminate in 1990.

ALBA's major product was standard ingot, but it also provided T-ingot and hot metal to local downstream (see Glossary) industries. As of early 1984 it had a billet capacity of 60,000 metric tons per year (mtpy) and a rolling slab capacity of 16,000 mtpy.

The governments of Bahrain and Saudi Arabia market their ALBA product shares, representing 78 percent of ALBA's total output, through the Bahrain-Saudi Aluminum Company (BALCO), owned by both governments. BALCO sells to 122 customers in 22 countries, including the Middle East, South Asia, Southeast Asia, and East Asia. Total shipments for 1983 were over 215,000 tons.

Early in 1983 a rise of 30 percent in world aluminum prices gave BALCO sales revenues of US$288.3 million in 1983, a 52-percent increase from 1982. This gave BALCO a 1983 profit of US$29.9 million, which contrasted starkly with a record loss of US$22.2 million the previous year.

A new and related industry planned for Bahrain is the Gulf Aluminum Rolling Mill Company (GARMCO), a joint venture of all Gulf Arab governments, including Iraq. Aluminum strip and sheets will be produced by a 40,000-ton mill expected to be operational by November 1985. As of mid-1984 BD13.7 million of GARMCO's authorized capital of BD24 million was paid up.

Bahrain Extrusion Company (BALEXCO), the first extrusion plant in the Gulf, is 100 percent government owned and a major customer of ALBA. The company increased its output of aluminum extrusion from 3,300 tons in 1981 to 4,200 tons in 1982 and 4,400 tons in 1983. The bulk of its output was unfinished systems (cladding, doors, window frames, etc.) supplied directly to the construction industry. BALEXCO supplied Bahrain's total needs for aluminum extrusion and in 1983 exported the remaining 57 percent to Saudi Arabia (26 percent); Kuwait (10 percent); Qatar (12 percent); UAE and Oman (6 percent); and Iraq and Pakistan (3 percent).

Founded in 1980 by Arab public and private shareholders, Bahrain's first steel company, the Arab Iron and Steel Company (AISCO), was expected to start production by the end of 1984. Kobe Steel Company of Japan was awarded a US$220 million con-

tract to build an iron ore pelletizing plant having an expected production capacity of 4 million tons a year. At the plant site a 300-
meter jetty with a capacity for ships up to 100,000 tons has been
built. Approximately 1.2 million square meters of land was being
reclaimed for the plant project, one-half of which will be for the
pelletization plant and one-half for either a downstream project or
another pelletization plant, for experts predicted that one plant
cannot meet the demands for steel from the Arabian Peninsula
and Iraq.

Ship Repair

Bahrain's location adjacent to one of the world's busiest shipping routes makes ship repair a logical local venture. In addition
to having three small repair yards, Bahrain is the site of the large
Arab Shipbuilding and Repair Yard (ASRY). Built in 1977, ASRY
is owned and financed by seven members of the Organization of
Arab Petroleum Exporting Countries (OAPEC): Bahrain, Iraq,
Kuwait, Libya, UAE, Qatar, and Saudi Arabia (see Appendix B).
As a result of the worldwide reduction in business and of government subsidies to repairers in such countries as Japan, Greece,
and Spain, ASRY had not made a profit as of early 1984.

Since its inception ASRY has repaired some 500 vessels, one-
half of which were in the super-tanker class. To diversify its industrial base and utilize spare capacity at the yard, ASRY took a 15-
percent shareholding in the Kuwait Desalination Plant Company.
As a result ASRY hoped for a major role as a steel fabricator for desalination and petrochemical projects in the area. ASRY management anticipated that a larger proportion of members' national
shipping fleets will be repaired at the yard.

ASRY's general manager announced that of the 68 super
tankers repaired at ASRY in the first 11 months of 1982, only 40
percent were Arab owned. In 1982 dry-dock occupancy was close
to maximum (almost 90 percent) while ship-repair revenues rose
by 5 percent to nearly US$25 million. For several reasons, includ-
ing the Iran-Iraq War and the reduced shipping caused by the
world oil glut, only 41 vessels were dry-docked and nine were repaired alongside in 1983.

Far from being conceived as merely a commercial venture,
ASRY was intended, and has proved, to be a major vehicle for
technology transfer to the Gulf. It has benefited both from the
spin-off of additional service industries and associated contracts
and from intensive staff-training programs aimed at maximum
Arabization. In mid-1984 about 65 percent of the 1,200-person

work force and one-half of the top management team were Arab.

The Causeway

Work began in early 1982 on the single largest construction project in the history of the Gulf—the building of a road link between Bahrain and Saudi Arabia. The construction contract was awarded to a Saudi-Dutch consortium called Bandar Ballast, led by the Dutch firm, the Ballast Nedam Group. The project was scheduled to be completed by National Day, December 16, 1985. The causeway will be a 25-kilometer-long, four-lane highway running over 22 kilometers of sea and three kilometers across Bahrain's Umm Nasan Island. It will run from Jasra in the northwest of Bahrain to Al Aziziyah, 10 kilometers south of Al Khubar in Saudi Arabia (see fig. 8).

Government officials and leading Bahraini businessmen were very optimistic about the project's positive benefits for Bahrain. In addition to assisting Bahrain to remain prosperous and, therefore, more likely to remain politically stable, Saudi Arabia will also benefit from the causeway, which will constitute the necessary transportation link to enable Bahrain's work force and light industry to develop in a manner complementary to Saudi Arabia's huge industrial development projects in its eastern regions.

Banking and Finance

No sector of the economy has witnessed a more dramatic growth rate than that of banking and finance, and no sector is more responsible for Bahrain's economic transformation. Banking in formal, if rudimentary, form began in 1921, when a branch of the Eastern Bank (currently the Chartered Bank) opened as Bahrain's first commercial bank; it was followed two decades later by the British Bank of the Middle East. In 1957 the Bank of Bahrain was founded; its name was subsequently changed to the National Bank of Bahrain. This was the first commercial bank on the island that was completely owned by Bahrainis. In the early 1960s several other banks opened branches in Bahrain, but banking activity was desultory; demands on the banks were fairly elementary, consisting chiefly of the financing of trade and the provision of deposit facilities for customers. Foreign exchange surpluses were invested in British treasury bills and government securities.

The modernization of the banking sector began in 1965, when the standard currency, the Indian rupee, was replaced by the Bahraini dinar. Also, Bahrain's already highly educated elite had begun to explore alternatives to reliance on oil, their single but declining commodity, and informally invited banks to establish branches. In response, 15 commercial banks opened branches in Bahrain between 1969 and 1977.

The increase in the number of banks in the early 1970s made it apparent that a central monetary institution with the ability to direct, supervise, and control banks was needed. In 1973 a decree by the amir created the Bahrain Monetary Agency (BMA) as a legal entity that possessed extensive central banking powers. As an independent juristic personality and fiscal agent of the government, the BMA enjoys wide discretionary powers. In 1984 it issued currency, was recognized as the government banker and depository of government funds, and was entrusted with investment of the government's foreign reserves, among other powers.

The accelerated economic growth of 1973 and 1974 required an even more sophisticated banking sector, both to finance construction and trading in the private sector and to channel the increasing volume of liquid funds into the international market. Further, bankers began to realize Bahrain's considerable potential for development as a regional banking center, ideally catching the fallout from the banks that were leaving the turbulence of Lebanon. Located midway between the time zones of East and West, Bahrain had the potential to do business with both and to work through the Western weekend of Saturday and Sunday. The government decided to expand the telecommunications systems, upgrade airport facilities, enhance the service sector, and construct residential housing attractive to expatriate professionals.

In 1975 the BMA announced the government's plan to develop a banking center by offering a host of attractive advantages, including exemption from maintaining reserves with the BMA or from observing liquidity ratios; no withholding of taxes on interest by depositors; no tax of banking income; and freedom from exchange and trade controls. The enthusiastic response to the BMA's invitation resulted in the establishment of 26 offshore banking units (OBUs) by 1976. OBUs pay only an annual license fee of US$25,000. They are prohibited from carrying on commercial banking operations in dinars in Bahrain, but their economic contribution to the island's economy is immense. In rents, salaries, license fees, and other local expenditures, OBUs annually add approximately US$75 million in foreign-exchange income to Bahrain. They have also created more than 1,000 jobs for Bahrainis and offered substantial training in banking and financial services.

By mid-1984 Bahrain, despite its relatively low per capita income (US$9,000) relative to the other Gulf states, had become the premier banking and financial center of the Gulf. It was estimated that about 3 percent of the work force was engaged in banking. Ancillary markets in insurance, commodities, and securities had also been developed. As of January 1984 Bahrain had 145 licensed banks, some with more than one type of license: 75 offshore banks (OBUs), 19 full commercial banks, 54 representative offices, and nine investment banks. Banks from virtually every geographical area of importance in the world economy were represented within the market. Fourteen American banks had offices in Bahrain.

The major Western banks, well established in Bahrain, were soon joined by new and aggressive Arab banks with large amounts of public funds at their disposal, reflecting the trend among Arab financial institutions to play a larger role in investing government funds. Bahrain had the headquarters of two major Arab banking consortia—the Gulf International Bank (GIB—an OBU owned by the governments of Bahrain, Kuwait, Oman, Qatar, UAE, Iraq, and Saudi Arabia), with US$21 billion in assets, and the Arab Banking Corporation (ABC), a Kuwait-Libya-Abu Dhabi joint venture that had paid-in capital of US$1 billion.

For nearly a decade Bahrain's banking community experienced spectacular growth. Bahrain has not been immune, however, from the downturn in the region's economic health or the worldwide banking malaise. Bahrain's slowdown became apparent by April 1983, when BMA figures showed a drop in total assets of OBUs to US$55.6 billion, in contrast with a peak of US$61.1 billion in April of 1982. OBUs did close 1983 at a record US$62.7 billion, but by January 1984 assets had fallen to US$59 billion. An additional factor in the downturn had been restrictions that the Saudi Arabian Monetary Authority (SAMA) had placed on the lending operations of Bahrain's OBUs in Saudi Arabia. Also, project lending into Saudi Arabia, the mainstay of OBUs, dried up in 1984, both because of the decrease in Saudi Arabia's oil revenues and spending and because the kingdom's major infrastructural projects, such as Yanbu and Al Jubayl, were largely completed.

Banking specialists believed that the latter half of the 1980s would see the OBUs concentrating on correspondent banking with Saudi institutions and on portfolio management. Experts opined that after a period of consolidation, Bahrain's banking community was likely to emerge with a broader base and a more modest growth rate, a pattern typical of matured banking centers.

As of mid-1984 domestic banking in Bahrain had not suffered

the difficulties experienced by the OBUs. Commercial bank profits at the end of 1983 were sufficiently high that in March 1984 the BMA requested commercial banks to begin publishing their best lending rates. It was hoped that such a hitherto unknown publication (for Bahrain) would stimulate competition as well as lower interest rates. The National Bank of Bahrain, which was the top performer and had the largest assets (US$354.4 million) of the locally owned banks, reported a profit of US$33.1 million in 1983, an increase over a profit of US$30 million for 1982.

The successful experiment with offshore banking led to the introduction in 1977 of the offshore company system. Businesses that plan long-term activity in the area can be incorporated in tax-free Bahrain for a period of up to 25 years and can acquire Bahraini nationality. The company must have capital of at least BD20,000 (US$53,000), and, although the company can be owned partly or wholly by Bahrainis, neither majority Bahraini ownership nor a local sponsor is necessary. The company is officially barred from interaction with the domestic economy, but there are even various exemptions from the rule.

The company pays a registration fee of BD2,500 (US$6,625), renewable annually. When the system was first introduced, the companies had to take the form of closed, joint-stock companies and could not offer shares for public subscription. In 1979, however, the law was changed to allow for public subscription, and in late 1983 some 13 of the total of 152 exempt companies were public shareholding companies. All of the 13 were owned exclusively by Arabs. The registration fee for such a company is BD10,062 (US$26,666), payable annually.

In late 1983 exempt firms included 11 investment companies, 13 OBUs, and 15 insurance companies, plus accountants, equipment lessors, engineers, catering services, and oil field and industrial services. Such companies provided jobs for Bahrainis, spent locally for rents, goods, and services, and amplified Bahrain's reputation as a financial and service center.

Budget

The annual budget was both the government's principal instrument of economic development and its barometer of progress. It included neither large projects in Bahrain financed by other Arab governments nor international financial and investment institutions, including the causeway, cracking plant, twin ammonia and methanol plant, and the Arabian Gulf University. It did, however, include yearly appropriations for Bahrain's share of such projects.

For more efficient planning the government presents biennial budgets, although until 1983 it had a four-year investment plan. In 1983 the government expanded the four-year program to six years because only BD175 million of the BD330 million earmarked for 1982 was spent. Clearly the absorptive capacity of the economy was more modest than had been thought. In 1982 the budget surplus dwindled to BD80 million.

Bahrain's economy performed well in 1983, despite the challenge proffered by the decline in oil prices. The 1981 growth rate of 9 percent dropped to 6 percent for both 1982 and 1983, a relatively small decrease in the face of a loss of between US$8 million and US$10 million a month following the OPEC price realignment.

The government's total revenue fell from approximately BD646 million in 1982 to BD607 million in 1983. This relatively small drop in revenue and the overall good performance of the economy was made possible by non-oil income and, particularly, by subventions from the wealthier GCC states. Although the oil sector represented 75 percent of government revenue, it was only 25 percent of the gross domestic product (GDP), exhibiting the foresight of Bahraini planners in early diversification of the economy.

Because of the premium investment in major project planning, the government decided to stretch out major projects over longer periods of time rather than cancel them. For example, the most expensive project—the heavy-oil cracking plant—was being reevaluated in mid-1984 (see Petroleum Industry, this ch.). Major government subsidies were also cut. Gasoline prices were doubled in 1983, easing, though not eliminating, a US$45.05 million government subsidy.

Government economists expected that government revenues in 1984 would total BD545 million. Although the industrial sector's percentage of GDP dropped from 13.7 percent in 1981 to 12.3 percent in 1982, it was expected to perform better by the end of 1984, when such major projects as the aluminum rolling mill and the steel and petrochemical plants should be in operation.

Increases in both the development program and recurrent expenditures rose from 1983 to 1984 and were expected to increase in 1985. The development budget of BD201 million ($532.6 million) in 1984 will rise to BD210 million, and recurrent expenditures will move from BD343 million to BD363 million.

The overall increase in the budget from BD545 million to

Street scene, Manama
Courtesy Ministry of Information, Bahrain

BD575 million was expected to occur without increasing medical or electricity costs or reducing food subsidies. One reason the Bahrainis may have felt confident about their budget was that the Saudis, among others, were expected to continue their economic support. The total in direct aid to Bahrain was expected to reach BD56 million in 1984. At the October 1983 GCC meeting in Qatar, the heads of state voted that Bahrain will share a US$1.8 billion defense fund for improvement of its defense facilities. In addition to paying for the causeway, Saudi Arabia will pick up the tab for a new and immense desalination plant, and Abu Dhabi will fund the cost of other projects. Kuwait was funding Bahrain's school-building program.

Foreign Trade and the Balance of Payments

Traditionally, Bahrain had been the entrepôt and the distribution center of the region. This position has been usurped to a great extent, however, by the development of Saudi ports and strong competition from Dubai. Oil continued to be the dominant factor in the trade account, representing 82 percent of visible export receipts and 50 percent of merchandise imports. The government strategy of diversifying the industrial base and encouraging the growth of local industries has contributed to a reduction of imports by 9.6 percent (value terms) in 1982, in contrast with an 18.1 percent increase in 1981. Bahrain will remain strongly dependent on the outside world, however, for its basic requirements for some years to come. Government officials hope that the opening of the Bahrain-Saudi causeway may bring in new business for Bahrain's deep-water port, Mina Salman. To this end a new access road has been planned that will run from the container terminal directly to the causeway's link road.

A surplus of US$59.63 million in 1982 characterized foreign trade, down from US$222.6 million in 1981 and US$117.93 million in 1980. The oil accounts surplus declined 6.9 percent from about US$1.4 billion in 1981 to about US$1.3 billion in 1982. The deficit in the non-oil account continued to increase, although the rate was lower. A deficit of US$1.2 billion was recorded in 1982, in contrast with US$1.2 billion in 1981 and US$1.1 billion in 1980, representing increases of 6.5 percent in 1981 and 5.7 percent in 1982.

Imports

The total value of imports in 1982 was approximately US$3.7 billion, a 9.6-percent decrease from the 1981 total of about US$4.1 billion. There was a 25.8-percent drop in crude oil imports from about US$2.5 billion in 1981 to about US$1.9 billion in 1982. Crude-oil imports to the end of the second quarter in 1983 were 37.9 percent lower than the same 1982 period. Non-oil imports increased 15.1 percent, from approximately US$1.6 billion to about US$1.9 billion. Machinery and transport equipment were the major non-oil imports, at US$702.8 million, followed by some other manufactured goods, including the raw material for aluminum, at US$393 million; chemicals, US$223.93 million; and food and live animals, US$186.03 million. Chemical imports rose by 42.9 percent, machinery and transport material by 19.2 percent, food and live animals by 16.4 percent, manufactured goods by 7.8 percent, and miscellaneous manufactured articles by 2.3 percent.

In 1982 Bahrain's chief trading partners were the United States, Japan, Britain, Australia, and West Germany, accounting for 20 percent, 15 percent, 13.8 percent, 10.4 percent, and 6.4 percent, respectively, of total non-oil imports. The United States share of the total declined slightly from 22.4 percent in 1981, although it increased in value from US$363.3 million to US$375.2 million. Japan also experienced a marginal decline from 15.7 percent in 1981, although the value rose from US$256.3 million to US$281.4 million. Britain's share also declined from 15.2 percent in 1981, rising in value from US$247.25 million to US$259.97 million. Australia and West Germany's respective shares increased. In value terms West Germany recorded a huge increase of 78.6 percent to US$120.8 million in 1982, followed by Australia's 50.8-percent increase to US$196.1 million.

Exports

Total exports of about US$3.8 billion were recorded in 1982, down 12.8 percent from 1981. As a consequence of the oil glut, the value of total exports of refined oil decreased by 19 percent, from about US$3.9 billion in 1981 to US$3.1 billion in 1982. Because of the surplus of oil on world markets, exports of refined oil decreased by 11.8 percent to reach a total of 86.8 million barrels in 1982, in comparison with 97.1 million barrels in 1981.

The government's policy of diversification is reflected in the 38.4-percent increase in non-oil exports from US$436.75 million in 1981 to US$643.16 million in 1982, compared with a 16-percent increase in 1981. This expansion was owing mainly to a 41.7-percent increase in ALBA's production.

In 1982 the chief non-oil exports were manufactured goods, including aluminum exports worth US$320.12 million (49.9 percent of total), up from US$255.73 million in 1981, and machinery and transport equipment worth US$251.48 million (39.2 percent), up from US$37.9 million (5.9 percent). The main markets for Bahrain's non-oil exports continued to be Arab countries, accounting for 46.8 percent of total exports, the value of which was US$303.3 million in 1982. The second largest market consisted of Asian countries, which recorded a 185.7-percent increase in exports, from US$85.33 million in 1981 to US$244.07 million in 1982—37.9 percent of the total. European countries represented the third most important market, amounting to 7.9 percent of Bahrain's non-oil exports.

By country, Saudi Arabia and Japan were Bahrain's largest markets, amounting to 20.5 percent (US$132.24 million) and 17.7 percent (US$113.95 million) of the total, respectively. Other key markets included the UAE (US$45.05 million); Hong Kong (US$40.02 million); Britain (US$33.92 million); Taiwan (US$33.66 million); and Kuwait (US$30.2 million).

In mid-1984 Bahrain was pressing for greater trading opportunities with countries of the Organisation for Economic Co-operation and Development (OECD), including greater concessions from Western Europe for Bahrain's refined products and aluminum exports. Under the generalized system of preferences, the European Economic Community (EEC) does give Bahrain reduced tariff rates on certain manufactured imports.

Customs and port taxes and duties amounted to the third largest source of government funds. Rates payable were manufactured goods, 10 percent; automobiles, 20 percent; tobacco products, 30 percent; alcoholic beverages, 100 percent; fresh fruits and vegetables, 7 percent; and all others, 5 percent. As of March 1, 1983, there were no duties on animal, agricultural, industrial, or natural wealth products from any GCC country. Non-oil trade with GCC countries has risen steadily to a total value of US$236.12 million (36.7 percent) in 1982. Imports from GCC countries have declined from 4.6 percent of total imports in 1978 to 3.1 percent in 1982. Trade with GCC countries in 1982 yielded a surplus of US$177.8 million, a 17.2-percent decline over 1981's surplus.

Balance of Payments

There was a contraction in the growth of net foreign assets, from US$805.6 million in 1981 to US$171.72 million in 1982, the first deceleration of growth since 1979. Components of the smaller surplus were a 73.1-percent reduction in the trade balance and a 97.2-percent shortfall in nontrade items.

Net accrual on services, unrequited transfers, and capital in 1982 were US$112.1 million, contrasting with a US$584.06 million accrual in 1981. Net income on travel and tourism increased in 1982 by 30.2 percent, in contrast with a 9.9-percent increase in 1981. This was attributed to a 12.6-percent rise in the number of foreigners arriving in Bahrain, in contrast with a 0.2-percent rise in the number of nationals traveling abroad.

Net investment income within the banking sector rose by 44.7 percent over 1981. Workers' remittances were only slightly higher than 1981 figures. The US$171.72 million increase in reserves consisted of a US$175.96 million increase in commercial banks' net foreign assets and a US$4.24 million decrease in net official reserves.

Government and Politics

The establishment of a formal government structure and a bureaucracy began in the 1920s, at the insistence of the Bahraini elite, with the introduction of free modern health facilities and a secular educational system. Officially, the treaties with Britain placed only foreign affairs and defense under British control, but British influence and tutelage in domestic affairs were extensive and restrictive. Until 1926, for instance, the governmental activities of the ruling family were limited to the registration of property through the British adviser and the collection of taxes.

Intensive petitioning not only by the ruling family but also by merchants and tradespeople opposed to British economic regulations led in 1926 to the establishment of the Merchants Association and the Irrigation and Agricultural Association. In addition to a discussion of common objectives, each group resolved commercial differences among its members. In 1927 the first municipality was established in Manama, its members being appointed by the deputy ruler, Hamad bin Isa, who became amir when his father, Shaykh Isa, died in 1935.

It was during the reign of Amir Hamad that the foundations of modern Bahrain were laid. During the first part of his rule, the pearling industry, though in decline, was still the mainstay of the economy. Hamad improved the conditions of the pearl divers, expanded the educational systems, and enlarged the municipality structure. In 1930 he signed a concession agreement with the Bahrain Petroleum Company. Three years later shipments of oil began to be exported from Bahrain, bringing in revenue at a critical point when the pearling industry had slumped disastrously.

Hamad died in 1942 and was succeeded by his son, Salman bin Hamad, who inaugurated numerous development projects during his 19-year reign. He is best remembered for the establishment of Mina Salman, which bears his name and which in 1958 became a free-transit port.

An administrative council that served as Bahrain's executive body between 1956 and 1970 was established by decree and headed by Khalifa bin Salman Al Khalifa, who in 1948 was prime minister. The five-member council was responsible for making recommendations to the amir and government departments and acted as the public relations arm of the government. The council supervised an administrative structure of 26 departments and offices, including the Israel Boycott Office, an office for petroleum affairs, and an office for economic development.

In 1970 the amir created the first formal executive authority, the Council of State, which replaced the administrative council. This 12-member body was the first high-level government body without a British member; it included four members of the royal family. Each council member headed a government department. Upon independence in 1971 the departments (two were merged) became ministries, and their heads, ministers. Decrees by the amir officially confirmed Bahrain's complete control over its lands and internal and external affairs.

According to the new structure, the ruler (amir) was the head of state. He had responsibility for appointing both the head and members of the Council of State, for sanctioning all major decisions, and for issuing decrees, which included those relating to administrative affairs as well as major laws. Day-to-day administrative affairs were dealt with by the members of the Council who were responsible to the ruler. Among the Council's responsibilities were the issuing of administrative decrees, their implementation, and the preparation of the state budget.

The incumbent amir, Isa bin Salman Al Khalifa, was born July 3, 1933, and became ruler of Bahrain in 1961 upon the death of his father. His first 10 years of rule were devoted to preparing Bahrain for its independence and preparing the diplomatic community for its acceptance. He initiated both official and unofficial discussions with leading politicians in Britain, the United States, France, Iraq, Saudi Arabia, and Kuwait. He was particularly active at the meetings intended to produce a union of all the Gulf amirates, although, ultimately, Bahrain chose to become independent. Internally, he was chiefly concerned, as was his father, with fostering social development. The development of housing at Isa Town became a favored project, as did the educational system.

Isa declared Bahrain's independence from Britain on August 14, 1971, and on December 16, 1971, his tenth anniversary of rule, he announced that henceforth Bahrain would manage both internal administration and international relations. Bahrain celebrates its National Day on December 16.

In 1984 the State of Bahrain was a traditional amirate with a cabinet-executive system (see fig. 10). Principal government officials included the amir; his eldest son and the heir apparent, Hamad bin Isa, who was also minister of defense; and the other 16 members of the Council of Ministers. Bahrain is unique among Gulf states in that it is the only one in which primogeniture has constitutional sanction. The office of amir passes from father to eldest son unless the amir designates another to succeed him; otherwise it is not subject to amendment.

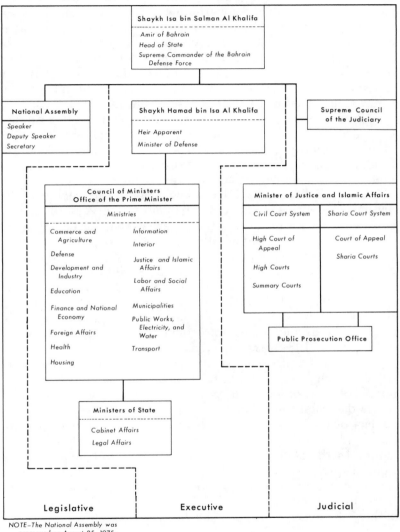

Shaykh Isa bin Salman Al Khalifa

Amir of Bahrain
Head of State
Supreme Commander of the Bahrain
Defense Force

National Assembly

Speaker
Deputy Speaker
Secretary

Shaykh Hamad bin Isa Al Khalifa

Heir Apparent
Minister of Defense

Supreme Council
of the Judiciary

Council of Ministers
Office of the Prime Minister

Ministries

Commerce and
Agriculture

Defense

Development and
Industry

Education

Finance and National
Economy

Foreign Affairs

Health

Housing

Information

Interior

Justice and Islamic
Affairs

Labor and Social
Affairs

Municipalities

Public Works,
Electricity, and
Water

Transport

Minister of Justice and Islamic Affairs

Civil Court System

High Court of
Appeal

High Courts

Summary Courts

Sharia Court System

Court of Appeal

Sharia Courts

Public Prosecution Office

Ministers of State

Cabinet Affairs

Legal Affairs

Legislative   Executive   Judicial

NOTE–The National Assembly was
prorogued on August 25, 1975;
as of August 1984 it had not been
reconvened.

Figure 10.   Bahrain. Government Structure, August 1984.

Of the 17 members of the Council of Ministers in mid-1984, eight were members of the Al Khalifa family. Of the nine remaining ministers, three were Shia. The prime minister, Khalifa bin Salman, was generally regarded as the most powerful figure in the Council and possibly the government. Although, as might be expected, the amir and the prime minister possess the authority to override a decision made by any other minister, in actuality the ministers have a great deal of autonomy. Ali Fakhru, the minister of education, for instance, initiated a revolutionary plan of his own devising for the educational system, which after minimal discussion was accepted by the Council (see Education, this ch.).

Both the royal and the nonroyal members of the Council were distinguished by an unusually high level of educational attainment and experience. Bahrain's minister of information, the articulate **Tariq Abdurahman al Muayyid, has called Bahrain** "a middle-class country." Lacking the financial resources of its neighbors, Bahrainis have had to work harder to establish their nation's credentials. In the opinion of most observers, this has inculcated a work ethic among the ministers that has given them a disproportionate amount of influence in Gulf forums.

In addition to the modern apparatus of state, the traditional majlis (pl., majlises), a form of appeal followed by generations of Arab rulers, continued to exist. The majlis is a form of open court that takes place for several hours a week in the ruler's palace. Any Bahraini or non-Bahraini subject may present a petition to the amir, who usually takes immediate action. The number of petitioners in 1984 was estimated at 60 per day.

Bahrain's amir is unusually accessible, even by traditional tribal standards. And, unlike many of the Gulf ruling elite who do not perceive a conflict of interest in holding a governmental position and engaging in business, Isa in no way involved himself in financial dealings. Many Gulf experts perceived him as the glue that holds together Bahrain's diverse society. He is highly regarded by the Shia, to whom he regularly gives land and money from his privy purse. The Shia recall his rescinding of the death sentence received by a Shia youth for murdering an Egyptian journalist in the 1970s, as well as his humane influence at the trial of those involved in the 1981 abortive coup d'etat.

The Constitutional Experiment

In December 1972 the members of a constituent assembly were elected in the country's first national assembly. In response to the amir's request, the Constituent Assembly, which included appointed members, prepared the draft of a constitution, which the amir issued on May 26, 1973.

Under the terms of the Constitution, a parliament—the National Assembly—was elected on December 7, 1973, for a four-year term of office and was established on National Day, December 16. More than 100 candidates stood for the 30 seats, and over 85 percent of the electorate of adult males exercised the franchise. The 10 nonelected members were, as provided in the Constitution, members of the cabinet and had no fixed terms. All those elected swore loyalty to the amir and the Constitution, which gave the Assembly the right to question the administration's policies and the decisions of the cabinet members and to withdraw confidence from any minister except the prime minister.

Theoretically, the candidates stood as individuals, because political parties have been prohibited. About 50 percent of those elected could be termed independent, nearly a quarter were Shia conservatives, and another quarter were left-wing radicals. Most of the candidates lacked education and firm political principles. Conspicuous by their absence were candidates from leading Bahraini familes. The *Financial Times* of London noted "that the leading families explained that they were too busy with business, and, more interestingly, that they felt that it would be undignified and embarrassing to have attention focused on them during the campaign."

This was not an excuse on the part of these families. One great stumbling block to the election process was, and remains, the absolute lack of such a tradition among tribal peoples. A man, for instance, did not seek to become shaykh but rather had it thrust upon him by something resembling popular acclamation. An American-educated son of a leading Bahraini family who wished to see such an assembly resuscitated nevertheless recoiled in horror when asked if he would run for office if given the opportunity. He replied: "To me and my family, it would be about the same as my entering the 'Miss World' contest!"

In addition to divisions between traditionalists and leftists, there was constant quarreling between the Sunni and Shia members. The leftists—comprising socialists, labor leaders, and some radicals who were committed to the overthrow of the monarchy—could agree on neither strategy nor platform.

The free elections and the resultant Assembly seemed to lessen the absolute authority of the monarch, but political parties were not permitted to organize within the country, and labor unions, promised by the Constitution, were still not sanctioned by the amir. The Assembly was in constant dispute with the prime minister and the cabinet. In 1974 new elections for the Assembly were held, but the new members produced even greater friction. The government barred a number of the newly elected radicals from taking their seats, stating that members of the Bahrain National Liberation Front did not have a place in the Assembly.

By mid-1975 the attempts to develop a constitutional monarchy had become a burden on the government's day-to-day activities, and the sharing of power that the government had hoped would produce stability was actually producing instability. On August 24, 1975, Prime Minister Khalifa resigned along with his cabinet in protest of the Assembly's interference in the running of the government. The following day Khalifa formed a new government, and Amir Isa dissolved the Assembly. In the three years in which it sat, the Assembly failed to pass a single piece of legislation.

After the dissolution of the Assembly, several dissidents were arrested, including at least one former Assembly member. Isa announced in August 1976 that the Assembly would remain dissolved for an indeterminate period. Since the dissolution of the Assembly, speculation about the possibility of the amir's resuscitating it has continued unabated in Bahrain, particularly after the institution of appointed consultative councils in Qatar and Oman, the reappointment of a council in the UAE, and the election of a new National Assembly in Kuwait. Most Bahrainis viewed the 1983 deliberations of the Kuwaiti National Assembly with revulsion, however. That, and the continuing concern with the Iran-Iraq War and Iranian intentions in general, appeared in 1984 to have muted active discussion relating to the reestablishment of the Assembly in Bahrain.

Workers' Representation

One of the issues that emerged frequently in the discussion of the National Assembly was the question of trade unionism and labor representation. Until 1976 the only labor law was the 1955 Labor Ordinance, which was based on British colonial practice. Bahrain had had a long history of labor activism, beginning during the 1920s, when it was still under British rule.

In 1973 at the ALBA plant Bahrain experienced its most traumatic strike. The new smelter had been beset with a seemingly endless series of mechanical problems that tended to dwarf, by comparison, the significance of the growing tension among workers in the plant. Welders who had legitimate grievances

were persuaded by a cell of the Popular Front for the Liberation of the Occupied Arabian Gulf (PFLOAG), which was backed by the People's Democratic Republic of Yemen (Yemen [Aden]), to use them as their sole grievance channel. The workers then went on strike and refused to engage in any discussions with management until they were granted official recognition to form a trade union. In sympathy, other workers joined the strike, occupied part of a plant, and threatened to throw into pots of molten aluminum anyone who tried to interfere. Eventually the strikers were ejected by the police, and 200 workers lost their jobs. Management offered double and even triple pay for nonmilitant workers to keep the smelter in operation, and support for a union gradually evaporated. The government realized, however, that the whole affair had been handled badly, and in 1976 it instituted a new and comprehensive labor law. At ALBA, workers were encouraged to elect representatives from each department, who were given direct access to the chief executive.

In July 1981 the minister of labor, Khalifa bin Salman bin Muhammad Al Khalifa, who had been in office for one year, issued an order designating eight of the major companies in the country to establish joint consultative committees between management and labor. Most of the eight companies had experience of some kind with workers' organizations. The refinery, formerly American owned, was American oriented. Departmental supervisors acted as channels of communication between workers and management, whereas ALBA was organized on the British model, using direct representation from the shop floor.

The labor ministry's system consisted of five appointed management representatives and five elected workers forming a joint committee to "cooperate in resolving disputes, securing improved social conditions for workers, determining wages, organizing social services, increasing productivity, and in any other matter of mutual interest to the two parties."

Workers' representatives for the first joint consultative committees were elected by a secret ballot of all employees. The election at ALBA, the first of the series, was held in November 1982, and by January 1983 the major companies—such as ALBA, Arab Shipbuilding and Repair Yard (ASRY), Bahrain Telecommunications Company, BP Arabian Agencies, and Gulf Air—had set up joint consultative committees representing nearly 80 percent of the island's work force. There was a high turnout of voters at all of the joint consultative committee elections.

In February 1983 workers' representatives from all the joint consultative committees elected an 11-member national body, the General Committee for Bahrain Workers, Bahrain's first officially sanctioned representative body. Membership in the joint consultative committees and the General Committee was restricted to Bahraini nationals. The General Committee nominates Bahrain's representative for Arab and International Labor Organization conferences.

Legal System

Bahrain was the first Gulf state to begin developing a non-Islamic legal system. This development was begun in the mid-1920s under the first of numerous British legal advisers, Sir Charles Belgrave; in the early 1950s a formal position of British judicial adviser was created to accelerate the codification of statutory law. In 1984 the process continued, but there remained remnants of many systems of law, including *urf*, or customary tribal law, two schools of Sunni sharia law (Maliki and Shafii), Shia sharia law, and civil law as defined in numerous codes and regulations.

At the pinnacle of the judicial system was the amir, who retained the power of pardon and whose office was the first step in the appellate procedure. By the mid-1950s Bahrain had developed a local court system effective enough to replace British jurisdiction at the local level in 1957. Since independence the minister of justice and Islamic affairs, acting for the amir, has exercised the judicial authority.

Theoretically, according to the modified 1973 Constitution, the judiciary is a completely independent and separate branch of government. The court system is extensive: the nature of an offense determines in which court a claimant appears. The formal dual court system, which has jurisdiction over all other court systems, comprises the civil court system and the sharia court system. Decisions handed down by courts of *urf* law, for instance, could be appealed to one of the appropriate recognized courts. Civil trials provide procedural guarantees, including open trial, right to counsel (including legal aid for indigents), and right to appeal.

Sharia courts were established in response to the Sunni-Shia division within Bahraini society. The courts, found throughout the country, deal primarily with personal status law, although the sharia Court of Appeal in Manama has final authority over the many sharia courts under the minister of justice and Islamic affairs. In 1984, however, the highest court was the High Court of Appeal, which was a part of the civil court system. The court's primary duty was to hear appeals from the high courts, but it was also competent to decide on the constitutionality of laws and regulations.

The high courts heard appeals from the network of summary courts throughout the country. The sharia court system and the civil court system constitute the formal unified court system, which was administered by an independent body called the Supreme Council of the Judiciary. The Supreme Council determined the jurisdiction of each court and of the Public Prosecution Office. In practice, however, it was probably the minister of interior who supervised the functions of prosecution. After the Assembly was dissolved in August 1975, a state security law that the Assembly had refused to enact was promulgated and remained in effect in 1984, providing for separate security courts.

It was in such courts that the dissidents who attempted the December 1981 coup d'état were tried. Those tried in security courts, normally reserved for high treason, lack the rights to a public trial or appeal but retain the right to counsel, including legal aid. Sentences imposed by the security court can be referred to the amir for clemency, which is not customarily allowed by the civil courts. For instance, in the case of the 1981 dissidents, the amir let it be known that capital punishment for the dissidents was unacceptable to him as a judicial option.

Most commercial cases fall under the authority of the Ministry of Commerce and Agriculture, which maintains for the purpose commercial law codes based on standard international commercial law. The ministry is empowered to adjudicate on most commercial matters, but litigants also have access to the civil court system.

Foreign Relations

Since the accession of Amir Isa in 1961, Bahrain has worked diligently to increase its involvement with other nations. Initially this was confined to cooperation with international specialist agencies to develop the health, educational, and nutritional needs of the populace. Additionally, Bahrain was active with League of Arab States (Arab League) committees, including the establishment of the Regional Boycott Office in 1964. In 1969 a department of foreign affairs was appointed by decree of the amir in preparation for the creation of a foreign ministry upon independence.

Following independence the first Bahraini embassy was established in Egypt in September 1971. Bahrain became a full member of the Arab League on September 11, 1971, and of the United Nations (UN) on September 21, 1971, when its first permanent delegation to the UN was appointed. In 1984 Bahrain had permanent representation in Canada, Egypt, France, India, Iraq, Jordan, Kuwait, Pakistan, Saudi Arabia, Tunisia, Britain, and the United States. Fifteen countries had embassies in Bahrain in 1984; 14 maintained consular agents, and two had consulate generals. Bahrain had not established diplomatic relations with the Soviet Union or its Warsaw Pact allies. Visa requests from such countries were routinely denied, and professional degrees received by Bahraini students in such countries were not acknowledged.

Bahrain participates in meetings of the Nonaligned Movement and the Organization of the Islamic Conference and takes part in the Euro-Arab Dialogue and the Euro-Arab African tripartite talks for aid to Africa. In mid-1984 Bahrain's major foreign policy objective was to work as harmoniously as possible with the other GCC states to ensure their mutual defense against aggression from Iran and fallout from the Iran-Iraq War (see Appendix C).

Iran had plagued Bahrain for centuries. In 1970, as Bahrain prepared for independence, Mohammad Reza Pahlavi had laid claim to Bahrain based on Iran's occupation of Bahrain for periods in the seventeenth and eighteenth centuries. Because Bahrain was not yet independent, UN representatives conducted a public opinion survey that conclusively demonstrated that the majority of Bahrainis did not wish to unite with Iran.

Shortly after the establishment of the revolutionary government in Iran in 1979, Iran chose Bahrain as the primary target for the export of the revolution. Radio Tehran, which has excellent reception in Bahrain, regularly exhorted the Shia population to rise against the Al Khalifa. Bahrain's worst fears were realized in late 1981, when security forces detected the arrival of some 72 mostly Bahraini dissidents whose goal was to assassinate the amir, the heir apparent, and the prime minister, and to seize the communications centers (see Bahrain, ch. 1; Bahrain, ch. 7). In mid-1984 experts opined that, although an indeterminate number of Bahraini Shia shared sympathies with Ayatollah Ruhollah Khomeini, most, nevertheless, had become disenchanted with the evolution of Iran's revolution and were disinclined to exchange their relatively high standard of living in Bahrain for the rigors of life in revolutionary Iran.

* * *

There are few works that focus solely on Bahrain. Fuad I. Khuri's *Tribe and State in Bahrain: The Transformation of Social and Political Authority in an Arab State* was in mid-1984 the only detailed sociopolitical analysis of Bahrain. The single most comprehensive source for Bahrain is Ahmed A. Fakhri's encyclopedic *Bahrain Business Directory,* which in 1984 was in its fifth edition. In addition to being the most comprehensive business directory in the region, including as it does the full text of the labor and commercial laws, it contains detailed histories of Bahrain's business and industrial ventures as well as critical analyses on many pertinent subjects. It is also the best single compilation of statistical information. Among the periodical literature, the annual "MEED Special Report: Bahrain," usually published in September, and the *Financial Times* "Survey" on Bahrain, usually published in May, provide superb, detailed, and current data and analyses. (For further information and complete citations, see Bibliography.)

189

Chapter 4. Qatar

Crest of the State of Qatar

Country

Formal Name: State of Qatar.

Short Form: Qatar.

Term for Citizens: Qatari(s); adjectival form, Qatari.

Capital: Doha (Ad Dawhah).
Flag: Three-fourths maroon field with serrated line separating white field on staff side.

Geography

Size: About 10,360 square kilometers.

Topography: Mostly low-lying, barren terrain.

Climate: Hot, limited rainfall, high humidity.

Society

Population: Estimates for mid-1984 ranged from 250,000 to 290,000.

Education: Free throughout 12-year public school system, which consists of six-year primary cycle, three-year preparatory cycle, and three-year secondary cycle. Most school-age children attend primary cycle; girls outnumber boys in subsequent cycle. Qatar University—which has more female than male students— also free.

Health: Excellent comprehensive public health system free. Almost all medical personnel foreigners.

Ethnic Groups: Most Qataris are Arabs, as are minority of foreigners. Largest expatriate communities consist of Iranians (23 percent of total population) and Pakistanis (19 percent).

Religion: Most Qataris adhere to Wahhabi (see Glossary) Islam; most Arab foreigners Sunni (see Glossary) as are most Pakistanis. Most Iranians presumably Shia (see Glossary). Indians included Muslims, Hindus, and a few Christians.

Economy

Gross Domestic Product (GDP): Estimated at roughly US$6 billion in 1981.

Industry: Hydrocarbons and associated industries, plus cement and embryonic iron and steel processes, contributed about 90 percent of GDP in early 1980s.

Agriculture: Contributed less than 1 percent of GDP in early l980s.

Exports: About US$5.8 billion in 1981; decreased in subsequent years. Japan major purchaser of oil exports, taking about 40 percent.

Imports: About US$1.6 billion in 1982, mostly machinery and foodstuffs. Japan, Britain and other West European states, and United States major suppliers.

Government and Politics

Government: Ruler (amir) head of state and head of government. Shaykh Khalifah bin Hamad Al Thani, who became amir in 1972, continued to rule in 1984. Two of his sons and three of his brothers dominate Council of Ministers; Advisory Council largely powerless. Independent (if circumscribed) judiciary.

Politics: No political parties. Al Thani family large and powerful. Foreign communities kept under close surveillance and control.

Foreign Relations: Major foreign policy efforts increasingly channeled through Gulf Cooperation Council (GCC), Organization of Arab Petroleum Exporting Countries (OAPEC), Organization of Petroleum Exporting Countries (OPEC), and Organization of the Islamic Conference. Also belongs to United Nations (UN) and most of its special agencies and to League of Arab States (Arab League). Strong supporter of Palestine Liberation Organization (PLO).

National Security

Armed Forces: Estimated strengths in early 1984: army, 5,000; navy, 700; and air force, 300. Service voluntary. Army used French AMX-30 main battle tanks and a variety of other armored vehicles. Navy had three French-built guided missile boats. Air force combat aircraft included Alpha Jets, Mirages, and FGS-6s.

A FEW HUNDRED adult males of the Al Thani ruling family continued to dominate Qatar's sociopolitical system in the mid-1980s. The broader Al Thani tribe was estimated to number several thousand, perhaps 40 percent of the indigenous Qatari population. Qataris were beduin from Najd in the interior of the Arabian Peninsula who came to the Qatar Peninsula in search of forage for their animals. Some continued their nomadic existence; others settled around wells to cultivate date palms and other crops, and some took up fishing. Doha (Ad Dawhah) became a small trading center but did not develop the entrepôt business and the importance of such ports as Manama, Dubai, and Kuwait City.

The discovery of oil in 1940 and the beginning of its commercial exploitation in 1949 doomed the traditional pattern of existence. The oil industry, unhampered by local constraints, developed much faster than the rest of the economy. Wage scales were set in other countries, not locally. Higher pay in the oil fields and subsequently in trade, construction, and government employment attracted workers from lower paying traditional pursuits in Qatar and from other countries. The economy was rapidly restructured, and economic growth was paced primarily by the flow of oil revenues.

Oil revenues made the country one of the world's richest in per capita terms, but income distribution was far from equal. There were extremes of poverty and wealth. The government's social welfare programs provided free schooling and health care, and subsidized food, utilities, and housing eased the lot of the poorest, although citizens fared better than expatriates.

In a 1916 treaty with Britain, Qatar agreed not to enter into any relations with foreign governments without British consent. In return, Britain agreed to protect Qatar from all attacks from the sea and to offer its good offices for negotiations in the event Qatar was attacked by land. Technically, the 1916 treaty and a subsequent one signed between the two countries in 1934 pertained only to foreign relations. In fact, Britain exercised considerable influence over Qatar's internal politics.

In 1968 Britain announced its intention of withdrawing from military commitments east of Suez, including those in force with Qatar, by 1971. Anticipating the country's complete independence, the ruler of Qatar issued a written provisional constitution in April 1970. The Constitution, which in 1984 remained in force, though still provisional, includes conditions for modern state administration in the form of a governmental ministry system, which reduced and consolidated the more than 30 departments into 15 ministries. The Constitution also provides for a very limited extension of political participation and decisionmaking. In the realm of foreign relations the Constitution committed Qatar to joining Bahrain and the Trucial Coast states in forming the proposed Federation of the Arab Amirates. The original federation became a moot issue when, in large part because of mutual rivalries and suspicions, Bahrain and Qatar decided not to join. In August 1971 Bahrain proclaimed its independence; Qatar followed suit on September 1. The Trucial Coast states eventually united to form the seven-member United Arab Emirates (UAE).

Geography

Qatar occupies a peninsula that extends north from the mainland of the Arabian Peninsula. The country contains about 10,360 square kilometers (see fig. 11). At various points the northwest coast is less than 30 kilometers from the main island of Bahrain, and the Hawar Islands immediately off the peninsular coast remained the subject of a territorial dispute between Qatar and Bahrain. The southern shoreline of the Khawr al Udayd forms part of the land boundary that Qatar and Saudi Arabia defined and delimited in 1965, but as of 1984 the UAE had not publicly recognized the delimitation.

The land is largely flat desert covered with loose sand and pebbles broken by occasional outcroppings of limestone. The western coast, where most of the oil fields are located, is marked by low cliffs and hills. In the south, sand dunes and salt flats predominate. What little natural vegetation and cultivated land exist is confined to the north.

Doha is the capital of the country and the major administrative, commercial, and population center. It is linked to other towns and development sites by a system of more than 900 kilometers of roads—about one-half of which are hard surfaced—and contains the country's international airport. Doha has a deepwater port that is used for most shipping, although oil exports are usually piped to Musayid (Umm Said), which is the major industrial center in the country. Limited port facilities are located at several other cities.

The climate is characterized by intense heat and humidity between June and September, when the temperature often

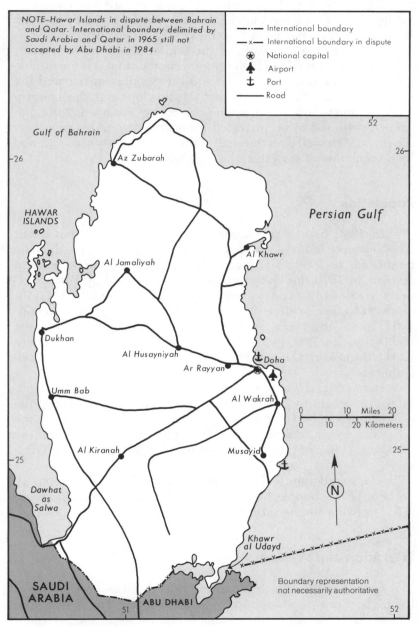

NOTE–Hawar Islands in dispute between Bahrain and Qatar. International boundary delimited by Saudi Arabia and Qatar in 1965 still not accepted by Abu Dhabi in 1984.

—·—·— International boundary
—x— International boundary in dispute
National capital
Airport
Port
Road

Gulf of Bahrain

Persian Gulf

Az Zubarah

HAWAR ISLANDS

Al Jamaliyah

Al Khawr

Dukhan

Al Husayniyah

Ar Rayyan

Doha

Umm Bab

Al Wakrah

Al Kiranah

Musayid

Dawhat as Salwa

Khawr al Udayd

SAUDI ARABIA

ABU DHABI

Boundary representation not necessarily authoritative

10   Miles   20
10   20   Kilometers

N

Figure 11.   Qatar, 1984.

reaches 40°C. The months of April, May, October, and November are more pleasant. During the winter the temperature may fall to 17°C, which is relatively cool for the latitude. Rainfall is negligible; it is confined to the winter months and falls in short storms that often flood small ravines and the usually dry wadis.

The scarcity of rainfall and the limited underground water, most of which has such a high mineral content that it is unsuitable for drinking or irrigation, restricted the population size and the extent of agricultural and industrial development the country could support until desalination projects were started. Although water continued to be provided from underground sources, by the mid-1980s well over one-half of the water supply was obtained by desalination of seawater.

Population

In 1950 British and other observers estimated that about 25,000 people (most of whom were indigenous Arabs) lived on the peninsula. In 1960 an educated guess placed the population at 40,000. In 1970 the Qatari government, assisted by British experts, carried out a census that reported a population of 111,113, of which 45,039, or 40 percent, were identified as Qataris. In mid-1984 most observers estimated the population at between 250,000 to 290,000, but some observers used figures that were markedly lower. Qataris accounted for 20 to 30 percent of all residents.

Iranians and Pakistanis made up the largest foreign communities, accounting for 23 percent and 19 percent of the population, respectively. In mid-1984 Qataris adhered to Wahhabi (see Glossary) Islam, and most Arab foreigners were also Sunni (see Glossary). Most of the Iranians presumably were Shia (see Glossary).

The population was overwhelmingly urban. Only about 10 percent of the people lived in rural villages; the remainder resided in Doha and its suburbs and in the few other large towns.

Education and Welfare

Qatar has shown a strong interest in education and has one of the highest per-pupil expenditures in the world. The first secular schools for boys were opened on a limited scale in 1952. Expansion and improvement of the educational system were under-

Qatar University graduates
Courtesy Embassy of Qatar, Washington

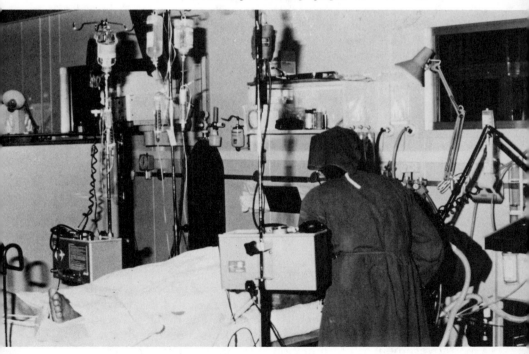

Health care
Courtesy Embassy of Qatar, Washington

taken by the government in 1955. Other developments in the mid-1950s included the establishment of separate schools for girls and the addition of secondary education. In the mid-1980s students continued to be segregated on the basis of sex. Education was free, and students received school supplies, clothing, meals, and transportation to and from school at no cost.

The educational system was composed of six years of primary school, three years of preparatory (intermediate) school, and three years of secondary school. In addition to general academic courses, secondary education included technical, vocational, commercial, and religious training. Instruction throughout the system was in Arabic, but English was introduced in the last two years of primary school, and there were special language training programs for government personnel. Private facilities were available for kindergarten instruction.

During the 1982–83 school year more than 46,000 students were enrolled in the 12-year system. The Ministry of Education, which was the largest government employer, announced that the number of schools would be increased from approximately 160 in 1983 to about 300 in 1990. Although a majority of the school-teachers and administrators were foreigners—mostly Egyptians and Palestinians—over 43.5 percent were Qataris, most of them women. The classes and often the schools were sexually segregated. Women taught in the boys' schools, however, particularly in the primary grades.

In the 1982–83 school year about 3,500 students were enrolled in Qatar University. Almost 60 percent of the students were Qataris, and over two-thirds of the Qataris were women. The university offers courses in the disciplines of education, sharia (Islamic law), science, humanities, and engineering. Approximately 58 percent of the students were majoring in education, and almost 69 percent of the students were women. The university did not enroll women in the engineering department; the dominance of women in education and their exclusion from engineering reflected the Wahhabi attitudes of the rulers of the country.

The 1983–84 government budget allocated approximately 5 percent of expenditures to the Ministry of Education and another 4.5 percent to Qatar University, evidence of the government's continuing commitment to education. The budget allocations for health and youth welfare totaled 5.1 percent, demonstrating the government's determination to expand and improve its free, comprehensive public health and welfare programs. The extent to which the program has been successful was indicated by the observation of a senior health official that "the biggest killers in Qatar are products of the twentieth century—such as heart-related disease, car accidents, and cancer."

In the mid-1980s most of the medical services personnel were foreigners. Most of the nurses were South Asians, as were many of the physicians. Although some Qatari women had pursued medical studies abroad and were serving in Qatar as physicians, few had become nurses.

The Economy

Oil continued to dominate the economy in mid-1984, as it had for the 30 previous years. Nonetheless, from the mid-1970s onward there had been dramatic changes in other sectors of the economy. Because of the enormous increases in oil revenues in the 1970s, the government embarked on an ambitious program of industrialization. By the early 1980s Qatar had a state-of-the-art iron and steel complex, a large petrochemical plant, and a growing fertilizer industry. Industrial capacity, especially that of heavy industry, had expanded tremendously. An increase in infrastructure—roads, power, port, transportation, and communications facilities—had accompanied the growth in industry.

All of this was part of the government's avowed policy to use Qatar's oil resources as effectively as possible to foster a strong, diversified economic basis for future growth. In addition, the government supported "Qatarization" of the labor force, i.e., employing Qataris whenever possible. Estimates put the proportion of expatriates in the work force at some 90 percent. All major firms had programs to train Qataris for skilled and managerial positions.

The government's economic policies depended, for their long-term success, on the ability of Qatari industries to secure foreign markets. The local economy could absorb only a fraction of the increased industrial output. Qatari products would inevitably have to find a place in regional or world markets. Further, in order to maintain a competitive edge Qatari industries needed cheap supplies of energy. The nation's North Field gas reserves, still untapped in mid-1984, held the key to the country's future. How and when they were to be developed was central in virtually all economic planning.

Oil and Natural Gas

Oil exploration began in Qatar with the granting, in 1935, of a 75-year concession to a precursor of British Petroleum (BP). BP immediately assigned the concession to the Iraq Petroleum company (IPC) for development. BP, the Royal Dutch Shell Oil Company—also a British concern—Compagnie Française des Pétroles (CFP), Standard Oil of New Jersey, Mobil Oil Company, and Participations and Explorations (Partex—a Gulbenkian Foundation) all held shares in IPC. At the time IPC had adequate supplies of crude oil, and exploratory drilling in Qatar was put off until 1938. IPC found oil in 1940, but World War II combined with the company's surfeit of crude oil to hold up actual production until 1949. In 1952 a Royal Dutch Shell subsidiary—Shell Company of Qatar (SCQ) obtained a 75-year concession for offshore exploration in the vicinity of Halul Island, some 90 kilometers east of Doha (see fig. 9).

Additional concessions, primarily in areas relinquished by the major concessionaires, IPC and SCQ, were let in the 1960s. Wintershall Company, a firm headquartered in the Federal Republic of Germany (West Germany), held concessions in the area north and west of the peninsula. Wintershall's concessions were adjacent to the North Field, a region rich in natural gas deposits. Wintershall began exploration in 1975; by mid-1984 there were no firm plans for developing the concessions.

Qatar joined the Organization of Petroleum Exporting Countries (OPEC) in January 1961, soon after the organization's founding (see Appendix B). The country has been a member of the Organization of Arab Petroleum Exporting Countries (OAPEC) since mid-1970. Qatar is an active and loyal supporter of both OPEC and OAPEC and follows their policies in most respects. In May 1981 OPEC set a 300,000 barrel per day (bpd) production quota for Qatar that had a striking impact on the government budget and, by extension, the domestic economy. Qatar has reportedly exceeded its quota on a more or less regular basis since 1983 by selling a large quantity of its oil on the spot market.

The Oil Affairs Department of the Ministry of Finance and Petroleum oversees the operation of oil companies in Qatar; the department is charged with protecting Qatar's interests as the oil industry affects them. Qatar follows OPEC guidelines on concessions closely. In 1973 the state purchased 25 percent each of Qatar Petroleum Company (QPC), which operated in the country's onshore oil fields, and SCQ, which worked offshore. Qatar increased its share of the companies to 60 percent in 1974. In 1976 Qatar announced its intention of acquiring the remaining 40-percent ownership of QPC and SCQ. Extended negotiations resulted in agreements whereby the state acquired QPC and provided for the formation of the Dukham Service Company to oversee the day-to-day operations of the onshore oil fields. Similar arrangements for the offshore fields followed in 1977. A wholly state-owned company, the Qatar General Petroleum Corporation (QGPC), established in 1974, deals with oil operations. The exploration, production, refining, transport, storage, and marketing of oil, natural gas, and their by-products all fall within QGPC's purview.

The lack of trained Qataris has meant that service companies and expatriate workers continue to play a prominent role in oil production, although there are a number of training programs aimed at giving Qataris the technical expertise and experience the industry requires. Two foreign-owned service companies produce oil for QGPC. The Dukhan Service Company Company lifts crude oil from Qatar's onshore oil fields, while the Qatar Shell Services Company directs offshore liftings. BP, CFP, Mobil, Exxon, and Partex own the Dukhan Service Company; Qatar Shell Services Company is an affiliate of the Royal Dutch Shell Group.

In 1984 crude oil production was handled under the terms of five-year contracts with the two companies; under these terms the companies received the equivalent of US$0.22 per barrel of crude oil produced and fixed-purchase allocations of oil at the official prices. The agreements actually expired in 1981, and since then neither side has been able to reach a satisfactory compromise; oil liftings continued under the terms of the expired contracts. QGPC reportedly wished to combine both onshore and offshore operations and bring the staff working in crude oil production into a single salary and benefit structure with the rest of the state-owned oil industries. The service companies were unhappy about their purchase quotas; in the face of the oil glut in the early 1980s they wished them lowered. No agreement had been reached by mid-1984.

Onshore production comes from the Dukhan field on the western side of the peninsula. Dukhan crude oil is rated at 41.50 degrees on the American Petroleum Institute's (API) gravity scale. The higher the API rating, the greater the amount of light and costly oil products, such as gasoline, obtainable per unit volume of crude oil. Thirty-four degrees is standard for the Gulf. Dukhan crude oil has a sulfur content rated at 1.1 percent. There are three offshore producing fields—Idd ash Sharqi, Maydan Mahzam, and Bul Hanine (Abu al Hunayn). Offshore crude oil has a lower API rating, 36.3 degrees, and a sulfur content of 1.4 percent.

Oil pipelines carry crude from the Dukhan field to the Musayid refinery and export terminal. Terminal facilities for the offshore operations are located on Halul Island. The island's storage capacity is roughly 4.5 million barrels; it also has two high-capacity pumping stations, power generators, and a water distillation plant. A final offshore field, the small Bunque field, was shared equally with Abu Dhabi. Although the Bunque crude oil has a high API rating, the field itself was plagued by a variety of technical problems and ceased production in 1979.

Crude oil production began in 1949 with a minimal 730,000 barrels for the year; it increased steadily through the mid-1970s (see table 14, Appendix A). Until mid-1984 the maximum annual production had been in 1973, when liftings had averaged some 570,000 bpd. From 1974 through 1980 production was in the range of 410,000 to 520,000 bpd. Lowered production reflected the government's desire to conserve Qatar's oil reserves. In early 1983 experts rated the life expectancy of Qatari oil fields at about 40 years, given an average daily production of 300,000 bpd, and at a scant 25 years at 400,000 bpd.

Production of crude oil declined in the early 1980s. Production in 1980 was less than in 1979, and in 1981 it was lower still; 1982 production was the lowest in more than a decade. 1983 offered little improvement; production averaged 280,000 bpd, even less than Qatar's OPEC quota. Liftings were higher in the last months of the year; production in the early weeks of November was reportedly more than 400,000 bpd. In mid-1984, in the midst of a general improvement in oil prices, production was reputed to be nearly 400,000 bpd.

The OPEC production quota of 300,000 bpd was considerably down from the high production rates of the mid-1970s; it made Qatar OPEC's third smallest producer. Oil production was hard to maintain in the face of a glut on the world market and a general economic slowdown. Most of QGPC's customers were not taking their full purchase allotments, although the country did manage to inspire a measure of customer loyalty. In 1982 QGPC's main buyers took an estimated 70 to 90 percent of their contracted purchases of crude oil. Observers credited customer loyalty to Qatar's extensive natural gas reserves in the North Field; oil importers were anxious not to foreclose a possible long-term supply of liquefied natural gas (LNG).

Production would have been even lower, given the weakness of the world oil market, had not the government resorted to barter payments in crude oil for some budget expenditures. Barter payment for a number of large-scale development projects shored

Offshore oil platform

up oil production and helped to maintain liftings at slightly less than the 300,000 bpd quota for most of 1983. Payment for the second phase of construction on the new university was made in crude oil. In late 1983 the government was reportedly considering direct barter payments for a power and desalination complex as well as the expansion of the Musayid export facilities and multiproducts pipeline. Experts suggested that of slightly less than 300,000 bpd lifted in 1983, 100,000 to 120,000 bpd were disposed of in cash sales, the rest in barter payments. Direct payments generated some controversy. The price for oil on which the payments were made was reportedly discounted from OPEC's official prices, although there were official denials of this.

Until the early 1980s virtually all crude oil was exported, so that export earnings, the balance of payments, and government spending reflected the fluctuations in production. Exports peaked in 1973, when Qatar exported more than 200 million barrels of crude oil (see table 15, Appendix A). In 1982 crude oil exports stood at less than two-thirds of their 1979 levels. Exports remained low in the first three quarters of 1983. More than one-half of all oil exports went to Asia. Japan alone bought more than the countries of Western Europe combined; more than 40 percent of all oil exported in 1982 was destined for Japan. West European countries purchased slightly more than one-third. France accounted for roughly 13 percent of crude oil exports and Italy a little less than 9 percent.

Oil revenues climbed precipitously with increases in the prices of crude oil in 1973 and again in 1979. The increases leveled off in the early 1980s and then fell, ending a decade of bonanza. In 1974 revenues were nearly five times those of 1973. Between 1978 and 1979 they nearly doubled again; oil earnings rose slightly in 1981, but in 1982 revenues fell by some 25 percent.

Local production of petroleum products began with a small QPC-owned refinery that started up in 1953; it had a capacity of approximately 600 bpd. Production and distribution of petroleum products for the local market is the domain of the National Oil Distribution Company (NODCO), a QGPC subsidiary established in 1968.

By 1975 refinery capacity had expanded to some 6,000 bpd, and after further modifications the plant was able to handle over 10,000 bpd in the early 1980s. In 1981 work began on a new refinery near the Musayid facility, and the plant began actual production on a limited basis in late 1983. The new refinery had a capacity of 50,000 bpd; it raised domestic refining capacity above 60,000 bpd. Projections indicated that the plants should be able to meet local demand for refined petroleum products through the late 1980s. Indeed, since Qatari use of refined products was averaging 18,000 to 20,000 bpd in the mid-1980s, officials expected a surplus that could be exported. Officials were waiting for market conditions to improve before increasing the plant's output. In mid-1984 QGPC was still in the process of completing plans for a multiproducts terminal at Musayid and a pipeline connecting that city with Doha, as well as a spur to the Doha airport.

In the early 1970s Qatar flared roughly 80 percent of the 16.8 million cubic meters of natural gas produced daily in association with crude oil liftings. In that decade the country made extraordinary strides in making use of its natural gas resources. Nearly two-thirds of onshore gas was flared in 1974; by 1979 the proportion had fallen to less than 5 percent. Use of offshore gas had encountered greater obstacles; nonetheless, QGPC had made great efforts to assure its utilization. Qatar had gone from flaring most of its gas to using it in a wide variety of associated industries producing fertilizer and petrochemical products and as a source of power in a number of other industries, as well as in power and desalination plants.

Two natural gas liquids/liquefaction (NGL) plants were

operating by mid-1984. NGL-1 in Musayid was designed to make use of the gas produced in association with the crude oil of the onshore Dukhan field. When it began production in 1981, its daily production capacity was rated at 1,200 tons of propane, 750 of butane, and 450 of gasoline. NGL-2 was built nearby to make use of existing infrastructure. It processed the gas associated with Qatar's offshore fields; the plant's estimated daily capacity was 1,100 tons of propane, 900 of butane, and 900 of gasoline. It also began production in 1981. Together the NGL plants were expected to provide ample feedstocks of ethane and methane to Qatar's fledgling petrochemical industries.

Developing the capacity to make use of natural gas resources had not been easy. In April 1977 an explosion largely destroyed a precursor to NGL-1 at Musayid. Six people were killed, and experts put the cost of damage above US$500 million. Arbitration to settle QGPC's claim against Shell Internationale Petroleum Maatschappij (SIPM—a company associated with the plant's building) continued in 1984.

NGL-2 had problems with the 12-inch-diameter and 24-inch-diameter pipelines that connected the plant with the offshore oil fields. The plant shut down late in 1981 in an attempt to diagnose the problems. Both pipelines showed excessive corrosion and had built up debris. Consultant SIPM had agreed to replace the onshore section of the 24-inch pipeline. QGPC officials initially thought that all of the 12-inch pipeline would have to be replaced because in 1982 the NGL-2 plant's 12-inch line was transporting only slightly more than half the gas for which it was designed. Officials, having witnessed one plant explode, took the "once burned . . . twice careful" approach to the problem. Nevertheless, by late 1983 throughput was substantially higher, despite the drop in oil production in the offshore fields, but the reasons for the increased flow remained unclear.

The drop in oil production had a more severe impact at NGL-1. NGL-1 was shut down for nearly two months for lack of feedstock. Industries, power stations, and desalination plants that relied on gas associated with oil also suffered. Planning projections for production of NGL had assumed crude oil production in the range of 400,000 to 500,000 bpd—well above 1982 and 1983 levels. The oil slump underscored the weakness in Qatar's ready supplies of natural gas. Aside from associated gas, the country had easy access to only the gas located beneath the onshore oil fields; projections estimated this gas would last only until 1988.

The two plants produced some 500,000 tons of propane and butane in 1982—slightly more than one-half plant capacity. Condensate production lagged even further at 138,000 tons, 40 percent of capacity. Figures for 1983 remained low: 521,000 tons of propane and butane, 184,000 tons of natural gasoline, and 419,000 tons of ethane-rich gas.

The massive gas reserves of the North Field, also called the North Dome or Northwest Dome, were widely acknowledged to be the key to Qatar's future development. The North Field promised to be as central to the country's economy in the coming decades as oil had been over the previous 30 years. In early 1984 experts put the field's proven reserves at 4.5 trillion cubic meters; probable reserves were much greater, nine to 12 trillion cubic meters. The higher estimates would give Qatar about one-eighth of the world's known natural gas reserves. Defining the precise approach to the North Field's development was a top priority from 1983 to 1984. The cost of development was sure to be high and the market for Qatari natural gas uncertain. Europe, the nearest buyer and in many ways the most logical market, was probably lost because of its long-term gas deals with the Soviets.

Other large-scale LNG projects were under development in Australia, Canada, and Indonesia, and these will compete vigorously for the major Asian LNG markets, the Republic of Korea (South Korea), and Japan. The Australian and Indonesian projects were due to begin production before LNG from the North Field would be ready to market. Qatar was further handicapped because of its greater distance from the Asian markets, to say nothing of the relatively greater cost of developing and producing offshore gas. Finally, the general political instability of the Middle East, especially the seemingly endless Iran-Iraq War, made possible buyers leery of relying too strongly on Qatari LNG.

Japan was formally committed to other LNG suppliers; nonetheless, QGPC remained hopeful that the Japanese might adjust their gas-purchasing plans to accommodate Qatari LNG. Such a deal would offer the Japanese the advantage of diversifying its sources of supply. The principals had not reached an agreement in mid-1984, and Japanese planners had projected that Japan's energy requirements would decline by some 20 percent in the late 1980s.

The Qataris were also reportedly considering acting as LNG supplier for the Gulf region as a whole. These markets would be close to home, and demand for LNG would likely rise as more and more industries and power stations began production. This approach demanded that there be a coherent pricing policy for regional supplies of LNG. In late 1983 the Gulf Cooperation Council (GCC) was reportedly considering construction of a natural gas pipeline to deliver North Field LNG to Saudi Arabia and Kuwait.

The need for long-term supplies to meet domestic needs figured into development plans for the North Field as well. The likelihood that supplies of unassociated gas might be depleted by 1988 made some sort of development of the North Field increasingly urgent. Officials estimated that work would have to begin sometime in 1984 if the country's budding industries and power plants were not to experience shortfalls in feedstock later in the decade. Even this would not be the total answer to local needs, because the low ethane content of the North Field gas made it inappropriate for some petrochemical industries (see Industry, this ch.).

By mid-1984 Qatar had reached an agreement for large-scale development of the North Field with BP and CFP-Total (the successor to CFP). There would be a 6-million-ton-a-year LNG plant and wells in the North Field to supply some 600 million cubic meters of gas daily. Such production would vastly exceed domestic needs; as of the initial agreement there was no buyer firmly committed to purchasing the LNG.

According to the terms of the agreement, QGPC would finance the wells and platforms to supply the LNG plant. QGPC would like to hold 70 percent of the plant, giving 7.5 percent each to BP and CFP-Total. QGPC hoped that either Wintershall or a Japanese firm would hold the remaining interest. Both cases reflected the Qataris' concern over the problem of marketing the gas.

Plans called for plant construction at Musayid rather than a more northerly location closer to the gas fields. This was an attempt to cut the costs of development by making use of the industrial and port facilities already in existence at Musayid. QGPC wanted strict liability for all gas facilities and pipeline installations. QGPC hoped to begin construction in 1985; using an optimistic timetable that would give priority to supplying domestic needs, North Field gas could be on-line for Qatari factories and plants by 1987 or 1988, and the country could begin exporting by the early 1990s.

Industry

Industrialization in Qatar began only after the discovery and exploitation of the country's oil resources. Growth of the manufacturing sector moved slowly at first because roads, ports, utilities, and other infrastructure were lacking. The small indigenous labor force was uneducated and unskilled. There were consistent efforts at Qatarization of the work force, and the number of Qataris in management and skilled positions expanded over the years. Nonetheless, most of the labor force for both technical and menial work was expatriate. In the mid-1980s an effort to "Arabize" the labor force—to substitute Arabs for the large number of Asian and South Asian workers—was added to the drive for Qatarization. Industrialization faced further obstacles in that the domestic market was negligible; most manufacturing was of necessity oriented to the export market, where there were already established competitors.

The government actively encouraged industrial and manufacturing projects in order to diversify the basis of the economy and make the best use of Qatar's natural resources. Oil revenues provided the capital to finance infrastructure and capitalize a number of large-scale oil-related industries. Natural gas resources provided a relatively cheap source of power. Gas was used as the direct reductions agent in the iron and steel industry; it provided feedstock for the petrochemical industries producing nitrogenous fertilizers, ethylene, and a variety of by-products. Musayid had a deep-water port capable of accommodating 100,000 deadweight-ton vessels; it was also the center of heavy industry.

Cheap power gave Qatari industry a competitive edge in fields dominated by more established industries. The government followed a strategy of import substitution, looking for capital-intensive industries with low labor requirements to limit the need to import foreign workers. The drop in oil production in the early 1980s, coupled with the prospective end of onshore supplies of nonassociated gas by as early as 1988, spelled problems for Qatari industries. As oil production declined, existing supplies were stretched to meet the needs for fuel and feedstock of industries already in place. Further development of large-scale industry awaited the North Field gas (see Oil and Natural Gas, this ch.). The government's priority was to develop small- to medium-scale manufacturing, especially enterprises finishing products using materials from the country's heavy industries.

Provision of water and electricity was a growth industry throughout most of the 1970s. Peak loads grew more than sevenfold between 1971 and 1981. Observers expected demand to triple by the early 1990s, although the projected growth curve leveled off in the late 1980s. Most power came from 618-megawatt and 210-megawatt stations. The Ministry of Electricity and Water Resources, charged with providing power, was adding generating capacity at several smaller new stations. These stations were initially intended as an emergency back-up supply; there were indications, however, that they would have to fill the gap until a planned 1,500-megawatt power station and desalination plant began producing. Most power went to domestic use; efforts to connect residences to the national power grid suffered in the budget cuts. Electricity was substantially subsidized; customers paid roughly one-half the cost of production.

A 1980 law related to organizing industries provided generous incentives to those ventures receiving the government's go-ahead. They were eligible for loans of up to 40 percent of capital outlay to a maximum of QR20 million (for value of the Qatari riyal—see Glossary); the credit was subsidized at 3 to 4 percent interest. The government offered further assistance by arranging credit at local banks and guarantees for foreign loans. Road, electricity, and water hookups were free. Companies received services at cost; the government provided land leases at minimal rates. On large projects the government participated by holding roughly 70-percent equity. The 1980 law also provided for protective tariffs, exemption from income tax and import duties (for raw materials and equipment), and preferential purchasing by the government from Qatari industries.

The Industrial Development Technical Center (IDTC), formed in 1973, directed much of the country's industrialization. IDTC identified industries to meet Qatar's medium- and long-term needs; it coordinated industrial planning. In addition, IDTC monitored the performance of all industries on a monthly basis. In the early 1980s IDTC began to assess the environmental impact of the industrial plants and production. It was involved in a wide variety of experimental projects ranging from desalination plants to growing coolhouse vegetables to solar energy farms to more conventional manufacturing pilot programs.

Industrial output increased substantially in the late 1970s as new factories came on-line and older ones increased their capacity (see table 16, Appendix A). Industrial production remained high despite the economic downturn in the early 1980s. Steel production rose at an average 8 percent annually between 1979 and 1982, fertilizer exports were up nearly 50 percent annually during the same period, and cement rose by close to 25 percent a year. The gains dropped off as government contracts dried up and markets became harder to find. Manufacturing increased only 6 percent in 1982—in contrast with a hefty 58 percent in the previous year. Industry did, however, increase its share of gross domestic product (GDP—see Glossary), mostly because of increased production of fertilizers.

Several large, partially state-owned firms dominated the industrial sector. The Qatar Iron and Steel Company (QASCO) was among the largest. Established in 1974, QASCO was 70 percent state-owned, the remaining shares being divided between two Japanese concerns—Kobe Steel Company and Tokyo Boeki. The Japanese companies handled plant construction, production, marketing, and export. The plant began production in 1978 with a design capacity of 330,000 tons a year; it has exceeded that for most years of its operation. Its efficiency both at the direct reduction stage and rolling mill stage was rated highly.

Most of QASCO's steel has been sold to Saudi Arabia and the UAE; together in 1981 they accounted for nearly three-fourths of total sales. Saudi Arabia alone represented roughly one-half of 1981 and 1982 sales. QASCO's competitive advantage lies in its closeness to Gulf markets and its ability to manage on-site truck deliveries promptly. The expectation was that even with increasing Saudi steel production the kingdom would be able to accommodate Qatari steel products.

QASCO faced declining prices for its products in the early 1980s. In 1980 the price of the steel reinforcing bars that the plant produced stood at US$350 per ton; it had dropped to US$200 by 1982. The company kept production high in its effort to make up for the drop in prices, and in 1982 QASCO produced 485,000 tons of steel reinforcing bars, 144 percent of the plant's design capacity; still, the company registered its first losses. Production was down slightly in 1983 but still well above rated plant capacity.

In part QASCO was having problems competing with cheaper South Korean and Japanese imports. The government imposed a 20-percent tariff on imported steel products that were similar to those made domestically. Plans to double plant capacity were put on hold until the market stabilized, and a supply of gas from the North Field was more certain.

QGPC and Compagnie de France Chimie (C de F Chimie) were joint owners of the Qatar Petrochemical Company (QAPCO), in which QGPC held 84 percent of the shares. QGPC also had part interest with C de F Chimie in Compagnie Pétrochemique du Nord, a petrochemical plant at Dunkerque, France, that began operations in 1979. QAPCO's petrochemical complex at Musayid started production in 1981. The complex has an annual capacity to produce 280,000 tons of ethylene, 140,000 tons of low-density polyethylene, and small amounts of sulfur and propylene.

The drop in supplies of feedstock hit QAPCO particularly hard. To reach operating capacity the complex required some

600,000 tons of ethane-rich gas annually from the NGL plants. Production in 1982 was down by one-half because of the problems with the pipelines (see Oil and Natural Gas, this ch.). The long-term prospects were clouded as well because samples from the North Field were low in ethane content. By mid-1984 QAPCO had negotiated loans to consolidate its debt and improve its ethane recovery plant.

The Qatar Fertilizer Company (QAFCO), established in 1969, was 75-percent state owned. A Norwegian firm, Norsk Hydro, owned 25 percent and managed the plant and handled marketing. QAFCO used methane-rich gas to produce ammonia and urea. Production grew dramatically. Between 1974 (the plant's first full year of operation) and 1979, ammonia production more than tripled, while that of urea grew more than sevenfold. Plant capacity expanded as well.

QAFCO has not been as handicapped by the drop in natural gas production as have some other industries, because most of its supplies are made up of nonassociated onshore gas. Production was still nearly at plant capacity in 1981 and 1982, although officials estimated a loss of 20 percent of ammonia production and 8 percent of urea output because of gas shortages. Steep declines in prices offered more serious problems, and long-term market uncertainty might well pose more intractable ones. Ammonia sold for US$480 per ton in 1975, when QAFCO decided to construct another plant. By 1982 the price hovered between US$200 and US$260 per ton, and in 1983 it fell still further, to US$165 per ton.

QAFCO's strategy was to maintain production at high levels to try to generate income. Profits fell despite high sales. Profits in 1981 were one-half those of the previous year, and 1982 profits fell again by roughly 50 percent. Virtually the entire stock was exported. India was the principal buyer, accounting for 45 to 50 percent of total sales in 1981, followed by China with 10 to 15 percent. The Indian purchases declined as India's own production capacity increased. Indeed, Indian imports of Qatari urea dropped in 1982, although roughly two-thirds of ammonia sales still went to India. QAFCO faced the prospect of more intense competition as other regional producers either upgraded their facilities or started producing.

Qatar also had a variety of other industries, prominent among which were a flour mill and two cement companies. The Qatar Flour Mills Company processed flour and bran from wheat; its production has increased steadily since the first mill began operations in 1972. Two local firms that produced cement were favored in that the country had ample raw materials for cement production. Qatar National Cement Company (QNCC) was owned by government and private shareholders. Although originally intended for export, most of the plant's output has gone to meet local demand. QNCC expanded production in 1974 and 1976 and in 1982 was capable of producing 330,000 tons a year. In 1982 its production met perhaps one-half of local demand. By 1983 both firms faced competition from foreign firms, principally from Japan, Europe, and the UAE; Qatari cement companies responded by cutting prices by 14 to 22 percent.

Agriculture and Fishing

Prior to the discovery and growth of oil production, agriculture and fishing provided a livelihood for most Qataris. The limits of traditional technology and the difficulties of desert farming meant low incomes and a bare subsistence for most farmers and fishermen. Rising oil production and the subsequent expansion of construction, trade, and government employment drew Qataris in droves to these higher paying jobs. In the early 1980s, perhaps 2,500 people found employment in agriculture, which contributed on the order of 0.5 to 0.7 percent of GDP. The majority of foodstuffs were imported.

Qatari agriculture faced severe limiting factors. Rainfall was scarce, and there were no streams on the peninsula. Agriculture depended on irrigation from wells and springs. Fertile soil and arable land were limited; estimates put the amount of cultivable land at anywhere from 16,000 to 30,000 hectares.

An adequate supply of irrigation water was perhaps the most intractable and critical problem. All future planning for increased agricultural production hinges on adequate water—by no means a readily available commodity. The northern aquifer was the source of most irrigation water. In 1980 it was being overdrawn at the rate of 26 million cubic meters a year, and the groundwater table was dropping rapidly. Problems arising from soil salinity, relatively rare in the mid-1970s, were increasingly acute by the mid-1980s. Salt water was encroaching at the rate of a kilometer a year in some places. The Food and Agriculture Organization (FAO) suggested that the level of salinity could preclude planting all but the most salt-resistant crops by the year 2000, although groundwater supplies might last another 20 to 30 years. The more pessimistic reports imply projected depletion of the groundwater by 2000. The government's first priority was to halt depletion of the groundwater or face irreversible salinity problems with existing farmland.

Agriculture development center
Courtesy Embassy of Qatar, Washington

The government had considered or undertaken a variety of steps to alleviate the problem. Threats to shut down farms that were inefficient in using water received little credence because their owners typically possessed political influence. Improved irrigation techniques, such as the use of sprinklers, had the potential to cut water use by 30 to 50 percent, and partial shade netting could cut evaporation rates. According to an FAO report, improved irrigation practices could increase the area under cultivation to more than 17,000 hectares and quadruple the value of farm produce by the year 2000.

There were alternate sources of irrigation water. An FAO report suggested that of the 90 million cubic meters of water used annually in farming, one-third could come from treated sewage effluent (TSE) and another one-third from desalination. TSE was already available in substantial quantities in the mid-1980s. Much went to water the gardens and parks of the capital (where it had been so used since the mid-1970s), but an estimated 12 to 14 million cubic meters were available for crop irrigation. By 2000 the government expected to have roughly 35 million cubic meters of TSE available annually for use in farming.

There was an ambitious project to use TSE to grow fodder for dairy cows. The farm would be connected by pipeline with a treatment plant located near the capital. When fully operational, the farm could produce 4,000 tons of milk annually—7 percent of projected local demand. Funding had been allocated for a two-year experimental project to use solar power and condensed seawater to keep sand moist and so irrigate crops.

The number of farms has grown astronomically since 1960. In that year there were 120 farms in the country; a decade later the figure had tripled, and by 1979 the number had risen another 60 percent. Most were small, on average some 2.5 hectares (see table 17, Appendix A).

In the mid-1980s farming was rarely seen as a commercial venture by landowners. Most farms were, in fact, country estates where their owners enjoyed a weekend away from the capital. The Ministry of Agriculture and Industry estimated that perhaps two-fifths of all holdings were little more than "amenity farms." The backbone of agricultural production consisted of tenant farmers, mostly Palestinians who had migrated to Qatar in the 1950s. As a rule their holdings were inefficient and undercapitalized, and they bore the brunt of the rising levels of soil salinity. Little of the available credit found its way into the hands of tenants; non-Qataris were not eligible for the government soft loans, nor were banks or landlords willing to subsidize the tenants' needs for production credit. Theirs was—and continues to be—generally a hand-to-mouth existence.

The agricultural ministry made its contribution to economic diversification by developing Qatar's farming and fishing industries. Self-sufficiency—a goal throughout much of the 1970s—was by the mid-1980s widely viewed as unattainable. The recognition of the limited extent of Qatar's arable land and water resources contributed to the scaling down of the agricultural targets. Assuming reasonably adequate water supplies, the country might cut its food imports by perhaps 80 percent by 2000; even this is a very optimistic projection. Any improvement in agricultural production would be welcome. Some 90 percent of all foodstuffs was imported and represented roughly 10 percent of the import bill in the early 1980s.

Agricultural production was subsidized. Farms of less than five hectares received seeds, fertilizer, chemicals, and a variety of mechanized services free. Larger farms received inputs at 8 percent of cost. IDTC has given considerable support by applying capital-intensive methods and technologies to Qatari agricultural production. The FAO has recommended input subsidies for poorer farmers, using traditional technologies as well as price supports for cereal and mutton.

Crop production as a whole rose in the 1970s to early 1980s (see table 18, Appendix A). Vegetable yields peaked at more than 25,000 tons in 1978, a nearly 50-percent rise from 1973, but then fell off in the early 1980s. Vegetable production was the one area in which the government had real hopes of achieving self-sufficiency; in 1983 approximately 60 percent of vegetables were locally produced. IDTC was involved in an experimental project of growing coolhouse vegetables in air-conditioned greenhouses, using aquifer water that had been treated at a small reverse-osmosis plant. The project's fields—3.2 hectares—were expected to produce about 700 tons of vegetables a year.

Livestock and poultry production had increased as well (see table 19, Appendix A). Meat production nearly doubled from 1979 to 1982. Milk and milk products grew by a dramatic five times in the same period, so that dairy production met more than a third of local demand.

Fish was traditionally a source of protein in the local diet and fishing a major source of income. Shrimping was relatively modernized by the 1970s, but most fishing continued to use traditional techniques and equipment. There were efforts to modernize the industry in the late 1970s and early 1980s, including an experimental fish farm. In 1980 the government assumed control of the Qatar National Fishing Company. The fish catch was down slightly from mid-1970s levels (of nearly 3,000 tons annually) in the early 1980s; the decline was part of the government's efforts to prevent overfishing. The catch still met 80 to 90 percent of local demand.

Budget

Oil revenues made up the bulk of government receipts, and government spending was the primary means of injecting oil earnings into the local economy. Given the small size of the local market, government spending generated most of domestic economic activity. National and foreign companies alike awaited the annual budget with anticipation.

Following the lead of other oil-rich Gulf states, Qatar's budget funded health, education, housing, and a number of other social welfare programs designed to improve living conditions and increase the number of Qataris trained to play technical and managerial roles in oil and other industries. There was, as well, extensive spending to establish the country's infrastructure and to diversify the economy against the time when Qatar's oil reserves were depleted. The government built roads, upgraded port facilities, and constructed power and desalination plants. There were massive outlays on industrial plants in the mid- to late-1970s; the spending bunched capital expenditures in a short period and raised inflation levels.

Government budgets followed an expansionary policy from 1974 to 1977. In an effort to build infrastructure, the government pumped a large portion of the increases from the 1973 hike in oil prices into costly, large-scale projects and underwrote a plethora of social welfare programs and measures. Nationals received free education, health care, electricity, and water. The government invested massive amounts in school buildings, land reclamation, industrial plants and equipment, and utilities.

From 1974 through 1977 current spending more than doubled, and capital outlays increased five times. The budget surplus dropped from QR4.9 billion in 1974 to QR.8 billion three years later. In order to reduce the inflationary pressure caused by such high levels of spending, the government adopted deflationary budgets in the 1978-80 period. A number of large projects were rescheduled, payments to contractors were delayed, and advances for contracted projects were harder to come by. Overall, these measures succeeded in reducing the estimated rate of inflation.

Budgets for 1980 and 1981 were moderately expansionary. The government directed its efforts to encouraging the development of the non-oil sectors of the economy without causing either another round of high inflation or a demand for large numbers of foreign workers. The 1979 increases in oil revenues did not give rise to the frenetic spending typical of the 1974–77 era, though spending was up in 1980 and 1981 (see table 20, Appendix A).

In the 1980s, published budgets continued to be descriptive rather than statements of the govenment's actual expenditures. Foreign aid and stipends to members of the royal family were both excluded; defense was included for the first time in the 1983–84 budget. Although all of these were probably limited in their impact on the Qatari economy, foreign aid and defense increased in the 1980s with the prolonged conflict in the Gulf (see Regional Problems, ch. 7). Estimates put defense spending in 1982 at roughly 8 percent of the total budget. There were also more exclusions from published budgets. QGPC's budget was not on the roster of the long 1981–83 budget, nor was an addition to the amir's palace.

As a rule, budgets have been underspent. Official statements indicate that during the 1979–82 period, budget spending averaged 80 to 90 percent of allocations. Unofficial figures put the rate of underspending much higher, more in the range of 50 percent in 1980 and 1981. Budgets were based on the hijra (lunar) calendar, and the years given correspond only roughly to Western years. The government followed an 18-month budget from October 1981 through March 1983; it was designed to bring the fiscal year into line with the periods of peak economic activity. The 1983–84 budget began mid-hijra year in Rajab 1403; on the Gregorian calendar it ran from April 14, 1983, to April 2, 1984. The change, perhaps not coincidentally, brought the fiscal year in line with that of Saudi Arabia.

Because of the government's tendency to underspend allocations, the decline in revenues caused by the reduction in oil exports seems to have had limited impact on spending. The government frequently instructed its departments to reassess their programs to see where spending might be cut. The government has geared its efforts to complete those projects already under way, to scale down new undertakings, and to limit new projects to those deemed absolutely essential.

The 18-month 1981–83 budget called for allocations 7 percent below its 12-month predecessor. In the 1983–84 budget only oil sector spending and plans to upgrade Musayid's export facilities were high priorities. The government used direct payments in crude oil to contractors both to shore up oil production and to continue work on essential projects (see Oil and Natural Gas, this ch.).

Substantial budget surpluses in 1980 and 1981 cushioned the impact of falling revenues. The government projected a deficit for the 1983–84 budget. Revenues in 1982 and 1983 had been low in comparison with earlier years. Nonetheless, the government managed to show a small surplus for the first half of the 1983–84 period. Some observers suggested that the government had overstated its financial straits as a way of limiting its contributions to the Iraqi war effort. The 1984–85 budget called for a 27- to 37-percent increase in capital outlays. If the initial projections were correct, total spending in 1984 would be up by 18 percent.

Money and Banking

The Indian rupee was the principal currency until 1959, when the government replaced it with a special Gulf rupee in an effort to halt gold smuggling into India. In 1966 Qatar and Dubai jointly established a currency board to issue a Qatar-Dubai riyal.

Finally, in 1973 the country introduced its own Qatari riyal (QR). The Qatari riyal is pegged to the International Monetary Fund's (IMF—see Glossary) special drawing rights (SDR). Its exchange rate in terms of real money is QR3.64 per US$1.00. The Qatari riyal appreciated slightly in 1980; since then the exchange rate relative to United States dollars has declined slightly.

The Qatar Monetary Agency (QMA) dates from 1973; it has most of the traditonal powers and prerogatives of a central bank. The QMA regulates banking, credit, and finances; issues currency; and manages the foreign reserves necessary to support the Qatari riyal. Unlike many central banks, the QMA shares control over the country's reserves with the Ministry of Finance and Petroleum. The QMA does not act as the state's banker, which is the preserve of the Qatar National Bank (QNB). Limited staff hampered the QMA's operations.

In 1984 there were 15 banks licensed to operate in Qatar. The largest and typically the most profitable—one of the few whose profits were up in 1983—was QNB. Founded in 1965 with full Qatari capital, QNB was 50 percent state owned. QNB had substantial deposits of Qatari riyals; it functioned in many ways as a central bank, supplying riyals to the local economy.

Banks operated with fixed interest rates. In late 1983 the rates were 7 percent for time deposits and 9.5 percent for commercial bank lending. Bankers would have preferred a variable interest rate structure, and they blamed low fixed interest rates for the flow of capital out of the country. In the early 1980s there had been a general decrease in private deposits of Qatari riyals in favor of those in foreign currencies. In 1983, however, the trends changed; as international interest rates lowered, foreign deposits declined slightly.

Some observers blamed the interest rate structure, in part, for the lack of liquidity and tight credit locally. Low interest rates at home sent private deposits abroad; at the same time, reduced government spending cut the amount of money and credit available locally. Delays in state payments to contractors put more pressure on the system because government contractors relied on local banks to tide them over until the government paid them.

The QMA instituted controls on finance and exchange houses in 1982 and 1983 and wanted to tighten up on banks' reserves and capital requirements. In 1984 it was also considering measures to assist banks through short-term liquidity shortages. Controls over finance houses came in the wake of the collapse of one of the largest houses and indications that several others were on shaky financial footing. The QMA was also considering controls on foreign banks operating in Qatar.

Trade and Balance of Payments

The country depended on imports for most foodstuffs and items of consumption. Although industrial and manufacturing plant capacity had increased under the aegis of government investments in the 1970s, Qatar could anticipate a substantial import bill for years to come, if not indefinitely. The composition of Qatar's imports changed with the increase in investment in industrial plants and infrastructure in the 1970s. The share of machinery in the total value of imports climbed from 1975 through the end of the decade. As the expanded refinery, petrochemical, and NGL plants began operation, the contribution of refined products and fuels to the import bill, already small, dropped still further.

More customs duties were minimal; Qatar raised tariffs from 2.5 to 4 percent in November 1983, in keeping with a GCC agreement. There was a 20-percent import duty on steel products that were similar to those produced by QASCO. A unified GCC tariff policy might help Qatar's fledgling industries by opening new markets, but it could also hinder them with competition from other Gulf industries. Qatar played a small role in regional entrepôt trade. Most imports were for local use; only a small portion was destined for reexport to Saudi Arabia and the UAE. Most imports arrived by sea.

Increases in oil revenue financed the import bill, and imports grew dramatically with the oil price hikes of the 1970s. From 1969 through 1979 the value of imports grew an average of nearly 40 percent annually. In 1979 imports were more than 20 times their 1969 value. Imports remained high in the early 1980s, despite the fall in oil prices, production, and exports. The 1982 value of imports rose by approximately 25 percent, although 1983 gave evidence of the slowdown and imports fell to roughly their 1980 level. The largest declines were in construction materials, and this trend lasted into early 1984; the fall reflected the drop in government spending on major building projects. Plants, machinery, vehicles, manufactured goods, and food imports all registered declines.

Until the mid-1970s Britain had been Qatar's main supplier of imports, but then Japan became Qatar's principal trading partner. Japan bought some two-fifths of the country's crude oil and furnished about 20 percent of its imports. In 1983 Britain was second with 16 percent. Britain and France were the main beneficiaries of Qatar's increased defense spending, but France nonetheless dropped from third to sixth place as a supplier of imported goods in the 1982–83 period. Qatar and India maintained a significant trading relationship. In 1982 Qatar imported food, textiles, and manufactured goods to the value of QR100 million from India, while India was a primary market for QAFCO's ammonia and urea. In 1982 India's purchases of ammonia and urea were valued at QR95 million.

Crude oil accounted for most export earnings—on the order of 95 percent between 1975 and 1982 (see table 21, Appendix A). Efforts to diversify the economy brought a rise in exports of such goods as ammonia, urea, steel, and cement; Qatar anticipated exporting more refined oil products in the future. Observers expected some form of regional protectionism as more and more industries came on-line. Qatar's position was particularly difficult because the local market was so small as to be negligible for many manufacturers. Qatari firms, in the struggle for markets, required at least regional outlets for their goods. In late 1983 QASCO and the Saudi Iron and Steel Company were consulting about coordinating sales and keeping regional markets safe from foreign imports (see Industry, this ch.).

The dominance of the oil sector meant that a large portion of GDP was in foreign exchange. Oil earnings financed a hefty import bill throughout the mid-1970s and early 1980s. Declines in oil revenues ate into the country's reserves. In 1981 the IMF estimated Qatar's reserves at QR10 billion; by 1984 they were one-half that amount. By mid-1984 the estimated reserves could finance about 26 months of imports at 1983 levels.

Political Dynamics

Under the terms of the 1916 and 1934 treaties between Qatar and Britain, British interests in Qatar were within the purview of the British political agent posted in Bahrain. In 1949, when Qatari oil production began, the British assigned a separate political agent to Doha. He was joined by other diplomatic and support personnel in the early 1950s and by a special British financial adviser to the Qatari amir. Other British nationals served as commanders of the army and the police force. British extraterritorial legal jurisdiction was extended to cover not only British subjects in Qatar but also all non-Arab and non-Muslim foreigners.

British political and financial advisers provided assistance in organizing the state administration, as did an Egyptian, Hasan Kamil. When the post of British financial adviser was replaced with that of director of government in the late 1950s, Kamil filled the new position. He still held the post (retitled technical adviser to the ruler) in mid-1984. By early 1970 more than 30 major governmental departments had been established. An effective vertical chain of command did not exist, however. Each of the departments was equal, and each department head reported directly to the ruler. The lack of hierarchical organization, absence of adequate communications between departments, and considerable duplication of functions led to significant bureaucratic inefficiency.

During the 1950s and 1960s the Qataris began developing state administrative organs, a development that was both necessitated and facilitated by increasing petroleum revenues, related industrial and commercial growth, and the desire to redistribute a major portion of the national income through various social welfare schemes. Modern state administrative machinery was also necessary because Qatar was assuming an increasingly important role in regional Arab political and economic affairs.

The Ruling Family and the Succession of
Shaykh Khalifah bin Hamad Al Thani

In mid-1984 the Al Thani ruling family comprised three main branches: the Bani Hamad, headed by Khalifah bin Hamad Al Thani (1972–); the Bani Ali, headed by Ahmad bin Ali Al Thani (1960–72); and the Bani Khalid, headed by Nasir bin Khalid Al Thani (the minister of commerce and economy in 1984) (see fig. 12).

Ahmad had succeeded his father, Ali bin Abdallah Al Thani (1949–60), as Qatar's ruler, but neither had any particular interest in supervising daily government. Thus, somewhat by default, those duties had been assumed, beginning in the 1950s, by Ahmad's cousin Khalifah, the heir apparent and deputy ruler. By 1971 Khalifah not only had served as prime minister but also had headed the ministries or departments of foreign affairs, finance and petroleum, education and culture, and police and internal security.

On February 22, 1972, with the support of the Al Thani family, Khalifah assumed power as ruler of Qatar. Western sources frequently refer to the event as an overthrow, a takeover, even a bloodless coup d'état. The Qataris, at least officially, regarded Khalifah's assumption of full power as a simple succession. This was because the Al Thani family notables had declared Khalifah the heir apparent on October 24, 1960, and it was their consensus that Ahmad should be replaced.

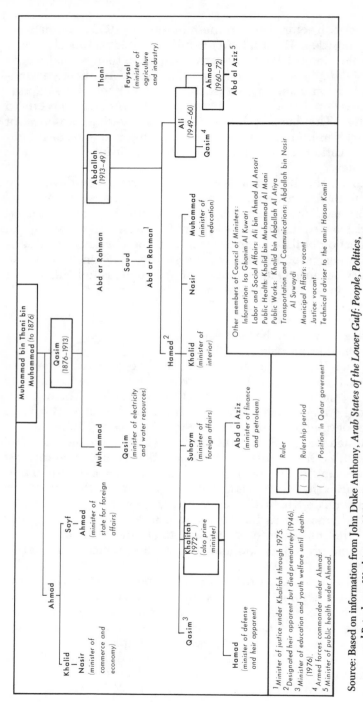

Source: Based on information from John Duke Anthony, *Arab States of the Lower Gulf: People, Politics, and Petroleum,* Washington, 1975, 78.

Figure 12.   Qatar.   Abridged Al Thani Genealogy, with Government Positions, August 1984

The reasons for the transfer of power are not entirely clear. Khalifah has reportedly stated that his assumption of power was intended "to remove the elements which tried to hinder [Qatar's] progress and modernization." Khalifah has consistently attempted to lead and control the process of modernization caused by the petroleum industry boom and the concomitant influx of foreigners and foreign ideas so that traditional mores and values based on Islam could be preserved. He and other influential members of the ruling family notables were known to have been troubled by financial excesses on the part of many members of the Al Thani family. Ahmad was reported to have drawn one-fourth, and the entire Al Thani family between one-third and one-half, of Qatar's oil revenues in 1971. The new ruler severely limited the family's financial privileges soon after taking power.

Family intrigue may also have played a part in the change of rulers. Factionalism, jealousies, and rivalries are not uncommon within ruling families, particularly those as large as the Al Thani. Western observers have reported rumors to the effect that Khalifah acted when he learned that Ahmad might be planning to substitute his son, Abd al Aziz, as heir apparent, a move that would have circumvented the declared consensus of the Al Thani family.

Government Process and Constitution

Qatar is governed by a regime that generally resembles a traditional monarchy. Because of the modernization process it probably is in some stage of transition, but to what is not yet clear. Qatar is a unitary state; it has no subnational political units possessing inherent authority. Municipal councils (in Doha, Al Wakrah, Al Khawr, Ar Rayyan, and Musayid), however, plan their own development programs although remaining directly responsible to the Ministry of Municipal Affairs. Sovereignty is, according to the 1970 Constitution (sometimes called the Basic Law), vested in the state, but to all intents and purposes it is vested in the head of state, or ruler. Although the ruler is supreme in relation to any other individual or insititution, his rule is not in practice absolute.

Rule of Qatar is hereditary within the Al Thani family, but it is not automatically passed from father to son. Instead the ruler is designated by the consensus of family notables. Once a ruler loses that consensus, he is replaced, as was illustrated in the transfer of power from Ahmad to Khalifah. A Qatari ruler is also guided, and to some degree constrained, by the ethics of Islam—particularly by the strictures of Wahhabi Islam—that emphasize fairness, honesty, generosity, and mutual respect. Islamic religious and ethical values are applicable both to the ruler's personal life and to his conduct of the amirship. Thus the ruler must retain the support of the religious community.

The state political organs include the ruler, the Council of Ministers, and the Advisory Council. The ruler makes all major executive decisions and legislates by decree. The Constitution institutionalizes the legislative and executive processes in the functions of the ruler, in effect formalizing his supremacy. The more important of the ruler's duties enumerated in the Constitution include convening the Council of Ministers, ratifying and promulgating laws and decrees, commanding and supervising the armed forces, and appointing and dismissing senior civil servants and military officers (by decree). Finally, the Constitution provides that the ruler possess "any other powers with which he is vested under this provisional constitution or with which he may be vested under the law." This means, in short, that the ruler may extend or modify his own powers by personal decree.

The Constitution also provides for a deputy ruler, who is to assume the post of prime minister. The prime minister is to formulate government programs and exercise final supervisory control over the financial and administrative affairs of government. Although when the Constitution was promulgated Khalifah was concurrently the heir apparent and the prime minister, the Constitution did not specify that the post of prime minister must be held by the heir apparent. Khalifah retained the prime ministership when he became amir and continued to do so in 1984. In 1977 he designated his eldest son, Hamad, as heir apparent. In 1984 Hamad continued to serve as minister of defense (see Qatar, ch. 7).

The Council of Ministers, which resembles similar bodies in the West, forms the amir's cabinet. In mid-1984 the Council included the amir as prime minister, the heads of the 15 ministries, and the technical adviser to the amir, Hasan Kamil, who headed what was called the Technical Office. (The posts of minister of justice and minister of municipal affairs were vacant.) Nine of the ministers were Al-Thani, and five of the nine were members of the amir's branch of the family. They included two sons—Hamad as defense minister and Abd al Aziz as minister of finance and petroleum—and three brothers: Suhaym bin Hamad Al Thani, minister of foreign affairs; Khalid bin Hamad Al Thani, minister of interior; and Muhammad bin Hamad Al Thani, minister of education. In terms of revenues, expenditures, and the power of the

*His Highness, Khalifah,
ruler of Qatar
Courtesy Embassy of
Qatar, Washington*

state, the five family members headed up the most powerful and influential ministries.

The Council of Ministers was responsible collectively to the ruler, as was each minister individually. The ruler appointed and dismissed ministers (technically on the recommendation of the prime minister when that post was occupied by someone other than the ruler). Only natural-born Qataris could become ministers, and the Constitution prohibited the prime minister and other ministers from engaging in business or commercial activities while holding state office.

The Advisory Council debated laws proposed by the Council of Ministers before they were submitted to the ruler for ratification. If approved by the ruler, a law becomes effective on publication in the official gazette of Qatar. In 1975 the amir empowered the Advisory Council to summon individuals to answer questions on legislation before promulgation. The Advisory Council also debated the draft budgets of major public projects and general policy on political, economic, social, and administrative affairs, as referred to it by a minister or by the prime minister. The Advisory Council could request from the Council of Ministers information pertaining to the policies it was debating, direct written questions to particular ministers, and summon ministers to answer questions on proposed legislation. Ministers had the right to attend and address Advisory Council meetings in which policy matters within their purview were being discussed. This constitutional guarantee seemed unnecessary because members of the Council of Ministers were also members of the Advisory Council.

The Constitution stipulates that for purposes of forming the Advisory Council, Qatar would be divided into 10 electoral districts. Each district would elect four candidates, of whom the ruler would select two, making a total of 20; these constituted the relatively representative portion of the Advisory Council. The members would represent all the Qatari people, not their specific districts. The Advisory Council was increased to 30 members in December 1975. Membership was limited to natural-born citizens of at least 24 years of age. The Constitution states that the members will serve three-year terms; in May 1975, however, the members' terms were extended for an additional three years, in May 1978 for another four years, and in May 1982 for a further four years. As of mid-1984 elections to the Advisory Council had never been held. Abd al Aziz bin Khalid Al Ghanim was the chairman of the Advisory Council.

The constitutional provisions for the Advisory Council indicate a recognition of the desirability of extending political participation, albeit in a very limited fashion. The Constitution also stipulates that the ruler may postpone Advisory Council meetings for only a limited period and only once without the consent of the Advisory Council during any given session. Although in practice such provisions in no way limit the real power of the ruler, they do exhibit at least an embryonic recognition of the principle of institutional constraint of the individual leader—a novel principle, even if only in theory, in the Arabian Peninsula.

Before the implementation of the Constitution, the ruler's legislative authority frequently overlapped or encompassed judicial functions, because he personally adjudicated disputes and grievances brought before him. The Constitution apparently marked the beginning of an attempt to organize the judiciary.

The secular courts included a higher and a lower criminal court, a civil court, an appeals court, and a labor court. Civil and criminal codes, as well as a code of judicial procedure, were introduced in 1971. All civil and criminal law falls within the jurisdiciton of these secular courts. The labor court was created in 1962, primarily because few of Qatar's existing judicial customs and codes were applicable to contemporary labor relations.

The sharia court was the oldest element in Qatar's judiciary. The court's law was based on the Hanbali school of Islam, wherein judges (qadis) adhere to a narrow and rigid interpretation of the Quran and the Sunna (see Tenets of Islam, ch. 1). Originally the sharia court's jurisdiction covered all civil and criminal disputes between Qatari nationals and between all other Muslims. Beginning in the 1960s this jurisdiction was successively restricted by decree. In 1984 its responsibilities were confined primarily to family matters, including property, inheritance, divorce, and religious morality. Non-Muslims were tried in the secular courts unless they were married to Muslims. In mid-1984 Qatar had six sharia judges working in three courts. The judges also acted as notaries.

The Constitution establishes the legal presumption of innocence and prohibits ex post facto laws. The Constitution also stipulates that "judges shall be independent in the exercise of their powers, and no party whatsoever may interfere in the administration of justice." The judiciary was apparently independent, not so much because of the constitutional guarantee as because its jurisdiction was most unlikely to confront the ruler's exercise of power. The secular courts adjudicated on the basis of the ruler's past decrees, and the religious courts were restricted to questions of family life and personal behavior. There was no provision for judicial review of the constitutionality of legislation or for landmark judicial decisions that might run afoul of the ruler's plans and wishes.

According to the preamble to the 1970 Constitution, the government was undergoing a transitional or experimental stage of development. The Constitution is thus provisional and is to be replaced with a new constitution based on the results of the transitional period. Khalifah usually legitimates government changes that he decrees by reference to the Constitution. By mid-1984, however, there was no indication that the full implementation of the Constitution was imminent (for example, the electoral aspects of selection to advisory council membership) or that the transitional period was ending and a new constitution forthcoming.

In addition to formally describing and delineating governmental authority, the Constitution sets forth such protections as equal Qatari citizenship regardless of race, sex, or religion; freedom of the press; sanctity of the home; and recognition of both private and collective ownership of property. Such guarantees, however, are limited by the public interest and must be in accordance with the law—which is determined by the ruler.

The Constitution also includes a commitment to certain economic, social, and cultural principles, including state provision of health care, social security, and education. Housing, pension, medical, and educational programs were begun in the 1960s and expanded by Khalifah in the 1970s and 1980s as increasingly substantial portions of the state's petroleum revenues were used to improve the living standards of Qatari citizens. No state taxes of any kind were imposed on individuals, and the state subsidized basic food prices to minimize inflationary rises. Although these programs appeared to reflect West European welfare statism, they were practical manifestations of the ruler's sense of duty, based on obligations inherent in Islamic ethics.

Domestic Political Problems

Like other modernizing countries, Qatar faces two basic political problems as it attempts to develop. These are the lack of a skilled and fully organized administration and the possibility that impatience on the part of some quarter of the population with the slow rate of controlled change might result in political instability. The Al Thani family, the basis of any Qatari ruler's strength, also limits the ruler in that he must use appointments to government posts to retain family support and to balance diverse family factions. Estimates of the number of adult male Al Thanis who in 1984 received government stipends ranged from 2,000 to 3,000. Although attempts had been made to improve government administration, clear lines of interorganizational authority and responsibility had not been fully established. The resulting inefficiency was further underscored by the ruler's continuing to make all major decisions. He undoubtedly slighted the needs of some agencies while deciding the more pressing policies or issues of another. Amir Khalifah, who was highly respected for his financial acumen, personally signed or countersigned each check or government expenditure in excess of QR25,000. This degree of centralization drastically slowed down the governmental process. In the opinion of experts, a further block on government operations was the growing power of the amir's Technical Office, which tended to encroach upon the responsibilities of other departments.

The organized civil service is a relatively new phenomenon in Qatar, and it thus lacks a tradition of public service. Furthermore, the lack of educated personnel plagues the entire system. The lack is partly offset by the employment of relatively skilled administrators from Egypt and other Arab countries and by the use of advisers, particularly from Britain. There has been grave discontent over the employment of foreign nationals, and observers believe that pressure to staff the administrative and social services solely with Qataris will increase.

The necessity of providing jobs for the approximately 800 Qatari university graduates who enter the job market each year has created another problem in public administration. The first graduates of Qatar University were immediately drafted into high positions in government and industry. By 1984 these individuals were still in their twenties or early thirties, and new graduates had scant prospects of displacing those already at work and decades away from retirement. The new graduates nevertheless expected to receive a high-status position of some sort. As of 1984 the government was continuing to create places for them within the civil service. In the opinion of many specialists these inexperienced and often unqualified bureaucrats contributed to the increasing paralysis of government.

Political parties and labor unions remained prohibited in Qatar in 1984, although workers' committees, which attempted to settle grievances by means short of collective bargaining, were permitted. Most Qatari citizens were apparently satisfied with the social welfare programs of the ruler and had few grievances. Foreign nationals, however, who made up almost the entire unskilled work force and perhaps three-fourths of the total population, were not eligible for Qatari citizenship and did not receive any benefits. Third-generation Qataris of foreign national origin were legally eligible for citizenship but at a status significantly lower than that of indigenous citizens. Foreign Arab elements of the population included Palestinians, Egyptians, Omanis, and Yemenis; the non-Arab elements were much larger, comprising primarily Iranians, Pakistanis, and Indians (see Population, this ch.). In 1980 approximately 300 Indians and Pakistanis were arrested for not having their work visas in order.

At least two revolutionary groups, the National Liberation Front of Qatar and the Organization for the National Struggle of Qatar, were reported to be operating in Qatar in the early 1980s. Observers have also noted that the Pan-Arab, nationalist, and socialist (but noncommunist) Baath Party had an organized branch in Qatar as late as 1983. If any of these or similar movements and groups did exist in Qatar in mid-1984, their impact appeared to be insignificant and their support negligible.

Foreign Relations

Qatar's primary foreign policy concern is the stability of the Gulf area. The nation has consistently supported some form of unity among the Arab states of the Gulf to foster regional stability. During the mid-1960s Qatar began advocating a unified monetary and customs policy and the creation of a common market. After the collapse in 1971 of plans for a political union comprising the Trucial Coast states, Bahrain, and Qatar, Khalifah began to reemphasize the original idea of regional economic unity, which during the 1970s remained one of his major policy goals. Qatar joined the general Arab condemnation of the Camp David Agreements of 1978 and the Egypt-Israel peace treaty of 1979. Like other oil-rich states of the Arabian Peninsula, Qatar has supported Iraq with huge subventions in its war with Iran, although its direct support declined markedly in late 1983 (see Impact of the Iran-Iraq War, ch. 7). In 1984 Qatar continued to perceive the GCC, which it helped to found in 1981, as the best hope for regional peace and security (see Appendix C).

Qatar and Saudi Arabia share the conservative, even puritanical, Wahhabi strain of Islam, which provides a positive link between the two countries. Qatar was one of the few Arab countries that observed the full 40-day mourning period after the assassination of Saudi Arabia's King Faisal in March 1975 and the death of King Khalid in 1982. Qatar has generally followed Saudi Arabia's lead in foreign affairs.

Like other states on the Arabian Peninsula, Qatar has publicly opposed a naval buildup in the Gulf and the adjacent Indian Ocean by either the United States or the Soviet Union. Since the increase of attacks on tankers sailing to and from nonbelligerent ports in the spring of 1984, Qatar has placed greater emphasis on the GCC's collective defense capabilities and efforts. Relations with the United States in 1984 were amicable; no major treaties were in force between the two countries. In the past, relations have been strained because of strong American support for Israel. The Islamic religion, particularly Wahhabism, is antithetical to communist ideology; consequently Qatar did not recognize any communist countries, although it did engage in some relatively minor trade with East European nations and China.

Qatar has emphasized close relations with Arab states and has championed Arab causes, particularly Palestinian claims. It has contributed unknown, but reportedly quite significant, amounts of financial assistance to the Palestine Liberation Organization (PLO) and has demanded that the PLO be represented in any peace talks between the Arab states and Israel. Qatar has demonstrated great interest in the needs of the lesser developed countries, providing over US$1.4 billion in development aid between 1975 and 1980.

Among the industrialized countries Britain continued to enjoy a special relationship with Qatar. The two countries maintained numerous economic and commercial ties, and Britain supplied training and technological assistance. When the 1916 treaty between the two countries was nullified by Qatar's proclamation of independence, it was immediately replaced by a new treaty of friendship. Qatari commercial and financial arrangements with France increased during the 1970s and early 1980s. France was the only industrialized country that had received a loan (the equivalent of about US$150 million) from Qatar. The relationship with France reached an apogee in early 1984, when Qatar received three Mirage FICs, the first installment of a purchase of 14 (see Qatar, ch. 7).

Some observers have noted that the Arab states are favorably disposed toward France because France has been the most sympathetic of the major Western nations to Arab and Palestinian positions in confrontations with Israel. France has also played an intermediary role between petroleum exporters and importers and has consistently refused to join a united front of petroleum-importing nations, an idea periodically suggested as a means of resisting oil price increases by the Organization of Petroleum Exporting Countries (OPEC). Qatari-Japanese commercial ties, particularly in the realm of heavy industrial contracts, were strong. Japan was a major importer of Middle East oil during the 1970s and early 1980s.

Chad was the first African country to receive financial assistance from Qatar. By 1984 most African countries had received aid in varying amounts. Qatar usually supports the African causes of anticolonialism and antiapartheid in return for African support against Israel's occupation of Arab territory after the June 1967 War. India and Pakistan were the major non-African Third World nations that had received Qatar financial aid in 1984.

Qatar is a member of the League of Arab States (Arab League) and has extensive multilateral relations with other Arab countries. It has made major contributions to the Arab Fund for Economic and Social Development (headquartered in Kuwait) and has fully supported the Arab commercial boycott of Israel. A member of the Organization of Arab Petroleum Exporting Countries (OAPEC), Qatar adopted the oil production cutback and embargo policies established by that group after the October 1973 War. Qatar has joined Saudi Arabia, Bahrain, Oman, Kuwait, the UAE, and Iraq in multistate commercial ventures, including an Arab maritime company. Other multilateral organizations to which Qatar belonged were the Arab Civil Aviation Organization, the Arab Labor Organization, and the Arab Union of Tourism.

As a member of OPEC, Qatar has consistently recognized the interdependence of petroleum-exporting and -importing countries and thus the necessity of cooperation between them. At the same time, Qatar has stressed the connection between the price of oil and the price of consumer goods. Its basic policy has been to favor rises in oil prices to counter inflationary price rises in the consumer goods and industrial equipment that it imports from industrialized countries.

Qatar became a member of the United Nations (UN) in September 1971, shortly after it proclaimed independence. It is a member of several specialized agencies of the UN, including the International Atomic Energy Agency; International Civil Aviation Organization; Food and Agriculture Organization (FAO); International Labor Organization; World Health Organization; Universal Postal Union; United Nations Educational, Scientific and Cultural Organization; International Monetary Fund (IMF); and the World Bank (see Glossary).

Problems between Qatar and Bahrain continued to exist in 1984, although dwarfed by the Iran-Iraq War. They were based on historical rivalry and jealousy between the ruling families of the two countries. In 1937 Qatar took full control of the town of Az Zubarah, located on the northwestern Qatari coast. The ruling family of Bahrain, the Al Khalifa, had established a settlement at Az Zubarah and had begun their invasion and conquest of Bahrain from that point in the late nineteenth century. The Al Khalifa family, believing that it had retained sovereignty over the Az Zubarah area, has never accepted its loss to the Al Thani.

Bahrain also continued to claim the Hawar Islands, located off the west coast of Qatar. Third parties have periodically attempted to mediate the dispute, but to no avail. In the interests of regional unity, the Qatari ruler downplayed the Hawar problem in a January 1976 Bahraini magazine interview and stressed both the closeness of relations between the two countries and his personal regard for Bahrain's ruler. In March, however, Foreign Minister Suhaym pointedly denied a claim reportedly made by his Bahraini counterpart to the effect that there was no longer a dispute over the islands. Suhaym stressed both Qatari sovereignty over the islands and confidence that fraternity between the two countries would ensure an eventual fair solution.

Nevertheless, Bahrain has refused to relinquish its claim to the Hawar Islands. In 1982 it named a vessel after the islands, thus reviving the issue. Not to be outdone, the Qatari amir periodically wades to the islands at low tide to demonstrate Qatari possession. Although muted by more pressing regional concerns, the dispute hinders the expansion of bilateral economic relations.

* * *

In the early 1980s little authoritative information was available on the society and the economy of Qatar. The *Financial Times* and the *Middle East Economic Digest* provide regular reports on economic developments, and their annual special supplements and surveys on events in Qatar are extremely valuable. *IMF Survey* articles are useful, as are *Arab Oil* and *Standard Chartered Review*.

The scarcity of English source material on the politics of Qatar reflects the general lack of interest by Western scholars in the lower Persian Gulf area until the region's petroleum exports became a topical issue. John Duke Anthony's *Arab States of the Lower Gulf: People, Politics, and Petroleum* and Muhammad T. Sadik and William P. Snavely"s *Bahrain, Qatar, and the United Arab Emirates: Colonial Past, Present Problems, and Future Prospects* provide a good grounding on the politics of the region. Legal and constitutional information are provided in Husain M. Al Baharna's "Qatar" in the *International Encyclopedia of Comparative Law*, edited by Viktor Knapp. (For further information and complete citations, see Bibliography.)

Chapter 5. United Arab Emirates

Crest of the United Arab Emirates

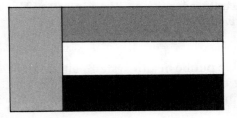

Country

Formal Name: United Arab Emirates.

Short Form: UAE.

Term for Citizens: No generally accepted term; some Western writers use Emirians.

Capital: Abu Dhabi (Abu Zaby).

Flag: Vertical red stripe on staff side and three horizontal stripes (green, white, and black from top to bottom) on right.

Geography

Size: Probably about 82,000 square kilometers, although some estimates as low as 77,000 square kilometers.

Topography: Largely desert, although mountainous in north.

Climate: Desert regions hot and dry; coastal cities experience frequent high humidity.

Boundaries: External boundaries mostly undefined; several internal boundaries subjects of dispute between and among amirates.

Society

Population: Probably about 1.2 million in mid-1984. Foreigners accounted for over 70 percent—possibly as high as 80 percent—of population. Majority of foreigners males.

Education: In 1981–82 school year over 126,000 students (almost one-half female) attended free 12-year public schools. Most of 10,000 teachers and administrators foreigners. In same year National University of the UAE had more than 3,100 students, almost one-half women.

Health: Free, comprehensive public health system, although in 1984 government preparing to charge foreigners. Most medical personnel foreigners, primarily Egyptians, Indians, and Pakistanis.

Ethnic Groups: Almost all citizens indigenous Arabs. Foreign community includes numerous Arabs (Egyptians, Omanis, and Palestinians) and large contingents from India, Iran, and Pakistan.

Religion: Most citizens Sunni (see Glossary) Muslims. Most but not all Arab expatriates also Sunni, as are Pakistanis. Indians mostly Hindu and Sunni Muslim. Iranians and some others Shia (see Glossary) Muslims.

Economy

Gross Domestic Product (GDP): US$26.7 billion in 1983, about US$20,550 per capita. GDP declining since 1981 (US$32.5 billion—US$29,000 per capita) because of world oil glut and lower production.

Oil Industry: In 1983 oil and gas extraction contributed nearly 48 percent of GDP, oil revenues supplied over 90 percent of public sector revenues, and petroleum products accounted for over 80 percent of exports. Abu Dhabi had largest reserves and most of production. Crude oil production was 424 million barrels in 1983 (68 percent from Abu Dhabi), down from 626 million barrels in 1980.

Industry: 11 percent of GDP in 1983. Oil refining and gas processing most important, followed by petrochemicals, utilities, and cement, all of which used oil or gas as fuel and feedstock. Government owned at least one-half interest in these plants. Dubai Dry Docks one of world's largest and most modern. Bulk of industrial workers expatriates.

Agriculture: 1 percent of GDP in 1983. Production mostly vegetables, fruit, livestock, and poultry. Shortages of water and labor restrict farming.

Exports: US$15.4 billion in 1983, of which US$12.7 billion oil and gas. Remainder largely propane-butane and reexports. Petroleum markets primarily Japan and Western Europe.

Imports: US$7.9 billion in 1983, of which 45 percent consumer goods and 39 percent machinery and transport equipment. Japan, United States, and Western Europe supplied bulk of imports.

Government and Politics

Government: Federation of seven amirates, as defined in 1971 Provisional Constitution. Powers divided between federal and amirate governments. Head of state is UAE president, chosen by Supreme Council of the Union composed of rulers of the seven amirates. Federal National Council has consultative function.

Politics: No political parties. Amirs and their families, particularly those of Abu Dhabi and Dubai, most important political actors; technocrats and commercial interests play lesser role.

Foreign Relations: Member of United Nations (UN) and its specialized agencies, League of Arab States (Arab League), and Organization of the Islamic Conference. Active in Gulf Cooperation Council (GCC), founded in 1981. Member of the Organization of Arab Petroleum Exporting Countries (OAPEC), and Organization of Petroleum Exporting Countries (OPEC).

National Security

Armed Forces: Known as Union Defense Force. Estimated strengths in early 1984: army, 46,000; navy, 1,500; and air force, 1,500. Army uses British, French, and West German main battle tanks and wide assortment of other armored vehicles. In addition to several gun boats, navy also operates six Exocet-equipped guided missile boats. Combat aircraft includes Mirages, Alpha Jets, and Aeromacchi MB-326s.

BETWEEN THE MID-SEVENTEENTH and mid-eighteenth centuries, first Portugal and then Holland—which had been the dominant European commercial and naval powers in the Persian Gulf area since about 1500—were displaced by Britain as part of the surge of expansionism in which the British established their empire in India. In the Gulf region British interests were primarily commercial and strategic—trade and naval stations for security of the sea route to India. The coast of the United Arab Emirates (UAE), in a stretch about 320 kilometers along the Gulf from the town of Abu Dhabi northeast to the tip of the peninsula jutting into the Strait of Hormuz, was known as the Pirate Coast, harassed by both European and seafaring Arab marauders. With the rise of the Islamic Wahhabi movement in the Arabian Peninsula in the early nineteenth century, Arab seaborne depredations increased. In response, Britain conducted punitive operations in 1806, in 1809, and, notably, in 1818. A treaty for suppression of piracy and the slave trade was concluded in 1820 between Britain and the Arab tribal shaykhs, and for a time a strong British naval squadron was based at Ras al Khaymah. Intertribal sea and land raiding broke out again, however, and Britain negotiated a successful and lasting maritime truce with the shaykhs, who, in the further agreements of 1839 and 1847, undertook to prohibit slave traffic in their vessels and agreed to British enforcement of this prohibition.

This long series of treaties and agreements climaxed in May 1853 in the Treaty of Maritime Peace in Perpetuity between Britain and the Arab tribal rulers of what then became known as the Trucial Coast or Trucial Oman. By consensus—the traditional, usually difficult, but more effective and necessary mode of joint action among the Arabs—the shaykhs, unable to trust one of themselves, entrusted an outsider, Britain, to supervise and enforce this maritime peace and to adjudicate alleged violations. Britain, in turn, undertook to perform this enforcement and to secure the Trucial Coast shaykhdoms against external attacks. Britain refrained from outright seizure or colonization of the inhospitable coast and from interference in the internal affairs and disputes of the shaykhs ashore. By the late nineteenth century, however, when France, Germany, and Russia began showing interest in the Gulf area, the British imperial preeminence established effectively by the treaty of 1853 was strengthened further by identical, separate treaties between Britain and each of the Trucial

Coast rulers. These prohibited the sale or disposal of any territories to any party except Britain and in effect gave the British control of the foreign relations of these states.

British control of the Gulf in World War II was of major strategic importance to the Allied powers, although bases and stations in the Trucial Coast states had only a supporting role to the large Allied logistical installations at Abadan and other Iranian ports on the opposite side of the Gulf. After the war Britain maintained a joint task force in the Trucial Coast area, in continuation of its earlier obligations, which were unchanged. As part of the postwar adjustment period, however, and with a view to an eventual federation or union of the small shaykhdoms, Britain in 1951 set up the Trucial States Council of the seven rulers, who were to meet at least twice annually under the chairmanship of the British political agent at Dubai.

As a result of changes in policy, the British government in early 1968 announced that it would withdraw its force and terminate its special positions and obligations in the Gulf by the end of 1971; in fact, it did so. Representatives of Bahrain, Qatar, and the seven Trucial Coast states met in February 1968 and on March 30 announced the provisional formation of the Federation of the Arab Amirates. This arrangement did not last long, however, because of various boundary disputes, old dynastic quarrels, and inability to agree on details of precedence and organization. Bahrain and Qatar chose to remain separate and independent. Six of the shaykhdoms formed the UAE and adopted its Provisional Constitution on December 2, 1971; the seventh, Ras al Khaymah, acceded to the union in February 1972. (Although the name of the country is usually given as United Arab Emirates, the member units are referred to here as amirates or as shaykhdoms.)

Geography

The federation, including its numerous islands in the Gulf, encompasses approximately 82,800 square kilometers. Because of disputed claims to some of the islands, the lack of precise information on the size of many of them, and several undefined land boundaries, the exact size of the country is unknown. Although all territorial disputes between and among the seven amirates had theoretically been resolved, the several enclaves, some of which were under so-called shared or joint administration, retained considerable potential for interamirate disputes (see fig. 13).

Despite the nearly 650 kilometers of coastline, the country

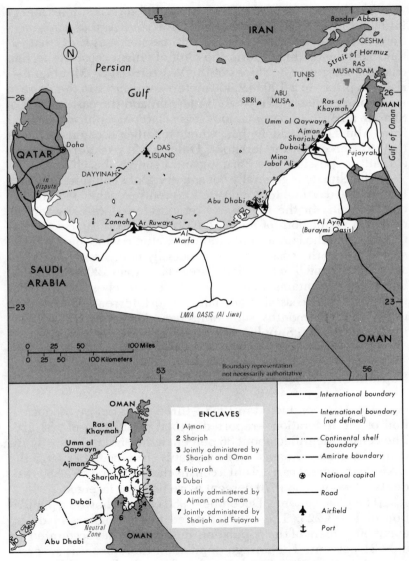

Figure 13.   United Arab Emirates (UAE), 1984

had only one large natural harbor, Dubai. Other ports have been built since the mid-1970s, both on the Persian Gulf and on the Gulf of Oman. Numerous small islands, reefs, and shifting sandbars menace navigation, and strong tides and occasional windstorms further complicate ship movements near the shore.

South and west of Abu Dhabi, vast, rolling sand dunes merge into the Rub al Khali (Empty Quarter) of Saudi Arabia. Large sections of the Abu Dhabi coast are salt marshes *(sabkhat)* that extend far inland. Inland from the Gulf of Oman coast the terrain changes sharply. The slopes of the Western Hajar Mountains—rising in places to 2,100 to 2,400 meters—run close to the shore in many places. Ras al Khaymah, Fujayrah, and the eastern part of Sharjah are hilly or mountainous regions, topographically distinct from Abu Dhabi and Dubai, which together account for more than 87 percent of the territory. Only in a few scattered areas is agriculture possible (see Farming and Fishing, this ch.).

The climate is generally hot and dry. Between June and September the daytime temperature frequently reaches 48°C on the coastal plain. In the mountains temperatures are considerably cooler, a result both of increased altitude and of sparse vegetation. During the late summer months a humid wind known as the *sharqi* makes the coastal region especially unpleasant. The average annual rainfall in the coastal area is less than 120 millimeters, but in the mountains annual rainfall often reaches 350 millimeters. Rain in the coastal region falls in short, torrential bursts during the summer months, sometimes resulting in floods in ordinarily dry wadi beds. Supplies of groundwater are very limited.

Population

A census conducted in 1968—three years before the formation of the federation—reported a total population of 182,226. The census identified about 36 percent as foreigners—mostly Indians, Iranians, Omanis, and Pakistanis. In December 1975 the UAE government carried out a census that reported 557,887 residents, of whom about 70 percent were listed as foreigners.

The government's December 1980 census showed a population of 1,043,225. The data indicated that foreigners made up about 80 percent of the population and that females accounted for only 31 percent. The foreign population therefore was severely skewed in the ratio of males to females, which created various social problems.

Estimates of the mid-1984 population varied considerably.

The United States embassy reported in early 1984 that the population was undergoing a gradual decline from a peak of 1.2 million. The figure of 1.2 million was about the same as unofficial UAE estimates but was markedly lower than the estimates of various agencies of the United States government. As examples, the Bureau of the Census in 1983 projected a mid-1984 population of over 1.5 million, and the United States Central Intelligence Agency (CIA) suggested a mid-1983 population of 1,374,000 and an annual rate of growth of 10.7 percent, which would also yield a mid-1984 total of over 1.5 million.

It seemed probable that although the population was not experiencing a decrease in the mid-1980s, it was growing at a rate well below the 8- to 10-percent annual average of the late 1970s and early 1980s. The indigenous population was growing, presumably at a rate of about 3 percent, but the number of foreigners entering the country was slowing dramatically. The construction sector of the economy slowed considerably in the post-1982 period, and the government was making determined efforts to compel foreign construction workers to depart the country as soon as their current projects were completed (see The Economy, this ch.).

The 1980 census reported that 43.2 percent of the people lived in Abu Dhabi, 26.7 percent in Dubai (Dubayy), 15.3 percent in Sharjah (Ash Shariqah), 7.1 percent in Ras al Khaymah, 3.4 percent in Ajman, 3.1 percent in Fujayrah, and 1.1 percent in Umm al Qaywayn. Estimates by foreign observers in early 1984, however, presented different percentages, suggesting either some significant population shifts, errors in the 1980 census, or mistakes in the estimates. According to these calculations, 37.3 percent of the population lived in Abu Dhabi, most of them in the cities of Abu Dhabi (Abu Zaby) and Al Ayn, and 33.6 percent lived in Dubai, most of them in Dubai city. The amirate of Sharjah accounted for 11 percent, followed by the amirates of Ras al Khaymah (7.7 percent), Fujayrah (3.9 percent), Ajman (3.5 percent), and Umm al Qaywayn (2.9 percent).

Education and Health

Except for a few schools of religion attached to mosques, there were no schools in the seven shaykhdoms in 1952. In 1953 a school was opened in Sharjah that provided free education to about 450 boys. By the 1972–73 school year there were an estimated 140 schools, 12 of which offered boarding facilities. In the

1981–82 school year there were more than 126,000 students—almost one-half of them girls—and more than 10,000 teachers and school administrators (see table 22, Appendix A). In addition, there were a few private schools for the relatively small number of foreign children.

The National University of the UAE (also called the UAE University) opened in 1977 in Al Ayn, enrolling more than 400 students in four faculties or departments: arts, science, education, and public administration and politics. In the 1981–82 school year more than 3,100 students—almost one-half of them women—were registered, and, in addition to the four original faculties, the university provided courses in law and sharia, engineering, and agriculture (see table 23, Appendix A).

The university's goals were to ensure that 85 percent of the student body were UAE nationals, that the remainder of the students be selected primarily from surrounding Arab states, that the size of the university be limited to about 7,000 students, and that the teaching and administrative posts be filled by UAE nationals as soon as possible. In mid-1984 most of the teachers and staff were Egyptians, Lebanese, or Palestinians, and observers anticipated that their numerical dominance would continue for many years.

Education in the public schools was free, as were medical services. In 1984, however, the rapidly escalating cost of the comprehensive health program was causing government officials to examine plans to charge foreign workers for at least some services. The argument against charging the expatriates has been that because many of the seriously debilitating diseases—such as malaria—are brought into the country by the workers, it is prudent for the government to treat the workers not only to return them to productive labor but also to prevent the spread of the diseases to the indigenous population.

Spending on health rose from about UD55 million in 1972 to more than UD1 billion in 1982 (for value of the dirham—see Glossary). In the mid-1980s the administration and financing of public health services reflected the general confusion of federal-amirate administrative arrangements (see Progress in Political Integration, this ch.). In the amirate of Abu Dhabi—where over one-half of the health facilities were located—foreign firms operated the hospitals, clinics, and health centers under contract, and this seemed to be the case in Fujayrah and Sharjah. The amirate of Dubai, however, directly operated its three major hospitals. The funding for all public health facilities presumably came from the federal Ministry of Health, although the amir of Abu Dhabi re-

*Traditional wind tower,
private dwelling*

portedly gave direct assistance to public health projects in some of
the poorer amirates.

The Economy

Before the discovery of oil, economic life in the separate
amirates that constitute the UAE was largely the same. People
clustered around those few places where water was available.
Where water was relatively plentiful, such as the Buraymi and
Liwa oases and the plains of Ras al Khaymah, settled agriculture
developed. Cultivation of date palms and fodder predominated.
Nomadic herdsmen also used the wells and oases for their base
camps, moving their animals to various forage areas during the
course of a year. Settlement also occurred on the coast, where the
water supply permitted. These inhabitants usually looked to the
sea for a livelihood. Boatbuilding, fishing, pearling, and trade became major sources of income. Pearling was an important occupation until the worldwide depression and Japanese cultured pearls
disrupted markets in the early 1930s; pearling in the Gulf never
recovered. The people who clustered around the water sources

251

formed relatively isolated and autonomous communities. Production was geared to the small markets and was nearly subsistence in nature.

Some of the coastal towns, particularly Dubai and Sharjah, turned to trade and merchant activities to break out of the isolation and economic stagnation imposed by the harsh environment. By the late 1800s Sharjah was the commercial center in what became the UAE. By the turn of the century, however, Dubai began to take over commercial leadership because of shrewd maneuvers by its rulers. In the 1920s, for example, Dubai attracted a number of Iranian traders, who, with their capital, were fleeing unsettled conditions in Iran. In the 1950s Dubai's ruler managed to obtain loans to dredge Dubai Creek, facilitating shipping, while the inlet at Sharjah remained silted and constricted. In the early 1960s Sharjah decided to tax imports of gold, which further centered the gold trade in Dubai. Gold was flown in from London, where it was loaded onto dhows and smuggled to India. The trade flourished in the 1960s and made several merchant houses very wealthy. In 1970 Dubai imported a record 259 tons of gold, about one-fifth of the supply of new gold marketed in the noncommunist world, mostly for smuggling to India. Actions by Indian authorities and the sharp rise in the price of gold in the early 1970s permanently disrupted the trade, but Dubai was firmly established as the main commercial center by the time oil revenues began and the UAE was formed.

Even though foreign trade afforded opportunities beyond the small local markets and some wealthy merchants emerged, the amirates that formed the UAE were poor and backward before the discovery of oil. Health care and schools were almost nonexistent. Electricity and modern transportation and communications were unavailable. Traditional mud houses sheltered the population, and there were few large buildings. The diet was inadequate, and the bulk of the population existed much as earlier generations had, and on incomes that were quite low by international standards.

Oil supplied the wherewithal for the rapid transformation of the amirates in which it was found. Foreign oil companies provided the management and technical expertise, the financing and construction of necessary facilities, and the marketing of output. The amirs, who constituted the government in the amirates where oil was found, simply received the payments for exploitation of their oil, spending the revenue as they deemed appropriate. In 1963 oil revenues became significant in Abu Dhabi, in 1970 in Dubai, in 1975 in Sharjah, and in 1984 in Ras al Khaymah.

Abu Dhabi was not only the first to receive oil revenues but it also furnished the bulk of the UAE's oil and gas reserves and production (see Oil Industry, this ch.). The disparity in resource endowment and timing of oil discoveries led to uneven economic development in the individual amirates, a condition that was only partially modified by the creation of the UAE.

Abu Dhabi and Dubai had a slight head start in economic development before the formation of the UAE. Although Abu Dhabi's oil revenues began mounting earlier, it was mainly after 1966, when Shaykh Zayid bin Sultan Al Nuhayyan replaced his brother as amir, that economic and social spending began. In the 1960s Dubai was expanding its economy through commercial activities before oil revenues started in 1970. These two amirates, however, continued to develop more rapidly in the 1970s because they were the recipients of oil revenues and had more money to spend. The other amirates, also wishing to expand services and undertake projects, were largely dependent on funding from the federal budget after the UAE was formed or direct financial assistance from the amirs who received oil revenues (see Role of Government, this ch.). Some amirates also borrowed abroad to speed up their own development.

With the creation of the UAE in 1971, collection of statistics on a national basis began, but some amirates provided less than full cooperation. By the 1980s a limited number of statistics were published, some of which were little better than educated guesses. Others had a better foundation, but few were overly precise. When time series were available, the data indicated orders of magnitude and trends.

The 1970s was a period of rapid growth that all the amirates shared in varying degrees. After the sharp increase of oil prices and revenues in 1973, the federal government embarked on an ambitious program to build up the social and economic base. Between 1975 and 1980 the gross domestic product (GDP) in constant 1980 prices increased by an average of 16 percent a year. The non-oil economy grew more rapidly than the oil sector—19 percent a year, in comparison with 14.5 percent a year for oil and gas extraction. Although oil production declined after 1977—initially because of conservation efforts by Abu Dhabi and later because of surplus oil in world markets—the sharp rise of world prices in 1979 and 1980 increased budget revenues and government spending through 1981. GDP peaked in 1981 at US$32.5 billion, a per capita GDP of over US$29,000 (assuming a population of about 1.1 million), which was among the highest in the world.

In 1982 and 1983 the economy contracted by about 8 percent in real terms. The major cause was diminished government expenditures as oil revenues declined. Contributing factors included completion of some large infrastructure and industrial projects, efforts to lower the number of foreign workers, a freeze on government hiring, and the Iran-Iraq War, which affected the reexport trade and investment. In 1983 GDP was about US$26.7 billion, a per capita GDP of about US$20,550 (assuming a population of about 1.3 million). Although the UAE still had one of the highest national incomes on a per capita basis, income was not distributed evenly. The earnings of those who followed traditional pursuits—such as farming and fishing—were still low by international standards. Many urban dwellers, particularly in the northern amirates, earned only slightly more. Nonetheless, the opportunity for higher incomes existed for citizens of the UAE because they had preference in employment and the government stood ready to provide them with a job.

Economic life in the UAE changed drastically after it became a federation. By 1984 modern roads and telecommunications linked all of the amirates and provided access to other countries. Feeder roads reached many isolated communities. Larger towns were rebuilt and expanded, and included in the process was the construction of numerous modern high-rise buildings. Two industrial cities were built on barren wastes, and the number of ports and airports was increased substantially. The number of schools and hospitals multiplied as social services were extended and were usually provided without charges. Electricity and pure water became increasingly available. Imported foods, some at subsidized prices, improved the average diet. Subsidized housing and utilities were available to citizens. Aid to agriculture and industry provided jobs, increased earnings, and opened investment opportunities.

By 1982 the structure of the economy had changed substantially, although figures from the early years were unavailable to quantify the shift. Production of oil and gas, plus minor amounts of quarrying, contributed 48 percent of GDP. Manufacturing, including utilities, accounted for 11 percent, largely because of processing of crude oil and gas into other products. Construction's share of GDP was 9 percent. Agriculture, including fishing, accounted for only 1 percent. Of the various services, trade contributed 9 percent to GDP; government, nearly 9 percent; finance, 8 percent; and transportation, 5 percent. Although the oil sector continued to dominate the economy, especially if refining and gas processing were included, considerable expansion had occurred in utilities, manaufacturing, transportation and communications, and a variety of other services.

Rapid economic development was not without problems. The boom conditions that followed the 1974 jump in oil revenues overtaxed the economy. Long lines of ships carrying imported goods waited months to unload. The internal distribution system also became clogged. Many shortages occurred, and inflation rates exceeded 30 percent a year. In 1977 the government began to contain growth of expenditures—the main determinant of economic activity—and this was accompanied by increases in capacity in ports and internal distribution. The rate of inflation diminished to about 15 percent a year. By 1982 it was down to about 10 percent, although the Central Bank of the UAE acknowledged that adequate price statistics were not available. The government resumed expansionary spending in 1980 and 1981 as oil revenues jumped, but the absorptive capacity of the economy had improved. The rise in government spending created few difficulties.

The most vexing problem for the UAE was that rapid economic growth could be achieved only by importing labor. Although official figures were unavailable, by 1983 observers usually guessed that nearly 80 percent of the population consisted of aliens and perhaps up to 90 percent of the labor force of approximately 600,000 persons consisted of expatriates. Imported labor was used for all kinds of positions. The bulk of the work force was Asian, mostly Indians and Pakistanis. Arabs from several Middle Eastern countries also had an important role in the economy. Foreign workers were largely males, unaccompanied by family, often illiterate, and frequently unable to speak Arabic. Imported labor was concentrated in Abu Dhabi, Dubai, and Sharjah, where development activity had been greatest; UAE citizens were a majority in the three most northern amirates. Citizens in the work force were employed primarily by the federal or local governments or engaged in such traditional pursuits as farming and fishing. Although growing numbers of citizens had achieved university degrees by the mid-1980s, the skill level in the local population remained low, and many were illiterate.

By the early 1980s resentment of the large number of foreign workers was growing among citizens. This resentment probably influenced officials at the same time that oil revenues declined. In any event, development expenditures slowed, resulting in a diminished need for imported labor. In 1983 and early 1984 the authorities increased their efforts to catch foreign workers without proper credentials and deported them as illegal aliens. In addition, a controversial law was instituted in 1983, forbidding a foreign worker from changing employers without first leaving the UAE for at least six months. Many local employers disliked the law because it increased costs of obtaining foreign workers, requiring them to recruit abroad and pay the cost of bringing workers to the UAE. In mid-1984 the law was modified, providing greater flexibility for employers to hire foreign workers already in the country. Nevertheless, the law also had the effect of making many foreign workers (who had work permits but who had already changed employers) illegal aliens. By early 1984 observers noted increased departures of foreign workers and feelings of uncertainty among those remaining. Nonetheless, the number of work permits issued in 1983 appeared to exceed the number of departures of foreign workers, although the net influx was small and far less than earlier years. The fact remained that the UAE economy will long require large numbers of foreign workers to operate at current levels, although further growth of the alien population could be slowed through moderation of the development effort.

Oil Industry

Discovery of major oil fields preceded formation of the UAE. Although only Abu Dhabi and Dubai possessed known reserves in 1971, all the amirs hoped for oil and gas discoveries in their amirates. Ras al Khaymah held off joining the UAE for some months because of an oil strike that subsequently proved uneconomical to develop; the ruler thought he would better his position in the federation if he had oil revenues of his own.

When the UAE was formed, control of oil and other mineral resources was left with the individual amirates and was not a matter for which the federal government had responsibilities. Nonetheless, the Ministry of Petroleum and Mineral Resources was established in the federal government, but it had been virtually powerless outside Abu Dhabi through 1983. Abu Dhabi became a member of the Organization of Petroleum Exporting Countries (OPEC) in 1966. When the amirates united, the membership was changed to the UAE; Abu Dhabi officials represented the rest of the amirates but exercised no power over them. Dubai, for example, provided little information about its oil industry and revenues and in 1983 continued to produce at near-normal levels—not diminishing output in accordance with the UAE's quota under OPEC's efforts to limit oil production by its members (see Appendix B). The other amirates handled arrangements for concessions, exploration, and oil field development in their territory and published limited information about such arrangements.

Offshore oil platform

Although official figures on proven reserves were not published, UAE crude oil reserves were usually reported in the neighborhood of 32 to 33 billion barrels. The authoritative *Oil and Gas Journal* estimated that proven recoverable reserves at the beginning of 1984 were 30.4 billion barrels of crude oil and 615 billion cubic meters of gas in Abu Dhabi, 1.4 billion barrels of crude oil and 129.6 billion cubic meters of gas in Dubai, 400 million barrels of crude oil and 180 billion cubic meters of gas in Sharjah, and 100 million barrels of condensate (wet gas containing petroleum products, such as natural gasolines) and 12 billion cubic meters of gas in Ras al Khaymah. The same journal reported that a newly discovered field in Ajman would provide that amirate with a small but undetermined amount of reserves of condensate and gas in 1985. In 1984 considerable exploration and drilling were under way in most of the amirates, and additional discoveries were probable.

Oil production began first in Abu Dhabi in 1962. Subsequently, 10 additional fields were discovered—the most recent in the early 1980s. Production began in Dubai in 1970, and in Sharjah in 1974 (see table 24, Appendix A). Ras al Khaymah began production in January 1984, less than a year after the field was discovered.

Oil production in the UAE climbed steadily as new fields were developed and production facilities expanded. Peak production was reached in 1977, at nearly 730 million barrels, of which 83 percent was from Abu Dhabi. In 1977, when Abu Dhabi's production reached about 603 million barrels, officials began to implement a conservation policy so that the amirate's reserves would last longer. As surplus oil supplies emerged on world oil markets after 1979, output began to decline at an accelerating pace. By 1983 Abu Dhabi's crude oil production was down to 288 million barrels, less than one-half of 1977 production. In contrast, Dubai continued to maximize oil production, consistent with good management of the fields. Thus output for the UAE declined more slowly than that of Abu Dhabi, reaching 424 million barrels in 1983, of which 68 percent was from Abu Dhabi.

In 1983 the UAE's crude-oil production quota under the OPEC system to limit members' output was 1.1 million barrels per day (bpd). Within the UAE Abu Dhabi's 1983 ceiling was 800,000 bpd and Dubai's was 300,000 bpd. Preliminary production figures for 1983 indicated that Abu Dhabi produced slightly below its ceiling (789,000 bpd) while Dubai exceeded its ceiling by about 11 percent (334,000 bpd). In early 1984 estimated crude oil production capacity that could be sustained for several months was 2.4 million bpd for the UAE, which included 2 million bpd for Abu Dhabi and 370,000 bpd for Dubai. Sharjah had very limited production capacity, although it increased substantially in 1983 as a result of development of a new gas-condensate field.

In 1980 the Emirates General Petroleum Corporation (EGPC) was established as a wholly federal government-owned company. Its purpose was to distribute petroleum products to the other amirates, except Abu Dhabi. EGPC's initial activities focused largely on the supply and marketing of refined products for local consumption. Its largest project, to be completed in 1984, was a US$200 million pipeline to distribute gas from Sharjah's field to fuel power stations, cement plants, and other installations in the northern amirates. In late 1983 the federal government announced that 30 to 40 percent of EGPC's shares were to be sold to the public (only to UAE citizens). Abu Dhabi had its own oil company to distribute petroleum products within the amirate.

Abu Dhabi

The first oil concession in the amirates was granted in 1939 by Abu Dhabi for 75 years to the Iraq Petroleum Company (IPC). The latter created a wholly owned subsidiary, the Abu Dhabi Petroleum Company (ADPC), to develop the concession, which covered most of the amirate's onshore area. Oil was discovered in 1960; production and export started in 1963. A sea terminal at Jabal Dhanna (Az Zannah), about 224 kilometers south and west of Abu Dhabi city, and subsequently a refinery and industrial town at nearby Ar Ruways processed the output from the onshore fields, which remained Abu Dhabi's most productive oil fields in the early 1980s. Onshore production was about 267 million barrels in 1980.

In 1953 a concession was granted for a term of 55 years to the Abu Dhabi Marine Operating Company (ADMA) for a large offshore area. ADMA was originally wholly owned by international oil companies. ADMA made its first commercial strike in 1958, and production and export started in 1962. Das Island became the center for much of the offshore operations (see fig. 9). Submarine pipelines led from the fields, some distance away, to the island, where various facilities were constructed. ADMA's fields were Abu Dhabi's other major oil area, producing 187 million barrels in 1980.

In the 1960s and 1970s Abu Dhabi granted additional concessions, largely from areas relinquished by ADPC and ADMA. The Abu Dhabi Oil Company (ADOC), owned by Japanese oil firms, discovered oil offshore in 1969 and commenced production and export in 1973. The Total Abu Al Bukhoosh Oil Company was formed in 1973 by several international oil companies to develop an offshore field discovered by ADMA in 1969. Production started in 1974. In the early 1980s a couple of additional companies were producing small amounts of oil from offshore fields.

Like many other fields in the Middle East, most of Abu Dhabi's oil fields had sufficient gas pressure to cause the crude oil to flow to the surface. Only a few wells required pumps. Nearly all of the amirate's fields produced very light crude oils of low sulfur content. These oils commanded premium prices, which, at times, as in the early 1980s, made marketing more difficult.

The Abu Dhabi National Oil Company (ADNOC) was formed in 1971 as the amirate's wholly government-owned national oil company. A shortage of qualified citizens resulted in heavy reliance on foreign personnel, even in the early 1980s. ADNOC first undertook through a subsidiary the supplying and marketing of petroleum products, imported largely from Kuwait, in Abu Dhabi. In 1975 a subsidiary for shipping bought its first tanker, and in 1976 a small refinery near the capital was completed for ADNOC, the UAE's first. By the mid-1970s ADNOC was also marketing abroad part of the amirate's oil production. In a few short years ADNOC had emerged as an integrated international oil company.

Abu Dhabi officials supported Saudi Arabia's gradual approach to the takeover of the foreign oil companies operating in their area, rather than employing nationalization measures adopted by some Arab OPEC members. Abu Dhabi, representing the UAE, joined other Gulf oil exporters in 1972 in negotiating participation agreements with the international oil companies. Effective January 1, 1973, Abu Dhabi acquired 25-percent-ownership participation in ADCP and ADMA in return for an undisclosed payment. In September 1974 negotiations raised Abu Dhabi's ownership in ADCP and ADMA to 60 percent, effective from the beginning of 1974. Unlike Kuwait and Saudi Arabia, which subsequently acquired 100-percent ownership of the main oil-producing companies in their countries, Abu Dhabi in 1983 still owned only 60 percent of the major operating companies. In the meantime, the name of the onshore operating company was changed from ADPC to the Abu Dhabi Company for Onshore Oil Operations (ADCO). Government participation in the other, smaller producing companies varied from none to 88 percent in the costly Upper Zakum (Az Zaqqum) offshore field. The government's equity interests were held by ADNOC. Observers ascribed Abu Dhabi's slowness in acquiring full ownership of the oil producing companies in the amirate to the complexities and difficulties of operating the amirates' fields, the large investments required to develop and operate the fields, and the shortage of technically trained citizens in the amirate.

Like other Arab oil exporters, Abu Dhabi officials deplored the flaring of gas associated with the production of crude oil. In 1973 construction of a gas-gathering system for major offshore fields and processing facilities on Das Island was started. In March 1976 Abu Dhabi proclaimed all gas the property of the government and gave ADNOC the responsibility of exploiting the gas resources. The announcement merely formalized what had been apparent earlier. In 1977 gas processing began. The Abu Dhabi Gas Liquefaction Company (ADGAS) was formed to operate and market the gas products from the offshore fields. ADGAS was 51 percent owned by ADNOC; the remaining shares were owned by international oil companies, Japanese companies predominating. In 1983 ADGAS capacity was 2.3 million tons of liquefied gas a year, 13,000 bpd of propane, 8,000 bpd of butane, and 4,000 bpd of heavier natural gas liquids. Production in 1983 was near capacity for liquefied gas because cap gas was drawn from a nearby field; reduced output of crude oil lowered the availability of associated gas. Production of propane and butane totaled about 10,000 bpd (about half of capacity), and output of heavier natural gas liquids was 3,400 bpd. ADGAS marketed its own products, the bulk being delivered to the Tokyo Electric Power Company under a long-term contract. In mid-1984 development of an offshore natural gas field appeared to be starting facilities which, when completed, will provide for the Das Island a flow of gas that will be unaffected by the level of crude oil production.

In 1981 a gas-gathering and processing system was completed for the major onshore crude oil fields. The Abu Dhabi Gas Industries Company (GASCO) was formed to process the gas. GASCO was owned by ADNOC (68 percent) and international oil companies. Field facilities removed the associated gas from the crude oil and then stripped the dry gas (methane), which was piped through ADNOC's gas system to various fuel facilities and to ADNOC's fertilizer plant at Ar Ruways for use as feedstock. The remaining natural gas liquids were sent by pipeline to a fractionation plant at Ar Ruways that had a capacity of 24,000 bpd of propane, 28,000 bpd of butane, and 42,000 bpd of other natural gas liquids. In 1983 the fractionation plant was operating at about 50 percent of capacity because the low production of crude oil restricted the availability of associated gas. By 1984 ADNOC was developing an onshore natural gas field to supplement the flow of associated gas and to stabilize the gas supply for the Ar Ruways power station and liquefaction plant. GASCO's shareholders marketed their shares of production. ADNOC sold a considerable portion of its share in Japan.

Abu Dhabi officials also expanded oil refining, partly to gain the added value from processing a portion of its crude oil before export. The Umm al Nar refinery, owned by ADNOC and located near the capital, was completed in 1976, and its capacity was 15,000 bpd of crude oil input. In mid-1983 an expansion of the refinery was completed, raising capacity to 75,000 bpd. A second refinery located at Ar Ruways and also owned by ADNOC was completed in 1982, its capacity 120,000 bpd throughput. About three-fifths of its refined products in 1982 were sold in the UAE. In 1983 the refinery operated at less than half capacity because of weak markets at home and abroad.

Dubai

The Dubai Petroleum Company (DPC), owned by a multinational group, obtained a 56-year concession in 1963 for offshore exploration and production. Oil in commercial quantities was found in 1966, and production commenced in late 1969. Subsequently, three additional offshore fields were located. In 1982 the first onshore oil field was discovered—the Margham field near the Sharjah border. This field was being developed by an American oil company; production was expected to start in early 1985 and eventually to peak at about 75,000 bpd. Discovery of the onshore field renewed interest in Dubai; by 1984 the amir had granted exploration concessions to nearly all of the amirate's available onshore and offshore areas.

In 1984 the DPC was the amirate's only producing company. The amirate had no refinery, and all production was exported as crude oil. The shipping terminal was offshore near the fields. The bulk of the crude oil consisted of heavy, less desirable grades. The fields had been operated at near maximum capacity throughout their life. Observers anticipated that production from the main fields would begin to decline soon. Little information was available about the terms of the oil production agreement or the amirate's equity in DPC. Even the revenues paid to the ruler were unknown.

In the mid-1970s a gas-gathering system and facilities to process the gas were started to conserve the gas that previously had been flared. Facilities at the fields separated the associated gas, which was pumped ashore to the new port of Mina Jabal Ali. The Dubai National Gas Company (DUGAS) was formed, wholly owned by the Dubai government, although actual operations were managed by a Canadian company under contract. DUGAS' processing facilities came onstream in 1980; its capacity was 20,000 bpd of natural gas liquids (propane, butane, and heavier liquids) and 2.1 million cubic meters of dry gas (methane) a day. The supply of gas associated with crude oil production was supplemented by gas from an offshore condensate reservoir. In 1983 production of natural gas liquids was near capacity because production at Dubai was reduced only marginally on account of the supplemental gas unassociated with crude oil. The dry gas was piped to the Dubai Aluminum Company (DUBAL) at Mina Jabal Ali, where it was to fuel the large electric power and desalination plant (see Industrialization and Other Development Activities, this ch.). A small part of the natural gas liquids was locally bottled and consumed, but most was exported, largely to Japan.

Dubai officials anticipated a declining supply of gas—particularly for electric power plants—as offshore crude oil production began to fall when the fields passed their peak. Early discussions concerned a gas pipeline from Abu Dhabi. Discovery in Dubai of the onshore Margham field and a gas-condensate field in Sharjah relieved Dubai of the necessity of turning to Abu Dhabi. Although the amount of gas available from the Margham field was not known in mid-1984, Dubai officials had sufficient gas for several years from their own new field. Dubai electric plants were converted to use gas instead of distillate fuel.

The Other Amirates

In 1969 the amir of Sharjah granted a 40-year concession for offshore exploration and production to a group of small American oil companies. Oil was discovered in 1973 in the Mubarek field off Abu Musa Island, and production began in July 1974. Because of conflicting territorial claims, revenues were equally shared with Iran. Umm al Qaywayn and other northern amirates reportedly received up to 30 percent of Sharjah's oil revenues from the field because of their claims to the area. The Mubarek field was small, and production peaked in 1975 at about 14 million barrels; production declined thereafter, amounting to about 3 million barrels in 1982. By 1984, if not earlier, Iran reportedly ceased transferring to Sharjah its half-share of oil revenues, presumably because of the financial drain of the war with Iraq, as well as Arab support of Iraq.

Sharjah's economic prospects picked up dramatically with the discovery in 1980 of an onshore field, Sajaa, containing gas and condensate. By late 1983 output varied between 30,000 and 35,000 bpd of condensate, which was exported; production reached about 55,000 bpd of condensate in 1984. The field was predominantly gas, however, and the gas had to be flared in 1983, for facilities were not yet available to handle it. In 1984 a 224-kilometer pipeline, owned by EGPC and extending from Sajaa to Ras al Khaymah and other northern amirates, was completed to supply dry gas (methane) to power plants and some other industries. The pipeline was to be operated and maintained by a foreign firm under contract to EGPC. By 1984 or 1985 gas production at Sajaa was expected to be about 12 to 15 million cubic meters per day, 9 million cubic meters of which was to be supplied to EGPC for distribution. In mid-1984 it was unclear what would be done with the remaining dry gas. Reinjection into the field appeared too costly. Construction of a urea or methanol plant was a possibility under discussion. Construction of a liquid petroleum gas plant, which would process the wet gas into a wider variety of products, was expected to start in 1984.

Discovery of the Sajaa field was under an old-fashioned concession agreement with an American oil company. Reportedly the amirate received royalties of 14.5 percent and taxes of 77 percent of the oil-operating company's net profits, without any participation arrangements. Nonetheless, the estimated oil revenues were likely to be above US$400 million by 1985 and perhaps reach US$600 million a year later, much higher than the approximate US$15 million in 1982 from the old offshore field. The amirate's economic prospects were altered substantially because of the new field. In addition, observers believed that part of Dubai's Margham field extended into Sharjah territory, which in the future might yield some production- or revenue-sharing arrangement between the two amirates.

The fortunes of Ras al Khaymah also improved when a gas-condensate field was discovered offshore in 1983. Under the amirate's concession arrangements, it becomes a 50-percent shareholder when oil or gas in commercial quantities is found. The Ras al Khaymah National Oil Company held the amirate's 50-percent share of the field, and several international firms held the other half. The amirate, short of funds, found it difficult to provide its share of investments. The field appeared small and presumably would not produce very long. Nonetheless, the decision was made to begin production as rapidly as possible—probably so the amirate's equity share could be largely paid out of incoming revenues.

Production from the first well began in January 1984 at a rate of 5,000 bpd of condensate containing some crude oil. Two additional wells were to be drilled and were expected to raise production to about 30,000 bpd by late 1984 or 1985. A moored tanker provided storage and loading facilities for exports. The rush to begin production meant that large amounts of gas would be flared. By mid-1984 it was not known whether the gas would be eventually piped ashore or even if other processing facilities would be constructed. Meanwhile, Ras al Khaymah claimed that two additional oil fields had been discovered and that oil production would reach 500,000 bpd in 1985. Confirmation of these claims was lacking in mid-1984.

Experts believed that oil and gas finds were quite possible in the remaining amirates, although as of mid-1984 none had been found, except for a gas-condensate field of undetermined size in Ajman. A private company based in Ajman, however, was reportedly buying a used refinery in Britain in June 1984—to be dismantled and reconstructed in Ajman. It was to use Abu Dhabi or Saudi Arabia crude oil brought in by tanker; refined products were to be sold in the Gulf. Also in mid-1984, a 240-kilometer pipeline with an initial capacity of 500,000 bpd of crude oil from Abu Dhabi's onshore fields to a port in Fujayrah on the Gulf of Oman reportedly was to be built and was scheduled for completion by 1986. The line was intended to permit export of Abu Dhabi crude to tankers loading outside of the Persian Gulf in case the Strait of Hormuz was blocked by some aspect of the Iran-Iraq War.

Role of Government

Formation of the UAE brought federation, not unity. The amirs were long accustomed to independence, particularly financial autonomy, which they found difficult to relinquish. Historically each amir had income, however slight, whether it came from property, trade, raids on neighbors, or taxes on traders passing through his territory on land or sea, that he disposed of as he saw fit. Collecting taxes from passing British ships in the eighteenth and nineteenth centuries led to the British government's presence in what became known as the Trucial Coast (see The Entrance of the Europeans into the Gulf, ch. 1). In more recent times the rulers received income from additional sources, such as operation of a British base in Sharjah, issue of unusual stamps purchased by philatelists in foreign countries, and rental payments from oil companies for exploration concessions. The British, the Kuwaitis, the Saudis, and others also provided particular amirs with funds at times. Although the amirs agreed to form a federal government in 1971, each retained as much financial autonomy as possible.

Government organization in the amirates was largely a function of the amount of funds available. Abu Dhabi, which had the earliest and largest oil revenues, had to expand government to provide the services and facilities needed by its people. As government grew, so did the need for financial controls. By 1984 Abu Dhabi had developed the most modern public administration and budgetary process in the UAE, even though the amir still retained considerable independence. In Dubai public funds and the ruler's purse were indistinguishable. A budgetary process was in place, and some financial information was available, but revenues were those the amir passed on to finance expenditures. The amir financed some projects personally and at times gave his personal guarantee for government commitments. Government was less well developed in the other amirates, and little was known of their finances. The amirs in each of the amirates had considerable say about economic development in their areas.

The jump in Abu Dhabi's oil revenues between 1972 and 1974 (from US$760 million to US$3.5 billion) as a result of OPEC's increase in the price of crude oil ushered in a boom period in all of the amirates that lasted into 1977. Several factors contributed to a burst of construction. Abu Dhabi increased its contribution to the budget, which allowed the federal government to undertake many projects throughout the country, such as schools, hospitals, roads, and a communications system. Dubai's oil revenues also jumped, allowing the amir to expand the port and airport and build new ones, finance a huge dry dock, build an aluminum smelter, and begin other projects. The other amirs, wishing to create jobs, facilities, and business opportunities in their amirates and probably being unduly optimistic about the future, obtained funds wherever they could to undertake projects. Some, such as Ras al Khaymah and Sharjah, borrowed heavily, given their resources, to finance projects and were still trying to service the debts in the early 1980s. The amount of the remaining indebtedness in 1984 was unknown, but the recent oil discoveries in the two amirates dispelled any concern about inability to repay the debts.

Simple project coordination did not exist between the amirates through the 1970s. Unfortunately, competition and duplication of effort occurred. Dubai, Sharjah, and Ras al Khaymah built large international airports, even though they were within a half-hour drive of each other and less than a two hours' drive away from Abu Dhabi's large international airport. Duplicative investments and excess capacity also developed in port facilities, hotels, office buildings, and cement plants, among others. By 1984 only part of the capacity was employed productively and earning a return on the investment.

The sharp rise in public expenditure—federal and amirates—from 1974 to 1977 led to severe difficulties. The UAE economy could not absorb the inflow of goods and labor. High rates of inflation followed. Excessive credit expansion by banks and speculation in the currency—the dirham—caused financial difficulties, leading to the closing of two banks and, eventually, to creation of a central bank. Officials became aware that more coordination and cooperation were needed in economic development. Planning at the federal level was strengthened. Amirs began to concede functions to the federal government, and the growth of public expenditures was restrained in 1978 and 1979.

The federal government's economic authority increased gradually, partly because of increased spending power. According to the UAE Provisional Constitution, each amirate was to contribute to the federal budget, but through the 1970s Abu Dhabi financed almost all of the expenditures. The other amirates held on to whatever revenue sources they had. In the early 1980s Dubai began contributing to the federal budget—reportedly one-half of the amirate's oil revenues. The federal government was empowered to levy taxes and charge fees. By 1984 federal taxes had not been imposed but reportedly were under consideration because of deficits. Small sums, amounting to about 4 percent of total revenues, were collected from fees from government departments, such as passport and immigration and the postal service. Additional fees were under discussion, such as imposing charges—particularly on aliens—for health services and education. In 1983 domestic prices for petroleum products were raised substantially (higher than in the United States) in order to curtail subsidies formally provided local customers. Federal government revenues totaled UD12.9 billion in 1983.

Spending by the federal government has been the main incentive for greater integration or unity in the UAE. The effectiveness has been somewhat undercut by the high proportion of federal expenditures for defense, which approached one-half of total expenditures for several years (see table 25, Appendix A). Although national security was a federal function, the two most important amirates had considerable power. In 1983, for example, the Abu Dhabi regional command reportedly ordered important quantities of planes and tanks from France while the Dubai regional command was said to have ordered nearly as many planes from British companies, and both orders were charged to the federal defense budget (see United Arab Emirates, ch. 7). Nonetheless, capital expenditures by the federal government have been responsible for much of the development of the economic and social infrastructure in the amirates that lacked oil revenues. Perhaps more important has been the federal government's acceptance of operation and maintenance costs of some schools, power plants, and other projects that poorer amirates started but could not maintain or, in some instances, even complete. In 1984 difficult decisions remained to be made on the extent that federal help would be forthcoming for those projects that were started by individual amirates and that subsequently encountered difficulties.

The major outlines of public revenues and expenditures in

the UAE can be derived from the federal and Abu Dhabi budgets and the available financial information from Dubai (see table 26, Appendix A). Although five amirates and some important public corporations could not be incorporated because of lack of data, the major components of public spending were included. Public expenditure tended to follow revenues, but with a lag. Authorities tried to avoid sharp swings in expenditures as oil revenues changed. Surplus funds accrued after the first crude oil price increases of 1974 and again in the early 1980s. By 1984 the surplus belonging to Abu Dhabi appeared to exceed US$20 billion, largely held in assets abroad. Dubai's surplus was undoubtedly considerably less, but its amount was unknown. The federal government's surplus amounted to US$3.4 billion in foreign currency reserves plus whatever other reserves it might have from earlier budget surpluses.

The sharp rise in crude oil prices in 1979 and 1980 caused public sector revenues to increase by 70 percent between 1979 and 1981, when they peaked at about US$13.2 billion. The subsequent world oil glut and declining production caused public revenues to fall by 40 percent by 1983, amounting to just under US$8 billion. Public spending rose less rapidly than revenues, reaching US$11.9 billion in 1981. Expenditures also declined less rapidly on the downswing, falling 22 percent to US$9.3 billion in 1983. The consolidated public sector budget incurred its first deficits in about a decade in 1982 and 1983, amounting to 5 percent of GDP in the latter year. Because public spending is the major determinant of economic activity, its decline, and particularly the component of development expenditures, caused a business recession in the UAE. The various levels of government canceled, postponed, and stretched out projects in order to bring expenditures in line with revenues. Also instituted were payment delays, which created severe difficulties for contractors who had completed jobs.

Another means of lowering public expenditures was to sharply reduce foreign aid. The UAE, and particularly Abu Dhabi, has been especially generous in providing financial aid to developing countries since oil revenues shot up in 1974. Foreign aid grants and loans peaked in 1981 at over US$2.7 billion, 8 percent of GDP. By 1983 financial assistance to other countries had been reduced to nearly US$1 billion, but this remained a remarkable 4 percent of GDP. The bulk of the aid was provided by Abu Dhabi, although partly in the name of the UAE. The ruler of Abu Dhabi personally provided additional amounts of aid to other countries that were not included in budget data. Much of the

UAE financial aid went to other Arab countries, such as to the frontline states confronting Israel and Iraq, which was at war with Iran.

Economists expected the oil glut to persist into 1984 and perhaps 1985, continuing the budget constraints on UAE officials. Preliminary data on the 1984 budget indicated further efforts to reduce public expenditures in order to lessen the deficit. Business conditions were not expected to improve while public spending was restrained. Some stimulus was anticipated from Sharjah and Ras al Khaymah, and perhaps Ajman, as production from their new oil fields boosted revenues and some development expenditures. It was not clear whether these new oil-producing amirates would contribute part of their revenues to the federal budget, although the amirs reaffirmed in June 1984 a pledge of 50 percent of each amirate's revenues to the federal budget.

Industrialization and Other Development Activities

Apart from oil and gas, the UAE had few known natural resources. Limestone was abundant and was exploited to make cement. Ajman had a high-grade marble that was quarried, mostly for local use. Ras al Khaymah possessed rock that was used in construction, such as at Abu Dhabi's port and Saudi Arabia's new industrial city of Al Jubayl. Surveys had located deposits of chrome, manganese, copper, bauxite, magnesium, gold, and asbestos in small quantities, mostly in the Hajar Mountains, but there was very little mining.

With limited other natural resources it was economically sound for the UAE to concentrate development around oil and gas. Construction of two industrial towns, started on barren wastes and centered on hydrocarbon resources, was the largest development project in the country.

Dubai's new port and industrial facilities at Mina Jabal Ali, 35 kilometers southwest of the city, was the largest and most comprehensive in the UAE. The port itself, comprising 66 berths and 15 kilometers of quays, is the largest in the Gulf. In 1983 it included more than 50,000 square meters of covered storage and a large container port that could hold 6,000 containers. Started in 1976, the basic port was completed in 1979, although facilities were added as needed. Adjacent to the port was a large (over 2,000 hectares) industrial zone, intended eventually to contain all of Dubai's industry. Twenty-three companies had located in the industrial zone by the beginning of 1984. One company in a highly automated plant produced up to 16,000 tons a year of fabricated steel for structures, partly for export. An aluminum extrusion plant had a capacity of 4,000 tons of sections a year, mainly for doors and windows. Some companies leased facilities for use as a storage and distribution center for the Middle East. The port also had a free-trade zone. A bagging company was established in 1983, for example, that bagged bulk cargo for reshipment to neighboring countries. In 1983 the port handled about 3.3 million tons of cargo; 6.1 million tons were handled at Port Rashid, Dubai's other port, which was adjacent to Dubai city. The two ports accommodated about 80 percent of the UAE's cargo, other than oil products.

Close to Mina Jabal Ali were the gas-processing facilities of the Dubai National Gas Company (DUGAS), owned by the Dubai government (see Oil Industry, this ch.). Dry gas from this facility provided the fuel for the smelter and power station of the nearby Dubai Aluminum Company (DUBAL), wholly owned by the Dubai government. Completed in 1979, DUBAL achieved full production in 1982. Although design capacity was 135,000 tons of very high purity aluminum a year, production exceeded that capacity, reaching 151,000 tons in 1983, of which 45 percent went to Japan, 24 percent to Iran, 12 percent to the Republic of Korea (South Korea), and 11 percent to the United States. Alumina was imported from western Australia. The US$1.4 billion cost of DUBAL was split about equally between the smelter and the power-desalination plant. The power plant had 515 megawatts of capacity as well as a capacity of 114 million liters of desalinated water a day. The power plant was tied in with Dubai Electricity Company, and 100 megawatts could be transferred either way between the two facilities. Desalinated water (about 87 million liters a day in summer) was supplied to the Dubai Water Department for distribution. Although successful in keeping production costs down, the low world price for aluminum in recent years kept DUBAL from yielding a profit in 1982 and 1983.

The other large facility near Mina Jabal Ali was the Dubai Dry Docks, owned by the Dubai government. One of the largest and most modern in the world, the three dry docks could handle any vessel up to 350,000 deadweight tons, super tankers up to 500,000 deadweight tons, and extra-large tankers (which had not yet been built by 1984) up to 1 million deadweight tons. The dock cranes were among the largest in the world. Modern, fully equipped workshops for machinery, plate and pipes, rigging, and electric repair (some of the largest and best in the Middle East), could be used for work other than just ship repair. The laboratory was the most sophisticated in the region and could be used by a variety of additional users. The dry docks were completed in 1979 but a contract for an operator was not signed until 1983 because of the amir's ailing health and indecision. Substantial maintenance costs were incurred while the docks sat idle. Business was better than expected by early 1984, and there was hope that the docks would produce a profit by 1985.

Abu Dhabi's industrial town and port complex at Ar Ruways, reportedly costing about US$20 billion, was 224 kilometers southwest of the capital. The port facilities were not as large as those at Mina Jabal Ali, nor was the industrialization as extensive. A large refinery and gas fractionation plant produced petroleum products intended mainly for export. The other major plant was the Ruways Fertilizer Industries (Fertil), which used gas as fuel and feedstock to produce ammonia and fertilizer. The plant, two-thirds owned by ADNOC and the rest owned by a French company, had a capacity to produce 100 tons a day of liquid anhydrous ammonia and 1,500 tons a day of urea. The plant was fully operational in November 1983. Output was mostly for export; long-term contracts existed with India, Japan, and some Gulf states for about one-half of anticipated production. Sulfur, extracted from oil and gas processing, was exported at a special bulk terminal. For several years an iron and steel plant that was to use gas reduction of imported ore had been discussed for Ar Ruways, but construction had not started by 1984. The other industrial plants in the complex were on a much smaller scale.

Production of electricity was a rapidly growing industry, reflecting the rapid increase of the population and extension of service to more distant consumers. Abu Dhabi's generating capacity expanded from eight megawatts in 1973 to 845 megawatts in 1982, and planned capacity was 1,340 megawatts for 1985. A consultant's study showed demand for electricity increasing by 25 percent a year between 1973 and 1982 in Abu Dhabi. Demand in Dubai increased at about 15 percent a year. The other amirates were less well supplied with electricity and needed additional generating capacity. Sharjah and Ras al Khaymah suffered power disruptions in 1983 because of overloaded facilities.

Abu Dhabi, Dubai, Sharjah, and Ras al Khaymah had their own electrical companies when the UAE was formed and the Ministry of Electricity and Water created. This administrative nightmare remained in 1984 and contributed to the problems of planning and development. Because of their substantial oil revenues, Abu Dhabi and Dubai were able to increase capacity and extend service. The more northern amirates were increasingly dependent on the federal government for construction and operation of electrical generators. Ras al Khaymah, for example, in the 1970s started, but was unable to finish, a power plant because of lack of funds; the federal ministry finally reached an agreement with the amir to complete the plant and hookups and operate the facility. Because of the several administrative bodies, there were no national statistics on generating capacity or production. But electricity was cheap in all areas of the UAE. It was viewed as an essential service by most authorities, and according to many observers, the most expensive subsidy provided by the various levels of government. Higher charges for electricity and effective collection were recommended by economists as a means of reducing public expenditures.

By 1984 population growth had exceeded the supply of fresh water. Increasingly the UAE has had to turn to the costly desalination of seawater to meet the population's needs. Abu Dhabi and Dubai had installed capacity to meet demand. Some of the amirates to the north were in need of desalination units because their wells had drawn down the water table so heavily that intrusion of salt water was threatening irreversible damage. Although data on capacity and production were not available, the UAE had installed a substantial amount of desalination equipment in association with power plants, and additional capacity was planned.

The other major manufacturing industry in the UAE was production of cement. Cement plants were located in several amirates; some of the plants were owned by the amirate government or amirs in association with Kuwaiti or Saudi investors. During the construction boom of the 1970s in Middle East oil-exporting countries, cement was often a critical item in short supply; it looked like a good investment until the oil glut on world markets in the early 1980s reduced development expenditures. By 1984 UAE reportedly had capacity to produce nearly 7 million tons of cement, but local needs were about 2 million tons. Actual cement production was unknown, but press articles indicated that foreign sales faced increasing competition.

Industrialization in the UAE met with serious constraints. The very small local market, although with substantial buying power plus easy access for imports from established competitors, made domestic manufacturing difficult and attempts at large-scale production, without marketing help abroad, nearly impossible. The largest number of UAE's manufacturing industries produced such goods as foods, beverages, furniture, printed products, and cement tiles and blocks for the local market. But the value added in manufacturing came mostly from the large, capital-intensive industries processing the country's hydrocarbon resources.

Farming and Fishing

Agriculture, including some fishing, contributed about 1 percent of GDP in the early 1980s and reportedly employed about 25,000 workers. Farming was a minor part of the UAE economy. In spite of its diminishing importance over the years (relative to other sectors of the economy), farming probably covered a greater area and was more productive than ever before. By the early 1970s agricultural activity was on the upswing. Although shortages of water and labor precluded the country's ever being self-sufficient in foods, great productivity from agriculture lessened the economy's dependence on oil, improved living conditions for and spread the wealth to rural inhabitants, and provided a means to settle the beduin.

The bulk of the land in the UAE is either mountainous or desert, and all of it is arid. Even Ras al Khaymah, which receives the most rainfall, does not have enough to support cropping. Farming required irrigation. Most irrigation water originally fell as rain on the Hajar Mountains. Some cultivation used the direct runoff for irrigation, and by the early 1980s several dams had been built to impound more of the runoff. Most irrigation, however, tapped underground reservoirs created by impervious rock trapping the runoff of rainfall as it sank through the porous strata above. The underground reservoirs were dispersed, accounting for the isolated patches of cultivation. Abu Dhabi and Ras al Khaymah had the more important agricultural areas.

The underground reservoirs were frequently in areas unsuitable for cultivation because of topography or soil conditions. Centuries ago the inhabitants had developed a primitive but ingenious system of tunnels *(falaj)* to lead water to fertile soils. Some were as much as 32 kilometers long and more than 16 meters underground. The tunnels sloped gently from the water source to the fields. Vertical shafts, which provided air for the diggers, a means of removing dirt from the excavation, and openings to obtain water and to clear silt after the tunnel was in operation, were placed about 10 meters apart. It had required 18 years alone to complete a 1.5-kilometer segment of one tunnel under construction in the 1940s. About 80 such tunnels were known in various parts of the country, although only about 25 were still functioning in the early 1980s. Drilling wells and installation of pumps was the more important method of irrigating in recent years.

Increasing use of wells and pumps permitted a tremendous expansion of the cultivated area. Statistics for the UAE were generally difficult to obtain, but agricultural data were the scarcest and appeared the least reliable. Official 1981 figures showed 26,000 hectares to be the total area of farms, 7,700 hectares of which were in Abu Dhabi. The cultivated area reportedly expanded from about 4,000 hectares in 1970 to 8,500 hectares in 1973, and 16,000 hectares in 1977. The number of farms increased from 7,500 in 1977 to more than 12,500 in 1981. Farm production in 1981 was 160,000 tons of vegetables, 60,000 tons of fruits, including dates, and 123,000 tons of field crops, presumably including fodder, according to official statistics. In 1973 farm production included at least 22,000 tons of vegetables, 8,000 tons of tobacco, and 15,000 tons of alfalfa. In addition, by 1983 some 25,000 hectares of trees had been planted to lessen soil erosion and provide protection from dust storms; most afforestation was in Abu Dhabi, much of it irrigated by reclaimed water from the sewage system.

Raising animals was an important adjunct to farming. Before the discovery of oil, nomadic herdsmen, primarily raising camels and goats, had depended on settled communities for some food and equipment, even though they ranged widely to find forage for their animals. During the hottest months the nomads stayed around perennial wells and springs, where there usually was some settled farming by tribe members. Government efforts to settle the beduin are believed by observers to have reduced the number of nomads and the livestock population, but by how much was uncertain. Many farms maintained a variety of animals. In addition, commercial dairy and poultry farms had expanded considerably, adding to the supply of milk, eggs, and meat.

By 1984 agricultural production was making a remarkable contribution toward meeting the nation's food needs. According to the minister of agriculture and fisheries, the UAE produced about half of the country's supply of vegetables and a quarter of the supply of dairy products; there was near self-sufficiency for fish, poultry, and eggs. Seasonal surpluses permitted some exports of vegetables. The country remained almost completely dependent on imports for grains, however.

The expansion of agricultural productivity resulted from substantial government support. The extension of roads had been an important factor in opening up agricultural areas and providing access to markets. Many inputs and long-term loans to agriculture were subsidized, and some amirates supported farm prices. Abu Dhabi provided farmers extensive incentives. The country had

*International Trade
Center, Dubai*

experimental, research, and training facilities that assisted farmers.

Continued agricultural expansion will be difficult. The increases in the area cultivated and in yields were the result of rapid and uncontrolled well drilling. By the early 1980s the water table had been dropping at an alarming rate in most aquifers for nearly a decade. Many wells have shown increasing salinity. Although a comprehensive water survey had not been undertaken, computations indicated that irrigation annually used nearly 7.5 times the aquifer recharging supplied by average rainfall. One expert predicted that, if depletion rates of the early 1980s continued, the country would run out of underground water in 13 years. Others were less pessimistic, but all agreed that conservation measures were needed quickly. In 1983 a federal authority was finally given complete control of drilling (which was formerly shared with the amirates) and eventually of supervising water use. Replacement of the traditional practice of flood irrigation with drip systems could reduce water use by about two-thirds.

Fish were plentiful in the waters around the UAE, and fishing traditionally provided employment to a substantial part of the population, particularly in the more northern amirates. In the 1970s the UAE participated in a regional fishing survey by the United Nations (UN) Food and Agriculture Organization to de-

275

termine the fish available, the size of catches to avoid overfishing, and the equipment best suited to local conditions. The federal government provided fishing equipment to fishermen at subsidized prices and on concessionary repayment terms and built roads and assisted in developing shore and marketing facilities. The motorized boats and improved equipment had raised the fish catch. The fish catch amounted to 70,075 tons in 1982, in contrast with 64,400 tons in 1977.

Money and Banking

Various foreign coins long circulated for local monetary use in the area that became UAE, but the Indian rupee became the main medium of exchange in much of the twentieth century. When the rupee was devalued in 1966, Abu Dhabi adopted the Bahraini dinar as legal tender. Dubai and the other northern amirates opted for the riyal, issued jointly by Dubai and Qatar in 1966. The dinar and the riyal were the principal currencies in circulation when the UAE was formed.

The amirs agreed that a common currency was needed. Legislation was enacted, and in May 1973 the federal Currency Board was established and issued the UAE dirham (UD—sometimes Dh) as the national currency. The board had some of the functions of a central bank but was not given full authority. The board was responsible for note issue and had some control over commercial banks, but it lacked full control of commercial banking and credit.

A few banks, mainly British, had been active in the amirates for many years, particularly in Dubai and Sharjah. Gradually, local banks were formed, and at least one in each amirate had part ownership by, or a special relationship to, the ruling family. These in effect became the amirate (state) banks. The amirs refused to grant the Currency Board full control over banks because it might interfere with their own financial activities. Credit expansion was rapid after 1973, along with extensive speculation in real estate. In 1977 a financial crisis emerged that also involved speculation in the dirham. It led to the failure of two banks and additional pressure that had been building since the mid-1970s to establish a central bank. It took until 1979 for the amirs to agree to grant the necessary power to a central monetary authority. In December 1980 the Central Bank began operations with increased responsibility for regulation of banks and control of credit.

The number of banks increased rapidly after the formation of the UAE. After the mid-1970s the licensing of new banks slowed to a trickle. Nonetheless, by 1983 there were 52 commercial banks (51 in operation) and a total of 325 branches in the UAE, which, with its small population, often received from journalists the dubious distinction of being the world's most over-banked country. Twenty-three of the commercial banks were locally owned, and 29 were foreign banks. Four additional foreign banks had restricted licenses, which excluded current transactions in dirhams (making these banks offshore banking units), and 13 foreign banks had representative offices in the UAE. The National Bank of Abu Dhabi and the National Bank of Dubai, plus a few other commercial banks, accounted for the bulk of the banking business. The remaining commercial banks were mostly small, and many were considered unsound.

A basic aim of the Central Bank policy has been to strengthen the banking structure. One means was to encourage mergers to reduce the number of banks and to make more viable those that remained. By 1984 the number of banks had not diminished, but individual foreign banks had been required to close all but eight of their branches in the country. To strengthen the banking structure, increased reporting by banks was required; audits and inspections were expanded; a Central Bank risk department was established with computer facilities to keep track of banks' loans to customers (so that individual banks could inquire about loans already outstanding to applicants); minimum capital requirements for commercial banks were set; and a bank's liabilities were limited to 15 times its capital and reserves. In July 1982 Central Bank regulations required that loans and guarantees by a bank to any single director of the bank must not exceed 5 percent—or 25 percent for all directors and managers—of the bank's paid-up capital. Time was allowed for borrowers to adjust their position to this requirement. The intent of the Central Bank regulation was to force sounder lending policies on a number of banks that had been formed to finance activities of major builders and traders. The actions of the Central Bank by 1984 indicated a determined effort to improve the country's banking practices to protect depositors while not reducing lending for justified undertakings.

The Central Bank's regulations on a bank's loan to directors resulted in a serious upheaval in banking. In November 1983 Abdul Wahhab Galadari and the rest of his board of directors resigned at the Union Bank of the Middle East (UBME, the country's third largest) because of the bank's difficulties; they were replaced by a government team to administer the bank. Galadari was a prominent Dubai businessman who had to hand over part of his assets as collateral, including the Dubai Hyatt Regency Hotel and adjoining Galleria office and shopping complex, for his loans from UBME. Unofficial estimates of his loans from UBME amounted to US$325 to US$380 million, plus bank guarantees of US$135 to US$270 million, whereas the bank's capital was about US$130 million. The Central Bank and Dubai government reportedly pledged about US$380 million to UBME at 2 percent interest to ensure the soundness of the bank until settlement of Galadari's affairs. Galadari reportedly commented that many banks were in a similar position and why pick on him! In mid-1984 it was unclear whether more disruptions were likely or what effect the troubles at UBME would have on the rest of the banking system.

In 1983 the commercial banks faced difficult times because of the recession. The decline in public sector spending slowed financing requirements for trade and construction, although bank loans were needed by contractors waiting to be paid by government for work completed. Government deposits were down, and deposits by individuals were sought aggressively by small banks. An important part of wage payments was transferred home by foreign workers, often through banks of their home country operating in the UAE. Control of credit in 1983 was not a problem.

Commercial banking concentrated largely on short-term financing—mostly for construction in Abu Dhabi and trade in Dubai. A number of specialized public and private financial institutions provided credit for such things as consumer durables, housing, and industrial and agricultural projects. Specialized loans from the federal or amirate institutions often had concessionary terms. In most years credit for reasonable undertakings appeared easily accessible because of the lack of investment opportunities relative to funds available.

The wealth of the UAE, and particularly Abu Dhabi, generally exceeded the domestic investment opportunities. Several investment firms, public and private, helped place funds of government entities and private investors. The Abu Dhabi Investment Authority, established in 1976, was the most important, handling the amirate's surplus funds invested abroad, amounting to probably over US$20 billion. Large UAE commercial banks and some mainly government-owned institutions engaged in arranging syndications for, and participation in, loans in the UAE and in other countries. UAE institutions were quite active in international finance.

In 1984 the UAE financial system was only partially developed. So far government institutions and private firms had not

Dhows in creek in Dubai

relied on bonds or shorter term securities for financing, and the Central Bank could not use rediscount rates to affect the credit system. Although some stocks were traded, the country lacked an official stock exchange. Plans were formulated, however, to establish an exchange in 1985 or 1986, although it was not expected to have many stock shares to be traded initially because companies had not relied on this method for equity financing. The amirates were struggling to develop the financial sector, along with the other parts of the economy.

Foreign Trade and Balance of Payments

The UAE maintained an open economy with few restrictions on trade or foreign exchange transactions. Goods from almost any area of the world could be imported, and tariffs were low. Customs administration and rates were a function reserved to the individual amirates, and duties and regulations therefore varied among them. In November 1983 a 4-percent general import tariff was imposed to conform to agreements among the Gulf Cooperation Council (GCC) members on minimum duties; previously, most UAE imports had been subject to lower duties or none at all. Further changes were possible if the GCC moved toward a common market and a unified currency (see Appendix C).

Imports increased rapidly in the 1970s after the jump in oil revenues largely removed any balance of payments constraint. Imports peaked at US$8.6 billion in 1981 and fell to US$7.9 billion in 1983. Import statistics were not available for the UAE because each amirate kept its own information. Data had to be compiled from various sources, using different categories and methodologies. Nonetheless, data from Abu Dhabi, Dubai, and Sharjah covered the bulk of imports. In 1982 some 45 percent of imports were consumer goods, of which food, beverages, and tobacco products accounted for 11 percent of total imports. Capital goods, consisting mostly of machinery and transport equipment, amounted to 39 percent. Intermediate goods, which included a large proportion of refined petroleum products, including lubrication oils, composed almost all of the remainder. Stated another way, more than 75 percent of imports were manufactured articles. The industrialized countries of Western Europe, Japan, and the United States were the source of 76 percent of UAE imports. Japan was the largest supplier (19 percent), followed by the United States (14 percent), Britain (12 percent), the Federal Republic of Germany (West Germany) (9 percent), and France (7 percent). The remaining sources of imports were concentrated largely in Western Europe.

Exports were reported only by a portion of the amirates, and the direction of petroleum exports was not given in value terms. In addition, sales of liquid petroleum gases (LPG) were not treated in a consistent manner. Moreover, the value of exports of petroleum products represented neither the revenues actually received by the amirates nor their share of the foreign exchange proceeds from such sales. In spite of difficulties with statistics, a general picture of UAE exports was possible.

UAE exports were rising in the 1970s and peaked at US$22 billion in 1980, of which oil and gas exports accounted for US$20 billion. Declining oil and gas sales reduced exports to US$15.4 billion by 1983, of which oil and gas exports were US$12.7 billion. In 1981 the destinations of exports of crude oil from Abu Dhabi and Dubai (in terms of quantity) were Japan, 37 percent; France, 11 percent; United States, 7 percent; Netherlands, 6 percent; Spain, 4 percent; West Germany, 4 percent; and Italy, 4 percent. The remainder was sold to many countries, none of which accounted for more than 3.5 percent of total crude oil exports, and most were considerably less.

Non-oil exports from the UAE were largely reexports, particularly through Dubai, although all of the amirates probably had some reexport trade. Iran was the main reexport market in the late 1970s, but this trade declined after the outbreak of the Iran-Iraq War in 1980. Nearby GCC countries, particularly Saudi Arabia and Qatar, were the other main recipients of the UAE's reexports in 1982. Reexports consisted primarily of manufactured articles, especially machinery and transportation equipment that may have been predominantly consumer durables. Non-oil exports from the UAE actually included substantial amounts of liquid petroleum gases because of Dubai's classification system. Another important UAE export was aluminum from Dubai's smelter. In future years exports of fertilizer from Abu Dhabi should become important.

The large increase in crude oil prices in 1974 and in 1979 and 1980 supplied the UAE economy with an inflow of foreign exchange that allowed officials great flexibility regarding payments abroad. Through much of the 1970s foreign payments were substantially less than receipts, building up surpluses in foreign assets, most of which accrued to Abu Dhabi. The surplus on current account peaked in 1980 at US$10.1 billion (see table 27, Appendix A). In the early 1980s, as exports—essentially oil exports—declined, payments for imports, services, and remittances home by foreign workers declined less rapidly, reducing the current account balance to US$4.5 billion in 1983. Government capital flows declined with falling oil revenues in 1982 and 1983, and the outflow of private funds slowed greatly in 1983 as foreign interest rates came down. Nonetheless, in 1983 the UAE experienced its first overall balance of payments deficit in a decade, although it was only US$400 million. Economists expected a small improvement in the country's external accounts in 1984—one that would probably yield a small surplus. But as long as oil exports remained low, officials would need to watch the outflow of foreign exchange more closely than at any time since 1974.

Government and Politics

Although Lord Curzon, as viceroy of India, declared to the rulers of the Trucial States in 1903 that "we found strife and we have created order," British policy in the lower Gulf, from the signing of the 1853 Treaty of Maritime Peace in Perpetuity to the withdrawal of their presence in 1971, was focused on narrow objectives. These were confined essentially to keeping the sea-lanes open, preventing other European powers from establishing a substantial presence in the Gulf, and, in the twentieth century, arranging favored access to the region's oil for British companies (see The Trucial Coast: The Qawasim and the Bani Yas; Gulf Developments Before Independence, ch. 1). Interference in the internal affairs of the amirates was directed solely to the preservation of British interests. The British preferred to deal with the rulers on an individual basis rather than promote modern alternatives to traditional political institutions, although they did not remain uninvolved in the frequent succession struggles within ruling families.

The official British presence was generally confined to naval contingents and a system of political agents and officers responsible for directing the Trucial State rulers on matters related to foreign affairs and defense. These were under the British viceroy of India until 1947 and the British Foreign Office thereafter. It was not until 1946, however, that a political officer was established on a year-round basis in the Trucial States, at Sharjah.

The limited nature of the British presence enabled the amirs to maintain virtually intact the prerogatives of personal rule, though their ambitions seaward were blocked by the British navy. The inherent conservativism of the system and centuries-old suspicions and antagonisms retarded the integration of the Trucial States outside the framework of shaykh rule. But in 1951 the British established the Trucial Oman Levies (later known as the Trucial Oman Scouts), a peacekeeping force that drew recruits from and operated in all the amirates (see United Arab Emirates, ch. 7). The following year the Trucial States Council, a consultative body composed of the seven amirs and presided over by the British political officer, was organized. Through its semiannual meetings, the Council afforded the amirs an unprecedented opportunity to define areas of common interest. The Development Fund, under the jurisdiction of the Trucial States Council, was established during the 1960s and received grants from Britain, Qatar, Bahrain, and, most significantly, Abu Dhabi. Abu Dhabi's newfound oil wealth enabled it to contribute as much as 80 percent of the fund's total revenue by 1970.

Britain's announcement in early 1968 that it was withdrawing from its bases east of the Suez Canal by 1971 entailed an abrogation of its treaties with the Trucial States. This obligated the seven amirs and the rulers of Qatar and Bahrain to begin the process of forging a new political arrangement serving mutual interests in areas such as security and development. They regarded some form of federation as most desirable, as this would allow them to retain their independence to a substantial degree while enabling the smaller and poorer amirates to benefit from association with those possessing oil reserves. Shaykh Zayid, ruler of Abu Dhabi—the largest and richest of the Trucial States—and in mid-1984 the president of the UAE, was particularly active in promoting the idea of establishing a federation that would be an independent state rather than a regional arrangement of several independent states.

On July 18, 1971, rulers of six of the Trucial States ratified the Provisional Constitution of the United Arab Emirates, the product of more than three years of bargaining among the rulers, and it was promulgated on December 2, 1971, when the UAE became independent. The rulers of Qatar and Bahrain refused to join, and the ruler of Ras al Khaymah postponed joining until February 1, 1972. The Provisional Constitution, as its name indicates, was meant to be a transition document that would be replaced by a permanent constitution after a five-year period. This was predicated on substantial progress in political integration. The conservatism of rulers jealous of their traditional prerogatives and the lack of articulate political constituencies among UAE citizens, however, impeded the implementation of constitutional provisions and the development of effective federal institutions. The Provisional Constitution was extended for a period of five years in December 1976 and for a further five years in December 1981.

Constitutional Framework

The constitutional framework of the UAE, as defined in the Provisional Constitution, provides for the separation of powers into executive, legislative, and judicial branches. Additionally, it separates legislative and executive powers into federal and local jurisdictions. Certain powers are expressly reserved for the central government, residual powers being exercisable by the individual shaykhdoms.

The separation of powers remained nominal in 1984, for the Supreme Council of the Union (SCU) continued to function as the highest federal authority in executive and legislative capacities. Narrowly, the executive branch consists of the SCU, the Council of Ministers (the cabinet), and the Presidency (see fig. 14). The SCU is composed of the rulers of the seven amirates; it elects from among its members a chairman and vice chairman, who serve for a term of five years. Its responsibilities include formulation of general policy; ratification of federal laws and decrees, including those relating to annual budget and fiscal matters; ratification of international treaties and agreements; and assent to the appointment of the prime minister and Supreme Court judges.

The rulers make decisions by a simple majority, except on substantive issues; in that case a majority of five, including the votes of Abu Dhabi and Dubai, is mandatory. This requirement is in deference to the weighty role that the richest amirates were expected to play in the federation. Presumably any federal venture lacking the support of either Abu Dhabi or Dubai would be an exercise in futility. The SCU carries out its work through a secretariat and may appoint an ad hoc committee.

The chairman of the SCU is automatically the president of the UAE and the head of state. He is also the supreme commander of the federation in his capacity as the chairman of the Supreme Defense Council. The president convenes the SCU and appoints the prime minister, deputy prime minister, cabinet ministers, and other senior civil and military officials. He is also empowered to proclaim martial law and to carry out a host of other functions usually associated with the chief executive of a modern nation-state.

The day-to-day management of federal affairs is the function of the Council of Ministers. By mid-1984 its original membership of 14 in 1971 had expanded to 25, including the prime minister and two deputy prime ministers. The ministers must be citizens of the UAE and are individually and collectively answerable to the president and the SCU. In addition to its executive duties, the Council of Ministers is responsible for drafting bills for formal enactment.

Under the Provisional Constitution the Federal National Council (FNC) is the principal legislative authority, but its actual role in the governmental process is limited to consultation. Its 40 members are appointed for two years by the ruler of each amirate, according to procedures appropriate to local conditions and in accordance with a constitutionally fixed quota that reflects, albeit imperfectly, the wealth and size of Abu Dhabi and Dubai. The quota calls for eight members each from Abu Dhabi and Dubai; six each from Sharjah and Ras al Khaymah; and four each from Ajman, Umm al Qaywayn, and Fujayrah. The members must be citizens of the respective amirates, 21 years of age or older, and literate. They may not hold any other public offices. In an attempt to foster a spirit of federation, these members are urged, under the Provisional Constitution, to represent the people not only of their respective amirates but also of the federation as a whole.

The FNC meets in a regular session for a minimum of six months, beginning in the third week of November; when neces-

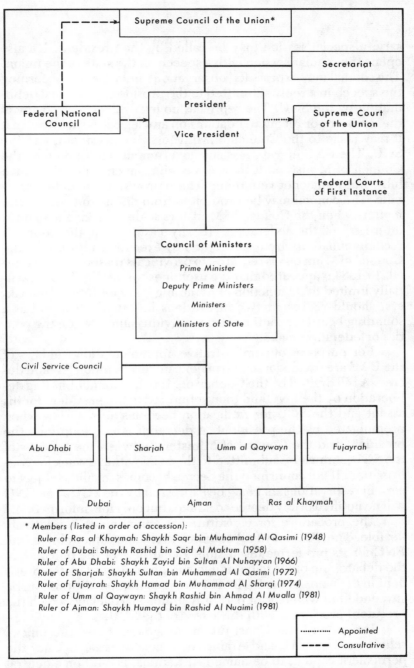

Figure 14. *United Arab Emirates (UAE). Government Structure, 1984.*

sary, a special session may be called by the president. He also opens the regular session with a speech on the state of the union. The council may express its "observations and wishes" concerning the speech in a reply submitted to the president for formal deliberation by the SCU. The reply has no legal effect, nor do any of the decisions or recommendations on any legislative matters that it may make to the Council of Ministers, the president, and the SCU. The FNC may discuss any government bills drafted by the Council of Ministers; it may agree with, amend, or reject such bills, but it may not veto them. These provisions include money bills. The council may be prohibited from discussing any federal matters when the Council of Ministers so decides in "the highest interests" of the federation. In any case, when the council's recommendations are not accepted by executive authorities, the Council of Ministers is required to provide its reasons to the council. In 1984 it appeared that the usefulness of the FNC was essentially limited to its function as a training body for future lawmakers, should representative institutions be established, and as a sounding board for sentiments in individual amirates on the politics of federation making.

For purposes of administrative implementation the laws of the UAE are divided into two major categories: union law and decree. A bill drafted by the Council of Ministers for nonbinding deliberation by the FNC and then submitted to the president for his assent and the SCU for ratification becomes a union law when promulgated by the president. A decree is issued jointly by the president and the Council of Ministers between the sessions of the SCU; it must be submitted to the SCU within a week for confirmation. If not confirmed the decree becomes invalid, subject to certain reservations that may be expressed by the SCU. The FNC will be notified of any decree so issued, but only for "information."

The procedure for constitutional amendment is relatively flexible. The SCU may first submit a draft amendment bill to the FNC for its pro forma discussion. Regardless of the outcome of the debate, the bill is to be signed and promulgated by the president in the name of the SCU. The Provisional Constitution can be suspended in whole or in part only under martial law, which the president proclaims, with the assent of the SCU.

The Provisional Constitution designates Islam the official religion of the UAE and Arabic the official language. Until the permanent capital, to be named Al Karama, is built on a neutral site on the border between Abu Dhabi and Dubai, the provisional capital is the city of Abu Dhabi.

Among the basic social and economic principles of the UAE are those prescribing education as "compulsory in its primary stage" and "free at all stages." A comprehensive health care program is guaranteed "by the society for all its citizens." Private property is inviolable and may be expropriated only for due cause and on payment of fair compensation. The natural resources and wealth of each amirate are to be considered the public property of that amirate. The Provisional Constitution also lists fundamental rights and liberties that are familiar to most modern nations.

Division of Powers

Article 120 of the Provisional Constitution assigns the federal government "exclusive legislative and executive jurisdiction" over foreign affairs, national defense, internal security, federal finances and taxes, communications, highways and aviation, nationality, education, public health, public information, the taking of censuses, currency, electric power, and weights and measures. In addition, the Constitution assigns the federal government responsibility for legislation on labor relations, social security, banks, the penal code, civil and criminal proceedings in courts, printing and publications, copyright, the protection of cultural, technical, and industrial property, the delimitation of territorial waters, and navigation on the high seas.

Although the individual amirates are charged in the Provisional Constitution with seeing that laws and international agreements ratified by the federal government are properly implemented, they retain responsibility for all areas not expressly reserved to the federal government. Moreover, they are granted significant concurrent powers. These include the power of each amirate to conclude "limited agreements of a local and administrative nature with the neighboring states or regions," although such agreements must be consistent with the interests of the UAE and the circumstances relating to these accords must be provided in advance to the SCU and other federal authorities. Article 138 of the Provisional Constitution provides for federal defense forces under a single command, but Article 142 gives the amirates the authority to establish their own local security forces. Both the federal and the amirate governments have the authority to levy taxes and borrow money.

The intent of the framers of the Provisional Constitution is nevertheless clear concerning the primacy of federal authority over the amirates; federal laws and international agreements are theoretically binding on all amirates. Any laws of the amirates inconsistent with the Provisional Constitution or federal laws and decrees are to be declared null and void through the judicial review of the Supreme Court of the Union. There is to be only a single UAE citizenship. All amirates are expected to contribute to the annual budget of the federal government.

The Judiciary

Article 94 of the Provisional Constitution guarantees the independence of the judicial branch under the Supreme Court of the Union. This body consists of a president and no more than five judges appointed by the UAE president, following approval by the SCU. The Supreme Court is vested with the power of judicial review and original jurisdiction over federal-amirate as well as interamirate disputes; the court is also empowered to try cases of official misconduct involving cabinet and other senior federal officials. The Provisional Constitution as well provides for the establishment of union courts of first instance to handle certain civil, commercial, criminal, and administrative cases, judgments from these courts being appealable to the Supreme Court. Local courts in each amirate have jurisdiction over areas not specifically allotted to the union courts in the Provisional Constitution. In 1978 judicial authority was transferred formally from the amirates to the federal government.

The Provisional Constitution designates sharia as the basis of all legislation. In mid-1984 the compiling of a legal code based on sharia was in progress, though the date on which it would be implemented was uncertain. There are four major schools of Islamic law—Hanafi, Shafii, Maliki, and Hanbali—and three of the four are present in the societies of the UAE. The majority of the indigenous population adheres to the Maliki legal school, but many of the residents of Fujayrah observe the guidelines of the Shafii school, and perhaps one-half of the population of the city of Al Ayn are Wahhabis (see Glossary) and therefore follow the precepts of the Hanbali school. Observers believed that, if and when a legal code is adopted, it will conform to the Maliki school but will not be objectionable to adherents of other interpretations.

In mid-1984 judicial procedures in the UAE were based on a synthesis of Anglo-Saxon, Continental European, and Islamic models. Many of the magistrates were Egyptian nationals, pending their replacement with qualified UAE citizens.

The Ruling Families

Traditional rule in the Arab polities of what is now the UAE has always been family-based and patriarchal. Political allegiance was defined in terms of loyalty to the amir and his family rather than in terms of belonging to a nation-state with clearly defined borders. This was particularly evident in the northeastern region of the UAE, facing the Gulf of Oman, which in mid-1984 still consisted of a patchwork of small, noncontiguous territories whose inhabitants were tied by links of loyalty to the north-coast amirates and to Fujayrah on the east coast (see fig. 13). Disputes over territory containing wells, forage areas for grazing, or, more recently, oil reserves, have been a recurrent feature of relations between the different amirates, and land was valued primarily for its economic potential rather than its association with a national territory. The strongest and most prestigious families were those who, through prowess in war and success in forging political marriage alliances, were able to gain control of economic resources with which they could support a large number of followers. The discovery of oil in the 1960s both reaffirmed and distorted this traditional pattern. Because the amirs of Abu Dhabi and Dubai had the most wealth at their disposal in the mid-1980s, they could create new constituencies outside of their traditional followings, although the rulers of the smaller amirates strove to retain a significant measure of independence.

The amirs customarily came from the senior ranks of the most powerful families and were expected to possess strong personal qualities of piety, good character, intelligence, and generosity. Links between ruler and subject were reaffirmed through the holding of frequent majlises (sing., majlis), or audiences, where the amir personally met with petitioners. In mid-1984 the majlis continued to be an important political institution, despite the growth of more formal administrative organs. One observer remarked that majlises held in the northern amirates by Shaykh Zayid in his role as president of the UAE were particularly well attended, given the large amounts of money at that ruler's disposal.

The senior members of the ruling families of the amirates—the Al Nuhayyan family in Abu Dhabi, the Al Maktum in Dubai, the Al Qasimi in Sharjah and Ras al Khaymah, the Al Mualla in Umm al Qaywayn, the Al Nuaimi in Ajman, and the Al Sharqi in Fujayrah—remained the most important political actors in the UAE in mid-1984; no other group enjoyed a comparable measure of power and prestige. Constitutional arrangements, forged by the rulers during the 1968–71 period, focused power on themselves as members of the SCU, with its wide-ranging executive and legislative authority. Many cabinet ministers were family members, and none could be appointed unless considered suitable by the rulers.

Although the increasing complexity of governmental tasks in a rapidly developing society required a more formal and impersonal style of administration—and a loosening of traditional ties could be expected—the political process in the mid-1980s was dependent upon personalities and a delicate balancing of ruling-family interests. Personal qualities of the rulers remained an essential factor in gaining them effective popular support. Thus, the question of succession was crucial as the time approached when a new generation of rulers would come to power and the founders of the UAE would pass from the scene.

The Al Nuhayyan Family of Abu Dhabi

The Al Nuhayyan family, a branch of the Al Bu Falah clan of the Bani Yas tribe, traces its origins to the Liwa Oasis. Originally beduin, they established themselves at Abu Dhabi on the coast and Al Ayn in the Buraymi Oasis during the eighteenth and nineteenth centuries. Before the discovery of oil in the early 1960s, the economic base of Al Nuhayyan power was control of the water resources of the inland oases. Oil revenues gave the family new opportunities to extend their power and influence.

The amir in mid-1984, Shaykh Zayid, came to power in 1966 following the deposition of his elder brother, Shaykh Shakhbut bin Sultan. Shakhbut was regarded by powerful members of the family as excessively conservative, his attachment to the traditional beduin way of life making him reluctant to spend oil revenues on modernization. By contrast, Zayid had established a reputation as modernizer while he was governor of Abu Dhabi's Eastern Province. Both as amir and, after 1971, as president of the UAE, he has combined traditional appeals—strong character and a personal style of rule—with policies designed to build stable government institutions transcending the latent instability of family politics. Following his installation as amir, he set up specialized organs of government in Abu Dhabi, there being in mid-1970 some 28 government departments, organized the following year into 13 ministries. The National Consultative Council was established in 1971, on the eve of the creation of the UAE, and in mid-1984 served Abu Dhabi as a consultative body of 50 appointed members.

Zayid, the most powerful of the seven amirs in the UAE, has also been the principal force behind the development of the UAE as a federal entity. To provide benefits to UAE citizens and to support the evolution of federal institutions, he pledged in 1971 to use Abu Dhabi's oil revenues to underwrite 85 percent of the UAE federal budget, although the reluctance of the other amirs to contribute has meant that he has had to contribute as much as 95 percent. Much of this has been used for the development of the poorer northern amirates. Resources and personnel have been transferred from Abu Dhabi to the federal structure. In 1973 the amirate's ministries were demoted to department status, a number of former ministers being incorporated into the federal Council of Ministers. In 1976 the Abu Dhabi Defense Forces were absorbed into the Union Defense Force (UDF).

In the interests of promoting stability, the traditional practice of senior members of the ruling family choosing a successor at the time of the ruler's death has been abandoned in favor of the ruler himself designating a successor. The crown prince, Khalifah bin Zayid Al Nuhayyan, Zayid's eldest son, served in mid-1984 as chairman of Abu Dhabi's Executive Council (the amirate equivalent of a cabinet), head of the Social Services Department, and, on the federal level, as deputy commander in chief of the UDF. During the early 1980s he became actively involved in the amirate's oil policy while presiding at meetings of the board of the Abu Dhabi National Oil Company (ADNOC) and has encouraged the replacement of foreign ADNOC managers with qualified UAE nationals. In mid-1984 none of his younger brothers played an active political role, though Muhammad bin Zayid Al Nuhayyan was a colonel in the UAE air force.

Other prominent members of the Al Nuhayyan family in mid-1984 included Tahnun bin Muhammad Al Nuhayyan, chairman of ADNOC and governor of Abu Dhabi's Eastern Province since Zayid's accession in 1966; Sarur bin Muhammad Al Nuhayyan, president of Zayid's ruler's diwan and chairman of the Central Bank, and Hamdan bin Muhammad Al Nuhayyan, one of two deputy prime ministers of the UAE. All were members of the Bani Muhammad, a branch of the ruling family distinct from that of Zayid. Their inclusion in the highest ranks of the Abu Dhabi and UAE government reflected the need to maintain unity within the Al Nuhayyan, lest the Bani Muhammad emerge as a rival to Zayid's line (see fig. 15).

The Al Maktum Family of Dubai

The Al Maktum family, a branch of the Al Bu Falasah clan of the Bani Yas tribe, migrated from Abu Dhabi and established it-

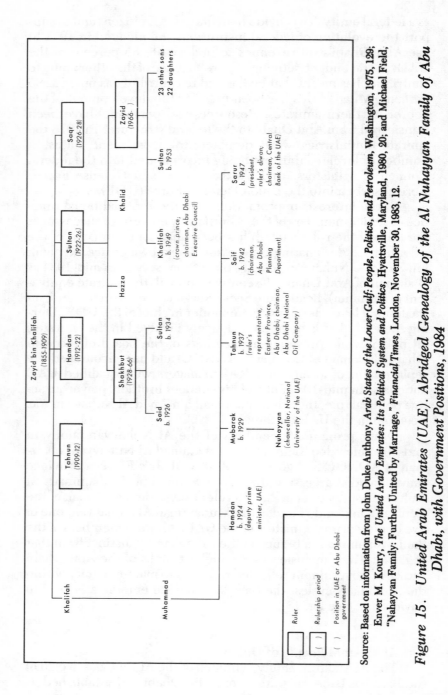

Source: Based on information from John Duke Anthony, *Arab States of the Lower Gulf: People, Politics, and Petroleum*, Washington, 1975, 129; Enver M. Koury, *The United Arab Emirates: Its Political System and Politics*, Hyattsville, Maryland, 1980, 20; and Michael Field, "Nahayyan Family: Further United by Marriage," *Financial Times*, London, November 30, 1983, 12.

Figure 15.   United Arab Emirates (UAE).   Abridged Genealogy of the Al Nuhayyan Family of Abu Dhabi, with Government Positions, 1984

self along Dubai Creek during the 1830s. Dubai's excellent port attracted merchants from Iran and India during the nineteenth and twentieth centuries, and the amirate had a large non-Arab population even before the discovery of oil and the influx of foreign workers. Commerce gave the Al Maktum a secure economic base and an outward-looking perspective somewhat different from that of the beduin Al Nuhayyan. Shaykh Rashid bin Said Al Maktum, amir since 1958, remained the second most powerful figure in the UAE, serving as vice president of the federation since 1971 and prime minister since 1979; in mid-1984, however, he was suffering from a serious illness, and many of his responsibilities had been taken over by his four sons. The eldest, Maktum bin Rashid Al Maktum, was designated crown prince. He had served as UAE prime minister until 1979, when his father assumed that post, and in mid-1984 was a deputy prime minister. Of his younger brothers, Hamdan bin Rashid Al Maktum was UAE minister of finance and industry, Muhammad bin Rashid Al Maktum was minister of defense, and Ahmad bin Rashid Al Maktum was commander in chief of the UDF (see fig. 16). Observers regarded the close and cooperative arrangement among the brothers as relatively stable, in part because all of them had been born to the same mother and thus lacked the traditional animosities of half-brothers.

Although comparatively smaller in area than Abu Dhabi, Dubai had a population in mid-1984 that was almost as large, and its status as a trade center and possession of oil revenues gave the Al Maktum a degree of independence not enjoyed by the poorer northern amirates. This was reflected in the Dubai rulers' enhanced powers, as conferred by the Provisional Constitution, and the inclusion of Al Maktum family members in the highest levels of the UAE government. Rivalry between the two amirates impeded Zayid's plans for more ambitious political integration, including the adoption of a permanent constitution. In mid-1984 Dubai maintained its own separate armed forces, and a major issue between Zayid and the Al Maktum had been the latter's reluctance to contribute to the federal budget. Despite its oil wealth, Dubai had funded few federal projects outside its own borders.

The Al Qasimi Family of Sharjah

Tracing its origins to the Qawasim maritime confederation of the eighteenth and nineteenth centuries, the amirate of Sharjah enjoyed a special status as the center of the British presence in the

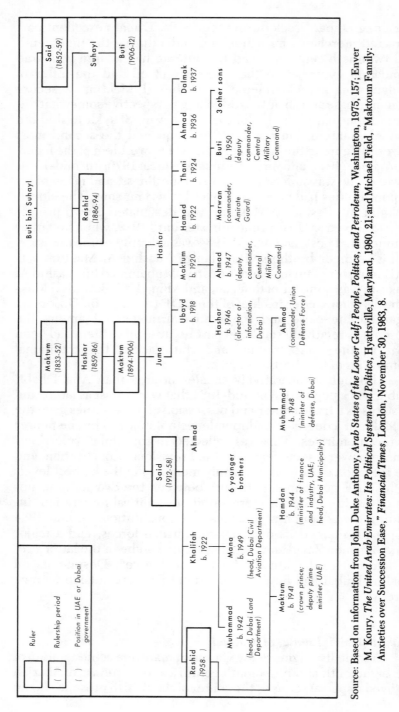

Source: Based on information from John Duke Anthony, *Arab States of the Lower Gulf: People, Politics, and Petroleum*, Washington, 1975, 157; Enver M. Koury, *The United Arab Emirates: Its Political System and Politics*, Hyattsville, Maryland, 1980, 21; and Michael Field, "Maktoum Family: Anxieties over Succession Ease," *Financial Times*, London, November 30, 1983, 8.

Figure 16.   United Arab Emirates (UAE). Abridged Genealogy of the Al Maktum Family of Dubai, with Government Positions, 1984.

Trucial States, the headquarters of the first attempts at regional integration—the Trucial Oman Levies and the Trucial States Council—and the site of the first modern boys' school during the 1950s. The amir, Shaykh Sultan bin Muhammad Al Qasimi, came to power in 1972, following the assassination of his brother Khalid (see fig. 17). Educated at the University of Cairo during the era of Gamal Abdul Nasser, Sultan was exposed to modernist and Pan-Arab ideas. Observers have characterized Sharjah as a center of relative "progressivism" in the conservative federation, largely because of Sultan's support or at least acquiescence. *Al Khaleej,* an influential UAE newspaper that has supported Palestinian and other Arab causes, opposed the "neo-colonialism" of the superpowers, and advocated elective institutions within the UAE, was published in the mid-1980s in Sharjah. A second publication emanating from Sharjah, *Al Azmina Al Arabiya,* strongly criticized the status quo in the UAE and had a wide following among the younger generation of students and civil servants until it was banned in the early 1980s. In 1975 Sultan had been the first amir to adopt the UAE flag in place of his own and transferred control of his militia, police, and courts to federal jurisdiction. In the mid-1980s he remained a strong proponent of political integration and a critic of those wishing to preserve the amirates' traditional independence.

The Ruling Families of the Northern Amirates

Lacking substantial oil revenues, the rulers of the four northern amirates—the Al Qasimi of Ras al Khaymah, the Al Nuaimi of Ajman, the Al Mualla of Umm al Qaywayn, and the Al Sharqi of Fujayrah—were limited in terms of the power they could exercise in their own domains and the influence they could wield in the UAE as a whole. On the one hand, their financial dependence on the richer amirates, particularly Abu Dhabi, tied the interests of the northern amirates to the federal institutions of the UAE. On the other hand, because of their small size and populations, the political dynamics of the northern amirates retained a strongly traditional character. The ruler of Ras al Khaymah, Shaykh Saqr bin Muhammad Al Qasimi, belonged to the same family as that ruling in Sharjah and took pride in the Qawasim's former dominance of the coast. In mid-1984 his son, Khalid bin Saqr Al Qasimi, who had been educated in the United States, was crown prince (see fig. 18).

Ajman, Umm al Qaywayn, and Fujayrah—the smallest and poorest amirates—were sometimes likened to village states or de-

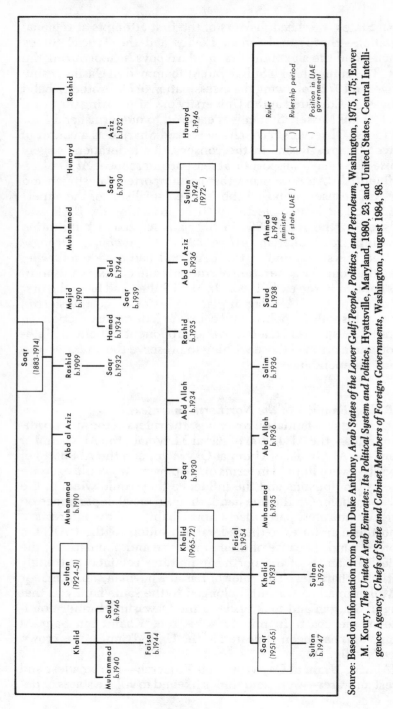

Source: Based on information from John Duke Anthony, *Arab States of the Lower Gulf: People, Politics, and Petroleum,* Washington, 1975, 175; Enver M. Koury, *The United Arab Emirates: Its Political System and Politics,* Hyattsville, Maryland, 1980, 23; and United States, Central Intelligence Agency, *Chiefs of State and Cabinet Members of Foreign Governments,* Washington, August 1984, 98.

Figure 17.   United Arab Emirates (UAE). Abridged Genealogy of the Al Qasimi Family of Sharjah, with Government Positions, 1984.

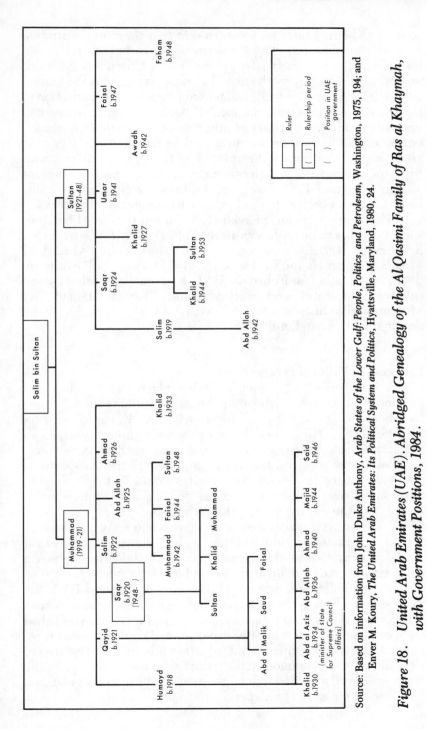

Source: Based on information from John Duke Anthony, *Arab States of the Lower Gulf: People, Politics, and Petroleum,* Washington, 1975, 194; and Enver M. Koury, *The United Arab Emirates: Its Political System and Politics,* Hyattsville, Maryland, 1980, 24.

Figure 18.   United Arab Emirates (UAE). Abridged Genealogy of the Al Qasimi Family of Ras al Khaymah, with Government Positions, 1984.

scribed as being under one-man rule in that their administrative functions were exercised by the amirs' kinsmen in their name and by a handful of expatriate advisers. Reform, where it was initiated, was prompted mainly by the need for coordination with the federal authorities responsible for development projects. Administration in the smaller amirates was complicated because these amirates had enclaves inside the territory of other amirates. In those enclaves, characteristically containing villages, date palm oases, or grazing areas, representatives of the rulers had the right to collect taxes from the various beduin groups migrating between the different amirates. By mid-1984, however, the building of extensive roads had tied these enclaves to the UAE's urban centers on the coast.

The amir of Ajman, Shaykh Humayd bin Rashid Al Nuaimi, succeeded his father, Shaykh Rashid bin Humayd Al Nuaimi, in September 1981. A new amir, Shaykh Rashid bin Ahmad Al Mualla, was proclaimed ruler of Umm al Qaywayn following the death of his father in February 1981. Fujayrah was ruled by the relatively youthful and well-educated Shaykh Hamad bin Muhammad Al Sharqi, who, at 35 years of age, presided over the dominant Al Sharqi family.

Progress in Political Integration

A basic operating principle under which the founders and promoters of the UAE believed political institutions would evolve has been described by political scientist Enver Koury as "functionalism." He defined this as a process beginning with the integration of relatively noncontroversial areas, such as communications and social services, into the federal framework. As a sense of national identity developed, the amirates would, in stages, surrender control over more controversial political and administrative areas to the center. In Koury's words, "as the proposed federal system acquired more powers and responsibilities in the social, economic, and technical fields, the consequences for political integration would be enhanced." Functionalism assumed a convergence, rather than an identity, of interests among the different ruling families and other UAE citizens. By the mid-1980s the process had advanced to the point where significant federal institutions, such as a central judicial structure and a central bank, had been established. Interamirate suspicions and rivalry, however, remained a significant impediment to further integration. There were clear differences of opinion on the merits of functionalism, and some amirs preferred a limited federalism in which the amirates retained a significant measure of independence.

Tensions between the two major actors in the political system—the ruling families of Abu Dhabi and Dubai led, respectively, by Zayid and the sons of Rashid—persisted over the issue of the pace and nature of political integration. These reached crisis proportions after February 1978, when UAE president Zayid, impatient with the progress of federalization of the armed forces, appointed his second son, Sultan, commander in chief of the UDF, without consulting with Vice President Rashid. This was perceived by many as a means of limiting the influence of Rashid's son, Maktum, who was minister of defense. The Dubai and Ras al Khaymah armed forces refused to take orders from the new commander in chief, and there were apprehensions that the two amirates might secede from the union.

Divisions between advocates of strong and limited federalism were still more clearly defined in March 1979, when the FNC, presided over by its speaker, Taryam Omran Taryam of Sharjah, issued a memorandum to the SCU, recommending such pro-union measures as the abolition of all amirate boundaries, a consolidation of all amirate revenues, complete federalization of the armed forces, an economy more free of foreign influences, and the removal of non-UAE citizens from the army. These recommendations and other proposals, such as granting the FNC genuine legislative powers and providing for the popular election—not the appointment—of its members, were regarded by the rulers of Dubai and Ras al Khaymah as attempts by Abu Dhabi (and to a lesser degree, Sharjah) to undermine their traditional autonomy, and they boycotted SCU meetings.

A new balance was restored when Rashid agreed to assume the post of prime minister in July 1979. In the compromise that he and Zayid worked out, they pledged to give one-half of their oil revenues to the federal budget and to continue certain aspects of the process of federalization, such as the creation of the Central Bank in 1980. The amirs did not agree, however, on a permanent constitution to replace the provisional document at the end of the latter's second five-year term in December 1981, citing their support for further "unity through evolution."

Obstacles to greater unity among the amirates remained considerable in mid-1984. Two important areas of contention were disputes over amirate subsidies from the federal budget to the poorer amirates and conflicting territorial claims. Despite the compromise of 1979, there was only partial progress on the part of some rulers to surrender revenues to a common budget. Conflicting territorial claims, both on land and on water, were pursued with some vehemence because of potential oil and natural gas reserves, the most important dispute being between Dubai and Sharjah.

Politics and Society

In mid-1984 there were no significant groups or parties of an expressly political nature operating in the UAE. Constitutional arrangements provided no outlet for mobilized public opinion, even if such had existed, and traditional tribal and family links remained reasonably effective in meeting the articulated needs of UAE citizens. In the larger amirates, however, especially Abu Dhabi, there was a large and at times inefficient bureaucracy in charge of the institutions of a modern welfare state. Citizens of the UAE were a relatively small, privileged elite, forming only 20 to 30 percent of the total population of 1.2 million in 1984. Practically all benefited from the development projects and subsidies made possible by oil revenues. Those classes that in other countries formed the nucleus of radical dissent—high school and, especially, university students—were not alienated from the political system insofar as they could anticipate promising careers in public administration or business, particularly because the government sought to replace experts with qualified nationals. But students, younger members of the civil service, and educated persons in general tended to identify with causes, such as the establishment of an effective, popularly elected legislature and a greater measure of political integration. Although these opinions were particularly widespread in the relatively liberal atmosphere of Sharjah, they were expressed by an increasing number of persons in the other amirates as well. For example, during the crisis months of early 1979, a committee of citizens in Ras al Khaymah petitioned the ruler, Shaykh Saqr, requesting that he be more active in supporting the federation, endorse the March 1979 recommendations of the FNC, and liberalize Ras al Khaymah's economy and administration. Another group with perhaps a greater measure of political influence in the mid-1980s consisted of long-established commercial interests, particularly in Dubai. Prominent merchants maintained traditionally close relationships with the amirs.

The UAE's Arab identity and the large numbers of foreign experts and laborers brought into the country, mostly in the wake of the oil boom, precluded the comfortable isolation of Trucial States' days. Fears about the presence of foreigners tended to have political and cultural dimensions. Political apprehensions were directed toward the Arab nationals, particularly Palestinians, Yemenis, Egyptians, and Jordanians, who occupied positions of responsibility as magistrates, civil servants, teachers, and other professionals. They were regarded by conservatives as importers of radical, potentially subversive, ideas and were also feared for their tendency to settle inter-Arab disputes on UAE soil. A Palestinian gunman had killed the UAE minister of state for foreign affairs, Sayf bin Said Al Ghubash, in October 1977 in an abortive attempt to assassinate the Syrian foreign minister; during the early 1980s several bomb incidents occurred and were attributed to mutually hostile Iraqis and Syrians, and there was evidence that expatriates and nationals were involved in smuggling arms into the country.

The movement commonly described as Islamic fundamentalism had strong support among students and teachers at the National University of the UAE at Al Ayn. Many teachers were Egyptian nationals who were members of the radical Al Ikhwan al Muslimun (Muslim Brotherhood). Fundamentalist ideas were also gaining currency among the *qutuba* (Islamic preachers), and the government, through the Ministry of Islamic Affairs and Awqaf, was tightening supervision of their activities.

Non-Arabs formed the majority of expatriates. In Dubai there was an Iranian minority, mostly merchant families who had lived there for several generations and had close ties with Iranian ports across the Gulf. They were Shiite Muslims, but the extent to which they and other Iranians in the UAE were receptive to the ideas of the Islamic revolution in Iran was unclear. There had been a demonstration supporting Ayatollah Ruhollah Khomeini in February 1979, but many of the more established Iranians were apparently UAE citizens with some interest in the status quo.

Apprehensions concerning other non-Arabs centered on their numbers and their very different cultural orientations. Pakistanis, the second largest foreign group (100,000 persons in 1981), were Muslims. Many Indians, representing the largest group (140,000 persons in 1981), were adherents of non-Muslim religions, as were most of the small number of workers from East Asia. The government attempted to exercise maximum control over these groups by limiting their terms of stay in the UAE, preventing any form of organization among workers, and segregating them as much as possible from nationals. Individuals deemed undesirable were deported on short notice. In the mid-1980s the role of non-Arab foreigners remained severely limited. High wages, the threat of deportation, and the fact that they were not able to bring their families with them generally ensured their political acquiescence, although resentment among foreigners against nationals was sometimes expressed.

Foreign Relations

The UAE, calling itself a nonaligned and developing nation, joined the League of Arab States (Arab League) on December 6, 1971, as its eighteenth member and was admitted to the UN three days later as its one hundred thirty-second member nation. It has since joined a number of international organizations, including the Organization of the Islamic Conference, the World Bank (see Glossary), the International Monetary Fund (IMF), the Food and Agriculture Organization (FAO), the International Labor Organization (ILO), the World Health Organization (WHO), and the United Nations Educational, Scientific and Cultural Organization (UNESCO). The UAE is also a member of the Organization of Arab Petroleum Exporting Countries (OAPEC) and the Organization of Petroleum Exporting Countries (OPEC).

Diplomatic relations in the early 1980s were maintained with more than 60 countries, and some 44 countries maintained embassies in Abu Dhabi in 1984. Formal ties were established with all Middle Eastern countries, save Israel and Egypt, and with selected states in Western Europe, the Western Hemisphere, Asia, and Africa. In 1984 the UAE did not have full relations with the Soviet Union or any other communist country; it had, however, trade ties with Hungary, the German Democratic Republic (East Germany), Bulgaria, Romania, and China; Hungary, East Germany, and Bulgaria maintained trade offices in the UAE.

The conduct of foreign relations has been geared to the Arab world, of which the UAE regards itself as an integral part because of a shared religion, language, culture, and history. The federation has unflaggingly supported the Palestine Liberation Organization (PLO) against Israel, and it broke diplomatic ties with Egypt as a result of Egyptian president Anwar al Sadat's rapprochement with that country. Within the region the UAE claims for itself the role of an active mediator, playing an important part in normalizing relations between Oman and the People's Democratic Republic of Yemen (Yemen [Aden]), accomplished in November 1982, and being involved in ongoing negotiations to unify Yemen (Aden) and the Yemen Arab Republic (Yemen [Sanaa]). As part of its comprehensive, nonaligned stance, the UAE has made statements opposing foreign military presence in the Gulf region.

Ruins of old fort on east coast

The more than two-decades-old dispute with Saudi Arabia and Oman over the Buraymi Oasis was settled in 1974 with the agreement on a new border between the UAE and Saudi Arabia. The UAE was given six villages in the Buraymi Oasis, and Oman three; Saudi Arabia secured a corridor to the Gulf through UAE territory. In the mid-1980s a territorial dispute with Oman was still unresolved. The amirate of Ras al Khaymah and Oman both claimed a 16-kilometer strip of land along the coast, the offshore area of which was believed to hold oil resources. Because of this conflict, Oman did not maintain an embassy in the UAE.

Through the decade of the 1970s, the UAE participated in efforts by the Arab states of the Persian Gulf to forge a regional consensus based upon perceptions of common economic, social, and cultural interests. Ministers of the UAE and the other Gulf states began meetings in 1973 to deliberate on issues related to education, health, information, communications, finance, commerce, agriculture, labor, and social affairs. During this period there was a growing realization that the countries shared common problems, such as the existence of large and potentially destabilizing foreign worker populations within their territories, the solution or amelioration of which required joint effort.

Progress toward the establishment of a comprehensive regional arrangement proceeded at a halting pace, however, until the outbreak of the Iran-Iraq War in September 1980. This new source of instability made the Gulf Arab countries more urgently aware of common security concerns. In early 1981 the groundwork was laid for the establishment of the GCC, which was inaugurated in May 1981, with the meeting in Abu Dhabi of the heads of state of the UAE, Saudi Arabia, Kuwait, Qatar, Bahrain, and Oman.

Relations with Iran had been strained when Mohammad Reza Pahlavi's armed forces occupied the Greater and Lesser Tunb Islands, claimed by the amirate of Ras al Khaymah, and the island of Abu Musa, previously recognized as part of Sharjah, on November 30, 1971. Although a compromise was reached between Sharjah and Iran and stated principally that they would share whatever oil revenues Abu Musa might possess, there was loss of life in the occupation of the Tunbs and a reaction from Arab countries—especially Libya, Iraq, and Yemen (Aden)—over alleged Iranian expansionism (the shah claimed that these islands had been part of Iran before the period of British dominance). After the outbreak of the Iran-Iraq War, Iraq demanded the return of these islands to the UAE, a gesture designed to gain that country's support. UAE president Zayid, however, stressed that although the UAE still claimed them, this territorial dispute had to be settled in a peaceful manner.

Of the six GCC states, the UAE came closest to neutrality in regard to the Iran-Iraq War. This was in large measure attributable to the long historical contact between Dubai and Iranian ports and to Dubai's Iranian population. In the mid-1980s Dubai was an important transshipment point for goods going to Iran. However, observers commented that differences between the amirates contributed a measure of ambiguity to UAE-Iran relations. Abu Dhabi has on its own given contributions to Iraq's war effort.

In the mid-1980s a central component of the UAE's foreign policy was its use of oil revenues for overseas assistance, probably exceeding US$3 billion in 1981. The country's aid disbursements, amounting to more than 8 percent of GDP in 1981, made it the world's most generous aid donor and in absolute terms the third most generous among oil exporters. Almost all of this came from Abu Dhabi. Although a portion of this assistance was channeled through the Abu Dhabi Fund for Arab Economic Development (ADFAED), most was given in the name of the federation as a whole (a total of around US$3 billion in 1981). Contributions were made bilaterally or through regional and international agencies, such as the Arab Fund for Economic and Social Development, the Arab Bank for Development in Africa, the Arab Monetary Fund, the IMF, and OPEC's Special Fund for International Development. Official statements stressed the UAE's interest in helping the poorest countries, and concessionary loans were granted for infrastructure projects in those countries.

Following the formation of the UAE in 1971, relations with the United States were close and friendly. The United States was one of the first countries to recognize the UAE, and it sent a resident ambassador in 1974 to Abu Dhabi. Relations have been strained, however, by the UAE government's perception of a lack of "evenhandedness" on the part of the United States in resolving the Arab-Israeli conflict. A second source of differences was the growing United States military presence in the Gulf region, particularly after the signing of an agreement by Washington and Muscat in June 1980 giving United States forces access to military facilities in Oman. The United States declaration of "vital interest" in the Persian Gulf was described by some officials as a threatening form of interventionism, though the escalation of the Iran-Iraq War in 1984 inspired less criticism of the United States.

*   *   *

Few recent books are available on the economy of the UAE. Ragaei El-Mallakh's *The Economic Development of the United Arab Emairates* surveys the progress of all sectors through the 1970s. More recent developments are reviewed in the *Financial Times'* "Surveys," usually published annually, and the *Middle East Economic Digest's* "MEED Special Report: UAE." The UAE Central Bank's *Annual Report* and more frequent *Bulletin* are additional useful sources of information and statistical data. The foregoing sources also offer the most accessible information on demographic and social matters.

John Duke Anthony's *Arab States of the Lower Gulf: People, Politics, Petroleum* describes the amirates and their ruling families in some detail, though its 1975 publication date precludes discussion of recent developments. Good discussions of federal institutions and their evolution after 1971 are found in Ali Mohammed Khalifa's *The United Arab Emirates: Unity in Fragmentation*, published in 1979, and Enver M. Koury's *The United Arab Emirates: Its Political System and Politics*, published in 1980. (For further information and complete citations, see Bibliography.)

Chapter 6. Oman

Crest of the Sultanate of Oman

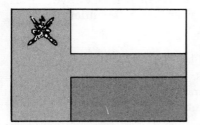

Country

Formal Name: Sultanate of Oman.

Short Form: Oman.

Term for Citizens: Omani(s); adjeetival form, Omani.

Capital: Muscat.

Flag: Three horizontal stripes (broad white and green at top and bottom, respectively, thinner red in center) joining broad red vertical stripe at staff side; national emblem (a *khanjar* dagger in its scabbard superimposed on two crossed swords in scabbards) is at top of vertical stripe.

Geography

Size: About 212,000 square kilometers, although estimates vary.

Topography: Mostly desert and mountainous. Four major regions: Musandam Peninsula, Al Batinah coastal plain, Oman interior, Dhofar Province (or region).

Climate: Hot and dry, except for Dhofar, which has light monsoon.

Boundaries: Mostly undefined.

Society

Population: Mid-1984 estimates ranged from 950,000 to over

1 million. Foreigners variously estimated at 25 to 48 percent of population.

Education: Free public schools consist of primary level of six years, preparatory level of three years, and secondary level of three years. Most teachers foreign.

Health: Reliable data unavailable, but life expectancy reportedly ranges from 45 to 50 years. Infant mortality high at about 130 per 1,000. Improvement and expansion of health care facilities major ongoing government priority.

Ethnic Groups: Most Omanis are Arabs, although numerous citizens of non-Arab African origin. Foreign community includes Egyptians, Pakistanis, Indians, and others.

Religion: Most Omanis are Muslim; Ibadis constitute largest group.

Economy

Gross Domestic Product (GDP):   In 1982 about US$7.17 billion; per capita US$7,500.

Oil Industry: Accounted for 57 percent of GDP, 95 percent of export earnings, and about 90 percent of government revenues.

Agriculture: Contributed about 2 percent of GDP in early 1980s.

Government and Politics

Government: Sultan as head of state and prime minister presides over Council of Ministers. State Consultative Council (SCC) has advisory role but no legislative powers. No constitution.

Politics: No political parties. Important political actors are persons close to sultan, including Western-educated administrators and special advisers.

Foreign Relations: Member of United Nations (UN) and its specialized agencies, League of Arab States (Arab League), Organization of the Islamic Conference, and Gulf Cooperation Council (GCC), formed in 1981. June 1980 agreement allows United States use of military facilities in Oman.

National Security

Armed Forces: Sultan of Oman's Land Forces, Sultan of Oman's Air Force, and Sultan of Oman's Navy. Estimated strengths in early 1984: army, 20,000; navy, 2,000; and air force, 2,000. Army primarily infantry force but has some tanks and armored cars. Navy a coastal patrol force, expanding and modernizing by acquisition of guided missile (Exocet) boats and new gunboats. Air force has 41 combat aircraft, all of British manufacture.

IN MID-1984 OMAN'S RULER, Sultan Qaboos bin Said bin Taimur Al Bu Said, continued to function as an absolute monarch. He served as prime minister, minister of defense, minister of foreign affairs, and commander in chief of the armed forces. The country had no constitution—the sultan was the final source of new legislation and the embodiment of the highest judicial power.

Since deposing his father in a coup d'état on July 23, 1970, Qaboos has set in motion sweeping socioeconomic reforms and has introduced important, if limited, political changes. The number of children in school has increased dramatically, and the availability of medical and social services, still inadequate by United Nations standards, has sharply improved the health and welfare of many of the people. Although the nation's oil reserves were relatively modest, oil export earnings have enabled the sultan to launch numnerous projects to promote the welfare of his people and to enhance the nation's economic prospects.

In 1976 Qaboos married a daughter of his father's only brother, but he subsequently terminated the marriage. Observers doubted that the sultan, who was born in November 1940, would marry again. Because he does not have any offspring or close male relatives, the matter of a successor to the office of the sultan becomes of greater moment each year. Although Qaboos has relinquished no real power and carefully preserves his political autonomy, observers have speculated that over the years Qaboos will assign additional power and authority to the new governmental institutions—such as the State Consultative Council—that he established in the early 1980s.

Geography

Because the country's boundaries remain unfixed, Oman's size was unknown (see fig. 19). The government used an estimate of 300,000 square kilometers, but most foreign observers suggested an area of about 212,000 square kilometers, roughly the size of Kansas. Geography has made the sultanate virtually an island, bordered mostly by the sea and the Rub al Khali (Empty Quarter) of Saudi Arabia. Historically, the country's contacts with the rest of the world have been largely by way of the sea, which not only provided access to foreign states but also linked the

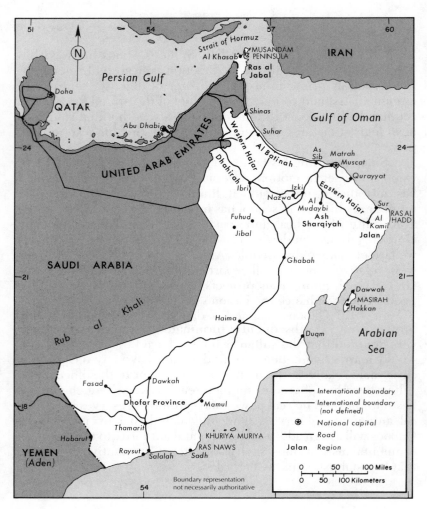

Figure 19.   Oman, 1984

coastal towns of Oman. The Rub al Khali, difficult to cross even
with modern desert transport, has served as a barrier between the
sultanate and the Arabian interior. Insularity has been reinforced
by the formidable Hajar Mountains, which form a belt between
the coast and the desert, from the Musandam Peninsula (Ras
Musandam) to the city of Sur. The desert and the mountains have
combined to keep Oman remarkably free of foreign encroach-

ments—either military or cultural—from the interior of the peninsula.

The country is divided by natural features into several distinct areas: the Musandam Peninsula; the Al Batinah plain; the Muscat-Matrah coastal area; the Oman interior, comprising the Jabal Akhdar (Green Mountain), its foothills, and the desert fringes; Dhofar Province (also called the Dhofar region) in the south; and the offshore island of Masirah.

The northernmost area, Ras al Jabal, extends from the Musandam Peninsula to Dibbah. It touches the Strait of Hormuz, which links the Persian Gulf with the Gulf of Oman, and is separated from the rest of the sultanate by a belt of territory belonging to several states of the United Arab Emirates (UAE). This area consists of low mountains forming the northernmost extremity of the Western Hajar. Two inlets, Elphinstone and Malcolm, cleave the coastline about one-third of the distance from the Strait of Hormuz and at one point are separated by only a few hundred meters of land. The coastline is extremely rugged, and the Elphinstone Inlet, 16 kilometers long and surrounded by cliffs 1,000 to 1,250 meters high, has frequently been compared with fjords in Norway.

The UAE territory separating Ras al Jabal from the rest of Oman extends almost as far south as the coastal town of Shinas. From the point at which the sultanate is entered again to the town of As Sib, about 140 kilometers to the southeast, runs a narrow, well-populated coastal plain known as Al Batinah. Across it a number of wadis, which are heavily populated in their upper courses, descend from the Western Hajar to the south. A ribbon of oases, watered by wells and underground channels (*falaj*), extends the length of the plain, about 10 kilometers inland from the coast.

South of As Sib the coast changes character. For about 175 kilometers, from As Sib to Ras al Hadd, it is barren and is bounded by cliffs almost its entire length; there is no cultivation and little habitation. Although the deep water off this coast renders navigation relatively easy, there are few natural harbors or safe anchorages. The two best are at Muscat and Matrah, where natural harbors gave rise to the growth of cities centuries ago.

With the exception of Dhofar Province, which has a monsoon climate and receives cool winds from the Indian Ocean, Oman's climate is extremely hot and dry most of the year. Summer begins in mid-April and lasts until October. The highest temperatures are registered in the interior, where readings of over 50°C in the shade are common. On the Al Batinah, summer temperatures seldom exceed 46°C, but because of the low elevation the plain experiences up to 90 percent humidity. The mean summer temperature in Muscat is 33°C, but the *gharbi* (literally, western), a strong wind that blows from the Rub al Khali, can raise temperatures for the towns on the Gulf of Oman by 6°C to 10°C. Winter temperatures are mild and pleasant, ranging between 15°C and 23°C.

Precipitation on the coasts and on the interior plains ranges from 20 to 100 millimeters a year and falls during mid- and late winter. Rainfall in the mountains, particularly over the Jabal Akhdar, is much higher and may reach 700 millimeters. Because the plateau of the Jabal Akhdar is porous limestone, rainfall seeps quickly through it, and the vegetation, which might be expected to be more lush, is extremely meager. A huge reservoir under the plateau provides springs for low-lying areas, however. Additionally, an enormous wadi channels water to these valleys, making the area agriculturally productive in years of good rainfall. Dhofar, benefiting from a southwest monsoon between June and September, receives heavier rainfall and has constantly running streams, which make the province Oman's most fertile area.

West of the coastal areas lies the tableland of central Oman. The Hajar Mountains form two ranges: the Western Hajar (Hajar al Gharbi) and the Eastern Hajar (Hajar ash Sharqi). They are divided by Wadi Samail, a valley that forms the traditional route between Muscat and the interior. The general elevation is about 1,200 meters, but the peaks of a high ridge known as Jabal Akhdar—which is considered a separate area but is actually part of the Western Hajar—rise to over 3,000 meters in some places. The Jabal Akhdar is the only home for a unique species of wild goat, the Arabian *tahr*. In hopes of saving this rare animal, Sultan Qaboos has declared part of the Jabal Akhdar a national park.

Behind the Western Hajar are two inland regions, Dhahirah (Az Zahirah) and inner Oman, separated by the lateral range of Jabal al Khawr. Both regions become stony desert before meeting the Rub al Khali. Adjoining the Eastern Hajar are the sandy regions of Ash Sharqiyah and Jalan, which also border the desert.

The desolate coastal tract from Jalan to Ras Naws has no specific name. Low hills and wastelands meet the sea for long distances. Halfway along this coast and about 15 kilometers offshore is the barren island of Masirah. It is about 70 kilometers long, virtually uninhabited, but distinguished by various military facilities (see Oman, ch. 7).

Dhofar Province extends from Ras ash Sharbatat to the border of the People's Democratic Republic of Yemen (Yemen

*Zawawi Mosque,
Muscat*

[Aden]). Its exact northern limit has never been defined but the territory claimed by the sultan includes the Wadi Muqshin, about 240 kilometers inland. The southwestern portion of Dhofar's coastal plain is regarded as one of the most beautiful in Arabia, and its capital, Salalah, was the permanent residence of the former sultan and the birthplace of Sultan Qaboos. The highest peaks are about 1,000 meters. At their base lies a narrow, pebbly desert adjoining the Rub al Khali to the north.

Population

As of mid-1984 the government had never carried out a census, and the data on population were educated guesses. In 1974 the government decided to use the figure of 1.5 million for purposes of formulating an economic plan, but domestic and foreign observers soon agreed that the figure was far too high.

In mid-1984 population estimates ranged from 950,000 to slightly over 1 million. Most observers agreed that the annual rate of growth was 3 percent or somewhat higher. There is wide disagreement over the number of resident aliens, ranging from estimates of about 25 percent to over 48 percent. On the one hand, *International Demographics* reported in April 1983 that almost 460,000 out of an estimated population of 978,000 were foreigners. On the other hand, Professor James A. Bill of the University of Texas suggested in early 1984 that approximately 250,000 out of a total population of 950,000 were foreigners.

Whatever the population, an estimated one-third lived in the Al Batinah coastal region between Muscat and Shinas. Dhofar Province remained sparsely settled, having only 50,000 to 90,000 people. About one-half the population lived in the small towns and villages of inner Oman. Fewer than 10,000 lived on the Musandam Peninsula.

Education

By mid-1984 government-supported educational facilities had greatly increased in both quantity and quality since the impoverished period before the accession of Sultan Qaboos in 1970. In early 1970 there were only three primary schools in the sultanate—in Mascat, Matrah, and Salalah. These were reserved for approximately 900 boys handpicked by the sultan from among many applicants. Additionally, in Muscat there was a religious institute with an enrollment of 50 boys, three private schools for Hyderabadis (Indians), and one American missionary school serving 50 foreign girls.

In the 1982–83 school year a reported 140,582 students attended 455 government schools that were staffed by 6,575 teachers (see table 28, Appendix A). The school system consisted of a primary level of six years, a preparatory level of three years, and a secondary level of three years. The government hoped to possess enough schools, equipment, and teachers by 1985 to provide primary education to all children at the primary level. Government data available in mid-1984 did not indicate what percentage of school-age children were in school.

The government reported in 1983 that 1,399 students were enrolled in foreign universities—369 in Egypt, 260 in the United States, 177 in Jordan, 147 in Britain, and 446 in other countries. Of the 311 female students, almost all went to institutions in neighboring Arab countries. Engineering, business administration, and science were the favored courses of study, accounting for 278, 261, and 153 students, respectively.

The overwhelming majority of teachers were foreigners. In the 1983–84 school year 709 out of 6,817 teachers were Omanis. Egyptians held 62 percent of the teaching positions, and Jordanians (probably of Palestinian origin), 12 percent. About 42 percent of the teachers were women.

Health and Medical Facilities

In 1984 there were neither morbidity nor mortality statistics available for Oman, but experts presumed that the average life span was between 45 and 50 years and that the infant mortality rate was about 130 per 1,000. The disease characteristics of the country were incompletely understood. Typical diseases of the Arabian Peninsula, such as trachoma, enteric diseases, and helminthiasis, were prevalent, particularly in Dhofar Province. In addition, poliomyelitis, tuberculosis, protein-calorie malnutrition, and diseases caused by vitamin deficiencies were common. There was also a small incidence of leprosy and cholera. Free medical facilities were provided for the population as quickly as the government could afford to build and staff them, but the government's explanation for the high incidence of disease before 1970 remained applicable in 1984 for many areas, particularly in the hinterland: "Diseases [are] caused mainly by primitive living conditions, non-existent sanitation and insufficient knowledge of personal hygiene."

In 1970 the country had only three small clinics, but by 1982 medical facilities included 14 hospitals, 19 health centers, and 63 dispensaries and medical centers. Together they provided about 2,000 beds. A 600-bed hospital bearing the sultan's name was scheduled for opening in 1986. It will contain the country's only psychiatric unit and will provide other special services not previously available in the sultanate.

The government announced in early 1984 that it was moving

ahead on the design and construction of 17 additional health facilities. The projected units will include six small health centers, two dispensaries, one maternal-child care center, three major health clinics, and an expansion of services in two existing hospitals.

The availability of competent medical staff remained a serious problem in a country with only a 14-year history of primary schools. Of the 379 physicians working in the country in 1982, only a handful were Omanis, and they had received their entire education outside the country. Most physicians, who on the average earned twice what they would in their homelands, were Pakistani or Indian. Several score Indians and Pakistanis maintained private practices, but most of them were government sponsored. Most nurses and medical technicians were also from India or Pakistan. Oman's sole nursing school, which was founded in 1971, had graduated 100 students by 1983—65 females and 35 males. The country had no medical school.

The Public Health Department of the Ministry of Health, formerly perceived as less important than the primary-care facilities, received increasing attention after 1974. Because a majority of the country's fatalities, particularly those seen at hospitals, are caused by diseases that are largely preventable, development of public health services received paramount attention during the late 1970s and early 1980s. In 1971 public health authorities were eventually able to control a cholera epidemic that had spread throughout the country. Since 1971 they have carried out mass immunizations for smallpox and other infectious diseases. Their area of responsibility has been enormous, including all inoculations and vaccinations, disease control, maternal and child care, health education, school health programs, sanitation, food hygiene control, antimalaria campaigns, and nutrition.

Economy

In 1984 the economy was heavily dominated by the oil industry, which accounted for 57 percent of the gross domestic product (GDP), 95 percent of export earnings, and about 90 percent of government revenues. This situation contrasted sharply with conditions before 1967, when the stagnant economy was based almost entirely on subsistence agriculture and fishing.

Commercial production and export of oil began in 1967, and the industry subsequently generated relatively large amounts of foreign exchange earnings and government revenues. These resources provided the means for rapid economic development during the 1970s and early 1980s. Because the oil industry had a later start in Oman than in neighboring countries, the latecomer was in a position to benefit from experiences of its neighbors in both the development of the oil industry and the general development of its economy.

When Sultan Qaboos seized power from his father in 1970, he immediately pressed forward an economic development and modernization program. Priority was devoted to building up the country's almost nonexistent infrastructure. In the early 1970s substantial progress was made in developing an economic and social infrastructure, mainly in the form of roads, a new deep-water port, an international airport, electricity-generating plants, and desalination plants, as well as schools, hospitals, and low-cost housing.

By 1983 the country had 2,200 kilometers of asphalt roads; there had been only 10 kilometers in 1970; another 14,700 kilometers were classified as motorable tracks. A deep-water port, Mina Qaboos, built in Matrah during the early 1970s and later expanded, had 12 berths within a protected harbor. A specialized oil port, Mina al Fahl, near Mina Qaboos, handled all of the country's oil exports. In the south, near Salalah, a smaller general cargo port, Mina Raysut, featuring six berths, was developed to serve the Dhofar region. An international airport was built at As Sib, and modern airport facilities have also been contructed near Salalah. Some 960 kilometers of crude oil pipeline and 390 kilometers of natural gas lines were in operation by 1983.

The electric-generating capacity was increased substantially, reaching 611,300 kilowatts in 1982. Numerous government office buildings were erected in the 1970s and early 1980s. By 1983 two desalination plants had been completed. A number of new hotels were constructed, and a major one was under construction in 1984 at Seeb (As Sib) International Airport.

In 1974 the government established the Development Council and gave it the responsibility for approving a national development plan for the 1976–80 period, defining overall strategy, and setting priorities. In 1984 the Development Council was composed of the governor of Dhofar and the ministers of foreign affairs, communications, interior, health, commerce and industry, agriculture and fisheries, petroleum and minerals, social affairs and labor, and land affairs and municipalities (see Government Institutions, this ch.). In contrast to the emphasis on infrastructure during the first half of the decade, priority for the 1976–80 period was given to income-generating projects. Each ministry was responsible for development projects within its sphere.

Oman has sought technical guidance from numerous foreign sources. Emphasis has been placed on resource surveys and industry feasibility studies. Most have been carried out by well-known international corporations. For technical aid Oman has turned to the United Nations Development Programme (UNDP). Over the years numerous UNDP experts have served in the country on such diverse assignments as agriculture, education, telecommunications, public administration, and postal services.

Although Oman's economy is in many respects market oriented because of the income it receives from oil, the government accounts for over one-half of the national income and spending (see table 29, Appendix A). The momentum for economic growth has therefore been provided primarily by government development programs, and government ownership and control predominates in most large-scale enterprises, such as oil, utilities, ports, and mining. But the government generally prefers joint ventures to wholly government-owned firms, and its policy is to leave the establishment and operation of most small-scale business to private enterprise. Private merchants have tended to broaden their activities beyond traditional trading to real estate, repair facilities, and light assembly plants.

The government welcomes foreign investments, but participation by Omani citizens in several kinds of business is required by law. Omani participation in capital and profits may not be less than two-thirds for press and information companies; 51 percent for public utility, real estate, shipping, and airline companies; and 35 percent for other business endeavors. The sultan has the power to decree exemptions, and in the mid-1970s foreign firms operating in Oman under contract with the government were exempt.

The country's foreign exchange and trading systems favored the growth of private enterprise. Neither import nor export licenses were required, and there were no controls on the exchange of currencies. The gold content of the Omani rial had not been changed since it was instituted as the national currency in 1970. In early 1984 US$1 equaled OR 0.3454 (for value of the Omani rial—see Glossary).

Although it made its first contribution to the Omani economy as late as 1967, oil accounted for an estimated 57 percent of the nation's GDP in 1982; fewer than 5,000 were employed in this sector, however. Apart from oil, in 1982 the largest contribution to GDP—12 percent—was made by wholesale and retail trade and hotels. Public administration and defense accounted for 11 percent, construction 6 percent, and transportation and communications 3 percent.

Because of the acute shortage of trained Omanis, the country's economic progress has largely depended on expatriate managers and workers. As of 1982 the government had issued about 187,000 labor cards for expatriates. Although the expatriate labor force had increased sharply during the 1970s and 1980s, the government was pressing for gradual replacement of expatriates by Omani citizens, and by 1984 some trained Omanis had returned from abroad to take up newly developed employment opportunities.

Because of their isolation from the rest of the world, Omanis until recently felt little need to collect statistics. Therefore, the quantitative estimates of the various sectors of the Omani economy must be used with caution.

Agriculture

Although agriculture in 1984 was overshadowed by the dynamic and prosperous oil industry, at least half of the population remained directly dependent on farming and livestock for its livelihood. Agriculture has declined in relative sectorial importance, as indicated by the fact that in 1967 agriculture and fisheries together contributed about 34 percent of GDP, but by the early 1980s they represented a mere 2 percent. Before the oil era, farm products dominated export trade, but by 1980 they accounted for less than 2 percent of total exports.

Subsistence farming dominates Omani agriculture. In an effort to assist farmers in improving the distribution and storage of local produce, the government created the Public Authority for Marketing of Agricultural Produce. Farming units are almost universally small, and most family holdings consist of two or more separate plots.

Farmland ownership and tenancy rights continued to be based largely on tradition. Three main forms of land tenure prevail: short-term lease of land for the growing of annual crops, long-term lease for the planting of tree crops, and full ownership. In addition, nomadic herdsmen possess a vague but generally recognized right to move their herds over certain areas. Traditional tribal grazing ranges often cross the ill-defined national frontiers. Some increase in absentee landlordism occurred in the 1970s as a result of investments in land by owners of newly acquired wealth.

About 40,000 hectares of land—little more than 0.1 percent

of the land surface—was under cultivation in the mid-1980s. Approximately the same quantity of additional land may be cultivable without discovery of major new water resources. Water for irrigation is essential for crop production because rainfall is scanty.

Nearly 50 percent of all presently cultivated land is used for production of dates—estimated at 38,000 tons in 1977, when they accounted for about one-fourth of the value of all crops harvested. Dates are an important item in the Omani diet and are traditionally an export product. Date cultivation, however, requires heavy watering and is low in profitability. Yields declined during the 1970s.

Alfalfa, which is cut and used as forage for livestock, ranked second in area and accounted for nearly one-half the value of all crop production. Alfalfa production in 1975 was estimated at 140,000 tons. The crop is extremely important to the mixed crop-livestock systems that prevail in most areas.

About 10 percent of the cultivated area was devoted to limes, the principal non-oil export commodity. About the same acreage was in onions. Between 3 and 4 percent of the cultivated area was in wheat; annual production totaled about 5,000 tons. Other crops included bananas, coconuts, grapes, mangoes, oranges, papayas, sorghum, millet, tobacco, okra, cucumbers, eggplant, peppers, melons, and tomatoes.

Although estimates of Oman's livestock population vary, it appears that in 1978 there were approximately 217,000 goats, 140,000 cattle, 73,000 sheep, 26,000 donkeys, and 16,000 camels. There were also some horses. Until recently many livestock were owned by nomads, but as these migrant people have become more sedentary, herds have declined rapidly.

Goats were raised throughout the country for milk and meat, and sheep for meat and wool. The hides of both were valuable by-products. Donkeys were used primarily for transportation; camels were used for both transportation and plowing. In the latter function, however, camels have been largely replaced by tractors provided by the government for a nominal rent. Cattle were kept primarily for milk production. Dhofar Province was the cattle raising area of Oman; elsewhere very few were seen.

There are five distinct agricultural regions. These are the interior oases; the valleys and the high plateau of the eastern region; the Al Batinah coast; Dhofar Province in the south, along the narrow coastal strip from the border with Yemen (Aden) to Ras Naws and the mountains to the north; and the Musandam Peninsula.

Interior farming areas account for over one-half of the country's cultivated land. Rainfall, though greater than along the coast, is insufficient for the production of crops. Most of the water for irrigation is obtained by the use of the millennia-old *falaj* system. This system consists of a vertical shaft dug from the surface to reach water in porous rock. From the bottom of this shaft a gently sloping tunnel is dug to tap the water and allow it to flow to a point on the surface at a lower level or into a cistern or underground pool from which it can be lifted by bucket or pump.

A *falaj* may be many kilometers in length and requires numerous additional vertical shafts in order to provide fresh air to the tunneler and to permit the removal of the excavated rock and soil. A *falaj* requires a tremendous expenditure of human labor for maintenance as well as for construction. Because of the dwindling labor supply for such work during the 1970s and early 1980s, the condition of the *falaj* system deteriorated. Beginning in 1981 the government undertook a major task of repairing and rebuilding the system in an effort to increase by 30 percent the quantity of water available to cultivated areas in 1985. With some modernization the *falaj* will apparently continue to play an important role.

Subsistence farming by 1984 continued in the interior, although the growing opportunities to market agricultural produce, particularly in oil-producing areas, were causing some change in farm practices. Nevertheless, the leading crop was dates. Wheat, millet, and sorghum were grown as well. Alfalfa for forage was extremely important because practically every family kept a few goats to produce milk and meat for family consumption. Donkeys and sheep were also common. Many men from rural areas of the interior, searching for employment, left the farm and their families behind; they were unlikely to return to farming.

The cooler climate on the high plateau of the Jabal Akhdar allows production in its more favored spots of apricots, grapes, peaches, and walnuts. These products were transported down steep trails, by donkey, to the markets of the small towns at the foot of the mountains.

The Al Batinah coastal plain, accounting for nearly two-fifths of the land under cultivation, is the most concentrated farming area of the country. The annual rainfall along the coast is meager, but moisture falling on the mountains percolates through permeable strata to the coastal strip and provides a source of underground water only about two meters below the surface. Diesel motors are used to pump water from these shallow wells for irrigation.

By 1984 the water table along the Al Batinah coast dropped to a low level, and the salt content of the water in the wells increased, thus reducing the quality of water significantly. The joint causes of this were the cultivation of land too close to the sea and the pumping of more well water than was being resupplied by nature, thus permitting seawater to seep in. The use of medium-lift irrigation pumps had increased twentyfold in 20 years. In an effort to remedy the problem, the government tried to persuade villagers to move their fields and wells back from the coast.

The section of Dhofar Province inland from Salalah has more rainfall than any other region. Good, natural grazing is made possible by the monsoon rains that move inland from the Arabian Sea from June to September. As a consequence, in the early 1980s some 50,000 head of cattle were maintained in the area. Although vegetation dries up quickly after the seasonal rains, cattle can get along by grazing on dried grass until the next rainy season brings renewed growth.

Insufficient drinking water for stock during the long dry season has limited the growth of the cattle industry. In its attempt to overcome this handicap, the government included as part of its development program a project for drilling wells at key centers.

Little more than 2 percent of the cultivated area of the country is in Dhofar. This land is largely some 8,000 hectares on the Salalah plain. Perhaps the greatest improvement in Omani agriculture took place in Dhofar during the 1970s. Coconuts were the most important crop. Alfalfa, sorghum, millet, and bananas made up the bulk of the remaining farm production, but such vegetables as okra and tomatoes were also grown. For millennia Dhofar was the world's leading source of frankincense, an incense resin that is obtained by cutting the bark of the low, squat trees of the *Boswellia* genus and collecting and drying the gum that oozes from the gash.

The rudiments of experimental and extension programs in agriculture were launched in Oman in the first half of the 1970s. Experimental farms were in operation at Rumays, Suhar, Al Ghubrah, and Al Khaburah on the Al Batinah coast, at Nazwa in the interior, and at Rabat and Salalah in Dhofar. In 1983 there were 48 administrative centers in Dhofar, designed to provide farm advisory service and other services to rural areas.

Because cattle have been kept mainly for milk, the practice in Dhofar has been to slaughter bull calves shortly after birth. In its development program for that province, the government established a cattle-feeding center at Salalah. Bullocks were purchased from the herdsmen, castrated, and raised for meat. It is believed that, by this means, Dhofar can produce enough beef to satisfy the nation's requirements and that Oman can even export

Fishing dhow near Khasab
Courtesy
Aramco World Magazine

beef to nearby countries. In 1977 the feeding center became a joint venture as government sought to attract investment capital into agricultural development.

One of the primary goals of the government under the 1981–85 development plan was to reduce the country's growing dependence on food imports. It has been estimated that in 1980 Oman's import share of various staple articles of food consumption was 100 percent of rice, 90 percent of wheat, and 40 percent of vegetables and meat; a generation earlier the country was virtually self-sufficient in food. The principal cause of this trend has been the migration of labor from the farms to other types of employment. Opportunities for introducing laborsaving production methods were limited by the small size of most farms and by the nature of the crops grown. Nevertheless, under the 1981–85 development plan the government sought to encourage farm mechanization and to reduce the movement of agricultural labor from the farm by making rural life more profitable and satisfying. Given the relatively attractive opportunities for nonagricultural employment and the constraints on agricultural development, such as the lack of water, it seemed unlikely that Oman would be able to reduce significantly its heavy dependence on food imports in the near future. Probably the best prospects for increased ag-

327

ricultural production were in more intensive cultivation of existing producing areas rather than in expansion of cropping into new
lands.

The 1976–80 development plan allocated 4.4 percent of total
government expenditures to the Ministry of Agriculture and
Fisheries and lagged in achieving its targets. In the 1981–85 plan
10.3 percent of government expenditures were allocated to this
ministry.

Fisheries

Fishing has historically been second only to farming as an
economic activity in Oman. Both the Gulf of Oman and the Arabian Sea abound in a variety of fish within easy reach of the country's 1,700-kilometer coastline. Among the plentiful kinds of fish
are sardines, bluefish, mackerel, shark, and tuna. Abalone,
lobsters, and oysters reportedly are also abundant.

Fish are important in the diets of the peoples of the coast and
of the interior. Although the fresh fish are available only to those
living near the sea, dried and salted fish are sold throughout the
country. Dried sardine meal has long been used for fertilizer and
cattle feed.

Fishermen harvested their catch in the waters near the
coast, using a traditional, small, seagoing canoe, to which an out-
board motor had been added. By 1975 more than 80 percent of
the wooden fishing craft had been motorized. Ready-made nylon
nets have largely replaced handcrafted cotton nets.

The annual catch was about 84,000 tons in 1982, and sardines
were by far the predominant species caught. The tonnage of fish
caught in the early 1980s was lower than during the mid-1960s because many fishermen turned to more remunerative employment
provided by the oil boom. The number of fishermen declined
from 15,000 in early 1970 to only 7,000 by the end of 1980. Although the catch declined as a result of fewer fishermen, local demand expanded. As a consequence, exports of salted and dried
fish, once substantial, became negligible.

In its long-term economic planning the government has
stressed modernizing and expanding the fishing industry and developing it into an important export industry that will provide expanded employment opportunities. A foreign consulting firm,
Mardela International, was employed to investigate the fishing
potential. After a four-year survey, the consultants confirmed that
there were substantial resources in the seas bordering Oman and
suggested the possibility of a tenfold increase in the annual catch.

The first major fishing project was launched in April 1976, when a consortium of Japanese firms was awarded a three-year concession for deep-water fishing off Oman's southeast coast. Within two years, however, the Japanese pulled out and were replaced by a South Korean company. Under the agreement with the South Koreans, 65 percent of the catch is turned over to the Omanis.

In 1980 responsibility for the concession agreements, government trawlers, and land facilities was transferred to the newly formed National Fisheries Corporation. This company, 60 percent owned by private Omani investors, 20 percent by the government, and 20 percent by traditional fishermen, became the principal agency for fisheries development. In 1983 it acquired its first trawler, which joined four chartered trawlers operated by the company.

In the late 1970s the Ministry of Agriculture and Fisheries provided inducements to traditional fishermen to remain in their occupations by distributing more than 1,000 aluminum craft and motors on a grant-loan basis. Later, low-interest loans became available to fishermen from the Bank for Agriculture and Fisheries.

Despite various forms of governmental assistance for fisheries development during the 1970s and early 1980s, signs of progress were hard to find. Just as it had occurred in the agricultural sector, manpower tended to shift to fields offering better immediate opportunities. Nevertheless, in the long term the abundant fish resources available to Omanis should provide the basis for significant development.

Industry

At the beginning of the 1970s there were no modern industries in Oman, with the exception of the oil industry. By 1984, however, some light industries had been established. In operation were date-packaging plants in Nazwa and Rustaq, each of which had daily capacities of 50 tons. New factories manufacturing furniture, aluminum products, soft drinks, milk products, flour, fish products, and industrial gases had also gone into operation. In 1984 Russayl Industrial Estate, covering 90 hectares and located 15 kilometers from Seeb International Airport, was under development, and 11 factories—seven of them new—were about to move into the area. One of the major occupants of the estate was the Oman Cement Company, which had a US$180 million investment in a cement plant, the annual capacity of which was

624,000 tons. The plant reportedly began operation in late 1983. Another cement plant with a planned capacity of 210,000 tons a year was nearing completion in 1983 at Raysut, near Salalah.

Still operating by primitive methods were a few small-scale, traditional industries, such as the production of ghee (clarified butter) and the drying of fish, dates, and limes. Some handicraft industries remained, but their importance was steadily declining. Silversmiths continued to ply their trade in almost every town. Bahlah was an important center for the production of household pottery, the capital area and its surroundings were the location of goldsmiths, and a few areas turned out low-quality, handmade cloth from locally produced wool. Boats were still being built in the coastal towns.

The government strongly encouraged private sector development as well as joint ventures between government and private firms. Foreign investments were actively being sought for vegetable oil and soap, ceramic products, nails and screws, paints and varnishes, plastic products, and others. An aluminum extrusion plant costing US$15 million was, in 1983, apparently soon to be established in Russayl Industrial Estate.

Development of new industry will probably be slow and for some time will be oriented toward the home market. The government will, however, undoubtedly press hard to diversify the economy, and small industry will provide some further opportunities for diversification.

Oil Industry

Discovery of oil in Oman occurred late, and proven reserves were small. Nevertheless, the petroleum industry dominated the economy. The oil sector contributed about 57 percent of GDP, about 95 percent of foreign exchange earnings, and about 90 percent of government revenues. Oil production peaked in 1976 at 135 million barrels, declined from 1977 to 1980, but rose thereafter as new producing areas were developed (see table 30, Appendix A). Proven reserves at the end of 1982 were estimated at almost 3 billion barrels, sufficient to permit 23 years of output at about 337,000 barrels a day, the production rate in that year.

Oil prospecting began in 1937, when the first concession agreement was signed with Petroleum Concessions, a company formed by the owners of Iraq Petroleum Company (IPC). In 1951 the concessionaire's name was changed to Petroleum Development (Oman) (PDO). After several years of costly and unsuccessful exploratory drilling, most IPC partners wanted to get out. In

1960 Royal Dutch Shell bought 85 percent of PDO; Participations and Explorations (Partex—a Gulbenkian foundation) held the remaining 15 percent. In 1967 a French company bought 10 percent of PDO from Partex. In December 1973 the government of Oman, following the participation agreements negotiated by several Gulf countries, acquired a 25-percent share of PDO. In July 1974 the government's share was raised to 60 percent, effective January 1, 1974; in mid-1984 the government's participation remained at 60 percent, and three foreign companies owned 40 percent. A management committee consisting of two government and four oil company representatives operated PDO. This company accounted for more than 95 percent of Oman's crude oil production in 1984. The other producers were a group of foreign companies.

Most of Oman's land area was included in the original 1937 concession. In 1951 PDO relinquished its rights in Dhofar Province, and the sultan then assigned the rights to a friend, an American archaeologist who was unfamiliar with the oil industry but who nevertheless was able to interest several American companies in the concession. Oil was discovered in 1957 in eastern Dhofar, but it was too heavy for fuel and was primarily suited for road construction. In isolated Dhofar it possessed no commercial value. By the late 1960s more than US$50 had been invested in this concession, without any return. In 1969 PDO again obtained concession rights in eastern Dhofar Province and subsequently disovered good-quality oil but not in commercial quantities. In the early 1980s PDO developed the Mamul, Rima, and other fields in southern Oman, producing about 100,000 to 150,000 barrels per day (bpd).

The new finds encouraged other international companies to prospect for oil in Oman. Among the four companies that took up concessions in 1981 was a group headed by a French company. This consortium included the Kuwait Petroleum Corporation (KPC), the International Energy Development Corporation, and the Sumitomo Corporation of Japan. It undertook exploration in eastern Oman. Japex Oman Company signed a concession agreement in 1982. The same year another Japanese consortium, Japan Petroleum Development Company (Oman), signed a production-sharing agreement with the government. Amoco Oman Oil Company was granted two concessions in Oman's northern mountains. PDO's development expenditure under the 1981–85 plan was estimated at US$2.7 billion, and a total of US$555 million was projected for the other oil companies.

Oil in commercial quantities was discovered by PDO in

1964, about 240 kilometers southwest of Muscat. The main fields were located at Fahud, Natih, Yibal, and Huwaisah adjacent to the Rub al Khali (see fig. 9). When the fields were developed, PDO constructed a pipeline to Mina al Fahl, where a tank farm and a deep-water offshore-loading terminal were built. In 1983 the pipeline capacity was about 400,000 bpd, and the sea terminal consisted of three offshore, single-buoy moorings; a project was under way to replace the 15-year-old pipeline by 1986, after which it would have a capacity of 650,000 bpd.

A proposal was presented to the Gulf Cooperation Council (GCC) in 1983 to build a pipeline from Kuwait to the Omani port of Salalah and to construct a 200,000 bpd refinery at that port (see Appendix C). A principal motivation behind the proposal was concern over the safety of shipping in the Persian Gulf and through the Strait of Hormuz. No decision had been announced as of mid-1984.

Production and regular export of crude oil began in August 1967. Production and export amounted to 20.9 million barrels in 1967 and 87.9 million barrels in 1968. By 1976 production reached 135 million tons, after which a decline occurred until 1981, when the trend was reversed, primarily because new fields in south Oman began to produce oil. Production in 1983 was expected to increase to about 125 million barrels, all by PDO, the only producing company.

Japan was the main purchaser of Oman's crude oil, accounting for over half the exports from 1977 through 1981 and 40 percent in 1982. Singapore ranked second, with 22 percent in 1982. The Netherlands, the Federal Republic of Germany (West Germany), and the United States each took from 5 to 7 percent of oil exports in that year. Because all petroleum exports were crude oil, exports to refining centers, such as Singapore and the Netherlands were not necessarily for use in those countries. Although Oman was not a member of the Organization of Petroleum Exporting Countries (OPEC), the government implemented most OPEC decisions on royalties, income taxes, and participation (see Appendix B).

Income tax payments by PDO were the main source of oil revenues until 1974. Participation agreements with PDO gave the government a 60-percent share, effective January 1, 1974. In 1974 the government paid PDO the equivalent of US$110 million for its share and paid an additional US$60 million for company operations during that year. In return, the government received 60 percent of the crude oil produced, the bulk of which was sold back to PDO for marketing abroad, forming the main source of oil revenue. In 1981 the government's oil revenues consisted of 49 percent from direct sales, 18 percent from buy-back sales, and 33 percent from royalty and income tax. The participation agreements sharply diminished the importance of royalties and taxes as sources of oil revenues.

The quality of Omani crude oil from the older fields of the central area is good, having an American Petroleum Institute gravity ranging between 30 degrees and 34 degrees, less than 1 percent sulfur content, and little wax. Shipping distances from Oman to major markets were shorter than from the oil exporters of the Gulf. Omani fields, however, required considerable gas and water injection to maintain reservoir pressure. This factor, the relatively small scale of production, and the need for extensive pipelines combined to make Oman's crude among the most costly to produce in the Middle East.

In the 1970s the government made plans for major industrial projects based on hydrocarbon resources. A 50,000 bpd refinery was completed in 1982 at Mina al Fahl. Its purpose was to meet domestic needs for petroleum products. The refinery was operated by the Oman Refinery Company, which was 99 percent owned by the government and 1 percent by the Central Bank of Oman. Refined products were sold to private companies engaged in distribution of these products in Oman.

Additional industrial projects were developed, based largely on natural gas. In 1983 reserves of natural gas were estimated at 6.3 trillion cubic feet. Most of the gas produced was associated with oil production and was reinjected into the oil fields—particularly Fahud—to boost production. In Yibal a natural gas liquids plant derived 3,500 bpd of gasoline from gas. A new pipeline bringing associated gas from PDO's fields to the capital area came into operation in 1978. This led to the use of gas in the power station and desalination plant at Al Ghubrah, construction of two additional gas liquids plants, and the use of gas at Russayl Industrial Estate. A spur line of the gas pipeline was built from PDO's fields to Suhar, thus providing energy for a copper project that began operations in 1983.

Other Mineral Resources

In 1983 Oman became a producer of copper, chromite, and limestone, thus realizing important development plans that had been initiated several years earlier and signaling some success in diversification of the economy. Although the accomplishments were modest, they encouraged further development in this field.

Surveys in the 1970s by Prospection of Canada indicated copper reserves of 12 million tons. Oman's main copper reserves are at Bayah, Arga, and Liasail in the Suhar area on the Al Batinah coast. The resources there, containing 11 million tons of ore with a copper content of 2.1 percent, were opened in 1979; processing of the ore began in 1983. The Suhar complex had facilities for crushing, concentrating, smelting, pelletizing, and refining the material. Production capacity for copper ingots was about 20,000 tons annually. The government-owned Oman Mining Company, which operated the complex, identified other sizable reserves of copper ore in the general area, and further exploration was continuing. The company expected to begin exports of some of the product in late 1983 through the new port of Majis Kabirah, 17 kilometers south of Suhar. Also, the organization was studying the prospects for downstream (see Glossary) products, such as copper tubes and wire.

Chromite production by the Oman Mining Company also began in 1983 in the Rajmi and Nakhl areas. A new road to carry the ore from the mines to the port of Majis Kabirah was nearing completion in 1984. Overseas markets for the product were being explored.

Limestone for cement production was mined in both northern and southern areas to feed the Oman Cement Company plant in the Russayl Industrial Estate and the Raysut Cement Corporation's plant near Salalah. Tile and marble were produced for local construction. Some observers regarded marble as having a high export potential.

Surveys have indicated deposits of numerous other materials—asbestos, coal, iron ore, lead, manganese, nickel, silver, and zinc. Whether commercially exploitable quantities of any of these materials exist will not be known until further surveys have been completed.

Water and Power

The country's water resources are a key to its economic future, and development will require much more water than has been available in the past. Rainfall is so scant that crop production is not possible without irrigation. Livestock raising is restricted to areas having a dependable supply of drinking water for animals. Any substantial expansion of agricultural production will therefore necessitate the development of new sources of water. Industrial expansion, the development of tourism, and an increasing standard of living will combine to boost the requirements for water.

Rural Omani

Several preliminary surveys have been carried out, but in 1984 there were still few data on the water resources of Oman. Such survey data as were available led to the tentative conclusion that the country does have some valuable underground water deposits, especially in the interior, but the discoveries to date have not been in the quantities hoped for.

The government has pushed projects to make more water available. Wells for village water supplies have been drilled throughout the country, and supplies in the capital area and in Salalah have been expanded and improved. Plans have been drawn up for catching floodwater at the bases of the mountains before it flows into the sea and for improving the efficiency of the *falaj* system by making it less leaky, but by 1984 little had been done.

By 1984 much had been accomplished toward improving and expanding the water distribution and sewerage systems of the capital area and in Salalah and Raysut. Early in 1983 the second desalination plant in Oman began operation at Al Ghubrah in the capital area. This plant had a capacity to produce 6 million gallons of drinking water daily, based on conversion of seawater to salt-free water.

In 1969 Oman had only one electric power generating station; it produced one megawatt of electricity for the capital area. By August 1982 the Riyam and Al Ghubrah power plants of the capital area produced over 290 megawatts of electricity. A third power plant was expected to be completed in the Russayl Industrial Estate in 1984. The principal fuel for power generation was natural gas. Electricity was introduced in Salalah in 1970, on Masirah Island in 1976, and in Nazwa, Sumail, Saham, and Ibri in 1978. Two electric power stations in the Musandam Peninsula were completed in 1982.

Tourism

Oman has the potential for developing a tourist industry, but as of 1984 the policy of the government was to proceed cautiously with such a program. Government officials, particularly Sultan Qaboos, have expressed concern that mass tourism may jeopardize Oman's cultural heritage. Thus the intention was to approach this field step by step and to assess carefully visitor responses and the effects on the local community.

The Department of Tourism of the Ministry of Commerce and Industry was implementing a comprehensive program for tourism development in 1983, placing greater emphasis on domestic tourism than tourism from abroad. Included in the program were construction of a four-star hotel at Seeb International Airport, four rest houses along the Muscat-Salalah road, a chain of gasoline stations, a recreation center at Dawwah, and a national museum at Bait al Falaj.

Tourist attractions are many, for the country's winter climate is nearly ideal. There are vast stretches of clean, sandy beaches, colorful towns, historical sites, a variety of natural scenery, a growing number of good hotels, and superb fishing.

Public Finance

Before the accession of Qaboos, virtually no distinction was made between the finances of the sultan himself and those of the sultanate. Oman's first government budget, therefore, dates back only to 1971.

Between 1978 and 1982, budgeted revenues increased from OR502 million to OR1.2 billion, current expenditures more than doubled, from OR437 million to OR970 million, while development expenditures more than tripled, from OR123 million to OR395 million (see table 31, Appendix A). Deficits occurred in

1978, 1980, and 1982, but surpluses developed in 1979 and 1981. Provisional figures issued in January 1984 indicated that both revenue and expenditures increased sharply in 1983 from those of 1982 and resulted in a further deficit in 1983. Moreover, a budget deficit was projected for 1984 (see table 32, Appendix A).

Petroleum revenues, representing 90 percent of total revenues, increased in each year from 1978 to 1981 but declined to OR1.1 billion in 1982 as a result of a reduction in international oil prices. According to provisional data, oil revenue in 1983 reached a record level of OR1.2 billion.

In 1982 revenues from non-oil sources accounted for about 10 percent of the total. They consisted mainly of customs duties levied on imports, income tax on corporate bodies, charges for public utilities, and investment income on government assets placed abroad. Although a relatively small part of the total, revenues from these sources seem destined to increase as a result of anticipated growth in imports and rapid expansion of the commercial sector. Nevertheless, in anticipation of the time when oil revenues will decline, analysts have suggested that it would appear prudent for Oman to widen its tax base by introducing personal income taxes and property taxes.

The high level of expenditures for defense placed a heavy burden on the government's financial resources in the 1978–82 period. In 1982 defense and security represented 60 percent of current expenditures, or 42 percent of total expenditures. Despite the termination of hostilities in Dhofar in the mid-1970s, defense expenditures continued at relatively high levels into the early 1980s.

Money, Credit, and Prices

In 1984 the Omani rial, which replaced the Gulf Indian rupee in May 1970, continued to be a freely convertible currency. The gold content of the rial has remained unchanged since its introduction. The rial was in effect pegged to the United States dollar, whereas the exchange rates for other currencies were based on the London market (see table 33, Appendix A).

Under a banking law issued in November 1974, the government in April 1975 established the Central Bank of Oman. The institution replaced the Oman Currency Board, which since 1972 had been responsible for issuing currency, managing government accounts, and carrying out banking transactions with commercial banks and international institutions. The Central Bank, capitalized at OR2 million, was placed under the management of a board of governors appointed by the sultan. The board possessed full authority to discharge all the functions required for the operation of the Central Bank and the supervision of commercial banking.

The Central Bank's responsibilities included the management of the government's foreign assets. It could make advances to the government to cover temporary deficiencies in recurrent revenues (up to the maxima of 90 days and an estimated 10 percent of recurrent revenues). It could purchase government treasury bills and securities with a maximum maturity of 10 years. It also could make advances to commercial banks and was empowered to buy, sell, discount, and rediscount commercial paper.

The number of commercial banks operating in Oman increased from three in 1972 to 14 in 1976 and 25 in 1982. Ten were subsidiaries of foreign-owned banks. The 25 commercial banks in 1982 had 162 branches, many of which were in the capital area. Under the 1974 banking law, in addition to the initial capital requirement of OR500,000 and the reserve requirement of 5 percent of deposits, each bank must maintain an interest-bearing account with the Central Bank of 0.1 percent of its resources, including, for foreign institutions, the total assets of the parent bank. The minimum deposit is OR50,000 and the maximum OR500,000. In 1982 the Central Bank issued regulations setting a maximum limit for foreign exchange exposure for each bank. In 1980 the Central Bank set targets for "Omanization"—a government policy of replacing foreign personnel with Omanis—in commercial banks.

Commercial bank lending increased from OR208 million in 1976 to OR407 million in 1982. Credits to the private sector increased from OR122 million in 1976 to OR402 million in 1982. Loans to the government, which were 44 percent of commercial lending in 1976, were only 1 percent of the total in 1982. Deposits rose sharply. About one-half of the lending to the private sector has been channeled to import trade, 16 percent to construction, 15 percent to personal loans, and 4 percent to wholesale and retail trade.

The Oman Development Bank was created in 1976, primarily to make loans for industrial development. The government owns 40 percent of the shares, regional and foreign institutions own another 40 percent, and 20 percent is open for private Omani subscription. In 1981 the bank approved OR5.6 million financing for 31 projects.

The Bank for Agriculture and Fisheries was established in

1981, and the government owned 98.9 percent of the capital. Its purpose is to make short-, medium-, and long-term loans to individuals or enterprises for financing activities in agriculture and fisheries. By mid-1983 the bank had six branches and planned to open eight more by 1985. The Oman Housing Bank, established in 1977, has grown steadily and in 1981 made loans totaling OR30 million. Loans to low- and medium-income borrowers represented 67 percent of the total value of loans in 1981. Beginning in 1981 interest rates on mortgages were subsidized by the government. Rates were as low as 2 percent per annum for low-income borrowers.

Oman experienced a high rate of inflation in the 1970–76 period. During the 1975–76 period inflation ran at rates of 15 to 20 percent but fell below 10 percent from 1978 to 1979, mainly as a result of the controls on growth of government expenditures. The rate accelerated to 10 to 15 percent from 1980 to 1981, principally because of increases in rents, but slowed again to well under 5 percent in 1982. A decline in import prices in 1982 exerted downward pressure on domestic prices, and the housing shortage also eased considerably in 1982.

Foreign Trade and Balance of Payments

Oil shipments have accounted for the bulk of the value of Oman's export trade. Development goods and defense items dominated imports; increasing personal incomes, however—especially among the large number of expatriates—resulted in a rapid boost in the demand for, and importation of, consumer goods in the early 1980s.

Nearly all of Oman's petroleum is exported as crude oil; only a small proportion of the production is refined locally for the domestic market. Oil exports for 1982 were 119 million barrels, down from 134 million in 1976 but higher than in some more recent years. Payments to the Oman government for the oil extracted totaled OR1.4 billion in 1982 and OR1.5 billion in 1981.

Exports of commodities other than oil totaled OR7.7 million in 1982, a substantial increase over previous years. Frozen fish accounted for nearly one-half of the total value of non-oil exports, and dried limes were in second place. Other non-oil exports were flour, fresh fruits and vegetables, dried dates, and tobacco.

In 1982 shipments to Dubai and Abu Dhabi in the UAE accounted for a high proportion of the total non-oil exports. India and Iraq were the only other export destinations. Small amounts were shipped to Bahrain, Iran, Kuwait, Qatar, and Yemen (Aden) in some years.

Oman's recorded imports of OR927 million in 1982 probably understated actual imports by at least 50 percent. Imports of defense goods were not reported, and a substantial amount of other imports were unrecorded.

Although a few light industries have been established, Oman must still import most industrial goods and a growing proportion of its food requirements. Since 1973 the category of machinery and transport equipment has been the leading one, but there has been a phenomenal increase in imports of all categories.

Britain, traditionally Oman's leading source of imports, moved back to first place in 1975 after being displaced for some years by the UAE. In 1982 Western Europe was the leading source of imports, but Japan and India were important Asian suppliers.

Nonmetallic mineral manufactures—largely cement—were the leading import category by weight in 1982, totaling over 1 million tons. Other outstanding imports included 684,000 tons of petroleum products, 262,000 tons of iron and steel, 221,000 tons of cereals and cereal preparations, and 117,000 tons of wood, lumber, and cork. A wide range of food and consumer products, as well as industrial goods, were imported.

Oman's balance of payments position has undergone changes essentially in response to changes in oil export receipts and, to a similar extent, to the growth in import payments (see table 34, Appendix A). After recording a deficit of US$100 million in 1978, mainly owing to a fall in oil export receipts, the overall balance turned into increasing surpluses during the next three years, culminating in a peak surplus of US$1.4 billion in 1981 and ending with a somewhat reduced surplus in 1982. Oman is highly dependent on imports of consumer and capital goods and maintains no import controls. Total import payments grew at an average annual rate of 23 percent in the 1973–81 period, much lower than the rate of the increase in export receipts.

The services and private account is characterized by substantial outflows of workers' and profit remittances and payments for other services, which together rose on average by 24 percent during the 1979–82 period. In addition to surpluses on current account, Oman has also enjoyed surpluses on its capital account, resulting from inflows of official loans and grants and of investments in the oil sector. Despite outflows of private capital, the surpluses on current and capital accounts were large enough to produce overall surpluses that helped build up official reserves to a level of US$3.3 billion at the end of 1982, equivalent to more than 12 months of imports.

His Majesty Sultan Qaboos
Courtesy Ministry of
Information, Oman

Government and Politics

On July 23, 1970, a coup d'état ended the 38-year rule of Sultan Said bin Taimur Al Bu Said. The ouster had been organized around his son, Qaboos, with the support of British officers seconded to the Oman army. There was a minimum of bloodshed. The sultan was wounded, but after hospitalization he was allowed to reside in comfortable exile in London, until his death in 1972. Although there had been no popular uprising associated with the coup, the change of rulers was greeted enthusiastically by Omanis, who had grown tired of Said's stinginess, inflexible conservatism, and despotic rule. His harsh and inept handling of the insurgency in Dhofar Province had given the Yemen (Aden)-backed guerrilla movement considerable popular support. By the time of the coup it was a major threat to national unity and the continuity of the Al Bu Said dynasty.

The British government, the principal official foreign presence in Oman at that time, acquiesced in the coup d'état, recognizing that Said's growing incompetence could prove a major destabilizing factor in the region after the British withdrawal from

341

bases east of the Suez Canal, planned for late 1971. They placed their trust in Qaboos, who had expressed his desire to implement a substantial reform of political institutions and a program of equitable development, to be funded by Oman's modest oil revenues. Though his education and experience overseas had given Qaboos a more cosmopolitan outlook than that of his father, the new sultan was, in the early 1970s, inexperienced in political matters and the effective use of the wide-ranging powers accorded him as an absolute monarch. His success in growing into that demanding role, combining the traditional prerogatives of a sultan with a commitment to modernization, were in the mid-1980s a major factor in Oman's large measure of political stability.

Qaboos' active interest in promoting the development of his country stemmed in part from the experiences of his childhood and youth, both in Oman and abroad. Born in 1940, he spent his earliest years isolated within the walls of the royal palace. At the urging of his father's British advisers, however, Qaboos was allowed to go to Britain in 1958 for his education. He spent two years at a small private school, where he acquired mastery of the English language and an appreciation for English literature. In 1960 he went to the military academy at Sandhurst and, after graduating from a two-year course of study, served for several months with British units stationed in West Germany. After a world tour and studies in London, he returned to Oman in December 1964. His hopes of acquiring a responsible role in the government or military were frustrated by his father, who, suspicious that he had been "corrupted" by foreign influences, kept him under virtual house arrest in the palace at Salalah. Rivalry between father and son provided a personal dimension to Qaboos' involvement in the coup d'état, concurrent with his conviction that his father's isolationist policies would spell disaster for the country.

Qaboos' most pressing concerns after his assumption of power were to gain support for his coup and to bring peace to Dhofar. One of the new sultan's first political acts was to call out of exile his uncle, Tariq bin Taimur Al Bu Said, and appoint him prime minister on August 9, 1970. Tariq had been educated in Germany, was married to a German, and had extensive experience working in the Middle East as the representative of a construction firm. He had been an outspoken critic of his elder brother's despotic rule and had been forced into exile in 1958. Tariq formed his first cabinet on August 16, 1970. It consisted of ministers of interior, justice, health, and education. Other ministers, including those in charge of foreign affairs, the economy, communications and transportation, and information, were appointed in late 1970 and 1971.

Tariq enjoyed great popularity among the people because he was the only member of the royal family to have fought against the imamic insurgency in the 1950s (see Internal Developments in Oman, ch. 1). He was known and respected more than the young sultan, who, because of the house arrest imposed upon him by his father, had seldom been seen by the people. However, soon after his return, Tariq became a controversial figure. He wished the country to have a formal written constitution, and he hoped that in time Oman would become a constitutional monarchy. He believed the institution of the sultanate to be anachronistic and intrinsically ill designed to serve Oman's entry into the modern world. In December 1971 Tariq resigned his post, and his duties as prime minister were assumed by the sultan. Qaboos reorganized the cabinet, which then included interior and justice, foreign affairs, health, education and culture, economy, defense and communications, labor, and agriculture.

The end of Tariq's brief career as prime minister, however, did not mark the eclipse of his formative influence on the evolution of the Omani political system. Qaboos made him a senior adviser, and ties between the ruler and his uncle were further strengthened when, in March 1976, Qaboos married Tariq's daughter Kamilla, though the marriage did not last. Tariq also served as governor of the Central Bank until his death in 1980. Observers agree that the adviser's greatest successes were in diplomacy—establishing relations with countries both inside and outside the region and with international organizations, such as the League of Arab States (Arab League) and the United Nations (UN). Before the coup d'état only Britain and India had diplomatic representatives in Muscat, the capital—a reflection of the British colonial sphere of influence that extended to the early nineteenth century. The progressive departure from dependence on Britain in the sphere of foreign relations marked both a recognition of a changed balance of power following the country's withdrawal from the region in 1971 and a growing assertion of Oman's role as an Arab state involved in regional and Pan-Arab issues.

Qaboos, whose mother was a Dhofari of the Qara tribe, took a personal interest in ending the insurgency in that province, led by the Popular Front for the Liberation of the Occupied Arab Gulf (PFLOAG), known after August 1974 as the Popular Front for the Liberation of Oman (PFLO). This was accomplished through a combination of a military strategy designed to penetrate the guerrillas' mountain strongholds and cripple their effectiveness in isolated villages and a development program intended to win popular support for the government. The latter included a civil aid program that built wells, clinics, schools, and other facilities in the highlands of Dhofar and made investments in local agriculture, particularly the raising of cattle. Roads were built, and electrification, both on the coast and in the highlands, was initiated. Overall, Dhofar was favored in terms of investment over the northern region of Oman proper. Between 1971 and 1975 about one-quarter of all investments in development, totaling US$1.75 billion, was spent on projects in Dhofar, although the population of the province was only about 50,000—small in comparison with a northern Omani population of 400,000 in the mid-1970s. An amnesty with generous terms was declared soon after the 1970 coup d'état, and by the mid-1970s as many as 2,000 rebels had surrendered, been retrained, and been incorporated into the Sultan's Armed Forces (SAF). In 1973 the shah of Iran, fulfilling his self-perceived role as guardian of the Persian Gulf following the departure of the British, sent ground forces (eventually numbering more than 3,000 men) and air units to Dhofar to assist the sultan. By December 1975, when the coastal town of Dhalqut was captured from the guerrillas, the entire province was effectively under government control, though mopping-up operations were continued thereafter, and Omani positions near the Yemen (Aden) border were threatened by Yemeni bombardment. The PFLO had been effectively neutralized and no longer posed a substantial threat to national security (see Oman, ch. 7).

A fatal weakness of the insurrection was a rift between Arab nationalist leaders, religious conservatives who could enlist the support of tribal shaykhs in a common struggle against Said, and Marxist revolutionaries who envisioned Dhofar as the starting point for an anti-imperialist movement that would spread throughout the Middle East. The movement in the province had originally been organized, in 1963, under the Dhofar Liberation Front. In 1968 the Marxists gained leadership, having the support of Yemen (Aden), the Soviet Union, and China. Conservative Dhofaris broke with it, and when Qaboos seized power in 1970, many agreed to support him against the insurgency.

One significant aspect of the Dhofar war was Qaboos' success in gaining support from neighboring countries that perceived a common interest in stopping the insurgency before it spread beyond Oman's borders. In addition to the long-standing support of Britain and the more recent matériel and manpower sent by the shah, Oman received annual financial aid of around US$200 million from Abu Dhabi, largest amirate of the UAE, to assist military and civil development projects and received around US$2.5 billion from Saudi Arabia, with whom relations had been much improved. Training spaces in military schools were provided for armed forces personnel by Britain, Jordan, Saudi Arabia, Egypt, and Pakistan. The UAE and Jordan occasionally provided troop units for guard duty in the north, thereby releasing Omani units for service in Dhofar. The war thus proved the wisdom of Qaboos' repudiation of Oman's long-standing isolationism.

After the insurgency had become a less urgent issue in the late 1970s, the sultan was able to concentrate his attention on the development of the country as a whole and the refinement of modern governmental and administrative institutions. By the mid-1980s practically all regions of the country were linked by well-maintained roads and a network of telecommunications, and the standard of living had risen substantially, generating popular support for his regime and the idea of Oman as a unified nation. Ministerial government and the civil service were expanded, and limited participation in the political process broadened with the establishment of the State Consultative Council (SCC) in November 1981. In mid-1984 succession had become an important, though not pressing, question because Qaboos did not have an heir, and observers wondered how long the institution of the sultanate as an absolute monarchy could be maintained, given the growth of a more educated and articulate population that might demand a more active political role of its own.

Government Institutions

In the mid-1980s Oman was one of the few states in the world preserving a system of absolute monarchy. Qaboos was the source of all authority, not so much head of state as the embodiment of the state itself. There was no constitution and no legislature. All government enactments, laws, and appointments had ultimately to be approved by the ruler. This system was essentially the same as that which had existed under his father, although Qaboos, responding to the requirements of a rapidly modernizing society, had expanded the scope of governmental activity far beyond the rudimentary institutions maintained by his predecessor. Moreover, through establishing the SCC in 1981, the sultan gave sections of the population the opportunity to comment on, but not actively participate in the decisionmaking process.

Government institutions on the national level included the Council of Ministers and three other bodies; the National Defense Council, the National Development Council, and the

Ministry of Diwan Affairs (see fig. 20). In 1984 the Council of Ministers had 28 members, including the prime minister and three deputy prime ministers and the governors of the capital area and Dhofar, who held ministerial rank. The sultan occupied the key posts of prime minister, minister of defense, minister of foreign affairs, and minister of finance. He appointed the other ministers and in the mid-1980s customarily presided over the weekly meetings of the Council of Ministers and the other national-level bodies, although ministers had considerable latitude in running their own ministries, and the council sometimes met with the ruler in absentia. Policy formulation consisted, for the most part, of person-to-person negotiations between the sultan and individual ministers.

The National Defense Council, working in conjunction with the Ministry of Defense and the Ministry of Interior, coordinated the activities of the SAF and the Royal Oman Police (ROP). The National Development Council was responsible for economic planning, and all projects involving more than a certain minimum expenditure required its review. In 1984 Muhammad bin Zubayr was designated a special adviser to the sultan, having responsibility to advise on economic planning.

In the mid-1980s there was no majlis (pl., majlises—see Glossary) on the national level, the traditional institution of the Arabian Peninsula wherein citizens can directly petition the ruler. The majlis was discontinued in 1958, when Said ensconced himself in his palace at Salalah. Qaboos had not revived it, perhaps because of the danger of assassination. The *diwan,* or royal court department, was the main forum for petitioners. The minister of *diwan* affairs was assisted in this function by a deputy and an administrative director, there also being a head of the protocol department and a press adviser. The Ministry of Diwan Affairs was also responsible for Oman's civil service. In 1982 the number of government employees in the country was 44,087, of which about 62 percent were Omani nationals (this figure excluded the armed forces, police, *diwan,* and Central Bank). It was a larger percentage than in previous years, principally because of the government's program of Omanization.

The State Consultative Council

On October 18, 1981, the sultan issued a decree establishing the State Consultative Council (SCC). This followed a year of discussion and preparation by the ruler and his ministers, who had perceived the necessity of setting up a formal advisory body with

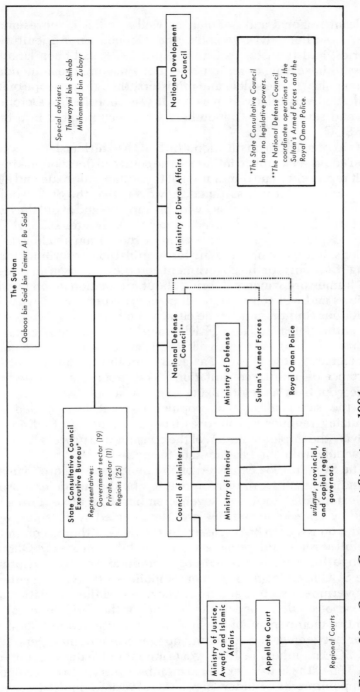

Figure 20. Oman. Government Structure, 1984

347

significant regional and popular, as well as official, representation. An earlier advisory body, the Council on Agriculture, Fisheries, and Industry, set up in April 1979, had been largely successful in serving as an "outside" body making recommendations on policy to the sultan and ministers, though the scope of its consultation was relatively narrow. It was abolished in October 1981, and seven of its 12 members were incorporated into the larger SCC.

As a consultative institution, the SCC had no legislative powers and could seek only to influence the course of decisionmaking. Thus it represented no diminution of the sultan's ultimate and absolute authority. It was assumed, however, that the SCC would help the ruler maintain contact with his subjects and avoid the isolation into which Said had retreated, particularly after 1958. High officials depicted it as an expression of the nation's values and traditions, a deputy prime minister in mid-1983 describing it as placing "the efforts of the government and the citizens in an integrative framework which will bring about interaction among various views and will concentrate all powers and efforts on what is good for our country and for the citizen and his welfare." According to anthropologist Dale F. Eickelman, "'consultation,' a bland term in English, is as evocative in the Islamic context as the idea of democracy in the West." Passages from the Quran stress the importance of "mutual consultation." This process is regarded in Islamic countries as legitimizing even an absolutist regime in much the same sense that popular consent is regarded as legitimizing regimes in countries having democratic traditions. However, the implementation of the consultative process has differed widely from one Islamic state to another.

The SCC in 1984 consisted of 55 members, 10 more than at its founding in 1981. All were appointed by the sultan for a two-year, extendable term. A seven-member Executive Bureau, headed by a president and vice president named by the ruler, set priorities on issues to be discussed by the SCC, either in committee or full session. Full sessions were scheduled quarterly. Of the Executive Bureau's five remaining members, who were chosen by the SCC itself from the sultan's appointees, two represented the "government sector" and three represented the population at large, variously described as the "public" or the "private sector." The entire membership of the SCC was apportioned in a similar manner between government and nongovernment members. Of the 55 SCC members in 1984, government delegates accounted for 19. Ten of these were ex officio members, serving as a result of their appointments as under secretaries of various ministries, and

*Guard at governor's
residence, Musandam
Courtesy
Aramco World Magazine*

nine were high officials appointed as individuals. The latter have included former ministers, ambassadors, provincial governors, and other high officials. "Popular" delegates, 36 in all, were divided among 11 representing the "private sector" (mostly prominent merchants from the Muscat capital area) and 25 representing the "region." Eickelman points out that there have been some ambiguities involved in these designations. In early 1982 eight regional delegates, supposedly representing the people, were government officials, while the concept of "regional" representation was somewhat clouded by the Executive Bureau's resolution, approved by the sultan, that members chosen from different parts of the country nevertheless had to represent "all" of Oman.

The consultation process was initiated by discussion within the Council, guided by the Executive Bureau, and concluded with the presentation of recommendations by the council president to the sultan, who could reject them or pass them on to the appropriate ministry. These proceedings were kept secret. The decree establishing the SCC guaranteed its members freedom of speech while participating in its deliberations, a right not explicitly granted Omani citizens. By mid-1983 there were five internal committees, dealing (as named) with legal affairs, economic affairs, services (concerned with health, welfare, education, and labor), utilities (water, electricity, communications, land, and municipal affairs), and education and training.

At the end of the SCC's first two-year term in November 1983, Qaboos granted it a second term and expanded its membership from 45 to 55, apparently to achieve greater regional balance. The body was also granted the responsibility of examining and commenting on proposals in the social and economic spheres before those proposals become law, as well as making general recommendations.

Whether or not the SCC is a first step in the direction of broadening genuine participation in the political process remained unclear in 1984. The sultan has described it as a "political experiment," and in the *Financial Times* in October 1983 he was quoted as saying that it was a "first step," there being "no limits to what development may mean. . . . It will be a happy day for me when more people will take responsibilities from my shoulders. But we have to take into consideration the situation of our culture, our religious heritage and guidance, our traditions, and not to import a system that is already made and put in a package." Within a specifically Omani context, the issue of "consultation" is controversial. In many minds it was more closely associated with the Ibadi imams, who were elected by the elders of the community, rather than with the Al Bu Said dynasty and its history of absolutism (see Internal Developments in Oman, ch. 1). However, in the mid-1980s the threat of a restored imamate challenging central rule was sufficiently remote for the sultan to co-opt certain aspects of the consultative tradition.

Regional and Local Government

In 1984 Oman was organized into 36 divisions, called *wilaya* (pl., *wilayat*), two provinces—Dhofar and the Musandam Peninsula—and the municipality of the capital. The latter, including Muscat, Matrah, Ruwi, Bashur, and As Sib, was administered by a powerful wali, or governor; in mid-1984 the sultan also appointed a deputy prime minister for governance of the capital, that post being filled by his distant cousin and longtime personal adviser, Thuwayyni bin Shihab Al Bu Said. Dhofar Province was administered by a governor, who was minister without portfolio. A third important regional official was the governor of the *wilaya* of Nazwa, the center of the old imamate. The *wilaya*, a system borrowed from the Ottoman Turks, has prevailed in Oman for many centuries. The wali was a civil servant—not a local tribal leader—who was appointed by the sultan and was under the Ministry of Interior. He was responsible for representing the national government, implementing the sultan's decrees and ministerial directives, and administering justice. Each wali was assisted by a qadi, or Islamic judge. The wali held majlises, where individuals could present petitions.

In the mid-1980s Dhofar Province had a municipal council whose members met at the provincial capital of Salalah. Towns acquiring the status of municipality included Nazwa, Sur, Suhar, Sumail, Rustaq, Ibri, Buraymi, and Masirah, although they still came under the *wilaya* system.

The wali of an area worked closely with the *tamimah*, the paramount shaykhs of his area. The *tamimah* were the walis' chief avenue of communication with the tribes, many of which were widely scattered over inhospitable terrain. Many tribes continued to function as autonomous units when a matter purely of internal tribal interest occurred. The tribes, however, were being drawn slowly into the network of the state. The walis were sensitive to tribal concerns and interfered in tribal affairs only when necessary. In turn, the tribes recognized the wali as their political superior. A wali's suzerainty over the tribes was reinforced chiefly because of his sole ability (acting with a qadi) to settle intratribal disputes and because he lobbied with the central government for the needs of his people. Because the tribes were finally experiencing beneficial effects from the state, the old animosities toward Muscat appeared to be softening.

The Judicial System

Oman's legal system is based on the Ibadi interpretation of sharia—Islamic religious law—containing very precise dicta for virtually every aspect of a Muslim's personal and private life. Sharia varies from school to school, but the Ibadi interpretation is similar to that of the four orthodox schools (see Islam: Emergence and Development, ch. 1). Jurisdiction in the mid-1980s was administered regionally by the wali, in conjunction with the qadi, a judge who has attained that position either by graduating from an Islamic law college or by taking advanced study with local religious legal experts. The majority of all cases was decided on this level. Although primarily guided by sharia, jurisdiction was aimed at arriving fairly at a decision or compromise that would be acceptable to all parties involved. Invariably, tribal law has become mixed with religious law at that level.

In late 1983 there were 50 regional courts throughout the

country. Each qadi had his own staff, including deputies and clerks. The Ministry of Justice, Awqaf [religious endowments] and Islamic Affairs, the national body responsible for the administration of the courts, periodically made it a practice to transfer qadis to different posts. It maintained a court of appeal, the three-member Appellate Court, in the capital. There were proposals to establish a supreme court, but these had not been acted on in mid-1984. In extraordinary cases an appeal could be made directly to the sultan.

Political Dynamics

Qaboos had no brothers, and as of 1984 no successor had been designated. His 1976 marriage to his cousin Kamilla was short-lived, and observers considered it uncertain whether he would marry again and produce an heir. To perpetuate the monarchy, a successor would have to be chosen from another branch of the Al Bu Said family. The succession issue, however, was not considered urgent in 1984, given the fact that Qaboos at that time was only 44 years old. He continued to play the central decisionmaking role in the political process, devoting several hours daily to public affairs though expressing both in words and in actions a willingness to delegate substantial responsibilities to trusted subordinates.

The sultan's relatives do not have the political influence or power enjoyed by members of many royal families on the Arabian Peninsula. Thuwayyni bin Shihab served in the mid-1980s as one of four deputy prime ministers and as an influential adviser to the sultan, and several family members held ministerial positions. A number of walis were related—some quite distantly—to the sultan. Members of the royal family were mentioned frequently in the press, the title sayyid preceding their names. This was meant to be a token of respect and did not have the usual connotation of the title—a descendant of the family of the prophet Muhammad.

The royal relatives who were in politically responsible positions were described by observers as men of proven ability, and those who were walis or were employed in lesser positions in the civil service held these positions not as a mark of the sultan's acquiescence in the nepotism typical of traditional Arabian Peninsula societies but as a result of the sultan's patronage. It was understood that they were only his representatives. As one Omani official observed, "for us there is only one member of the royal family and that is the Sultan."

Thus political influence, particularly on the national level, was gauged in terms of relationships of trust built up over the years with the sultan rather than politically sensitive balances of power within the ruling family. Prominent in the ruling circle were men who had assisted Qaboos in his July 1970 takeover, including some expatriate officers and advisers. Others were Omanis who had been forced to go abroad during the last, tyrannical years of Said's reign or had sought a modern education and had returned to the country after the coup d'état.

Returnees included Tariq bin Taimur, who served as first prime minister and who subsequently served as special adviser to the sultan and as governor of the Central Bank (until his death in 1980), and Abdul Hafidh Salim Rajab, a Dhofari who had studied automotive engineering in the Soviet Union. Rajab had begun serving in Qaboos' government in late 1971 and in 1984 was minister of agriculture and fisheries. By virtue of their education, a number of Omanis from Zanzibar (the island off the coast of East Africa that had been a possession of the Omani ruler in the nineteenth century [now part of Tanzania]) were appointed high officials after the coup d'état. Their influence provoked some resentment among native Omanis, particularly because many had not lived in the country before 1970. Nevertheless, they continued to be prominent in government and the professions in the mid-1980s.

Politics and Society

Among the most important groups, in terms of political influence in the mid-1980s, were prominent merchants of the capital area, most of whom were of foreign origin and whose families had been settled in Muscat for several generations. These merchants, including both Hindus and Muslims from the Indian subcontinent and Shia (see Glossary) from Iran, had consolidated their power during the reign of Said and continued to amass fortunes after 1970, largely through monopolistic or quasi-monopolistic franchises. None were directly involved in the oil business, but together they were the major suppliers of goods to the government, local contractors, expatriate firms, local consumers, and the oil industry. Valuable distributorships for consumer and capital services were under their aegis. Close cooperation between the merchants and Said has evolved into a mutually protective relationship with civil servants in Qaboos' government.

Tribes and tribal leadership were of considerable but declining importance in the political process in the mid-1980s. The society outside the capital and other large towns remained tribally oriented, the *tamimah* playing the role of political authorities on the local level. Eickelman reveals that 15 of the 18 regional delegates to the SCC were the sons or nephews of shaykhs in 1982, although only three of the 15 were themselves shaykhs. According to Eickelman, the latter fact suggests the government's determination not to perpetuate tribal elites that were largely identified with the old regime.

The power of tribes to function as pressure groups within their regions remained strong in the mid-1980s, although that function was increasingly undermined by the inevitable extension of the power of the central government and its growing ability to provide for the needs of individuals outside the traditional tribal framework. Increasing mobility vitiated tribal ties. The construction of good roads and a countrywide telecommunications network brought tribesmen into contact with the outside world and exposed them to new influences. Economic opportunities existed, for the most part, around the capital and even outside the country (it was estimated in 1981 that 111,000 Omanis worked in neighboring Persian Gulf states), resulting in movement of the population. Observers remarked, however, that modern highways made it feasible for villagers to work in the capital or even in the UAE and then return to their villages for the weekend, maintaining, though in diluted form, social cohesion.

Two of Qaboos' most important political and social objectives have been to bring the peripheral regions of Oman into the mainstream of national life and to organize new constituencies--particularly women and youth, who were disadvantaged under the old regime—for the goals of national construction. Dhofaris, for instance, were well represented in the national government in the mid-1980s, and an important rationale for the formation of the SCC in 1981 was the need for a medium through which regional concerns—including not only those of Dhofar but also those of the interior regions of the north and the neglected Musandam Peninsula—could be voiced.

Although women were not members of the SCC in 1984, Oman appeared to have the greatest success among the states of the Arabian Peninsula in initiating women into the developmental process of an emerging nation. Although illiteracy and traditional perceptions held by both men and women about the proper, and limited, sphere of women's activities hampered the government's attempts to integrate them into the full life of the society, the sultan's intent was clear, and efforts by various government ministries through the 1970s and early 1980s yielded significant and positive results. Women are a potentially important labor resource, and, because the country has only a small income from oil and limited resources, Qaboos deemed it necessary that women enter the labor market as quickly as possible. More important, it was vital to demonstrate that a traditional absolute monarchy need not have the anachronistic social and economic trappings generally associated with it.

Women were prominent in communications, banking, the foreign service, and the domestic civil service. Like many Omani civil servants in responsible positions, most of the women conspicuous in public service were raised and educated outside the country. A new generation of Omani women was being educated in the country's recently established school system, however, and it was hoped that professional women would serve as important role models and demonstrate that women in the work force need not behave in ways antithetical to Islamic mores.

Omani youths—who in the 1980s were the first generation to have the opportunity of a secular education—were perceived by the government as the country's most important resource. In 1974 Omanization was begun. Moreover, the age-range of candidates for various jobs was lowered to accommodate students and school dropouts. The Ministry of Information and Culture noted that "a country in a hurry cannot afford to wait too long for practical skills to be polished or academic excellence to remain theoretical." In addition to a wide range of employment opportunities, Omani youths were encouraged to identify with the goals of the state through a program of community affairs and social activities that stressed shared responsibility and decisionmaking. Planning was in progress for the establishment of a national university, the Sultan Qaboos University, that would admit both male and female students and would open by 1986. According to a government spokesman, the institution was designed "to play an effective role in meeting the needs of Omani society at its present and future stages of growth."

Potential Factors in Instability

In the mid-1980s Oman enjoyed a large measure of political stability. The PFLO Executive Committee remained based in Yemen (Aden), receiving support from radical Arab states, such as Libya, and the Soviet Union and Cuba. It was divided internally, however, could maintain only a handful of guerrilla fighters in the interior of Dhofar Province, and was largely cut off from sources of supply in Yemen (Aden), receiving little assistance from the local populace. Its activities increased during the late 1970s, but this did not signal the beginning of a new insurrection. In 1978 guerrillas attacked a party of British engineers near Salalah, and in June 1979 the governor of Dhofar was assassinated. Although the prospects for improved relations between Oman and Yemen (Aden) through "normalization" of relations were uncertain, it was possible that it would result in less support on Aden's part for insurgency (see Foreign Relations, this ch.). The PFLO maintained close ties with the Popular Front for the Liberation of Palestine (PFLP), sharing with it information, training facilities, and an arms-smuggling network. Relations were also maintained with Libya and Syria. Contacts with Iraq were ended in March 1981, when the government of President Saddam Husayn shut down its offices in Baghdad. The PFLO was regarded as insufficiently supportive of Iraq's war with Iran, while Iraq was criticized by PFLO leaders, who disapproved of its lack of militance and its closer relations with Saudi Arabia.

The large number of foreign workers in Oman aroused considerable apprehension in government and private circles, as it did in other countries of the peninsula. A 1981 estimate placed the foreign population at 459,700, or 48 percent of a total population of 948,000. The majority (175,000) were from the Indian subcontinent (Pakistan, Bangladesh, and India). However, 43,000 nationals from Yemen (Aden) were a special cause of concern, given their country's involvement with the PFLO. Omanization remained in the mid-1980s a central component of government policy. Foreigners remained in all levels of the labor force, including those of civil servants and professionals. In 1983 restrictions were placed on the hiring of foreigners for certain occupations, and programs of educational development for Omanis were being implemented with continued urgency. The government maintained tight control over noncitizens, and the fact that most foreign workers did not bring their families to Oman, planned to remain only a few years, and were primarily concerned with saving their earnings for investment in their own countries, minimized their involvement in the political system (see Foreign Workers, ch. 1).

With the fall of the shah of Iran in 1979 and Ayatollah Ruhollah Khomeini's call to Shiite populations in the region to support his Islamic revolution, there were fears that Oman's small Shiite minority, concentrated along the Al Batinah coast and around the capital, might be a source of instability. There were demonstrations in 1979 and 1980, but they were limited in scope. Many Omani Shiites were from the Indian subcontinent rather than from Iran and occupied a relatively privileged position as a result of their activity in trade. According to Eickelman, 16 percent of the membership of the SCC was Shiite, larger than their percentage of the total population.

Foreign Relations

Oman's foreign relations have been shaped by Qaboos' determination to free his country of its traditional isolationism and play a more active role both regionally and internationally; its strategic position on the southern shore of the Strait of Hormuz; the threats posed by revolutionary regimes in Yemen (Aden) and Iran; and the imperatives of an economy already dependent on exports of petroleum. By the mid-1980s a coherent foreign policy—significantly, in concert with that of other moderate Arab states—had evolved, though there was disagreement on important issues, and Oman was not a member of OPEC. Oman has been a member of the GCC since its formation in May 1981 and has both contributed to and benefited from that six-nation body's efforts to maintain stability in the region. However, the country's historic links with Britain, the education and background of its ruler, and its experience as what one writer has called a "front-line state" facing communist insurgency, have been contributing factors in the evolution of a foreign policy that was more Western oriented than that of its neighbors. It was criticized by the latter as violating the principle of nonalignment and noninvolvement in competition between the superpowers. In mid-1984 these criticisms were muted, however, as the six GCC states faced the prospect of growing escalation in the war between Iran and Iraq and perceived the need for closer collaboration with Western countries, particularly the United States, in order to ensure the integrity of their borders and the continued flow of oil shipments through the Strait of Hormuz.

Regional Relations

On the eve of Qaboos' assumption of power, formal diplomatic relations between Oman and Saudi Arabia and the shaykhdoms of what would become in December 1971 the UAE were nonexistent, and contact was minimal. Only Britain and India maintained representatives in Muscat. Unclear boundaries and the fluidities of tribal politics stoked hostility and suspicions, particularly with Saudi Arabia. Saudi Arabia claimed the Buraymi Oasis region, and from the early 1950s the kingdom served as a base from which the imam continued to challenge the authority of the Al Bu Said dynasty. After the coup d'état, Qaboos sought to improve and normalize relations. He offered the imam-in-exile, Ghalib bin Ali, the option of returning to Oman and functioning in a purely religious capacity, one that the imam refused. In December 1971 Qaboos made a state visit to Saudi Arabia; formal relations were established thereafter. The Buraymi Oasis issue was resolved with an agreement on July 29, 1974, between Oman, Saudi Arabia, and the UAE. It stipulated that Oman would receive three villages in the region and Abu Dhabi—one of the states of the UAE—six, and that the two countries would share the oil field at Shaybah. Saudi Arabia, in turn, was to receive an outlet to the Gulf through UAE territory. Although the boundary between Saudi Arabia, the UAE, and Oman in the mid-1980s remained largely undefined, the countries involved did not regard boundary resolution as a pressing issue. There were conflicting claims, however, advanced by Oman and Ras al Khaymah, an amirate of the UAE, over a strip of territory having potential oil reserves.

In the course of the Dhofar war, Oman received substantial financial support from Saudi Arabia, the UAE, and Kuwait—countries that feared the spread of subversive activities by the Popular Front for the Liberation of the Occupied Arab Gulf (PFLOAG) to their own territories. During the decade of the 1970s, Omani officials participated in a series of ministerial meetings of Gulf Arab states. These dealt with various topics, such as education, labor and social affairs, agriculture, communications, and finance, and paved the way for the establishment of the GCC. This was formed in February-March 1981, largely in response to the threat posed by the war between Iran and Iraq (see Appendix C). One of its first acts was the formation of the Mediation Committee, consisting of the UAE, Saudi Arabia, and Kuwait, to assist in settling long-standing disputes between Oman and Yemen (Aden). Defense, particularly as related to oil fields and facilities, was a primary concern of the GCC. In September 1981 Omani officials presented a position paper on defense to the foreign ministers of the GCC, stressing the importance of counteracting the Soviet threat in the region by developing joint security forces and collaborating with the United States and other Western countries. Oman had, in June 1980, signed an agreement with the United States permitting the latter to use Oman's military facilities as approved by the sultan on a case-by-case basis. Oman's view of security problems was a cause of disagreement with GCC states—particularly Kuwait—that favored a nonaligned stance oriented toward Islamic and Pan-Arab concerns and the exclusion of all foreign forces from the Gulf.

A second cause of friction between Oman and other Arab states was the former's support of the peace treaty between Egypt and Israel. In 1977 Qaboos praised Egyptian president Anwar al Sadat's visit to Jerusalem as a "courageous and bold step aimed at driving the wheel of peace forward." Oman and Sudan were the only two Arab states to maintain relations with Egypt after the signing of the Camp David Agreements in September 1978. This was regarded by other states in the region as a betrayal of the Palestinian cause, a criticism that the ruler strongly denied. In an interview in December 1983, Qaboos expressed his consistent support for Palestinian rights, reaffirmed his belief in the constructiveness of the Camp David Agreements, and criticized "Israeli intransigence" for the slowdown in progress toward peace. He criticized other Arab states for not supporting what was called "Cairo's right to wage the 'war' of negotiations on the peace front" and in concert with Egypt called for Israel's withdrawal to its pre-June 1967 boundaries and its recognition of the right of the Palestinians to establish their own independent state. Ties between Oman and Egypt remained close and friendly in the mid-1980s.

The People's Democratic Republic of Yemen

Since the 1960s Yemen (Aden) has been the center of Oman's security concerns because of its support for insurgency and its role as a base of Soviet-bloc military forces and influence in the region. In 1980 and 1981 the two states traded accusations and protested to the Arab League about border violations and the presence of foreign troops on each other's soil. Throughout 1982 the foreign ministers of Kuwait and the UAE, acting on behalf of the GCC, arranged consultations between high-level Omani and Yemen (Aden) officials. In October 1982 an agreement on a "declaration of principles" was reached, including a commitment to normalize relations. Other provisions included the establishment of a "technical committee" to deliberate on border disagreements (including Kuwaiti and UAE mediators), a statement that foreign forces were not to be used by either country for aggressive acts against the other, a moratorium on hostile propaganda, and a promise to exchange diplomats. Although the committee on border problems met in January 1983, as of mid-1984 diplomatic representatives had not been exchanged.

Relations with the United States

Relations between Oman and the United States grew close during the 1970s as Qaboos supported United States initiatives for peace in the Middle East and shared Washington's apprehensions over the growth of the Soviet presence in Yemen (Aden) and other states along the Indian Ocean littoral. The Iranian revolution and the danger of that country, seemingly on the brink of civil war, falling under the Soviet sphere of influence led to a more active collaborative relationship in 1979 and 1980. Given its strategic position on the Strait of Hormuz, through which tankers passed to and from the oil-rich Gulf states, Oman played a central role in United States strategic planning, particularly after President Jimmy Carter declared the Gulf an area of vital United States interests.

Following several months of negotiations, the two countries signed an agreement on June 4, 1980, giving the United States the use of installations in Oman at such times when it served the security interests of both parties. This was part of a larger regional strategy that also included facilities in Somalia and Kenya. The air bases at As Sib and Thamarit (Thumrait) and on Masirah Island (the latter abandoned by the British in 1977) and the port facilities at Matrah and Salalah were specifically mentioned by official United States spokesmen as being upgraded for use by the newly formed Rapid Deployment Force (by 1984 the United States Central Command). The agreement included a United States commitment of military and economic aid. The United States administration stressed at that time that the security arrangements with Oman did not entail a permanent and extensive United States military presence in the country. During the early 1980s United States troops participated in joint military exercises in Oman (see Oman, ch. 7).

The Joint United States-Oman Commission was established to fund and administer economic assistance programs in the country. Between 1981 and 1983 a total of US$31.2 million was transferred to Oman in the form of loans and grants; military assistance during the same period totaled US$85.2 million.

Relations with Other Countries

Given the existence of old trade routes, historical ties developed during the period of British maritime dominance, and because large numbers of foreign workers came from the Indian subcontinent, ties with India, Pakistan, and Bangladesh were substantial. Another factor in Oman-Pakistan relations was the Islamic orientation of Pakistani president Mohammad Zia ul Haq, who stressed the building of solidarity between Muslim countries. Official Omani statements described the two countries as enjoying a substantial community of interests and perspective that in the mid-1980s formed the basis for long-term cultural, technical, and economic collaboration.

Relations with Britain remained close, though the British military presence—officers seconded to the Sultan's Armed Forces—was being phased out as part of a comprehensive Omanization program. In May 1978 Oman established diplomatic relations with China. China had ended its support of the PFLO and was regarded by Qaboos and his advisers as a potential counterweight to Soviet influence in the region. Recognition of China as the "sole legal government representing the entire Chinese people" brought an end to relations with the government on Taiwan. Suspicion of the Soviet Union remained high, given the 1979 invasion of Afghanistan, a Muslim country, and continued support for Yemen (Aden) and the PFLO insurgency. In the mid-1980s, there seemed little prospect of relations being established.

*   *   *

Sources of information on Oman are relatively scanty, confined to general surveys rather than to detailed, scholarly monographs. Donald Hawley's *Oman and Its Renaissance*, published in 1977, provides both an introduction to the country's history, society, economy, and government and a striking pictorial presentation. J. E. Peterson's *Oman in the Twentieth Century: Political Foundations of an Emerging State* gives historical background for the changes that came with the accession of Sultan Qaboos, while John Townsend's *Oman: The Making of a Modern State* focuses on the building of governmental institutions after 1970. Majid Khadduri's chapter on Sultan Qaboos in *Arab Personalities in Politics* gives a good overview of developments before and after 1970 and a biographical sketch of the sultan. Other useful books include Frank A. Clements' *Oman: The Reborn Land* and Liesl Graz' *The Omanis: Sentinels of the Gulf*, published in 1982, which includes a short but useful annex dealing with United States-Oman security arrangements. Dale F. Eickelman's article "Kings and People: Oman's State Consultative Council," appearing in the *Middle East Journal,* is an interesting discussion of institutional reforms in the early 1980s and their possible future direction. (For further information and complete citations, see Bibliography.)

Chapter 7. Regional and National Security Considerations

Crossed scimitars

PERSPECTIVE DETERMINES WHETHER the body of water between the Arabian Peninsula and Iran is called the Persian Gulf or the Arabian Gulf. It is important to keep in mind that, from the perspective of the Gulf Arabs, it is—emphatically—the Arabian Gulf.

Iran, Iraq, and Saudi Arabia are the regional "superpowers" of the Gulf. Although this study concerns the five other Gulf states—Kuwait, Bahrain, Qatar, the United Arab Emirates, and Oman—all Gulf activities are heavily influenced by the three major powers. This influence has been felt particularly since the start of the fundamentalist revolution in Iran in 1978, the outbreak of war between Iran and Iraq in 1980, and the joining of Saudi Arabia with the five smaller states in the Gulf Cooperation Council in 1981.

In the mid-1980s the Iran-Iraq War was the dominant issue facing the eight Gulf states. The two belligerents at the top of the Gulf had been battling each other for almost four years, but their war was not confined to their own territories or shores and, because of the constant danger of full-scale warfare spreading to any or all of the other states, the peoples of the Gulf lived under that pall. Milton Viorst in the *Washington Post* of March 20, 1984, said, "If Iran's army vanquishes Iraq, it would almost surely turn south, to swallow up the pro-Western oil states—Kuwait, Qatar, Bahrain—on the shore of the Persian Gulf."

A few months after the start of the Gulf war, the six nonbelligerents banded together in the Gulf Cooperation Council. Advertised as an economic, social, and political association of likeminded states, the council also quickly identified itself as a military alliance. It made it clear, however, that its reason for being was completely defensive. Gulf Arab leaders feared that a decisive victory by Iran would simply fuel the drive of the Iranian Shia Muslims to spread their Islamic fundamentalism. Ayatollah Ruhollah Khomeini, who had replaced the shah as the Iranian leader, had openly broadcast his disdain for monarchies, predicting that the sultans, amirs, and shaykhs would eventually be overrun by his revolution. Iraq had disposed of its monarch years before, but President Saddam Husayn was a particular target of Khomeini's hatred, dating from the ayatollah's residence in Iraq during several years of exile. The founders of the Gulf Cooperation Council hoped that, in alliance, they would find a measure of security.

Iraq, recognizing that it could not win a long war of attrition, decided to attack the Iranian economy in the hope of bringing the enemy to the negotiating table. Saddam Husayn evidently believed that if Iran's oil supplies were threatened, the countries of Western Europe and Japan would, of necessity, pressure Iran to end the war. Because a world oil glut had occurred coincidentally with the war, oil consumers were reluctant to get involved in the Gulf, and Iran, instead of rushing into negotiations, began tit for tat attacks on tankers servicing other Gulf producers. In mid-1984 the Gulf oil trade remained at the mercy of a religious fanatic in Iran and a military tyrant in Iraq, both of whom sought the destruction of the other's regime, and neither of whom seemed willing to give an inch.

Regional Problems

Impact of the Iran-Iraq War

According to archaeologists, warfare was a common activity 50 centuries ago among the peoples of the area of the Middle East that in modern times became Iran, Iraq, Saudi Arabia, and the smaller Gulf states. Intermittent hostilities among the peoples of the area have occurred ever since. Sargon, Hammurabi, Nebuchadrezzar II, and Alexander the Great were only some of the best known kings who led warring armies in the area during the 2,500 years before the birth of Christ. After the rise of Islam, hostilities pitted Arab against Persian and, later, Sunni (see Glossary) Muslim against Shia (see Glossary) Muslim. In mid-1984 Khomeini (leader of Iran since the overthrow of Shah Mohammad Reza Pahlavi in 1979) and Saddam Husayn al Takriti (Iraqi strongman since 1968 and president since 1979) had their countries locked in a stalemated war of attrition in which neither side seemed capable of mustering sufficient strength to defeat the other. After almost four years the war had taken a terrible toll of lives on both sides and had devastated the economies of both countries. The other Gulf states lived in fear of the possibility of a spillover of the hostilities, either by accident or design. Then, in late spring 1984, both belligerents attacked tankers of neutral countries, seemingly to widen the war for their own arcane purposes.

Mark A. Heller, in the *New Republic* of April 23, 1984, began an article on the Iran-Iraq War by describing it as "a war between two barely distinguishable four-letter countries. It is fought with the weapons of the 1980s, the tactics of World War I, and the pas-

sions of the Crusades." The two countries are very distinguishable—their religious and ethnic differences have kept them at
odds for centuries—but the war is aptly characterized by Heller.
It began after a period of seriously deteriorating relations between the two countries, dating from the fall of the shah and the
rise of Khomeini. Full-scale warfare erupted on September 21,
1980, as Iraqi military units swept across the Shatt al Arab, apparently intending to occupy key positions in the Iranian province of
Khuzistan, Iran's richest oil-producing area. Using blitzkrieg-like
tactics at the outset, the Iraqi forces moved rapidly toward their
objectives, taking the Iranian port of Khorramshahr and almost
surrounding Abadan, the oil refining center. In addition to his designs on Khuzistan (the so-called Arab province of Iran), Saddam
Husayn obviously hoped to overthrow Khomeini, who had been
overtly attempting to spread his fundamentalist revolution into
Iraq, where the Sunni regime ruled a majority Shia population.

At the time, the Iraqi armed forces, numbering approximately 220,000, were drawn from a population of about 13 million. The Iranian forces numbered about the same but came from
the much larger population of about 40 million. Exact estimates of
Iranian strength were difficult to make because of the upheaval
caused by the revolution. Mass desertions more than halved the
enlisted ranks, estimated at about 415,000 during the final days of
the shah's reign; purges and executions then eliminated most
high-ranking officers, including all generals and admirals.

During late 1980, in addition to the fighting along the Shatt al
Arab, both sides used aircraft to attack strategic, i.e., economic,
targets far from the battlefield. Baghdad and Tehran, the capitals,
were repeatedly bombed. Attacks and counterattacks were followed by charges and countercharges concerning the bombing
and shelling of civilians and targets of no military importance.
Both belligerents prohibited foreign observers and correspondents from entering the war zones, thus forcing them to rely on official communiqués for information. By mid-1981 the battlelines
were about the same as they had been in the early days of the war.
Iraqi forces still held Khorramshahr and a few other Iranian towns
and still surrounded Abadan, but they had not been able to consolidate their gains or deliver a decisive blow. Oil, the economic
lifeblood of both countries, was flowing at far below the prewar
rates, and huge oil facilities had been reduced to rubble.

Although staggered by the reduction of its oil income, Iran
was able to maintain much more production than its enemy and
also had more non-oil assets to fall back on. Iraq, without substantial outside support, could not maintain its capacity to wage war.

In early 1981 the Iranian news agency claimed that Saudi Arabia, Kuwait, Bahrain, Qatar, and the United Arab Emirates (UAE) had agreed on September 19, 1980—two days before the Iraqi attack—to support Iraq financially in its military adventure. A Kuwaiti newspaper later confirmed that the countries named had indeed pledged to lend Iraq about US$14 billion. As the lines were drawn, most Arab states vowed support for Arab Iraq in its war against non-Arab Iran. Notable exceptions were Libya and Syria, whose leaders, Muammar al Qadhaafi and Hafiz al Assad, respectively, accused Iraq's Saddam Husayn of being an agent of the "imperialist West." Thus, in addition to the Arab-Persian and Sunni-Shia elements that were already at play in the Gulf war, the East-West superpower threat was introduced.

In backing Iraq the other Arab Gulf states apparently chose the lesser of what they considered to be two evils. The rulers of these conservative monarchies did not approve of the republican ideas propounded by revolutionary Iraq, but they feared more the religious extremism of revolutionary Iran. Although aggressive actions by Iraq had caused problems in the past, the Gulf Arabs felt most threatened by Iran in 1980; it was therefore easy for them to support Iraq, a brother Arab country. Kuwait, closest to the war, was sufficiently worried to order general mobilization on October 5, 1980, although its objective was probably more the registration of resident aliens (slightly more than half the population) than an actual call to the colors.

Two days after the outbreak of hostilities, President Jimmy Carter announced that the United States would observe strict neutrality in the war, and he called upon the Soviet Union to follow a similar policy. Within the week United States secretary of state Edmund S. Muskie met with the Soviet foreign minister, Andrey A. Gromyko, for a long discussion of the Gulf war and the role of the superpowers in the area. Muskie later met with Sadun Hammadi, Iraq's foreign minister, to state the strong United States desire that the hostilities not be spread to other countries of the Gulf. Hammadi was quoted in the press as saying that his government was also against escalation and had "limited objectives" and reportedly requested that the United States not "interfere in the conflict in any way." Eight days after the outbreak of the war, the Carter administration announced that it was sending four E-3A airborne warning and control system (AWACS) aircraft to Saudi Arabia to enable the worried Saudis to detect threatening Iranian aircraft movements.

The deputy secretary of state, Warren Christopher, speaking officially for the United States, declared that the prevention of escalation of the war and the restoration of peace to the Gulf region were the principal American objectives. He stated that the United States was neutral in the war but had vital interests in the area that it would defend if necessary; it would also respond to "requests for assistance from nonbelligerent friends in the area" who feared the spread of hostilities. At the time, the United States had 30 ships in the Indian Ocean, including the aircraft carriers U.S.S. *Eisenhower* and U.S.S. *Midway,* which were joined by about 30 additional ships from Australia, Britain, and France, presenting a formidable Allied fleet near the troubled Gulf. The Western Allies stated succinctly that it was their intention to ensure that nothing interfered with the vital flow of oil. Despite American-Iranian problems in the wake of the shah's overthrow and, particularly, after the taking of hostages at the United States embassy in Tehran, the Carter administration made it clear that it did not want to see territorial changes (meaning it did not want to see Soviet-backed Iraq dismember Iran, which appeared to be a possibility in the early days of the war).

The Soviet Union also pledged itself to the restoration of peace in the Gulf and stressed noninterference by outside powers, but, seeking a propaganda advantage, it accused the West of meddling in Gulf affairs and later accused the United States of having provoked the conflict. Although Iraqi armaments were practically all of Soviet manufacture, Moscow did not openly support its former client in the early days of the war but tried to remain on good terms with both sides. For the Iranians the Soviet press had praise for the "anti-imperialist" tone of Khomeini's fundamentalist revolution while mildly criticizing its "religious fanaticism." *Pravda,* the official newspaper of the Central Committee of the Communist Party of the Soviet Union, called for an early end to the war, stating that its continuation "plays into the hands of imperialism," and President Leonid I. Brezhnev loosed a propaganda shot at the West, saying that there existed "those who want to establish their control over Near and Middle East oil, who again dream of turning Iran into a military base and gendarme post of imperialism." The American decision to send AWACS aircraft to Saudi Arabia was also denounced in Moscow as interference in Gulf affairs. Six weeks after the outbreak of the war, the Kremlin announced that arms shipments to Iraq had been halted and that 800 Soviet military advisers had been recalled.

Other than the lifting of the siege of Abadan, there was no major change in the status of the belligerents on the battlefield during 1981; neither was there any lessening of the threat to the other Gulf states. The quick, successful strike that the Iraqi leadership hoped for in September 1980 (and that many outside observers expected because of the chaos in revolutionary Iran) had not been possible; the conflict had become a high-casualty war of attrition that seemed unresolvable as long as both sides could avoid utter exhaustion. Iraq, having lost the possibility of achieving the aims that prompted its attack, proclaimed its desire for peace, stating that it wanted only its own sovereignty and the establishment of decent relations between revolutionary Iran and the Arab states of the area. Several countries (including the Gulf states) and international organizations attempted to mediate between the antagonists, but all attempts foundered, usually on Iranian obduracy. Iran—holding American hostages from November 1979 to January 1981—was undergoing considerable inner turmoil between moderates who wanted to negotiate peace terms and hard-liners who, before anything else, wanted to destroy Saddam Husayn and his regime. The other Gulf states continued to support Iraq and continued to worry about escalation.

From the time that the Iranians forced the lifting of the siege of Abadan late in 1981, the initiative—which had been with the Iraqis since their surprise attack—seemed to be on the side of the Iranians. At the beginning of the holy month of Muhurram (during which the Quran forbids fighting between Muslims), Saddam Husayn reportedly attempted to arrange a cease-fire for the month or longer, whichever the Iranians would agree to, but because of their newly acquired initiative and the fanaticism of Khomeini, the Iranians pressed for a military solution.

Both belligerents, after two years at war, were suffering from lack of replacements for lost weapons and equipment and were particularly hampered by the lack of spare parts. Iran's forces used American matériel, Iraq's used Soviet; both superpowers had embargoed armaments and spare parts, forcing the warring countries to seek other sources of supply. If, according to the old adage, politics makes for strange bedfellows, war too brings about strange relationships. In this case, Israel and Libya were on the same side providing support to Khomeini. Strong evidence pointed to Israel as a major supplier of arms and equipment to Iran despite Khomeini's open hostility toward the "occupiers of Jerusalem." The Libyan government of the mercurial Qadhaafi was able to set aside its Pan-Arabist sentiments to become a supplier of arms to Iran for use against Arab Iraq. The Democratic People's Republic of Korea (North Korea) and Taiwan were also reportedly supplying arms and equipment to Iran during the early period of the war. On the other side, Iraq received a steady flow of arms traffic from Eastern Europe. After Israel bombed the

Iraqi nuclear plant in June 1981, the Soviet Union resumed its direct support of Iraq. Brazil became a major supplier of armored vehicles to Iraq in 1981 but also sold some to Iran. France began sending Mirage aircraft in exchange for Iraqi oil. Britain contracted to repair Chieftain tanks for the Iraqis, stating that such a maintenance deal would not impinge on British neutrality. China was called opportunistic in dealing with both sides in the Gulf war.

The other Gulf states—those not engaged in the hostilities—were adversely affected by the actions taken by the belligerents to restrict shipping not only in the war zone but also in the entire Gulf. Several foreign ships had been trapped in the Shatt al Arab at the outbreak of the war; others entering the Gulf were harassed by the navies of the combatants. In August 1981 Iran seized a Danish freighter suspected of carrying a military cargo to Iraq. The ship, when seized, was in the Strait of Hormuz, about 800 kilometers from the active combat area. Iraq attacked ships leaving Iranian ports and mined navigation channels from those ports to the Gulf. Both governments warned foreign shipping interests that vessels anywhere in the Gulf were at risk. In effect the noncombatant states were involved despite their expressed desire to stay out of the war.

In May 1981 Saudi Arabia, Kuwait, Bahrain, Qatar, the UAE, and Oman banded together in the Gulf Cooperation Council (GCC) to protect their interests and, if necessary, to defend thsmselves (see Appendix C). All GCC members backed Iraq, although they remained ostensibly neutral. Iranian aircraft intruded into Kuwaiti airspace in June 1981, Iranian revolutionaries were involved in troubles in Mecca in October, and Iranian subversives attempted a coup in Bahrain in December, all of which bolstered the prevalent attitude that Iran was the greater threat to the smaller Arab states. Potential mediators from the United Nations (UN) and from various Islamic organizations were unable to bring the warring states together for talks.

By the second anniversary of the outbreak of the war, it had become obvious that there had been a change in the roles of the participants. Iraq, the aggressor of September 1980, had been forced into defensive positions during the summer of 1982 as the Iranians retook the city of Khorramshahr and continually pushed the Iraqi forces back toward their own border. Iraq called for cease-fire negotiations, but the Iranians, gaining strength and confidence, repeatedly upped the ante for any talks by demanding, primarily, the ouster of Saddam Husayn.

As Iran assumed an offensive posture during 1982, various

Arab countries expressed concern that Khomeini might become unstoppable. Syria, which had supported the Iranians from the first, warned Khomeini that an invasion of Iraq would be unacceptable in Damascus. The foreign ministers of the GCC countries at a meeting in Riyadh applauded Syria's stance, stating that "a unified Arab position is the basic factor in ending the bloodshed between the two Moslem countries." Khomeini warned the Gulf states that their support of Iraq could bring on retribution, saying in May 1982, "I have a piece of brotherly advice for you—do not do anything which will oblige us, under the tenets of the Koran, to treat you according to divine law." His foreign minister was more direct, stating that Iran would not countenance the continued flow of arms from the Gulf states to Iraq.

After the initiative changed hands, Western observers expected that Iran would launch a major offensive, but it was not until February 1983 that the long-awaited attack occurred. Relying on waves of massed infantry with limited armored support and little air cover, the Iranian offensive encountered Soviet-built T-72 tanks under the cover of fighter aircraft and helicopter gunships. Iranian casualties were heavy, and it was later reported that the troops rebelled against the "human wave" tactics ordered by the leadership in Tehran. But thousands of untrained volunteers—many of them as young as 14 years old—were thrown into battle against heavily defended Iraqi positions; casualties among the teenagers were staggering. The offensive, which had been heralded in the Majlis (the Iranian legislature) as the decisive engagement of the war, ended in failure.

The war again impinged on the well-being of all Gulf states in March 1983 when Iraqi air-to-surface missiles hit two Iranian oil wells in the Norwuz field, about 190 kilometers northwest of Kharg Island (see fig. 3). The resulting oil slick endangered marine life and coastal communities around the Gulf. The Regional Organization for the Protection of the Marine Environment, which included Iran and Iraq in addition to the six GCC states, held meetings during April that were attended by representatives from all member states; no plans to fight the oil slick were adopted, however, because the two combatants could not agree on the necessary cease-fire. At the end of the year two oil leaks continued, and the slick grew larger. Environmental damage was extensive, but a major ecological disaster had been avoided because favorable winds blew the slick away from the shore and dispersed large portions of it.

A fall offensive by the Iranians in the Penjwin area, about 300 kilometers northeast of Baghdad, was considerably more successful than the February operation. The attackers claimed (and the Iraqis subsequently confirmed) that they had penetrated several kilometers into Iraqi territory and had knocked out several military positions as they captured stragetic high ground. Iraq then attacked several Iranian towns using missile-firing aircraft, claiming that the raids were in retaliation for the deliberate destruction of Penjwin by Iranian troops. The Iranians then asserted that the Iraqis had destroyed their own town in order to have a pretext for the air raids against civilian targets. Because foreign correspondents and observers were still banned from war zones, the claims and counterclaims could not be sorted out.

The complexion of the air war was altered in October 1983, when the French government sold the Iraqi air force five Super Etendard aircraft. Iraq immediately started an air offensive against merchant shipping in the Gulf, which, although intended to undercut Iranian trade, posed a threat to all Gulf interests. The Exocet-equipped Super Etendards attacked ships using Iranian ports, regardless of flag, and, before the end of the year, Greek and Panamanian vessels had been hit by missiles. In addition, a Japanese construction firm was warned by the Iraqis not to resume its contract work on a petrochemical complex at Bandar Khomeini (formerly Bandar Shapur). The Super Etendards roamed as far as the Strait of Hormuz to intercept shipping.

In early 1984 the two belligerents were issuing threats to bomb each other's civilian populations, and Iran threatened to close the Strait of Hormuz, which the United States had already pledged to keep open. Iraq threatened to increase its attacks against the oil terminus at Kharg Island. Iran also massed a huge army, consisting mostly of untrained or poorly trained volunteers who had been promised by Khomeini that they would go directly to heaven if killed in battle. When summer arrived and the Iranian offensive had still not occurred, observers speculated that there were divisions in the Iranian leadership. There seemed to be no end in sight for the long war of attrition, and even as Iraq again sought to arrange some kind of a cease-fire, it also stepped up its attacks on the enemy's economy, particularly its oil industry.

As the war dragged on, newspapers in the GCC states claimed that Iranian intransigence kept the hostilities going. The amir of Kuwait, Shaykh Jabir al Ahmad al Jabir, appealed to Prime Minister Indira Gandhi of India to use her influence as chairperson of the Nonaligned Movement to attempt mediation again. Other Gulf leaders held conferences to search out new methods of getting the combatants to the negotiating table. Sultan Qaboos

bin Said bin Taimur Al Bu Said of Oman stressed that the problems were Gulf problems and should be resolved by Gulf states
without interference from the superpowers. Khomeini held to
the course that he had set at the time of the Iraqi invasion, that is,
that Saddam Husayn be deposed. The ayatollah, certain that his
country was strong enough to outlast the enemy, would not consider negotiating on terms other than his own. Those terms included the overthrow of the Iraqi government and the payment of
heavy reparations.

Writing in the March 1984 issue of *Defense and Foreign Affairs,* Frederick Axelgard of Georgetown University's Center for
Strategic and International Studies said that "from the war's outset the small Arab sheikhdoms have been torn over how to give
fraternal Arab support to Iraq without overexposing themselves
to Iran's military and ideological arsenal." The quandary for the
Arab Gulf states continued as the war entered a new, more
dangerous phase in late spring 1984, when Iraq began determined attacks on Iranian oil facilities and the foreign tankers servicing them. Instead of attempting to close the Strait of Hormuz
as it had earlier threatened, Iran chose to reply in kind by attacking tankers leaving the ports of other Gulf oil producers. To close
the strait would have been a direct challenge to President Ronald
Reagan, who had vowed to keep it open. Attacking tankers was an
indirect way of reaching the same goal, i.e., disrupting the flow of
oil, without openly challenging the Americans.

At the beginning of May, Saddam Husayn announced that
his country was increasing its efforts to stem the tide of oil flowing
from Iran to the noncommunist world and the flow of goods and
money into Iran. In February the Iraqi president had warned all
shipping interests that he intended to interrupt all trade with
Iran. Iraqi aircraft then attacked several foreign vessels, including
Saudi-owned ships chartered by other countries to carry Iranian
oil from Kharg Island. The Iraqi attacks on ships owned by Saudi
Arabia—one of Iraq's benefactors—raised political questions for
Gulf leaders that they were obviously uncomfortable in answer-
ing, e.g., what to do about a brother Arab state—Iraq—that was
attacking Arab-owned ships carrying oil for non-Arab Iran? There
were also international ramifications to the attacks on oil tankers;
Liberian or Panamanian flag vessels, for example, were owned by
American, Italian, Saudi, Swedish, or other interests; were cap-
tained by Spaniards or Britons, among others; and were crewed
by Yugoslavs, Moroccans, or seamen from dozens of other countries. Meanwhile, every attack sent insurance rates soaring as
Lloyds of London assumed ever-increasing risks for the mul-

timillion dollar ships and cargoes.

When the war on tankers heated up, Arab newspapers in the Gulf countries reiterated their oft-expressed fear that attacks on the Gulf oil economy invited outside interference, and they pleaded with the belligerents to end this war between "Muslim brothers." Some of the newspaper comments were moderate in tone; others were radical and virulently anti-American. Most of the editorialists chose to ignore indiscriminate Iraqi attacks on shipping and concentrated instead on condemning Iran, whose attacks on tankers were only technically different from Iraq's. An example of the extremist views circulating in Gulf countries appeared in a Kuwaiti newspaper, which stated that the Iranian attacks on neutral ships had been planned and instigated by the United States as a cause for intervention. Another Kuwaiti daily claimed that "the rulers of Tehran are paving the way for a foreign, namely American, intervention in the Gulf," and that the American fleet was poised to fulfill that goal. In addition to blaming the United States for the Gulf tragedy, some Arab spokesmen said that the Iranian attacks were "Zionist" inspired.

The United States in late May maintained its position of ostensible neutrality in the war. When asked at a press conference if the United States would provide air power to protect shipping in the Gulf, President Reagan noted that the Gulf states had not requested direct United States military support although the United States had made clear its support for their security. There was much speculation about the role of the United States in the escalating crisis as both belligerents stepped up their attacks on ships of neutral countries, but the American reaction remained low key. In keeping with that approach, the U.S.S. *La Salle*, flagship of the five- or six-ship Gulf flotilla that had been visiting Indian Ocean ports, continued on its way to Diego Garcia, giving the impression of an American hands-off attitude. At the same time, an American naval force led by the aircraft carrier U.S.S. *Kitty Hawk* continued to steam "over the horizon" in the Arabian Sea.

In July 1984 the costly war of attrition continued, but neither side seemed willing to invest sufficiently in the conflict to secure immediate victory. Iraq continued its attacks on tankers and cargo ships serving Iran, which it referred to as "naval targets," and Iran retaliated by attacking tankers serving the other Gulf oil producers. Iran also kept a huge army massed near the Shatt al Arab. Iraq had sufficient air power to attack Kharg Island but held back; Iran, conceivably, could have captured Basrah, but it also held back. The danger of the war's spreading to the Gulf Arab states in-

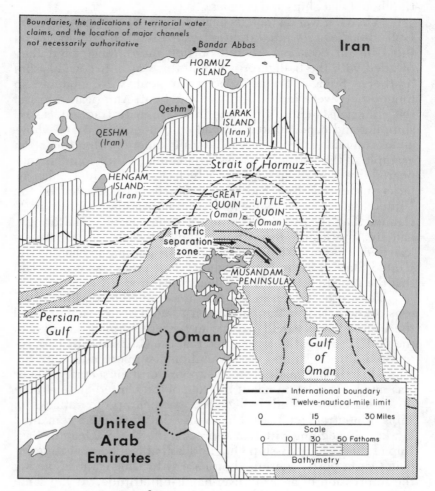

Figure 21. Strait of Hormuz

creased as both belligerents went outside the war zone to attack shipping targets of opportunity. The United States expedited shipment of 400 Stinger antiaircraft missiles to the worried Saudi Arabians but refused a Kuwaiti request for the same weapon, promising, however, to assist the Kuwaitis with other air defense systems.

Saudi Arabian F-15s, guided by American-manned AWACS, shot down two Iranian F-4s, putting Tehran on notice that it could not attack Gulf Arab targets without retaliation and indicating that the GCC countries had a limit on how much they would take before responding in kind. After 46 months the war seemed no closer to resolution than it had in its early days in late 1980. Ned Temko, writing for the *Christian Science Monitor* from Baghdad, quoted an Iraqi policeman whose words seemed to assess accurately the situation. "The war is no good," he said, "but as long as Khomeini and Saddam Hussein are around, it will go on."

Vulnerability of the Strait of Hormuz

Until the start of the Iran-Iraq War in late 1980, the Strait of Hormuz was well known only to geographers and navigators. After the outbreak of the war, however, the strait became a vital waterway because it was perceived as a choke point for any power that might desire to interrupt the flow of oil out of the Gulf. Much of the noncommunist world's oil supply passes through the 38-kilometer-wide strait that separates the Musandam Peninsula—the tip of which is owned by Oman—from Iran (see fig. 21).

Even before the outbreak of hostilities, the United States had pledged to keep open the Strait of Hormuz. Deputy Secretary of State Warren Christopher stated on September 18, 1980, that the United States would ensure free passage of ships in and out of the Gulf, even to the taking of naval action if that became necessary. Christopher said that his government wanted to keep the war from spreading to other countries of the Gulf and wanted to prevent the interruption of the flow of oil until peace could be restored between Iran and Iraq. President Valéry Giscard d'Estaing of France proclaimed his country's intention of aiding in maintaining freedom of navigation in the area. A powerful armada of American, Australian, British, and French warships was assembled in the Indian Ocean to back up Western statements. The deputy prime minister of Iraq declared that his country had no intention of interfering with ship traffic through the strait.

As the war progressed (or more precisely, as the land war became stalemated), Iraq declared that the northern end of the Gulf was a war zone in which it would attack ships servicing Iranian ports. Iran declared its right to halt ships anywhere in the Gulf that it suspected of carrying war cargoes to Iraq. During 1982, as the initiative in the war passed to the Iranians, the Iraqis stepped up their attacks on foreign ships. Saddam Husayn proclaimed an "exclusion zone" extending about 65 kilometers out from Kharg Island, and he warned foreign shipping interests that they would have only themselves to blame if ships were hit by Iraqi missiles in that area. An Iranian spokesman replied to the new proclamation by again threatening to close the Strait of Hormuz, stating that "the whole of Europe will be deprived of Gulf oil," but Iran made no move to carry out the threat. The acquisition by Iraq of Super Etendard aircraft armed with Exocet missiles in November 1983 also prompted the ayatollah's government to issue another threat to close the strait to all shipping.

The escalation of threats as well as of hostile actions worried the other Gulf states, particularly because the United States had asserted that it would take action to keep the strait open. At a press conference in October 1983 President Reagan said, "I do not believe the free world could stand by and allow anyone to close the Strait of Hormuz and the Persian Gulf to the oil traffic through those waterways." Arab newspapers around the Gulf continually expressed the concern that the Gulf war could easily become a superpower war.

When the Super Etendard deal was consummated, Iran again condemned the French and once more threatened to block all oil shipments. It also increased its naval and air patrol activities in the strait and reportedly moved artillery to its islands in that area of the Gulf. Many Western analysts had concluded by this time, however, that Iran was not capable of carrying out its oft-repeated threats to block the strait. Leaders of the other Gulf states, concerned about constant threats to close the strait—and thus cut off their economic lifeline—generally have been cautious in their public statements concerning what their own reactions would be in the event that Iran carried through on its threat. Sultan Qaboos of Oman told interviewers in March 1984 that his government would act only in concert with the other states of the GCC. Qaboos had signed an agreement in June 1980 by which the United States would be allowed to use bases in Oman, but he said that such use would need GCC approval. The sultan, however, did not believe that Iran would close the strait, because it depended on its own shipments through the waterway. Shaykh Muhammad bin Mubarak Al Khalifa, foreign minister of Bahrain, said that his government would support any effort to ensure that the Strait of Hormuz remained open to all traffic.

In February 1984 a spokesman for the Reagan administration reiterated the president's earlier avowal that the United States had every intention of maintaining free passage for all vessels through the strait. Prime Minister Margaret Thatcher of Britain stated that "it might be in Britain's interests to join with U.S. forces to protect that part of the world, and the oil supplies which are vital to the West." The United States Navy issued a statement to ships and aircraft in the Gulf area to the effect that its "forces operating in international waters within the Persian Gulf, Strait of Hormuz, Gulf of Oman, and Arabian Sea north of 20 degrees are taking additional defensive precautions against terrorist threats" and requested that ships coming within five nautical miles of an American naval vessel identify themselves. The navy also warned that aircraft approaching American ships at altitudes under 600 meters might be placing themselves at risk. TASS, the Soviet press agency, said that American naval actions and declarations in the Gulf and Arabian Sea were violations of international law and were "dramatically escalating tension and provoking a conflict situation with the involvement of the U.S. armed forces there." The American and Soviet statements heightened the nervousness of the Arab press.

By late spring 1984 closure of the strait had become a moot point as constant Iraqi attacks on Iranian oil facilities and ships lifting oil or delivering cargoes brought an Iranian response but not the blocking of the strait. Instead. Iran attacked tankers carrying oil from Kuwait or Saudi Arabia. Such attacks resulted in skyrocketing insurance rates, making shipowners wary and, in effect, impeding the free flow of oil out of the Gulf without blocking the strait. Crews of ships entering the Gulf began to express doubts that the bonuses they had received since the war started were still adequate after both belligerents declared open season on Gulf shipping. Japan, which gets 80 percent of its oil from the Gulf, stopped sending Japanese-owned or -crewed ships into the northern Gulf, although it continued to charter ships of other owners.

Disputes and Perceived Threats

Until 1971 Britain's armed forces had maintained peace and order in the Gulf, and British officials had arbitrated local disputes; but after the withdrawal of those forces and officials, old territorial claims and suppressed tribal animosities rose again to the surface. Anthony H. Cordesman contends in *The Gulf and the Search for Strategic Stability* that "there is nothing new about military crises in the Gulf. The states in the region have been at war with one another for the last thousand years, and few Gulf states have had the opportunity to change rulers peacefully or without some form of military intervention." He continues in a footnote that "from 1890 through 1974, no Trucial State changed rulers without family strife, a coup d'état, or civil war." So it came as no surprise when old hostilities reemerged. Some of the conflicts continued into the mid-1980s, but added to such localized problems were concerns about the possible spread of the Iran-Iraq War, the potential for superpower involvement in the Gulf, and the ever-present worry about Israel.

Territorial Disputes

Iran, Iraq, and Saudi Arabia are the dominant powers of the Gulf. Kuwait, Bahrain, Qatar, the UAE, and Oman—smaller and less powerful—often are referred to collectively as "the other Gulf states." Since the start of the Iran-Iraq War, Saudi Arabia frequently has been included in that grouping. The small states have been intimidated at times by their more powerful neighbors. Among many examples, Iran has often laid claim to Bahrain; Iraq to Kuwait; and Saudi Arabia to large areas of the UAE. But territorial animosities have just as often arisen between or among the lesser states: Bahrain continues to claim the Hawar Islands, just off the Qatari shore, as well as a coastal strip of Qatar itself.

The Iranian claim to Bahrain was based on the seventeenth-century defeat of the Portuguese by the Iranians and their subsequent occupation of the Bahraini archipelago. The Iranians were in turn pushed out in the late eighteenth century by the Arab clan known as Al Khalifa, which has provided the ruling family of Bahrain ever since. But the Iranians have refused to give up their revanchist claims. The late shah, Mohammad Reza Pahlavi, raised the Bahraini question again after the British announcement of withdrawal from east of Suez, but he supposedly laid the matter to rest after a UN-sponsored plebiscite showed that the Bahrainis much preferred independence to Iranian hegemony. By showing reasonableness over Bahrain, the shah was better able to press his demand for the lower Gulf islands of Abu Musa and the Tunbs, claimed respectively by Sharjah and Ras al Khaymah. There was no great outcry in the West over the occupation of the islands because the shah was a friend and ally, and the affair was written off as a local dispute that should not concern the West. When the friendly shah was replaced by the hostile ayatollah, there were some belated misgivings about Iranian control of the strategically located islands, but Iranian possession was a fait accompli. The religious leaders of Iran's Islamic Revolution resurrected the claim to Bahrain, but secular leaders were able to set the claim aside in an attempt to establish better relations with the Bahrainis.

The United States had fostered close ties to Iran under the shah at the time of the British departure, hoping that Iran could police the Gulf as Britain previously had; but Iran was too heavily involved as a player to be an effective umpire. The increasing power of the shah, under American auspices, worried some Arab rulers, who saw the seizure of the Gulf islands as only a harbinger of what might happen. At the same time that the United States was building its close relationship with Iran, the Soviet Union was striving to create a client state in Iraq, and some Arab Gulf rulers openly worried about further Soviet advances in the region.

Another point of contention in the Gulf was the Bahraini claim to Az Zubarah on the Qatari coast and to the Hawar Islands, claims that stemmed from former tribal areas and dynastic struggles. The Al Khalifa had settled at Az Zubarah before driving the Iranians out of Bahrain in the eighteenth century, but the Al Thani, ruling family of Qatar, vigorously disputed the Al Khalifa claim to the old settlement area as well as the claim to the Hawar Islands, a stone's throw from the Qatari mainland but over 20 kilometers from Bahrain. The seven entities that became the UAE in 1971 might well have been nine if Bahrain and Qatar could have settled their territorial disputes.

Another territorial dispute involved Abu Dhabi, Qatar, and Saudi Arabia. This long-standing controversy centered on the Khawr al Udayd, a meandering inlet once occupied by a tribe of the Bani Yas confederation of Abu Dhabi. The inlet had been placed under the sovereignty of the Al Nuhayyan of Abu Dhabi by British decree, but the British ruling was contested by the Al Thani of Qatar and the Al Saud of Saudi Arabia, both of whom put forth their own bases for ownership. Sovereignty over the inlet had supposedly been part of the agreement that settled another long-lived dispute involving the Buraymi Oasis, a dispute in which Abu Dhabi, Oman, and Saudi Arabia had been embroiled since the late nineteenth century. Whatever the agreement, to international geographers the borders at the base of the Qatari Peninsula (adjacent to the Khawr al Udayd) were still in dispute, and the three countries involved had not published definitive boundaries (see Regional Relations, ch. 6).

The Buraymi Oasis, which had succored various tribes since the second or third century A.D., became an area of dispute among the Abu Dhabians, Omanis, and Saudis in 1869 when an Omani force expelled the Wahhabi (see Glossary) governor. The oasis had been under control of Wahhabis from the Najd region of central Arabia since 1800. After 1869, even though the tribes remaining in residence in the several settlements of the oasis were from Oman and Abu Dhabi, the dominant religious influence among them continued to be Wahhabism. On the basis that Wahhabism was native to Saudi Arabia and that the people of the oasis continued to follow the Wahhabi doctrine in the mid-twentieth century, King Abd al Aziz bin Abd ar Rahman Al Saud, the great hero-king of Saudi Arabia, sent a small constabulary force to reassert Saudi control of Buraymi in 1952. The king's action led to a confrontation with the British, who eventually sent their Trucial Oman Scouts to expel the Saudi constabulary. The dispute dragged on into the post-British period and presented a barrier to good relations between Saudi Arabia and the newly created UAE, as well as between Saudi Arabia and Oman. An ambiguous agreement in 1974 left various boundary disputes unresolved, but the principals seemed to prefer a certain amount of ambiguity; in the succeeding 10 years, the oasis continued to be occupied peacefully by Abu Dhabian and Omani tribes, and the Saudis seemed content to let their very tenuous claim lie dormant.

The physical separation of Oman from its enclave on the Musandam Peninsula has been a continuing source of friction between Oman and various neighboring amirates for more than a century (see fig. 19). Oman is larger than the UAE, Qatar, Bahrain, and Kuwait combined, but in the 1980s the tiny segment of Oman's territory on the peninsula gained great international significance because of its position on the Strait of Hormuz. This small enclave also gives Oman its shoreline on the Gulf. The division of Oman dates back to the nineteenth-century reign of Sultan Sayyid Said, who, despite his prowess in gaining footholds on the African and Indian coasts, was forced to give up territory on his own borders to the Wahhabis. That ceded territory was included in the amirates that joined to become the UAE in 1971 and was a source of friction between Oman and the new state until the early 1980s. Since the start of the Iran-Iraq War and the subsequent formation of the GCC, Oman and the UAE have stopped arguing about the disputed territory.

Because of the vast oil wealth of the Gulf seabed and the potential for future discoveries of new oil fields under the Gulf waters, the delimitation of the continental shelf has been of extreme importance to all of the littoral states. The entire seabed of the Gulf is considered to be continental shelf under international law, and much of the shelf has been delimited, but sovereignty disputes over several islands have resulted in a lack of demarcation in those areas. The most notable island disputes continuing in 1984 were those involving Iran and the UAE over the Tunbs and Abu Musa, and Bahrain and Qatar over the Hawar Islands. Land boundaries and delimitations of the continental shelf that would have had little or no importance before the discovery of oil have taken on great importance in the late twentieth century.

Concern over Superpower Involvement

In the early 1980s the Iran-Iraq War captured the attention of the United States and the Soviet Union, in addition to all Western oil-consuming nations and Japan. Neither of the superpowers benefited from the war, and both wanted to be instrumental in bringing it to an end, but neither had sufficient influence in the area to end the hostilities. From the beginning of the war, many Gulf Arab editorial writers have expressed fears that the superpowers would turn it into an East-West confrontation. More often than not the remarks have been aimed at the United States rather than the Soviet Union, probably because the former has had a visible presence in the Gulf region since World War II and has interests in the area that have been described as vital by both the Carter and the Reagan administrations. In May 1984 a spokesman for the United States Department of State reiterated that the Gulf "is an area of vital interest to us" and that "we are prepared to defend our vital interests."

Some of the press warnings about superpower involvement seemed to be expressions of genuine concern, but most were pure propaganda. One UAE editor, for example, offered the opinion that the United States and the Soviet Union preferred that the war continue "so that arms factories can continue work." A Kuwaiti newspaper editorial in March 1984 said that the greatest service that the United States could provide to the Gulf countries would be to refrain from intervening in the war, adding that American involvement would present greater dangers than the continuation of the war. Some of the anti-United States tirades in the Gulf Arab press were obviously motivated by the American-Israeli relationship. One UAE newspaper in April 1984 said that "only the United States and its allies—and above all Israel, which is usurping Arab lands including Jerusalem—stand to gain." In this all-too-common Arab opinion the United States is a stalking-horse for Israel, poised to intervene in the Gulf war to advance the Israeli cause in the Middle East.

Soviet interest in the area began in imperial times as part of the general Russian expansionism of the early nineteenth century as the tsars moved into Central Asia. These moves eventually brought the Russians into confrontation with the British, who had already established themselves in the Gulf. Competition for influence in the area grew after the British discovered oil in Iran in 1908, and soon the United States was also a party to the confrontation. The East-West struggle continued after the Russian Empire

had become the Soviet Union, and even though the pro-
tagonists—Britain, the Soviet Union, and the United States—
were allies during World War II, the contest for economic and
political influence in the area did not diminish. Rather, with the
onset of the Cold War, that contest accelerated considerably.
British withdrawal in 1971 removed the force that had maintained
stability, thus heightening tensions in the entire region and between the world's two superpowers.

The chaos in Iran brought on by the overthrow of the shah
and the subsequent war with Iraq prompted some observers to
conclude that the country was ripe for subversion by its Soviet-
supported Tudeh (Masses) Party. In that event the United States
would have to become involved in order to prevent Iran from becoming a Soviet satellite. If such a scenario were to evolve, the
superpower confrontation dreaded by the Gulf states would be
unavoidable. The potential was lessened measurably when the
Tudeh Party, as an instrument of subversion, was dealt a severe
blow by the Khomeini regime, which executed several Tudeh
leaders in the spring of 1984.

In weighing its Gulf options, the United States let it be
known that it would be in close contact with its European allies
and with Japan before taking any action toward intervention.
American spokesmen had stated consistently that the United
States would not intervene unless requested to do so by Gulf Arab
countries, which would have to be willing to provide facilities,
and that if such action were contemplated, the United States preferred that its allies (who were much more dependent on Gulf oil)
also become involved. As attacks on oil tankers continued, some
Kuwaiti officials announced a 180-degree turn in policy, stating
that it would be proper for Western countries to intervene in the
Gulf war if their vital interests were threatened. Despite the
change of opinion, however, a Kuwaiti cabinet minister reiterated the standard admonition that foreign powers should not establish military bases on Arab soil.

In the *Christian Science Monitor* of June 14, 1984, David D.
Newsom offered the opinion that it was possible that the Gulf
Arabs actually mean what they have been saying regarding their
desire for nonintervention by foreign powers. He presented the
idea that American strategists have believed that the Arabs repeat
their requests that the superpowers stay out of the Gulf but in fact
want the Americans to stand by in case they are needed. Newsom
contended that this notion may be a misreading of the true Arab
position. In his view, strong support for Israel, congressional
statements about not involving American troops in overseas

View of Doha, Qatar
Courtesy Embassy of Qatar, Washington

troubles, and continuing efforts to free the country from dependence on Middle East oil have made the Arabs wary of depending on American help. Newsom argued that Washington might need to reassess its position in Gulf affairs and, perhaps, to place more credence in the statements of Arab Gulf leaders.

Concern over Perceived Israeli Threat

Despite territorial disputes and conflicts with neighbors, despite the acknowledged threat of Khomeini's Islamic Revolution, and despite the fear of superpower intervention, the primary concern of Gulf Arabs—as they see it—is the threat emanating from Israel. Conservative leaders of the small Gulf countries fear that they could be overthrown from within if they fail to demonstrate continually their hostility to Israel. Most of the small Gulf states have numerous Palestinian refugees residing in their countries. But it is not only the Palestinians who pressure governments to show hostility to Israel. All Arabs appear to be very conscious of the Arab-Israeli conflict, and young Arabs have been educated to consider practically every aspect of life in the light of how it affects or is affected by that conflict.

Events such as the Israeli attack on the Iraqi nuclear plant in 1981 and the Israeli invasion of Lebanon in 1982 serve to convince Arab countries that they live in constant danger from what Arab newspapers invariably refer to as "the Israeli enemy." In past Arab-Israeli wars the support provided the Arab cause by the Gulf states has been limited, and it appeared unlikely that they would be able to provide much support in a future war. Furthermore, an Israeli assault against any Gulf country seemed more than remote in 1984. Nevertheless, the perception that they live under the Israeli gun was very real to Gulf Arabs.

Military Aspects of the Gulf Cooperation Council

In 1984 the GCC continued to include as members all of the countries having Gulf shorelines, except Iran and Iraq. Actually, it was the danger to the entire Gulf brought on by the war that motivated the nonwarring countries to unite in the GCC in May 1981. A regional organization of some sort had been discussed frequently among the Gulf states, but it took a few months of the war between two of them to cause the others to become serious in such discussions. Although the GCC has also been concerned with foreign affairs, education, and other matters affecting the member societies, security had a high priority in the minds of its creators when they agreed to organize for cooperation. In the words of John Duke Anthony of the Johns Hopkins University Foreign Policy Institute, "The need to find a more credible and effective means to deal with the pressing problem of security was, indeed, one of the most compelling reasons for establishing the GCC."

The statutes of the GCC, signed at Abu Dhabi by the heads of state of the six founding members on May 24, 1981, proclaim the aims of the organization to be "co-ordination, integration and co-operation among the member-states in all fields." Article 4 of the statutes entitled "Aims" lists six areas in which the Council would cooperate: economic and financial affairs; trade, customs, and transportation; education and cultural affairs; health and social affairs; information and tourism; and judicial and administrative affairs. Noticeable by its absence in the statutes was any reference to mutual defense; and, of the five committees established by the GCC on its second day of existence, none dealt with defense. This seeming lack of attention to security matters belied the concern that the six rulers shared about the dangers presented to all by the Iran-Iraq War (see Appendix C).

In the final communiqué of its first meeting, the Supreme Council of the GCC stated: "Their majesties and highnesses reviewed the current situation in the area. They reaffirm that the region's security and stability are the responsibility of its peoples and countries and that this Council expressed the will of these countries and their right to defend their security and independence. They also affirm their absolute rejection of foreign interference in the region from any source. They call for keeping the entire region free of international conflicts, particularly the presence of military fleets and foreign bases, in order to safeguard their interests and the interests of the world." The communiqué also reiterated the position that stability in the Gulf was related to stability in the Middle East as a whole, and peace in the entire area was linked to the Palestinian question and Israeli occupation of Arab lands.

In September 1981, only four months after the establishment of the GCC, the chiefs of staff of the armed forces of the six member states met in Riyadh to discuss regional military cooperation. Two months later, at the scheduled meeting of the Supreme Council, the six heads of state studied the reports prepared by the chiefs of staff and decided to order a meeting of their respective defense ministers "to set the priorities" for mutual defense. The principal conferees and their staffs were welcomed to that meeting in January 1982 by Prince Sultan bin Abd al Aziz Al Saud, minister of defense and aviation of the host country, Saudi Arabia. The other ministers in attendance were Shaykh Salim al Sabah al Salim Al Sabah of Kuwait; General Hamad bin Isa Al Khalifa, Bahraini crown prince and commander of the Bahrain Defense Force; Shaykh Hamad bin Khalifah Al Thani, Qatari crown prince and defense minister; Shaykh Muhammad bin Rashid bin Said Al Maktum, UAE defense minister; and Prince Fahr bin Taimur Al Bu Said, Omani deputy prime minister for security and defense.

Although working sessions of the defense ministers' meetings were held in camera, Sultan and Abdullah Yakub Bisharah, secretary general of the GCC, held a press conference at the conclusion of the talks. Sultan stated that there had been no differences of opinion and that agreement and harmony had characterized the conference. Bisharah stressed that the GCC was determined to maintain the security of the Gulf with its own forces and without intervention from outside. No official communiqué was issued concerning results of the conference, but some news reports indicated that joint air defense of the six member countries had been discussed, as had joint production of arms. Sultan and Bisharah were noncommittal when asked specifically about these subjects. Some newspapers also reported that an Arab rapid deployment force would result from the conference but, as is customary, military developments were not publicized nor was there any public speculation on such subjects by the principals.

The first major field exercise by the armed forces of the six member states took place in October 1983 when Shield of the Peninsula (Dir al Jizira) brought together about 6,500 troops in the UAE. The exercise, under the command of Brigadier General Ahmad Salim of the host country, was designed to test units of the ground, sea, and air forces of the member states operating under a joint command. The chiefs of staff of the individual armed forces, plus other high-ranking defense officials, visited Abu Dhabi to view the final stage of Dir al Jizira. Referring to the combined force as the GCC's Rapid Deployment Force, military officials pointedly remarked that their own RDF was capable of defending any member country from external aggression without calling for any outside assistance.

A few days after the conclusion of Dir al Jizira, the chiefs of staff of the armed forces of the GCC members assembled in Riyadh for two days of meetings at which they listened to critiques of the exercise and discussed a number of pertinent military matters. According to news reports the chiefs of staff discussed the establishment of a joint military command, but nine months later no further news had appeared on that subject. Saudi Arabia, the largest and most powerful of the GCC states, would be the natural leader of such an organization. In the past, discussions of Gulf cooperation often were hung up on the fear that Iran or Iraq would try for hegemony over any regional association. If the smaller states have held similar fears concerning the Saudis, expressions of those fears have been muted since the establishment of the GCC; nevertheless, a joint command under Saudi generalship might be expected to cause concern among the leaders of the smaller states.

Various kinds of military cooperation are possible under the GCC umbrella. For example, air defense stands out as one area of immediate concern, and steps have been taken to standardize procedures and to cooperate on defense; but, as of mid-1984, progress had been relatively slow. Other potential areas of military cooperation might be intelligence gathering and analysis, arms procurement, and arms manufacture. There have also been news reports of discussions concerning the possibilty of a joint military academy and the sharing of military training facilities. It is possible that progress has been made in some of these areas without coming to public attention; all member states are very chary about publishing military developments. Furthermore, the individual states—half of them independent only since the British departure in 1971—remained jealous of their prerogatives, and agreements that appear to impinge on sovereignty were difficult to achieve.

In May 1984 a Kuwaiti newspaper, without naming its source, stated that the goal of the GCC Defense Council, i.e., the collective defense ministers, was to establish a "strike force." At a time when the Gulf war was again heating up and discussions of possible United States military bases were again prominent in the news, a leak concerning a joint GCC strike force might have been a ploy designed to offset speculation about outside intervention. Well into the summer of 1984, no integrated GCC force or joint command had appeared.

The chiefs of staff met in late June 1984 to discuss how best to protect tankers in the lower Gulf from Iranian attack. Again, no public mention was made of Iraqi attacks on shipping outside the war zone. At the meeting (described by Kuwaiti officials as the most significant of its kind to date), the chiefs reportedly decided that constant air cover, in conjunction with early warning provided by the American AWACS, would provide the best possible protection. The conferees also ratified a plan to increase air defense installations along the coastal areas that are exposed to hostile air attack, particularly in Kuwait, which was closest to the war zone.

Kuwait

Background

From 1899 until 1961 Kuwait remained, in effect, a British protectorate. During those six decades the country was ruled by a succession of shaykhs of the Al Sabah family, but the handling of its foreign affairs was a British prerogative, and the security of the shaykhdom was guaranteed by the British Empire (see British Governmental Transition, ch. 1; The Political System, ch. 2). Kuwaiti forces consisted of the shaykh's royal guard plus a small domestic police force—constabulary—under the British administration. British protection became particularly important during the 1920s and 1930s in deterring Saudi encroachment and later in blocking Iraqi territorial claims.

After World War II, as thoughts of independence became more prevalent among the Kuwaiti people, the need for the formation of national armed forces became obvious. By the mid-1950s Kuwait had become a major producer of oil, and revenues from that production ensured that there would be ample funds to pay for as much military expansion as the Al Sabah desired. By Independence Day—June 19, 1961—the British had converted the 600-man constabulary into a combined arms brigade of 2,500 men that was trained by a British military mission. Small air and naval forces were also established under British tutelage in 1961.

Six days after the exchange of diplomatic notes between the governments of Britain and Kuwait that established the latter's independence, the prime minister of Iraq laid claim to the newly independent neighboring state. The Iraqis based their claim on the assertion that Kuwait was properly a part of Iraq that had been stolen by British "colonial imperialists" in 1899. The Kuwaiti ruler, Shaykh Abdallah al Salim Al Sabah, immediately appealed to the UN, the League of Arab States (Arab League) and, more important, to Britain, which was committed to come to his aid under the terms of the independence agreement. British troops began landing on July 1, 1961, and within a week 6,000 had been brought in from Aden, Cyprus, Kenya, and Britain. Kuwaiti forces were mobilized, and all were placed under joint British-Kuwaiti command.

Over objections by the government of Iraq, independent Kuwait was admitted to membership in the Arab League later in July. Iraq then moderated its pressure on its neighbor but refused to give up its claim to sovereignty. By October the British forces had been replaced by Arab League contingents from Jordan, Saudi Arabia, Sudan, and Egypt, all under the command of a Saudi general. The Arab League forces remained in Kuwait until a military coup in Iraq resulted in a government that was willing to recognize Kuwaiti independence. By early 1963 the Arab League troops had been withdrawn, and, in October of that year, the new Iraqi government recognized Kuwait as an independent state.

After the crises attending its establishment as an independent state, Kuwait sought to play a moderating role among Arab countries, using its vast oil wealth generously in grants and loans to many Arab states and causes (including, for example, support to the Palestine Liberation Organization [PLO]). After Britain's declaration on May 13, 1968, of its intent to cancel its defense commitments and withdraw its armed forces from east of Suez by the end of 1971, the government in London further announced its intention to terminate its commitment of assistance to Kuwait to become effective on May 13, 1971, three years from the date of the announcement. The decision had been preceded by two events: a troublesome border incident with Iraq in 1967, in which Britain was involved in its role as protector; and the 1969 negotiated division of the Kuwaiti-Saudi Arabia Neutral Zone, in which the British were similarly involved (see The Oil Industry, ch. 2). Such incidents pointed to the increased responsibilities that the Kuwaiti armed forces would have after the British departure.

A new politico-military crisis developed on March 20, 1973, when Iraqi forces occupied the Kuwait border post of Al Samitah and shelled another post. Each side blamed the other for provoking the incident. Kuwait immediately declared a state of emergency, reinforced its border guards, and appealed to Arab and world opinion for condemnation of Iraq as the alleged aggressor. Under pressure from the Arab League, Iraq withdrew its forces from the occupied areas in early April. A major factor reportedly motivating the withdrawal was a Kuwaiti threat to withhold financial aid to several Arab countries in their continuing confrontation with Israel if Iraq did not desist in its aggression. Inconclusive talks between the two principals in the border dispute dragged on for several months, during which the Iraqi foreign minister further clouded the issue by laying claim to the Kuwaiti offshore islands of Al Warbah and Bubiyan (see fig. 4). The incursion at Al Samitah and the subsequent claim to the islands served to remind Kuwaitis that Iraqi threats to their sovereignty were still alive even after 12 years of independence. In June the Kuwaiti National Assembly voted to spend US$1.2 billion on building up the armed forces. The border dispute with Iraq was not settled until mid-1978, when a two-kilometer buffer zone was established between the two countries.

The development of Kuwait's armed forces has taken place in the context of the national development of a traditionalist Arab state that in 1984 had been fully independent for slightly under a quarter of a century. It is a country unique in the world because of its small size but enormous welalth; a country that is administered as a welfare state but is also a family preserve run by a paternalistic, constitutionally established monarchical line; and a country in which only 50 to 60 percent of the residents are citizens. Its armed forces have been characterized by small size and a defensive posture, as well as by professionalism, high pay and perquisites, and high morale. The forces have also been noted for their close identification with, and complete support of, the ruling house—Al Sabah—which has provided generous funds for weapons and equipment. The British influence on organization, equipment, and training under which the forces were established and developed were still strong in the 1980s, but American and French equipment and influence had also been introduced.

In June 1984 the United States refused to sell Stinger antiaircraft missiles to Kuwait on the grounds that they might fall into the hands of terrorists. At the same time, however, the United States did agree to upgrade Kuwait's existing HAWK antiaircraft defense system. In early July the Kuwaiti defense minister, Shaykh Salim, traveled to Moscow on a weapons-buying trip, denying to reporters that the trip was a result of the American refusal to sell the Stingers. On August 15 Kuwait signed a relatively modest arms purchase agreement with the Soviets that included various air defense weapons and provided for a small number of Soviet advisers for a short period of time. Kuwait, the only GCC member maintaining diplomatic relations with the Soviet Union, had dealt with that country before, purchasing SA-7 and SA-8 antiaircraft missiles, but it had not previously employed resident Soviet personnel as trainers and advisers. Spokesmen for the United States said that it would follow through on its commitment to improve the Kuwaiti air defenses.

External and Internal Threats

Kuwait's small size and limited military power effectively preclude aggressive policies. Its vast oil wealth, however, makes it vulnerable to aggression by its much larger neighbors. British protection shielded Kuwait for the first half of the twentieth century and for two and one-half decades after World War II during which the smaller Gulf states were gaining independence and seeking national stability. The grave political consequences of disturbing the recognized balance in the region (which had existed under British protection and was passed on to the new national entities) appeared to be a deterrent to adventurism by distant powers or to expansionism at Kuwait's expense by its more powerful neighbors—Iraq, Saudi Arabia, and Iran. The other small Gulf amirates do not present conceivable threats and, of course, in the 1980s these small states and Saudi Arabia allied themselves in the GCC.

An additional external threat to Kuwait has arisen from its extensive political and economic involvement in the Arab-Israeli conflict. Kuwait has been very active in Middle Eastern affairs, using its wealth to create favorable relations, mediating inter-Arab disputes, supporting Arab nationalist causes in general, and contributing huge amounts of money to the states and movements that have been most actively involved in the conflict with Israel (see Foreign Relations, ch. 2). Although separated from Israel by more than 1,200 kilometers, Kuwait's military officials feared that Kuwait could be a target of Israeli preventive strikes in the event of a renewal of actual Arab-Israeli hostilities.

Internally, the principal threats to security have lain not in ordinary crime or possible coups d'état but in political agitation and public disturbances generated by radical activists from among the large Palestinian minority (estimated to account for more than half of the large, non-Kuwaiti population). In addition, by the mid-1980s terrorism by Islamic radicals had become a real threat to the regime. In 1976 a combination of internal stresses and external factors produced a domestic crisis in which the amir dissolved the National Assembly, closed down opposition newspapers, and instituted a period of rule by royal decree (see The Constitutional Monarchy, ch. 2). During this constitutional crisis the amir and his supporters—apprehensive about the security of the regime and fearful that the bitter conflict in Lebanon could spread into Kuwait—confronted the legislature and the Palestinian elements in the population. The National Assembly remained suspended until February 1981.

Organization and Mission of the Forces

Under the Constitution, "the Amir is the Supreme Commander of the Armed Forces. He appoints and dismisses officers in accordance with law." The Constitution further states that "the Amir shall declare defensive war by decree. Offensive war is prohibited." The amir also has constitutional power to decree martial law for up to 15 days; periods in excess of that time require approval by the National Assembly. If that body has been dissolved, the condition of martial law must be considered by the successor body at its first sitting. The Constitution states that safeguarding the integrity of the country is a trust for every citizen; that military service shall be regulated by law; that only the state may form armed forces and public security forces; that mobilization must be regulated by law; and that a supreme defense council shall be set up to conduct defense affairs, to safeguard state integrity, and to supervise the armed forces. As prescribed, the Supreme Defense Council was established in November 1963; its original membership included the amir, the prime minister, the foreign minister, the defense minister, some top-ranking military officers, and several other cabinet ministers whose duties might have a bearing on national security.

Because the army is by far the largest of the three services, the minister of defense directs the armed forces through the army chief of staff. The small air force has a limited functional autonomy under its own commander, but he is responsible to the army chief of staff. Somewhat similarly, the National Guard has its own commander, but he reports directly to the minister of defense. The public security forces, all under the minister of interior, who is director of national security, include the police and the coast guard. The coordination of military and security affairs was greatly simplified for many years because the same man—Shaykh Said al Abdallah al Salim Al Sabah—headed both ministries. When Said became prime minister, other members of Al Sabah took over the defense and interior portfolios. In mid-1984 Shaykh Salim al Sabah al Salim Al Sabah headed the Ministry of Interior. The ruling family maintained a tight grip on the organs of power, including many senior posts in the security services. The army/armed forces chief of staff in 1984 was Major General Abdallah Farraj al Ghanim.

The classic missions of defense of the state from attack by land, sea, or air are applicable to the armed forces of Kuwait; adaptations were occasioned by the country's particular circumstances. The preservation of national sovereignty and national honor requires armed forces to validate a national identity and independence. The small size of the country and of its population, however, provide a correspondingly small base for the development of military strength. It is clearly not militarily rational to suppose that Kuwait alone could successfully defend itself indefinitely against a sustained, determined attack from an aggressor; its defense strategy, therefore, must be one of developing friendly alignments, such as it has done by joining the other nonwarring Gulf states in the GCC. Kuwait, with its limitations of small size and population and exposed location, has built armed forces that might possibly inflict initially heavy casualties on an invader; but those forces would function primarily as a trip wire.

They would be an immediate deterrent to an invader, but there would have to be other forces brought in for rapid reinforcement; otherwise, a powerful aggressor could be expected to overrun the country in a very short time. This, of course, explains Kuwait's eagerness to ally itself with the other states of the GCC.

The army's mission is to contain or delay a ground attack as far forward as possible and to defend the capital. The primary mission of the air force is air defense in conjunction with the ground-to-air missile system. Additional air force missions include interdiction of an invading force, close air support of ground troops, reconnaissance, and air transport. Ground and air forces would seek to impose rapid and heavy initial casualties on an invader. (The development of a credible, recognized capability for so doing is inherent in the organization, equipping, and training of the forces in peacetime.) The navy has been essentially a coastal defense force; in the early 1980s it has been increasing its firepower and would have a role in turning back any aggressor. The ground element of the air defense system is structured around American-made I-HAWK missiles, and the entire system has been tied into the Saudi air defense in order to take advantage of information supplied by the four American AWACS aircraft that have been on loan to Saudi Arabia since the start of the Iran-Iraq war.

The army at the beginning of 1984 had a strength estimated at 10,000 officers and enlisted men. The principal combat formations were one armored brigade, two mechanized infantry brigades, and one surface-to-surface missile battalion. Simple arithmetic demonstrates that a total force of 10,000 would be spread rather thinly in three brigades and a missile battalion when the necessary headquarters and support forces are also considered. Of necessity, some units must be held at reduced manning levels. Organizational patterns, administrative structures, and logistical systems revealed the legacy of the long and continuing British influence.

Armor in use by the army in 1984—all British-made main battle tanks—included 160 Chieftains, 70 Vickers, and 10 Centurions. On order were an unknown number of Scorpion light tanks, also from Britain. Other armored vehicles included 175 American-made M-113 armored personnel carriers (APC), 130 Saracen APCs, 100 Saladin armored cars, and 80 Ferret scout cars. The Saracen, Saladin, and Ferret vehicles are all of British manufacture. On order from the United States were 188 additional M-113 APCs and 56 M-113 chassis mounting TOW antitank weapons. Also on order were 4,800 improved TOW missiles. The principal tube artillery held by the army were 80 French-made

AMX 155mm self-propelled (SP) howitzers, 18 American-made M-109 SP 155mm howitzers, and 10 British-made 25-pounder artillery pieces. The surface-to-surface missile battalion was equipped with Soviet-made FROG-7s. Army antiaircraft units also had Soviet-made SA-7 missiles and ZSU 23x4 SP guns.

Air force strength was estimated at 1,900 in early 1984, but that figure did not include a number of expatriate technicians employed by the service. The inventory included about 60 combat aircraft, five transports, 40 helicopters, and nine British Strikemasters used as trainers. Two fighter-bomber squadrons used 36 McDonnell-Douglas A-4KU Skyhawks, and an interceptor squadron was equipped with 20 Dassault-Breguet Mirage F-1s. Helicopters—all of French manufacture—included 30 SA-342K Gazelle for reconnaissance and assault missions; some were armed with HOT missiles for antitank use. Also in the helicopter force were nine SA-330 Pumas for transport use. On order were 12 additional Mirage F-1s, four C-130H Hercules (Lockheed), and six Super Puma helicopters. An official announcement in July 1984 declared that, for better coordination and greater efficiency, all air force and air defense elements had been drawn together into a single command to be known as the Air Force and Air Defense Forces.

The navy had a strength estimated at 500 officers and enlisted men. Primarily a coastal defense force with police responsibilities, the navy was undergoing enhancement of its combat capabilities during 1984 that should change its complexion considerably. Previously operating a wide variety of patrol craft, the navy had on order six TNC-45 guided missile boats being built by the West German company of Friedrich Lürssen Werft in Bremen for delivery in 1984. The TNC-45s will be equipped with Exocet missiles. Two larger FPB-57 fast attack craft were on order from the same company and will be used for command ships of the new combat navy. The navy has also ordered six landing craft, six Hovercraft, two fireboat/tugs, and six service launches.

The National Guard—a semiautonomous body—has guard duties on the border and at the oil fields and performs public security functions in inland rural areas. The Guard acts as a reserve for the regular forces, reinforces the metropolitan police as directed and, in times of war or emergency, would have rear area security responsibilities. The national police, operating in the capital and other rural areas, performs the usual police functions of crime prevention and investigation, maintaining order, guarding officials and government buildings, traffic control, and public assistance. The navy performs police coast guard functions and has the usual missions of preventing smuggling and illegal entry. In emergencies, if police capabilities prove insufficient, the National Guard and regular forces may be used to restore order.

Although the armed forces would be expected to play a role in any extraordinary internal emergency, maintaining public order is a function of the public security force, i.e., the police. Each of the country's four governorates—Al Ahmadi, Al Jahrah, Hawalli, and Kuwait City—has a director of security, appointed by the minister of interior, who is the overall supervisor of security.

For several years social and political unrest have been much more apt to draw police attention than ordinary crime, and a very large expatriate population (which, in 1984, included 350,000 Palestinians, 150,000 Egyptians, 120,000 Iraqis, and 80,000 Iranians) has fostered extremist terrorism and inter-Arab radical intrigue. There were also about 200,000 from the Indian subcontinent. The Palestinians have presented problems for the Al Sabah rulers for several decades, but in the early 1980s militants and terrorists advancing the Khomeini brand of Islamic fundamentalism somewhat overshadowed the Palestinians as troublemakers.

Public order was shattered on December 12, 1983, when terrorists bombed the American and French embassies, an American housing complex, and three Kuwaiti public installations. Although there were fatalities, none was American or French. The Kuwaiti police quickly began rounding up suspects and imposed a ban on leaving the country against Palestinians and nationals of Iran, Iraq, Jordan, Lebanon, and Syria. A week after the bombing, Kuwaiti investigators attributed the terrorists' acts to Iraqi nationals who belonged to an Islamic fundamentalist group. The *Financial Times* of London said that "there can be little doubt that the Iranian regime was behind the attacks," an assessment widely held by observers.

About three months after the bombings, 25 suspects (four in absentia) were tried by the State Security Court. Of the 25 accused, 17—including the four who had not been captured—were Iraqis, three were Kuwaitis, three were Lebanese, and two were stateless. Six of those convicted received death sentences (three in absentia), seven were sentenced to life imprisonment, others received from five to 15 years at hard labor, and five were acquitted. After the trial, observers indicated that the entire episode would cause reverberations in the Kuwaiti security system that would be long lasting, particularly in the treatment of expatriates (see Introduction).

Bahrain

After more than 150 years of British presence and protection, Bahrain gained full independence in 1971. The agreement granting independence contained no provision for British defense in an emergency, but it did provide for "consultation." British authorities had hoped that Bahrain, the most economically and socially advanced of the small Gulf states, might take the lead in a federation, i.e., the United Arab Emirates, but both Bahrain and Qatar eschewed confederation, opting instead for complete independence. Shaykh Isa bin Salman Al Khalifa, leader of the Al Khalifa since the death of his father in 1961, became the newly independent country's first amir and continued in that role in mid-1984.

The Constitution designates the amir supreme commander of the armed forces. In 1977 Amir Isa chose his eldest son and heir apparent, Shaykh Hamad bin Isa Al Khalifa, to be minister of defense and commander in chief of the Bahrain Defense Force (BDF), and Hamad retained those positions in 1984. Other members of the Al Khalifa in prominent military positions included Brigadier General Shaykh Khalifa bin Ahmad Al Khalifa, BDF chief of staff, and Shaykh Abdallah bin Salman Al Khalifa, BDF assistant chief of staff for operations. As in all of the other Arab Gulf states, the ruling family kept a tight hold on important governmental positions.

The total strength of the BDF in 1984 was about 2,700: army, 2,300; navy, 300; and air force, 100. The Bahraini army was organized into one mechanized infantry battalion, one independent armored car company, one artillery battery, and assorted small support units. Weapons included 20 AML-90, French-built Panhard four-wheel armored cars mounting 90mm guns, eight towed 105mm howitzers, 60 TOW antitank missile launchers, and various mortars and recoilless rifles. Weapons on order for the army at the end of 1983 included eight American-made M-198 towed 155mm howitzers and additional TOW launchers. Equipment on hand included 110 Panhard M-3 APCs, eight Saladin armored cars, and eight Ferret scout cars. The British-made Saladin and Ferret vehicles have been in inventory for several years.

Until 1979, when four combat craft were ordered, Bahrain's maritime force was a coast guard under the supervision of the minister of interior. The combat vessels, ordered from the West German Lürssen Werft, for the first time gave the navy a capability for sea warfare; that part of the force has been placed under the ministry of defense. Two Lürssen craft already commissioned

*Omani naval officer
on duty in Strait
of Hormuz
Courtesy
Aramco World Magazine*

were FPB-38 fast attack gunboats. Each was 38 meters long, mounting one Bofors 40mm gun and two Oerlikon 20mm guns, and employing a complement of about 30 to 35. The two other Lürssen craft awaited by the Bahraini navy in mid-1984 were TNC-45 fast attack missile boats. These were 45 meters in length, mounting four single-launcher Exocet missiles, one 76mm OTO Melara gun, one Bofors 40mm gun, and three 7.62mm machine guns and carrying a complement of 40. The coast guard, which operates a wide variety of patrol craft, was also enhancing its capabilities with new acquisitions in the early 1980s.

The Bahraini air force began operations in 1977 with two MBB (Messerschmitt-Bölkow-Blohm) BO 105 light utility helicopters. Subsequent acquisitions included one additional BO 105, two Hughes D-500 (United States military OH-6), and 12 Agusta-Bell AB-212s (military UH-IN). The only fixed-wing aircraft operated by the air force was a twin turbofan Gulfstream II, used for executive travel. In mid-1984, however, the Bahrainis were still reviewing their options for acquiring a fixed-wing fighter aircraft. Acquisition of such combat aircraft will greatly enhance the capability of the tiny air force, but it will also demand considerable expansion in trained personnel and facilities.

An official news release in April 1984 disclosed that Bahraini air units had concluded joint exercises with units from the air forces of Kuwait, Qatar, and Saudi Arabia. Presumably, these were routine GCC maneuvers but, as is customary in newspaper stories dealing with military affairs in the region, no details were provided on the kind of exercises or the kind of aircraft involved. Earlier in the year Bahraini and Qatari helicopters had held joint exercises under GCC auspices.

At the time of the British withdrawal in 1971, the United States entered into an arrangement with the newly independent government of Bahrain to lease port and docking facilities for the United States Middle East Force. This was, in fact, an extension of the American-British agreement that had been in effect since the early 1950s by which United States ships used facilities at Al Jufayr, a port section of Manama. The agreement was quietly arranged and, at the request of the Bahraini officials, not publicized because of the strong nationalistic feelings that accompanied independence. No Gulf Arab, newly freed from British overlordship, wanted to give the impression of submitting to some new form of colonialism or of becoming involved in the East-West conflict. In addition, the June 1967 War between Israel and three Arab states was too recent, and the United States was too closely linked with Israel for any Arab state to be overly casual in its relations with Washington.

After the October 1973 War between Israel, Egypt, and Syria, the American presence on the 40-hectare site near the Bahraini capital became even more sensitive to the host government, which began openly discussing the cancellation of the lease. During the mid-1970s the United States had reduced its naval strength and sent many dependents home. In 1977 the issue again came to the fore, and the amir's government terminated the lease. American vessels were subsequently permitted to resupply at Al Jufayr, but the headquarters of the United States Middle East Force was compelled to move aboard one of the three ships that constituted that force. Operationally, little changed as a result of the termination of the lease, but the American profile was lowered and the Bahrainis supposedly felt better about the foreign military presence being at sea rather than on their shore.

The issue of United States use of Bahraini port facilities for naval operations in the Gulf was just as sensitive for the amir's government in early 1984 as it had been when the arrangement was initially concluded more than a dozen years earlier. Neither the landlord nor the lessee referred to the facilities at Al Jubayr as an American "base." That term had connotations in the Gulf that all governments tried to avoid. *USA Today*, in its issue of March 16, 1984, referred to the American establishment in Bahrain as "a minibase manned by fewer than 100 U.S. sailors responsible for providing everything from communications to supplies." American personnel wore civilian attire when ashore and tried to maintain a very low profile, acknowledging the sensitivity of their presence to their hosts and the importance of the small facility to the United States Middle East Force.

In 1981 Bahrain became a founding member of the GCC, an alliance on which it continued to rely in mid-1984 as a deterrent to any nation having aggressive intentions against the small Arab Gulf states. It also retained its ties to Britain and the United States, in addition to various moderate Arab countries. The country's small, moderately equipped armed forces could not be expected to operate in any independent military role; of necessity they would have to be a part of a larger allied force. Bahrain's national security policies, therefore, rested on the assumption that, should it be invaded, it would have to depend on its friends and allies to respond immediately.

The Bahraini minister of information, Tariq Abdurahman al Muayyid, announced in early 1984 that Bahrain would receive special funds from the GCC for improvement of its defenses. The GCC had decided to allocate money to Bahrain and Oman for defense purposes because these countries had much smaller oil revenues than the other members. The minister stated that first priority for use of the GCC funds would be enhancement of air defense capabilities. Bahrain expected to spend US$700 million in GCC funds over a 3-year period, whereas its own defense budget over the same period would probably have amounted to about US$450 million. News reports said that part of the GCC funds would be spent on construction of an air base that would have the longest military runway in the Gulf.

In 1984 the Bahraini Security Force, which included a small detachment of policewomen working in investigation, had an estimated strength of about 2,000. A few British expatriates still held high postiions in the force. The mission of the police included all of the usual police functions, but one of the most important tasks was maintaining peace between the Sunni and Shia elements of the population. Since the rise of Khomeini in Iran, the Shia Muslims of Bahrain—making up about 60 percent of the native population—have been much more aggressive, even to the point of attempting a coup d'état in December 1981. The foiled coup resulted in arrests of as many as 300 Shia dissidents, most of whom were expelled from the country rather than tried. The 72 who were brought to trial were convicted and sentenced to prison terms ranging from life for three persons, 15 years for 60, and seven years for the remaining 10. It was brought out at the trial that almost all of the defendants had received guerrilla training in Iran and had been armed and supplied by sympathetic elements in that country.

The Al Khalifa rulers, who are Sunni, are continually faced with the potential explosiveness of religious division. They must constantly allay the fears of both communities and assure each that it is not being discriminated against.

Qatar

In company with other Gulf shaykhdoms, Qatar had long-standing ties with Britain but had remained under nominal Ottoman hegemony until 1916, when the British took over Qatari foreign affairs and defense. During the next five decades Britain also exercised considerable influence in the internal affairs of the shaykhdom, and when the announcement came that it would withdraw its military forces from the Gulf by 1971, the Qatari leadership was forced to contemplate how to survive without British protection. Obviously, the small shaykhdom could not defend itself singlehandedly against a full-scale attack by a powerful aggressor. The ruling family, therefore, concluded that national security would be dependent on the stability of the entire Gulf region: that stability depended particularly on the balance of power among Qatar's more powerful neighbors—Saudi Arabia, Iraq, and Iran. The acceptance of its status as a ministate alleviated the necessity of trying to compete in the regional arms race. Rather than a large military establishment, Qatar has sought to maintain small, mobile forces that could preserve internal order and protect the borders against minor incursions.

The ruler in 1984, Amir Khalifah bin Hamad Al Thani, had taken control of the country 12 years earlier, when the leading members of the Al Thani ruling family decided that Khalifah's cousin, Ahmad bin Ali Al Thani, should be replaced because of his many shortcomings as amir. Khalifah, who had been named heir apparent when Ahmad became amir in 1960, had been the de facto ruler for several years because of his inherent abilities and his cousin's general lack of interest in ruling. Amir Ahmad, as supreme commander of the armed forces, had left the routine

Qatari Military Band
Courtesy Embassy of Qatar, Washington

supervision of the military to his brother, Qasim bin Ali Al Thani, but the de facto commander of the forces was Ronald Cochrane, a British expatriate who had converted to Islam and taken the name Muhammad Mahdi.

Qasim's connection with the armed forces was ended in 1977 when Amir Khalifah issued a decree appointing his son and heir apparent, Shaykh Hamad bin Khalifah Al Thani, to the post of commander in chief. The same decree created the Ministry of Defense and named Hamad as minister. Hamad was a graduate of Sandhurst and had attained the rank of major general. In 1984 Hamad continued in his dual role as minister of defense and commander in chief of the armed forces. Mahdi was retained as military adviser. Brigadier General Muhammad Abdallah al Atiyah had been named deputy commander in chief. Colonel Mubarak bin Abd al Rahman Al Thani was armed forces chief of staff.

The armed forces, which had consisted of little more than the Royal Guard Regiment and some scattered units equipped with a few armored cars and four aircraft at the time of independence, had grown into an army of 5,000 men, a navy of 700, and an air force of 300 by early 1984. The Royal Guard Regiment continued in the duties that the name implies, but the army had expanded to include a tank battalion, five infantry battalions, and one or two artillery batteries. The tank battalion operated 24 French-made AMX-30 main battle tanks. Artillery units were equipped with eight British-made 25-pounders and six American-made 155mm SP howitzers. Other army equipment included 30 AMX-10P APCs, 25 Saracen armored cars, and 10 Ferret scout cars.

In a major step to upgrade its naval capabilities, Qatar in 1980 placed an order with Construction Mécanique de Normandie of Cherbourg, France, for the construction of three La Combattante III guided missile boats. All three had entered service by 1984, joining six Vosper Thornycroft large patrol boats and a variety of smaller coastal patrol craft. The new French boats carry eight Exocet missiles each, in addition to two twin Emerlec Ex-30s (American-made 30mm antiaircraft guns). Although referred to as large patrol craft, the Vosper Thornycroft boats are much smaller than the La Combattante IIIs—120 tons displacement as opposed to 430. These six boats—all commissioned in the mid-1970s—mount two 20mm guns as main armament and carry a complement of 25. With the exception of two older (1969) patrol boats that also mount 20mm guns, the remaining boats are smaller, usually carry four to six men, and are armed with 7.62 machine guns. All were commissioned in the 1970s or early 1980s. The Qatari naval force, about 48 vessels in 1984, was modest considering the relatively long coastline of the peninsula country, but the coast was also defended by army units equipped with trucks mounting four Exocet missiles.

The air force had 14 combat aircraft: eight Alpha Jets, three Mirage F-1Cs, two Hawker Hunter FGA-6s, and one Hawker Hunter T-79. Eleven additional Mirage F-1Cs were on order. Transport aircraft included two Boeing 707s, one Boeing 727, and one Britten Norman Islander. The helicopter inventory included four Westland Commandos, three Westland Lynx, two Westland Whirlwinds, and two Aérospatiale SA-341 Gazelles. All of the aircraft were based at the military airfield near Doha, the capital. Although training of Qataris as pilots and aircraft technicians has been going on for some time, seconded British pilots remained on duty with the air force, and many technician slots were filled by expatriates.

The Qatari police force was organized under the Ministry of Interior, which in 1984 was still headed by the amir's brother,

Shaykh Khalid bin Hamad Al Thani (see Political Dynamics, ch. 4). Another member of the ruling family, Shaykh Hamad bin Qasim Al Thani, commanded the police force. Hamad was a graduate of the Hendon Police College in Britain and reportedly operated a competent, efficient security force. As in the other small states of the Gulf, the size of the population of foreign workers was the source of most police problems, but compared with some of the other countries, Qatar's dissidents seemed quiet. The largest single group of foreign workers (and the one causing most of the police problems) was the Iranian group, but aggressive police responses had held down serious troubles. The resident Iranians complained about police harassment, but, fearing deportation, many foreign workers would not lend their voices to those who sought to make official complaints against the police.

United Arab Emirates

Background

The numerous treaties that Britain concluded with the several Gulf shaykhdoms in the nineteenth century provided, inter alia, that the British were responsible for defense and foreign relations. Until the early 1950s the principal military presence in the Trucial Coast States (sometimes referred to as Trucial Oman) consisted of British-led forces that were literally Arab security police and personal bodyguard units of the ruling shaykhs. The colorful bodyguards were still maintained in the UAE in the early 1980s, but they were armed with automatic rifles rather than the long-barreled beduin muskets of earlier days.

In 1951 the British formed the Trucial Oman Levies (later called the Trucial Oman Scouts), replacing an earlier security force that had been maintained in the area. By the time the UAE became independent in 1971, the Scouts had been made into a mobile force of about 1,600 men, trained and led by about 30 British officers. Arabs from the Trucial Coast made up only about 40 percent of the strength; Omanis made up about 30 percent, and the remaining 30 percent included Iranians, Pakistanis, and Indians. The British personnel were on assignment (seconded) from the Royal Marines, and Britain paid the total bill. Organized as light armored cavalry, the Scouts used British weapons, trucks, and armored cars in performing the assigned mission of maintaining order among the tribes of the various shaykhdoms. The commander of the force reported to the British political agent of the Gulf. During its approximately two decades of existence, the unit was well respected and considered generally successful, which British observers attributed to the Scouts' autonomy (that is, to its independence from the ruling shaykhs).

In 1966, anticipating the end of the colonial era in Aden, the British stepped up development of the military installations at Sharjah to supplement and eventually replace the base at Aden. By 1968 the British joint task force, headquartered in Bahrain, had reached a strength of 9,000. The army component, a reinforced brigade group, maintained a battalion at Sharjah, which had been built up into the principal British base in the Gulf. The Royal Navy maintained a squadron of three destroyer escorts and six coastal minesweepers, using various Gulf ports as home ports. The Royal Air Force (RAF) component consisted of two jet fighter squadrons and supporting elements, one at Bahrain and the other at the Sharjah airbase that the RAF had been using since 1940.

As independence approached, plans for the defense and security forces that would be necessary after the British withdrawal received serious attention. The first British defense adviser to the UAE, Major General John Willoughby, proposed that the Trucial Oman Scouts should be the nucleus for the forces of the federation. Under the Willoughby plan top control was to be vested in the UAE Supreme Council of the Union and exercised in practice by a commander or a chief of staff designated by the council. Conservative British opinion held that the only way the force could be accepted by the ruling shaykhs—and therefore be successful—would be if military command was in non-Arab hands. Although considerable verbal support for unified UAE forces was expressed by the shaykhs, sufficient resources to support the project were not forthcoming, and the separate entities of the union—especially Abu Dhabi—made it clear that they intended to maintain their individual forces.

Abu Dhabi had acquired tremendous oil wealth in the early 1960s, and, later in the decade, when the British withdrawal from the Gulf was announced, the amir of Abu Dhabi ordered that high priority be given to the development of the Abu Dhabi Defense Force (ADDF). Officered primarily by British and Jordanians on contract, the force was composed of two infantry battalions, an armored car battalion, and an artillery battery. British-supplied equipment included Saladin armored cars, Ferret scout cars, and 25-pound guns for artillery support. An air wing—two transports and two helicopters—was added in 1968, and the acquisition of air defense missiles and fighter aircraft began. Training and maintenance services were provided by a British firm under contract, and British and Pakistani pilots were contracted to fly the 12 rebuilt Hawker Hunter fighter-bombers acquired in 1970. Two years earlier the ADDF had been augmented by a sea defense wing when four fast patrol boats were purchased from Britain and several former Royal Navy officers were engaged on contract to command and operate the budding navy.

Independence and Unification

At the time of independence and federation, the creation of a viable defense structure for the new federal entity required compromise on the part of the ruling shaykhs. The Trucial Oman Scouts became the Union Defense Force (UDF), maintaining its headquarters at Sharjah, and became responsible to the federal minister of defense, the Supreme Council of the Union (SCU), and—ultimately—to the president of the federation, Shaykh Zayid, who retained that office in mid-1984. Although British officers and noncommissioned officers (NCOs) continued to provide operational leadership, training, and management of logistics and maintenance, their gradual withdrawal was set as a goal.

Despite the formation of the UDF, separate shaykhdom forces were also authorized by the Provisional Constitution to allay initial apprehensions concerning the power of the central government as well as the fears that British personnel might suddenly be withdrawn. The largest separate force was the ADDF; Dubai had a much smaller force, and Ras al Khaymah and Sharjah even smaller. The mission of the UDF and the separate shaykhdom forces, which were subject to call by the central government, continued to be essentially the same as that of the former Trucial Oman Scouts (that is, police and paramilitary patrolling of the villages and desert regions to maintain order and prevent local disputes from escalating into intertribal or intershaykhdom conflicts).

Because of the small populations of the seven shaykhdoms that federated as the UAE, personnel for the UDF and the separate forces were recruited from several different countries of the region, but soon after independence enlistments from the Dhofar Province of Oman and from the People's Democratic Republic of Yemen (Yemen [Aden]) were halted on the grounds that personnel from those areas might spread dangerous revolutionary doctrines. A short time later, in January 1972, the UDF was instrumental in suppressing a coup attempt in Sharjah and in settling a classic tribal altercation over water rights between tribesmen of Sharjah and Fujayrah. The UDF was assisted in that action by the ADDF, and a UDF battalion was stationed in the area to prevent a recurrence.

As the largest in territory and population and by far the richest of the shaykhdoms, Abu Dhabi bore the brunt of funding the new federation and its military establishment (see Progress in Political Integration, ch. 5). It followed that Abu Dhabi should become the predominant—although not exclusive—political power center and that President Zayid should seek to enhance the central authority. In time the separate Abu Dhabi government structure was downgraded, and several cabinet ministers were shifted to the central government. By the mid-1970s Sharjah had merged its police and small military force with the UDF, and Sharjah, Fujayrah, and Abu Dhabi had given up their separate flags and adopted the UAE colors. A major step toward unification occurred in May 1976 when Abu Dhabi, Dubai, and Ras al Khaymah announced the merger of their separate armed forces with the UDF. Zayid, as president, remained supreme commander of the unified force; Major General Wallid Muhammad al Khalidi of Jordan was contracted to be chief of staff, providing the outside influence that some observers believed necessary for cohesion in the UDF.

Despite the promises and pledges of 1976, true integration and unification of the UAE armed forces did not occur. Centuries-long intertribal hostilities and suspicions could not be put aside casually, in addition to which the individual amirs viewed their warriors as symbols of sovereignty no matter the size or combat capability of the units. The idea of giving up their royal guards to a central authority did not sit easily with some amirs, even as they cooperated in several other spheres of development of the new federation. The UDF was seen by some, particularly the amir of Dubai, as merely an extension of Abu Dhabi power, and there was apprehension about losing the separate identity that is so important to the people, the clans, and the tribes of the entire region. The separate forces therefore continued as they had earlier, but they were called regional commands and, ostensibly, were part of the UDF.

The unity of the armed forces was shaken to its uneasy foundations in January 1978 when Zayid, without prior conferences, announced the appointment of his second son, Shaykh (Brigadier General) Sultan bin Zayid Al Nahayyan, to be commander in chief of the UDF. Even though the defense minister, Shaykh Muhammad bin Rashid bin Said Al Maktum—son of the amir of Dubai—continued in that office, the appointment of Zayid's son to the top military post was seen as a raw grab for power by the Abu Dhabians. The ruling families of Dubai and Ras al Khaymah were particularly affronted, and some threatened withdrawal from the union, but the crisis eventually passed. The episode strengthened the resolve of the Dubaians to maintain the autonomy of their own regional military command (the Central Military Command), which was placed under the control of Shaykh Ahmad bin Rashid Al Maktum, another son of the amir of Dubai. Ahmad retained that position in mid-1984, and his brother Muhammad continued as federal minister of defense. The controversial commander in chief of the UDF, Sultan, resigned in February 1982.

Organization of Forces

The total strength of the UAE armed forces in early 1984 was about 49,000, overshadowing the combined forces of Kuwait, Bahrain, Qatar, and Oman, and coming very close to the 51,500 of Saudi Arabia. The UAE total included the Dubai contingent of 6,000, which enjoyed considerable autonomy. The UDF army, numbering 46,000 in 1984, has always been by far the largest component of the armed forces. Principal army units included the brigade-size Royal Guard, five armored battalions (mixed tanks and other armored vehicles), nine mechanized infantry battalions, three artillery battalions, and three air defense battalions. Major weapons included 100 French AMX-30 and 18 West German OF-40 main battle tanks and 60 British Scorpion light tanks; 90 French AML-90 armored cars and a number of British Shorland and Saladin armored cars; and 20 British 25-pound guns, 50 American 105mm howitzers, and 20 AMX 155mm SP howitzers. APCs and other infantry combat vehicles included a number of AMX-10Ps, 30 AMX VCIs, and 300 Panhard M-3s. Several older Saladin armored cars, Ferret scout cars, and Saracen APCs were kept in storage. On order at the end of 1983 were 18 additional OF-40 tanks, 20 Scorpions, 54 TOW antitank missile launchers, 42 I-HAWK SAM launchers, and over 300 I-HAWK missiles.

The pride of the 1,500-man UDF navy in 1984 consisted of six Lürssen TNC-45 fast attack missile boats, each mounting two twin Exocet launchers. The TNC-45s, in addition to the Exocets, also mount a 76mm gun forward and two twin 40mm antiaircraft guns aft. The six missile boats, ordered from the West German builder in 1977, were delivered and commissioned in the early 1980s. Other naval vessels included six large patrol boats built by Vosper Thornycroft of Britain and commissioned in 1975 and 1976 and three Keith Nelson-type coastal patrol craft built in Britain and commissioned in 1969. The coast guard, operating under the direction of the Ministry of Interior, had a fleet of about 50 small patrol craft of various types.

The 1,500-man air force was equipped with combat aircraft, trainers, utility aircraft, and transports from several different countries. Two interceptor squadrons were equipped with 30 Dassault-Breguet Mirage 5s, a ground attack squadron had six Alpha Jets, and a counterinsurgency squadron had 12 MB-326s built by Aeromacchi of Italy. The air transport fleet of 24 aircraft included American, British, Canadian, and Spanish aircraft; seven missile-firing Alouette IIIs were included among the 48 helicopters of various American, British, and French makes. Trainers included 14 Swiss Pilatus PC-7s and 16 British BAC Hawks. Among the large orders for aircraft that were placed for delivery in 1985 and 1986 were 36 Mirage 2000 fighters. Given the number of aircraft in inventory and the number on order, the air force in 1984 reportedly needed to upgrade its personnel in order to meet the demands of constantly advancing technology. Many UAE pilots and technicians have been trained, but there was still heavy reliance on British, Jordanian, and Pakistani personnel.

The *Financial Times* of London estimated in 1979 that there were 28 different ethnic groups represented in the UDF. The small number of locals in the overall population and the minuscule number in the armed forces must, of necessity, be cause for worry among military planners. There has been a continuing effort to train citizens of the UAE to become officers in the armed forces; the Zayid Military College, which turns out second lieutenants for the UDF, has been in operation since 1970. Manning the forces with citizens would probably require all adult males. Traditionally, Omanis have made up a large percentage of the men in the ranks and that situation continued in 1984. When Ras al Khaymah had a border dispute with Oman in 1979, President Zayid ruled in favor of Oman and against his constituent amirate. Actually, the case for Ras al Khaymah had little merit, making Zayid's decision easier, but it could have been a difficult time for the UAE if its Omani soldiers had to be tested against their own homeland.

The Provisional Constitution authorizes federal police and security guard forces that are subordinate to the Ministry of Interior. The strength of the police force in 1984 was not known, but observers estimated that it was relatively large because of the federal nature of the country. As with the military, the individual ruling shaykhs had their own police forces before independence and maintained those forces after unification. Jealous of their own prerogatives, the shaykhs sometimes had their security forces duplicate the efforts of the federal police but at other times augmented them.

Sultan Qaboos
in field with troops
Courtesy Ministry of
Information, Oman

The federal police are constitutionally mandated to maintain public order and to combat crime throughout the union. The force included a border coast guard charged with the prevention of infiltration by illegal immigrants. There are citizenship and educational requirements for applicants to the federal force, and a number of British expatriates were still retained in advisory positions. In January 1984 the government approved a law that would provide for the establishment of a police academy for the development of cadres and the training of personnel in modern police technologies.

Oman

Background

As a regional commercial power in the nineteenth century, Oman held territories in Zanzibar and Mombasa along the east coast of Africa and at Gwadar on the coast of Baluchistan (in present-day Pakistan) across the Arabian Sea. When the African possessions were lost, Oman withdrew into isolationism in the southeast corner of the Arabian Peninsula. Another of the Gulf states with long-standing ties to the British, Oman had become important in the British-French rivalry at the end of the

411

eighteenth century, when Napoleonic France challenged the British Empire for control of the trade routes to the East. Although nominally a fully independent sultanate, Oman enjoyed the protection of the empire without being, de jure, in the category of a colony or a protected state. A treaty in 1891, however, gave the British significant influence in Omani internal as well as foreign affairs.

In 1952, when the Saudis occupied Omani territory near the Buraymi Oasis, it was British force that fought the incursion and retook the territory for the sultan. Later in the same decade, British troops were again called on to aid the sultan in putting down a rebellion at Jabal Akhdar (Green Mountain). The uprising was led by the former imam (see Glossary) of Oman, who attempted to establish a separate state, free of rule from Muscat. The sultan, believing that his own forces were too weak to contain the rebellion, requested and received aid from the British. Trucial Oman Scouts from Sharjah and three companies of British Cameronians from Kenya were dispatched to aid the Muscat and Oman Field Force in putting down the rebels. The British part in assisting the sultan was condemned by the Arab League as "aggression," but the UN Security Council voted against an Arab motion to take action against Britain. Instead of a minor intertribal affair in Oman's hinterland, the Jabal Akhdar rebellion had been blown up into an international incident, one of a series of incidents caused by the highly nationalistic and antimonarchist attitudes prevalent in the Middle East at the time.

An agreement between Sultan Said bin Taimur Al Bu Said and the British government in 1958 led to the creation of the Sultan's Armed Forces (SAF) and the promise of British assistance in military development. The agreement included the promise of secondment of British officers to help command and advise the Omani forces, which were to have an air wing for the first time. The British received confirmation of the Royal Air Force's rights to continue use of facilities at Salalah in Dhofar Province and at Masirah, an island off the Omani coast in the Arabian Sea (see fig. 19).

Sultan Said was ultraconservative and isolationist, and abhorred change of any kind. Even as revenues increased, his subjects continued to exist in terrible poverty, disease, and ignorance. Said also abhorred education. Kindled by the Arab nationalism that had been rampant in the Middle East since the overthrow of King Faruk of Egypt in 1952 and ignited by the oppression of Said, a rebellion in the province of Dhofar challenged the British-led SAF and changed the course of Omani history.

412

The Dhofar Rebellion, or Dhofar Insurgency as it is called, began in 1964 and was not finally quashed until 1975. For Oman the most important event of the entire period was the overthrow of Said by his son Qaboos bin Said Al Bu Said, who replaced his father as sultan and began taking the steps necessary to bring Oman into the twentieth century (see Internal Developments in Oman, ch. 1; Government and Politics, ch. 6).

Rebellion and Coup

Oman was regarded as one of the most backward countries in the world under the reactionary reign of Said, and Dhofar was the most backward and exploited area of Oman. The rebellion began as a tribal separatist movement against a grossly oppressive ruler, but the Dhofar rebels soon received aid from leftist elements in Aden and formed the Dhofar Liberation Front (DLF). The original intent of the DLF was the overthrow of Said, but by 1967 it had changed its name to the Popular Front for the Liberation of the Occupied Arab Gulf (PFLOAG), signifying an expansion of its goals far beyond the overthrow of the Omani sultan. PFLOAG was committed to a leftist ideology, supported by the Soviet Union through Yemen (Aden), and hoped to spread revolution throughout the conservative regimes of the Arabian Peninsula. In 1972 PFLOAG became the Popular Front for the Liberation of Oman (PFLO).

Said's strategy to crush the insurgency consisted of a program of brutal reprisals against the Dhofari people, which did little other than to drive them into the camp of the rebels. At what had to be one of the lowest points in Omani history, Qaboos, assisted by British officers, deposed his father and began the long, difficult development of the country and its armed forces, an effort that would eventually end the insurgency. Along the way, in addition to the invaluable contributions of troops, commanders, and advisers provided by the British armed forces, the new sultan was assisted by troops sent by the shah of Iran; aid also arrived from India, Jordan, Pakistan, Saudi Arabia, and the UAE, all interested in ensuring that Oman did not become a "people's republic."

Qaboos, a Sandhurst graduate and veteran of British army service, requested British assistance—primarily through expatriates—in his efforts to modernize the country. He also called on educated Omanis who had emigrated to return to the homeland to aid in its development. Under the new sultan, Oman joined the Arab League and the UN and established its own diplomatic relations around the world. But the major problem facing Qaboos was the ongoing Dhofar Rebellion and the perceived need to restructure the SAF in order to end that long-lasting conflict. By late 1975 Qaboos was able to declare that the insurgency had been defeated.

The commanders of the SAF at the time of the Qaboos accession were seconded British officers or retirees on contract. Qaboos held nothing against the seconded and contract officers—in fact he increased their numbers—but he was convinced that his country needed its own defense force if it were to play a part in the Gulf as well as in the world arena. He therefore initiated a program of "Omanization" designed to create an Omani officer corps and NCO corps, and before the end of the Dhofar Rebellion, some SAF units were commanded by Omani officers and employed Omani NCOs. By the end of the decade, the first Omani had reached the rank of brigadier. Qaboos also initiated a program for the reequipping of the SAF with up-to-date weapons and equipment, and Britain became the major supplier of armaments.

Organization and Missions of the Forces

The missions of the armed forces have been the defense of the realm by land, sea, and air; the protection of the monarchy; and the maintenance of internal order. Sultan Qaboos has been his own prime minister and defense minister and, as the absolute monarch, he has also been supreme commander of the SAF. His graduation from Sandhurst and subsequent service as a junior officer in a British regiment, plus his intensive personal involvement in the prosecution of the war against the Dhofar Insurgency, have given him a close identification with the armed forces. Active in the role of supreme commander, Qaboos has been the main channel of communication between the civil and military arms of the Omani government.

The operational command and administration of the armed forces were vested in a commander in chief who was also principal defense adviser to the sultan in the latter's capacity as minister of defense. In early 1984 the commander in chief of the SAF was General Timothy Creasy, seconded from the British army. He was assisted by the staff of the Ministry of Defense in Muscat and the armed forces general staff, which maintained its principal field headquarters at Raysut, west of Salalah in Dhofar. The armed forces general staff was concurrently the army general staff; the air force and the navy had only limited autonomy and were responsible to the army general staff. British officers were still prominent in the forces at the beginning of 1984, but the process of Omanization continued at a steady, productive pace, and Omani officers were filling more and more command slots as each year passed.

The total strength of the armed forces commanded by General Creasy at the beginning of 1984 was about 24,000. More than 200 British officers were still posted to Oman as advisers, and many still commanded units as the training of Omani officers continued. Several Pakistani military advisers were still present in the country, and a few thousand Baluch from Pakistan served in the Omani ranks. Because Gwadar on the Pakistan coast had been an Omani possession until 1958, it was a common recruiting ground for the Omani forces, and the Baluch were not thought of as foreigners or expatriates. Nevertheless, there has been a successful drive to enlist more native Omanis into the ranks. Military pay scales were kept high enough to maintain desired strength levels, and the defense share of the budget has run as high as 45 percent in some years. Oman has received aid in its military financing from Saudi Arabia and some of the other Gulf states whose oil income is higher and who see a strong Oman as a wise investment.

As in all of the other Gulf states, the army is the largest of the armed services. Known as the Sultan of Oman's Land Forces (SOLF), the army at the beginning of 1984 had a strength of almost 20,000, or 85 percent of the total. The SOLF was organized into the Royal Guard brigade, an armored regiment composed of two tank squadrons and three armored car squadrons, one independent armored car squadron, eight infantry battalions, three artillery regiments, one paratroop squadron, one special forces company, and support units of varying sizes. Two brigade headquarters have been maintained since the end of the Dhofar Rebellion to make expansion of the SOLF easy, if it were to become necessary.

The two tank squadrons were equipped with six American M-60A1s and 12 British Chieftains. The armored car squadrons have been using British Saladin vehicles, but at the end of 1983 they were in the process of changing over to British Scorpion light tanks. The artillery regiments were equipped with 36 British-made 105mm guns, 12 Soviet-made 130mm guns (acquired from Egypt), 12 American-made 155mm SP howitzers, some British 25-pound guns, and a variety of mortars. Additional Chieftain tanks have been ordered, as well as TOW antitank weapons, American I-HAWK antiaircraft missiles, and 200 Steyr cross-country vehicles.

Oman's small naval element—the Sultan of Oman's Navy (SON)—had a strength of almost 2,000 in early 1984 and reportedly would have liked to build its strength to about 3,000 in order to man properly the vessels already in inventory and those on order. Omani personnel have been trained, and more were being trained, to replace British personnel, who have been essential to naval operations since the inception of the SON. As the navy expands and modernizes, even more trained Omanis have been needed; according to *United States Naval Institute Proceedings* of March 1984, "The Omani Navy has a particularly well-organized training structure." The Institute publication also stated that the former royal yacht (930-ton displacement) had been returned to its builder, Brooke Marine of Britain, for conversion into a fleet training ship, which will considerably enhance the afloat training capability of the SON.

The navy had received delivery of two Province-class missile boats built by Vosper Thornycroft of Britain, one of which carried six Exocet launchers and the other eight. A third boat of the same class to be delivered in 1984 will also carry eight Exocets. These boats also mount a 76mm OTO Melara gun and a Breda twin 40mm antiaircraft gun. The navy also operated two Brooke Marine 37.5-meter fast attack missile boats, each mounting two Exocets, a 76mm OTO Melara gun, and a Breda twin 40mm gun; four Brooke Marine fast attack gun boats; and seven landing craft.

The Sultan of Oman's Air Force (SOAF) in 1984 also had a strength of 2,000 and, reportedly, would also be building toward a strength of 3,000 during the mid-1980s. The 41 combat aircraft that were operational in early 1984 were assigned to two ground attack squadrons and one counterinsurgency squadron. The inventory of combat aircraft included 14 Jaguar S(O) Mk-1s, 15 Hawker Hunter FGA-6s and T-7s, and 12 BAC-167 Strikemasters. Twelve additional Jaguars were on order. The aircraft flown by three transport squadrons included one Mystère Falcon, two De Havilland DHC-5 Buffalo, two C-130H Hercules, three BAC One-Elevens, seven Britten Norman Defenders, and 15 Short Skyvans. SOAF helicopters included two Agusta Bell AB-206s, five AB-214Bs, six Super Pumas, and 15 AB-205s. Military airfields were located at Khasab on the Musandam Peninsula, Masirah, Muscat, Nazwa, Salalah, and Thamarit (Thumrait).

The Royal Oman Police, commanded by the inspector general of police and customs, was under the supervision of the Ministry of Interior. The size of the force in mid-1984 was not accurately known, but estimates ranged between 7,000 and 8,000, and observers assessed it as being well trained and efficient. As in the armed forces, some British officers still served the Royal Oman Police in command positions, but more frequently Omanis had assumed command of the units, and the British were retained as advisers. The principal internal security problem for several years had been political terrorism and subversion rather than ordinary crime, and the public security branch of the police had gained proficiency in dealing with the problem. After many years of the Dhofar Insurgency and the turmoil of its aftermath, the internal security situation of the early 1980s seemed calm by comparison.

Some problems have resulted from feuding among *firqat* (Home Guard) units, which had been raised and trained for irregular counterinsurgency operations by troops of the British Army's Special Air Services. Armed with rifles and other small arms, the *firqat* units provided excellent service as tribal police and defense forces for the mountain people and their cattle in areas infiltrated by the insurgents during the rebellion. Because of their knowledge of the terrain, they also made excellent scouts for regular forces. After the insurgency they remained as paramilitary tribal police and, reviving ancient tribal feuds, have presented some problems to the Royal Oman Police, but no widespread troubles had occurred as of mid-1984.

* * *

The annual editions of *The Military Balance*, published by the International Institute for Strategic Studies, are useful in studying the size and holdings of armed forces, and Jane's publications—*Jane's Fighting Ships, Jane's All the World's Aircraft, Jane's Weapon Systems*, and *Jane's Armour and Artillery*—are particularly helpful in sorting out the myriad weapons and items of military equipment used in the region. Three books important for background reading are John Duke Anthony's *Arab States of the Lower Gulf* (1975), David E. Long's *The Persian Gulf* (1978), and J.B. Kelly's *Arabia, the Gulf, and the West*. A new book, *The Gulf and the Search for Strategic Stability* by Anthony H. Cordesman, published in mid-1984 when this study was well under way, appears to be comprehensive and has good capsule descriptions of the military forces of the Gulf countries and assessments of the security situations in each. For the most part, periodical literature is the best source for information on the Iran-Iraq War and how it has affected the other Gulf countries up to the mid-

1980s. (For further information and complete citations, see Bibliography.)

Appendix A

Table 1.   *Metric Conversion Coefficients*

When you know	Multiply by	To find
Millimeters	0.04	inches
Centimeters	0.39	inches
Meters	3.3	feet
Kilometers	0.62	miles
Hectares (10,000 m)	2.47	acres
Square kilometers	0.39	square miles
Cubic meters	35.3	cubic feet
Liters	0.26	gallons
Kilograms	2.2	pounds
Metric tons	0.98	long tons
. . . .	1.1	short tons
. . . .	2,204	pounds
Degrees Celsius	9	degrees Fahrenheit
(Centigrade)	divide by 5 and add 32	

Table 2. Kuwait. Public Education, 1981/82

Level and Sex	Students	Teachers[1]	Classrooms	Schools
General education				
Kindergarten				
Male	10,134	0	n.a.	n.a.
Female	9,628	1,432	n.a.	n.a.
Total kindergarten . . .	19,762	1,432	750	73
Primary				
Male	66,370	3,618	2,047	93
Female	63,014	3,589	1,958	89
Total primary	129,384	7,207	4,005	182
Intermediate				
Male	59,554	4,244	1,896	79
Female	49,127	4,016	1,550	66
Total intermediate . . .	108,681	8,260	3,446	145
Secondary				
Male	30,091	3,086	945	41
Female	26,455	3,173	841	35
Total secondary	56,546	6,259	1,786	76
Total general education				
Male	166,149	10,948	4,888	213
Female	148,224	12,210	4,349	190
	314,373	23,158	9,987[2]	476[2]
Vocational education				
Equivalent education[3]	375	89	36	2
Religious[3]	896	92	32	2
Teachers Training				
Institute				
Male	845	160	n.a.	1
Female	1,180	132	n.a.	1
Total Teachers Training Institute . . .	2,025	292	n.a.	2
Commercial Institute				
Male	403	88	n.a.	1
Female	1,312	58	n.a.	1
Total Commercial Institute	1,715	146	n.a.	2
Public Health Institute				
Male	0	5	0	0
Female	190	32	n.a.	1
Total Public Health Institute	190	37	n.a.	1

Table 2. (Continued)

Level and Sex	Students	Teachers[1]	Classrooms	Schools
Special training (handicapped)				
Male	1,220	233	100	12
Female	794	187	78	12
Total special training (handicapped)	2,014	420	178	24
Technological institute[3]	924	133	n.a.	1
Total vocational education				
Male	4,663	800	168	19
Female	3,476	409	78	15
Total	8,139	1,209	246	34
All public education				
Male	170,812	11,748	5,056	232
Female	151,700	12,619	4,427	205
Total all public education	322,512	24,367	10,233	510

n.a.—not available.
[1]545 female teachers were instructors in various male schools.
[2]Totals as published.
[3]Only males listed.

Source: Based on information from Kuwait, Ministry of Planning, Central Statistical Office, *Annual Statistical Abstract, 1982*, Kuwait, 1983, Table 247.

Table 3.   Kuwait. Private Education, 1981/82

Type and Sex	Kindergarten	Primary	Intermediate	Secondary
Arabic schools				
Male	4,797	7,268	5,496	3,858
Female	4,245	6,059	4,783	3,478
Total Arabic schools	9,042	13,327	10,279	7,336
Foreign schools				
Male	2,206	6,385	4,542	2,252
Female	2,128	5,676	4,097	2,026
Total foreign schools	4,334	12,061	8,639	4,278

Source: Based on information from Kuwait, Ministry of Planning, Central Statistical Office, *Annual Statistical Abstract, 1982*, Kuwait, 1983, Table 258.

Table 4. Kuwait. Enrollment in the University of Kuwait, 1981/82

Field of Specialization	Freshman		Sophomore		Junior		Senior		Total	
	Male	Female	Male	Female	Male	Female	Male	Female	Male	Female
Sciences	460	501	122	260	71	195	48	158	701	1,114
Literature	779	971	281	746	141	586	168	509	1,369	2,812
Law	207	93	116	75	108	66	54	31	485	265
Commerce, economics, and political science	213	200	249	204	282	235	220	197	964	836
Engineering and petroleum	212	141	173	128	113	87	106	69	604	425
Medicine	32	34	33	34	33	45	48	83	146	196
Allied health	16	43	10	37	5	41	2	12	33	133
Total	1,919	1,983	984	1,484	753	1,255	646	1,059	4,302	5,781

Source: Based on information from Kuwait, Ministry of Planning, Central Statistical Office, *Annual Statistical Abstract, 1982,* Kuwait. 1983, Table 265.

Table 5. Kuwait. Gross Domestic Product by Sector,
Selected Years, 1972–81
(in millions of Kuwaiti dinars at current prices)[1]

Sector	1972	1975	1979	1980[2]	1981[2]
Oil Industry[3]	942	2,532	4,802	5,286	4,254
Agriculture and fishing	4	9	17	17	19
Mining and quarrying	1	2	6	7	7
Manufacturing[4]	37	120	187	210	236
Utilities	11	13	27	25	28
Construction	38	74	210	220	263
Trade	111	221	426	468	505
Transportation and communications	35	60	106	124	146
Financial services	95	150	347	401	477
Public administration and defense	81	114	234	263	329
Community and social services	102	169	333	365	428
Import duties	7	23	48	65	72
TOTAL	1,464	3,487	6,743	7,451	6,764

[1]For value of the Kuwaiti dinar—see Glossary.
[2]Preliminary.
[3]Includes crude oil and gas production and refining.
[4]Excludes oil refining.

Source: Based on information from Kuwait, Ministry of Planning, Central Statistical Office, *Annual Statistical Abstract, 1982*, Kuwait, 1983, 236–37.

Table 6. Kuwait. Oil Production, Revenues, and Exports,
Selected Years, 1946–82

Year	Crude Oil Production[1] (in millions of barrels)	Oil Revenue (in millions of Kuwaiti dinars)[2]	Petroleum Exports[3] (in millions of barrels)
1946	6	n.a.	n.a.
1947	16	n.a.	n.a.
1950	126	5	n.a.
1955	403	101	n.a.
1960	619	159	n.a.
1965	862	216	n.a.
1970	1,091	298	1,063
1971	1,167	354	1,129
1972	1,202	507	1,217
1973	1,102	531	1,113
1974	929	2,403	962
1975	761	2,380	761
1976	785	n.a.	802
1977	718	n.a.	723
1978	777	2,575	764
1979	911	3,036	895
1980	607	5,940	571
1981	411	4,434	381
1982	299	2,786	n.a.

n.a.—not available.
[1]Includes Kuwait's share of production from the former Kuwait-Saudi Arabia Neutral Zone.
[2]Calendar years through 1959. Fiscal years beginning April 1 through 1974. Fiscal years ending June 30 after 1974. For value of the Kuwaiti dinar—see Glossary.
[3]Includes refined products but excludes liquid petroleum gases.

Table 7. Kuwait. Budget Summary, FY 1980–83[1]
(in millions of Kuwaiti dinars)[2]

| | Actual | | Proposed | |
	FY 1980	FY1981	FY 1982	FY 1983
Revenues				
Oil and gas	5,942	4,450	2,786	2,967
Investment income	880	1,744	1,364	1,600
Other	101	157	130	239
Total revenues	6,923	6,351	4,280	4,806[3]
Expenditures				
Current	1,247	1,434	1,670	n.a.
Development	423	489	663	n.a.
Transfers abroad	213	262	245	n.a.
Other	495	692	1,136	n.a.
Total expenditures .	2,378	2,877	3,714	3,970
SURPLUS	4,545	3,474	566	836

n.a.—not available.
[1]Fiscal year begins July 1 and ends June 30.
[2]For value of the Kuwaiti dinar—see Glossary.
[3]Partially estimated for investment income and net lending in Kuwait.

Source: Based on information from International Monetary Fund, "Kuwait Adopts Measures to Adjust to the Impact of Reduced Oil Revenues," *IMF Survey*, August 8, 1983, 237.

Appendix A

Table 8. Kuwait. Employed Labor Force by Sector, Census Years 1970, 1975, and 1980 (in thousands)

Sector	Kuwaiti			Non-Kuwaiti			Total[1]		
	1970	1975	1980	1970	1975	1980	1970	1975	1980
Agriculture[2]	0.8	4.0	3.9	3.3	3.5	5.2	4.1	7.5	9.1
Mining and quarrying	1.7	1.8	2.6	5.5	3.1	4.4	7.2	4.9	7.0
Manufacturing	6.1	2.3	3.0	26.0	22.2	37.9	32.1	24.5	40.9
Utilities	2.1	2.0	2.1	5.1	5.2	6.1	7.3	7.3	8.2
Construction	2.2	1.8	1.2	31.5	30.5	95.8	33.7	32.2	97.0
Trade	7.3	6.3	4.6	25.7	33.2	54.2	33.0	39.6	58.8
Transportation and communications	2.4	4.6	7.9	9.8	11.1	22.3	12.1	15.7	30.2
Other services	37.1	64.3	78.3	67.9	103.5	154.7	105.0	166.8	232.9
TOTAL[1]	59.6	87.0	103.5	174.7	211.4	380.6	234.4	298.4	484.1

[1]Figures may not add to total because of rounding.
[2]Includes fishing.

Source: Based on information from Kuwait, Ministry of Planning, Central Statistical Office, *Annual Statistical Abstract, 1982,* Kuwait, 1983, 104.

429

Table 9. Kuwait. Value of Petroleum Exports by Destination,
1976–80[1]
(in millions of Kuwaiti dinars)[2]

Destination	1976	1977	1978	1979	1980
Arab countries	70.1	67.1	64.3	144.6	204.6
Africa	1.9	2.4	8.2	32.6	26.0
Western Hemisphere	195.1	230.9	116.8	163.6	400.2
Asia	1,276.5	1,277.7	1,308.6	2,529.3	2,804.3
European Economic Community	837.2	788.8	953.6	1,668.6	1,356.8
Other West European countries	91.1	35.8	31.6	46.2	74.6
Eastern Europe . . .	37.7	33.5	28.0	1.1	39.6
Oceania	79.8	60.6	57.4	95.0	122.3
Other[3]	69.4	60.4	60.1	99.8	90.7
TOTAL[4]	2,658.7	2,557.1	2,628.7	4,781.0	5,119.2

[1]Exports include crude oil, refined products, and liquefied petroleum gas.
[2]For value of the Kuwaiti dinar—see Glossary.
[3]Includes ships' bunkers.
[4]Figures may not add to total because of rounding.

Source: Based on information from Kuwait, Ministry of Planning, Central Statistical Office, *Annual Statistical Abstract, 1982*, Kuwait, 1983, 212.

Table 10.   Kuwait. Imports by Commodity Group, 1977–80[1]
(in millions of Kuwaiti dinars)[2]

Commodity Group	1977	1978	1979	1980
Food and live animals				
Live animals	11	14	20	23
Meat products	19	20	19	24
Dairy products	16	18	18	26
Grains	10	17	20	23
Other	92	93	117	134
Total food and live animals	148	162	194	230
Beverages and tobacco	14	18	25	22
Crude materials (inedible)	21	24	30	29
Fuels and lubricants	10	7	10	13
Vegetable oils and fats	3	3	3	7
Chemicals	42	44	85	74
Manufactured products				
Rubber tires	14	10	18	34
Textiles (cloth and products)	71	66	79	91
Cement	22	24	38	48
Iron and steel products	49	65	81	81
Other	144	125	142	179
Total manufactured products	300	290	358	433
Machinery and equipment				
Cars and trucks	125	114	128	166
Consumer appliances	58	39	35	60
Other	448	347	347	412
Total machinery and equipment	631	500	510	638
Miscellaneous manufactured articles	208	204	236	307
Unclassified commodities	10	12	16	10
TOTAL	1,387	1,264	1,437[3]	1,765[3]

[1]Imports reported on a c.i.f. (cost, insurance, and freight) basis.
[2]For value of the Kuwaiti dinar—see Glossary.
[3]Total as published.

Source: Based on information from Kuwait, Ministry of Planning, Central Statistical Office, *Annual Statistical Abstract, 1982*, Kuwait, 1983, 193–96.

*Table 11. Kuwait. Import Suppliers by Area
and Major Countries, 1977–80[1]*
(in millions of Kuwaiti dinars)[2]

Area	1977	1978	1979	1980
Arab countries	33	43·	55	65
Africa	4	5	5	3
Western Hemisphere				
United States	189	165	208	256
Other	25	21	33	37
Total Western Hemisphere	214	186	241	293
Asia				
Japan	275	247	262	371
South Korea	83	37	47	73
Taiwan	33	35	42	60
China	37	27	37	40
India	53	43	47	41
Other	73	70	85	97
Total Asia	554	459	520	682
Western Europe				
West Germany	129	115	115	152
Britain	137	129	144	152
Italy	70	79	80	99
France	42	47	48	68
Other	140	133	153	173
Total Western Europe	518	503	540	644
Eastern Europe	43	38	37	32
Oceania	21	29	39	45
Unspecified	0	1	0	1
TOTAL	1,387	1,264	1,437	1,765

[1]Imports reported on a c.i.f. (cost, insurance, and freight) basis.
[2]For value of the Kuwaiti dinar—see Glossary.

Source: Based on information from Kuwait, Ministry of Planning, Central Statistical
Office, *Annual Statistical Abstract, 1982*, Kuwait, 1983, 199–201.

Table 12. Kuwait. Summary of Balance of Payments, 1978–82
(in millions of Kuwaiti dinars)[1]

	1978	1979	1980	1981	1982[2]
Current account					
Receipts					
Exports					
Oil	2,584	4,702	5,153	3,888	2,428
Other commodities	231	303	416	558	644
Total exports	2,815	5,005	5,569	4,446	3,072
Investment income	798	988	1,483	2,343	1,908
Other receipts	193	327	331	388	308
Total receipts	3,806	6,320	7,383	7,177	5,288
Payments					
Imports	-1,189	-1,346	-1,826	-1,879	-2,064
Other	-710	-887	-1,189	-1,208	-1,393
Total payments	-1,899	-2,233	-3,015	-3,087	-3,457
Total current account . . .	1,907	4,087	4,368	4,090	1,831

Table 12. (Continued)
(in millions of Kuwaiti dinars)[1]

	1978	1979	1980	1981	1982[2]
Capital account					
Foreign aid	-274	-265	-366	-335	-334
Government investment	-1,131	-2,585	-2,805	-2,214	-912
Other transactions (net)[3]	-619	-1,124	-916	-1,464	-20
Total capital account	-2,024	-3,974	-4,087	-4,013	-1,266
BALANCE OF PAYMENTS	-117	113	281	77	565

[1]For value of the Kuwaiti dinar—see Glossary.
[2]Preliminary.
[3]Includes errors and omissions.

Source: Based on information from International Monetary Fund, "Kuwait Adopts Measures to Adjust to the Impact of Reduced Oil Revenues," *IMF Survey,* August 8, 1983, 238.

Table 13. Kuwait. Exports of Crude Oil
by Area and Major Countries of Destination, 1978–81
(in millions of barrels)

Area	1978	1979	1980	1981
Arab countries	8.2	17.4	6.6	10.0
Europe				
Britain	72.0	57.5	45.4	16.3
France	20.2	32.3	22.8	7.1
Netherlands	68.2	94.8	59.8	27.6
Italy	65.1	73.8	1.8	2.5
Ireland	25.9	24.3	4.1	1.0
Other	22.2	14.8	15.7	13.3
Total Europe	273.6	297.5	149.6	67.8
Western Hemisphere				
United States	5.5	5.4	7.5	0.0
Brazil	25.5	18.1	25.7	9.0
Other	4.1	7.9	5.9	2.4
Total Western Hemisphere . . .	35.1	31.4	39.1	11.4
Asia				
Japan	176.7	208.5	84.2	89.9
South Korea	54.9	58.6	49.7	36.4
Taiwan	49.7	55.4	55.6	50.3
Singapore	9.3	42.5	44.8	19.2
Other	24.9	31.1	13.4	7.8
Total Asia	315.5	396.1	247.7	203.6
Africa	0.7	5.2	3.0	0.5
Oceania	9.7	11.7	6.1	3.8
Other	0.0	1.0	9.3	0.0
TOTAL	642.8	760.3	461.4	297.1

Source: Based on information from Kuwait, Ministry of Planning, Central Statistical
Office, *Annual Statistical Abstract, 1982,* Kuwait, 1983, 161.

Table 14.   Qatar. Crude Oil Production,
Selected Years, 1950–82
(in millions of barrels)

Year	Quantity	Year	Quantity
1950	12.1	1975	159.5
1955	40.4	1976	178.3
1960	60.4	1977	158.8
1965	83.9	1978	176.5
1970	132.5	1979	184.8
1971	156.9	1980	172.3
1972	176.5	1981	147.8
1973	208.2	1982	119.7
1974	189.2		

Source: Based on information from Qatar, Industrial Development Technical Centre, *Achievements in Industrial Development*, Doha, February 1981, 21; and Qatar, Central Statistical Organization, *Annual Statistical Abstract*, Doha, July 1983, 162.

Table 15.   Qatar. Exports of Crude Oil, 1972–82
(in millions of barrels)

Year	Quantity	Year	Quantity
1972	176.3	1978	174.8
1973	208.2	1979	180.9
1974	186.7	1980	170.4
1975	156.6	1981	142.7
1976	178.1	1982	117.8
1977	153.6		

Source: Based on information from Qatar, Central Statistical Organization, *Annual Statistical Abstract*, Doha, July 1983, 162.

Table 16. Qatar. Production of Major Industrial Firms, 1977–82
(in thousands of tons)

Firm	Product	1977	1978	1979	1980	1981	1982
Qatar Fertilizer Company	Ammonia and urea	293	427	868	1,128	1,022	1,190
Qatar National Cement Company	Cement	176	210	248	208	257	229
	Quick lime	---	---	14	19	21	20
Qatar Iron and Steel Company	Reinforcimg steel bars	---	86	380	440	453	485
	Oxide iron ore	---	---	1	13	37	15
Qatar Flour Mills Company	Flour	16	13	20	22	21	25
	Bran	4	4	5	6	6	6
Qatar Petrochemical Company	Ethylene	---	---	---	---	133	127
	Low-density polyethylene	---	---	---	---	111	120
	Sulfur	---	---	---	---	9	13

---means none.

Source: Based on information from Qatar, Central Statistical Organization, *Annual Statistical Abstract*, Doha, July 1983, 170.

Table 17.   Qatar. Land Distribution, 1979

Size of Holding (in hectares)	Percentage of All Farms
0.0–1.0	37
1.1–3.0	39
3.1–9.0	20
Over 9.1	4
TOTAL . .	100

Source: Based on information from Qatar, Ministry of Information, Press and Publications Department, *Yearbook, 1980–81*, Doha, n. d., 135.

Table 18.   Qatar. Agricultural Production, 1979–82
(in tons)

Product	1979	1980	1981	1982
Cereals	530	640	735	1,368
Vegetables	20,655	17,868	18,291	17,851
Root beets	36	48	36	28
Fruits and dates . . .	3,819	3,942	6,860	9,534
Forage	26,950	36,400	38,680	42,003

Source: Based on information from Qatar, Central Statistical Organization, *Annual Statistical Abstract*, Doha, July 1983, 193–94.

Table 19. Qatar. Meat, Fish, Poultry, Egg, and Dairy Production, 1979–82
(in tons)

Product	1979	1980	1981	1982
Meat	817	1,402	1,235	1,515
Fish	2,690	1,762	2,273	2,315
Poultry	913	700	776	923
Eggs	307	276	318	313
Dairy products . . .	1,210	3,501	5,575	6,208

Source: Based on information from Qatar, Central Statistical Organization, *Annual Statistical Abstract*, Doha, July 1983, 195.

Table 20. *Qatar. Budget Summary, FY 1975–82*[1]
(in millions of Qatari riyals)[2]

	FY 1975	FY 1976	FY 1977	FY 1978	FY 1979	FY 1980	FY 1981	FY 1982
Revenues								
Oil	6,623	8,020	7,458	7,421	11,220	17,454	17,189	11,682
Non-oil	512	907	696	804	870	1,550	2,054	1,989
Total revenues .	7,135	8,927	8,154	8,225	12,090	19,004	19,243	13,671
Expenditures								
Capital	1,209	2,034	3,022	2,536	2,430	3,260	3,630	5,067
Other	3,224	3,775	4,296	3,936	5,843	7,677	11,113	7,552
Total expenditures	4,433	5,809	7,318	6,472	8,273	10,937	14,743	12,619
Surplus	2,702	3,118	836	1,753	3,817	8,067	4,500	1,052

[1]The fiscal year is based on the hijra calendar; the year corresponds only roughly to its Gregorian counterpart.
[2]For value of the Qatari riyal—see Glossary.

Source: Based on information from Qatar, Central Statistical Organization, *Annual Statistical Abstract*, Doha, July 1983, 240.

Table 21. Qatar. Estimated Balance of Payments, Selected years, 1975–82
(in millions of Qatari riyals)*

	1975	1978	1979	1980	1981	1982
Exports						
Oil	6,923	8,936	13,933	19,645	20,006	15,339
Other	210	313	722	1,142	1,266	1,066
Total exports	7,133	9,249	14,655	20,787	21,272	16,405
Imports	1,800	4,590	5,378	5,265	5,524	7,100
Trade balance	5,333	4,659	9,277	15,522	15,748	9,305
Services and private transfers	891	1,079	4,419	5,843	7,069	5,214
Current account balance	4,442	3,580	4,858	9,679	8,679	4,091
Capital and official transfers	3,577	2,167	2,112	7,055	5,392	6,866
CHANGE IN RESERVES	865	1,413	2,746	2,624	3,287	−2,775

*For value of the Qatari riyal—see Glossary.

Source: Based on information from Qatar, Central Statistical Organization, *Annual Statistical Abstract*, Doha, July 1983, 247.

Table 22. United Arab Emirates. Schools, Classes, Students, and Staff, 1977/78, 1979/80, and 1981/82

	Male	Female	Coed	Total
1977/78				
Schools	104	88	36	228
Classes	1,440	1,177	218	2,835
Students	43,085	35,896	n.a.	78,981
Teachers and				
administrative staff	3,170	3,177	n.a.	6,347
1979/80				
Schools	118	98	39	255
Classes	1,718	1,454	288	3,460
Students	51,631	44,446	n.a.	96,077
Teachers and				
administrative staff	3,789	4,025	n.a.	7,814
1981–82				
Schools	150	132	41	323
Classes	2,276	2,006	401	4,683
Students	66,584	59,782	n.a.	126,366
Teachers and				
administrative staff	4,806	5,646	n.a.	10,452

n.a.—not available.

Source: Based on information from United Arab Emirates, Ministry of Education, Central Statistical Department, *Statistical Yearbook*, Abu Dhabi, 1983.

Table 23. United Arab Emirates. Enrollment in the National University of the UAE, 1977/78, 1979/80, and 1981/82

Faculty	1977/78			1979/80			1981/82		
	Male	Female	Total	Male	Female	Total	Male	Female	Total
Arts	81	65	146	231	277	508	406	569	975
Science	42	40	82	138	150	288	215	294	509
Education	42	61	103	170	197	367	178	294	472
Public administration and politics	97	19	116	341	108	449	453	215	668
Law and sharia ...	---	---	---	122	14	136	260	64	324
Engineering	---	---	---	---	---	---	81	22	103
Agriculture	---	---	---	---	---	---	52	---	52
TOTAL	262	185	447	1,002	746	1,748	1,645	1,458	3,103

---means none.

Source: Abu Dhabi, Department of Planning, Statistical Section, *Statistical Yearbook, 1982*, Abu Dhabi, 1983, Table 59.

Table 24. United Arab Emirates.
Oil Production and Exports, 1962–83
(in millions of barrels)

Year	Abu Dhabi Production	Dubai Production[1]	Sharjah Production[2]	Total Production	Exports
1962	6.0	---	---	6.0	5.4
1963	18.2	---	---	18.2	18.1
1964	69.2	---	---	69.2	67.8
1965	102.9	---	---	102.9	102.1
1966	131.3	---	---	131.3	132.5
1967	139.4	---	---	139.4	137.4
1968	182.4	---	---	182.4	181.4
1969	218.8	---	---	218.8	222.5
1970	253.2	12.5	---	265.7	284.5
1971	341.0	31.3	---	372.3	384.4
1972	384.1	45.8	---	429.9	439.8
1973	475.6	55.8	---	531.4	553.3
1974	515.2	80.2	8.5	603.9	608.3
1975	512.4	92.8	13.9	619.1	619.7
1976	580.6	114.8	13.5	708.9	710.0
1977	602.8	116.4	10.3	729.5	724.2
1978	527.9	131.8	8.1	667.8	665.0
1979	534.1	129.3	5.1	668.5	654.7
1980	494.2	127.8	4.0	626.0	617.4
1981	412.8	131.0	3.7	547.5	n.a.
1982	329.0	131.0	3.0	463.0	n.a.
1983[3]	288.0	122.0	14.0	424.0	n.a.

n.a.—not available.
[1]Oil production in Dubai began in 1970.
[2]Oil production in Sharjah began in 1974.
[3]Preliminary data.

Table 25. United Arab Emirates. Federal Government Budget, 1979–82
(in billions of dirhams)[1]

Budget	1979	1980	1981	1982[2]
Revenues				
Amirates' contributions . . .	8.5	17.1	22.6	15.7
Other	0.2	0.3	0.6	0.4
Total revenues	8.7	17.4	23.2	16.1
Expenditures				
Current expenditures				
Defense and interior . . .	4.5	7.8	9.3	8.9
Education and youth . . .	0.9	1.0	1.2	1.3
Electricity and water . . .	0.2	0.2	0.3	0.4
Other	1.8	3.2	6.9	6.5
Total current expenditures	7.4	12.2	17.7	17.1
Development expenditures				
Electricity and water . . .	0.1	0.1	0.3	0.5
Other	0.5	0.8	1.0	1.0
Total development expenditures	0.6	0.9	1.3	1.5
Equity participation	0.5	2.0	1.6	0.7
Total expenditures	8.5	15.1	20.6	19.3
Surplus or Deficit (–)	0.2	2.3	2.6	–3.2

[1]For value of the dirham—see Glossary.
[2]Preliminary figures.

Source: Based on information from United Arab Emirates, Central Bank, *Bulletin*, Abu Dhabi, 3, No. 2, June 1983, 124.

Table 26. United Arab Emirates.
Consolidated Government Budget Summary, 1979–83[1]
(in billions of dirhams)[2]

	1979	1980	1981	1982	1983[3]
Revenues					
Oil and gas[4]	26.9	44.6	45.9	34.7	26.5
Other	1.8	2.1	2.9	2.8	2.7
Total revenues	28.7	46.7	48.8	37.5	29.2
Expenditures					
Current spending	11.8	18.2	22.2	22.1	20.6
Development expenditures . . .	9.0	8.3	9.5	10.4	8.6
Domestic loans and investments	1.5	2.6	2.2	2.3	1.1
Foreign equity investments . . .	0.5	0.6	0.6	0.1	0.3
Foreign loans and grants	3.3	7.5	9.3	5.9	3.7
Total expenditures	26.1	37.2	43.8	40.8	34.3
SURPLUS	2.6	9.5	5.0	–3.3	–5.1

[1]Primarily budgets of Abu Dhabi, Dubai, and federal governments.
[2]For value of the dirham—see Glossary.
[3]Preliminary data.
[4]Includes those revenues turned over to Abu Dhabi and Dubai governments.

*Table 27. United Arab Emirates. Summary
of Balance of Payments, 1980–83*
(in billions of United States dollars)

	1980	1981	1982	1983[1]
Current account				
Exports (f.o.b.)[2]	22.0	21.8	18.2	15.4
(Oil and gas)	(20.0)	(19.5)	(16.0)	(12.7)
Imports	–7.6	–8.6	–8.1	–7.9
Government grants	–1.7	–1.1	–0.7	–0.4
Private transfers	–2.2	–2.3	–2.2	–1.9
Investment income (net) . .	1.4	1.9	2.0	1.6
Other service payments (net)	–1.8	–2.5	–2.2	–2.3
Total current account . .	10.1	9.2	7.0	4.5
Capital movements				
Foreign aid (net)	–0.5	–1.6	–1.0	–0.8
Government capital				
movements (net)	–3.2	–1.3	–0.7	–0.6
Private capital movements				
(net)[3]	–4.6	–4.0	–4.3	–3.5
Total capital movements .	–8.3	–6.9	–6.0	–4.9
CHANGES IN FOREIGN				
ASSETS[4]	–1.8	–2.3	–1.0	0.4

[1]Preliminary figures.
[2]f.o.b.—free on board.
[3]Includes errors and omissions.
[4]A minus sign indicates an increase in foreign assets.

Table 28.   Oman. Government Schools, Students, and Teachers,
Selected Years, 1969/70–1982/83[1]

	1969/70	1974/75	1978/79	1982/83
Schools[2]				
Primary				
Male	3	88	73	72
Female	---	44	50	56
Co-education	---	31	134	76
Total primary	3	163	257	204
Preparatory				
Male	---	9	55	107
Female	---	2	20	45
Co-education	---	---	11	67
Total preparatory . . .	---	11	86	219
Secondary				
Male	---	1	7	13
Female	---	1	2	19
Total secondary	---	2	9	32
Total schools	3	176	352	455
Students				
Primary				
Male	909	36,351	53,025	72,311
Female	---	12,225	24,949	44,156
Total primary	909	48,576	77,974	116,467
Preparatory				
Male	---	437	5,765	14,541
Female	---	134	1,513	5,444
Total preparatory . . .	---	571	7,278	19,985
Secondary				
Male	---	63	529	2,899
Female	---	19	156	1,231
Total secondary	---	82	685	4,130
Total students	909	49,229	85,937	140,582
Teachers				
Male	30	1,610	2,762	4,430
Female	---	505	1,103	2,145
Total teachers	30	2,115	3,865	6,575
Average number of				
teachers per school	10.0	12.0	11.0	14.5
Student-teacher ratio	30.3	23.3	22.2	21.4

---means none.
[1]The school year begins in September and ends in May.
[2]The number of schools is not the number of buildings. A building may be used for two schools, morning and afternoon.

Source: Based on information from Oman, Directorate General of National Studies, *Statistical Yearbook,* Muscat, November 1983, 15.

Table 29. Oman. Gross Domestic Product by Type
of Economic Activity, Selected Years, 1976–82[1]
(at current prices in millions of Omani rials)[2]

Economic Activity	1976	1980	1981	1982
Oil sector				
Crude petroleum	530.4	1,225.3	1,456.6	1,394.2
Natural gas	n.a.	15.7	17.6	18.2
Total oil sector	530.4	1,241.0	1,474.2	1,412.4
Mining and quarrying . . .	n.a.	0.9	2.3	3.3
Production sector				
Agriculture and livestock . .	15.4	26.3	28.8	30.7
Fishing	6.0	10.2	11.2	15.0
Manufacturing	4.0	22.3	26.3	35.6
Total production sector .	25.4	58.8	66.3	81.3
Services sector				
Construction	83.0	111.3	129.3	153.4
Transport	20.4	45.2	59.4	70.9
Communication	5.1	6.6	12.0	15.1
Electricity	3.3	13.7	14.4	14.9
Water	1.7	5.6	7.5	9.6
Wholesale and retail trade and hotels[3]	50.3	185.6	234.2	298.7
Banking	11.2	29.5	42.4	49.6
Insurance	n.a.	2.0	4.3	9.3
Ownership of dwellings . .	13.8	72.1	91.3	111.6
Public administration and defense	71.0	184.9	239.1	263.2
Other services	11.4	17.6	20.0	22.1
Total services sector . . .	271.2	674.1	853.9	1,018.4
TOTAL	827.0	1,974.8	2,396.7	2,515.4
Less (–) imputed bank service charge	n.a.	27.5	36.7	42.1
Plus (+) import duties	4.5	8.6	11.3	14.7

Table 29. Continued.
(at current prices in millions of Omani rials)[2]

Economic Activity	1976	1980	1981	1982
Gross domestic product				
in purchaser's values	831.5	1,955.9	2,371.3	2,488.0
Less (–) indirect taxes	11.6	21.5	21.5	31.7
Gross domestic product				
at factor cost	819.8	1,934.4	2,346.2	2,456.3
Less (–) other current				
transfers from the rest				
of the world (net)	147.9	150.1	179.8	217.4
Gross national product				
at factor cost	672.0	1,784.3	2,166.4	2,238.9

n.a.—not available.
[1] From 1980 revised figures; are not comparable with figures for earlier years.
[2] For value of the Omani rial—see Glossary.
[3] Figures for hotels from 1980 and later.

Source: Based on information from Oman, Directorate General of National Studies, *Statistical Yearbook*, Muscat, November 1983, 172.

Table 30. Oman. Petroleum Statistics, 1973–82
(in millions of barrels)

Year	Crude Oil Production	Crude Oil Exports	Oil Revenues (in millions of Omani rials)*
1973	107	107	114
1974	106	106	419
1975	125	125	488
1976	135	134	544
1977	124	122	546
1978	115	116	522
1979	108	108	746
1980	103	102	1,245
1981	120	120	1,526
1982	123	119	1,410

*For value of the Omani rial—see Glossary.

Source: Based on information from Oman, Directorate General of National Studies, *Statistical Yearbook,* Muscat, November 1983.

Table 31.   Oman Government Expenses, 1978–82
(in millions of Omani rials)*

	1978	1979	1980	1981	1982
Internal revenue					
Oil revenue	457.7	634.6	831.2	1,125.4	1,057.3
Other revenue	44.6	57.6	92.5	136.8	118.1
Total internal revenue	502.3	692.2	923.7	1,262.2	1,175.4
Expenditures					
Current expenditures					
Defense and national security	264.5	269.0	406.8	521.9	581.3
Civil ministries	138.1	144.5	214.8	272.5	315.7
Interest on loans	16.2	19.7	21.1	15.5	17.5
Government contribution in operating cost					
of Petroleum Development (Oman)	18.6	24.1	35.3	47.1	55.7
Total current expenditures	437.4	457.3	678.0	857.0	970.2

Table 31. Continued.
(in millions of Omani rials)*

	1978	1979	1980	1981	1982
Development expenditures					
Civil ministries	89.0	129.4	168.9	241.0	289.0
Government contribution in development cost					
of Petroleum Development (Oman)	33.7	63.7	77.8	76.4	106.2
Total development expenditures	122.7	193.1	246.7	317.4	395.2
Participation in local, international,					
and regional enterprises	25.0	11.4	25.1	49.4	47.5
Total expenditures	585.1	661.8	949.8	1,223.8	1,412.9
SURPLUS OR DEFICIT (−)	−82.8	30.4	−26.1	38.4	−237.5

*For value of the Omani rial—see glossary.

Source: Based on information from Oman, Directorate General of National Studies, *Statistical Yearbook*, Muscat, November 1983.

Table 32. Oman. Government Budget,
1983 and 1984
(in millions of Omani rials)*

	1983	1984
Expenditures	1,650	1,765
Revenue		
Oil	1,181	1,100
Non-oil	262	461
Total revenue	1,443	1,561
Deficit	207	204
Major allocations		
Defense and security	612	677
Petroleum Development, Oman	135	59
Private sector development	n.a.	9
Oman Bank for Agriculture		
and Fisheries	n.a.	5
Oman Housing Bank	n.a.	4
Total major allocations	747	754

n.a.—not available.
*For value of the Omani rial—see Glossary.

Source: Based on information from *Middle East Economic Digest*, London, January 6,
1984, 32.

Table 33.   Oman.   Factors Affecting Changes in Money and Quasi-Money, 1978–82
(in millions of Omani rials)[1]

Factor	1978	1979	1980	1981	1982
Money and quasi-money					
Money	2.9	9.0	31.5	58.0	27.8
Quasi-money	20.9	6.9	47.2	67.7	84.1
Total money and quasi-money	24.0[2]	15.9	78.7	125.7	111.9
Foreign assets (net)	−34.5	102.6	150.1	155.4	98.1
Domestic assets					
Claims on government (net)	34.5	−91.3	−83.2	−47.8	5.3
Claims on private sector	31.2	24.2	60.7	51.6	42.4
Other items (net)	−7.2	−19.6	−48.9	−33.6	−33.9
Total domestic assets (net)	58.5	−86.7	−71.4	−29.8	13.8

[1]For value of the Omani rial—see Glossary.
[2]Figures do not add to total because of rounding.

Source: Based on information from International Monetary Fund, *IMF Survey,* July 25, 1983, 223.

455

Table 34. Oman. Balance of Payments, 1978–82
(in millions of United States dollars)

	1978	1979	1980	1981	1982[1]
Trade balance					
Oil exports	1,510.7	2,158.9	3,603.4	4,419.3	4,081.1
Other exports and reexports	87.4	120.7	144.8	276.5	341.9
Imports	−1,269.0	−1,428.1	−2,065.1	−2,722.1	−3,147.4
Total trade balance	329.1	851.5	1,683.1	1,973.4[2]	1,275.6
Services and private transfers					
Profit remittances	−114.9	−126.8	−172.2	−302.2	−331.5
Official interest (net)	4.6	−22.0	63.1	229.9	385.6
Other services (net)	−66.3	−92.1	−134.6	−276.5	−331.2
Workers' remittances (net)	−241.2	−281.4	−361.9	−448.2	−683.6
Total services and private transfers	−417.8	−522.3	−605.6	−797.0	−960.7
Current account balance	−88.7	329.2	1,077.5	1,176.4	314.9
Official capital and grants					
Grant receipts	20.3	179.2	101.9	144.8	42.3
Net drawings on loans	−23.7	−11.0	13.6	145.9	120.7
Other official capital	−3.8	−28.1	−10.7	15.0	−55.0
Total official capital and grants	−7.2	140.1	104.8	305.7	108.0

Table 34. Continued.
(in millions of United States dollars)

	1978	1979	1980	1981	1982[1]
Oil sector capital (net)					
Direct investments	27.2	76.4	85.4	74.4	134.1
Oil export credits (net)	18.0	−50.4	−7.5	−46.6	−1.2
Total oil sector capital (net)	45.2	26.0	77.9	27.8	132.9
SDR allocations[3]	---	4.1	2.9	---	---
Errors and omissions (net)[4]	−49.7	−202.2	−323.0	−109.3	303.9
Overall balance	−100.4	297.2	940.1	1,400.6	859.7

---means none.
[1]Provisional.
[2]Figures do not add to total because of rounding.
[3]SDR—special drawing rights (see Glossary).
[4]Includes non-oil private capital.

Source: Based on information from International Monetary Fund, *IMF Survey*, July 1983, 222.

Appendix B

Summary of Developments in the International Oil Industry

The era of cheap energy ended in the early 1970s when members of the Organization of Petroleum Exporting Countries (OPEC) took control of the pricing of crude oil from international oil companies and subsequently increased prices rapidly. This caused a tremendous growth in revenues for oil exporters and serious balance of payments difficulties and recession for many oil importers. National oil companies also took over other functions from the large multinational oil companies that had dominated the industry for about a century. The international oil industry drastically changed during the 1970s.

One factor contributing to the sharp change in the price of energy was the steeply rising world demand caused by the mechanization of so many activities during the previous 100 years. One estimate indicated that the fuel and power consumed by an average American in the 1980s amounted to the energy equivalent of 200 full-time servants. Between 1962 and 1971 the estimated world demand for energy increased at an annual rate of 4.8 percent, a rate that would result in a doubling of demand every 15 years. Energy requirements were accelerating so rapidly that observers predicted critical energy shortages in the twenty-first century and the exhaustion of known oil deposits relatively soon. World oil production was expected to peak about 1990 and decline thereafter. The primary energy sources—coal, oil, and natural gas—were being depleted at an astonishing rate.

Accompanying the growth in energy demand was a radical shift in the source of energy. When the world's first oil well began producing in 1859, men and animals supplied much of the world's power needs, supplemented by waterwheels, windmills, and steam generated by burning coal and wood. Coal powered an early part of the Industrial Revolution; in 1910, for example, coal supplied 90 percent of American commercial energy requirements. Coal still made up over half the world's commercial sources of energy in 1960, but oil was rapidly displacing it as the world's primary fuel.

Petroleum was used long before the Christian Era. Noah allegedly waterproofed his ark with bitumen, an asphalt of Asia Minor also used in ancient times in mud bricks and mortar. Early man used oil for medicinal purposes and as fuel for lamps. Remains of roads paved in antiquity with natural asphalt are still found today in Iraq. Until modern times, petroleum was collected from natural seepage. Not until 1859, when a drilling rig was set up on Oil Creek near Titusville, Pennsylvania, was oil sought commercially.

The oil industry grew rapidly after the first well came in. Within a decade Russia, Romania, Canada, Italy, and the United States were producing oil. Several more countries began producing soon afterward, and oil was discovered in Iran in 1908.

During the late nineteenth century, petroleum was used primarily as a lubricant and as lamp fuel. In 1900 about 58 percent of petroleum consumption in the United States—the largest producer and consumer of oil—was in the form of kerosine for heaters and lamps; most of the rest was used as fuel oil for heating and in power plants.

Development of the internal-combustion engine vastly expanded the demand for petroleum products. World War I and World War II greatly accelerated engine development. Improvements in petroleum refining accompanied diversification and refinement of engines. Research added to the uses for petroleum products; a whole new field of petrochemicals emerged, producing dyes, fertilizers, and other products and increasing the demand for crude oil.

Petroleum was cleaner, more convenient, and cheaper than other fuels. In addition, it was the unique fuel for internal-combustion engines, feedstock for petrochemicals, and the only base for lubricants. As a result, the market for oil grew much more rapidly than the total demand for energy. World consumption (excluding communist countries) increased from 1 million barrels per day (bpd) in 1915 to more than 5 million bpd in 1940 and 48 million bpd in 1976. Between 1962 and 1971 world consumption of petroleum increased at an annual rate of 7 percent, a doubling of consumption in 10 years. Of the energy consumed in 1970 by noncommunist countries, a little more than one-half came from oil. Coal accounted for nearly one-fourth, natural gas supplied about one-fifth, and nuclear power provided less than 0.5 percent; hydropower contributed the remainder.

Another factor contributing to the sharp rise in the price of energy was the growing international trade in petroleum products. The Soviet Union surpassed the United States as the largest producer of crude oil in 1974 as a result of the declining output of American fields (4 percent a year) that set in at the end of the 1960s. Both countries, however, consumed most of their own production. The Soviet Union began exporting relatively small amounts of petroleum in the 1950s; the United States had begun importing increasing quantities of oil to meet consumption needs some years before. The main stimulus for the international petroleum trade came from the rapid economic growth and increased oil consumption in Western Europe and Japan after World War II, supplemented by rising energy needs in developing countries. These countries lacked significant crude oil deposits and required large and increasing imports to satisfy growing consumption needs. Between 1962 and 1971 the petroleum imports of Western Europe more than doubled, and Japan's increased more than fourfold. Petroleum became the most important commodity in value in international trade, and by the mid-1970s petroleum products accounted for more than one-half of all seaborne commerce.

Geologists have determined the outlines of a large basin extending from the Taurus Mountains in southeast Turkey to the Arabian Sea in the south and underlying western Iran, eastern Saudi Arabia, Iraq, and most of the Persian Gulf. In 1976 this basin held 55 percent of the world's proven reserves. The development of these Middle Eastern fields after World War II made them the world's most important crude oil source, supplying about 37 percent of world production in 1976. Crude oil production costs have been low because pressure in these prolific fields is fairly high; transportation costs have been low because the fields are relatively close to water routes. The countries owning these reserves have small populations, little domestic oil consumption, and an interest in exporting oil. As a result, these states became the most important exporters of petroleum products, supplying nearly two-thirds of the oil in international trade by the mid-1970s.

Structure of the International Oil Industry

Another factor contributing to the sharp rise in the price of energy was the changing structure of the international oil industry. The industry is divided into several distinct phases—exploring, producing crude oil, refining into usable products, transporting, and marketing—and each phase requires costly investments. Even with modern techniques, for example, only 10 percent of the wells drilled in new fields produce oil or gas, and only 2 percent of the wells are significant producers. The industry, as first developed, consisted of a few very large companies vertically integrating all phases from exploration to marketing.

The petroleum industry before World War II was dominated by seven or eight major oil companies. Five of these were American; the others were European. These major companies held most of the foreign concession agreements for exploration and development. This gave the companies a degree of horizontal integration; they could adjust the output of crude from various areas to match overall marketing needs.

Before World War II the dominance of these companies, vertically and horizontally integrated, gave them a high degree of influence over supply and price through mutuality of interests, if not collusion. The major oil companies were able to exert considerable control for some years after World War II; output from prolific, low-cost Persian Gulf fields was phased into world markets without excessive disruption to pricing, petroleum investments, or employment in the United States and in other high-cost crude oil areas. Throughout most of the world, coal mining, which had become costlier as the richer seams were depleted, was less disrupted than it might have been had there been a forced adjustment to cheaper oil. The price of energy diminished in relation to other prices but less rapidly than it would have with quicker exploitation of Persian Gulf crude and competitive pricing; the adjustment process was eased for many countries, but at the cost of windfall profits to the oil companies.

By the 1950s the dominance of the major oil companies was gradually decreasing. The booming oil business encouraged the entrance of smaller oil companies. Some, such as the Getty Oil Company, were private firms; others, such as the French and Italian national petroleum companies, were state-owned businesses. The smaller companies won concessions in oil-producing countries by offering the host governments more favorable terms than those of the major oil companies. The Soviet Union also began to export oil—an action over which the major companies had no control. These developments occurred within the broader framework of the bipolar relations between the leading communist and noncommunist countries. Some developing countries were asserting more control over their own destinies and natural resources at the insistence of domestic nationalistic groups. Diminishing dominance by the major oil companies meant an increasing inability to match petroleum supplies to consumption needs. By the end of the 1950s, a growing supply of oil caused prices to fall. The downward pressure on petroleum prices was favored by the consumer, but it reduced revenues for the oil-producing states.

Oil Pricing

Oil pricing before the 1970s was a vast and controversial subject complicated by the vertical integration of much of the industry and the secretiveness of the companies involved. Price can simply match supply and demand, or it can incorporate political decisions to achieve some possibly noneconomic goal. The United States, though an avowed advocate of free enterprise and free trade, had long interfered in the pricing of some commodities—as in price supports for major agricultural crops—and regulated phases of the domestic oil and gas industry for particular goals that, to a degree, affected international prices of petroleum. Other oil-producing countries have also sought to exert various controls over their petroleum resources with the result that oil pricing and trade have reflected forces other than just supply and demand.

The major international oil companies were largely housed in the United States, where they had domestic fields, refineries, and outlets. There had been many United States congressional investigations of the oil companies, and their operations in foreign countries have been watched, threatened, and, in some instances, taken over by the host government. Contrary to their popular image, the oil companies have not been free agents concerned only with maximizing profits. This is not to say, however, that they have not wielded considerable domestic as well as international power, done unsavory things, or secured huge profits.

Early in the 1900s the United States was the world's major oil exporter, and international crude oil pricing by the major oil companies was based on the United States price plus transportation costs. This was a base-point pricing system in which the price to the buyer was equivalent to the price of oil shipped to him from the Gulf of Mexico, regardless of actual source. There were other oil-exporting countries at the time, but the oil companies' price was the same to India, for example, even if the oil was shipped from the Persian Gulf, where transportation costs were substantially less than those from the Gulf of Mexico. This system worked when there were only a few oil companies with mutual interests; it protected their investments in the United States and other areas and provided a high return for developing fields, such as those in the Persian Gulf regions. How much the oil company kept and how much the government owning the field received depended on the concession agreement, but there was not a downward pressure on the price of crude oil produced in the new foreign fields in the Caribbean and Middle East.

Between 1945 and 1950 the increased supply of crude from foreign fields, the emergence of independent oil companies, and United States pressure applied through its help in rebuilding postwar Europe brought about major modification of the single base-point price system. The major oil companies set crude oil prices in conjunction with transportation costs from actual point of shipment to establish a series of equalization points—points where the landed price of Middle East oil was the same as crude from the Gulf of Mexico and Venezuela. The equalization point was first southern Europe, then London, and eventually New York. The shifting of the equalization point northward and westward increased transportation costs, thereby requiring lower quotations for Middle East crude and revenues for these countries. When the equalization point was New York, Middle East oil had a competitive advantage in European markets formerly held by United States, Mexican, and Venezuelan crude.

The oil companies were caught in conflicting pressures. The cost of producing oil in the Middle East was a fraction of that in Venezuela. which in turn was substantially less than that in the United States. If prices were based on cost of production, Middle East crude would have forced other countries out of the market. The oil companies, American politicians, and American businesses did not want this. An effective coalition in the United States limited imports of foreign oil for the large American market for at least 10 years before official import quotas were established in 1959. The major oil companies would have profited from more imports, and the Middle Eastern oil-producing countries would have been happy—at least for a while—if the companies had taken more oil, for their revenues would have gone up. American, Venezuelan, and other relatively high-cost producers, however, did not want to be forced out of production of crude. Each producing country wanted to remain in the oil business and earn more money but did not want to suffer competition from cheap suppliers or have the price of its oil go down. The dominance of the major companies over the industry reduced for all producers the pain of adjustment to the large supply of low-cost Middle East crude entering the market.

From about 1950 to the early 1970s, there was a system of posted prices for each country—prices at which oil companies would sell crude oil to anybody. Transportation costs were not included. Because "anybody" generally meant independent oil companies that the major oil companies did not want to encourage, posted prices were higher than the actual price at which the bulk of crude oil sales took place. Moreover, a short-term oversupply of crude developed in the late 1950s as newly discovered fields began to produce, causing a downward pressure on crude oil prices. By the 1960s, if not earlier, the posted price became only a reference point for calculating the taxes and royalty payments due oil-producing states under the concession agreements.

The posted price per barrel of Saudi Arabian light (34 degrees on the American Petroleum Institute [API] gravity scale) marker crude oil was US$2.05 in June 1948, US$1.70 in November 1950, US$2.08 in June 1958, US$1.80 in August 1960, and US$2.18 in February 1971. The marker price is the basic price for a typical regional crude—in this case Arabian light used for the Gulf—from which regional prices are derived.

Although the major oil companies exerted considerable influence on crude oil prices, the oil industry was not a closed system, and market forces had an impact. Before 1973 crude oil was priced largely in the context of supply and demand; after 1973 crude oil pricing took into consideration the costs of other energy sources and the long-term supply of petroleum. The frame of reference for pricing decisions was vastly broader and less favorable to consumers than the one that had previously prevailed.

Organization of Petroleum Exporting Countries
The sheer size and integrated nature of the major international oil companies afforded them considerable advantages when negotiating original concession agreements with countries having known or probable deposits. Moreover, many of the concession agreements were arranged with developing countries generally lacking in sophistication and usually hard pressed for funds. The governments of these countries often failed to appreciate the value of their resources and were frequently so desperate for funds that they lacked bargaining power even if they understood the value of their oil. The oil states of the Gulf region were certainly in this position when the concession agreements were let before World War II.

Efforts by oil-producing countries to exercise control over their resources without causing excessive domestic economic and financial disruption were difficult because of the pressures the oil companies brought to bear. Mexico nationalized its oil industry in 1938, but it was a costly and prolonged experience. When Iran nationalized its oil industry in 1951, the oil companies refused to buy or transport the oil, causing a severe financial and political crisis in the country for some years.

OPEC was more than a decade in gestation. Part of the initial impetus came from Venezuela, which in 1943 began to press the international oil companies for more control over, and a better return on, its oil resources. Conscious of Mexico's difficult experience, Venezuela established contacts with Gulf oil states in an attempt to develop coordinated efforts among oil exporters. Some analysts have interpreted the rapid development of the Gulf oil fields after World War II by the major oil companies as both a means of forcing Venezuela to temper its demands and as an expansion of an alternative source of oil should the Venezuelan government's demands become unreasonable. Other observers stressed the low cost and other advantages inherent in Gulf oil as a natural cause for development of Middle East fields.

The Middle East countries recognized the usefulness of concerted action to protect their interests. Many of the countries, however, were desperately in need of revenues and, as a means to increase their incomes, independently pushed the oil companies to take more of their oil. Not until the oil companies unilaterally cut the posted price in the spring of 1959 (to reflect the glut of oil on the market and the growing discounts that they had been giving on posted prices) did a movement begin toward joint action. In response to the price cuts, the League of Arab States (Arab League) sponsored the first Arab oil conference in the summer of 1959; Venezuela and Iran attended as observers.

As a result of the contacts developed during the 1959 conference, Saudi Arabia and Venezuela issued a joint statement in May 1960 urging all oil-producing countries to adopt common policies to safeguard their economic interests. In August 1960 the oil companies further cut the posted prices of Middle East crude oil. The price reduction lopped off US$30 million from Saudi Arabia's estimated income for the year and thus severely hampered efforts to balance the budget and execute development programs. When the Saudi Arabian minister of petroleum attended an emergency meeting in Baghdad of authorities from oil-exporting states, he argued vigorously and successfully for the founding of OPEC.

OPEC was formed in September 1960 by Iran, Iraq, Kuwait, Saudi Arabia, and Venezuela to develop some bargaining power among oil-exporting countries vis-à-vis the international oil companies. Other countries joined subsequently. By 1984 Algeria, Ecuador, Gabon, Indonesia, Libya, Nigeria, Qatar, and the United Arab Emirates (UAE) were members, and applications for membership from other oil-producing countries were under consideration.

The foundation document of the organization noted the dependence of its members on revenue from oil exports, the wasting nature of the petroleum resources, and the interdependence of all countries. The first objectives of OPEC were to restore crude oil prices to the 1958 level and to stabilize prices through mutual cooperation with the oil companies. OPEC acknowledged the need for oil prices that balanced the interests of producing and consuming nations and provided a fair return on investments to the oil companies. The founding members agreed to stick together against efforts by the oil companies to woo any member country or apply sanctions against one that was following a unanimous decision of OPEC. In 1977 OPEC countries controlled about 70 percent of the world's crude oil reserves, over 50 percent of world oil production, and more than 80 percent of petroleum exports.

OPEC was unsuccessful during the 1960s in restoring crude oil prices to the level preceding the cuts of 1959 and 1960, but it won half the battle in that the oil companies did not make further cuts. OPEC also fostered negotiations with the oil companies to increase the revenues of the oil-exporting states. The negotiations concerned methods of calculating and increasing royalty payments and taxes due the host government, which raised the costs of producing crude oil. The added costs at least partly explained the absence of further price cuts in a situation fostering oversupply in the international crude oil markets.

The payments due host governments were spelled out in the concession agreements granted the oil companies. The more important concessions had been granted before World War II, when the host governments had little bargaining power. As a result, the financial return to the host governments was usually quite low. Venezuela started a major and important adjustment in concession agreements in 1943 by legislating a 50-percent tax on the net income earned by oil companies in the country; it became effective in 1947. A similar arrangement was discussed in Iran in 1948 but was not put into effect until 1954. The so-called 50–50 profit sharing was negotiated by Saudi Arabia with the Arabian American Oil Company (Aramco) in 1950, and it had become standard in the Persian Gulf by 1952. Profit-sharing arrangements substantially increased oil revenues for host governments. OPEC helped refine the calculations of taxes and royalties to the advantage of the host governments during the 1960s. OPEC also helped the oil-exporting governments negotiate considerably better terms in concession agreements granted after its founding.

The June 1967 War between Israel and several Arab states started a chain of events that led to a transformation in the world energy market. The war damaged and closed the Suez Canal, and several Arab oil states briefly embargoed oil exports. The canal remained closed until June 1975. The transportation problems of the much longer haul around Africa to Europe were partly offset by the use of new supertankers and by the increasing oil production in Africa—particularly in Algeria and Libya—which were close to southern Europe. Dependence on North African oil became even greater in 1970 as a result of civil war in Nigeria and disruption of operations of the pipeline from Saudi Arabia to the Mediterranean coast in Lebanon. The new military regime in Libya seized the opportunity of its enhanced position to cut back crude oil production and to secure higher posted prices and tax rates from the oil companies under the threat of cessation of exports if their demands were not met. An independent oil company, Occidental, agreed to the much more favorable terms for Libya, and other oil companies acceded to Libyan demands in September 1970.

Meanwhile, in a July 1970 speech, the Algerian representative to OPEC requested that other members seize control of pricing their internationally traded crude oil, a policy also strongly advocated by Iraq. OPEC followed with a unanimous resolution in December 1970 calling for substantial revisions and increases in crude oil pricing. Negotiations were held in Tehran in February 1971 for the Gulf region. The posted price of Gulf oil was raised by more than one-third, provision was made for yearly price increases of about 5 percent a year until 1975 to compensate for inflation, and the tax rate was raised to 55 percent. Libya negotiated an agreement in April 1971 whereby it won a substantially larger increase in the posted price, plus an increase of the tax rate to 55 percent. Algeria pressed for an increase in crude oil prices above that won by the Gulf but less than that won by Libya. Venezuela legislated, rather than negotiated, price and tax increases in March 1971.

These assorted actions effectively transferred control over crude oil prices from the oil companies to the producing states. When the United States dollar was devalued in 1971, a clause in the Gulf and Libyan agreements was invoked for new negotiations. An 8.5-percent increase in posted prices was established in Geneva in January 1972 to compensate for the devaluation, but officials of the producing nations thought the increase was insufficient. Further negotiations again took place after another devaluation in 1973.

OPEC members had long discussed having a hand in oil operations, but the oil companies made only token gestures. Discussion switched to taking control of the oil industries in their countries, and it was evident that some members would eventually act. Action came suddenly. Algeria and Libya seized properties of some concessionaires in 1971, and Iraq nationalized some of its fields in 1972. In January 1972 some Arab OPEC members from the Gulf region, particularly Saudi Arabia, began negotiations with the oil companies for a gradual takeover of company operations through participation. Participation—essentially buying part ownership of the operating company—was far less drastic than nationalization, and it had the particular advantage that the services, technical skills, and marketing chains of the oil companies were retained during the takeover. Participation avoided a problem faced by nearly all of the Arab oil states on the Gulf—an acute shortage of highly trained personnel capable of managing their oil fields and marketing petroleum products.

The Saudi oil minister, Shaykh Ahmad Zaki Yamani, led OPEC participation negotiations during several months of hard bargaining in 1972. The result was an immediate 25-percent participation in ownership by the oil states and 51-percent participation by 1983 through annual 5-percent increments starting in 1979. Individual Gulf oil states negotiated actual arrangements, such as compensation to the oil companies for the equity they yielded, as well as the process of phasing the country into marketing so that the companies could continue to meet their sales contracts. Some of the arrangements were not completed until 1974, but they were backdated to January 1, 1973.

The Kuwait National Assembly upset the schedule for a gradual increase in ownership when it refused to ratify the 25-percent participation agreement. Some members demanded 100-percent Kuwaiti ownership. Kuwait's negotiators arranged for 60-percent ownership, effective in 1974. In early 1975 the Kuwait government announced its intention to buy 100-percent ownership in the main producing company, and negotiations were completed in December but backdated to March 1975. Saudi Arabia negotiated 100-percent participation in Aramco in early 1976. Other Gulf oil states negotiated for full ownership.

The October 1973 War between Israel and Arab states created further disarray in oil markets. A selective embargo and phased cutback in crude production were imposed by several Arab countries. Iraq, however, increased rather than cut back oil exports, even though Iraqi officials had long argued the use of the oil weapon to counteract other countries' support of Israel. No oil-consuming country was seriously hurt by the embargo because the oil companies juggled supplies to keep oil flowing to all countries, but all consumers felt the threat and the supply pinch. Bidding for oil from Iran, for example, reportedly reached US$17 per barrel.

OPEC, and particularly the six member states in the Gulf region, took the opportunity to raise the price of crude oil twelve times in 1973 and then unilaterally raised it by more than 100 percent at the beginning of 1974. The posted price for Arabian marker crude, on which other Gulf prices were based, was US$5.12 per barrel in October 1973; the price became US$11.25 effective January 1, 1974. The posted price remained a reference price for assessing taxes and royalty payments. The actual selling price of crude was 93 percent of the posted price, or US$10.46 per barrel. A 10-percent increase decreed by OPEC in September 1975 raised Arabian marker crude to US$12.38 posted price and US$11.51 actual price per barrel. OPEC justified the more than fourfold increase in prices of crude between 1971 and 1975 as necessary to approximate the true cost of energy, compensate the oil producers adequately for depletion of their limited resources, and make up for the long period when oil prices were kept low while prices for manufactured goods continuously increased.

Several times during 1974, the Arab states of the Gulf also increased the royalty rates on each barrel of oil produced and the tax rates on foreign oil companies. The purpose of the increase was to diminish the wide differential between the costs to the oil companies of equity oil (the oil resulting from their equity in the producing company) and oil bought back from the host governments. Equity oil was much cheaper than buy-back oil. As a result of a meeting in Abu Dhabi, the UAE, Qatar, and Saudi Arabia increased the royalty rate to 20 percent and the tax rate on foreign oil companies to 85 percent while dropping the posted price for Arabian marker crude by US$.40 per barrel effective November 1, 1974. The changes raised the cost of equity oil close to the price of buy-back oil and resulted in an average return to the governments of just over US$10 per barrel. In a December 1974 meeting, OPEC members agreed to move toward such a unitary price system. OPEC members and most other oil-producing countries adopted the same royalty and tax rates.

The impact of all these changes on oil revenues of the producing countries was tremendous. Saudi Arabia illustrated the situation for the oil states on the Gulf. Saudi revenues per barrel increased from US$0.22 in 1948 to US$0.89 in 1970. By 1973 they had reached US$1.56 per barrel, and in 1974 they were above

US$10.10 per barrel. By the beginning of 1976, revenues were US$11.15 per barrel because of the OPEC price increase in October 1975.

Major Developments, 1973–83

In the decade after 1973, substantial changes occurred in the world oil industry. In many oil-exporting countries, ministries and national companies took over functions formerly performed by international oil firms. This practice was not limited to OPEC members but included Britain, Norway, Egypt, and Mexico, as examples. Governments and national oil companies usually set export prices and production limits. Many engaged in limited oil and gas exploration and oil field development. In the Gulf region, government-owned companies, sometimes with minority private investments, established export refineries, petrochemical plants manufacturing for foreign markets, and tanker fleets to carry their petroleum products to customers abroad. Kuwait bought a portion of Gulf Oil Corporation's European marketing system. In 1983 Saudi Arabia indicated it might also seek marketing outlets. International oil companies retained a high level of expertise, which was used by oil-exporting nations often under service contracts, and continued to market much of the world's oil products, but their impact in the world oil industry was greatly diluted from a decade earlier.

OPEC exerted considerable influence on petroleum prices but did not control them. Members increased crude oil prices several times with particularly large increases between 1979 and 1981. These increases were usually referred to as the second crisis; the weighted average of OPEC's crude oil export prices per barrel rose from US$12.93 in 1978 to US$30.87 in 1980, and to US$34.50 in 1981. Saudi Arabia's Arabian light marker crude per barrel increased from US$12.70 in 1978 to US$34 in November 1981 as a result of OPEC price decisions. The sharp rise in energy prices contributed to an economic recession in many nations, a result that some OPEC members had wanted to avoid.

In 1983 OPEC remained a loose confederation of diverse nations that first united to combat the power of international oil companies and then hung together after 1973 to force increases in crude oil prices. OPEC's diversity had been its salvation thus far in the difficult task of controlling crude oil supplies to maintain prices. There were two main groups within OPEC. One consisted of oil exporters having large reserves and small populations, such as Saudi Arabia, the UAE, Qatar, and Kuwait. This group might be called the moderate price group because during much of the 1970s they earned more oil revenues than they could invest profitably. They argued against sharp jumps in oil prices because that would intensify development by industrialized countries of new technology and energy sources. This group's interest was in moderate price increases and a slow rate of exploitation so that their oil reserves would continue to finance economic development long into the future.

The second group might be called the high price advocates. It was made up of such countries as Iran and Indonesia, which had relatively small oil reserves, large populations, and economic potentials other than oil. Because their reserves would not last long, they wanted to maximize current earnings on their limited reserves through high prices. They would then invest the earnings primarily in their own country to develop other resources and industries for self-sustaining growth. Some of tthese countries—Iran, for one—had pushed for substantially higher oil prices since 1973 than those adopted by OPEC members. Although Iraq was in an in-between position in terms of oil reserves, other resources, and the size of its population, Iraqi officials for many years have strongly advocated higher crude oil prices. Libya also usually favored maximum price increases.

Saudi Arabia, which has about one-quarter of the world's known oil reserves and a sustainable production capacity of over 10 million barrels per day (bpd), was capable of substantially affecting world oil supplies. In 1981 Saudi Arabia accounted for 18 percent of the world's crude oil production, 43 percent of that produced by OPEC members, and nearly half of the tonnage of petroleum exported by OPEC countries. In 1976 Saudi Arabia, joined by the UAE, refused to go along with the other OPEC members in raising crude oil prices by 10 percent on January 1, 1977. Instead, Saudi Arabia and the UAE raised prices by only 5 percent and increased production. Saudi officials defended their break with the rest of OPEC as necessary to promote economic recovery in industrialized countries and to return stability to the world's oil markets. By mid-1977 a compromise emerged whereby Saudi Arabia and the UAE increased the price of their oil by 5 percent while the rest of OPEC abandoned a scheduled 5-percent rise. OPEC again had a unified price base, forced in part by increased Saudi oil production.

Political turmoil in Iran that led to the fall of the shah disrupted oil production during 1978 and 1979, contributing to shortages in world markets. Buyers panicked and bid up crude oil prices to as much as US$40 a barrel in Europe's spot markets. The outbreak of the Iran-Iraq War in 1980 perpetuated the disarray in world oil markets. OPEC members voted a series of price increases that raised the average OPEC cost of a barrel from US$12.93 in 1978 to US$34.50 in 1981. Non-OPEC oil exporters raised prices by similar amounts and increased production and exports. By the early 1980s development of oil fields in Alaska, Mexico, and the North Sea had added about 6 million bpd to world production.

The 267-percent rise in crude oil prices in 1979–81 spurred efforts to increase supply. Exploration and drilling expanded rapidly throughout the world, resulting in the discovery of some new fields, although world reserves were falling as consumption remained greater than the amount of discoveries. Large projects employing new technology were started to produce petroleum products from various materials—coal and shale, for example. Greater attention was given to oil extraction from existing fields, such as the injection of steam and solvents. Standard extraction practices usually resulted in recovery of only about 25 percent of the oil in a field; injection of natural gas or water increased recovery to about 30 to 35 percent of the original oil. The higher crude oil prices made some investments in additional recovery techniques profitable. Experts expected an average of 40- to 45-percent recovery rate to be achieved eventually, and perhaps more than 70-percent recovery in some fields. Enhanced recovery added little to immediate oil supplies, however. Consumers substituted other sources of energy for oil. The rapid increase in use of wood for heating in the United States was an example, but substitution in the industrialized countries—such as greater use of coal and nuclear power—encountered various difficulties that slowed the substitution process.

High oil prices prompted growing conservation measures by consumers. Fuel-efficient cars, reduced energy use in homes and offices, and improved energy efficiency in industrial processes made each unit of energy more effective. Economists for the Organisation for Economic Co-operation and Development (OECD) estimated that between 1973 and 1982 noncommunist industrialized nations improved their energy efficiency by 31 percent. The United States, the largest consumer of commercial energy by far, used nearly 5 percent less energy in 1982 than in 1973; in the same period consumption of energy per dollar of the United States gross national product declined 19 percent. Energy conservation turned out to be more effective than originally thought, but skeptics argued that economic recession in the industrialized countries, partly induced by the rapid increase of oil prices, accounted for an important part of the reduced energy consumption. Energy conservation and economic recession had a strong impact on oil production. Consumption of petroleum products by noncommunist nations dropped from a peak of over 52 million bpd in 1979 to 45 million bpd in 1982, a decline of 14 percent.

The soft oil market posed problems for OPEC members. Between 1977 and 1980 Saudi Arabia and some other Gulf exporters had produced above-normal levels to meet world demand and to ease the pressure on prices; at times these exporters maintained lower prices than other countries. Antagonisms between OPEC's moderate and high price groups increased, particularly between Iran and Saudi Arabia. In 1981 world oil demand weakened, and prices on spot markets declined. At the October 1981 OPEC meeting, members agreed on unified prices based on US$34 a barrel for Arabian light marker crude oil. Saudi Arabia raised its price by US$2 a barrel to achieve the agreed level, but the agreement resulted in a decline of the average OPEC crude oil export price. Demand and prices continued to weaken. In April 1982 OPEC members established a production ceiling of 17.5 million bpd for all members in order to halt sagging prices. Saudi Arabia cut back production the most within OPEC. Iran and Libya argued for an even greater reduction by the Saudis so other members could have higher production quotas.

During 1982 oil supplies substantially exceeded demand. Production in Saudi Arabia averaged only 6.5 million bpd in 1982, the lowest level in a decade and only about 65 percent of the 9.9 million bpd produced in 1980. Non-OPEC producers increased output and cut prices to increase their share of the market. In 1982 noncommunist oil consumption declined 5 percent from the level in 1981, but OPEC production declined 17 percent. OPEC production fell more sharply during the last half of the year. Many members of OPEC produced above their quotas, however, and lowered prices to sustain sales and revenues to finance large development programs. By late 1982 a surplus of oil existed, and many exporters—including some OPEC members—offered substantial discounts on posted prices.

The oil glut continued in 1983. During the first quarter Saudi Arabia reduced production below 4 million bpd, and its share of OPEC production fell below 25 percent, compared with 43 percent in 1981. In March 1983 OPEC members reduced prices by 15 percent, the only decrease of price by the organization. The price for Arabian light marker crude decreased from US$34 to US$29 a barrel. Members again agreed on an OPEC production ceiling of 17.5 million bpd. Quotas for nearly all members increased (see table A, this Appendix). Saudi Arabia was not given a quota but was to adjust production to demand, although a nominal quota of 5 million bpd was implied. Some members exceeded their production ceilings which, along with increased sales by non-OPEC producers, continued the surplus of oil and forced spot prices down below the OPEC level. By November 1983 the equivalent of Arabian light was being sold for around US$28 a barrel compared with the OPEC reference price of US$29 a barrel. Although Saudi Arabia accepted the role of swing producer and sharply reduced output, OPEC members had again failed to adhere to their self-imposed production limits. Several members sought to maintain their oil income rather than limit output to attain price stability.

Table A.   *Production Quotas of Organization of Petroleum Exporting Countries, 1982 and 1983*
(in millions of barrels per day)

Country	1982	1983	Country	1982	1983
Algeria	0.65	0.73	Nigeria	1.30	1.30
Ecuador	0.20	0.20	Qatar	0.30	0.30
Gabon	0.15	0.15	Saudi Arabia	7.00	5.00[1]
Indonesia	1.30	1.30	United Arab		
Iran	1.20	2.40	Emirates	1.00	1.10
Iraq	1.20	1.20	Venezuela	1.50	1.67
Kuwait	0.80	1.05			
Libya	0.75	1.10	TOTAL	17.50[2]	17.50

[1]Saudi Arabia did not have a specific quota but was to adjust output to demand.
[2]Individual quotas do not add to total because they were obtained by reporters from unofficial sources who did not have a complete set of the final agreed quotas.

As the OPEC oil ministers met in December 1983, they faced a continuing glut of oil in the market, as well as declining prices. Iran announced prior to the meeting that it wanted a US$5 a barrel increase in OPEC prices. The other members rejected a price increase, recognizing that it would lose them customers in the depressed world market. All OPEC members were experiencing financial difficulties because of reduced oil revenues. Many, particularly Iran and Iraq, wanted higher quotas to improve their financial positions, but increased quotas could only come at the expense of production by Saudi Arabia, which also experienced deficits. After difficult sessions, the OPEC ministers compromised by freezing prices at US$29 a barrel (for Arabian light) and retaining the 17.5 million bpd production ceiling into 1984.

Economists noted that the winter of 1983–84 in Europe and North America would significantly affect OPEC's ability to hold the line on oil prices. A cold winter would increase demand for crude oil, perhaps removing the downward pressure on prices. Extension of the Iran-Iraq War that disrupted rising exports from these countries would have the same effect. More disastrous for world oil supplies would be a closing of the Strait of Hormuz, which Iran threatened to do if Iraq attacked Iranian oil installations (see fig. 21). The absence of factors increasing demand or reducing supplies would exacerbate the difficulties of maintaining unity in OPEC. If the market remained depressed, financial pressures on individual countries were expected by many observers to lead to continuing price discounting and efforts to increase production and exports by several members. OPEC lacked the means to enforce discipline, and mutual interest had so far proved insufficient. In 1984 OPEC confronted a potentially serious divisive situation. Many cartels of the past collapsed from the inability to enforce market sharing among participants.

Organization of the Arab Petroleum Exporting Countries

The Organization of Arab Petroleum Exporting Countries (OAPEC) was founded in January 1968, not as a rival to OPEC but as a supplemental organization for the major Arab oil exporters. Some Arab League members had frequently advocated the use of the oil weapon against supporters of Israel. In the June 1967 War, Arab oil exporters, except Libya and Iraq, embargoed oil shipments to the United States and a few other countries. The cutback in production and exports produced serious financial difficulties, particularly for Saudi Arabia and other exporters on the Arabian Peninsula. By midsummer Saudi officials had concluded that the embargo was hurting Arab oil exporters more than the targets of the policy. In September 1967 the partial embargo was lifted.

Saudi Arabia, Kuwait and Libya, all conservative monarchies at the time, created OAPEC partly as a mechanism to establish a unified oil policy for Arab countries. Membership in OAPEC was originally limited to Arab states whose principal and basic source of national income was oil, in order that the countries most affected by a joint oil policy would make that policy. The intent was to forestall a more militant organization dominated by Arab extremist nations, such as Algeria, Syria, and Iraq, whose economies were not as dependent on oil exports. Iraq, as a major Arab oil exporter, was invited to join as a founding member, although it hardly qualified in terms of dependence on oil for national income. Iraq refused to join, however, fearing it would be the single and isolated voice for militancy in oil affairs in an organization devoted to a cautious approach and dominated by the Saudis. Iraq instead developed closer bilateral relations with more extremist oil states.

The overthrow of the monarchy in Libya in 1969 began a shift in the nature of OAPEC. Libya's new revolutionary regime was more militant in its oil policies. In 1970 OAPEC voted to participate as individual members in oil meetings of the Arab League instead of as the former single unified entity. Libya sponsored membership for militant Algeria, which was accepted along with Qatar, Bahrain, and the UAE. Iraq applied for membership in 1970 but was not accepted until 1972 and then only after prolonged controversy stemming more from the question of the kind of organization OAPEC would be rather than the issue of Iraqi membership. Saudi Arabia finally agreed to Iraq's membership and sponsored a resolution, accepted by the other members, which amended the constitution. It was no longer necessary for oil to be the principal source of national income as a prerequisite for membership. Syria and Egypt subsequently became members, although Egypt was expelled in 1979 for signing a peace treaty with Israel. In March 1982 Tunisia became a member after Libya withdrew its objections. Except for Egypt, the aforementioned countries were members of OAPEC in 1984. The compromise by the oil moderates in 1972 permitted OAPEC to continue functioning, but at the expense of unity. The growing diversity of interests in OAPEC largely precluded future development of a joint oil policy that would be followed by all major oil exporters or that would forcefully influence Arab League or OPEC decisions.

An attempt to achieve a unified oil policy was initiated during the 1973 war. At first, Iraq militantly advocated nationalizing United States oil interests in Arab countries and suspending oil exports to the United States for its support of Israel. Instead, OAPEC oil ministers formulated a plan to make progressive cuts in oil production (until Israel withdrew from occupied territories) and to embargo oil exports to the United States. Most OAPEC members implemented the plan for a few months, although the timing varied. Iraq was an important exception, however, and neither cut production nor embargoed exports; this resulted in severe criticism for not supporting the Arab cause.

During the 1970s OAPEC's primary focus became economic and commercial activities. The organization facilitated the exchange of information on the petroleum industry and promoted coordination of oil policies among members. A petroleum library and various publications, including an annual statistical report on the petroleum industry in member countries, aided in the collection and dissemination of information. OAPEC sponsored various forms of training for Arab nationals, including introductory classes for new workers entering the oil industry and specialized seminars for trained technicians. In 1978 OAPEC established the Arab Petroleum Training Institute, which opened its first classes in 1980 in Baghdad. Training of Arab nationals was one of the intended objectives for the creation of several OAPEC businesses.

OAPEC, as a juridical entity, was empowered to form commercial companies to engage in activities associated with the petroleum industry. These were joint projects in which members desiring to participate purchased shares. Once formed, the companies became legally independent of OAPEC and of the member governments, which were the shareholders. These OAPEC companies, even when registered as national firms in one or more participating countries, were exempted from taxes, duties, and some other obligations imposed on other firms by the host country. The OAPEC companies were a mechanism to foster economic development in one or more Arab states, while also providing training for Arab nationals from almost any source.

The first OAPEC joint venture was the Arab Maritime Petroleum Transport Company. None of the members had tanker fleets when this company was established. In time, however, several member states created their own fleets to carry their petroleum exports. The duplication of investment caused underutilization of the OAPEC fleet and required subsidization from OAPEC resources rather than producing profits. The OAPEC Arab Shipbuilding and Repair Yard, located in Bahrain, began operations in 1978. Since then, it has operated near capacity, servicing tankers—including very large ones—but has incurred financial losses because the depressed market required prices below costs. The Arab Petroleum Investments Corporation (APICORP) provided capital, in the form of equity or loans, to downstream (see Glossary) petroleum development. The prohibitions in several OAPEC nations to external participation in its oil industry limited APICORP's aid to loans in those countries. APICORP helped finance projects to produce lube oils, detergents, natural gas, and fertilizers; some projects were in nonmember Arab states, such as Jordan. The Arab Petroleum Services Company was formed in 1976 to act as a holding company for operational subsidiaries. By the early 1980s a drilling company and other companies were established subsidiaries. The drilling company was quite active in Libya in the early 1980s, for example, In 1980 a fifth joint venture, the Arab Engineering Consulting Company, was formed, headquartered in Abu Dhabi.

January 1984

Gulf Cooperation Council

In January 1981, shortly after a summit meeting of the Organization of the Islamic Conference in Saudi Arabia, the Saudi leadership officially announced the formation of the Gulf Cooperation Council (GCC), an enterprise initiated by Saudi Arabia and long in the planning stage. The GCC includes the six states of the Arabian Peninsula that have similar political institutions, social conditions, and economic resources: Saudi Arabia, Kuwait, Qatar, the United Arab Emirates (UAE), Bahrain, and Oman. The aim of the GCC is to coordinate and unify economic, industrial, and defense policies. On May 24, 1981, the founding of the GCC was announced at the first meeting of the six heads of state, which was held in Abu Dhabi, capital of the UAE (see fig. 1).

The GCC states have a combined population of 12 to 15 million, a land area of about 2,653,000 square kilometers, and a combined annual gross domestic product (GDP) of about US$210 billion. Rich in economic resources and land, they are generally poor in trained manpower and also are beset by problems endemic to nations with (in some cases) only a decade of independence behind them. Most of the GCC population originates from the same region, Najd in central Arabia, whence tribal migrations propelled many of them to the Persian Gulf coast during the eighteenth century. The GCC states must still contend with rivalries from that period as well as new conflicts and competitiveness that have developed since the creation of their modern states. Because the similarities and common interests far outweigh the differences, the notion of a comprehensive, cooperative effort appeared a natural one.

Organization and Structure

The organization and structure of the GCC closely model the political systems and hierarchies of the member states. Essentially, the combined ministers of any single portfolio may function as a council. The Supreme Council, composed of the six heads of state, is the principal policymaking body of the GCC. The presidency of the group changes from year to year in alphabetical order. The Supreme Council is enjoined to meet every six months, but extraordinary meetings may be called by any of the six heads of state. Biannual meetings are commonly referred to as summit meetings.

The Supreme Council is responsible for overall planning, policy, and setting of priorities. The council reviews and must approve the deliberations or recommendations of any secondary body or committee within the GCC. The six foreign ministers, together called the Ministerial Council, meet bimonthly but may also choose to meet for extraordinary sessions.

In addition to a secretary general, who has overall suzerainty, there are two deputy secretary generals—one to concentrate on economic matters and the other on political matters. At the council's inauguration in Abu Dhabi in May 1981, Abdullah Yakub Bisharah was announced as the GCC's first secretary general, the head of the secretariat to be based in Riyadh. The unanimous choice of the articulate Bisharah was a felicitous one. A Kuwaiti, he had represented Kuwait for more than a decade at the United Nations (UN). He is known as a thorough but conciliatory negotiator who has always espoused a supranational approach to problem solving. Because of his advocacy of Arab causes, particularly the Palestinian issue, it was hoped that his appointment would blunt criticism from the left. Although he is aware, as any Gulf statesman must be, of the inherent rivalries within the GCC, he has preferred to concentrate on the similarities. At the GCC summit in Bahrain in November 1982, Bisharah noted that "the GCC is a modern articulation of an old legitimacy for future unification. . . . The concept of national borders and customs barriers are alien imports from the West."

Initially, reaction to the formation of the GCC was largely negative. As expected, Iran castigated its formation. President Saddam Husayn of Iraq, who had previously sought to form a similar grouping with Iraq as the preeminent member, was undoubtedly displeased. In view of the enormous financial subventions from the GCC states, however, Iraq was now in an embarrassingly dependent financial position, and any displeasure was muted.

Both the Yemen Arab Republic (Yemen [Sanaa]) and the People's Democratic Republic of Yemen (Yemen [Aden]) vociferously protested the formation. Each cited the fact that only the two states of the Yemen were excluded among the states of the Arabian Peninsula. They accused the GCC of essentially forming a rich clique that would gang up on the two impoverished Yemeni states. Yemen (Sanaa) was particularly disgruntled in view of its long and close relationship with Saudi Arabia. The Palestine Liberation Organization (PLO) excoriated the group's formation as a right-wing alliance of antiquated political entities.

Diligent activity characterized the GCC's first year. The Ministerial Council met in Oman in March 1981, in the UAE in May, and in Saudi Arabia in August. At the initial meetings, the council commissioned Oman to draw up a study of regional security and Kuwait to prepare a paper on regional economic issues.

As of early 1984 there had been nine meetings of the Ministerial Council and four GCC summits (meetings of the Supreme Council). The summit conferences were held in May 1981 in Abu Dhabi, November 1981 in Riyadh, November 1982 in Bahrain, and November 1983 in Doha, Qatar. The November 1983 summit was preceded by a meeting of the Ministerial Council in which members approved a working budget of US$25 million for the year. In addition to its hierarchy, the GCC by that time had 238 full-time employees at its headquarters in Riyadh.

In the decade before its founding, there had been several attempts to form a group composed in part of the states that would ultimately compose the GCC. The shah of Iran and Saddam Husayn of Iraq had individually and together proposed such an alliance at various times. In each case, the smaller Gulf states presumed that the overture was a thinly disguised attempt at Gulf hegemony, and they were wary of certifying, or even appearing to acquiesce to, the pretensions of hegemony of Iraq or Iran. The proposals were usually coolly received, although some desultory discussions did take place.

The outbreak of war between Iraq and Iran in September 1980 provided precisely the catalyst needed for the GCC states to create their own group. The war itself reinforced the GCC cognizance of its own vulnerability. Pan-Arab fellowship aside, in the opening days of the war the GCC states were as concerned with the prospect of a victorious and possibly adventuristic Iraq as they were with revolutionary Iran. Preceding Iraq's attack on Iran, Iraq had been vociferous in its verbal forays against the GCC states. Sultan Qaboos of Oman was particularly singled out and castigated for his relations with Britain and the United States.

As the war alternately intensified and stalemated (with no clear victory in sight for Iraq), GCC fears of aggressive Iraqi ambitions faded, to be replaced by a pragmatic decision to opt for the lesser of two evils. Because of increasing GCC vocal support for Iraq and concomitant indispensable funding for the Iraqi war effort, a considerably humbled Saddam Husayn made an about-face, even going to far as to congratulate Oman publicly for its tough domestic policy on resident foreign workers.

Once committed to open support of Iraq in both cash and arms supplies, the GCC states had no recourse but to continue their subventions, despite the fact that overt Iranian threats against them intensified. They had, however, purchased at least tacit acceptance from Saddam Husayn to form an alliance that excluded Iraq.

Mounting internal pressures, as well as such alarming regional developments as the Iran-Iraq War, prompted Saudi Arabia to institute discussions among those states with which it had a natural political affinity. Saudi Arabia urged them to shelve their petty rivalries in the major interest of mutual survival. Although the nature of the internal threats to each of the states differed, all, to a greater or lesser extent, faced the same external threats. Nearest to home, Yemen (Aden) was actively engaged in the training of terrorists and was viewed as a Soviet proxy, particularly by Saudi Arabia and Oman. All the GCC states were concerned about the level of leftist activity in Yemen (Aden) and presumed that at least some of the terrorist trainees were destined to undertake subversion and terorist acts in the Gulf states. The high level of Soviet military activities in and around Yemen (Aden)—particularly in the wake of the Soviet loss of Berbera, Somalia, as a major naval logistics support base—increased Saudi apprehensiveness, despite concurrent Soviet diplomatic overtures to the Gulf Arabs.

The Soviet Union was also increasing its presence in Yemen (Sanaa), which by the early 1980s had purchased large amounts of Soviet arms and had more than 300 Soviet advisers in the country. The Soviets were actively encouraging the two Yemens once again to consider unification. Rhetoric on the subject from both Sanaa and Aden filled their newspapers and dominated political statements. Despite the unlikelihood of actual unification, the Saudis viewed with alarm even the possibility of such a union.

The GCC states could not rely on revolutionary Iran as the "Gulf policeman," and they remained at odds with Egypt because it had signed a peace treaty with Israel. The only major power they could rely on was the United States, but this option was also fraught with problems. Even potentially close relations with the United States added fuel to Iran's enmity against GCC members (providing ammunition for barrages by Iranian propagandists against "Satanic" alliances) and generated internal pressures. Many Islamic fundamentalists perceived the United States in an unfavorable light because of the question of suzerainty of

Jerusalem. More secular elements within each Gulf society continued to be adamantly opposed to close relations with the United States because of its perceived open-ended support of Israel. Thus, it was obvious to the governments of the Gulf states that a highly visible alliance with the United States could create a lightning rod of internal discontent on virtually the only issue capable of uniting both right and left.

Further, many within the GCC states questioned the altruism of United States intentions. As analyst Joseph Malone observes: "the Arabs of the Gulf, whose memories are long, have a propensity for comparing British policy in the Gulf during World War II to the United States concept of a Rapid Deployment Force (RDF) in the 1980s. . . . Despite avowals of support for conservative, anticommunist regimes, the United States—and therefore the RDF—arouses suspicions based upon hidden agendas and side letters."

Another perceived threat was Israel, acting either on its own or as a surrogate, because of "secret protocols" with the United States. When knowledge of Israeli sales (primarily of spare parts for warplanes) to revolutionary Iran became public, several newspapers within the GCC states opined that an Iranian-Israeli alliance was in the offing and would be directed primarily against them.

Among the plethora of perceived threats, none ranked as high as the Iranian threat, and none was more realistic. Ayatollah Ruhollah Khomeini made no secret of his loathing for the GCC states and of his determination and mission to export his revolution to them. The large concentration of Shia in the critical oil-producing Eastern Province (Ash Sharquiyah) of Saudi Arabia, as well as the majority Shia population in Bahrain, felt particularly vulnerable. In December 1981 an Iranian-sponsored coup attempt was staged in Bahrain. The attempt was thwarted, but the fact that the Shia elements who staged the attempt had the confidence even to try it caused consternation among the Gulf governments. This, when coupled with sporadic agitation among the Saudi Shia after the Iranian revolution, starkly pointed out the need for immediate cooperative action among the Gulf states to ensure their survival.

Many observers agree that the major triumph of the GCC as of early 1984 was in foreign policy. An agreement between Oman and Yemen (Aden) was signed October 27, 1982, under GCC aegis. This rapprochement signaled, at least theoretically, an end to the hostile relations that had characterized their bilateral association since 1967 when the British quit Aden and Yemen (Aden) gained independence under a leftist banner. Yemen

(Aden) had sponsored the Dhofar Rebellion in Oman and continued a campaign of subversion and propaganda for more than a
decade. Even before the formal inauguration of the GCC, both
Kuwait and the UAE had attempted to effect a reconciliation between these two states. Also, Saudi Arabia occasionally dangled
the carrot of financial subvention before Yemen (Aden) in an attempt to defuse the situation and cool the rhetoric. None of these
efforts met with success. Insofar as the incumbent Yemen (Aden)
premier, Ali Nasir Muhammad al Hasani, was most probably the
first Yemeni head of state amenable to such an accord, it was unlikely that it could have been accomplished outside of the GCC
aegis. As part of this accord, Oman and Yemen (Aden) agreed to
establish normal relations based on nonintervention, resolve
their border disputes through peaceful means, end propaganda
campaigns, renounce ambitions against the other's territories,
and prohibit foreign troops from mounting aggressions against the
other from their territories.

Economic Cooperation

A feature of economic development in the 1970s was the re-
dundancy of much of the very expensive infrastructure of the Gulf
states. Within the UAE, for example, two contiguous states,
Dubai and Sharjah, built international airports within a few
kilometers of each other. Both Bahrain and Dubai have major
dry-docking facilities, although one would be sufficient to service
Gulf shipping interests. The flush of independence, the enormity
of the task of nation building, and the sudden and seemingly un-
limited funds to accomplish it prompted lavish undertakings.

Once the basics of their infrastructures were in place, the decisionmaking elites could observe the superfluity and the uneven-
ness of much of their development. It became clear that economic
cooperation among the six not only would be cost-effective but
also would ensure more rational and orderly development, which
in turn would promote social stability. Comparing the GCC with
the post-World War II situation in Europe, Malone notes that "if
the GCC hardly requires a Marshall Plan, it is significant that it
has in its actions supported the European view that comprehensive economic cooperation is the necessary preliminary to political stability."

When the GCC signed its Unified Economic Agreement in
June 1981, economic cooperation appeared desirable but did not
have the urgency it would acquire by the spring of 1983, when
even the most obtuse officials accepted the fact that a staggering

oil glut was inundating world markets. There were already joint-venture projects in place in the peninsula, most notably in Bahrain and Oman. The richer peninsular states viewed such joint ventures as sound investments, as well as a way to shore up stability in those states that possessed significantly fewer economic resources.

The financial and social success of these ventures encouraged planners to magnify the concept of cooperative planning. Because oil revenues had been significantly reduced, the necessity of unifying development strategies became obvious. The hopes and, some experts say, the fantasies, of Gulf economic planners are contained in the GCC's Unified Economic Agreement. The 28 articles of the agreement include provisions for the elimination of customs duties between GCC states where goods have 40 percent of their value added in the exporting GCC country (Articles 2 and 3); establishment of a common minimum external tariff set at 4 percent and rising to 20 percent (Article 4); coordination of import and export policies and regulations and the creation of a "collective negotiating force" to strengthen the GCC's position in dealing with foreign suppliers; free movement of labor and capital (Article 9); coordination of oil policies (Article 11); coordination of industrial activities and standardization of industrial laws; efforts to allocate industries to states according to "relative advantages" (Article 12); coordination of technology, training, and labor policies (Articles 14–17); a coordinated approach to sea, land, and air transport policies (Articles 18–20); and the development of a unified investment strategy to coordinate monetary, banking, and financial policies, including the possibility of a common currency (Articles 21–23).

The vehicle for developing a unified investment strategy is the Gulf Investment Corporation (GIC), which is based in Kuwait. The GIC's purpose is to finance joint-venture projects in all sectors of the economy. The GIC is also directed to seek investment opportunities worldwide. Working capital, which will ultimately total in excess of US\$2 billion, will be derived from individual contributions of US\$350 million—to be paid into the GIC in five increments—from each of the six member states. On November 15, 1983, the first incremental payment date was honored by all the states. GIC assets will be one of the largest investment funds in the area. According to reports, Kuwait was chosen as the venue for the GIC as a sign of faith from other members after the near disastrous collapse of the unofficial Kuwaiti stock market (the Souk al Manakh) in August 1982. Despite the collapse of that market, Kuwait remained the GCC state having the greatest investment expertise. For several years returns from Kuwaiti investments, worldwide and domestic, had exceeded its oil revenues.

Article 11 of the economic agreement, which aims to coordinate oil and gas strategies, is one of the most problematic but potentially rewarding of the articles. GCC members own about two-fifths of the world's proven oil reserves. Because of the divisiveness within the Organization of Petroleum Exporting Countries (OPEC), a smaller, tighter, and better disciplined association that dovetailed production with development needs could be useful to member states. However, because of the buyers' market that was expected to prevail through the 1980s, some experts opined that the short-term effect on the world's oil markets would be negligible.

Problems existed in that the distribution of oil reserves among the six states varied considerably. Neither Bahrain nor Oman possessed sufficient reserves to warrant membership in OPEC. Bahrain was unique among GCC states in that it exported no crude but depended on sales from refined products. The degree of control exercised over total oil resources also varied considerably from country to country. For example, only Kuwait had nationalized all levels of the industry. The Kuwaiti program demonstrated to the other GCC states that in the long run financial security may best be ensured by development that would control oil from the wellhead to the point of export. Because of the price slump of 1983 and 1984, it was also agreed among GCC members that downstream petrochemical development constituted the best utilization of the downstream resources; however, GCC states remained short of the refining and processing capacity necessary to transform this consensus into action. To this end, the GCC has approved the construciton of a catalytic refinery in Oman, the only GCC state with a refining capacity sufficient only for domestic needs.

Oman is also the only GCC state with free access to the Indian Ocean. This access through a member state would relieve many of the anxieties of Gulf governments, which are all too aware of the vulnerability of the Strait of Hormuz to overt or covert interdiction and the resultant denial of world markets to GCC oil exporters. The participants in the GCC summit in November 1983 approved funds for a full feasibility study of a pipeline from Kuwait to Salalah in Oman.

A feasibility study was also approved at the fourth summit for gas distribution systems from Sharjah (UAE) and Qatar. It was estimated that GCC natural gas reserves totaled more than 10.5 billion cubic meters, equal to about 12 percent of the world's total reserves. Yet, in 1982 combined GCC production was just over 1 percent of world demand. Another key area of GCC interest in gas associated with crude oil production was its use to run the many desalinization plants in the region. Closely related to gas distribution was the possibility of a regional GCC electrical grid, a project under study at the direction of the fourth summit.

Other feasibility studies recommended by the Ministerial Council that preceded the summit and subsequently endorsed by the Supreme Council included a trans-GCC highway that would run from Kuwait to Salalah, a railroad from Kuwait to Oman, and a strategic storage project. The storage project would include the bulk buying of such staples as sugar and flour. In 1983 rice—a major staple for GCC nationals—was bought in volume at a substantial saving.

Elements of Article 12 relating to standardization were in the process of implementation in early 1984. Saudi Arabia's University of Petroleum and Minerals, which already had a standardization facility, was designated to attempt to create industrial standards applicable to all GCC states. This presented an enormous task in view of the numbers and varieties of foreign vendors selling to GCC states. It is expected that the United States ultimately will benefit because United States standards were the prototypes used by the university.

Security and Defense

By far the most pressing priority of the GCC remained that of the physical security of its states from both internal extremism and external interference. Concern for their security was neither irrational nor overplayed but resulted from their relatively small indigenous populations, young military establishments, and natural resources, which were coveted by many. An important milestone in the direction of mutual and individual security was the September 1981 meeting in Riyadh of the GCC military chiefs of staff—the first instance of such a gathering. An Omani working paper on security issues presented at the meeting was closely studied by the participants who, according to one Western observer, agreed with most of the recommendations. Little more than a year later, on the eve of the third GCC summit in Bahrain in November 1982, GCC members were optimistic that a joint security pact would emerge. Prince Sultan bin Abd al Aziz Al Saud, the Saudi minister of defense and aviation, declared emphatically that the summit's main issue would be "defense coordination in the Gulf for collective security." Nevertheless, the Bahrain summit ended without a joint defense pact. Following the summit the foreign minister of Bahrain, Shaykh Muhammad bin Mubarak Al Khalifa, told the press, "We do not talk publicly about military aspects of our cooperation." He conceded, however, that there had been disagreements on some issues. According to press reports, a major stumbling block had been the possible role that the United States might play in case of a regional emergency. The polarities of this issue were represented by the stringently nonaligned Kuwait and the more Western-oriented Oman, which had engaged in one joint military exercise with United States forces and was preparing for another the month after the summit. A related failure of the third summit was the rejection by Kuwait and the UAE of a Saudi proposal to announce formally joint support of Iraq's war effort by means of GCC collective contributions to this effort.

In December 1982 Omani and United States armed forces carried out their second joint exercise, "Bright Star," less than two months after the Oman-Yemen (Aden) rapprochement. The Yemen (Aden) response to "Bright Star" was much more diplomatic that was customary and focused on blaming the United States. Radio Aden claimed that the exercise demonstrated the United States desire to bring the region "back to the era of direct imperialism, hegemony and imperialist control" of the resources of the region and warned that the exercise "will undoubtedly harm the good results of the positive efforts exerted during the negotiations" leading to the rapprochement.

In view of the lack of an overarching agreement, the GCC chose to concentrate on the practical aspects of military coordination and cooperation. Proof of their determination to police and protect their own shores and national interests was the participation, in October 1983, of troops from all GCC states in joint military exercises in Abu Dhabi that were labeled the Shield of the Peninsula (Dir al Jizira).

The maneuvers involved approximately 6,500 troops, one-twentieth of the GCC total military strength of about 130,000. According to reports, the Omanis were the stars of the exercise. Undoubtedly, the fact that the Omanis had already experienced two joint maneuvers with the United States gave them an edge over the other GCC forces. Additionally, the Omani military command initiated an award system for outstanding performance. One foreign observer noted that the sense of solidarity was so strong that the UAE military experienced no desertions, as had been expected. The UAE usually has no army on Thursdays and Fridays—the Gulf weekend—when the many Omanis in the UAE's armed forces return home. This was particularly noteworthy in that, because of Shield of the Peninsula, the UAE forces had been on alert for 18 consecutive days.

Future plans discussed during Dir al Jizira included two sets of joint exercises scheduled for January 1984—Kuwaiti-Saudi maneuvers and Omani-UAE exercises to test air defenses. At the conclusion of the Dir al Jizira operations, Chief of Operations Brigadier Ahmad Salim confidently noted that "the forces taking part in the exercises can participate in the defense of any GCC country when it is the target of external aggression, without the need to call for outside assistance."

One month after these exercises, as the fourth summit took place in Doha, Qatar, during November 1983, the aircraft carrier U.S.S. *Ranger* was positioned in the Indian Ocean. Apparently this move was taken in response to the escalation of Iranian threats against the GCC states during the summer and fall. In addition, President Husni Mubarak of Egypt, in an apparent effort to effect a reconciliation with the members of the GCC, suggested that Egypt's armed forces should participate in an "Arab Army" to resist Iran if necessary. A Jordanian force, reportedly sponsored by the United States, was also proposed.

Despite their awareness of a potential need for assistance, Gulf leaders appeared irritated by such offers. Secretary General Bisharah responded by observing that "gunboat diplomacy was unwanted and unneeded on the shores of the Gulf" and that the Gulf did not need "uncharitable volunteers." He later noted that "we appreciate Jordan's concerns over this, but it is not in line with our policy."

The fourth summit, which largely concentrated on economic matters, failed—as had the third—to conclude an overarching defense agreement. A petition to the UN Security Council did emerge, in which the GCC requested the Security Council to secure an instant cease-fire in the Iran-Iraq War. Presumably, the ongoing war was a major topic of discussion of the GCC defense ministers in January 1984, but the ministerial conference ended without any public pronouncement.

Despite the failure to conclude a major defense agreement, the success of the GCC military exercises and the amity that has characterized them bode well for further developments. Above all, GCC activity relating to security and defense in 1983 made clear, as Malone notes, that "leaders of the Arab states of the Gulf region have begun to see the merit of Benjamin Franklin's observation concerning the best strategy for confronting hegemonic power. Franklin's advice was that it was better to hang together than to hang separately."

*   *   *

Written sources for the GCC as of late 1983 were limited to periodical literature and press reports. Useful articles include Joseph J. Malone's "Security: A Priority for Gulf Council" in the *Journal of Defense and Diplomacy*. Two comprehensive studies are the October 28, 1983, edition of the *Middle East Economic Digest* (London) and "The Gulf, '83" in the *Far Eastern Economic Review* (Hong Kong). The single most useful overall study is John Duke Anthony's "The Gulf Cooperation Council" in the *Journal of South Asian and Middle Eastern Studies,* Summer 1982. Anthony's work is particularly useful because he is the only Western observer to have attended all four summit meetings. (For further information and complete citations, see Bibliography.)

January 1984

Bibliography

Abdulla, Saif Abbas. "Politics, Administration, and Urban Planning in a Welfare Society: Kuwait." (Ph.D. dissertation.) Bloomington: Department of Political Science, Indiana University, 1974.

Abdullah, Muhammad Morsy. *The United Arab Emirates: A Modern History*. London: Croom Helm, 1978.

Abdul-Rahman, Asad. "The Palestinians in Kuwait: Their Political Significance." Pages 14–17 in Ronald G. Wolfe (ed.), *The United States, Arabia, and the Gulf*. Washington: Center for Contemporary Arab Studies, Georgetown University, 1980.

ABECOR Group. *Country Report, Kuwait*. (Distributed by Barclays Bank, London.) London: November 1981.

―――. *Country Report, Kuwait*. (Distributed by Barclays Bank, London.) London: June 1983.

Abercrombie, Thomas J. "Oman: Guardian of the Gulf," *National Geographic*, 160, No. 3, September 1981, 344–77.

Abir, Mordechai. *Oil, Power, and Politics: Conflict in Arabia, the Red Sea, and the Gulf*. London: Cass, 1974.

Abu Dhabi. Department of Planning. Statistical Section. *Statistical Yearbook, 1982*. Abu Dhabi: 1983.

Abu-Hakima, Ahmad Mustafa. "The Development of the Gulf States." Pages 31–53 in Derek Hopwood (ed.), *The Arabian Peninsula: Society and Politics*. Totowa, New Jersey: Rowman and Littlefield, 1972.

―――. *History of Eastern Arabia, 1750–1800*. Beirut: Khayats, 1965.

―――. "Kuwait and the Eastern Arabian Protectorates." Pages 430–49 in Tareq Y. Ismael et al., *Governments and Politics of the Contemporary Middle East*. Homewood, Illinois: Dorsey Press, 1970.

Abu-Zahra, Nadia. "A Comment on Some Kuwaiti and Egyptian Anthropological Writings on Kuwait," (Review article.) *International Journal of Middle East Studies*, 15, No. 3, August 1983, 398–410.

Adelman, Morris A. "Politics, Economics, and World Oil," *American Economic Review*, 64, No. 2, May 1974, 58–67.

―――. *The World Petroleum Market*. Baltimore: Johns Hopkins Press, 1972.

Agwani, Mohammed S. *Politics in the Gulf*. New Delhi: Vikas, 1978.

Ajtony, M.A. *The Expanding Role of KNPC in the Oil Business*. Kuwait: Kuwait National Petroleum Company, n. d.

Akehurst, John. *We Won a War: The Campaign in Oman, 1965–1975*. London: Russell, 1982.

Al Baharna, Husain M. *The Legal Status of the Arabian Gulf*. Manchester, England: Manchester University Press, 1968.

———— "Qatar." Pages Q1-Q4 in Viktor Knapp (ed.), *International Encyclopedia of Comparative Law*. The Hague: Mouton, May 1972.

Al-Ebraheem, Hassan A. *Kuwait: A Political Study*. Kuwait: Kuwait University, 1975.

Alessa, Shamlan Y. *The Manpower Problem in Kuwait*. London: Kegan Paul International, 1981.

Ali, Sheikh R. "Holier Than Thou: The Iran-Iraq War," *Middle East Review*, 17, No. 1, Fall 1984, 50–57.

Allen, Robert C. "Regional Security in the Persian Gulf," *Military Review*, 63, No. 12, December 1983, 2–11.

Alnasrawi, Abbas. *Arab Oil and United States Energy Requirements*. Belmont, Massachusetts: Association of Arab-American University Graduates, 1982.

Al-Qudsi, Sulayman S. "Pre- and Post-Fiscal Distributional Pattern in Kuwait," *Middle Eastern Studies* [London], 17, July 1981, 393–407.

Al Rumaihi, Mohammad. "The Reformative Movement of 1938 in Kuwait, Bahrain, and Dubai," *Journal of Gulf and Arabian Peninsula Studies* [Kuwait], 1, No. 4, October 1975, 29–48.

Al-Sabah, Youssif S.F. *The Oil Economy of Kuwait*. London: Kegan Paul International, 1980.

Amirsadeghi, Hossein. *The Security of the Persian Gulf*. New York: St. Martin's Press, 1981.

Annual Statistical Bulletin, 1974. Vienna; Organization of Petroleum Exporting Countries, June 1975.

Anthony, John Duke. *Arab States of the Lower Gulf: People, Politics, and Petroleum*. (James Terry Duce Memorial Series, 3.) Washington: Middle East Institute, 1975.

————. "The Gulf Cooperation Council," *Journal of South Asian and Middle Eastern Studies*, 5, No. 4, Summer 1982, 3–18.

————. "The Impact of Oil on Political and Socioeconomic Change in the United Arab Emirates." Pages 79–98 in John Duke Anthony (ed.), *The Middle East: Oil, Politics, and De-*

velopment. Washington: American Enterprise Institute, 1975.

——. "Oman: Stable and Strategic," *Journal of Defense and Diplomacy*, November 1983, 12–14.

——. *Political Dynamics of the Sultanate of Oman*. (Department of State, Office of External Research, Foreign Affairs Research Paper, No. FAR 21070.) Washington: October 1974.

——. "The Union of Arab Amirates," *Middle East Journal*, 26, No. 3, Summer 1972, 271–88.

Anthony, John Duke (ed.). *The Middle East: Oil, Politics, and Development*. Washington: American Enterprise Institute, 1975.

"Arab Banking, Finance, and Investment," *Financial Times* [London], October 3, 1983, 1–20 (Survey).

"Arab Military Industries: A Reality," *Middle East* [London], No. 10, July 1975, 105–106.

Aramco Handbook. Dhahran: Arabian American Oil Company, 1968.

Axelgard, Frederick. "The Gulf States Gird Themselves Against an Iran-Iraq Spillover," *Journal of Defense and Foreign Affairs*, 12, No. 3, March 1984, 36.

Ayoob, Mohammed (ed.). *The Politics of Islamic Reassertion*. New York: St. Martin's Press, 1981.

Azar, Edward E. *Probe for Peace: Small-State Hostilities*. Minneapolis: Burgess, 1973.

Baaklini, Abdo I. "The Kuwaiti Legislature as Ombudsman: The Legislative Committee on Petitions and Complaints," *Legislative Studies Quarterly*, 3, No. 2, May 1978, 293–307.

——. "The Legislature in the Kuwaiti Political System." (Paper presented at Annual Convention of International Studies Association.) Toronto: February 1976.

——. "Legislatures in the Gulf Area: The Experience of Kuwait, 1961–1976," *International Journal of Middle East Studies*, 14, No. 3, August 1982, 359–79.

Baaklini, Abdo I., and Alia Abdul-Wahab. "The Role of the National Assembly in Kuwait's Economic Development: National Oil Policy." (Paper presented at Carmel Conference on Comparative Legislative Studies.) Carmel, California: August 1975.

Bacharach, Jere L. *A Near East Studies Handbook (570–1974)*. Seattle: University of Washington Press, 1974.

"Bahrain," *Foreign Economic Trends*, FET 83–055, September 1983 (entire issue).

"Bahrain," *Foreign Economic Trends*, FET 84–38, March 1984, (entire issue).

"Bahrain: A Special Survey," *Financial Times* [London], May 31, 1983, 1–12 (Survey).

"Bahrain: A Special Survey," *Financial Times* [London], May 8, 1984, 1–12 (Survey).

Bargar, Thomas C. *Arab States of the Persian Gulf*. Newark: University of Delaware, 1975.

Barth, Fredrik. "Factors of Production, Economic Circulation, and Inequality in Inner Arabia." Pages 53–72 in George Dalton (ed.), *Research in Economic Anthropology, 1*. Greenwich, Connecticut: Jai Press, 1978.

Beaumont, Peter. "Water Resources and Their Management in the Middle East." Pages 40–72 in John I. Clarke and Howard Bowen-Jones (eds.), *Change and Development in the Middle East*. London: Methuen, 1981.

Becker, Abraham S. "Oil and the Persian Gulf in Soviet Policy in the 1970s." (Rand Corporation Paper, No. P-4743.) Santa Monica: Rand, December 1971.

Becker, Abraham S., Bent Hansen, and Malcolm H. Kerr. *The Economics and Politics of the Middle East*. New York: American Elsevier, 1975.

Behbehani, Kazem, Maurice Girgis, and M.S. Marzouk (eds.). *Proceedings of the Symposium on Science and Technology for Development in Kuwait*. London: Kuwait Institute for Scientific Research-Longman, 1981.

Belgrave, Charles Dalrymple. *The Pirate Coast*. London: Bell and Sons, 1966.

Beling, Willard A. (ed.). *The Middle East: Quest for an American Policy*. Albany: State University of New York Press, 1983.

Bhutani, Surendra. "The Organizational Elite: Abu Dhabi, a Case Study." Pages 103–110 in Surendra Bhutani (ed.), *Contemporary Gulf*. New Delhi: Academic Press, 1980.

Bibby, Geoffrey. *Looking for Dilmun*. New York: Knopf, 1970.

Bidwell, Robin L. *The Arab World, 1900–1972*. London: Cass, 1973.

Bill, James A. "Resurgent Islam in the Persian Gulf," *Foreign Affairs*, 63, No. 1, Fall 1984, 108–27.

Bill, James A., and Carl Leiden. *The Middle East: Politics and Power*. Boston: Allyn and Bacon, 1974.

Bill, James A., and Robert W. Stookey. *Politics and Petroleum*. Brunswick, Ohio: King's Court Communications, 1975.

Blaustein, Albert P., and Gisbert H. Flanz (eds.). *Oman*. (Constitutions of the Countries of the World series.) Dobbs Ferry,

New York: Oceana, 1974.

————. *Qatar*. (Constitutions of the Countries of the World series.) Dobbs Ferry, New York: Oceana, July 1973.

Borthwick, Bruce M. "The Islamic Sermon as a Channel of Political Communication," *Middle East Journal*, 21, No. 3, Summer 1967, 299–313.

Brown, Michael P.(ed.). *Air Forces of the World: Part 2—North Africa and the Middle East*, 1 and 2. Geneva: Interavia Data, 1983.

Brown, William R. "The Oil Weapon," *Middle East Journal*, 36, No. 3, Summer 1982, 301–18.

Burrell, R. Michael. *The Persian Gulf*. Beverly Hills: Sage, 1972.

Burrell, R. Michael, and Keith McLachlan. "The Political Geography of the Persian Gulf." Pages 121–38 in Alvin J. Cottrell (ed.), *The Persian Gulf States: A General Survey*. Baltimore: Johns Hopkins University Press, 1980.

Central Banks and Monetary Agencies of the Arab Gulf States. *Economic Bulletin*, 4. Kuwait: December 1983.

Charles, Edward. "Kuwait," *New York Times*, November 21, 1983, D21–D24 (advertising feature).

Chisholm, Archibald H.T. *The First Kuwait Oil Concessions Agreement*. London: Cass, 1975.

Christie, John. "The GCC: A Preliminary Report," *Aramco World Magazine*, 35, No. 1, January-February 1984, 122–33.

Chubin, Shahram. "The Iran-Iraq War and Persian Gulf Security," *International Defense Review* [Geneva], 17, No. 5, June 1984, 705–12.

————. *Security in the Persian Gulf: The Role of Outside Powers*, 4. London: International Institute for Strategic Studies, 1982.

Chubin, Shahram (ed.). *Security in the Persian Gulf: Domestic Political Factors*, 1. London: International Institute for Strategic Studies, 1981.

Clarke, J.I., and W.B. Fisher (eds.). *Populations of the Middle East and North Africa: A Geographical Approach*. New York: Africana, 1972.

Clements, Frank A. *Oman: The Reborn Land*. London: Longman, 1980.

Cordesman, Anthony H. *The Gulf and the Search for Strategic Stability: Saudi Arabia, the Military Balance in the Gulf, and Trends in the Arab-Israeli Military Balance*. Boulder: Westview Press, 1984.

————. "The Iran-Iraq War in 1984: An Escalating Threat to the Gulf and the West," *Armed Forces Journal International*,

121, No. 8, March 1984, 22–30.

————. "Oman: The Guardian of the Eastern Gulf," *Armed Forces Journal International*, 120, No. 11, June 1983, 22–31.

————. "US Military Assistance to the Middle East: National Security or Election-Year Politics?" *Armed Forces Journal International*, 121, No. 6, January 1984, 27–33.

Cottrell, Alvin J. "Islam," *National Defense*, 68, No. 389, July-August, 1983, 36–39.

————. "The Political Balance in the Persian Gulf," *Strategic Review*, 2, No. 1, Winter 1974, 32–38.

————. "The U.S. Stake in the Persian Gulf," *National Defense*, 68, No. 382, November 1982, 22–26.

Cottrell, Alvin J. (ed.). *The Persian Gulf States: A General Survey*. Baltimore: Johns Hopkins University Press, 1980.

Cottrell, Alvin J., and Frank Bray. *Military Forces in the Persian Gulf*. (Washington Papers, 6.) Beverly Hills: Sage for The Center for Strategic and International Studies, Georgetown University, 1978.

Cottrell, Alvin J., Robert J. Hanks, and Frank T. Bray. "Military Affairs in the Persian Gulf." Pages 140–71 in Alvin J. Cottrell (ed.), *The Persian Gulf States: A General Survey*. Baltimore: Johns Hopkins University Press, 1980.

Crowe, Kenneth C. *Kutuayba Alghamin of Kuwait*. (Department of State, Office of External Research, Foreign Affairs Research Paper, No. FAR 24752-N.) Washington: May 1976.

Crystal, Jill. "Kuwait." Pages 602–606 in George Delary (ed.), *World Encyclopedia of Political Systems and Parties*. New York: Facts on File, 1983.

Curtis, Michael (ed.). *Religion and Politics in the Middle East*. Boulder: Westview Press, 1981.

Dafter, Ray. "World Oil Production and Security of Supplies," *International Security*, 4, No. 3, Winter 1979–80, 154–76.

Daniels, John. *Abu Dhabi: A Portrait*. London: Longman, 1974.

Darlow, Michael, and Richard Fawkes. *The Last Corner of Arabia*. London: Namara, 1976.

Dawisha, Adeed (ed.). *Islam in Foreign Policy*. Cambridge: Cambridge University Press, 1983.

Deakin, Michael. *Ras Al-Khaimah: Flame in the Desert*. London: Namara, 1976.

Delury, George E. (ed.). *World Encyclopedia of Political Systems and Parties*. 2 vols. New York: Facts on File, 1983.

Demir, Soliman. *The Kuwait Fund and the Political Economy of Arab Regional Development*. New York: Praeger, 1976.

Demographic Yearbook, 1974. (26th issue.) New York: Statistical

Office, Department of Economic and Social Affairs, United Nations, 1975.

Dostal, Walter. "The Shihuh of Northern Oman: A Contribution to Cultural Ecology," *Geographical Journal* [London], 138, No. 1, March 1972, 1–6.

"Dubai Dry Dock," *Financial Times* [London], February 26, 1979, 1–4 (Survey).

Dunn, Keith A. *Towards a US Military Strategy for Southwest Asia*. Carlisle Barracks, Pennsylvania: Strategic Studies Institute, United States Army War College, 1982.

Dunn, Roderic W. "A Rural Community Development Project in Oman." Pages 199–212 in John I. Clarke and Howard Bowen-Jones (eds.), *Change and Development in the Middle East*. London: Methuen, 1981.

Dyer, Gwynne. "Bahrain." Pages 42–43 in John Keegan (ed.), *World Armies*. New York: Facts on File, 1979.

––––––. "Kuwait." Pages 416–20 in John Keegan (ed.), *World Armies*. New York: Facts on File, 1979.

––––––. "Oman." Pages 524–27 in John Keegan (ed.), *World Armies*. New York: Facts on File, 1979.

––––––. "Qatar." Pages 585–86 in John Keegan (ed.), *World Armies*. New York: Facts on File, 1979.

––––––. "United Arab Emirates." Pages 747–52 in John Keegan (ed.), *World Armies*. New York: Facts on File, 1979.

Eickelman, Dale F. "Kings and People: Oman's State Consultative Council," *Middle East Journal*, 38, No. 1, Winter 1984, 51–71.

––––––. "Omani Village: The Meaning of Oil." Pages 211–19 in J.E. Peterson (ed.), *The Politics of Middle Eastern Oil*. Washington: Middle East Institute, 1983.

Eilts, Hermann F. "Sayyid Muhammad bin Aqil of Dhufor: Malevolent or Maligned?" *Historical Collections*, 109, No. 3, July 1973, 179–230.

––––––. "Security Considerations in the Persian Gulf," *International Security*, 5, No. 2, Fall 1980, 79–113.

El-Mallakh, Ragaei. *The Absorptive Capacity of Kuwait*. Lexington, Massachusetts: Lexington Books, 1981.

––––––. *The Economic Development of the United Arab Emirates*. London: Croom Helm, 1981.

Epstein, Edward Jay. "Kuwait Embassy Cables," *Atlantic Monthly*, 251, No. 5, May 1983, 16–19.

Fabian, Larry L. "The Middle East: War Dangers and Receding Peace Prospects," *Foreign Affairs*, 62, No. 3, Special Issue 1984, 632–58.

Fakhri, Ahmed A., (ed.). *Bahrain Business Directory*. Manama: Arab Communicators, 1984.

Farah, Tawfic E. "Alienation and Expatriate Labor in Kuwait," *Journal of South Asian and Middle Eastern Studies*, 4, Fall 1980, 3–40.

————. "Political Socialization in Kuwait: Survey Findings," *Journal of South Asian and Middle Eastern Studies*, 6, No. 2, Winter 1982, 38–47.

Farah, Tawfic E., and Faisal S.A. Al-Salem. "Political Efficacy, Political Trust, and the Action Orientations of University Students in Kuwait," *International Journal of Middle East Studies*, 8, No. 3, July 1977, 317–28.

Farley, Jonathan. "The Gulf War and the Littoral States," *World Today* [London], July 1984, 269–76.

Fenelon, K.G. *The United Arab Emirates: An Economic and Social Survey*. London: Longman, 1973.

Ferrier, R.W. *The History of the British Petroleum Company: The Developing Years, 1901–1932*, 1. Cambridge: Cambridge University Press, 1982.

Fesharaki, Fereidun, and David T. Isaak. *OPEC, the Gulf, and the World Petroleum Market: A Study in Government Policy and Downstream Operations*. Boulder: Westview Press, 1983.

Ffrench, G.E., and A.G. Hill, *Kuwait: Urban and Medical Ecology: A Geomedical Study*. (Geomedical Monograph Series, 4.) Vienna: Springer, 1971.

Field, Michael. "Al-Sabah Family Tree," *Financial Times* [London], February 22, 1984, Sec. 4, 3.

————. *A Hundred Million Dollars a Day*. London: Sidwick and Jackson, 1975.

————. "Maktoum Family: Anxieties over Succession Ease," *Financial Times* [London], November 30, 1983, 8.

————. "Nahayyan Family: Further United by Marriage," *Financial Times* [London], November 30, 1983, 12.

Financial Times [London], May 31, 1984 (Survey) (whole section).

Fisher, W.B. *The Middle East: A Physical, Social, and Regional Geography*. London: Methuen, 1971.

"Focus on Bahrain," *Middle East Education and Training* [Surrey, England], 6, No. 1, 1984, 14–22.

Freeman, S. David. *Energy: The New Era*. New York: Vintage Books, 1974.

Freeth, Zahra. *A New Look at Kuwait*. London: George Allen and Unwin, 1972.

Friedlaender, Israel. "The Heterodoxies of the Shiites in the Presentation of Ibn Hazm" (Pt. 1), *Journal of the American Oriental Society,* 28, 1907, 1–80.

Gawlik, Joseph Anthony. *Persian Gulf Security: The United States and Oman, the Gulf Cooperation Council, and Western Allied Participation.* (Master's thesis, No. AD-A127690.) Monterey: Naval Postgraduate School, December 1982.

Geadah, Sami. "Development Strategy of United Arab Emirates Seeks to Expand Economy's Productive Base," *IMF Survey,* October 4, 1982, 318–20.

————. "Qatar's Economic Program Aims at Balanced Growth While Containing Inflation," *IMF Survey,* 11, June 7, 1982, 171–73.

Gibb, H.A.R., and J.H. Kramers (eds.). *Shorter Encyclopedia of Islam.* Ithaca: Cornell University Press, 1953.

Glassman, Jon D. *Arms for the Arabs.* Baltimore: Johns Hopkins University Press, 1975.

Goodhind, Gilliam. "Iraq-Kuwait." Pages 222–25 in Alan J. Day (ed.), *Border and Territorial Disputes.* Essex, England: Longman, 1982.

————. "Kuwait-Saudi Arabia." Pages 229–32 in Alan J. Day (ed.), *Border and Territorial Disputes.* Essex, England: Longman, 1982.

Gordon, Murray (ed.). *Conflict in the Persian Gulf.* New York: Facts on File, 1981.

Graz, Liesl. *The Omanis: Sentinels of the Gulf.* London: Longman, 1982.

Griffith, William E. "The Great Powers, the Indian Ocean, and the Persian Gulf," *Jerusalem Journal of International Relations* [Jerusalem], 1, No. 2, Winter 1975, 5–19.

————. *The Middle East, 1982: Politics, Revolutionary Islam, and American Policy.* Cambridge: Center for International Studies, Massachusetts Institute of Technology, 1982.

"Gulf Co-operation—Theory or Practice?" *Middle East Economic Digest* [London], 27, No. 43, October 28, 1983, 14–24.

"The Gulf, '83" *Far Eastern Economic Review* [Hong Kong], 119, No. 9, March 3, 1983, 29–58.

"Gulf States Move Closer Together," *Middle East* [London], No. 16, February 1976, 35–36.

Gurfinckel, Mariano. "As Oil Prices Rise," *IMF Survey,* October 13, 1975, 297–305.

Habachy, Saba. "A Study in Comparative Constitutional Law: Constitutional Government in Kuwait," *Columbia Journal of Transnational Law,* 3, No. 2, 1965, 116–26.

Haddad, Wadi'd. "The Interaction Between Science and Society in the Arabic Press of the Middle East," *Science Education,* 58, No. 1, 1974, 35–49.

Halliday, Fred. *Arabia Without Sultans: A Political Survey of Instability in the Arab World.* New York: Vintage Books, Random House, 1975.

Hammond, Thomas T. "Afghanistan and the Persian Gulf," *Survey* [London], 26, No. 2, Spring 1982, 83–101.

Harrigan, Anthony. "Security Interests in the Persian Gulf and Western Indian Ocean," *Strategic Review,* 1, No. 3, Fall 1973, 13–22.

Hawley, Donald. *Oman and its Renaissance.* London: Stacey International, 1977.

———. "Some Surprising Aspects of Oman's History," *Asian Affairs* [London], 13, New Series, Pt. 1, February 1982, 28–39.

———. *The Trucial States.* New York: Twayne, 1970.

Heard-Bey, Frauke. *From Trucial States to United Arab Emirates: A Society in Transition.* London: Longman, 1982.

Heller, Mark A. "Turmoil in the Gulf," *New Republic,* April 23, 1984, 16–20.

Hensel, Howard M. "Soviet Policy Towards the Rebellion in Dhofar," *Asian Affairs* [London], 13, New Series, Pt. 2, January 1982, 183–207.

Hess, Andrew C. "Consensus or Conflict: The Dilemma of Islamic Historians," *American Historical Review,* 81, No. 4, October 1976, 788–99.

Hewish, Mark, et al. *Air Forces of the World.* New York: Simon and Schuster, 1979.

Hijazi, Ahmad. "Kuwait: Development from a Semi-Tribal, Semi-Colonial Society to Democracy and Sovereignty," *American Journal of Comparative Law,* 13, No. 3, Summer 1964, 428–38.

Hill, Allan G. "The Gulf States: Petroleum and Population Growth." Pages 242–74 in J.I. Clarke and W.B. Fisher (eds.), *Populations of the Middle East and North Africa: A Geographical Approach.* New York: Africana, 1972.

———. "Population Growth in the Middle East since 1945 with Special Reference to the Arab Countries of West Asia." Pages 130–53 in John I. Clarke and Howard Bowen-Jones (eds.), *Change and Development in the Middle East.* London: Methuen, 1981.

Hitti, Philip K. *History of the Arabs.* (6th ed.) London: Macmillan, 1956.

————. *Islam: A Way of Life*. Minneapolis: University of Minnesota Press, 1970.

Hoagland, Jim. "Oman's Leap into the Present," *Washington Post*, December 29, 1974, B2–B4.

Hodgson, Marshall G.S. *The Venture of Islam, I: The Classical Age of Islam*. Chicago: University of Chicago Press, 1974.

Hopwood, Derek (ed.). *The Arabian Peninsula: Society and Politics*. Totowa, New Jersey: Rowman and Littlefield, 1972.

Hottinger, Arnold. "Notes from the Gulf," *Swiss Review of World Affairs* [Geneva], 30, March 1984, 14–21.

————. "Political Institutions in Saudi Arabia, Kuwait, and Bahrain." Pages 1–18 in Shahram Chubin (ed.), *Security in the Persian Gulf, I: Domestic Political Factors*. Montclair, New Jersey: Allanheld, Osmun for the International Institute for Strategic Studies, 1981.

Hourani, George. *Arab Seafaring*. Beirut: Khayats, 1963.

Huneidi, Isa A. "The Transplants that Produced a Democratic Judiciary," *Kuwait Digest* [Kuwait], 4, No. 1, January-March 1976, 23–25.

Hurewitz, J.C. *Diplomacy in the Near and Middle East*. 2 vols. New York: Van Nostrand, 1956.

————. *The Persian Gulf: After Iran's Revolution*. (Headline series, No. 244.) New York: Foreign Policy Association, 1979.

————. "The Persian Gulf: British Withdrawal and Western Security," *Annals of the American Academy of Political and Social Science*, 401, May 1972, 106–15.

————. *The Persian Gulf: Prospects for Stability*. (Headline series, No. 220.) New York: Foreign Policy Association, April 1974.

International Bank for Reconstruction and Development. *The Economic Development of Kuwait*. Baltimore: Johns Hopkins Press, 1965.

International Institute for Strategic Studies. *The Middle East and the International System, Pt. II: Security and the Energy Crisis*. (Adelphi Papers, No. 115) London: 1975.

International Monetary Fund. *IMF Survey*, July 25, 1983, 221–23.

————. *International Financial Statistics*. Washington: November 1976, 318.

————. "Kuwait Adopts Measures to Adjust to the Impact of Reduced Oil Revenues," *IMF Survey*, August 8, 1983, 236–38.

International Petroleum Encyclopedia, 1970. Tulsa: Petroleum, 1970.

International Petroleum Encyclopedia, 1971. Tulsa: Petroleum, 1971.

International Petroleum Encyclopedia, 1972. Tulsa: Petroleum, 1972.

International Petroleum Encyclopedia, 1973. Tulsa: Petroleum, 1973.

International Petroleum Encyclopedia, 1974. Tulsa: Petroleum, 1974.

International Petroleum Encyclopedia, 1975. Tulsa: Petroleum, 1975.

International Petroleum Encyclopedia, 1976. Tulsa: Petroleum, 1976.

Ismael, Jacqueline S. *Kuwait: Social Change in Historical Perspective.* Syracuse: Syracuse University Press, 1982.

Ismael, Tareq Y., et al. *Governments and Politics of the Contemporary Middle East.* Homewood, Illinois: Dorsey Press, 1970.

————. *The Middle East in World Politics.* Syracuse: Syracuse University Press, 1974.

Iungerich, Raphael. "How Real Is the Soviet Threat to the Gulf Region?" *Armed Forces Journal International,* October 1984, 110–11.

————. "US Rapid Deployment Forces—USCENTCOM—What Is It? Can It Do the Job? *Armed Forces Journal International,* October 1984, 88–107.

Izzard, Ralph. "The Fight for Federation," *Middle East International* [London], No. 1, April 1971, 33–35.

Jaidah, Ali M. *An Appraisal of OPEC Oil Policies.* New York: Longman, 1983.

Jane's All the World's Aircraft, 1982–83. (Ed., John W.R. Taylor.) London: Jane's, 1982.

Jane's Armour and Artillery, 1983–84. (Ed., Christopher F. Foss.) London: Jane's, 1983.

Jane's Fighting Ships. (Ed., John Moore.) New York: Jane's, 1981.

Jane's Infantry Weapons, 1982–83. (Ed., John Weeks.) London: Jane's, 1982.

Jane's Military Vehicles and Ground Support Equipment, 1983. (Ed., Christopher F. Foss.) London: Jane's, 1983.

Jane's Surface Skimmers: Hovercraft and Hydrofoils, 1981. (Ed., Roy McLeavy.) New York: Jane's, 1981.

Jane's Weapon Systems, 1982–83. (Ed., Ronald T. Pretty.) London: Jane's, 1982.

Janke, Peter and Richard Sim. *Guerrilla and Terrorist Organiza-*

 ations: A World Directory and Bibliography. New York: Macmillan, 1983.

"Jebel Ali," *Financial Times* [London], May 27, 1982, 1–3 (Survey).

Johns, Richard, and Robert Graham. "Kuwait to Buy 150 Chieftain Tanks in £100m. Deal," *Financial Times* [London], February 16, 1976, 1.

Johnson, Maxwell Orme. *The Military as an Instrument of U.S. Policy in Southwest Asia: The Rapid Deployment Joint Task Force, 1979–1982.* Boulder: Westview Press, 1983.

Joint Publications Research Service—JPRS (Washington).

The following items are from the JPRS series:

Near East/South Asia Report

"Ambassador Interviewed on Egypt-Oman Relations," *Mayu,* Cairo, October 31, 1983. (JPRS 84005, January 11, 1984, 85–90.)

"Civil Service Report on Government Appointees," *Al Khalij,* Sharjah, September 21, 1983. (JPRS 84846, November 30, 1983, 117–18).

"Country's Borrowing Policy Explained," *Dubayy Times,* Muscat, December 9, 1983. (JPRS 84019, February 1, 1984, 13).

"Country's Expatriate Workforce Increases in 1982," *Khaleej Times,* Sharjah, August 28, 1983. (JPRS 84327, September 15, 1983, 89–91).

"Country's Judicial System Described," *Times of Oman,* Muscat, November 17, 1983. (JPRS 84986, December 20, 1983, 148–49).

"Deputy Prime Minister Discusses New Political Reforms, Policies," *'Uman,* Muscat, July 5, 1983. (JPRS 84395, September 23, 1983, 92–98).

"Editorial Casts Critical Eye on Federation," *Al Khalij,* Sharjah, January 14–19, 1984. (JPRS 84033, February 24, 1984, 112–20).

"Heir to Throne of Abu Dhabi Interviewed on Military, Political Issues," *Al Jazirah,* Riyadh, November 19, 1983. (JPRS 84008, January 13, 1984, 45–48).

"Iranair to Increase Tehran-Dubai Flights," *Khaleej Times,* Dubai, October 28, 1983. (JPRS 84792, November 22, 1983, 1–2).

"New Agricultural Techniques Reported," *Oman Daily Observer,* Muscat, January 11, 1984. (JPRS 84023, February 10, 1984, 7).

"New Ambassador Comments on Ties with India," *Oman*

Daily Observer, Muscat, July 28, 1983. (JPRS 84230, August 31, 1983, 56–57).

"Omanization of Banking Sector Described," *Times of Oman*, Muscat, December 29, 1983. (JPRS 84019, February 1, 1984, 5).

"Planning Moves Forward for Sultan Qabus University," *'Uman*, Muscat, May 17, 1983. (JPRS 83891, July 14, 1983, 56–57).

"Qabus Interviewed on Domestic, Foreign Issues," *Gulf Times*, Doha, December 23, 1983. (JPRS 84023, February 10, 1984, 104–05).

"State Consultative Council Enlarged," *Times of Oman*, Muscat, November 3, 1983. (JPRS 84986, December 20, 1983, 147).

"Steps to Streamline Civil Service Recommended," *Al Mujtama*, Kuwait, November 15, 1983. (JPRS 84016, January 30, 1984, 21–23).

"Student Society Election Results Detailed," *Al Mujtama*, Kuwait, November 1, 1983. (JPRS 84016, January 30, 1984, 17–20).

"Ties with Pakistan Described," *Oman Daily Observer*, Muscat, March 22, 1984. (JPRS 84069, April 27, 1984, 105–06).

"Ties with South Yemen," *Times of Oman*, Muscat, October 6, 1983. (JPRS 84660, November 1, 1983, 80).

Joyner, Christopher C. "The Petrodollar Phenomenon and Changing International Economic Relations," *World Affairs*, 138, No. 2, Fall 1975, 152–76.

Kabeel, Soraya. *Source Book on the Arabian Gulf States: Arabian Gulf in General, Kuwait, Bahrain, Qatar, and Oman*. Kuwait: Kuwait University Press, 1975.

Kassem, Oman. "The Gulf Needs Creative Financial Engineering," *Euromoney* [London], July 1981, 105–15.

Kaylani, Nabil M. "Politics and Religion in 'Uman: A Historical Overview," *International Journal of Middle East Studies*, 10, No. 4, November 1979, 567-79.

Kazziha, Walid. *Revolutionary Transformation in the Arab World*. New York: St. Martin's Press, 1975.

Kechichian, Joseph A. "Demographic Problems Facing the Gulf Cooperation Council," *International Demographics*, 2, No. 4, April 1983, 3, 12.

Kelly, John Barrett. *Arabia, the Gulf, and the West*. New York: Basic Books, 1980.

———. *Britain and the Persian Gulf, 1795–1880*. New York:

Oxford University Press, 1968.

————. *Eastern Arabian Frontiers*. New York: Praeger, 1964.

————. "A Prevalence of Furies: Tribes, Politics, and Religion in Oman and Trucial Oman." Pages 107–44 in Derek Hopwood (ed.), *The Arabian Peninsula: Society and Politics*. Totowa, New Jersey: Rowman and Littlefield, 1972.

Kelly, John Barrett, and Hermann F. Eilts. "Point/Counterpoint: Security in the Persian Gulf," *International Security*, 5, No. 4, Spring 1981, 186–203.

Kennedy, Gavin. *The Military in the Third World*. New York: Scribner's Sons, 1974.

Kergan, J.L. "Social and Economic Changes in the Gulf Countries," *Asian Affairs* [London], 62, New Series, 6, Pt. 3, October 1975, 282–89.

Key, Kerim K. *The Arabian Gulf States Today*. Washington: Asia Research Center, 1974.

Khadduri, Majid. *Arab Personalities in Politics*. Washington: Middle East Institute, 1981.

Khalid, Zulfikar A. "Straits of Hormuz, the Fulcrum of Persian Gulf Oil Security," *Asian Defence Journal* [Kuala Lumpur], February 1982, 36–38.

Khalifa, Ali Mohammed. *The United Arab Emirates: Unity in Fragmentation*. Boulder: Westview Press, 1979.

Khoury, Nabeel A. "The Pragmatic Trend in Inter-Arab Politics," *Middle East Journal*, 36, No. 3, Summer 1982, 374–87.

Khuri, Fuad I. *Tribe and State in Bahrain: The Transformation of Social and Political Authority in an Arab State*. Chicago: University of Chicago Press, 1980.

Kilner, Peter, and Jonathan Wallace (eds.). *The Gulf Handbook 1966–77*. London: Middle East Economic Digest, 1976.

Koury, Enver M. *Oil and Geopolitics in the Persian Gulf Area: A Center of Power*. Beirut: Catholic Press, 1973.

————. *The United Arab Emirates: Its Political System and Politics*. Hyattsville, Maryland: Institute of Middle Eastern and North African Affairs, 1980.

Kurian, George Thomas. *World Press Encyclopedia*. 2 vols. New York: Facts on File, 1982.

Kurtz, Richard A. "The Non-medical Use of Child Health Clinics: The Case of Kuwait," *Journal of Asian and African Studies* [London], 16, Nos. 3–4, 1981, 261–69.

Kurtz, Richard A., and A.M. Al-Rifal. "Kuwait: A Demographic and Economic Analysis," *Journal of the Kuwait Medical Association* [Kuwait], 13, 1979, 181–93.

Kuwait. Ministry of Planning. Central Statistical Office. *Annual*

Statistical Abstract, 1982. (19th ed.) Kuwait: 1983.

Kuwait. Planning Board. Central Statistical Office. *Annual Statistical Abstract, 1975*. Kuwait: 1975.

"Kuwait." Pages 157–68 in Anthony Axon et al., *Middle East Annual Review: 1975–6*. Great Chesterford, England: Middle East Review, 1975.

"Kuwait," *Financial Times* [London], February 25, 1981, 1–12 (Survey).

"Kuwait," *Financial Times* [London], February 24, 1982, 1–16 (Survey).

"Kuwait," *Financial Times* [London], February 23, 1983, 1–14 (Survey).

"Kuwait," *Financial Times* [London], February 22, 1984, 1–14 (Survey).

"Kuwait." Pages 598–620 in Amos J. Peaslee (ed.), *Constitutions of Nations*, 2. (rev. 3d ed.) The Hague: M. Nijhoff, 1966.

Kuwait Fund for Arab Economic Development. *20th Annual Report, 1981–82*. Kuwait: 1983.

Kuwait Petroleum Corporation. *Annual Report*. Kuwait: 1981.

Laliberté, Gérard. "La Guérilla de Dhofar," *Études internationales* [Quebec], 4, Nos. 1–2, March-June 1973, 159–81.

Landen, Robert G. "Gulf States." Pages 295–315 in Abid A. Al-Marayati et al. (eds.), *The Middle East: Its Governments and Politics*. Belmont, California: Duxbury Press, 1972.

————. *Oman since 1856: Disruptive Modernization in a Traditional Arab Society*. Princeton: Princeton University Press, 1967.

Laost, Henri. *Essai sur les Doctrines Sociales et Politiques de Taki-ad-Din Ahmad b Tamiya*. Cairo: Imprimerie de l'Institut Français d'Archéologie Orientale, 1939.

Lateef, Abdul. "A Security Pact in the Gulf?" *Middle East International* [London], No. 55, January 1976, 21–23.

Lawson, Fred H. "State of Bahrain." Pages 68–71 in George E. Delury (ed.), *World Encyclopedia of Political Systems and Parties*. New York: Facts on File: 1983.

Lederer, Ivo J., and Wayne S. Vucinich (eds.). *The Soviet Union and the Middle East: The Post World War II Era*. Stanford: Hoover Institution, Stanford University Press, 1974.

Leemans, W.F. *Foreign Trade in the Old Babylonian Period*. Leiden: Brill, 1959.

Legum, Colin (ed.). *Middle East Contemporary Survey, 1976–1977*. New York: Holmes and Meier, 1978.

————. *Middle East Contemporary Survey, 1977–1978*. New York: Holmes and Meier, 1979.

Levy, Reuben. *The Social Structure of Islam*. (2d ed.) Cambridge: Cambridge University Press, 1969.

Lewicki, T. "Ibadiyya." Pages 648–60 in Bernard Lewis et al. (eds.), *The Encyclopedia of Islam*, 3. Leiden: Brill, 1968.

Liebesny, Herbert J. "Administration and Legal Development in Arabia: The Persian Gulf Principalities," *Middle East Journal*, 10, No. 1, Winter 1956, 33–42.

―――. *The Law of the Near and Middle East: Readings, Cases, and Materials*. Albany: State University of New York Press, 1975.

Lippman, Thomas W. *Islam: Politics and Religion in the Muslim World*. (Headline series, No. 258.) New York: Foreign Policy Association, 1982.

Litwak, Robert. *Security in the Persian Gulf: Sources of Inter-State Conflict*. London: International Institute for Strategic Studies, 1981.

Long, David E. "Confrontation and Cooperation in the Gulf." (Middle East Problem Paper, No. 10.) Washington: Middle East Institute, 1974.

―――. *The Persian Gulf: An Introduction to Its People, Politics, and Economics*. Boulder: Westview Press, 1978.

Mackie, Alan. "Oman and South Yemen: A Gradual Rapprochement," *Middle East Economic Digest* [London], November 4, 1983, 33.

McLachlan, Keith. "The Oil Industry in the Middle East." Pages 95–112 in John I. Clarke and Howard Bowen-Jones (eds.), *Change and Development in the Middle East*. London: Methuen, 1981.

―――. "Oil in the Persian Gulf Area." Pages 195–224 in Alvin J. Cottrell (ed.), *The Persian Gulf States: A General Survey*. Baltimore: Johns Hopkins University Press, 1980.

McLachlan, Keith, and Narsi Ghorban. *Oil Production, Revenues, and Economic Development*. (Quarterly Economic Review Special Series, No. 18.) London: Economist Intelligence Unit, 1975.

McLaurin, R.D. *The Middle East in Soviet Policy*. Lexington, Massachusetts: Lexington Books, Heath, 1975.

McNaugher, Thomas L. "The Superpowers in the Persian Gulf," *Current*, No. 256, October 1983, 51–59.

Magnus, Ralph H. "International Organizations in the Persian Gulf." Pages 172–91 in Alvin J. Cottrell (ed.), *The Persian Gulf States: A General Survey*. Baltimore: Johns Hopkins University Press, 1980.

―――. "Middle East Oil," *Current History*, 68, No. 402, February 1975, 49–53.

Malik, Hafeez. "Islam and Women: Some Experiments in Qatar," *Journal of South Asian and Middle Eastern Studies*, 4, No. 2, Winter 1980, 3–9.

Malone, Joseph J. "America and the Arabian Peninsula: The First Two Hundred Years," *Middle East Journal*, 30, No. 3, Summer 1976, 406–24.

————. *The Arab Lands of Western Asia*. Englewood Cliffs: Prentice-Hall, 1973.

————. "Security: A Priority for Gulf Council," *Journal of Defense and Diplomacy*, 1, No. 6, September 1983, 15–17.

Mann, Clarence. *Abu Dhabi: Birth of an Oil Sheikhdom*. Beirut: Khayats, 1964.

Mansfield, Peter. *The New Arabians*. Chicago: Ferguson, 1981.

Mansur, Abdul Kasim. "The Military Balance in the Persian Gulf: Who Will Guard the Gulf States from their Guardians?" *Armed Forces Journal International*, 118, No. 4, November 1980, 44–86.

Martin, Leonore G. "Policy Implications of Boundary Disputes in the Persian Gulf," *Middle East Review*, 15, Nos. 1–2, Fall-Winter 1982–83, 25–32.

Maull, Hanns. *Oil and Influence: The Oil Weapon Examined*. (Adelphi Papers, No. 17.) London: International Institute for Strategic Studies, 1975.

"MEED Special Report: Bahrain," *Middle East Economic Digest* [London], September 1982 (entire issue).

"MEED Special Report: Bahrain," *Middle East Economic Digest* [London], September 1983 (entire issue).

"MEED Special Report: Kuwait," *Middle East Economic Digest* [London], May 1983 (entire issue).

"MEED Special Report: Kuwait," *Middle East Economic Digest* [London], May 1984 (entire issue).

"MEED Special Report: Kuwait and the Middle East," *Middle East Economic Digest* [London], May 1982 (entire issue).

"MEED Special Report: Oman," *Middle East Economic Digest* [London], November 1981 (entire issue).

"MEED Special Report: Oman," *Middle East Economic Digest* [London], November 1982 (entire issue).

"MEED Special Report: Oman," *Middle East Economic Digest* [London], November 1983 (entire issue).

"MEED Special Report: Qatar," *Middle East Economic Digest* [London], August 1982 (entire issue).

"MEED Special Report: Qatar," *Middle East Economic Digest* [London], August 1983 (entire issue).

"MEED Special Report: UAE," *Middle East Economic Digest* [London], November 1982 (entire issue).

"MEED Special Report: UAE," *Middle East Economic Digest* [London], December 1983 (entire issue).

Melamid, Alexander. "Boundary Disputes in the Persian (Arab) Gulf." (Paper presented at Annual Meeting of Middle East Studies Association.) Boston: 1974.

"Member Country Sketchbook: UAE," *OPEC Bulletin* [Vienna], February 1984, 20–31.

The Middle East and North Africa, 1981–1982. (28th ed.) London: Europa, 1981.

The Middle East and North Africa, 1983–1984. (30th ed.) London: Europa, 1983.

Middle East Economic Digest [London], October 28, 1983.

Middle East Economic Digest [London], January 6, 1984, 32.

"Middle Eastern, North African, and South Asian Navies," *United States Naval Institute Proceedings*, 110/3/973, March 1984, 48–54.

The Middle East Military Balance, 1983. (Ed., Mark Heller.) Tel Aviv: Jaffee Center for Strategic Studies, Tel Aviv University, 1983.

"Middle East Oil and Gas," *Financial Times* [London], November 3, 1980, 21–24 (Survey).

Miles, Samuel Barrett. *The Countries and Tribes of the Persian Gulf*. London: Cass, 1966.

The Military Balance. London: International Institute for Strategic Studies, 1983.

Mosley, Leonard. *Power Play*. New York: Random House, 1973.

Mossavar-Rahmani, Bijan. "The OPEC Multiplier," *Foreign Policy*, No. 52, Fall 1983, 136–48.

Mostyn, Trevor (ed.). *UAE: A MEED Practical Guide*. London: Middle East Economic Digest, 1982.

Nakhleh, Emile A. *Arab-American Relations in the Persian Gulf*. Washington: American Enterprise Institute, 1975.

———. *Bahrain: Political Development in a Modernizing Society*. Lexington, Massachusetts: Heath, 1976.

———. "Constitutional Development in the Arab Gulf." (Paper presented at Annual Meeting of Middle East Studies Association.) Boston: 1974.

Nath, Kamla. "Education and Employment among Kuwaiti Women." Pages 172–88 in Lois Beck and Nikki Keddie (eds.), *Women in the Muslim World*. Cambridge: Harvard University Press, 1978.

National Bank of Kuwait. *Annual Report, 1982: 30 Years of Pro-*

gress and Achievement. Kuwait: 1983.

Newsom, David O. Article in *Christian Science Monitor*, June 14, 1984.

Noyes, James H. *The Clouded Lens: Persian Gulf Security and U.S. Policy*. Stanford: Hoover Institution Press, 1979.

Oil and Gas Journal, 81, No. 52, December 26, 1983, 80–109.

"The Oil Crisis in Perspective," *Daedalus*, 104, No. 4, Fall 1975.

Olson, William J. "The Iran-Iraq War and the Future of the Persian Gulf," *Military Review*, 64, No. 3, March 1984, 17–29.

Oman. Directorate General of National Studies. *Statistical Yearbook*. Muscat: November 1983.

Oman. National Statistical Department. *Statistical Yearbook*. Muscat: 1974.

"Oman." *Middle East Economic Digest* [London], January 6, 1984, 32.

Oman: Current Economic Position and Prospects. (Report No. 2528-OM.) Washington: World Bank, October 1979.

Oman: Transformation of an Economy, 1, 2, and 3. (Report No. 1620-OM.) Washington: World Bank, October 1977.

Osborne, Christine. *The Gulf States and Oman*. London: Croom Helm, 1977.

O'Shea, Raymond. *The Sand Kings of Oman*. London: Methuen, 1947.

Ottaway, David B. "Kuwait Is Target of Islamic Reformers," *Washington Post*, April 24, 1984, A1, A8.

Owen, Roderic. *The Golden Bubble*. London: Collins, 1957.

Page, Stephen. *The USSR and Arabia: The Development of Soviet Policies and Attitudes Towards the Countries of the Arabian Peninsula*. London: Central Asian Research Centre, 1972.

Peterson, J.E. "Britain and 'The Oman War': An Arabian Entanglement," *Asian Affairs* [London], 63, New Series, 7, Pt. 3, October 1976, 285–98.

———. "Legitimacy and Political Change in Yemen and Oman," *Orbis*, 27, No. 4, Winter 1984, 971–98.

———, *Oman in the Twentieth Century: Political Foundations of an Emerging State*. London: Croom Helm, 1978.

———. *The Politics of Middle Eastern Oil*. Washington: Middle East Institute, 1983.

Phillips, Wendell. *Oman: A History*. New York: Revnal, 1968.

———. *Unknown Oman*. New York: McKay, 1966.

Plascov, Avi. *Security in the Persian Gulf: Modernization, Development, and Stability*, 3. London: International Institute for Strategic Studies, 1982.

Polk, William R. *The United States and the Arab World*. (3d ed.) Cambridge: Harvard University Press, 1975.

Price, D.L. "Building Bridges in the Gulf," *Middle East International* [London], No. 59, May 1976, 24–25.

————. *Oman: Insurgency and Development*. (Conflict Studies, No. 53.) London: Institute for the Study of Conflict, January 1975.

————. *Stability in the Gulf: The Oil Revolution*. (Conflict Studies, No. 71.) London: Institute for the Study of Conflict, May 1976.

"The Provisional Constitution of the United Arab Amirates," *Middle East Journal, 26, No. 3, Summer 1972, 307–25*.

Qatar. Central Statistical Organization. *Annual Statistical Abstract*. Doha: July 1983.

Qatar. Industrial Development Technical Centre. *Achievements in Industrial Development*. Doha: February 1981.

Qatar. Ministry of Information. *Qatar: A Forward Looking Country with Centuries Old Traditions*. Doha: 1974.

Qatar. Ministry of Information. Press and Publications Department. *Yearbook, 1980–81*. Doha: n. d.

Qatar. Presidency of the Council of Ministers. Central Statistical Organization. *Annual Statistical Abstract*. Doha: July 1983.

"Qatar." Pages 278–79 in Arthur S. Banks (ed.), *Political Handbook of the World, 1975*. New York: McGraw-Hill, 1975.

"Qatar." Page 319 in Jean Labayle Couhat (ed.), *Combat Fleets of the World, 1976–77: Their Ships, Aircraft, and Armament*. (Trans., James J. McDonald.) Annapolis: Naval Institute Press, 1976.

"Qatar: A Special Report." *Times* [London], June 23, 1975, 1–9.

"Qatar: A Special Survey," *Financial Times* [London], February 21, 1982 (Survey).

"Qatar: A Special Survey," *Financial Times* [London], February 22, 1983.

Ramazani, Rouhollah K. "Khumayni's Islam in Iran's Foreign Policy." Pages 9–33 in Adeed Dawisha (ed.), *Islam in Foreign Policy*. Cambridge: Cambridge University Press, 1983.

————. *The Persian Gulf: Iran's Role*. Charlottesville: University of Virginia Press, 1972.

————. *The United States and Iran: The Patterns of Influence*. New York: Praeger, 1982.

Rand, Christopher T. *Making Democracy Safe for Oil*. Boston: Atlantic Monthly Press, 1975.

Rentz, George. "A Sultanate Asunder." *Natural History*, 83, No. 3, March 1974, 58–66.

————. "The Wahhabis." Pages 270–84 in A.J. Arberry (ed.), *Religion in the Middle East: Three Religions in Concord and Conflict, II: Islam*. Cambridge: Cambridge University Press, 1969.

Report of the Directors and Balance Sheet. Doha: Qatar National Bank, 1976.

Report of the Directors and Balance Sheet, 31 December 1974. Doha: Qatar National Bank, 1975.

Roberts, John. "Oman Welcomes Vice-President Bush—and U.S. Assistance," *Middle East Economic Digest* [London], May 18, 1984, 44.

————. "Washington Moves to Support Its Gulf Allies," *Middle East Economic Digest* [London], June 1, 1984, 20, 21.

Rouleau, Eric. "My People Feel the Need of an Absolute Monarch to Protect Their Interests . . . " (Undated interview with Sultan Qaboos of Oman.) *Le Monde* [Paris], November 1976.

Rubin, Trudy. "What Do the Palestinians Want, III: The Palestinians in Kuwait." (Department of State, Office of External Research, Foreign Affairs Research Paper, No. FAR 22716.) Washington: June 1975.

Rubinacci, Roberto. "The Ibadis." Pages 302–17 in A.J. Arberry (ed.), *Religion in the Middle East: Three Religions in Concord and Conflict, II: Islam*. Cambridge: Cambridge University Press, 1969.

Rubinstein, Alvin Z. (ed.). *The Great Game: Rivalry in the Persian Gulf and South Asia*. New York: Praeger, 1983.

Sadik, Muhammad T., and William P. Snavely. *Bahrain, Qatar, and the United Arab Emirates: Colonial Past, Present Problems, and Future Prospects.* Lexington, Massachusetts: Heath, 1972.

Salisbury, Matthew. "End of a Rebellion," *Middle East International* [London], No. 57, March 1976, 18–20.

Sampson, Anthony. *The Seven Sisters: The Great Oil Companies and the World They Made*. New York: Viking Press, 1975.

Sapsted, David. *Modern Kuwait*. London: Macmillan, 1980.

Sayigh, Yusif A. *Arab Oil Policies in the 1970s*. Baltimore: Johns Hopkins University Press, 1983.

————. "Problems and Prospects of Development in the Arabian Peninsula," *International Journal of Middle East Studies*, 2, No. 1, January 1971, 40–58.

Scuka, Dario. *OPEC: Background, Review, and Analysis*. (Library of Congress, Congressional Research Service, HD9560 Middle East, 74–189E.) Washington: Library of

Congress, October 24, 1975.

Shehab, Fakhri. "Kuwait: A Super Affluent Society." *Foreign Affairs*, 42, No. 3, April 1964, 461–74.

Shwadran, Benjamin. "The Kuwait Incident," (Pt. 1), *Middle Eastern Affairs*, 8, No. 1, January 1962, 2?14..

————. "The Kuwait Incident," (Pt. 2), *Middle Eastern Affairs*, 8, No. 2, February 1962, 45–53.

Skeet, Ian. *Muscat and Oman: The End of an Era*. London: Faber and Faber, 1974.

"A Special Report: Focus on the United Arab Emirates," *Times* [London], April 19, 1982, 1–8.

"A Special Report: United Arab Emirates," *Times* [London], February 23, 1981, 1–20.

"Special Survey: Kuwait, Walking the Tightrope," *South: The Third World Magazine* [London], No. 27, January 1983, 33–47.

"Special Survey: Qatar," *South: The Third World Magazine* [London], No. 26, December 1982, 39–43.

Speece, Mark (comp.). "Draft Environmental Profile of the Sultanate of Oman." Tucson: Arid Lands Information Center, Office of Arid Lands Studies, University of Arizona, June 1981.

Stephens, R. *The Arabs' New Frontier*. London: Temple Smith, 1973.

Sterner, Michael. "The Iran-Iraq War," *Foreign Affairs*, 63, No. 1, Fall 1984, 128–43.

Stoakes, Frank. "Social and Political Change in the Third World: Some Peculiarities of the Oil Producing Principalities of the Middle East." Pages 189–215 in Derek Hopwood (ed.), *The Arabian Peninsula: Society and Politics*. Totowa, New Jersey: Rowman and Littlefield, 1972.

Stockholm International Peace Research Institute. *Arms Trade Registers: The Arms Trade with the Third World*. Cambridge: MIT Press, 1975.

Stookey, Robert W. *America and the Arab States: An Uneasy Encounter*. New York: Wiley, 1975.

Stork, Joe. *Middle East Oil and the Energy Crisis*. New York: Monthly Review Press, June 1975.

Swearingen, Will D. "Sources of Conflict over Oil in the Persian/ Arabian Gulf," *Middle East Journal*, 35, No. 3, Summer 1981, 314–30.

Sweet, Louise E. "The Arabian Peninsula." Pages 199–226 in Louise E. Sweet (ed.), *The Central Middle East*. New Haven: Human Relations Area Files Press, 1971.

Tachau, Frank (ed.). *Political Elites and Political Development in the Middle East*. Cambridge, Massachusetts: Schenkman, 1975.

Tahtinen, Dale R. *Arms in the Persian Gulf*. Washington: American Enterprise Institute, 1974.

Tétreault, Mary Ann. *The Organization of Arab Petroleum Exporting Countries: History, Policies, and Prospects*. Westport, Connecticut: Greenwood Press, 1981.

Thompson, W. Scott. "The Persian Gulf and the Correlation of Forces," *International Security*, 7, No. 1, Summer 1982, 157–80.

Tibawi, A.L. *Islamic Education: Its Traditions and Modernization into the Arab National Systems*. London: Luzac, 1972.

Tomkinson, Michael. *The United Arab Emirates*. London: 1975.

Townsend, John. *Oman: The Making of a Modern State*. London: Croom Helm, 1977.

Tremayne, Penelope. "Guevara Through the Looking Glass: A View of the Dhofar War," *Journal of the Royal United Services Institute for Defence Studies* [London], 119, No. 3, September 1974, 39–43.

"UAE: A Special Survey," *Middle East* [London], No. 110, December 1983, 71–80.

"UAE Banking in a State of Flux," *Banker* [London], 133, December 1983, 113–15.

"UAE 10th Anniversary: MEED Special Report," *Middle East Economic Digest* [London], November 1981 (entire issue).

United Arab Emirates. *The Petroleum Concession Agreements of the United Arab Emirates, 1939–81 (Abu Dhabi)*. London: Croom Helm, 1982.

United Arab Emirates. Central Bank. *Annual Report, 31 December 1982*. Abu Dhabi: 1983.

————. *Bulletin* [Abu Dhabi], 3, No. 2, June 1983 (entire issue).

United Arab Emirates. Ministry of Education. Central Statistical Department. *Statistical Yearbook*. Abu Dhabi: 1983.

United Arab Emirates. Ministry of Information and Culture. *United Arab Emirates*. n. pl.: n. d.

United Arab Emirates. Ministry of Information and Culture. Department of Press and Publications. *United Arab Emirates: A Record of Achievement, 1979–81*. Abu Dhabi: 1981.

United Arab Emirates. Ministry of Petroleum and Mineral Resources. Statistical Department, *UAE Oil Statistical Review, 1981*. Abu Dhabi: 1981.

"United Arab Emirates," *Financial Times* [London], June 26, 1978, 1–24 (Survey).

"United Arab Emirates," *Financial Times* [London], June 25, 1979, 1–20 (Survey).

"United Arab Emirates," *Financial Times* [London], June 22, 1981, 1–12 (Survey).

"United Arab Emirates," *Financial Times* [London], October 26, 1982, 1–12 (Survey).

"United Arab Emirates," *Financial Times* [London], November 30, 1983, 1–12 (Survey).

"United Arab Emirates," *Foreign Economic Trends*, FET 84–08, February 1984 (entire issue).

"United Arab Emirates: A MEED Special Report, 1973," *Middle East Economic Digest* [London], 17, No. 26, June 29, 1973.

"United Arab Emirates: A Special Report," *Times* [London], February 23, 1981, 1–20.

"United Arab Emirates, Economic Report," *Christian Science Monitor*, December 1, 1982, B1–B8.

United Nations. Economic Commission for Western Asia. *The Population Situation in the ECWA Region*. Beirut: 1980.

United States. Arms Control and Disarmament Agency. *Arms Control Report*. Washington: July 1976.

————. *World Military Expenditures and Arms Transfers, 1965–1974*. (ACDA Publication, No. 84.) Washington: GPO, 1976.

United States. Bureau of Reclamation. *Water Supply Augmentation for United Arab Emirates*. Washington: 1979.

United States. Central Intelligence Agency. *Chiefs of State and Cabinet Members of Foreign Governments*. Washington: August 1984, 98.

United States. Central Intelligence Agency. Directorate of Intelligence. *Economic and Energy Indicators*, DI EEI 84–007, March 30, 1984, 8.

————. *International Energy Statistical Review*, DI IESR 82–007, July 27, 1982 (entire issue).

————. *International Energy Statistical Review*, DI IESR 84–005, May 29, 1984, 1, 3.

United States. Congress. 97th, 1st Session. House of Representatives. Committee on Government Operations. *Federal Response to OPEC Country Investments in the United States (Pt. 1—Overview)*. (Hearings, September 22, 23, 1981.) Washington: GPO, 1981.

————. *Federal Response to OPEC Country Investments in the United States (Pt. 2—Investment in Sensitive Sectors of the U.S. Economy: Kuwait Petroleum Corporation Takeover of Santa Fe International Corporation)*. Washington: GPO, 1981.

United States. Congress. 97th, 1st Session. Joint Committee on Economics. *The Persian Gulf: Are We Committed? At What Cost? A Dialogue with the Reagan Administration on U.S. Policy.* Washington; GPO, December 1981.

United States. Department of Housing and Urban Development. *Housing and Urban Development in Kuwait.* Washington: GPO, 1977.

United States. Department of State. *Country Reports on Human Rights Practices for 1983.* (Report submitted to United States Congress, 98th, 2d Session, House of Representatives, Committee on Foreign Affairs, and Senate, Committee on Foreign Relations.) Washington: GPO, February 1984.

United States. Embassy in Kuwait. *Foreign Economic Trends and Their Implications for the United States, Kuwait.* (FET82–117.) Washington: International Trade Administration, Department of Commerce, December 1982.

USA Today, May 16, 1984.

Utaybah, Mani Said. *Essays on Petroleum.* London: Croom Helm, 1982.

Vaglieri, Laura Veccia. "The Patriarchal and Umayyad Caliphates." Pages 57–103 in P.M. Holt, Ann K.S. Lambton, and Bernard Lewis (eds.), *The Cambridge History of Islam, I: The Central Islamic Lands.* Cambridge: Cambridge University Press, 1970.

Van Hollen, Christopher. "Don't Engulf the Gulf," *Foreign Affairs,* 59, Summer 1981, 1064–78.

Venouss, Davar, C.K. Walter, and A. Frank Thompson. "OPEC's Goal and Strategies," *International Journal of Middle East Studies,* 16, No. 2, May 1984, 199–206.

Vreede-De Stuers, Cora. "Girl Students in Kuwait," *Bijdragen Tot De Taal-Land-En Volkenkunde* [Amsterdam], 130, 1974, 110–31.

Webman, Esther. "The Gulf States." Pages 458–520 in Colin Legum (ed.), *Middle East Contemporary Survey, 1980–81.* New York: Holmes and Meier, 1982.

Whelan, John (ed.). *Oman: A MEED Practical Guide.* London: Middle East Economic Digest, 1981.

Wilkinson, J.C. "The Origins of the Omani State." Pages 67–88 in Derek Hopwood (ed.), *The Arabian Peninsula: Society and Politics.* Totowa, New Jersey: Rowman and Littlefield, 1972.

Wilson, Arnold Talbot. *The Persian Gulf: An Historical Sketch from the Earliest Times to the Beginning of the Twentieth Century.* Oxford: Clarendon Press, 1928.

Winder, R. Bayly. *Saudi Arabia in the Nineteenth Century.* New

York: St. Martin's Press, 1965.

Winstone, Harry, and Zahra Freeth. *Kuwait: Prospect and Reality*. New York: Crane, Russak, 1972.

Wolfe, Ronald G. (ed.). *The United States, Arabia, and the Gulf*. Washington: Georgetown University, 1980.

World Factbook, 1982. Washington: Central Intelligence Agency, 1982.

"World Oil Industry," *Financial Times* [London], December 2, 1981, 1–8 (Survey).

"World's Air Forces," *Flight International* [Surrey, England], 124, No. 3874, August 6, 1983.

Wright, Denis. "The Changed Balance of Power in the Persian Gulf," *Asian Affairs* [London], 60, New Series, 4, Pt. 3, October 1973, 255–62.

Yager, Joseph A., and Eleanor B. Steinberg. *Energy and U.S. Foreign Policy*. Cambridge, Massachusetts: Ballinger, 1974.

Yodfat, Aryeh Y. *The Soviet Union and the Arabian Peninsula: Soviet Policy Towards the Persian Gulf and Arabia*. New York: St. Martin's Press, 1983.

Zabih, Sephr. "Iran's Policy Toward the Persian Gulf," *International Journal of Middle East Studies*, 7, No. 3, July 1976, 345–58.

Zahlan, Rosemarie Said. *The Origins of the United Arab Emirates: A Political and Social History of the Trucial States*. New York: St. Martin's Press, 1978.

(Various issues of the following publications were also used in the preparation of this publication; *Air Force; Arab Oil* [Bahamas]; *Arab World and Record* [London]; *Aramco World Magazine; Armed Forces Journal International; Baltimore Sun; Christian Science Monitor; Congressional Quarterly; Deadline Data on World Affairs; Defense and Foreign Affairs;* Department of State, *Background Notes; Economist* [London]; *Financial Times* [London], Foreign Broadcast Information Service, *Daily Report: Middle East and North Africa; IMF Survey; International Financial Statistics;* Joint Publications Research Service, *Near East/South Asia Report; Keesing's Contemporary Archives* [London]; *Kuwait Digest* [Kuwait]; *Manchester Guardian Weekly* [London]; *Middle East Economic Digest* [London]; *Middle East International* [London]; *Middle East Journal; Monthly Bulletin of Statistics; New York Times; Oil and Gas Journal, Oman News; Petroleum Intelligence Weekly; Standard Chartered Review* [London]; *Trade and Industry* [Dubai]; *U.S. News and World Report;* and *Washington Post*.)

Glossary

Al—Uppercased, it connotes family of or belonging to, as in Al
Sabah, Al Khalifa, Al Thani, Al Nuhayyan, Al Maktum, Al
Qasimi, and Al Bu Said. Lowercased, it represents the defi-
nite article *the*, as in Ras al Khaymah.

amir (pl., *umara*)—Literally, commander. In many of the Arab
states on the Gulf, amir often means ruler, king, or prince.

amirate—Political entity under the rule of an amir. Analogous to a
shaykhdom and, if an independent state, to a kingdom.

Bahraini dinar (BD)—Consists of 1,000 fils. Bahraini dinar notes
were first issued in October 1965 with a gold content of 1.866
grams of fine gold, which remained unchanged in 1984. The
gold definition of the Bahraini dinar kept it essentially constant at BD1 equal to 2.1 special drawing rights (SDR—*q.v.*)
through 1975. The Bahraini dinar's value in terms of United
States dollars was stable at BD1 equal to US$2.10 through
1971. Since then the yearly average exchange rate has fluctuated. Until 1972 the Bahraini dinar was pegged to the
British pound sterling, but in March 1972 the Bahraini dinar
was unofficially pegged to the United States dollar. In 1984
the Bahraini dinar had full foreign exchange backing and was a
strong, stable currency. Bahrain maintained no exchange restrictions and no restrictions on transfers of profits or capital.
In 1984 BD1 equaled US$0.37695.

barrels per day—Production of crude oil and petroleum products
is frequently measured in barrels per day, often abbreviated
bpd or bd. A barrel is a volume measure of 42 United States
gallons. Conversion of barrels to tons depends on the density
of the specific product. About 7.3 barrels of average crude oil
weigh one ton. Heavy crude would be about seven barrels per
ton. Light products, such as gasoline and kerosene, would average close to eight barrels per ton.

bin—Literally, son of; same as *ibn; bint* means daughter of and
bani (or *banu*) is literally sons of, hence clan or tribe.

dirham (UD or Dh)—National currency of the UAE, consisting of
100 fils, first issued on May 19, 1973. In 1978 the dirham was
officially pegged to the IMF's special drawing rights (SDR—
q.v.) at the rate of SDR1 per UD4.76. Since November 1980
the dirham has been effectively linked to the United States
dollar. The average value of the dirham per United States dollar was 4.00 in 1973, 3.96 in 1974, 3.96 in 1975, 3.95 in 1976,
3.90 in 1977, 3.87 in 1978, 3.82 in 1979, 3.71 in 1980, 3.67 in

1981, 3.67 in 1982, and 3.67 in 1983.

downstream—The oil industry views the production, processing, transportation, and sale of petroleum products as a flow process starting at the wellhead. Downstream includes any stage between the point of reference and the sale of products to the consumer. Upstream is the converse and includes exploration and drilling of wells. Term is also used in other industries.

gross domestic product (GDP)—A value measure of the flow of domestic goods and services produced by an economy over a period of time, such as a year. Only output values of goods for final consumption and investment are included because the values of primary and intermediate production are assumed to be included in final prices. GDP is sometimes aggregated and shown at market prices, meaning that indirect taxes and subsidies are included; when these have been eliminated, the result is GDP at factor cost. The word *gross* indicates that deductions for depreciation of physical assets have not been made.

hadith—Tradition based on the precedent of Muhammad's words and deeds that serves as one of the sources of Islamic law (sharia—*q.v.*)

hijra (pl., *hujar*)—Literally, to migrate, to sever relations, to leave one's tribe. Throughout the Muslim world hijra refers to the migration of Muhammad and his followers to Medina. In this sense the word has come into European languages as Hegira and is usually and misleadingly translated as "flight."

imam—Word used in several senses. In general use it means the leader of congregational prayers; as such it implies no ordination or special spiritual powers beyond sufficient education to carry out this function. It is also used figuratively by many Sunni *(q.v.)* Muslims to mean the leader of the Islamic community. Among Shiites *(q.v.)* the word takes on many complex and controversial meanings; in general, however, it indicates that particular descendant of the House of Ali who is believed to be God's designated repository of the spiritual authority believed to be inherent in that line. The identity of this individual and the means of ascertaining his identity have been the major issues causing divisions among Shiites. Among the Ibadites of Oman the imam was elected to office and was regarded by all as the spiritual leader of the community and by some as the temporal ruler as well. Claims of various Omani imams to secular power led to open rebellions as late as the 1950s.

International Monetary Fund (IMF)—Established along with the

World Bank *(q.v.)* in 1945, the IMF is a specialized agency affiliated with the United Nations and is responsible for stabiliz-
ing international exchange rates and payments. The main
business of the IMF is the provision of loans to its members
(including industrialized and developing countries) when
they experience balance of payments difficulties. These loans
frequently carry conditions that require substantial internal
economic adjustments by the recipients, most of which are
developing countries.

jihad—The struggle to establish the law of God on earth, often interpreted to mean holy war.

Kuwaiti dinar (KD)—The national currency, consisting of 1,000
fils, was first introduced in April 1961. The Kuwaiti dinar
equaled US$2.80 from its introduction through 1970. After
devaluation of the United States dollar in 1971, the Kuwaiti
dinar-dollar relationship began to fluctuate; in 1975 Kuwait
ceased linking the Kuwaiti dinar to the dollar and pegged it to
a weighted average of several currencies important in
Kuwait's foreign trade. The average annual Kuwaiti dinar-
dollar exchange rate, in terms of United States dollars per
KD1, was: US$2.82 in 1971, US$3.05 in 1972, US$3.39 in
1973, US$3.41 in 1974, US$3.45 in 1975, US$3.42 in 1976,
US$3.49 in 1977, US$3.64 in 1978, US$3.62 in 1979, US$3.70
in 1980, US$3.59 in 1981, US$3.47 in 1982, and US$3.43 in
1983.

majlis (pl., majlises)—Tribal council; in some countries the legislative assembly. Also refers to an audience with an amir or
shaykh open to all citizens for purposes of adjudication.

Omani rial—Monetary unit of Oman, abbreviated OR or RO (although OR is more common and is used in this study). Divided into 1,000 baizas. Its gold content has remained unchanged since it replaced the Gulf Indian rupee in May 1970.
In 1984 the Omani rial continued to be a freely convertible
currency. Average conversion rates to the United States dollar have been: before August 15, 1971, OR1 equal to US$2.40;
in 1972 OR1 equal to US$2.60; in 1983 OR1 equal to US$2.92.

qadi (pl., qadis)—Judge in sharia *(q.v.)* courts.

Qatari riyal—Had a gold value equal to 0.1866 gram of fine gold,
the same as the Qatar-Dubai riyal and the Gulf Indian rupee.
This made QR1 equal to 0.21 special drawing rights (SDR—
q.v.) through 1975. QR1 was equal to US$0.21 through 1971.
In 1972 QR1 was equal to US$0.228; in 1973 QR1 was equal to
US$0.25; in 1974 QR1 was equal to US$0.253; and in 1975

QR1 was equal to US$0.254. In March 1975 the Qatari riyal was pegged to the SDR, which resulted in an appreciation of the Qatari riyal of about 4 percent in terms of major currencies; previously, the United States dollar had been the peg. In 1984 QR1 equaled US$0.274.

sharia—Islamic law.

shaykh—Leader or chief. Word is used to mean either a political leader of a tribe or town or a learned religious leader. Also used as an honorific.

Shia (Shiite)—A member of the smaller of the two great divisions of Islam. The Shia supported the claims of Ali and his line to presumptive right to the caliphate and leadership of the world Muslim community, and on this issue they divided from the Sunni *(q.v.)* in the first great schism of Islam. Later schisms have produced further divisions among the Shia.

Shiism—One of the two great divisions of Islam *(see* Shia).

special drawing rights (SDR)—An International Monetary Fund (IMF—*q.v.*) unit of account made up of a basket of major international currencies.

Sunni—A member of the larger of the two great divisions of Islam. The Sunni, who rejected the claims of Ali's line, believe that they are the true followers of the Sunna, the guide to proper behavior composed of the Quran and the hadith *(q.v:)*

ulama (sing., alim)—Collective term for Muslim religious scholars.

Wahhabi—Name used outside Saudi Arabia to designate adherents to Wahhabism *(q.v.)*.

Wahhabism—Name used outside Saudi Arabia to designate official interpretation of Islam in Saudi Arabia. The faith is a puritanical concept of unitarianism (the oneness of God) that was preached by Muhammad bin Abd al Wahhab, whence his Muslim opponents derived the name. The royal family of Qatar and most indigenous Qataris are Wahhabis.

World Bank—Informal name used to designate a group of three affiliated international institutions: the International Bank for Reconstruction and Development (IBRD), the International Development Association (IDA), and the International Finance Corporation (IFC). The IBRD, established in 1945, has the primary purpose of providing loans to developing countries for productive projects. The IDA, a legally separate loan fund but administered by the staff of the IBRD, was set up in 1960 to furnish credits to the poorest developing countries on much easier terms than those of conventional IBRD loans.

The IFC, founded in 1956, supplements the activities of the IBRD through loans and assistance designed specifically to encourage the growth of productive private enterprises in the less developed countries. The president and certain senior officers of the IBRD hold the same positions in the IFC. The three institutions are owned by the governments of the countries that subscribe their capital. To participate in the World Bank group, member states must first belong to the International Monetary Fund (IMF—*q.v.*).

Index

527

Published Country Studies

550–65	Afghanistan		550–151	Honduras
550–98	Albania		550–165	Hungary
550–44	Algeria		550–21	India
550–50	Angola		550–154	Indian Ocean
550–73	Argentina		550–39	Indonesia
550–169	Australia		550–68	Iran
550–176	Austria		550–31	Iraq
550–175	Bangladesh		550–25	Israel
550–170	Belgium		550–182	Italy
550–66	Bolivia		550–69	Ivory Coast
550–20	Brazil		550–177	Jamaica
550–168	Bulgaria		550–30	Japan
550–61	Burma		550–34	Jordan
550–83	Burundi		550–56	Kenya
550–50	Cambodia		550–81	Korea, North
550–177	Cameroon		550–41	Korea, South
550–159	Chad		550–58	Laos
550–77	Chile		550–24	Lebanon
550–60	China		550–38	Liberia
550–63	China, Republic of		550–85	Libya
550–26	Colombia		550–172	Malawi
550–91	Congo		550–45	Malaysia
550–90	Costa Rica		550–161	Mauritania
550–152	Cuba		550–79	Mexico
550–22	Cyprus		550–76	Mongolia
550–158	Czechoslovakia		550–49	Morocco
550–54	Dominican Republic		550–64	Mozambique
550–52	Ecuador		550–35	Nepal, Bhutan and Sikkim
550–43	Egypt		550–88	Nicaragua
550–150	El Salvador		550–157	Nigeria
550–28	Ethiopia		550–94	Oceania
550–167	Finland		550–48	Pakistan
550–155	Germany, East		550–46	Panama
550–173	Germany, Fed. Rep. of		550–156	Paraguay
550–153	Ghana		550–185	Persian Gulf States
550–87	Greece		550–42	Peru
550–78	Guatemala		550–72	Philippines
550–174	Guinea		550–162	Poland
550–82	Guyana		550–181	Portugal
550–164	Haiti		550–160	Romania